CRIMINOLOGY

REVIEWERS

Jay Albanese, *Niagara University*

Bernard Cohen, *Queens College, New York*

Julius Debro, *Clark Atlanta University*

Albert Dichiara, *Eastern Illinois University*

Edna Erez, *Kent State University*

Franco Ferracuti, *University of Rome, Italy*

Edith Flynn, *Northeastern University*

Karen Gilbert, *University of Georgia*

Clayton Hartjen, *Rutgers University*

Joseph Jacoby, *Bowling Green State University*

Dennis Kenney, *University of Nebraska at Omaha*

Nicholas Kittrie, *American University*

Linda Lengyel, *Trenton State College*

Coramae Mann, *Indiana University, Bloomington*

Robert McCormack, *Trenton State College*

Lydia Rosner, *John Jay College of Criminal Justice*

Austin Turk, *University of California, Riverside*

Charles Wellford, *University of Maryland at College Park*

Frank Williams, *California State University, San Bernardino*

Marvin Wolfgang, *University of Pennsylvania*

CRIMINOLOGY

Freda Adler
Rutgers University

Gerhard O. W. Mueller
Rutgers University

William S. Laufer
University of Pennsylvania

McGRAW-HILL, INC.
New York   St. Louis   San Francisco   Auckland   Bogotá   Caracas
Hamburg   Lisbon   London   Madrid   Mexico   Milan   Montreal
New Delhi   Paris   San Juan   São Paulo   Singapore   Sydney   Tokyo   Toronto

This book was set in Palatino by the College
Composition Unit in cooperation with
Ruttle Shaw & Wetherill, Inc.
The editors were Phillip A. Butcher, Sylvia Shepard,
Bob Greiner, and Caroline Izzo.
The cover was designed by Carla Bauer.
Cover painting by William Low.
The photo editor was Barbara Salz.
Von Hoffmann Press, Inc., was printer and binder.

CRIMINOLOGY

2 3 4 5 6 7 8 9 0 VNH VNH 9 5 4 3 2 1

ISBN 0-07-000411-0

Library of Congress Cataloging-in-Publication Data is
available: LC Card #90-19144.

ABOUT THE AUTHORS

GERHARD O. W. MUELLER is Professor of Criminal Justice at Rutgers University, School of Criminal Justice. After earning his J.D. degree from The University of Chicago, he went on to receive the LL.M. degree from Columbia University. He was awarded the degree of the Dr. Jur. (h.c.) by the University of Uppsala, Sweden. He has been teaching criminal law, criminology, criminal justice, and international and comparative criminal justice since 1953. In the past he served as the Director of the United Nations Crime Prevention and Criminal Justice Branch, and as President of the American Society of Criminology. His published works include over 30 books and 200 articles.

FREDA ADLER is Professor of Criminal Justice at Rutgers University, School of Criminal Justice. She received her B.A. in sociology, her M.A. in criminology, and her Ph.D. in sociology—all from the University of Pennsylvania. Teaching since 1968, Dr. Adler's subjects include criminology, statistics, research methods, and international and comparative criminology. She has served as criminological advisor to the United Nations, as well as to federal, state, and foreign governments. Her published works include six books as author or co-author, six books as editor, and over fifty journal articles. She has served on the editorial boards of the *Journal of Research in Crime and Delinquency*, *Criminology*, and the *Journal of Criminal Justice*. Presently, Dr. Adler serves as editorial consultant to the *Journal of Criminal Law and Criminology*, and is co-editor of *Advances in Criminological Theory*.

WILLIAM S. LAUFER is Assistant Professor of Legal Studies and Associate Director of the Sellin Center for Studies in Criminology and Criminal Law at the Wharton School of the University of Pennsylvania. He received his B.A. degree in Social and Behavioral Sciences from the Johns Hopkins University before going on to earn his J.D. from Northeastern University School of Law, and his Ph.D. in Criminal Justice from Rutgers University. Dr. Laufer's research on crime-causation theory and behavioral assumptions underlying legal doctrine has been published in numerous journals, including the *Journal of Personality and Social Psychology*, *Journal of Research in Crime and Delinquency*, and *Criminal Law Bulletin*. He is co-editor of *Advances in Criminological Theory*; *Handbook of Psychology and Law*; *Crime, Values, and Religion*; and *Personality Theory, Moral Development, and Criminal Behavior*.

To our children and grandchildren

Mark J. Adler and Susan B. Weinstock-Adler with
  David S. Adler

Jill E. Adler-Donkersloot and Willem H.F.A.
  Donkersloot

Nancy D. Adler-Knijff and Robert F. Knijff

Mark H. Mueller and Constance Soboll Mueller with
  Nicholas Alexander Mueller

Marla L. Mueller and Lawrence Frederick Bentley

Monica R. Mueller

Matthew A. Mueller and Martha Sullivan Mueller
  with Lauren Elizabeth and Stephen William Mueller

Hannah Laufer

CONTENTS IN BRIEF

CONTENTS

SPECIAL FEATURES

PREFACE

Criminology is a young discipline. The term "criminology" is barely a century old, but in those one hundred years criminology has emerged as a major social and behavioral science. Criminology's contributions are essential for dealing with a crime problem in our society that many people consider to be intolerable. Problems as vital and urgent as those addressed in this book, *Criminology*, are challenging and exciting.

We invite the teacher and the student to trace the path which criminologists have traveled, and to join in mapping out the future of criminology in the twenty-first century—which is less than a decade away.

Organization

This book has four parts. Part I presents an overview of criminology, pointing to the vast horizon of this science. It explains techniques for measuring the characteristics of criminals, crime, and victims. It also traces the history of criminological thought through the era that witnessed the formation of the major schools of criminology: classicism and positivism (eighteenth and nineteenth centuries).

Part II explains criminal behavior on the basis of the various theories that were developed in the twentieth century. Among the subjects covered are theories that offer biological, psychological, sociological, sociopolitical, and integrated explanations.

Part III takes an innovative approach by explaining the types of crime not only from a legal-historical perspective but also on the basis of the contemporary theories of rational choice and routine activities. This approach permits an assessment of the motivations and activities of offenders, as well as the prevalence and distribution of crime. The familiar street crimes, such as assault and robbery, are assessed, and so are criminal activities that have been highlighted by researchers only in recent years.

"A Criminological Approach to the Criminal Justice System" (Part IV) emphasizes contemporary criminological research on the functioning and interaction of the various components of the system. It also explains the decision-making processes of all the participants.

Features

In our effort to provide the student with a pleasurable and rewarding learning experience, and the instructor with a teaching tool that is at once dynamic and effective, we have incorporated a number of special features:

• We highlight the evolution and interrelatedness of theories that explain criminal behavior.
• Throughout the text we demonstrate the interrelatedness of theory, policy, and practice. For example, in the theory chapters we include "Theory to Practice" sections, and in the criminal justice chapters, we consistently present the system within the context of contemporary criminological theory and research.
• In view of the dramatic effects of the globalization of society on contemporary crime, we highlight the international dimension of crime through international examples, cross-cultural

comparisons and a series of boxes called "Window to the World."

• We emphasize current issues in criminology including studies of family violence, stranger homicide, date rape, female criminality, environmental crime, abuse of power, local and transnational drug problems, and terrorism.

• To convey the excitement and relevance of the field of criminology, we use recognizable contemporary and historical examples and case studies. We also provide in-depth analyses of selected cases and research studies in our boxed feature called "Criminological Focus."

• The epilogue looks forward to the challenges of the twenty-first century.

Pedagogical Aids

By working together closely and cooperatively, the authors and the editors have developed a format for the book that is readable and informative. Numerous photographs, especially at chapter openings, highlight the textual coverage. A large number of graphs, charts, and maps amplify the textual presentation. Chapter outlines, key terms, reviews, the glossary, and name and subject indexes facilitate use of the book. The instructor's manual, prepared by Marie Henry, a respected and experienced college instructor of criminology at Sullivan County Community College, provides all the assistance an instructor may need to make this course a rewarding teaching experience.

A combined total of fifty-five years of teaching criminology provides the basis for the writing of *Criminology*. We hope that the result is a text that is intellectually provocative, factually rigorous, and scientifically sound, and that gives the student a stimulating learning experience.

In Appreciation

We gratefully acknowledge the assistance and support of a number of dedicated professionals. At Rutgers University, the librarian of the N.C.C.D./Criminal Justice Collection, Phyllis Schultze, has been most helpful in patiently tracking and tracing sources. We thank Prof. Sesha Kethanini, Illinois State University, for her tireless assistance throughout the project, and Joan Schroeder and Mary Gardner for their superb word processing of the manuscript. Included in the list of those to whom we are grateful are Rutgers University School of Criminal Justice research assistants Susanna Cornett, Dory Dickman, Lisa Maher, Susan Plant, and Mangai Natarajan, who provided helpful comment on the manuscript. We thank Jeff Ellis of the Wharton School, University of Pennsylvania, for compiling the glossary.

We owe a special debt to the team at McGraw-Hill. Phil Butcher orchestrated the production. Sylvia Shepard guided the book from thought to completion. Alison Husting launched the project. Mary Shuford shaped the final draft with patience and persistence. Bob Greiner's keen editorial judgment and devotion to *Criminology* deserve very special appreciation. Safra Nimrod, photography editor, deserves our thanks for pictorially enhancing the text. We also are grateful to Joan O'Connor, who supervised the design; Barbara Salazar, who edited the manuscript; Martha Wiseman for her thorough review of the manuscript; Cindy Booth for her tireless effort in producing galleys and pages; and Anita Kann for keeping the project on schedule.

Many academic reviewers (listed facing the title page) and survey respondents offered invaluable help first in the planning stage, and then in responding to chapter drafts. We thank them for their time and thoughtfulness, and for the wisdom which they brought from their teaching and research.

Freda Adler

Gerhard O. W. Mueller

William S. Laufer

CRIMINOLOGY

PART I

UNDERSTANDING CRIMINOLOGY

Criminology is the scientific study of the making of laws, the breaking of laws, and the reaction to the breaking of laws. Laws express the common interest of organized society. Sometimes the common interest is arrived at by consensus, sometimes it is imposed by those in power. In ancient times the common interest expressed by law was that of small groupings of people, clans, tribes, and kingdoms. Today the people of the entire world have many interests in common. Criminological research and crime prevention strategies are consequently becoming globalized (Chapter 1). Criminologists have adopted methods of study from all of the social and behavioral sciences. Like all scientists, criminologists measure. They assess crime over time and place, and they measure the characteristics of criminals, of crimes, and of victims by various methods (Chapter 2). Throughout history notable thinkers have philosophized about crime and criminals and the control of crime. Yet the term "criminology" is little more than a century old, and our subject has been of scientific interest for only two centuries. Two schools of thought contributed to modern criminology: the classical school, associated predominantly with Cesare Beccaria (eighteenth century), which focused on crime, and the positivist school, associated with Cesare Lombroso, Enrico Ferri, and Raffaele Garofalo (nineteenth and early twentieth centuries), which focused on criminals (Chapter 3). Contemporary American criminology owes much to these European roots.

1

AN OVERVIEW OF CRIMINOLOGY

Very little happens on earth that is not of interest to criminologists and to the criminal justice system. Most people think that criminologists deal only with crimes like murder, robbery, car theft, burglary, or perhaps shoplifting. This is a very narrow view because criminologists are, in fact, concerned with events that may not appear to have any criminological implication. Let us examine, for example, the people and events depicted in the photographs in the first photo essay, "The Universe of the Criminologist's Interest": Nelson Mandela, General Manuel Noriega, the *Exxon Valdez*, death at the Berlin Wall, and former Congressman Robert Garcia.

The photograph of *Nelson Mandela* shows the leader of the black majority of South Africa's population leaving prison. He had been held for twenty-seven years after his conviction for political crimes stemming from his vehement opposition to apartheid, the doctrine of racial segregation under which the country's white minority denies black Africans equality and a share in their own government. Apartheid itself is a crime, an international crime, recognized as such all over the world, except in South Africa. There apartheid is legal, although in February 1990 President F. W. de Klerk of South Africa began a process aimed at ending apartheid eventually. Nelson Mandela's release was the first step in that process. It took economic sanctions and the moral outrage of the rest of the world to persuade the South African government that by enforcing, often brutally, its criminal apartheid laws, it was offending the entire world.

Criminologists are interested in such questions as how criminal laws are created, who has the power to create them, what the purpose of such laws is, how they are enforced, and what role ethnicity plays with respect to crime and the criminal justice system. The Mandela case raises these and many more questions.

The photograph of *General Manuel Noriega* shows the former military dictator of Panama being arraigned in federal district court in Miami on an indictment of drug trafficking. In order to execute the warrant, the president of the United States launched a military invasion of Panama, in which hundreds of Americans and Panamanians were killed. Many Americans and Panamanians lauded this military action and saw nothing wrong with the use of military force against a sovereign country when it was considered necessary to capture a dictator charged with drug trafficking.

The case is of great interest to criminologists, who not only are studying the vast problem of worldwide drug trafficking and drug use but also are investigating the causes of drug addiction and its relation to all other forms of crime. Moreover, criminologists are interested in the limits of power to deal with the drug problem nationally and internationally. They are also concerned with questions of wrongdoing by government itself both before and during Noriega's capture and under both national and international law. Lastly, criminologists are concerned with how people like Noriega should be dealt with if they are convicted. What kind of disposition will best serve the cause of decreasing the international drug traffic? Criminological research may hold some answers.

The photograph of the supertanker *Exxon Valdez* shows crude oil exuding through a rupture in its hull after running aground in Prince William Sound, Alaska. The captain was brought to trial on charges of criminal negligence for causing North America's largest ecological disaster. Prosecutors and courts were interested in determining the guilt or innocence of the captain, his officers, and his crew. Was there negligence? Were some crew members intoxicated? Did maritime law enforcement agencies (the United States Coast Guard) contribute to the disaster? Should the Exxon Corporation be blamed for building tankers in a manner that puts profit above safety? Does that violate any laws?

Criminologists view the incident from a broad perspective. They study the kinds of sanctions or incentives that can best protect the environment. How can human behavior be controlled to safeguard the environment? Are new laws likely to provide greater protection against negligence and error? How much will new measures cost, and are they cost-beneficial? To make such studies, criminologists will have to select the most appropriate research methodology, and then assemble and analyze the results carefully.

The photograph of the *Berlin Wall*, which from 1961 until 1989 kept East Germans isolated from the Western world, was the scene of many violent deaths. Despite their hard work, East Germans suffered from severe shortages in every sector of their mismanaged economy. Corrupt political leaders controlled their thoughts; the wall controlled their movement. Over 150 people were killed by the police, attacked by guard dogs, or blown up by mines while trying to escape over the wall or through the death zone of the East German border. On November 9, 1989, seventy-one years to the day since their last rebellion (against the Kaiser), East Germans took to the streets, rebelled against their oppressors, and breached the wall.

It was a profound political event. People everywhere talked about the end of communism and the return to democracy. To criminologists the event has a deeper, more scientific significance, because criminologists study the relation between ideology and power in the making, enforcing, and breaking of laws. They research the effectiveness of law enforcement, its popularity and unpopularity, and its humaneness. They are interested in what happens on the streets and in the highest government offices. Their laboratory is the entire world.

The final photograph depicts what to many people was a sad, disheartening event. Congressman *Robert Garcia*, once a very popular and powerful politician who had made his way up the social and political ladder and who appeared to represent his minority constituency well, entered prison. He had been convicted of corruption, extortion, and bribery in the so-called WedTech scandal, involving government defense contracts.

To criminologists this is not just a sad news story. It is a far from isolated event in the area known as white-collar crime. Much research has been conducted in efforts to understand why prominent people commit crimes that affect broad sectors of the population. Criminologists are called upon by industry and government to explain and measure the cost of white-collar crime and to assist in devising strategies to curb it.

The five recent events described above demonstrate the wide-ranging subject matter of criminology. Before exploring the work of criminologists, we shall define what is meant by criminology, delineate its place among the sciences, and describe its major areas of concern: the making of laws, the breaking of laws, and society's reaction to the breaking of laws. For these purposes, we turn first to history.

WHAT IS CRIMINOLOGY?

In the Middle Ages human learning was commonly divided into four areas: law, medicine, theology, and philosophy. Consequently, the universities typically had four faculties, one for each of these four fields. Imagine a young person in the year 1392—a hundred years before Columbus discovered America—with a completed basic education, knocking at the portal of a great university with the request: "I would like to study criminology. Where do I sign up?" A stare of disbelief would have greeted the student, because the word had not yet been coined. Patiently the student would explain: "Well, I'm interested in what crime is, and how the law deals with criminals." The university official would smile and advise: "The right place for you to go is the law faculty. They will teach you everything there is to know about the law."

The student might feel discouraged. "That's a lot more than I want to know about the law. I really don't care about inheritance laws and the law of contracts. I really want to study all about crime and criminality. For example, why are certain actions considered wrong or evil in the first place, and..." The official would interrupt to explain, "Then you must go to the faculty of theology. They know all there is to know about good and evil, heaven and hell."

The student would persist. "But could they teach me what it is about the human body and mind that could cause some people and not others to commit crime?"

"Oh, I see," the official would say. "You really should study medicine."

"But, sir, medicine probably is only part of what I need to know, and really only part of medicine seems relevant. I want to know all there is to know about..." And then would come the official's last attempt to steer the student in the right direction: "Go and study philosophy. They'll teach you all there is to know!"

For centuries, all the knowledge the universities recognized continued to be taught in these four faculties. It was not until the eighteenth and nineteenth centuries that the natural and social sciences became full-fledged disciplines. In fact, the science of criminology has been known as such for only a little more than a century. In 1885 the Italian law professor Raffaele Garofalo coined the term (in Italian, *criminologia*).[1] The French anthropologist Paul Topinard used it for the first time in French (*criminologie*) in 1887.[2] "Criminology" aptly described and encompassed the scientific concern with the phenomenon of crime. The term immediately gained acceptance all over the world and criminology became a subject taught at universities. Unlike their predecessors in 1392—or even in 1892—today's entering students will find that there are not merely four disciplines at the university, but that teaching and learning are distributed among twenty or thirty disciplines and departments. And criminology or criminal justice is likely to be one of them.

Criminology is a science, an empirical science. More particularly, it is one of the social or behavioral sciences. It has been defined in various ways by its scholars. The definition provided in 1947 by Edwin H. Sutherland, one of the founding scholars of American criminology, is widely accepted:

> Criminology is the body of knowledge regarding crime as a social phenomenon. It includes within its scope the process of making laws, of breaking laws, and of reacting toward the breaking of laws....The objective of criminology is the development of a body of general and verified principles and of other types of knowledge regarding this process of law, crime, and treatment or prevention.[3]

This definition suggests that the field of criminology is narrowly focused on crime yet broad in scope. By stating as the objective of criminology the "development of a body of general and verified principles," Sutherland mandates that criminologists, like all other scientists, collect information for study and analysis in accordance with the research methods of modern science. As we shall see in Chapter 3, the first persons who conducted serious investigations into criminal behavior, in the eighteenth century, were not engaged in empirical research, although they based their conclusions on factual information. It was only in the nineteenth century that criminologists systematically gathered facts about crime and criminals and then evaluated their data in a scientific manner.

Among the first researchers to analyze empirical data (facts, statistics, and other observable information) in a search for the causes of crime was Cesare Lombroso (1835–1909) of Italy (see Chapter 3). His biologically oriented theories had wide influence on American criminology at the turn of the twentieth century. At that time the causes of crime were thought to rest within the individual: criminal behavior was attributed to feeblemindedness and moral insanity. From then on, psychologists and psychiatrists played an important role in the study of crime and criminals. By the 1920s other scholars saw the great influx of immigrants, with their alien ways of behaving, as the cause of crime. The search then moved to cultural and social interpretations. Crime thus was explained not only in terms of the offender but also in terms of social, political, and economic problems.

In increasing numbers, sociologists, political scientists, legal scholars, and economists entered the arena of criminology. But architects, too, have joined the ranks of criminologists in their efforts to design housing units that will be relatively free from crime. Engineers are working to design cars that are virtually theftproof. Pharmacologists have a role to play in alleviating the problem of drug addiction. Satellites put into space by astrophysicists can help us control the drug trade. Specialists in public administration are asked to improve the functioning of the criminal justice system. Educators have been enlisted to prepare children for a life as free from delinquency as possible. Social workers are needed to help break the cycle of poverty and crime. Biologists and endocrinologists have expanded our understanding of the relationship between the human body and deviant behavior. Clearly, criminology is a discipline composed of the accumulated knowledge of many other disciplines. Criminologists acknowledge their indebtedness to all contributing disciplines, but they strongly contend that theirs is a separate science.

WHAT DO CRIMINOLOGISTS STUDY?

According to Sutherland's definition, criminological study extends to the processes of "making laws, of breaking laws, and of reacting toward the breaking of laws." In explaining what is meant by "making laws," "breaking laws," and "reacting toward the breaking of laws," we shall take a contemporary as well as a historical look at these processes, and we shall frequently investigate their workings in other societies.

The Making of Laws

Until a few years ago, whenever a man entered an elevator anywhere in the United States, he would take his hat off. Just conjure up the picture of an elevator crowded with people, and all the men holding their hats in their hands. At the next floor another man enters the elevator and he does not take his hat off. Glowering stares from all those aboard warn the newcomer that he is in violation of a socially accepted practice, or custom. Blushing, he takes his hat off. Today we would not witness such a scene in an American elevator. Most men do not wear hats anymore, and the few who do rarely take them off in elevators. Customs—whatever their origin—come and go. Customs, social conventions carried on by tradition, are a gentle way of regulating human conduct. Criminologists are interested in studying the emergence of customs, reactions to violations of customs, and success or failure in inducing compliance with customs. They are also interested in learning what society does when customs no longer function to regulate conduct perceived as undesirable. New Yorkers' concern over the problem of dog droppings provides an example. Disciplined city dwellers had always observed the custom of curbing their dogs. But more and more dog owners failed to do that. Consequently, New Yorkers decided that the cleanliness of their sidewalks was an important issue. Laws were enacted making it

an offense not to clean up after one's dog. In Beijing, China, and Reykjavik, Iceland, dogs have been banned altogether. Criminologists are interested in studying whether the laws that replace customs have the desired effect.

What leads a society to designate some wrongs as crimes while it leaves other wrongs to be settled in private? For centuries, "natural law" philosophers, believing in the permanent rightness and wrongness of certain human behaviors, have held the view that some forms of behavior are innately criminal and that all societies condemn them equally. Homicide and theft were thought to be among these behaviors.

This notion is no longer supported. Raffaele Garofalo, who gave our discipline its name, defended the concept of "natural crime," by which he meant behavior that offends our basic moral sentiments, such as respect for the property of others and revulsion against infliction of suffering. Nevertheless, he admitted that although we might think such crimes as murder and robbery would be recognized by all existing legal systems, "a slight investigation seems to dispel this idea."[4] Neither the Roman Law of the Twelve Tables (451–450 B.C.) nor the Babylonian Code of Hammurabi (about 1700 B.C.) lists homicide or ordinary theft among crimes. Nor can we find these crimes among the listings of other very early legal systems. On the contrary, homicides appear to have been in a category of wrongs that could be righted by compensation or by the surrender of the perpetrator to the injured clan as a substitute worker for the slain victim. Theft was not a problem in societies that had not developed the concept of property, and it was a minor problem in societies that had little property to be concerned about or in which the few items of property in existence—a hammer, an ox, or a hoe—could be easily replaced or exchanged. In such societies, people resolved their problems by private arrangements rather than by resorting to legal punishment. Clearly the socioeconomic circumstances of a society determine which forms of behavior that society considers to be wrongs serious enough to be controlled by criminal law.

The overriding need of every society is to protect its own existence. Let us look at the story of Romulus and his brother Remus, the legendary founders of Rome. Romulus killed his brother after Remus had frivolously jumped over the protective city wall that Romulus and his workers had just constructed around the town that was to become Rome. Rather than being condemned for killing his brother, Romulus became the most revered figure among his people, who named their city after him: Rome. Why? Romulus had not killed Remus without just cause. By jumping over a certain part of the city wall, Remus had shown the town's enemies where the wall was most vulnerable to attack. That was treason, the one offense that threatens the very existence of a society. In every society, no matter how ancient or primitive, we find the only crime that all share is the one that threatens the society's existence—treason.

All of the earliest legal systems also recognized some other wrongs as crimes subject to punishment. Economic, social, and even environmental conditions influenced a society's choice of the wrongs it publicly condemned as crimes. To discover types of behavior that societies have outlawed for self-preservation, we have to look at specific societies. Among the pre-Columbian Incas of Peru, one of the most serious wrongs was the destruction of a bridge. In a country crisscrossed by ravines and canyons, bridges were the only means of communication. Among North American Plains Indians, theft of a horse or of a blanket was one of the most serious public wrongs. A person without a horse or a blanket was in danger of death. Among the ancient Germanic tribes, theft of a beehive was one of the most serious public wrongs. Beehives provided honey, which then was the only source of sugar for food and drink.

In order to study the emergence of the earliest concepts of crimes, which is part of Sutherland's inquiry into the making of laws, criminologists employ the research methods of anthropologists, ethnologists, and historians. Cross-cultural and historical comparison can teach us much about the making of laws in contemporary society.

The development of early legal systems
When we say that certain wrongful acts were considered to be crimes, we may seem to be saying that early societies actually had legal systems. Early societies had no legal system in the contemporary sense of the term. But they had ways of solving problems of wrongdoing. The information we have is sketchy. Many societies left no written records. Yet we do have some reports about preliterate societies by observers from more sophisticated cultures.

Germanic criminal law   In the first century A.D. the Roman writer Tacitus described crime control among the barbarian tribes then living in what is now Germany. Their approach was the forerunner of what ultimately became Anglo-Saxon and Anglo-American law. One way of dealing with wrongdoing, Tacitus wrote, was to institute a feud between the clans of the victim and the offender. Other wrongdoing could be settled by compensation.

It is also possible to make accusations and apply for the infliction of the death penalty before

the assembly. The differences of penalties depend on the [nature of the] crime. Traitors and deserters they hang on trees, cowards, war objectors and people bodily disgraced they drown in mud and swamps, even throwing wattlings on top.[5]

There are also records of a Germanic tribe, the migrant Goths, of the fourth century A.D. When their first native Christian bishop, Ulfilas, attempted to translate the Bible into Gothic, he could find no Gothic equivalent for the biblical text "They shall condemn him to death" (Mark 10:33). So he rendered it in Gothic as "They shall declare him to be a wolf." Among the Goths, the most serious punishment for a public wrong was a "wolf declaration." This punishment was tantamount to a sentence of death because the person so sentenced was, like the wolf, banished from the campfire and forced to flee into the wild forest.

Roman criminal law   There are two good reasons for examining early Roman criminal law. Not only are its sources well preserved, but it influenced most of the world's legal systems. By the time Tacitus wrote his report about the primitive Germanic approach to crime and justice, the Roman legal system was highly developed. But it, too, had humble beginnings. The earliest written form of Roman law was the Law of the Twelve Tables (451–450 B.C.). Here are some of its precepts:

• If anyone sings or composes an incantation that can cause dishonor or disgrace to another...he shall suffer a capital penalty.
• If anyone has broken another's limb there shall be retaliation in kind unless he compounds for compensation with him.
• If one commits an outrage against another the penalty shall be twenty-five asses.
• If a thief commits a theft by night, if the owner kills the thief, the thief shall be killed lawfully.
• If fruit from your tree falls onto my farm and if I feed my flock off it by letting the flock onto it...no action can lie against me either on the statute concerning pasturage of a flock, because it is not being pastured on your land, or on the

CRIMINOLOGICAL FOCUS

Fairy Tales and Crime

Have you ever wondered about the wolf who accosts Little Red Riding Hood as she makes her way through the forest to her grandmother's house? Later on he devours Grandma and Little Red Riding Hood. Who is that wolf who speaks like a man?

Scholarly research has revealed him to be a wolf of the two-legged variety. Fairy tales embody ancient folk wisdom and law. Before there were written legal codes, law was orally transmitted from generation to generation. This fairy tale tells us that the punishment for the most serious crimes was *to be a wolf*. Like the four-legged wolf, the offender was banished from human society and condemned to live in the forest, there to live or die among the four-legged wolves, to be shunned or hunted like one of them.

The ancient European tribes were ever on the move. Such societies could not rely on prisons as punishment for offenders. Outlawry seemed to be the perfect solution, and the wolf provided a model.

Source: Gerhard O. W. Mueller, "The Criminological Significance of the Grimms' Fairy Tales," in *Fairy Tales and Society: Illusion, Allusion, and Paradigm*, ed. Ruth B. Bottigheimer (Philadelphia: University of Pennsylvania Press, 1986), pp. 217–227.

statute concerning damage caused by an animal.
• Whoever is convicted of speaking false witness shall be flung from the Tarpeian Rock [on the Capitoline Hill in Rome].[6]

The laws put forth in the Twelve Tables had existed for centuries as unwritten law. To a large extent, however, they were kept secret by the ruling patrician class. The subjugated class, the plebeians, was nevertheless expected to conform to those laws.[7] The plebeians finally demonstrated their objection to this intolerable situation by gathering in protest on the holy mountain outside the city walls. Since the plebeians were the artisans and workers, the life of Rome was brought to a standstill. The plebeians demanded a written code of law to tell them what their duties, rights, and expectations were. The result was the first codification of Roman law. That law was written on twelve wooden tablets, which then were prominently displayed in the forum; hence the name, Law of the Twelve Tables.

In this code of laws we find three groups of wrongs. In the first group we find wrongs that were not considered criminal, such as battery (hitting another person). These were civil wrongs, for which the wrongdoer had to compensate the victim. In the second group we find wrongs for which the wrongdoer had to pay a fine in the amount of a multiple (double or triple) of the value of the injury inflicted. Only in the third group do we find the real crimes. These were offenses against the security of the state or the welfare of the people as a whole. These wrongs could be vindicated only by a purely criminal sanction, such as capital punishment.[8] This category of wrongs demonstrates that certain wrongs are so heinous that the offender cannot make amends by any kind of material compensation. The Romans called them sacral crimes, and they included treason, conspiracy, removal of sacred boundary stones, perjury, and offenses of a similar nature.

Other early legal systems   Many early cultures had legal codes, among them Babylon, with the Code of Hammurabi (about 1700 B.C.); the Israelites, with the Mosaic Code (1200 B.C.); Greece, with the Draconian Code (seventh century B.C.); India, with the Hindu Code of Manu (fifth century B.C.); and the Islamic societies, with the Koran (seventh century A.D.). When looked at closely, these codes show that the development of criminal laws generally followed the same pattern among all people everywhere. They all began with the recognition of some acts as wrong. All cultures regarded some law violations as minor and subject to private compensation. And all, according to the earliest records of their legal systems, considered some wrongs to be so serious that material compensation was not considered sufficient as a punishment or effective as a deterrent.

The influence of early legal systems on contemporary legal systems   The Code of Hammurabi had only faint influence on the later law of the Persians, but some of its principles, such as the government's duty to compensate victims of crime, live on. The Draconian Code of the Greeks had a heavy influence on later Greek laws, such as those formulated by Solon in 403 B.C. These laws in turn influenced the law of the Romans, most directly the Law of the Twelve Tables. These early Roman laws then contributed greatly to the highly sophisticated legal system of the Roman Empire. When the Roman Empire collapsed in the West in 476 A.D., the Roman codes were lost until the twelfth century, when they were rediscovered by accident. Thereafter they had a profound impact on the legal systems that developed all over continental Europe, and on criminal justice within those systems. From these legal systems the Roman (so-called civil law) system spread over a great part of the world. Today all of continental Europe, all of Latin America, most of the countries of Africa that once were French, Belgian, Spanish, or Portuguese colo-

The Code of Hammurabi (actually an ordered collection of judgments by Hammurabi, king of Babylonia) is the oldest intact legal code to have been discovered. Found in 1902 in Iran, the 8.2-foot diorite monument bearing most of Hammurabi's code is now on display at the Louvre Museum in Paris. An exact replica is displayed at the United Nations Building in New York.

THE UNIVERSE OF THE CRIMINOLOGIST'S INTEREST

Criminologists, so the general public believes, study crime. This belief immediately conjures up familiar pictures or experiences: a teenager shoplifting in a department store, a mugging victim lying unconscious on a street corner, a burglary in a housing development, a crack dealer selling illegal drugs, abandoned firearms and a puddle of blood—the leftovers at a murder scene. Criminologists do study crimes and criminals, but their horizons extend far beyond street corners and department stores. Indeed, very little happens anywhere in the world that does not challenge the criminological mind. To illustrate this point we have selected five major news events (for details, see Chapter 1).

Nelson Mandela's release from a South African prison (after 27 years!) raises profound criminological questions about the legitimacy of unjust laws, about the right to rebel against national laws permitting acts that are criminal under international law, about conditions of confinement in prison, and ultimately about the goals of correction.

General Manuel Noriega's trial on drug trafficking charges in a Miami federal court opens a Pandora's box of issues connected with international drug trafficking and its impact on street crime in the United States, money laundering and white collar crime, the propriety of American intelligence agencies' recruiting high-ranking foreign officials for illegal operations, the right of government to bring to trial a person apprehended abroad (perhaps illegally), and the status of a prisoner of war in facing criminal charges. These are only a few of the many issues brought into question by the Noriega trial.

The grounding of the supertanker *Exxon Valdez* (since renamed *Exxon Mediterranean*) in Prince William Sound, Alaska, created one of the greatest ecological disasters in human history. It also raises immense issues for criminological research and policy making: whether to use criminal sanctions for the protection of the environment, and if so, what sanctions; what legislation is needed to make shippers and shipyards build safer ships; how to control the sobriety of captains and crews; and how to police the police—in this case the U.S. Coast Guard—so that a proper balance can be struck in the deployment of resources for control of tanker traffic on the one hand and drug enforcement on the other.

The Berlin Wall is one of the harshest exemplifications of the police state. Hundreds tried to cross the wall, only to be shot by police without warning. Two fundamental questions that were raised by the wall—and its fall in a peaceful revolution on November 9, 1989—are the rule of law and the role of law enforcement.

The trial and conviction of Congressman Robert Garcia on corruption, extortion, and bribery charges and the prospect of further proceedings concerns criminologists greatly. Garcia's conviction, however, was overturned and he was released from prison.

Historically, politicians have been considered immune from the criminal process. Is this immunity a custom that has now been shattered? How does the criminal process work in an ordinary case, as distinguished from a case involving a congressman? Where should society draw the line between politicking and criminal activity? What are appropriate sanctions for political leaders or idols whose images have been destroyed by a finding of guilt?

We now invite you to make a test: Read today's newspaper and determine how many stories are of concern to criminologists, and how many are not.

A mugging victim lying unconscious on a street corner.

A burglary in progress.

A teenage girl shoplifting.

A crack dealer selling containers of crack.

Nelson Mandela leaving prison accompanied by his wife, Winnie.

Aftermath of a murder at an elementary school.

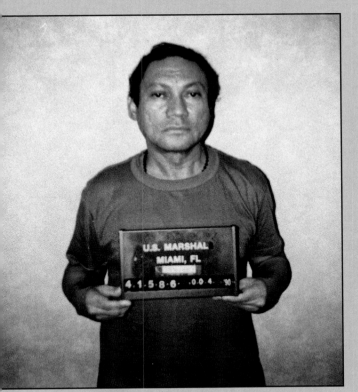

General Manuel Noriega being photographed by U.S. authorities after his "arrest."

Congressman Robert Garcia being interviewed during his trial.

A crew begins the cleanup.

The Exxon Valdez surrounded by leaking oil.

Crosses mark the area along the Berlin Wall where people were killed while trying to flee from East Berlin.

Jubilant celebrations as the Berlin Wall begins to come down.

nies, the countries of Asia that once were Dutch colonies, and Japan, China (to some extent), and South Africa are the heirs of the Greco-Roman system of law and justice.

As we shall explain in Part IV, even the Anglo-American system of justice derived some benefit from the Greco-Roman system, though its basis remains the Germanic (Anglo-Saxon) heritage of law and justice. The Anglo-Saxon (now called Anglo-American or common law) system of law and justice continues to be applied in all English-speaking countries with the exception of Scotland and—to some extent—South Africa.

India's Code of Manu lives on only in history and in some customs. The British colonial power imposed Anglo-Saxon law, modified to meet local conditions. The Koran of Islam continues in full force in Iran and Saudi Arabia (extended by regulatory legislation) and survives in large part in the legal systems of other Islamic countries, including Pakistan (otherwise a common law country), Sudan, several of the Persian Gulf states, and countries of Africa north of the Sahara.

In this book we are primarily concerned with crime and justice in the United States, one of the common law nations. Our historical references therefore deal primarily with the common law experience of justice and crime. But in Chapter 16 we juxtapose two medieval criminal law cases, one from the common law heritage and one from the Roman (civil) law heritage, in order to demonstrate the fundamental differences that to this day distinguish these two predominant systems of the world.

The consensus and conflict views of law and crime   In the traditional interpretation of the historical development of legal systems, and of criminal justice in particular, lawmaking is a smooth accommodation of interests in a society, whether that society is composed of equals (as in a democracy) or of rulers and ruled (as in a monarchy), so as to produce a system of law and enforcement to which everybody, basically, subscribes. This is the communal consensus model. According to this view, certain acts are deemed so threatening to the society's survival that they are designated as crimes. If the vast majority of the group shares this view, we can say the group has acted by consensus. The model assumes that members of society by and large agree on what is right and wrong, and that law is, in essence, the codification of social values, a mechanism of control that settles disputes that arise when some individuals stray too far from what is considered to be acceptable behavior. In Emile Durkheim's words, "We can...say that an act is criminal when it offends strong and defined states of the collective conscience."[9] Consensus theorists view society as a stable entity in which laws are created for the general good. Their function is to reconcile and to harmonize most of the interests that most of us accept, with the least amount of sacrifice.

However, some criminologists view the making of laws in a society from a different theoretical perspective. In their interpretation, known as the conflict approach, the criminal law expresses the values of the ruling class in a society, and the criminal justice system is a means of controlling the lower classes. Conflict theorists claim that a struggle for power is a far more basic feature of human existence than consensus. It is by means of power struggles that various interest groups manage to control lawmaking and law enforcement. Accordingly, the appropriate object of criminological investigation is not the violation of laws but the conflicts within society. Traditional historians of crime and criminal justice do not deny that throughout history there have been conflicts that needed resolution. Traditionalists claim that these differences have been resolved by consensus, while conflict theorists claim that the dominant group has ended the conflicts by imposing its power on the subjugated group. This difference in perspective marks one of the major criminological debates today, as we shall see in Chapter 8. It also permeates criminological discussion of who breaks the criminal laws and why.

The Breaking of Laws

Sutherland's definition of criminology refers to the task of investigating and explaining the pro-

Soccer Hooliganism: Beyond Public Tolerance

During the European Championship in Düsseldorf, West Germany, extra precautions were taken to avoid the invasion of English hooligans who have brought violence and death to their sport at home and abroad.

In an attempt to weed out known hooligans, every English ticket applicant was required to fill out a detailed application, giving travel plans and rooting interests. There were also checks at entry points to the European mainland.

Dutch hooliganism has become as well-developed in the last two decades as its counterpart in England, but the English have earned wider approbation for their despicable conduct ... after the May 29, 1985, horror at Heysel Stadium in Brussels, where Liverpool was playing Juventus of Turin, Italy, for the European club championship. Liverpool fans were considered largely responsible for a melee that left 39 dead and 450 injured when a wall collapsed under the weight of fans attempting to flee the riot.

In the wake of that tragedy, the Union of European Football Associations (UEFA) banned English club teams indefinitely from playing in any of the three tiers of European club championships contested every year. (The ban does not affect the national team.) That led the English football association to take antihooliganism measures at home, including the banning of alcohol in the stadiums, starting matches at 11:30 a.m. to limit drinking time before the matches, and separation of rival fans by seats left unsold. One club went so far as to bar visiting fans.

Hooliganism is not limited to a few countries, as evidenced by these recent incidents:

At a March 11 match in Libya between Malta and Libya, a fan brandishing a weapon caused a mass exodus that collapsed a wall, leaving 20 dead and 100 injured.

[At] an April 22 match in Zagreb between two Yugoslav club teams ...Zagreb police seized smoke bombs, firecrackers, knives, torches, and even two revolvers in searches before the game began. Despite that, the match was interrupted by firecrackers, smoke bombs, and flares thrown onto what the Yugoslav press called "a battlefield." There were 65 arrests.

A May 23 match between club teams in Nanchong, China, saw fans riot in protest over a referee's call, then stone police and visiting players and loot a hotel and police station. There were 135 injuries and 40 arrests.

After a May 27 match in Paris between two French club teams, several dozen "skinhead" fans attacked spectators with fists, feet, and tear gas, taking particular aim at blacks.

"I don't know whether there is more violence or more interest in reporting it," said Lode Walgrave, professor of juvenile criminology at the University of Louvain in Belgium.

He recently completed a report for the Belgian Government in which 306 Belgian league games were studied for incidents of fan violence. They produced 14 "heavy" incidents, in which "the aggressive meeting between two groups of opponents necessitated considerable deployment of police, resulting in arrests, injuries and so on."

The heavy incidents, according to Walgrave, "had no relation to what was happening on the field." One incident took place 25 miles from the stadium.

Hooligans have been generally identified as educationally deficient young bachelors who are frequently unemployed because the trades they once pursued (mining, for instance) provide fewer and fewer opportunities. Other studies have shown a surprising number to have steady jobs and families. Many hard-core hooligans have right-wing orientation and, as a natural consequence, are racist. Club teams in France, Holland, and England have many black stars, particularly from former African colonies of the countries involved.

"The right-wing feeling of the hooligans is visceral, not an elaborated ideology," Walgrave said. "The hooligans are attracted to the paramilitary image of many right-wing groups, which projects the macho image the hooligans like. These right-wing groups are, in some places, recruiting the hooligans to be their 'infantry' in demonstrations.

"Nationalistic impulses and racism are part of that picture. The racism has an ambivalence: a fan who doesn't like blacks will be sorry there are some on the club he roots for. On the other hand, he will say, 'All niggers aren't bad. Ours is an exception.' He feels the necessity of having these players for his club to win."

However complex the sociological and psychological causes of hooliganism may be, its effect is arrest, injury, or death.

Source: *C. J. International,* Vol. 4(6): 25, 1988.

cess of breaking laws. This may seem like a simple task, viewed from a purely legal perspective. A prosecutor, representing the law, is not interested in the fact that hundreds of people are walking on Main Street. But if one of those hundreds grabs a woman's purse and runs away with it, the prosecutor is interested, provided the police have brought the fact to the prosecutor's attention. What alerts the prosecutor is the fact that a law has been broken, that one of those hundreds of people on Main Street has turned from a law-abiding citizen into a lawbreaker. This event, if detected, sets in motion the legal process that ultimately will determine that someone is indeed a lawbreaker.

Sutherland, in positing that criminologists have to study the process of breaking laws, had much more in mind than the determination that someone has violated the criminal law. He was referring to the *process* of breaking laws. That process encompasses a series of events, perhaps starting at birth or even earlier, which result in the commission of crime by some people, and not by others. Let us analyze the following rather typical scenario: In the maximum security unit of a midwestern penitentiary is an inmate whom we shall call Jeff. He has been sentenced to life imprisonment, which in his case means that he will have to serve at least another twenty-five years on a felony murder conviction. He was one of three robbers who held up a check-cashing establishment. Another of the robbers killed the clerk.

Born in an inner-city ghetto, Jeff was the third child of an unwed mother. He had a succession of temporary "fathers." By age 12 he had run away from home—such as it was—for the first time, only to be brought back to his mother, who really did not care much whether he returned or not. He rarely went to school because, he said, "all the guys were bigger." After flunking two grades, at age 16 Jeff dropped out of school completely and simply hung around the street corners of his deteriorated, crime-ridden neighborhood. He had no job. He had no reason to go home, since usually no one was there. One night he was beaten up by members of a local gang. He joined a rival gang for protection, and soon began to feel proud of his membership in one of the toughest gangs in the neighborhood. Caught on one occasion

tampering with parking meters, and on another trying to steal a car radio, he was sentenced to two months in a county correctional institution for boys. By the age of 18 he had graduated from petty theft to armed robbery.

Many people reading the story of Jeff would conclude that he deserves what is coming to him, and that his fate should serve as a warning to others. Some would say that with his background, Jeff did not have a chance to turn into anything but a robber-killer. Some may even consider Jeff a folk hero who managed to survive for a while in a very tough world.

To the criminologist, such popular interpretations of Jeff's story do not explain the process of breaking laws in Sutherland's terms. Nor do these interpretations explain why people in general break this, that, or the other law. Sutherland demanded scientific rigor in researching and explaining the process of breaking laws. As we shall see (Parts II and III), scientists have thoroughly explored the story of Jeff, and of all other lawbreakers. Some scientists have researched the question of why some people who are inclined to do so engage in particular acts at particular times. They have demonstrated that opportunities to commit a crime play a great role in the decision to commit a crime. Opportunities consist simply of suitable targets inadequately protected. All that is required for a crime to be committed is a person motivated to offend in these circumstances. These claims are made by criminologists who explain crime in terms of two perspectives, called routine activities and rational choice. In our discussion of the many types of crime (Chapters 10–13) we use both a rational choice and a routine activities framework.

Criminologists, true to Sutherland's mandate, have also researched and explained the fundamental question: Why are some people prone to commit crime while others are not? Yet there is no agreement on the answer, because scientists have approached the question from different perspectives. Some have examined delinquents and criminals from a biological perspective in order to determine whether some human beings are constitutionally more prone than others to yield to opportunities to commit criminal acts. Are the genes to blame? the hormonal structure? the dietary patterns?

Others have explored the role played by the human mind and human emotions. What is it that affects the mind and the emotions in such a way as to make a person prone to crime? (Both of these approaches are discussed in Chapter 4.) Most contemporary criminologists look to such factors as economic and social conditions, which can produce strain among social groups, leading to lawbreaking (Chapter 5). Others point to many different types of subcultures committed to violent or illegal activities (Chapter 6). Another argument is that the motivation to commit crime is part of human nature. Consequently, some criminologists examine the ability of social groups and institutions to make their rules effective (Chapter 7). The findings of other researchers and scholars tend to demonstrate that lawbreaking depends less on what the offender does than on what society, including the criminal justice system, does to the offender (Chapter 8). This is the perspective of the labeling, conflict, and radical theorists, who had great influence on criminological thinking since the 1970s.

Up to this point, our emphasis has been on laws, in accordance with Sutherland's definition. But as we noted earlier, society also uses uncodified norms to govern its members: it uses customs. Some criminologists have argued that criminology is concerned only with lawmaking, lawbreaking, and reactions to lawbreaking, as Sutherland's definition seems to imply.[10] The overwhelming majority of criminologists, however, believe that criminology is concerned with the making and breaking of all norms, and with society's reactions to these activities. They have good reasons for taking this position. Most important, the difference between laws and customs is subject to constant change, and may vary from one state or country to another. What yesterday was only distasteful or morally repugnant may today be illegal as a result of legislative action. Criminologists are and must be interested in society's choices of all norms that regulate conduct. Making something that is distasteful into a crime may be counterproductive and detrimental to the social order. If everything deviant were to be made criminal, society would become very rigid. The more rigid a society, the more deviance, or behavior defined as violating social norms, is prohibited by law.

Jack D. Douglas and Frances C. Waksler have presented the continuum of deviance as a funnel (Figure 1.1). This funnel consists of definitions of deviance ranging from the most broad (a feeling that something is vaguely wrong, strange, peculiar) to the most narrow (a

The American People Finally Speak Up

FIGURE 1.1   The funnel of deviance

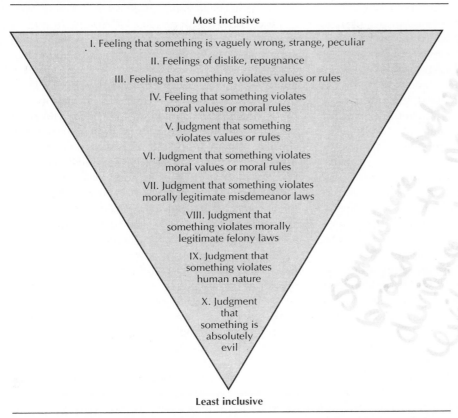

Most inclusive

I. Feeling that something is vaguely wrong, strange, peculiar

II. Feelings of dislike, repugnance

III. Feeling that something violates values or rules

IV. Feeling that something violates moral values or moral rules

V. Judgment that something violates values or rules

VI. Judgment that something violates moral values or moral rules

VII. Judgment that something violates morally legitimate misdemeanor laws

VIII. Judgment that something violates morally legitimate felony laws

IX. Judgment that something violates human nature

X. Judgment that something is absolutely evil

Least inclusive

Source: Adapted from Jack D. Douglas and Frances C. Waksler, *The Sociology of Deviance* (Boston: Little, Brown, 1982), p. 11.

judgment that something is absolutely evil). Somewhere between these two extremes, deviant behavior is made criminal; but the criminologist's interest in understanding the process of breaking of norms commences at the earliest point.[11]

The interest of criminologists in understanding the process of breaking a law or some social norm is tied to society's reaction to deviance, as every action invites reaction. The study of reactions to lawbreaking demonstrates that society has always tried to control or prevent norm breaking, whether by social policy or by revenge and retaliation.

Society's Reaction to the Breaking of Laws

Society's reaction to the breaking of laws is highly visible and seemingly omnipresent. The wayfarer of the Middle Ages entering a city had to pass the gallows, from which the bodies of the executed were swinging in the wind. At the city gate guardians would lower the drawbridge only during the daylight hours, eyeing the wayfarer suspiciously. The stocks and the pillory in front of the town hall warned dishonest vendors and pickpockets. Times have changed, but perhaps less than we think. Today penitentiaries and jails dot the countryside. Teams of work-release convicts clean the shoulders of highways under guard. Signs on posts proclaim "drug free school zone," and decals on doors announce that a "neighborhood crime watch" is at work. Police patrol cars are as visible as they are audible. These overt signs of society's concern about crime provide us with only a surface view of the large apparatus that society has created to deal with the breaking of laws. They tell us little of the vast amounts of research and policy making that have gone into the creation of this apparatus. True to Sutherland's mandate, criminologists have done much research on society's reaction to the breaking of laws, and much of the research has influenced policy making and legislation aimed at crime control. Such research has also revealed that society's reaction to lawbreaking has often been irrational, arbitrary, emotional, politically motivated, and counterproductive.

Criminological research on society's reaction to the breaking of laws began more recently than research on the causes of crime. It is more controversial, as it raises such questions as the objectivity of scientists, especially the danger that they are being co-opted by the power structure. Some criminologists assert that it is precisely the function of criminological research to assist the government in the prevention or repression of crime. Others insist that such a use of science only supports power structures that are corrupt. The position of most criminologists is somewhere between these extremes. In studying society's reaction to the breaking of laws, criminological researchers often bare inhumane and arbitrary practices and provide the data base and the ideas for the construction of humane, effective, and efficient crime control, both within and outside the criminal justice system.

The term "criminal justice system" is of relatively recent origin. It became popular only in 1967, with the report of the Task Force of the President's Commission on Law Enforcement and Administration of Justice: *The Challenge of Crime in a Free Society* (Chapter 14). The discovery that society's various ways of dealing with lawbreaking form a system was itself the result of criminological research. Further research into the functioning of the system and of its component parts, as well as of the operations of the many functionaries within the system, has provided many insights over the last few decades (Chapters 14–17). Scientists who study the functioning of the criminal justice system are frequently referred to as criminal justice specialists. This terminology suggests a separation between criminology and criminal justice. Such a separation is artificial. The two fields are closely interwoven, though their origins may differ.

Criminology has its roots in European scholarship, though it has undergone refinements, largely under the influence of American sociology. The discipline of criminal justice is a recent American innovation, unencumbered by European theory. The scholars of both disciplines use the same scientific research methods. They have received the same rigorous education and they pursue the same goals—those found in Sutherland's definition. Both fields rely on the cooperation of many other disciplines, including sociology, psychology, political science, law, management, and education.

The two fields are distinguished by the major focus of each. Criminology generally focuses on scientific studies of crime and criminality, whereas criminal justice focuses on scientific studies of decision-making processes, operations, and such justice-related concerns as the efficiency of the police, courts, and correctional systems, the just treatment of offenders, the needs of victims, and the effects of changes in sentencing philosophy. The interdependence of criminology and criminal justice is generally recognized.

In this book we analyze society's reaction to the breaking of laws through the operations of the criminal justice system. Our focus is on the findings of scientists who have studied the various sectors of the criminal justice system—the police, the courts, and the corrections system (Chapters 15–17)—and we shall preface this discussion with a description of the interaction of the three sectors as the process unfolds, from the report of a crime to the police to the disposition of the offender (Chapter 14).

The United States has well over fifty criminal justice systems—those of the fifty states and of the federal government, the District of Columbia, Puerto Rico, Guam, the Panama Canal Zone, and the military. They are very much akin to one another, all being based on constitutional principles and on the heritage of the common law, and all enjoy close working relationships. All were designed to cope with the problem of crime within their territories, on the assumption that crime is basically a local event calling for local responses. Crimes that have an interstate or international aspect are in the jurisdiction of federal authorities, and such offenses are prosecuted under the federal criminal code. Until fairly recently there was rarely any need to cooperate with foreign governments, as crime had few international connections. This situation changed drastically during the 1980s. Crime, like life itself, has become globalized, and our responses to the breaking of laws have inevitably extended beyond our local and national purviews.

THE GLOBAL APPROACH TO THE BREAKING OF LAWS

In the first three and a half decades after the end of World War II, from 1945 until the late 1970s, the countries of the world gradually became more interdependent. Commercial relations among countries increased. The jet age brought a huge increase in international travel and transport. Satellite communications facilitated public and private relationships.

Beginning in the 1980s, this process of internationalization accelerated sharply, as commercial statistics reveal:

- American purchases and sales of foreign stocks and bonds increased from $53 billion in 1980 to $595 billion in 1987.
- Purchases and sales of American securities by foreign investors increased from $198 billion in 1980 to $3,314.8 billion in 1987.
- Foreign assets in the United States increased from $40.9 billion in 1980 to $1,536 billion in 1987.

Such figures demonstrate the global linkage of most of the world's economies. As the Eastern European countries abandon or modify Marxist economic policies, their economies will become integrated with the European Economic Community (1992) and with those of the rest of the world.

The rapid integration of the world's economies has been facilitated by technology—the almost universal acceptance of computer networking, facsimile (fax) communications, TV networking—and by the easing of trade barriers and the proliferation of jet planes and air routes. These developments, which turned the world into what has been called a global village, have also had considerable negative consequences. As everything else in life became globalized, so did crime. The first criminal entrepreneurs to make use of the global market were the drug producers and traffickers (Chapter 13). Their worldwide operations affect every country, as producer, shipper, or consumer. The resulting problem of drug addiction in many countries affects their crime rates, largely because addicts tend to commit property crimes to support their habit; or, as research demonstrates, they engage in drug trafficking, thus contributing to the growth of the illegitimate market. Distributors turn to violent crime in order to protect or expand their markets. These seemingly local crime problems are simply the end products of the international illegal drug economy, which turns local crimes into international criminological events. Money laundering—the conversion of drug profits into "clean" money by transfer through unmarked accounts in some foreign countries—is yet another aspect of global criminality (Chapter 12).

Other forms of international crime include terrorism, maritime crime (including marine insurance fraud), ocean pollution through criminal negligence, criminal depletion of marine life, and modern forms of piracy (Chapters 10–12). Many forms of economic criminality became globalized with the internationalization of trade and commerce.

Other problems of international dimensions challenge criminological research. An industrial catastrophe or mismanagement in any one country may cause multiple deaths, destroy property, and damage the environment in surrounding countries and the entire world. Such catastrophes may be caused by criminal negligence or by avoidance or circumvention of protective laws. Often international entrepreneurs have influenced legislation in the countries of their operations so that they can engage in hazardous activities that are prohibited in other countries.

The criminal justice systems of individual countries were not designed to cope with criminal activities that extend beyond their borders or threaten harm to the world. There is no global criminal justice system. Though the interna-

WINDOW TO THE WORLD

Worldwide Crime-Control Efforts

Criminal justice officials from twenty-three countries met for a strategy planning session at the United Nations Asia and Far East Institute for the Prevention of Crime and the Treatment of Offenders (UNAFEI), at Fuchu, Tokyo, Japan, in March 1990. The network of United Nations crime-prevention institutes includes, besides UNAFEI, those located in San José, Costa Rica (for Latin America); Helsinki, Finland (for Europe); Kampala, Uganda (for

Africa); an affiliated institute in Riyadh, Saudi Arabia (for Islamic countries); and a worldwide research center in Rome, Italy. The work of the United Nations Secretariat in matters of crime prevention is carried out by the Crime Prevention and Criminal Justice Branch, located in Vienna, Austria.

The United Nations infrastructure in crime prevention and control has no legislative powers. But it monitors crime trends

(through world crime surveys conducted every five years) and developments in crime-control policies through-out the world; creates standards and guidelines for crime prevention and criminal justice based on the experiences of all nations; provides technical assistance to member states that request it; promotes sound, effective, and humane strategies for crime prevention and criminal justice; and provides a worldwide forum for international crime-control efforts. Every five years all member states participate at the United Nations Congress for the Prevention of Crime and the Treatment of Offenders, at which major policy decisions are made and major standards and guidelines, or draft conventions, are agreed upon. Among all United Nations activities, the efforts aimed at worldwide crime control have been among the most successful and least politically controversial.

tional community, through various United Nations agencies, has made substantial progress in harmonizing trade laws and facilitating international commerce, it has invested little money and effort in the task of dealing with global crime. Until recently, top-level policy makers and government officials were not fully alert to the threat that international crime poses for every country. Criminologists likewise have tended to view crime as a local or national rather than an international problem. These attitudes are changing. International comparative criminological research, until recently regarded as a luxury or curiosity, is now considered a ne-

cessity. The research literature on comparative and international aspects of lawmaking, lawbreaking, and needed responses to transnational crime is increasing rapidly. Many new journals have been added to the few that traditionally have been devoted to comparative criminology. The American Society of Criminology has established a very active international division. Research produced by the growing number of criminologists in America and abroad who deal with aspects of international and comparative criminology is likely to play a major role in responses to globalized crime.

REVIEW

Very little happens on earth without criminological implications. Yet criminology, as a science, is only a century old. Edwin H. Sutherland provided the most widely accepted definition of criminology: "the body of knowledge regarding crime as a social phenomenon. It includes within its scope the process of making laws, of breaking laws, and of reacting toward the breaking of laws."

In reviewing the history of some of the earliest criminal laws (namely those of the ancient Romans, to whom contemporary continental law is traceable, and to those of the Germanic tribes, to which the Anglo-American legal system is traceable), it becomes clear that custom often becomes law. In writing about history, it is necessary to distinguish between two conflicting views of interpreting the history of criminal law: the consensus view, which regards lawmaking as the result of communal consensus as to what is to be prohibited; and the conflict view, according to which laws are imposed by those with power on those without power.

The breaking of laws (to which subject much of this book will be devoted) is not merely a formal act that may lead to arrest and prosecution, but instead it is an intricate process by which some people violate some laws under some circumstances. Many disciplines are contributing to an understanding of the process of breaking laws or other norms. As yet there is no consensus on why people become criminals. While society has always reacted to lawbreaking (often quite brutally in the Middle Ages), the scientific study of lawbreaking is of very recent origin. Today criminologists analyze the existing methods and procedures that society uses in reacting to crime; they evaluate the success or failure of such methods; and on the basis of such research, they propose more effective and humane ways of controlling crime. Above all, criminologists have discovered that the various organs society has created to deal with lawbreaking constitute a system which, like any other system, can be made more efficient. Such research depends on the availability of a variety of data, especially statistics. The gathering and use of statistics on crime and criminal justice is itself a primary task of criminologists.

The province of criminology is the entire world. Every aspect of life on earth has become increasingly globalized in recent years as a result of the rapid advances in technology. Crime likewise has become globalized. Criminals have become, in fact, global entrepreneurs; and crime respects no international borders, whether it be the drug trade, terrorism, money laundering, or the criminal destruction of the environment. Consequently, society's reaction to the breaking of laws is becoming rapidly globalized. Therefore, this text will take an international view of crime and criminal justice.

NOTES

1. Raffaele Garofalo, *Criminologia* (Naples, 1885), published in English as *Criminology*, trans. Robert W. Millar (Boston: Little, Brown, 1914; rpt. Montclair, N.J.: Patterson Smith, 1968).

2. Paul Topinard, "L'Anthropologie criminelle," *Revue d'anthropologie* 2 (1887).

3. Edwin H. Sutherland, *Principles of Criminology*, 4th ed. (Philadelphia: Lippincott, 1947).

4. Garofalo, *Criminologia*, p. 5.

5. Tacitus, *Germania*, 1st century A.D., as quoted in Gerhard O. W. Mueller, "Tort, Crime and the Primitive," *Journal of Criminal Law, Criminology, and Police Science* 43 (1955): 303–310.

6. Allan Chester Johnson, Paul Robinson-Norton, and Frank Card Bourne, *Ancient Roman Statutes* (Austin: University of Texas Press, 1961), pp. 9–13.

7. Mueller, "Tort, Crime and the Primitive," p. 311.

8. Ibid., p. 312. Some writers refer to the latter

version of the law of wrongs as *fas* (religious) criminal law, while the remainder of the law of wrongs, subject to compensation or even punitive damages (a multiple of the injury caused), is referred to as *jus* (secular) criminal law.

9. Emile Durkheim, *Rules of Sociological Method,* trans. S. A. Solaway and J. H. Mueller (Glencoe, Ill.: Free Press, 1958), p. 64.

10. Paul W. Tappan, *Crime, Justice and Correction* (New York: McGraw-Hill, 1960). See also Jerome Michael and Mortimer J. Adler, *Crime, Law and Social Science* (New York: Harcourt Brace, 1933).

11. Jack D. Douglas and Frances C. Waksler, *The Sociology of Deviance* (Boston: Little, Brown, 1982).

2

MEASURING CRIME AND CRIMINAL BEHAVIOR PATTERNS

In one of many versions of Aesop's fable about the three blind men and the elephant, a circus comes to town, and the residents of a home for the blind are invited to "experience" an elephant. When one blind man is led to the elephant, he touches one of the beast's legs. He feels its size and shape. Another man chances to reach the tail, and still another feels the trunk. Back at their residence they hotly argue about the nature of the beast. Says the first man, "An elephant is obviously like the trunk of a tree." "No," says the second, "it's like a rope." "You're both wrong," says the third. "An elephant is like a big snake." All three blind men are partly right, for each has described the part of the beast he has touched.

The assessment of the nature and extent of crime often suffers from the same shortcomings as the three blind men's assessments of the elephant. Researcher *A* may make assessments on the basis of arrest records. Researcher *B* may rely on conviction rates to describe crime, while researcher *C* may use the number of convicts serving prison sentences. None of the researchers, however, may be in a position to assess fully the nature and extent of crime. Each is limited by the kinds of data collected.

Questions about how researchers measure crime and what those measurements reveal about the nature and extent of crime are among the most important issues of contemporary criminology. After we look at the objectives and methods of collecting information, we shall consider the limitations of the three sources of information that are used most frequently by criminologists to estimate the nature and extent of crime in the United States. We shall then explore the measurement of the characteristics of crimes, criminals, and victims.

MEASURING CRIME

Objectives of Measurement

There are three major reasons for measuring characteristics of crimes, criminals, and victims. First of all, researchers need to collect and analyze information in order to test theories about why people commit crime. A **theory** is a systematic set of principles that explain how two or more phenomena are related. One criminologist might record the kinds of offenses committed by offenders of different ages; another might count the number of crimes committed at different times of the year. But without ordering these observations in a meaningful way, without a theory, scientists would be limited in their ability to predict the future.

One theory of crime causation, for example, is that high crime rates may result if there is wide disparity between people's goals and the means available to them for reaching those goals. Some people who lack legitimate opportunities to achieve their goals try to reach them through criminal means. To test this theory, researchers might begin with the **hypothesis**—a testable proposition that describes how two or more factors are related—that lower-class individuals engage in more serious crimes and do so more frequently than middle-class individuals. (See Social Class and Crime later in this chapter.) Next they would collect facts, observations, and other pertinent information—called **data**—on the criminal behavior of both lower-class individuals and middle-class individuals. A finding that lower-class persons commit more crime than middle-class persons would lend support to the theory that people commit crimes because they do not have legitimate means, such as an adequate income, to reach their goals. The types of data that are collected and the way they are collected are crucial to the research process. Criminologists analyze these data and use their findings to support or refute theories. In Part II we shall examine several theories (including the one outlined briefly above) advanced to explain why people commit crime, and we shall see how these theories have been tested.

The second objective of measurement is to enhance our knowledge of the characteristics of various types of offenses. Why are some offenses more likely to be committed than others? What are the situational factors, such as time of day or type of place, that influence their commission? Experts have argued that this is the kind of information that is needed if we are to prevent crime and develop strategies to control it. (Part III deals with this subject.)

Measurement has a third major objective. Criminal justice agencies depend on certain kinds of information for daily operations and for anticipating future needs. Many questions must be answered. How many persons flow through county jails? How many will receive prison sentences? Besides the questions that deal with the day-to-day functioning of the system (number of beds, distribution and hiring of personnel, etc.), there are many other questions that affect legislative and policy decisions. If, for instance, a law changes in a given area, what effect does the change have on the amount of crime committed? Consider legislation on the death penalty. Some people claim that homicides decrease when laws establishing a death penalty are enacted. Others claim that they make no difference. Does fear of crime go down if we put more police officers in a neighborhood? Or does drug smuggling move to another entry point if old access routes are cut off? These and other potential changes need to be evaluated—and evaluations require measurement.

Given the importance of data for research, policy making, and the daily operation and planning of the criminal justice system, criminologists have been working to perfect data collection techniques. Through the years these methods have become increasingly more sophisticated.

Methods of Collecting Data

Depending on what questions they are asking, criminologists can and do collect their data in a variety of ways. One of the most widely used methods is survey research. This is a cost-effective method of measuring characteristics of both large and small groups. Experiments are used for a different purpose. They are studies in which groups of people are treated in different ways so as to determine the effects of the treatment. Experimental studies are difficult and costly to conduct and for that reason they are used infrequently, but they have been, and still are, an important means of collecting data on crime. Participant observation is quite different from either the survey or the experiment. This technique involves the direct participation of the researcher in the activities of the people who are the subjects of the research. A variation of this technique is nonparticipant observation, in which the researcher collects data without joining in the activity observed. Another way to collect information about crime, and especially about criminal careers, is to examine in detail the biographical and autobiographical accounts of individual offenders (the case study method). Other data can be found in a wide variety of sources, but the most frequently used sources are statistics compiled by government agencies and private foundations. Familiarity with the sources of data and the methods used to gather data will help in understanding the studies we will be discussing throughout this book. The facts and observations that researchers gather by their own measurements for the purpose of a particular study are **primary data.** Those they find in government sources, or data that were previously collected for a different investigation, are **secondary data.**

Surveys   Many people are familiar with the use of surveys in public opinion polls, marketing research, and election-prediction studies. Criminologists, too, use surveys to obtain quantitative data. A **survey** is the systematic collection of answers to questions that are asked of respondents in questionnaires or interviews; interviews may be conducted face to face or by telephone. Generally, surveys are used to gather information about the attitudes, characteristics, or behavior of a large group of persons. Such groups are called the **population** of the survey. Typical surveys conducted by criminologists measure the amount of crime, attitudes toward police or toward the sentencing of dangerous offenders, assessment of drug abuse and fear of crime, and so forth.

Instead of interviewing the total population that the researchers want to study, most researchers interview a selected, representative subset of that population—a **sample.** If a sample is carefully drawn, researchers are able to generalize their results from the sample to the population. Many samples are determined by random selection in a way that ensures that each person in the population to be studied has an equal chance of being selected. Such a sample is called a **random sample.** Thus one might study the relationship between drug abuse and high school grades in the United States by interviewing every tenth high school student in the country rather than interviewing them all.

While surveys are a cost-effective method of measurement, they have limitations. If the drug study of high school students, for example, were done one time only (a **cross-sectional study**), the finding of a relationship between drug use and poor grades would not tell us whether drug use caused bad grades, whether students with bad grades turned to drugs, or whether bad grades and drug taking result from some other factor, such as family ties. **Longitudinal studies,** by contrast, focus on a particular group repeatedly over a period of time.

Experiments   The experimental research technique is used primarily in the physical and biological sciences, as well as in the social sciences. In an **experiment,** an investigator introduces a change into a process and makes measurements or observations in order to evaluate the effects of the change. Through experimentation, scientists test their hypotheses about how two or more **variables** (factors that may change) are related to each other. The basic model for an experiment involves changing one variable, keeping all other factors the same (*controlling* them, or holding them *constant*), and observing the effect of that change on another variable. If you change one variable while keeping all other factors constant and then find that another variable changes as well, you may safely assume that the change in the second variable was caused by the change in the first.

Most experiments are done in laboratories, but it is possible to do them in real-world (field) settings. Such a **field experiment** was done at New Jersey's Rahway State Prison to test the hypothesis that if youngsters were shown the horrors of prison, they would not commit crimes. (The object was to scare young people out of crime; hence the project became known as the "Scared Straight!" project.) First, several agencies were asked to propose male juveniles for the experiment. All the juveniles proposed for the pool were given a series of tests to determine their attitudes toward crime, punishment, prison, the police, and so forth. Afterward some of the juveniles were randomly assigned to the experimental group, which would actually go to the prison, and the rest to a control group, which would not go. After the experimental group had participated in the program, both groups were again given the same attitude tests to find out if the prison experience had changed the attitudes of the experimental group. Six months later the juvenile records of the two groups were checked to find out how many of the youths in both the experimental and control groups had committed crimes during the six-month period. Had fewer of the youngsters who had supposedly been "scared straight" been arrested than those who had not made the visit? No, according to James Finckenauer's analysis. In fact, many more of the boys in the experimental group had been arrested than boys in the control group.[1]

Experiments in the real world are costly and difficult to carry out, but they have the advantage of increasing scientists' ability to establish cause and effect. Researchers who engage in participant and nonparticipant observation have different goals. These methods provide detailed descriptions of life as it actually is lived—in prisons, gangs, and other settings.

Participant and nonparticipant observation Observation is the most direct means of studying behavior. Investigators may play a variety of roles in observing social situations. When they engage in **nonparticipant observation,** they do not join in the activities of the groups they are studying. They simply observe the activities in everyday settings and record what they see. A researcher may sit in a police station, for example, recording what happens as suspects are brought in. Investigators who engage in **participant observation,** however, gather information through involvement in the social life of the group they are studying—they take part in many of the group's activities in order to gain acceptance, but generally make clear the purpose of their participation. Anne

Campbell, a criminologist who spent two years as a participant observer of the lifestyles of girl gang members, explains:

> My efforts to meet female gang members began with an introduction through the New York City Police Department's Gang Crimes Unit. Through one of their plain-clothes gang liaison officers, John Galea, I was introduced first to the male gang members of a number of Brooklyn gangs. On being reassured that I "only" wanted to talk to the female members, the male leaders gave their OK and I made arrangements to meet with the girls' leaders or "godmothers." At first they were guarded in their disclosures to me. They asked a lot about my life, my background and my reasons for wanting to hang out with them. Like most of us, however, they enjoyed talking about themselves and over the period of six months that I spent with each of three female gangs they opened up a good deal—sitting in their kitchens, standing on the stoops in the evenings or socializing at parties with allied gangs.[2]

Observations of groups in their natural setting afford the researcher insights into behavior and attitudes that cannot be obtained through such techniques as surveys and experiments. Another technique that is used to examine in detail the experiences of offenders is the case study.

Case study A **case study** is an analysis of all pertinent aspects of one unit of study, such as an individual, an institution, a group, or a community. The sources of information are such documents as life histories, biographies, diaries, journals, letters, and other records. A classic demonstration of criminologists' use of the case study method is found in Edwin Sutherland's *The Professional Thief,* based on interviews with a professional thief (see page 27). Sutherland demonstrates the kind of detailed information that a researcher can get using this technique. Sutherland learned about the relationship between amateur and professional thieves, how thieves communicate, how they determine whether to trust each other, and the process of networking. From discussions with the thief and an analysis of his writings on topics selected by the researcher, Sutherland was

CRIMINOLOGICAL FOCUS

The Indirect Language of Professional Thieves

Sometimes a professional thief is greatly embarrassed when he appears in public with an amateur who does not understand [the] indirect language of the professional thieves. A professional thief reported the following instance:

I was eating supper in a cafeteria with an occasional thief and drug addict who was a student in a law school. Two coppers were sitting at another table near by. The occasional thief had selected our table and had not recognized them as coppers. They were not in uniform, but a uniform is not needed to advertise to a professional that a copper is a copper. They could not possibly have been anything else. My friend said loud enough so the coppers could hear, "Did you hear what Jerry Myers got?" I knew alright that Jerry got four years, but I was not going to let the coppers know that we were talking about anyone who had received a bit, and I had to hush the youngster up. I could not say, "Nix!" as a thief might have said if the coppers had not been able to hear, for that word in itself would have informed the coppers that we were worth watching, and besides my friend would not have understood what the word meant in that connection. So I said, "I understand the doctor said he got tonsilitis." A professional thief would have sensed danger at once and would have carried on along that line, but my friend thought I must be hard of hearing or else a fool and he started in again, "No, I mean..." but I kicked him under the table and butted in again with some more information about tonsilitis. The police were watching us carefully, and I could not office (warn) my partner by moving my eyes toward them. As soon as I hesitated for a moment on the tonsilitis, he started in again on what Jerry got, so I had to get up and go to the counter for something more to eat. When I returned I picked up his book on Conveyances and looked at it a moment and then asked, "Have you seen the new book on Abnormal Psychology by Dr. Oglesby?" The policemen, who had finished eating some time before, immediately got up and reached for their hats. I nudged my partner to look at them, and as they stretched up you could see that each had a revolver in a holster. They doubtless went away thinking, "Just a couple of harmless university students or professors." My partner now understood why I had interrupted him and skinned his shins, and he asked, "Why didn't you tell me they were here?" I had told him a half-dozen times in language any professional thief would have understood but which he could not understand, principally because he did not have the attitude of suspicion which is the foundation of the indirect method of conversation, but also because he did not give me credit for good sense.

Language is not in itself a sufficient means of determining whether a person is trustworthy, for some people in the underworld are stool pigeons and some outsiders learn some of the language. Another method is by finding out what people the stranger knows. If he belongs to the underworld, he will know some of the important people in the underworld of Chicago, Baltimore, Kansas City, or some other city. It will not take long until a professional thief will find mutual acquaintances if the stranger really is a professional. What he knows about these mutual acquaintances will show whether he is trustworthy. If he knows someone in the local community, it is possible to ask this one about the stranger. He will either say, "He is alright" or else, "He is no good." That locates him so far as you are concerned. In the underworld a person's reputation quickly spreads to everyone, just as does everything that is done. There is no underworld newspaper, but there is complete communication among the members so that everyone knows about everyone else in his particular part of the underworld.

Source: Edwin H. Sutherland, *The Professional Thief* (Chicago: University of Chicago Press, 1937), pp. 19–21.

WINDOW TO THE WORLD

Measuring World Crime

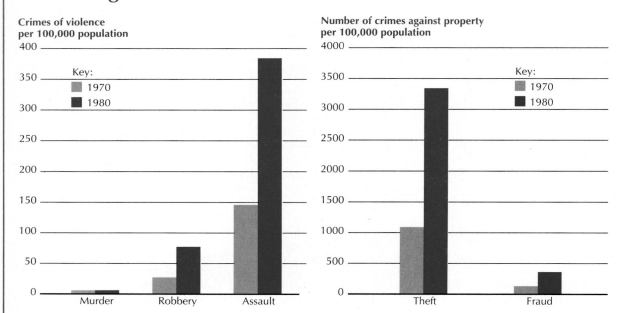

Crimes of violence per 100,000 population

Key:
▪ 1970
■ 1980

(Murder, Robbery, Assault)

Number of crimes against property per 100,000 population

Key:
▪ 1970
■ 1980

(Theft, Fraud)

We live in an age in which it has become necessary to measure everything. How much fuel is the population of the world consuming? How much fuel is available? When will the lights go out? At what rate is the world's population growing? How much more food can be produced to feed this growing population? When will starvation begin? (It has already.) All of these questions and their answers have worldwide significance. Crime is no exception. Crime has become as globalized as food shortages or the greenhouse effect that threatens our environment.

Researchers at the United Nations and elsewhere have undertaken the enormous task of measuring crime around the world, quantifying responses to crime, and measuring the relation-

able to draw several conclusions that other techniques of gathering data would not have yielded. For instance, a person is not a "professional thief" unless he is recognized as such by other professional thieves. Training by professional thieves is necessary for the development of the skills, attitudes, and connections required in the "profession."[3] One of the drawbacks of the case study method is that the information given by the subject may be biased or wrong, and by its nature is limited. For these reasons it is difficult to generalize from one person's story to other persons—in this instance, to all professional thieves.

Using available data in research   Besides collecting their own data by surveys, experiments, observation, and case study, researchers often depend on secondary data collected by private and public organizations for their own purposes. The police, the courts, and corrections

ships between crime and crime prevention strategies, formal and informal. But how can Nepalese crime be compared with American crime, Chinese crime with Norwegian crime? Suppose we wanted to compare transportation worldwide. How do one-half billion bicycles in China compare with ten thousand camels in Chad, ten thousand boats in Tonga, and twenty million automobiles in Germany? Crime differs almost as much under the laws of different nations. A formula had to be found to group the crimes of all nations into overall categories and then to count these crimes at a given stage in the criminal justice process (for example, at the stage of arrest).

In a crude manner this formula was finally achieved, and the United Nations published the first-world crime survey in 1977, based on the statistics of 64 countries for the years 1970 to 1975 (United Nations, *Report of the Secretary General on Crime Prevention and Control*, A/32/199, of 22 September 1977). A somewhat more sophisticated second-world crime survey, covering the years 1976 to 1980, was published in 1985 (United Nations, *Second United Nations Survey on Crime Trends, Operations of Criminal Justice Systems and Crime Prevention Strategies*, A/CONF. 121/18, of 30 May 1985). The third-world crime survey, which has not yet been released, will cover the years 1981 to 1985.

These surveys have demonstrated significant differences between the crime rates and trends of developed countries (proportionately more property crime) and developing countries (proportionately more violent crime), and between countries of various regions; thus, the socialist countries of Eastern Europe had significantly less street crime than the Western developed countries. The first two world crime surveys also showed that crime has been increasing significantly around the world, as the above graphs from the second-world crime survey demonstrate. Above all, beyond the importance of the specific data collected, researchers have learned that it is, indeed, possible to collect and compare statistics on a worldwide basis.

officials, for example, need to know the number of persons passing through the criminal justice system at various points in order to carry out day-to-day administrative tasks and to plan for the future. It is not always feasible to collect new data for a research project, nor is it necessary to do so when such vast amounts of relevant information are already available.

To study the relationship between crime and such a variable as income or a single-parent family, one might make use of the Uniform Crime Reports (national police statistics, discussed below), together with information found in the reports of the Bureau of the Census. Various other agencies, among them the Federal Bureau of Prisons, the Drug Enforcement Agency, the Treasury Department, and the Labor Department, are also excellent sources of statistics that are useful to criminologists. At the international level, United Nations world crime surveys contain information on crime,

criminals, and criminal justice systems in countries on all continents.

Researchers who use available data can save a great deal of time and expense. However, they have to exercise caution in fitting secondary data, not collected for the purpose of a particular study, into their research. Many official records are incomplete or have been collected in such a way as to make them inadequate for the research. It is also frequently difficult to gain permission to use agency data that are not open to the public because of a concern about confidentiality.

Ethics and the Researcher

In the course of their research, criminologists encounter many issues that call for evaluation on ethical grounds. Chief among such issues is that of confidentiality. Consider the dilemma faced by a group of researchers in the late

1960s. In interviewing a sample of 9,954 boys born in 1945, the team collected extensive self-reported criminal histories of offenses the boys had committed before and after they turned 18. Among the findings were four unreported homicides and seventy-five rapes. The researchers experienced at least two reactions to this information. They were naturally excited about capturing such interesting data. These findings supported the hypothesis of "hidden" delinquency (discussed below). More important, the researchers had feelings of grave concern. They faced ethical questions as to how they should handle their findings:

- Should the results of these interviews be published?
- Could the failure of the research staff to disclose names be considered the crime of "obstructing justice"?
- Does an obligation to society as a whole to release the names of the offenders transcend a researcher's obligation to safeguard a subject's confidentiality?
- What is the best response to a demand by the police, a district attorney, or a court for the researcher's files containing the subjects' names?
- Should criminologists be immune to prosecution for their failure to disclose the names of their subjects?
- Is it possible to develop a technique that can ensure against the identification of a subject in a research file?[4]

Such questions have few clear-cut answers, and fortunately most researchers never run into these issues. When they do so, however, they can now rely on standards that have been instituted to guide ethical human experimentation. Human experimentation review committees at most universities and government agencies check all proposals for research projects to ensure the protection of human subjects. In addition, researchers are required to inform their subjects about the nature of the study and to obtain their written and informed agreement to participate in it.

Despite researchers' heightened awareness of the ethical issues involved in human experi-

mentation—particularly in correctional institutions, where coercion is difficult to avoid—the field of criminology has not yet adopted a formal code of ethics. Some members of the discipline are arguing in favor of one. Frank Hagan, for example, has suggested that the code include guidelines on honoring commitments made to respondents, avoiding procedures that might harm subjects, exercising integrity in the performance and reporting of research, and protecting confidentiality.[5] In the end, however, as Seth Bloomberg and Leslie Wilkins have noted, "the responsibility for safeguarding human subjects ultimately rests with the researcher.... A code of ethics may provide useful guidelines, but it will not relieve the scientist of moral choice."[6]

THE NATURE AND EXTENT OF CRIME

As we have seen, criminologists gather their information in many ways. The methods they choose depend on the questions they want to answer. To estimate the nature and extent of crime in the United States, they rely primarily on data compiled by the police; on the National Crime Survey, which measures crime through reports by victims; and on various self-report surveys, which ask individuals about criminal acts they have committed, whether or not these acts have come to the attention of the authorities.

Police Statistics

In 1924 the director of the Bureau of Investigation, J. Edgar Hoover, initiated a campaign to make the bureau responsible for gathering national statistics. With support from the American Bar Association (ABA) and the International Association of Chiefs of Police (IACP), the House of Representatives in 1930 passed a bill authorizing the bureau (later renamed the Federal Bureau of Investigation, or FBI) to collect data on the number of crimes known to the police. These data are compiled into reports called the Uniform Crime Reports (UCR). At present approximately 16,000 city, county, and state law enforcement agencies, representing 97 percent of the total population, voluntarily contribute information on crimes brought to their attention. If the police verify that a crime has been committed, that crime goes into the report, whether or not an arrest has been made. Reporting agencies send data monthly on offenses in twenty-nine categories.

Part I and Part II offenses The UCR divide offenses into two major categories: Part I and Part II. Part I offenses include eight crimes, which are aggregated as crimes against the person (criminal homicide, forcible rape, robbery, and aggravated assault) and crimes against property (burglary, larceny-theft, motor vehicle theft, and arson). Collectively, Part I offenses are called **Index crimes.** Because they are serious, these crimes tend to be reported to the police more reliably than others, and therefore can be used in combination as an index, or indicator, of changes in crime over time. All other offenses, except traffic violations, are Part II crimes. These twenty-one crimes include fraud, embezzlement, weapons offenses, vandalism, and simple assaults.

Crime rates To analyze crime data, experts frequently present them as crime rates. Crime rates are computed by the following formula:

$$\text{Crime rate} = \frac{\text{Number of reported crimes}}{\text{Total population}} \times 100{,}000$$

Crime rates may be computed for groups of offenses (such as the Index crimes or crimes against the person) or for specific offenses (such as homicide). If we say, for example, that the homicide rate is 10.2, we mean that there were 10.2 homicides for every 100,000 persons in the population under consideration (total U.S. population, say, or all males in the United States). Expressing the amount of crime in terms of rates shows whether an increase or decrease in crime results from a change in population or a change in the amount of crime committed.

In addition to data on reported crimes, the UCR include the number of offenses "cleared by arrest." Crimes may be cleared in one of two ways: first by the arrest, charging, and turning over to the courts of at least one person for prosecution or second by disposition of a case when an arrest is not possible, as when the suspect has died or fled the jurisdiction. Besides "reported crime" and "crimes cleared by arrest," the reports contain extensive data on characteristics of crimes (such as geographical location, time, and place), characteristics of criminals (such as sex, age, and race), and distribution of law enforcement personnel. We shall look at the characteristics of crime and criminals in more detail shortly. But before we make use of these statistics, we must recognize their limitations.

Limitations of the Uniform Crime Reports Despite the fact that the UCR are among the main sources of crime statistics, their value for research has been questioned. The criticisms deal with methodological problems and reporting practices. Some scholars argue, for example, that figures on reported crime are of limited usefulness in those categories in which as much as 75 percent of crime is not reported. These statistics present the amount of crime known to law enforcement agencies, but they do not tell us how many crimes have actually been committed. Another serious limitation is the fact that when several crimes are committed in one event, only the most serious offense is included in the UCR; the others go unreported. At the same time, when certain other crimes are committed, each individual act is counted as a separate offense. If a person robs a group of six people, for example, the UCR list one robbery. But if a person assaults six people, the UCR list six assaults. The UCR data are further obscured by the fact that they do not differentiate between completed acts and attempted acts.

Police reports to the FBI are voluntary and vary in accuracy. In a study conducted on behalf of the Police Foundation, Lawrence Sherman and Barry Glick found that while the UCR require arrests to be recorded even if a suspect is released without a formal charge, all 196 departments surveyed recorded the arrest only after a formal booking procedure.[7] In ad-

dition, for political reasons police departments may desire to improve their image by showing that their crime rate has either declined (the streets are safer) or risen (justifying a crackdown on, say, prostitution).[8] Institution of new record-keeping procedures can also create significant changes (the New York robbery rate appeared to increase 400 percent in one year).[9] Many fluctuations in crime rates may therefore be attributable to events other than changes in the actual numbers of crimes committed.

Finally, the UCR data suffer from several omissions. Many arsons go unreported because not all fire departments report to the UCR.[10] Federal cases, too, go unlisted. Most white-collar offenses are omitted because they are reported not to the police but to regulatory authorities, such as the Securities and Exchange Commission and the Federal Trade Commission.[11]

To address some of these limitations in the UCR, the law enforcement community (including the International Association of Chiefs of Police, the National Sheriffs' Association, and the state-level UCR programs) has been working with the FBI on a revised UCR program. The establishment of the National Incident-Based Reporting System (NIBRS) marks the first attempt to improve the collection of crime data. The NIBRS views each crime as an "incident" and records vital information about the offender, victim, property, arrest, and so forth. Reporting standards have been expanded to include fifty-two items of information about crimes in twenty-two categories.

Official statistics gathered from law enforcement agencies provide us with the information available on the crimes actually investigated and reported by these agencies. But not all crimes appear in police statistics. In order for a criminal act to be "known to the police," the act first must be "perceived" by an individual (the car is not in the garage where it was left). It must then be "defined" or "classified" as something that places it within the purview of the criminal justice system (a theft has taken place), and it must be "reported" to the police. Once the police are notified, they classify it and often "redefine" what may have taken place before "recording" the act as a crime known to the police (Figure 2.1). Information about criminal acts may be lost at any point along this processing route, and many crimes are never discovered to begin with. To learn more about the gap between recorded and unrecorded incidents of crime ("the dark figure of crime," it has been

FIGURE 2.1 The processes of societal reaction to crime and recording by police

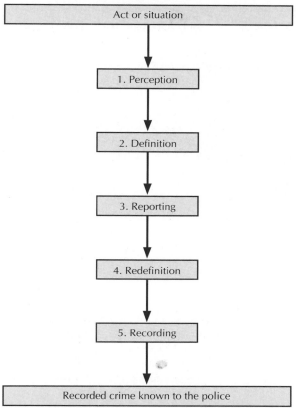

Source: R. F. Sparks, H. G. Genn, and D. J. Dodd, *Surveying Victims: A Study of the Measurement of Criminal Victimization, Perceptions of Crime, and Attitudes to Criminal Justice* (Chichester, Eng.: Wiley, 1977), p. 6.

called), criminologists rely on victimization surveys and self-report studies.

Victimization Surveys

Victimization surveys measure the extent of crime by interviewing individuals about their experiences as victims. The Bureau of the Census, in cooperation with the Bureau of Justice Statistics, collects information annually about persons and households that have been victimized (Table 2.1).[12] The report is called the National Crime Survey (NCS). Researchers for the NCS estimate the total number of crimes committed by asking respondents from a national sample of approximately 60,000 households,

representing 135,000 persons over the age of 12 (parental permission is needed for those below 14 years old), about their experiences as victims during a specific time period. Interviewers visit (or sometimes telephone) the homes selected for the sample. Each housing unit remains in the sample for three years. Every six months 10,000 households are rotated out of the sample and replaced by a new group.

Types of information collected The NCS measures the extent of victimization by rape, robbery, assault, larceny, burglary, and motor vehicle theft. Note that two of the UCR Part I offenses—criminal homicide and arson—are not included. Homicide is omitted because the NCS covers only crimes whose victims can be interviewed. The designers of the survey also decided to omit arson, a relative newcomer to the UCR, because measuring it with some validity by means of a victimization survey was deemed to be too difficult. Part II offenses have been excluded altogether because many of them are considered victimless (prostitution, vagrancy, drug abuse, drunkenness) or because victims are willing participants (gambling, con games) or do not know they have been victimized (forgery, fraud). The survey covers characteristics of crimes such as time and place of occurrence, number of offenders, use of weapons, economic loss, and time lost from work; characteristics of victims, such as sex, age, race, ethnicity, marital status, household composition, and educational attainment; perceived characteristics of offenders, such as age, sex, and race; circumstances surrounding the offenses and their effects, such as financial loss and injury; and patterns of police reporting, such as rates of reporting and reasons for reporting and for not reporting.

Limitations of victimization surveys While victimization surveys give us information about crimes that are not reported to the police, these data, too, have significant limitations. The NCS covers crimes in a more limited way than the UCR; the NCS includes only six offenses, whereas there are eight offenses in Part I of the UCR and an additional twenty-one in Part II.

TABLE 2.1   HOW DO THE UNIFORM CRIME REPORTS AND THE NATIONAL CRIME SURVEY DIFFER?

	UNIFORM CRIME REPORTS	NATIONAL CRIME SURVEY
Offenses measured:	Homicide Rape Robbery (personal and commercial) Assault (aggravated) Burglary (commercial and household) Larceny (commercial and household) Motor vehicle theft Arson	Rape Robbery (personal) Assault (aggravated and simple) Household burglary Larceny (personal and household) Motor vehicle theft
Scope:	Crimes reported to the police in most jurisdictions; considerable flexibility in developing small-area data	Crimes both reported and not reported to police; all data are for the nation as a whole; some data are available for a few large geographic areas
Collection method:	Police department reports to FBI	Survey interviews; periodically measures the total number of crimes committed by asking a national sample of 60,000 households representing 135,000 persons over the age of 12 about their experiences as victims of crime during a specified period
Kinds of information:	In addition to offense counts, provides information on crime clearances, persons arrested, persons charged, law enforcement officers killed and assaulted, and characteristics of homicide victims	Provides details about victims (such as age, race, sex, education, income, and whether the victim and offender were related to each other) and about crimes (such as time and place of occurrence, whether or not reported to police, use of weapons, occurrence of injury, and economic consequences)
Sponsor:	Department of Justice Federal Bureau of Investigation	Department of Justice Bureau of Justice Statistics

Source: U.S. Department of Justice, Bureau of Justice Statistics, *Report to the Nation on Crime and Justice,* Second Edition (Washington, D.C.: U.S. Government Printing Office, 1988), p. 11.

Although the NCS is conducted by trained interviewers, some individual variations in interviewing and recording style are inevitable, and as a result the information recorded may vary as well. Since the NCS is based on personal reporting, it also suffers from the fact that victims' memories may fade over time, so that some facts are forgotten while others are exaggerated. Moreover, some interviewees try to please the interviewer by fabricating crime incidents.[13] Respondents also have a tendency to telescope events—that is, to move events that took place in an earlier time period into the time period under study. Like the UCR, the NCS records only the most serious offense committed during an event in which several crimes are perpetrated.

Self-report Studies

Another way to determine the amount and types of crime actually committed is to ask people to report their own criminal acts in a confidential interview or, more usually, by completing an anonymous questionnaire. These investigations are called **self-report surveys.**

Findings of self-report studies Self-reports of delinquent and criminal behavior have produced several important findings since their development in the 1940s. First, they quickly refuted the conventional wisdom that only a small percentage of the general population commits crimes. The use of these measures over the last several decades has demonstrated very high rates of law-violating behavior by seemingly law-abiding people. Almost everyone, at some point in time, has broken a law. In 1947, James S. Wallerstein and Clement J. Wyle questioned a group of 1,698 individuals on whether or not they had committed any of forty-nine offenses that were serious enough to require a maximum sentence of not less than one year. They found that over 80 percent of the men reported committing malicious mischief, disorderly conduct, and larceny. More than 50 percent admitted a history of crimes including: auto misdemeanors (e.g., reckless driving and driving while intoxicated), indecency, gambling, fraud, and tax evasion. Notably, the authors acknowledged the lack of scientific rigor of their study. No attempt was made to ensure a balanced or representative cross-section of the individuals surveyed.[14] However, these findings do suggest that the distinction between criminals and noncriminals may be more apparent than real.

Studies conducted since the 1940s have provided a great deal more information. They suggest that there is a wide discrepancy between official and self-report data as regards the age, race, and sex of offenders.[15] Unrecorded offenders commit a wide variety of offenses, rather than specialize in one type of offense.[16] It also appears that only one-quarter of all serious, chronic juvenile offenders are apprehended by the police. Moreover, an estimated 90 percent of all youths commit delinquent or criminal acts, primarily truancy, using false identifications, alcohol abuse, larceny, fighting, and marijuana use.[17]

Limitations of self-report studies Self-report studies have indeed taught us a great deal about criminality. But they, like the other methods of data collection, have drawbacks. The questionnaires are often limited to petty acts, such as truancy, and therefore do not represent the range of criminal acts that people may commit. Thus Michael Hindelang, Travis Hirschi, and Joseph Weis argue that researchers who find discrepancies with respect to sex, race, and class between the results produced by official statistics and those collected by self-report methods are in fact measuring different kinds of behavior rather than different amounts of the same behavior. They suggest that if you take into account the fact that persons who are arrested tend to have committed more serious offenses and to have prior records (criteria that affect decisions to arrest), then the two types of statistics are quite comparable.[18] Another drawback of self-report studies is that most of them are administered to high school or college students, so that the information they yield applies only to young people attending school. And who can say that respondents always tell the truth? The information obtained by repeated administration of the same questionnaire to the same individuals might yield different results. Many self-report measures lack validity; the data obtained do not correspond with some other criterion (such as school records) that measures the same behavior. Finally, samples may be biased. People who choose not to participate in the studies may have good reason not to want to discuss their criminal activities.

Each of the three commonly used sources of data—police reports, victim surveys, self-report studies—adds a somewhat different dimension to our knowledge about crime. Thus all of them are useful in our search for the characteristics of crimes, criminals, and victims.

A U.S. marshal, far left, keeps his pistol trained on suspects as other marshals raid a crackhouse in Washington, D.C., July 1989.

MEASURING CHARACTERISTICS OF CRIME

On February 14, 1989, between 8:00 P.M. and midnight, police in the nation's capital notified the emergency room at D.C. General Hospital of eight shooting incidents. That night in the District of Columbia violent attacks left three people dead and ten injured. These numbers are not particularly unusual. In fact, Washington has been referred to as a city "under siege."[19] Between 1985 and 1989 the annual number of homicides rose from 148 to 372 (an increase of more than 150 percent), resulting in a murder rate of about 60 per 100,000—higher than that of New York or Detroit, the cities with a reputation for particularly high murder rates. More recent figures suggest that the situation continues to grow worse and that the homicide rate is increasing at an even faster rate.

Experts tie the mounting murder rate to crack cocaine, a drug almost unknown to the city before 1985. During that year one-fifth of all homicides were related to drugs. By 1989 that figure was four-fifths. Police sweeps of crack-infested areas accounted for 45,000 arrests over a thirty-month period. Areas with high levels of crack use lie primarily in the mostly poor, mostly black slums of the District's southeast corner.

These statistics tell us a good deal about the crime problem in Washington, D.C. They reveal not only a crack epidemic but also the number of homicides that have resulted, the changes in the homicide rate over time, the time of day when most homicides are committed, the high-risk areas, and the racial and economic composition of those areas. Criminologists use these kinds of data about crimes in their research. Some investigators, for example, may want to relate crack use to crime in major cities. Others may want to explain a decrease or an increase in the crime rate in a single city (Washington), in a single neighborhood (the southeast corner), or perhaps in the nation as a whole.

Crime Trends

One of the most important characteristics of any crime is how often it is committed. From such figures we can determine crime trends, the increases and decreases of crime over time. The UCR show that more than 13.9 million Index crimes (excluding arson) were reported to the police in 1988 (Table 2.2). Of the total number of Index crimes, violent crimes make up a small portion—11 percent—with a murder rate of 8.4 per 100,000. Most Index crimes are property offenses (89 percent), and 62 percent of these property offenses are larcenies.

The 1988 National Crime Survey presents a somewhat different picture (Table 2.3). Though the data presented in the NCS and the UCR are not entirely comparable because the categories differ, the number of crimes reported to the police and the number reported in the victimization survey are clearly far apart. According to the NCS's projections, there were nearly 36 million victimizations. Indeed, the NCS reports almost as many personal thefts as the total number of UCR Index offenses taken together. Later we shall investigate the reasons victims give for not reporting offenses to the police.

According to UCR data, the crime rate increased slowly between 1930 and 1960. After 1960 it began to rise much more quickly. This

TABLE 2.2 UNIFORM CRIME REPORTS: TOTAL NUMBER OF INDEX OFFENSES AND RATE PER 100,000 POPULATION, 1988

	NUMBER	RATE
Murder and nonnegligent manslaughter	20,680	8.4
Forcible rape	92,490	37.6
Robbery	542,970	220.9
Aggravated assault	910,090	370.2
Burglary	3,218,100	1,309.2
Larceny-theft	7,705,900	3,134.9
Motor vehicle theft	1,432,900	582.9
All index offenses	13,923,130	

Source: U.S. Department of Justice, Federal Bureau of Investigation, *Crime in the United States, 1988* (Washington, D.C.: U.S. Government Printing Office, 1989), p. 47.

TABLE 2.3 NATIONAL CRIME SURVEY: TOTAL NUMBER OF VICTIMIZATIONS AND RATE PER 100,000 POPULATION AGED 12 AND OVER, 1988

	NUMBER	RATE
Rape	167,450	80
Robbery	984,190	490
Aggravated assault	1,735,820	870
Simple assault	3,142,170	1,580
Personal theft	13,584,280	6,810
Burglary	6,061,230	6,490
Household larceny	8,707,990	9,330
Motor vehicle theft	1,614,900	1,730
All offenses	35,988,030	

Source: U.S. Department of Justice, Bureau of Justice Statistics, *Criminal Victimization in the United States, 1988: A National Crime Survey Report (Preliminary Findings)* (Washington, D.C.: U.S. Government Printing Office).

trend continued until 1980 (Table 2.4), when the crime rate rose to 5,950 per 100,000. From that peak the rate steadily dropped until 1984, when there were 5,031.3 crimes per 100,000. Since that year the crime rate has risen again. The NCS also shows that the victimization rate peaked from 1979 to 1981. These data, however, show a consistent decline since the early 1980s.[20]

The gradual decline in the crime rate after 1980 is an important phenomenon that requires a bit more analysis. One important factor is the age distribution of the population. Given the fact that young people tend to have the highest crime rate, the age distribution of the population has a major effect on crime trends. After World War II, the birth rate increased sharply in what is known as the baby boom. The baby-boom generation reached its crime-prone years in the 1960s, and the crime rate duly rose. As the baby-boom generation grew older, the crime rate became more stable and in the 1980s began to decline. Some researchers claim that the children of the baby boomers may very well once again expand the ranks of the crime-prone ages, and crime will once again increase.

During the period when the baby-boom generation outgrew criminal behavior, the society

TABLE 2.4   UNIFORM CRIME REPORTS: RATE OF ALL INDEX CRIMES PER 100,000 POPULATION, 1960–1988

YEAR	RATE
1960	1,887.2
1961	1,906.1
1962	2,019.8
1963	2,180.3
1964	2,388.1
1965	2,449.0
1966	2,670.8
1967	2,989.7
1968	3,370.2
1969	3,680.0
1970	3,984.5
1971	4,164.7
1972	3,961.4
1973	4,154.4
1974	4,850.4
1975	5,281.7
1976	5,266.4
1977	5,055.1
1978	5,109.3
1979	5,521.5
1980	5,950.0
1981	5,858.2
1982	5,603.6
1983	5,175.0
1984	5,031.3
1985	5,207.1
1986	5,480.4
1987	5,550.0
1988	5,664.2

Source: U.S. Department of Justice, Federal Bureau of Investigation, *Crime in the United States, 1975*; ibid., *1980*; ibid., 1988 (Washington, D.C.: U.S. Government Printing Office, 1976, 1981, 1989), pp. 49, 41, 47, respectively.

was undergoing other changes. We adopted a get-tough crime-control policy, which may have deterred some people from committing crimes. Mandatory prison terms permitted judges less discretion in sentencing, and fewer convicted felons were paroled. In addition, the growth of crime-prevention programs, such as Neighborhood Watch groups, became popular. These and other factors have been suggested to explain why the crime rate dropped, but we have no definitive answers. Nor can we explain with any certainty why it is once again rising.

Locations and Times of Criminal Acts

Statistics on the characteristics of crimes are important not only to criminologists who seek to know why crime occurs but also to those who want to know how to prevent it. Two statistics of use in prevention efforts are the locations of crimes and the times when they are committed.

Most crimes are committed in large urban areas rather than in small cities, suburbs, or rural areas (Figure 2.2). This pattern of variation can be attributed to a variety of factors—the density of the population, the age distribution of the residents, the stability of the population, economic conditions, and the quality of law enforcement, to name but a few. The statistics we have noted for Washington, D.C., showed that most of the arrests took place in the poverty-ridden ghetto areas. The fact that the majority of those arrests were made in what *Newsweek* has called the "open-air crack bazaars" fits the national picture, for almost half of all crimes occur on the streets.[21] The NCS data tell us that the safest place to be is inside one's home; according to victims' reports, only 14 percent of crimes were committed in their homes. The only crime that shows a significantly different pattern is rape: over half of such attacks were made in the victim's home or in the home of a friend or relative.[22]

As for the times when crimes are committed, the NCS data reveal that over 53 percent of all violent crimes are committed at night, between 6:00 P.M. and 6:00 A.M. The statistics for shooting incidents in Washington, D.C., reflect a similar time frame. Household crimes follow the same pattern: of crimes committed within a known period, 45 percent are committed at night. Most personal thefts, however, are committed during the day.[23]

Nationwide crime rates also vary by season. Personal and household crimes are more likely to be committed during the warmer months of the year, perhaps because in summer people spend more time outdoors, where they are more vulnerable to crime.[24] People often leave

FIGURE 2.2 Number of UCR index offenses per 100,000 population, by county

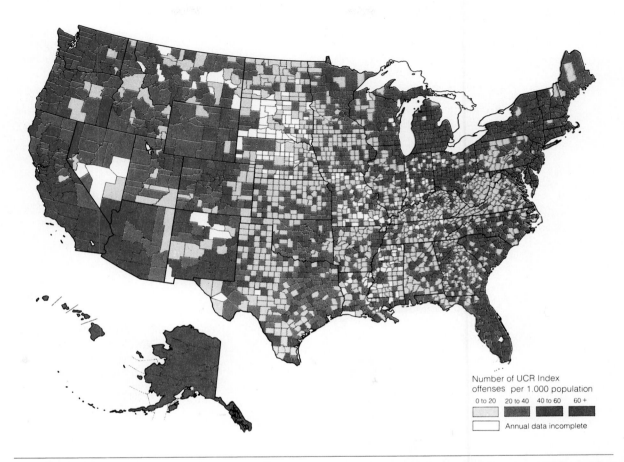

Number of UCR Index
offenses per 1.000 population

| 0 to 20 | 20 to 40 | 40 to 60 | 60 + |

Annual data incomplete

Source: U.S. Department of Justice, Bureau of Justice Statistics, *Report to the Nation on Crime and Justice*, Second Edition (Washington, D.C.: U.S. Government Printing Office, 1988), p. 18.

their doors and windows open when they go out in warm weather.

Severity of Crime

We have seen that crime rates vary in time and place. They also vary in people's perception of their severity. To some extent legislation sets a standard of severity by the punishments it attaches to various crimes. But let us take a critical look at such judgments of severity.

Do you believe that skyjacking an airplane is a more serious offense than smuggling heroin into the country? Is forcible rape more serious than kidnapping? Is breaking into a home and stealing $1,000 more serious than using force to rob a person of $10? A yes answer to all three questions conforms with the findings of the National Survey of Crime Severity, which in 1977 measured public perceptions of the seriousness of 204 events, from planting a bomb that killed twenty people to playing hooky from school.[25] The survey found that individuals generally agree about the relative seriousness of specific crimes (Table 2.5). In ranking the severity of crimes, people seem to base their decisions on

TABLE 2.5   HOW DO PEOPLE RANK THE SEVERITY OF CRIME?

SEVERITY SCORE	TEN MOST SERIOUS OFFENSES	SEVERITY SCORE	TEN LEAST SERIOUS OFFENSES
72.1	Planting a bomb in a public building. The bomb explodes and 20 people are killed.	1.3	Two persons willingly engage in a homosexual act.
52.8	A man forcibly rapes a woman. As a result of physical injuries, she dies.	1.1	Disturbing the neighborhood with loud, noisy behavior.
		1.1	Taking bets on the numbers.
43.2	Robbing a victim at gunpoint. The victim struggles and is shot to death.	1.1	A group continues to hang around a corner after being told to break up by a police officer.
39.2	A man stabs his wife. As a result, she dies.	0.9	A youngster under 16 years old runs away from home.
35.7	Stabbing a victim to death.	0.8	Being drunk in public.
35.6	Intentionally injuring a victim. As a result, the victim dies.	0.7	A youngster under 16 years old breaks a curfew law by being out on the street after the hour permitted by law.
33.8	Running a narcotics ring.		
27.9	A women stabs her husband. As a result, he dies.	0.6	Trespassing in the backyard of a private home.
26.3	An armed person skyjacks an airplane and demands to be flown to another country.	0.3	A person is a vagrant. That is, he has no home and no visible means of support.
25.8	A man forcibly rapes a woman. No other physical injury occurs.	0.2	A youngster under 16 years old plays hooky from school.

Source: U.S. Department of Justice, *Report to the Nation on Crime and Justice,* Second Edition, Bureau of Justice Statistics (Washington, D.C.: U.S. Government Printing Office, 1988), p. 16.

such factors as the ability of victims to protect themselves, the amount of injury and loss suffered, the type of business or organization from which property is stolen, the relationship between offender and victim, and (for drug offenses) the types of drugs involved. Respondents generally agreed that violent crime is more serious than property crime. They also considered white-collar crimes, such as consumer fraud, cheating on income taxes, polluting, and accepting bribes, to be as serious as many violent and property crimes.

Information on the characteristics of crimes is not the only sort of data analyzed by criminologists. They also want to know the characteristics of the people who commit those crimes.

MEASURING CHARACTERISTICS OF CRIMINALS

Behind each crime is a criminal, or several criminals. These criminals can be differentiated by age, ethnicity, gender, socioeconomic level, and other criteria. These characteristics enable us to group criminals into categories, and it is these categories that criminological researchers find useful. They study the various offender groups to determine why some people are more likely than others to commit crime, or particular types of crime. It has been estimated that 13.8 million arrests—a rate of 5,366 per 100,000 inhabitants—were made in 1988 for all criminal offenses except traffic violations. Table 2.6 shows how these arrests were distributed among the offenses. During the ten years between 1979 and 1988, the number of arrests rose 22 percent. Let us take a close look at the characteristics of the persons arrested.

Age and Crime

Six armed men who have been called the "over-the-hill gang" were arrested trying to rob an elegant bridge and backgammon club in midtown New York City. The robbery began at 10:25 P.M. when the men, wearing rubber gloves and ski masks and armed with two revolvers, a shotgun, and a rifle, forced the customers and employees to lie down in a back room while they loaded a nylon bag with wallets, players' money, and the club's cash box. A club worker slipped out a side door to alert police, who arrived within minutes. They surprised and disarmed one member of the gang, 48 years old, whom they found clutching a .22-caliber revolver. They took a .38-caliber revolver from another gang member, 41 years old. During the scuffle with the officers, one suspect tried to escape, fell, and broke his nose. The officers then found and arrested a 40-year-old man standing in the hallway with a 12-gauge Winchester shotgun. Meanwhile, the other gang members abandoned their gloves and masks and lay

TABLE 2.6   TOTAL NUMBER OF ARRESTS, 1988 (ESTIMATED)

TOTAL	13,812,300
Murder and nonnegligent manslaughter	21,890
Forcible rape	38,610
Robbery	149,100
Aggravated assault	416,300
Burglary	463,400
Larceny-theft	1,571,200
Motor vehicle theft	208,400
Arson	19,700
Violent crime	625,900
Property crime	2,262,700
Crime Index total	2,888,600
Other assaults	901,800
Forgery and counterfeiting	101,700
Fraud	366,300
Embezzlement	15,500
Stolen property: buying, receiving, possessing	166,300
Vandalism	295,300
Weapons: carrying, possessing, etc.	221,800
Prostitution and commercialized vice	104,100
Sex offenses (except forcible rape and prostitution)	106,300
Drug abuse violations	1,155,200
Gambling	23,600
Offenses against family and children	69,900
Driving under the influence	1,792,500
Liquor laws	669,600
Drunkenness	818,600
Disorderly conduct	760,500
Vagrancy	36,500
All other offenses (except traffic)	3,078,900
Suspicion (not included in totals)	14,000
Curfew and loitering law violations	72,200
Runaways	166,900

Source: U.S. Department of Justice, Federal Bureau of Investigation, *Crime in the United States, 1988* (Washington, D.C.: U.S. Government Printing Office, 1989), p. 168.

down among the people they had robbed. One of the suspects, aged 72, who wore a back

George Burns, Art Carney, and Lee Strassberg, in the Motion Picture Going in Style, *portray an "over-the-hill" gang of bank robbers.*

brace, complained of chest and back pain as police locked handcuffs on him. He was immediately hospitalized.[26]

This gang is extraordinary for at least two reasons. First, in any given year approximately half of all arrests are of individuals under the age of 25; and second, gang membership is ordinarily confined to the young. Though juveniles (young people under 18) constitute about 8 percent of the population, they account for almost one-third of the arrests for Index crimes. Arrest rates begin to decline after age 30 and taper off to about 2 percent or less from age 50 on.[27] This decline in criminal activities with age is known as the **aging-out phenomenon.** The reasons for it have sparked a lively scientific debate. Michael Gottfredson and Travis Hirschi contend that there is a certain inclination to commit crimes which peaks in the middle or late teens and then declines through life. This relationship between crime and age does not change, "regardless of sex, race, country, time, or offense."[28] Crime decreases with age, they add, even for people who commit frequent offenses. Thus differences in crime rates found among young people of various groups, such as men and women or lower class and middle class, will be maintained throughout the life cycle. If lower-class youths are three times more

likely to commit crimes than middle-class youths, for instance, then 60-year-old lower-class persons will be three times more likely to commit crimes than 60-year-old middle-class persons, though crimes committed by both lower-class and middle-class groups will constantly decline.[29] According to this argument, all offenders commit fewer crimes as they grow older because they have less strength, less mobility, and so on.

James Q. Wilson and Richard Herrnstein support this view that the aging-out phenomenon is a natural part of the life cycle.[30] Teenagers may become increasingly independent of their parents, yet they lack the resources to support themselves; so they band together with other young people who are equally frustrated in their search for legitimate ways to get money, sex, alcohol, and status. Together they find illegitimate sources. With adulthood, the small gains from criminal behavior no longer seem so attractive. Legitimate means open up. They marry. Their peers no longer endorse lawbreaking. They learn to delay gratification.[31] Petty crime is no longer adventurous.[32] It is at this time that the process of aging out of crime begins for most individuals. The ones who continue to commit offenses will also eventually slow down with increasing age.[33]

The opposing side in this debate argues that the decrease in crime rates after adolescence does not imply that the number of crimes committed by all individual offenders declines. In other words, the frequency of offending may go down for most offenders, but some chronic active offenders may continue to commit the same amount of crime over time. Why might this be so? Because the factors that influence any individual's entrance into criminal activity vary, the number and types of offenses committed vary, and the factors that eventually induce the individual to give up criminal activity vary.[34] The frequency of criminal involvement, then, depends on such social factors as economic situation, peer pressure, and lifestyle; and it is these social factors that explain the aging-out phenomenon. A teenager's unemployment, for example, may have very little to do with the onset of criminal activity because the youngster is not yet in the labor force and still lives at home. Unemployment may increase an adult's rate of offending, however, because an adult requires income to support various responsibilities. Thus the relationship between age and crime is not the same for all offenders. Various conditions that people go through in the life cycle affect their behavior in different ways.

To learn how the causes of crime vary at different ages, Alfred Blumstein and his colleagues suggest that we study criminal careers, a concept that describes the onset of criminal activity, the types and amount of crime committed, and the termination of such activity.[35] Longitudinal studies (studies of a particular group of people over time) should enable researchers to uncover the factors that distinguish criminals from noncriminals and those that differentiate among criminals in regard to the number and kinds of offenses they commit. Thus researchers who are involved in research on criminal careers assume that offenders who commit ten crimes may differ from those who commit one or fifteen. They ask: Are the factors that cause the second offense the same ones that cause the fourth, or the fifth? Do different factors move one offender from theft to rape or from assault to shoplifting? How many persons in a **birth cohort** (a group of people born in the same year) will become criminals? Of those, how many will become **career criminals** (chronic offenders)?

Starting in the 1960s, researchers at the Sellin Center of the University of Pennsylvania began a search for answers. Their earliest publication, in 1972, detailed the criminal careers of 9,945 boys (a cohort) born in Philadelphia in 1945. Marvin Wolfgang, Robert Figlio, and Thorsten Sellin obtained their data from school records and official police reports. Their major findings were that 35 percent of the boys had contact with the police; of those boys, 46 percent were one-time offenders and 54 percent were repeat offenders. Eighteen percent of those with police contact were chronic repeaters who had committed five or more offenses; they represented 6 percent of the total. The "chronic 6 percent," as they are now called, were responsible for more than half of all the offenses committed, including 71 percent of the homicides, 73 percent of the rapes, 82 percent of the robberies, and 69 percent of the assaults.[36]

Research continued on 10 percent of the boys in the original cohort until they reached the age of 30. This sample was divided into three groups: those who had records of offenses only as juveniles, those who had records only as adults, and those who were persistent offenders with both juvenile and adult records. Though they made up only 15 percent of the follow-up group, former chronic juvenile offenders represented 74 percent of all the arrests. Thus *chronic* juvenile offenders do indeed continue to break laws as adults.[37]

The boys in the original cohort were born in 1945. Researchers questioned whether the same behavior patterns would continue over the years. The criminologist Paul Tracy and his associates found the answer in a second study of 28,338 persons born in 1958; this birth cohort included women as well as men. The later cohort was involved in significantly more serious crimes than the 1945 group and had a larger percentage (7.5 percent) of chronic offenders.[38]

The policy implications of such findings are clear. If a very small group of offenders is committing a large percentage of all crime, the crime rate should go down if we incarcerate those chronic offenders for long periods of time. Many jurisdictions around the country are developing sentencing policies to do just that; but such policies are quite controversial, as we shall see in Chapters 16 and 17.

Gender and Crime ♀ compared to ♂

Except for such crimes as prostitution, shoplifting, and welfare fraud, males traditionally commit more crimes than females at all ages. According to the Uniform Crime Reports for 1988, the arrest ratio is typically about four male offenders to one female offender.[39] The National Crime Survey reports a wider gap: for personal crimes of violence involving a single offender, 85 percent of victims perceived the sex of the offender as male and 14 percent perceived it as female.[40] Self-report studies, too, which show more similarities in male and female criminal activity than official reports do, find that males commit more offenses than females.[41] Since the 1960s, however, there have been some interesting developments in regard to gender and crime data. In 1960 females accounted for 11 percent of the total number of arrests across the country. They now account for 18 percent. And while the female arrest rate is still much lower than that of males, the rate of increase for women has risen faster than the rate for men.[42]

Several self-report studies suggest that gender differences in crime may be narrowing. They demonstrate that the patterns and causes of male and female delinquent activity are becoming more alike.[43] John Hagan and his associates agree, but only with respect to girls raised in middle-class egalitarian families in which husband and wife share similar positions of power at home and in the workplace. They argue that girls raised in lower-class, father-dominated households grow up in a "cult of domesticity" that reduces their freedom and thus the likelihood of their delinquency.[44]

Because traditionally women have had such low crime rates, the scientific community and the mass media have generally ignored the subject of female criminality. Both have tended to view female offenders as misguided children who are an embarrassment rather than a threat to society. Only a handful of the world's criminologists have deemed the subject worthy of independent study. Foremost among them was Cesare Lombroso (whom we shall meet again in Chapter 3). His book *The Female Offender,* which appeared in 1895, detailed the physical abnormalities that would predestine some girls to be criminal from birth.[45] Lombroso's findings on male criminals, however, have not stood the test of later scientific research, and his portrayal of the female criminal has been found to be similarly inaccurate.

A little over a generation later Sheldon and Eleanor Glueck launched a massive research project on the biological and environmental causes of crime, with a separate inquiry into female offenders. Their conclusions were decidedly sociological. They said, in essence, that in order to change the incidence of their criminality, there would have to be a change in the social circumstances in which females grow up.[46] Otto Pollack shared the Gluecks' views on sociological determinants. In 1952 he proposed that female crime has a "masked character" that keeps it from being properly recorded or otherwise noted in statistical reports. Protective attitudes toward women make police officers less

willing to arrest them, make victims less eager to report their offenses, make district attorneys less enthusiastic about prosecuting them, and make juries less likely to find them guilty. Moreover, women's social roles as homemakers, child rearers, and shoppers furnish them with opportunities for concealed criminal activity and types of victims who are least likely to cooperate with the police. Pollack also argued that female crime was limited by the various psychological and physiological characteristics inherent in the female anatomy.[47]

A quarter of a century after Pollack's work, two researchers, working independently, took a fresh look at female crime in the light of the new roles of women in society. In 1975 Freda Adler posited that as social and economic roles of women changed in the legitimate world, their participation in crime would also change. According to this argument, the temptations, challenges, stresses, and strains to which women have been increasingly subjected in recent years cause them to act or react in the same manner in which males have consistently reacted to the same stimuli. In other words, equalization of social and economic roles leads to similar behavior patterns, both legal and illegal, on the part of both men and women. To steal a car, for example, one needs to know how to drive. To embezzle, one needs to be in a position of trust and in control of funds. To get into a bar fight, one needs to go to a bar. To be an inside trader on Wall Street, one needs to be on the inside.[48]

Rita Simon has taken a similar position. She, too, has argued that female criminality has undergone changes. But these changes, according to Simon, have occurred only in regard to certain property crimes, such as larceny/theft and fraud/embezzlement. Women are becoming more involved in these crimes because they have more opportunities to commit them. Simon hypothesizes that since the propensity of men and women to commit crime is not basically different, as more women enter the labor force and work in a much broader range of jobs, their property crime rate will continue to go up.[49]

Some criminologists have challenged the views of Adler and Simon on new roles for women in crime. Many questions have been asked about the so-called new female criminal. Does she exist? If so, does she commit more crimes than the old female criminal did? What types of crimes? Is she still involved primarily in offenses against property, or has she turned to more violent offenses? Researchers differ on the answers. Some contend that the extent of female criminality has not changed through the years but that crimes committed by women are more often making their way into official statistics simply because they are more often reported and prosecuted. In other words, the days of chivalry in the criminal justice system are over.[50] Others argue that female crime has indeed increased, but they attribute the increase to nonviolent, petty property offenses that continue to reflect traditional female sex roles rather than new, nontraditional roles.[51] Moreover, some investigators claim, the increased involvement in these petty property offenses suggests that women are still economically disadvantaged, suffering sexism in the legitimate marketplace.[52] Taking the opposite side of the argument, other researchers support the contention of Adler and Simon that female roles have changed and that these changes have indeed led women to commit the same kinds of crimes as men, violent as well as property offenses.[53]

Though scholars disagree on the form and extent of female crime, they do seem to agree that the crimes women commit are closely associated with their socioeconomic position in society. The controversy has to do with whether or not that position has changed. In any case, the association between gender and crime has become a recognized area of concern in the growing body of research dealing with contemporary criminological issues.[54]

Social Class and Crime

Researchers agree on the importance of age and gender as factors related to crime, but they disagree strongly as to whether social class is related to crime. First of all, the term "class" can have many meanings. If "lower class" is defined by income, then the category might include graduate students, unemployed stockbro-

kers, pensioners, welfare mothers, prison inmates, and many other persons who have little in common except low income. Furthermore, "lower class" is often defined by the low prestige associated with blue-collar occupations. Some delinquency studies determine the class of the young people by the class of their fathers, even though the young people may have their own jobs, which can be quite different from those of their fathers.

Another dispute focuses on the source of criminal statistics used by investigators. Many researchers attribute the relatively strong association between class and crime found in arrest statistics to class bias on the part of the police. If the police are more likely to arrest a lower-class suspect than a middle-class suspect, they say, arrest data will show more involvement of

AT ISSUE

Ivan Boesky, Millionaire Convict

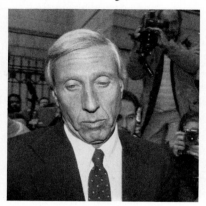

Ivan Boesky was the embodiment of the American dream. Son of a Russian immigrant, he earned a law degree, and by age 29 he had made it to Wall Street. Within ten years he had made a fortune of over $200 million, often betting millions on risky stocks—and winning. His wealth grew on the wave of a new business practice that developed in the 1960s and

1970s—the corporate takeover. Before the 1960s, when one company bought out another or when companies merged, the officers of the companies conducted the negotiations. But in the 1960s corporate raiders emerged. These raiders did not deal directly with the officers of the companies. Rather, when they learned of a takeover of one company by another, they bought up stock in the target company on the open market. Then, when news of the potential takeover spread, the price of the stock soared and the raiders made enormous profits. This practice is subject to one limitation: the Securities and Exchange Commission, which regulates the investment business, forbids insider trading—the use of nonpublic information about a company to trade in its stock.

Ivan Boesky was an expert at takeover financial deals. In one month, for instance, he bought

377,000 shares of Nabisco, and then sold them for a $4 million profit when Nabisco and R. J. Reynolds announced a merger. His successes mounted. He seemed always to buy the right stock at the right time. Was it instinct? Was he clairvoyant? Neither, as it turned out. He was building his fortune by insider trading. The story unfolded when an investment banker to whom Boesky had paid large sums for advance information about takeovers was charged with insider trading and named Boesky as an accomplice. Thus "Ivan the Terrible," as he was known in his heyday on Wall Street, once again became "Ivan the Bum," as his wealthy father-in-law had called him in his youth. He was fined $100 million, was debarred from security trading for life, and was sentenced to three years in prison.

lower-class people in criminality whether or not they are actually committing more crimes. When Charles Tittle, Wayne Villemez, and Douglas Smith analyzed thirty-five studies of the relationship between social class and crime rates, they found that little if any support exists for the claim that crime is primarily a lower-class phenomenon.[55] The data to support this contention came from self-report studies rather than arrest records. Many scholars have challenged this conclusion. They claim that self-report studies show few class differences because the studies ask only about trivial offenses, not serious ones. Delbert Elliott and Suzanne Ageton, for example, looked at serious crimes among a national sample of 1,726 young people aged 11 to 17. According to their responses to a self-report questionnaire, lower-class young people were much more likely than middle-class young people to commit such serious crimes as burglary, robbery, assault, and sexual assault.[56] In a follow-up study, Elliott and David Huizinga concluded that middle-class and lower-class youths differed significantly in both the nature and the number of serious crimes they committed.[57]

Controversies remain about the social class of people who commit crimes. There is no controversy, however, about the social class of people in prison. The probability that a person such as Ivan Boesky will get a prison sentence is extremely low. Boesky does not fit the typical profile of the hundreds of thousands of inmates of our nation's jails and prisons. He is educated. Only 28 percent of prison inmates have completed high school.[58] His income was in the millions. The average income of jail inmates who work is $5,600. He had a white-collar job. Eighty-five percent of prison inmates are blue-collar workers. He committed a white-collar offense. Only 18 percent of the persons convicted of such offenses go to prison for more than one year, whereas 39 percent of the violent offenders and 26 percent of the property offenders do.[59] Finally, Ivan Boesky is white in a criminal justice system where blacks are disproportionately represented.

Race and Crime

Statistics on race and crime show that while blacks constitute 12 percent of the population, they account for 29.6 percent of all arrests for Index crimes.[60] Other statistics confirm their disproportionate representation in the criminal justice system. Blacks account for 46 percent of all arrests for violent crimes. Fifty percent of black urban males are arrested for an Index crime at least once during their lives, compared to 14 percent of white males. The likelihood that any man will serve time in jail or prison is estimated to be 18 percent for blacks and 3 percent for whites. Moreover, the leading cause of death among young black men is murder.[61]

These statistics raise many questions. Do blacks actually commit more crimes? Or are they simply arrested more often? Are black neighborhoods under more police surveillance than white neighborhoods? Do blacks receive differential treatment in the criminal justice system? If blacks commit more crimes than whites, why?

Some data support the argument that there are more blacks in the criminal justice system because bias operates from the time of arrest through incarceration. Other data support the argument that racial disparities in official statistics reflect an actual difference in criminal behavior. Much of the evidence comes from the statistics of the National Crime Survey, which are very similar to the statistics on race found in arrest data. When interviewers asked victims about the race of persons who robbed them, nearly two-thirds identified the assailants as black.[62] Similarly, while self-report data demonstrate that less serious juvenile offenses are about equally prevalent among black and white youngsters, more serious ones are not: black youngsters report having committed many more Index crimes than do whites of comparable ages.[63]

If the disparity in criminal behavior suggested by official data, victimization studies, and self-reports actually exists, and if we are to explain it, we have to try to discover why people commit crimes. A history of hundreds of years of abuse, neglect, and discrimination against black Americans has left its mark in the form of high unemployment, residence in socially disorganized areas, one-parent households, and negative self images.[64]

In 1968, in the aftermath of the worst riots in modern American history, the National Advisory Commission on Civil Disorders alluded to the reasons that blacks had not achieved the successes accomplished by other minority groups that at one time or another were discriminated against as well. European immigrants provided unskilled labor needed by industry. By the time blacks migrated from rural areas to cities, the U.S. economy was changing and soon there was no longer much use for unskilled labor. Immigrant groups had also received economic advantages by working for local political organizations. By the time blacks moved to the cities, the political machines no longer had the power to offer help in return for their support. Though both immigrants and blacks arrived in cities with little money, all but the very youngest members of the cohesive immigrant family contributed to the family's total income. As slaves, however, black people had been forbidden to marry, and the unions they nevertheless formed were subject to disruption at the owner's convenience and tended to be unstable. We shall have more to say about the causal factors associated with high crime rates and race in Chapters 5 and 6.

The data reviewed here show that crime is an activity disproportionately engaged in by young people, males, and minorities. As we shall see, the characteristics of victims of violent crime tend to show a similar pattern.

MEASURING CHARACTERISTICS OF VICTIMS

After a night at the theater, Caroline Isenberg headed home alone. The 23-year-old aspiring actress entered the darkened lobby of her apartment house. Inside, Emmanuel Torres, son of the building superintendent, lurked in the shadows. At knifepoint he forced Isenberg into the elevator. On the roof he tried to rape and rob her. When she resisted, Torres stabbed her nine times. She screamed, "He's going to kill me! I'm bleeding to death!" Neighbors called police, who found the victim. She died five hours later at St. Luke's Hospital.[65] The story of Caroline Isenberg appeared in the national news media. It was newsworthy because the victim was so different from most victims of violent crime: she was white, female, a Harvard graduate. Victims of violent crimes are typically black males from lower-income families.[66]

Just as we can describe and categorize offenders, we can describe and categorize victims. The victims of burglaries own or occupy the premises burglarized. The victims of larcenies own or possess property. Victims of credit card frauds are store owners. It is more difficult to find common denominators among victims of crimes of violence. Nevertheless, victimological research tells us a lot about types and groups of human beings who are particularly vulnerable to crimes of various sorts.

Hans von Hentig, a victim of Nazi persecution, started us thinking about the significance of the victim in criminal activity. Indeed, his book *The Criminal and His Victim,* published in 1948, may be said to have started the criminological subdiscipline of victimology, which examines the role played by the victim in a criminal incident. People knew, for example, that tourist resorts were attractive to criminals who wanted to prey on unsuspecting vacationers.

But von Hentig actually gathered such information systematically.

Since that time the actual gathering of information about victims and the analyses of victim-offender relationships have become much more sophisticated with the creation of victimization surveys. We now know that the characteristics of victims of violent offenses differ from those of victims of theft. As we have noted, victims of violent offenses are predominantly black, male, and poor, whereas theft victims are primarily white persons with at least some college education and are in the highest income brackets.[67]

Crimes are directed against households as units as well as against individuals. Such crimes include burglary, larceny, and motor vehicle theft. Household victimization rates are highest among households that are headed by blacks, young people, and renters rather than owners; that include six or more persons; and that are located in urban areas rather than in suburbs or rural areas.[68]

Victimological research has shown that one-quarter of the 93 million households in the United States in 1988 were touched by a crime of violence or theft. The likelihood of such victimization, however, had gone down since 1975, when one-third of the households experienced such crimes. Households in the Northeast are least vulnerable to crime (19 percent) and those in the West most vulnerable (30 percent). Southern and midwestern households fall in between. The likelihood of car theft is low: it happens to only 1.5 percent of all households. Over the thirteen years from 1973 through 1986, crimes of violence decreased 14 percent, crimes of personal larceny with contact 11 percent, household burglary 33 percent, and motor vehicle theft 21 percent.[69] As people grow older their fear of crime tends to increase, but these fears are ungrounded because the chances of being victimized decrease with every age group after the age of twenty-four.[70] Finally, although violent crimes are typically associated with strangers who attack from behind to murder or assault an unknown victim, the reality is quite otherwise. In half of all homicides and assaults and in one-quarter of all robberies, victims know their assailants.[71]

REVIEW

Researchers have three main objectives in measuring crime and criminal behavior patterns. They need to collect and analyze data to test theories about why people commit crime, to learn the situational characteristics of crimes in order to develop strategies to prevent crime, and to run the criminal justice system on a daily basis. Data are collected by surveys, experiments, nonparticipant and participant observation, and case studies. It is often cost-effective to use repositories of information gathered by public and private organizations for their own purposes. The three main sources of data for measuring crime are the Uniform Crime Reports, victimization surveys, and self-report questionnaires. Though each source is useful for some purposes, all three have limitations.

By measuring the characteristics of crime, criminals, and victims, we can identify crime trends, the places and times at which crimes are most likely to be committed, and the public's evaluation of the seriousness of offenses. Current controversies concerning offenders focus on the relationship between crime and age throughout the life cycle, whether or not the role of women in crime has changed, and the effects of social class and race on the response of the criminal justice system. Crime is an activity disproportionately engaged in by young people, males, and minorities. These are also the people who are most likely to be victimized. Fear of crime increases with age but the chance of victimization actually decreases as people grow older. In a large proportion of violent crimes, offenders and victims know each other.

KEY TERMS

aging-out phenomenon
birth cohort
career criminals
case study
cross-sectional study
data
experiment
field experiment
hypothesis
Index crimes
longitudinal study
nonparticipant observation

participant observation
population
primary data
random sample
sample
secondary data
self-report surveys
survey
theory
variables
victimization surveys

NOTES

1. James O. Finckenauer, *Scared Straight and the Panacea Phenomenon* (Englewood Cliffs, N.J.: Prentice-Hall, 1982).

2. Personal communication from Anne Campbell. Based on *The Girls in the Gang: A Report from New York City* (New York: Basil Blackwell, 1984).

3. Edwin H. Sutherland, *The Professional Thief* (Chicago: University of Chicago Press, 1937).

4. Marvin E. Wolfgang, "Ethics and Research," in *Ethics, Public Policy, and Criminal Justice,* ed. A. F. Ellison and N. Bowie (Cambridge, Mass.: Oelgeschlager, Gunn & Hain, 1982).

5. Frank E. Hagan, *Research Methods in Criminal Justice and Criminology* (New York: Macmillan, 1989), p. 358.

6. Seth A. Bloomberg and Leslie Wilkins, "Ethics of Research Involving Human Subjects in Criminal Justice," *Crime and Delinquency* 23 (1977): 435–444.

7. Lawrence Sherman and Barry Glick, "The Quality of Arrest Statistics," *Police Foundation Reports* 2 (1984): 1–8.

8. Michael Couzens, "Getting the Crime Rate Down: Political Pressure and Crime Reporting," *Law and Society Review* 8 (1974): 457–493.

9. President's Commission on Law Enforcement and Administration of Justice, *The Challenge of Crime in a Free Society* (Washington, D.C.: U.S. Government Printing Office, 1967), p. 25.

10. Patrick Jackson, "Assessing the Validity of Official Data on Arson," *Criminology* 26 (1988): 181–195.

11. See Leonard Savitz, "Official Statistics," in *Contemporary Criminology,* ed. Leonard Savitz and Norman Johnston, pp. 3–15 (New York: Wiley, 1982).

12. For a comparison of victimization data with official police data, see Scott Menard and Herbert C. Covey, "UCR and NCS: Comparisons over Space and Time," *Journal of Criminal Justice* 16 (1988): 371–384.

13. James Levine, "The Potential for Crime Over-reporting in Criminal Victimization Surveys," *Criminology* 14 (1976): 307–330.

14. James S. Wallerstein and Clement J. Wyle, "Our Law-Abiding Law-Breakers," *Probation* 25 (March–April 1947): 107–112. See also Austin L. Porterfield, *Youth in Trouble* (Fort Worth, Tex.: Leo Potishman Foundation, 1946), for an early comparison of delinquents with college students.

15. Maynard Erickson and LaMar Empey, "Court Records, Undetected Delinquency and Decision-Making," *Journal of Criminal Law, Criminology, and Police Science* 54 (1963): 456–469; Martin Gold, "Undetected Delinquent Behavior," *Journal of Research in Crime and Delinquency* 3 (1966): 27–46; David Farrington, "Self-reports of Deviant Behavior: Predictive and Stable?" *Journal of Criminal Law and Criminology* 64 (1973): 99–110.

16. D. Wayne Osgood, Lloyd Johnston, Patrick O'Malley, and Jerald Bachman, "The Gen-

erality of Deviance in Late Adolescence and Early Adulthood," *American Sociological Review* 53 (1988): 81–93.

17. Franklin Dunford and Delbert Elliott, "Identifying Career Offenders Using Self-reported Data," *Journal of Research in Crime and Delinquency* 21 (1983): 57–86.

18. Michael Hindelang, Travis Hirschi, and Joseph Weis, *Measuring Delinquency* (Beverly Hills, Calif.: Sage, 1981).

19. *Newsweek,* March 13, 1989, p. 16.

20. U.S. Department of Justice, Bureau of Justice Statistics, *Households Touched by Crime, 1986,* NCF-105289 (Washington, D.C.: U.S. Government Printing Office, June 1987), p. 1.

21. *Newsweek,* March 13, 1989, p. 16.

22. U.S. Department of Justice, Bureau of Justice Statistics, *Criminal Victimization in the United States, A National Crime Survey Report,* NCJ-11456 (Washington, D.C.: U.S. Government Printing Office, August 1988), pp. 56–57.

23. Ibid., p. 54.

24. Derral Cheatwood, "Is There a Season for Homicide?" *Criminology* 26 (1988): 287–306; see also Steven P. Lab and J. David Hirschel, "Climatological Conditions and Crime: The Forecast Is...?" *Justice Quarterly* 5 (1988): 281–299. The article resulted in an interesting scientific exchange. See James L. Le-Beau, Comment, "Weather and Crime: Trying to Make Social Sense of a Physical Process," ibid., pp. 301–309; and Steven P. Lab and J. David Hirschel, "'Clouding' the Issues: The Failure to Recognize Methodological Problems," ibid., pp. 312–317.

25. U.S. Department of Justice, *The Severity of Crime,* Bureau of Justice Statistics Bulletin (Washington, D.C.: U.S. Government Printing Office, January 1984).

26. *New York Post,* April 20, 1989; *New York Times,* April 20, 1989.

27. See Kyle Kercher, "Causes and Correlates of Crime Committed by the Elderly," in *Critical Issues in Aging Policy,* ed. Edgar F. Borgatta and R. J. W. Montgomery (Beverly Hills, Calif.: Sage, 1987).

28. Michael Gottfredson and Travis Hirschi, "The True Value of Lambda Would Appear to Be Zero: An Essay on Career Criminals, Criminal Careers, Selective Incapacitation, Cohort Studies, and Related Topics," *Criminology* 24 (1986): 213–234.

29. Michael Gottfredson and Travis Hirschi, "Science, Public Policy, and the Career Paradigm," *Criminology* 26 (1988): 37–55; Travis Hirschi and Michael Gottfredson, "Age and the Explanation of Crime," *American Journal of Sociology* 89 (1983): 552–584; Lawrence Cohen and Kenneth Land, "Age Structure and Crime: Symmetry Versus Asymmetry and the Projection of Crime Rates Through the 1990's," *American Sociological Review* 52 (1987): 170–183; Michael Gottfredson and Travis Hirschi, "The Methodological Adequacy of Longitudinal Research on Crime," *Criminology* 25 (1987): 581–614. For a critique of Hirschi and Gottfredson's contentions, see Darrell J. Steffensmeier, Emilie Anderson Allan, Miles D. Harer, and Cathy Streifel, "Age and the Distribution of Crime," *American Journal of Sociology* 94 (1989): 803–831. For a test of those contentions, see Yossi Shavit and Arye Rattner, "Age, Crime, and the Early Life Course," *American Journal of Sociology* 93 (1988): 1457–1470.

30. James Q. Wilson and Richard Herrnstein, *Crime and Human Nature* (New York: Simon & Schuster, 1985), pp. 126–147; see also James A. Inciardi, "Crime and the Elderly: A Construction of Official Rates," in *The Elderly: Victims and Deviants,* ed. Carl D. Chambers, John H. Linquist, O. Z. White, and Michael T. Harter, pp. 177–190 (Athens: Ohio University Press, 1987).

31. Edward Mulvey and John LaRosa, "Delinquency Cessation and Adolescent Development: Preliminary Data," *American Journal of Orthopsychiatry* 56 (1986): 212–224.

32. Gordon Trasler, "Some Cautions for a Biological Approach to Crime Causation," in *The Causes of Crime: New Biological Approaches,* ed. Sarnoff Mednick, Terrie Moffitt, and Susan Stack, pp. 7–24 (Cambridge: Cambridge University Press, 1987).

33. Charles Tittle, "Two Empirical Regularities (Maybe) in Search of an Explanation: Commentary on the Age/Crime Debate," *Criminology* 26 (1988): 75–85.

34. Alfred Blumstein, Jacqueline Cohen, and David Farrington, "Criminal Career Research: Its Value for Criminology," *Criminology* 26 (1988): 1–35; David Farrington, Lloyd E. Ohlin, and James Q. Wilson, *Understanding and Controlling Crime: Toward a New Research Strategy* (New York: Springer-Verlag, 1986).

35. Alfred Blumstein, Jacqueline Cohen, Jeffrey Roth, and Christy Visher, *Criminal Careers and "Career Criminals"* (Washington, D.C.: National Academy Press, 1986). See also Alfred Blumstein, Jacqueline Cohen, Somnath Das, and Soumyo D. Moitra, "Specialization and Seriousness During Adult Criminal Careers," *Journal of Quantitative Criminology* 4 (1988): 303–345.

36. Marvin Wolfgang, Robert Figlio, and Thorsten Sellin, *Delinquency in a Birth Cohort* (Chicago: University of Chicago Press, 1972). For a discussion of how each delinquent act was weighted for seriousness, see Thorsten Sellin and Marvin Wolfgang, *The Measurement of Delinquency* (New York: Wiley, 1964).

37. Marvin Wolfgang, Terrence Thornberry, and Robert Figlio, *From Boy to Man, from Delinquency to Crime* (Chicago: University of Chicago Press, 1987).

38. Paul Tracy, Marvin Wolfgang, and Robert Figlio, *Delinquency Careers in Two Birth Cohorts* (New York: Plenum, 1990); Paul Tracy, Marvin Wolfgang, and Robert Figlio, *Patterns of Criminality in the 1958 Philadelphia Birth Cohort: Executive Summary,* for U.S. Department of Justice (Washington, D.C.: U.S. Government Printing Office, 1989). See also Rolf Loeber, "The Prevalence, Correlates, and Continuity of Serious Conduct Problems in Elementary School Children," *Criminology* 25 (1987): 615–642; Donald J. West and David P. Farrington, *The Delinquent Way of Life* (London: Heinemann, 1977); James Alan Fox and Paul E. Tracy, "A Measurement of Skewness in Offense Distribution," *Journal of Quantitative Criminology* 4 (1988): 259–274; Kimberly L. Kempf, "Crime Severity and Criminal Ca-

reer Progression," *Journal of Criminal Law and Criminology* 79 (1988): 524–540.

39. U.S. Department of Justice, Federal Bureau of Investigation, *Crime in the United States, 1988* (Washington, D.C.: U.S. Government Printing Office, 1989), p. 185; hereafter cited as Uniform Crime Reports.

40. U.S. Department of Justice, *Criminal Victimization in the United States, 1986,* p. 43.

41. Rosemary Sarri, "Gender Issues in Juvenile Justice," *Crime and Delinquency* 29 (1983): 381–397; Delbert Elliott and Suzanne Ageton, "Reconciling Race and Class Differences in Self-reported and Official Estimates of Delinquency," *American Sociological Review* 45 (1980): 95–110; Hindelang et al., *Measuring Delinquency.*

42. U.S. Department of Justice, *Report to the Nation on Crime and Justice,* 2d ed. (Washington, D.C.: U.S. Government Printing Office, 1988), p. 46.

43. Stephen A. Cernkovich and Peggy C. Giordano, "Delinquency, Opportunity, and Gender," *The Journal of Criminal Law and Criminology* 70 (1979): 145–151; Francis T. Cullen, Kathryn M. Golden, and John B. Cullen, "Sex and Delinquency: A Partial Test of the Masculinity Hypothesis," *Criminology* 17 (1979): 301–310.

44. John Hagan, John Simpson, and A. R. Gillis, "Class in the Household: A Power Control Theory of Gender and Delinquency," *American Journal of Sociology* 92 (1987): 788–816. See also Simon I. Singer and Murray Levine, "Power-Control Theory, Gender, and Delinquency: A Partial Replication with Additional Evidence on the Effects of Peers," *Criminology* 26 (1988): 627–647.

45. Cesare Lombroso and William Ferrero, *The Female Offender* (London: T. Fisher Unwin, 1895).

46. Sheldon Glueck and Eleanor T. Glueck, *Five Hundred Delinquent Women* (New York: Knopf, 1934).

47. Otto Pollack, *The Criminality of Women* (Philadelphia: University of Pennsylvania Press, 1950).

48. Freda Adler, *Sisters in Crime* (New York: McGraw-Hill, 1975), pp. 6–7.

49. Rita Simon, *The Contemporary Woman and Crime* (Rockville, Md.: National Institute of Mental Health, 1975).

50. Meda Chesney-Lind, "Female Offenders: Paternalism Reexamined," in *Women, the Courts, and Equality,* ed. Laura Crites and Winifred Hepperle (Newberry Park, Calif.: Sage, 1987).

51. Darrell J. Steffensmeier, "Crime and the Contemporary Woman: An Analysis of Changing Levels of Female Property Crimes, 1960–1975," *Social Forces* 57 (1978): 566–584, and "Organization Properties and Sex-Segregation in the Underworld: Building a Sociological Theory of Sex Differences in Crime," *Social Forces* 61 (1983): 1024–1025; Darrell J. Steffensmeier and Renée Hoffman Steffensmeier, "Trends in Female Delinquency: An Examination of Arrest, Juvenile Court, Self-report, and Field Data," *Criminology* 18 (1980): 62–85; Susan K. Datesman and Frank R. Scarpitti, "The Extent and Nature of Female Crime," in *Women, Crime, and Justice,* ed. Datesman and Scarpitti (New York: Oxford University Press, 1980); Lee H. Bowker, *Women, Crime, and the Criminal Justice System* (Lexington, Mass.: D. C. Heath, 1978). For a discussion of "masculine" characteristics and reported delinquency, see Stephen Norland, Randall C. Wessel, and Neal Shover, "Masculinity and Delinquency," *Criminology* 19 (1981): 421–433. For a description of the typical female offender (young, black, poorly educated, unskilled, unemployed, unmarried), see Nancy T. Wolfe, Francis T. Cullen, and John B. Cullen, "Describing the Female Offender: A Note on the Demographics of Arrests," *Journal of Criminal Justice* 12 (1984): 483–492. For a social-psychological discussion of the female offender, see Cathy Spatz Widom, "Female Offenders: Three Assumptions About Self-Esteem, Sex Role Identity, and Feminism," *Criminal Justice and Behavior* 6 (1979): 365–382.

52. Joseph Weis, "Liberation and Crime: The Invention of the New Female Criminal," *Crime and Social Justice* 6 (Fall 1976): 17–27;

Carol Smart, *Women, Crime, and Criminology: A Feminist Critique* (London: Routledge & Kegan Paul, 1977); E. Miller, "International Trends in the Study of Female Criminality: An Essay Review," *Contemporary Crisis* 7 (1983): 59–70; Jane Chapman, *Economic Reality and the Female Offender* (Lexington, Mass.: Lexington Books, 1980); Steven Box and Chris Hale, "Liberation/Emancipation, Economic Marginalization, or Less Chivalry," *Criminology* 22 (1984): 473–497. For a discussion of the internalization of gender roles by female prisoners, see Edna Erez, "The Myth of the New Female Offender: Some Evidence from Attitudes Toward Law and Justice," *Journal of Criminal Justice* 16 (1988): 499–509; Meda Chesney-Lind, "Girls' Crime and Woman's Place: Toward a Feminist Model of Female Delinquency," *Crime and Delinquency* 25 (1989): 5–29.

53. Nanci Koser Wilson, "The Masculinity of Violent Crime—Some Second Thoughts," *Journal of Criminal Justice* 9 (1981): 111–123; Josefina Figueira-McDonough, "A Reformulation of the 'Equal Opportunity' Explanation of Female Delinquency," *Crime and Delinquency* 26 (1980): 333–343; Ronald L. Simons, Martin G. Miller, and Stephen M. Aigner, "Contemporary Theories of Deviance and Female Delinquency: An Empirical Test," *Journal of Research in Crime and Delinquency* 17 (1980): 42–57; Roy Austin, "Women's Liberation and Increase in Minor, Major, and Occupational Offenses," *Criminology* 20 (1982): 407–430.

54. For a discussion of a unisex theory of crime, see Coramae Richey Mann, *Female Crime and Delinquency* (University, Alabama: University of Alabama Press, 1984). For an analysis of the relation of both gender and race to crime, see Vernetta D. Young, "Women, Race, and Crime," *Criminology* 18 (1980): 26–34. For a discussion of female crime in countries around the world, see Freda Adler, ed., *The Incidence of Female Criminality in the Contemporary World* (New York: New York University Press, 1984). See also Freda Adler and Rita James Simon, eds., *The Criminology of Deviant Women* (Boston: Houghton Mifflin, 1979).

55. Charles Tittle, Wayne Villemez, and Douglas Smith, "The Myth of Social Class and Criminality: An Empirical Assessment of the Empirical Evidence," *American Sociological Review* 43 (1978): 643–656.

56. Delbert Elliott and Suzanne Ageton, "Reconciling Race and Class Differences in Self-reported and Official Estimates of Delinquency," *American Sociological Review* 45 (1980): 95–110.

57. Delbert Elliott and David Huizinga, "Social Class and Delinquent Behavior in a National Youth Panel: 1976–1980," *Criminology* 21 (1983): 149–177.

58. The data on socioeconomic factors come from U.S. Department of Justice, *Report to the Nation*, pp. 48–49; Tittle et al., "Myth of Social Class and Criminality"; James Short and F. Ivan Nye, "Reported Behavior as a Criterion of Deviant Behavior," *Social Problems* 5 (1958): 207–213; Jay Williams and Martin Gold, "From Delinquent Behavior to Official Delinquency," *Social Problems* 20 (1972): 209–229.

59. U.S. Department of Justice, Bureau of Justice Statistics, *Annual Report, Fiscal 1986* (Washington, D.C.: U.S. Government Printing Office, April 1987), p. 39.

60. Uniform Crime Reports, 1988, p. 186.

61. Joan Petersilia, "Racial Disparities in the Criminal Justice System: A Summary," *Crime and Delinquency* 31 (1985): 15–34.

62. U.S. Department of Justice, *Criminal Victimization in the United States, 1986*.

63. Delbert Elliott and Harwin Voss, *Delinquency and Dropout* (Lexington, Mass: Lexington Books, 1974); Elliott and Ageton, "Reconciling Race and Class Differences."

64. Robert J. Sampson, "Urban Black Violence: The Effect of Male Joblessness and Family Disruption," *American Journal of Sociology* 93 (1987): 348–382; Charles Silverman, *Criminal Violence, Criminal Justice* (New York: Random House, 1979).

65. *Newsweek*, Dec. 17, 1984, p. 52.

66. U.S. Department of Justice, *Criminal Victimization in the United States, 1986*, pp. 3–6.

67. U.S. Department of Justice, *Report to the Nation,* p. 29.

68. U.S. Department of Justice, Bureau of Justice Statistics, *Criminal Victimization, 1986,* NCJ-106989(Washington, D.C.: U.S. Government Printing Office, October 1989), p. 3.

69. U.S. Department of Justice, Bureau of Justice Statistics, *Households Touched by Crime, 1988,* NCJ-117434 (Washington, D.C.: U.S. Government Printing Office, June 1989).

70. For a discussion of fear among the elderly, see Ronald L. Akers, Anthony J. La Greca, Christine Sellers, and John Cochran, "Fear of Crime and Victimization Among the Elderly in Different Types of Communities," *Criminology* 25 (1987): 487–505. See also Vincent J. Webb and Ineke Haen Marshall, "Response to Criminal Victimization by Older Americans," *Criminal Justice and Behavior* 16 (1989): 239–259; Mark Warr, "Fear of Victimization and Sensitivity to Risk," *Journal of Quantitative Criminology* 3 (1987): 29–46.

71. U.S. Department of Justice, *Report to the Nation,* p. 32.

3

SCHOOLS OF THOUGHT THROUGHOUT HISTORY

Children now love luxury. They have bad manners, contempt for authority. They show disrespect for elders. They contradict their parents, chatter before company, cross their legs and tyrannize their teachers.

The ideal condition would be, I admit, that men should be right by instinct; but since we are all likely to go astray, the reasonable thing is to learn from those who can teach.

When there is an income tax, the just man will pay more and the unjust less on the same amount of income.[1]

Criminologists traditionally consider that their field has its origins as a science in the eighteenth century, when Cesare Beccaria established what came to be known as the classical school of criminology. But when we look at what some much earlier thinkers had to say about crime, we may have to reconsider this assumption. Look again at the quotations above. The first may appear to be a modern description of delinquent youth, but Socrates made this observation over 2,300 years ago. The second quotation about instinct and learning and their association with criminality does not come from a modern criminology book on learning theory; rather, it was an observation made by Sophocles, who lived almost 2,500 years ago. The final quotation about income tax fraud is not taken from a study of American white-collar crime. It was Plato who voiced this insight, in his treatise *The Republic*, in the fourth century B.C.

Scholars have speculated about the causes of crime and possible remedies since ancient times. Modern criminology is based on their accumulated knowledge. The two leading schools of criminological thought are the classical and the positivist.

The **classical school of criminology,** which dates to the middle of the eighteenth century, is based on the assumption that criminals choose to commit crimes after weighing the consequences of their actions. According to classical criminologists, individuals have free will to choose legal or illegal means to get what they want; the fear of punishment can deter people from committing crime; and society can control behavior by making the pain of punishment greater than the pleasure of the criminal gains.

During the century that followed the presentation of the classical approach to crime causation, science underwent rapid development. By the middle of the nineteenth century scholars began to take a positivist approach to the causes of crime: they began to rely on the scientific method and empirical research. The **positivist school of criminology** assumes that human behavior is determined by forces beyond the control of individuals and that it is possible to measure those forces. Unlike classical criminologists, who claim (without scientific testing) that people rationally choose to commit crime, positivist criminologists view criminal behavior as stemming from biological, psychological, and social factors.

The earliest positivist theories of crime causation centered on biological factors. Such studies dominated criminology during the last half of the nineteenth century. In the twentieth century, biological explanations were ignored (and even targeted as racist after World War II). They did not surface again until the 1970s, when scientific advances in psychology shifted the emphasis from defects of criminals' bodies to defects of their minds. Throughout the twentieth century, psychologists and psychiatrists have played a major role in the study of crime causation.

A third area of positivist criminology focuses on the relation of social factors to crime. Sociological theories, developed in the second half of the nineteenth century, advanced throughout the twentieth, and continue to dominate the field of criminology today.

An understanding of the foundations of modern criminology helps us to understand contemporary developments in the field. Let us begin with the developments that led to the emergence of the classical school.

CLASSICAL CRIMINOLOGY

The Historical Context

Classical criminology grew out of a reaction against the barbaric system of law, punishment, and justice that existed before the French Revolution of 1789. Until that time, there was no real system of criminal justice in Europe. There were crimes against the state, against the church, and against the crown. Some of these crimes were specified, some were not. Judges had discretionary power to convict a person for an act not even legally defined as criminal.[2] Monarchs often issued what were called in French *lettres de cachet,* under which an individual could be imprisoned for almost any reason (disobedience to one's father, for example), or for no reason at all.

Many criminal laws were unwritten, and those that had been drafted, by and large, did not specify the kind or amount of punishment associated with various crimes. Arbitrary and often cruel sentences were imposed by powerful judges who had unbounded discretion to decide questions of guilt and innocence and to mete out punishment. "Due process" in the modern sense did not exist. While there was some general consensus on what constituted crime, there was no real limit to the amount and type of legal sanction the court commanded. Punishments included branding, burning, flogging, mutilation, drowning, banishment, beheading, and a host of others.[3] In England a person might receive the death penalty for any of more than two hundred offenses, including what we call today petty theft. Public punishments were popular events. When Robert-François Damiens was scheduled to be executed on March 2, 1757, for his attempted murder of Louis XV, so many people wanted to attend the one-and-a-half-hour spectacle that window seats overlooking the execution site were rented for high prices. Torture to elicit confessions was common. A criminal defendant in France might be subjected to the *peine forte et dure,*

> which consisted in stretching him on his back and placing over him an iron weight as heavy as he could bear. He was left that way until he died or spoke. A man would suffer these torments and lose his life in order to avoid trial and, therefore, conviction. In this way his lands and goods were not confiscated and were preserved for his family. This absurd proceeding was not abolished until the year 1772.[4]

AT ISSUE

Understanding Today What Happened Yesterday

Germany's only crime museum is located, appropriately, in a walled town. Behind ramparts perched above the winding Tauber River, Rothenburg ob der Tauber beckons visitors with its sixteenth-century atmosphere, complete with half-timbered houses, turrets and gables, and decorated shop signs. And, as with other picturesque towns encircled by nature or human artifice (Toledo, Venice, and Carcassonne are obvious European examples), tourists constitute the dominant industry.

The Medieval Crime Museum (Mittelalterliches Kriminalmuseum, as it is formally known) is a justly popular attraction. Housed in the former headquarters of the Order of the Hospital of St. John, a religious order of knights founded in the twelfth century, its present baroque building dates from 1718. Since 1977 the museum has offered the general public four floors of displays devoted to twelfth- through nineteenth-century European law, mostly German.

An illustrated guide to the museum accurately describes its holdings as including "instruments of torture and for the execution of sentences, costly books, graphic art, documents of emperors, princes, the nobility and towns, the law of coats of arms, seals and crafts and trades, patents of nobility and armorial bearings, caricatures of the judiciary," and the like. But if there is one subject matter that dominates all else, it is punishment—the calculated, brutal imposition of force when laws are infringed.

On entering the crime museum and descending to its basement and subbasement exhibition floors, one is immediately struck by the horrendous instruments of torture and punishment: a spiked chair from the time of witch trials; wheels used to break arms and legs and ultimately to cause death; a stretch ladder; finger and leg screws; a beheading block with the executioner's ax; tongue pliers; and other gruesome artifacts. The most direct deterrent warning is a "danger notice," a painting of a chopped-off hand which threatens those who might contemplate committing perjury and false witness.*

There are crime museums in all parts of the world. Austria has a curious relic of history north of Vienna, where a criminal court was sealed off a century-and-a-half ago. Recently, it was reopened to give a picture of what criminal justice was like in the early nineteenth century. In Milan, Italy, the ancient instruments of criminal justice are still in place in an old turret, where confessions were brutally extorted. In Rome, an ancient Vatican prison for noble prisoners has been restored for the display of ancient means of punishment. In many New England towns, foremost Sturbridge Village, the instruments of old criminal justice are also permanently on display.

These museums play a very important role in making us understand past efforts to control crime. What we are doing today to control crime will be displayed in the crime museums of the twenty-first century.

---

*Source: Timothy Stroup, *C. J. International*, Vol. 4 (1988): 5–6.

As Europe grew increasingly modern, industrial, and urban in the eighteenth century, it still clung to its medieval penal practices. With prosperity came an increasing gulf between the haves and the have-nots. Just before the Revolution, for example, a Parisian worker paid 97 percent of his daily earnings for a four-pound loaf of bread.[5] Hordes of unemployed people begged by day and found shelter under bridges by night. Social unrest grew. One of the few ways in which the established upper class could protect itself was through ruthless oppression of those beneath them; but ruthless oppression created more problems. As crime rates rose, so did the brutality of punishment. Both church and state grew increasingly tyrannical, using violence to conquer violence. The crime problem worsened.

The growing educated classes began to see the inconsistency in these developments. If terrible tortures were designed to deter crime, why were people committing even more crimes? The problem could not be insufficient punishment; there must be something wrong with the underlying reasoning. By the mid-eighteenth century, social reformers were beginning to suggest a more rational approach to crime and punishment. One of them, Cesare Beccaria, laid the foundation for the first school of criminology—the classical school.

Cesare Beccaria

Cesare Bonesana, Marchese di Beccaria (1738–1794), was rather undistinguished as a student. After graduating with a law degree from the University of Pavia, he returned home to Milan and joined a group of articulate and radical in-

Cesare Bonesana, Marchese di Beccaria, 1738–1794.

tellectuals. Disenchanted with contemporary European society, they organized themselves into the Academy of Fists. It was one of many young men's clubs that flourished in Italy at the time. Their purpose was to investigate the types of reforms that were needed to modernize Italian society.

In March 1763 Beccaria was assigned to prepare a report on the prison system. Pietro Verri, the head of the Academy of Fists, encouraged him to read the works of English and French writers—David Hume, John Locke, Claude Adrien Helvétius, Voltaire, Montesquieu, and Jean-Jacques Rousseau. Another member of the academy, the protector of prisons, taught him about the inhumanities that were possible under the guise of social control. Beccaria learned well. He read, observed, and made notes on small scraps of paper. These notes, Harry Elmer Barnes has observed, were destined to "assure to its author immortality and would work a revolution in the moral world" upon their publication in July 1764 under the title *Dei delitti e delle pene* (On Crimes and Punishment).[6] Beccaria presented to the world a coherent, comprehensive design for an enlightened criminal justice system that was to serve the people rather than the monarchy.

The tenor of the times was right. The controversy between the rule of men and the rule of law was raging. Some people defended the old order, under which judges and administrators made arbitrary or whimsical decisions. Others fought for the rule of law, under which the decision making of judges and administrators would be confined by precise legal limitations. The climate was ready for Beccaria's pen to provide the spark that ultimately exploded the barbaric traditions that had enslaved the people for centuries. Thus, with his small book, Cesare Beccaria became the "father of modern criminology."

According to Beccaria, the crime problem could be traced not to bad people but to bad laws. The arbitrary and capricious system that had been in place for generations needed to be torn down and replaced by a modern criminal justice system that would guarantee all people equal treatment before the law. Beccaria's book supplied a blueprint that defined and placed limits on the legal system. That blueprint was based on the assumption that people freely choose what they do and that they are responsible for the consequences of their behavior. Beccaria proposed the following principles:

- *Laws should be used to maintain the social contract:* "Laws are the conditions under which men, naturally independent, united themselves in society. Weary of living in a continual state of war, and of enjoying a liberty, which became of little value, from the uncertainty of its duration, they sacrificed one part of it, to enjoy the rest in peace and security."
- *Only legislators should create laws:* "The authority of making penal laws can only reside with the legislator, who represents the whole society united by the social compact."
- *Judges should impose punishment only in accordance with the law:* "[N]o magistrate then, (as he is one of the society), can, with justice inflict on any other member of the same society punishment that is not ordained by the laws."
- *Judges should not interpret the laws:* "Judges, in criminal cases, have no right to interpret the penal laws, because they are not legislators ....Every man hath his own particular point of view, and, at different times, sees the same objects in very different lights. The spirit of the laws will then be the result of the good or bad logic of the judge; and this will depend on his good or bad digestion."
- *Punishment should be based on the pleasure/pain principle:* "Pleasure and pain are the only springs of actions in beings endowed with sensibility ....If an equal punishment be ordained for two crimes that injure society in different degrees, there is nothing to deter men from committing the greater as often as it is attended with greater advantage."
- *Punishment should be based on the act, not on the actor:* "Crimes are only to be measured by the injuries done to the society. They err, therefore, who imagine that a crime is greater or less according to the intention of the person by whom it is committed."
- *The punishment should be determined by the crime:* "If mathematical calculation could be applied to the obscure and infinite combinations of human actions, there might be a correspond-

ing scale of punishments descending from the greatest to the least."
- *Punishment should be prompt and effective:* "The more immediate after the commission of a crime a punishment is inflicted, the more just and useful it will be.... An immediate punishment is more useful; because the smaller the interval of time between the punishment and the crime, the stronger and more lasting will be the association of the two ideas of crime and punishment."
- *All people should be treated equally:* "I assert that the punishment of a nobleman should in no wise differ from that of the lowest member of society."
- *Capital punishment should be abolished:* "The punishment of death is not authorized by any right; for...no such right exists.... The terrors of death make so slight an impression, that it has not force enough to withstand the forgetfulness natural to mankind."
- *The use of torture to gain confessions should be abolished:* "It is confounding all relations to expect...that pain should be the test of truth, as if truth resided in the muscles and fibres of a wretch in torture. By this method the robust will escape, and the feeble be condemned."
- *It is better to prevent crimes than to punish them:* "Would you prevent crimes? Let the laws be clear and simple, let the entire force of the nation be united in their defence, let them be intended rather to favour every individual than any particular classes....Finally, the most certain method of preventing crime is to perfect the system of education."[7]

Perhaps no other book in the history of criminology has had so great an impact as Beccaria's. Its ideas were so advanced for the times that Voltaire, who wrote the commentary for the French version, referred to Beccaria as "brother."[8] The English version appeared in 1767; by that time, three years after the book's publication, it had already gone through six Italian editions and several French editions. After the French Revolution, Beccaria's basic tenets served as a guide for the drafting of the French penal code, which was adopted in 1791. The Russian empress Catherine II (the Great) convened a commission to prepare a new code and issued instructions, penned in her own hand, to translate Beccaria's ideas into action. The Prussian king Frederick II (the Great) devoted his reign to revising the criminal and civil law. Emperor Joseph II had a new code drafted for Austria in 1787—the first code to abolish capital punishment. The influence of Beccaria's treatise spread across the Atlantic as well; it influenced the first ten amendments to the U.S. Constitution (the Bill of Rights).

Jeremy Bentham's Utilitarianism

Legal scholars and reformers throughout Europe proclaimed their indebtedness to Beccaria, but none owed more to him than the English legal philosopher Jeremy Bentham (1748–1832). Bentham devoted his life to developing a scientific approach to the making and breaking of laws. Like Beccaria, he was concerned with achieving "the greatest happiness of the greatest number."[9] His work was governed by utilitarian principles. **Utilitarianism** assumes that all of our actions are calculated in accordance with their likelihood of bringing happiness (pleasure) or unhappiness (pain). People weigh the probabilities of present and future pleasures against those of present and future pain. He proposed a precise pseudo-mathematical formula for this process, which he called "felicitous calculus." According to his reasoning, individuals are "human calculators" who put all the factors into an equation in order to decide whether or not a particular crime is worth committing. This notion may seem rather whimsical today, but at a time when there were 222 capital offenses, including the theft of 5 shillings' worth of goods from a shop, it provided a rationale for reform of the legal system.[10] Bentham reasoned that if prevention was the purpose of punishment, and if punishment became too costly by creating more harm than good, then penalties needed to be set just a bit in excess of the pleasure that one might derive from committing a crime, and no higher. The law exists in order to create happiness for its community. Since punishment creates unhappiness, it can be justified only if it prevents greater evil than it produces. Thus, Bentham suggested, if hanging a man's effigy produced the same preventive effect as hanging the man himself, there

would be no reason to hang the man, an act that surely increases the amount of cruelty in society.

Bentham had a long and productive career. He inspired many of his contemporaries, as well as criminologists of future generations, with his approach to rational crime control.

Sir Samuel Romilly, a member of Parliament, met Jeremy Bentham at the home of a mutual friend. He became interested in Bentham's idea that the certainty of punishment outweighs its severity as a deterrent against crime. Consequently, on February 9, 1810, in a speech before Parliament, he advocated Benthamite ideas:

> So evident is the truth of that maxim that if it were possible that punishment, as the consequence of guilt, could be reduced to an absolute certainty, a very slight penalty would be sufficient to prevent almost every species of crime.[11]

Although English conservatism prevented any major changes during Romilly's lifetime, the program of legislative pressure he began was continued by his followers and culminated in the complete reform of English criminal law between 1820 and 1861. During that period the number of capital offenses was reduced from 222 to 3: murder, treason, and piracy. Gradually, from the ideals of the philosophers of the Age of Enlightenment and the principles outlined by the scholars of the classical school, a new social order had been created, an order that affirmed a commitment to equal treatment of all people before the criminal law.

Evaluation of the Classical School

Classical criminology had an immediate and profound impact on jurisprudence and legislation. Substitution of the rule of law for human arbitrariness spread rapidly through Europe and the United States. Of no less significance was the influence of the classical school on penal and correctional policy. The classical principle that punishment must be appropriate to the crime was universally accepted during the nineteenth and early twentieth centuries. Yet the classical approach had weaknesses. Critics attacked the simplicity of the argument. The responsibility of the criminal justice system was simply to enforce the law with swiftness and certainty and to treat all people in like fashion, whether the accused persons were paupers or nobles. Government was to be run by the rule of law rather than at the discretion of its officials. In other words, the punishment was to fit the crime, not the criminal. The proposition that human beings had the capacity to choose freely between good and evil was accepted without question by the classicists. There was no need, then, to ask questions about why people behave as they do, questions about motive or about the specific circumstances surrounding criminal acts.

During the last half of the nineteenth century, scholars began to challenge these ideas. Influenced by the expanding search for scientific explanations of behavior in place of philosophical ones, criminologists shifted their attention from the act to the actor. They argued that people did not choose of their own free will to commit crime; rather, factors beyond their control were responsible for criminal behavior. Many scientific developments led up to this major shift in views about the causes of crime.

POSITIVIST CRIMINOLOGY

Biological Determinism

Following the emergence of the classical school, significant advances in knowledge of both the physical and the social world influenced thinking about crime. The intellectual climate became charged with the excitement of discovery. Auguste Comte (1798–1857), a French sociologist, firmly rooted the application of the modern methods of the physical sciences in the social sciences with his six-volume *Cours de philosophie positive* (Course in Positive Philosophy), published between 1830 and 1842. He argued that there could be no real knowledge of social phenomena unless it was based on a positivist (scientific) approach. Positivism alone, however, was not sufficient to bring about a fundamental change in criminological thinking. Not until Charles Darwin (1809–1882) challenged the doctrine of creation with his theory

of the evolution of species did the next generation of criminologists have the tools with which to challenge classicism. The turning point was the publication in 1859 of Darwin's *Origin of Species*. Darwin's theory was that God did not make all the various species of animals in two days, as we are told in Genesis 1:20–26, but rather that all had evolved through a process of adaptive mutation and natural selection. The process was based on the survival of the fittest in the struggle for existence. This radical theory seriously challenged traditional theological teaching. It was not until 1871, however, that Darwin publicly took the logical next step and traced human origins to an animal of the anthropoid group—the apes.[12] He thus posed an even more serious challenge to a religious tradition that maintained that God created the first man in his own image (Genesis 1:27).

The scientific world would never be the same again. The theory of evolution made it possible to ask new questions and to search in new ways for the answers to old ones. New biological theories rapidly evolved to replace older ones. Old ideas that demons and animal spirits could explain human behavior were replaced by new scientific principles as the social sciences came into being.

The nineteenth-century forces of positivism and evolution moved the field of criminology from a philosophical to a scientific perspective. But there were even earlier intellectual underpinnings of the scientific criminology that emerged in the second half of the nineteenth century.

The early search for criminal traits Throughout history a variety of physical characteristics and disfigurements have been said to characterize individuals of "evil" disposition. In the earliest pursuit of the relationship between biological traits and behavior, a Greek scientist who examined Socrates found his skull and facial features to be those of a person inclined toward alcoholism and brutality.[13] The ancient Greeks and Romans so distrusted red hair that even actors who wore red wigs were considered inferior. Through the ages cripples, hunchbacks, people with long hair, and a multitude of others have raised suspicion. Indeed, in the Middle Ages laws indicated that if two people were suspected of a crime, the uglier was the more likely to be guilty.[14]

The belief that criminals are born, not made, and that they can be identified by various physical irregularities is reflected not only in scientific writing but in literature as well. Shakespeare's Julius Caesar states,

> Let me have men about me that are fat;
> Sleek-headed men, and such as sleep o' nights.
> Yond Cassius has a lean and hungry look;
> He thinks too much: such men are dangerous.

Although its roots can be traced to ancient times, it was not until the sixteenth century that Giambattista della Porta (1535–1615) founded the school of human **physiognomy,** the study of facial features and their relation to human behavior. According to Porta, a thief had large lips and sharp vision. Two centuries later Porta's efforts were revived by the Swiss theologian Johann Kaspar Lavater (1741–1801).[15] They were elaborated by Franz Joseph Gall (1758–1828) and Johann Kaspar Spurzheim (1776–1832), whose science of **phrenology** posited that bumps on the brain were indications of psychological propensities.[16] In the United States these views were supported by a physician, Charles Caldwell (1772–1853), who searched for evidence that brain tissue and cells regulate human action.[17] Thus by the nineteenth century, the sciences of both physiognomy and phrenology had introduced specific biological factors into the study of crime causation.

Cesare Lombroso   Cesare Lombroso (1835–1909) integrated Comte's positivism, Darwin's evolutionism, and the many pioneering studies of the relation of crime to the body. In 1876, with the publication of *L'uomo delinquente* (The Criminal Man), criminology was permanently transformed from an abstract philosophy of crime control through legislation to a modern science of investigation into causes. Lombroso replaced the concept of free will, which had reigned for over a century as the principle that explained criminal behavior, with that of deter-

minism. Together with his followers Enrico Ferri and Raffaele Garofalo, Lombroso developed a new orientation, the Italian or positivist school of criminology, which seeks explanations for criminal behavior through scientific experimentation and research.

Cesare Lombroso was born in 1835. After completing his medical studies, he served as an army physician, became a professor of psychiatry at the University of Turin, and later in life accepted an appointment as professor of criminal anthropology. His theory of the born criminal states that criminals are a lower form of life, nearer to their apelike ancestors than noncriminals in traits and dispositions. They are distinguishable from noncriminals by various **atavistic stigmata**—physical features of creatures at an earlier stage of development, before they became fully human. He argued that criminals frequently have huge jaws and strong canine teeth, characteristics common to carnivores who tear and devour meat raw. The arm span of criminals is often greater than their height, just like that of apes, who use their forearms to propel themselves along the ground. An individual who is born with any five stigmata is a born criminal. This category accounts for about a third of all offenders. This theory

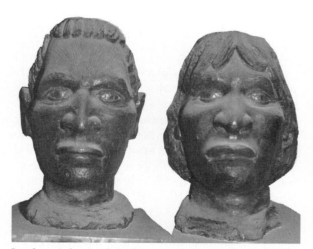

Lombroso's born criminal man and woman. Sculptures by an unknown Italian artist, commissioned by the Italian Ministry of Justice in the 1920s; now at the United Nations Interregional Research Institute for Crime and Justice (UNICRI), Rome.

became clear to Lombroso "one cold grey November morning" while he pored over the bones of a notorious outlaw who had died in an Italian prison:

> This man possessed such extraordinary agility, that he had been known to scale steep mountain heights bearing a sheep on his shoulders. His cynical effrontery was such that he openly boasted of his crimes. On his death...I was deputed to make the post-mortem, and on laying open the skull I found...a distinct depression ...as in inferior animals.

Lombroso was delighted by his findings:

> This was not merely an idea, but a revelation. At the sight of that skull, I seemed to see all of a sudden, lighted up as a vast plain under a flaming sky the problem of the nature of the criminal—an atavistic being who reproduces in his person the ferocious instincts of primitive humanity.[18]

Criminal women, according to Lombroso, are different from criminal men. It is the prostitute who represents the born criminal among them:

> We also saw that women have many traits in common with children; that their moral sense is different; they are revengeful, jealous, inclined to vengeance of a refined cruelty.... When a morbid activity of the psychical centres intensifies the bad qualities of women...it is clear that the innocuous semi-criminal present in normal women must be transformed into a born criminal more terrible than any man ....The criminal woman is consequently a monster. Her normal sister is kept in the paths of virtue by many causes, such as maternity, piety, weakness, and when these counter influences fail, and a woman commits a crime, we may conclude that her wickedness must have been enormous before it could triumph over so many obstacles.[19]

To the born criminal Lombroso added two other categories, insane criminals and criminoloids. Insane criminals are not criminal from birth; they become criminal as a result of some change in their brains which interferes with their ability to distinguish between right and wrong.[20] Criminoloids make up an ambiguous group that includes habitual criminals, criminals by passion, and other diverse types.

Most scientists who followed Lombroso did not share the exuberance he felt over the revelation that had come to him concerning the nature of criminality. As happens so often in history, his work has been kept alive more by criticism than by agreement. Though the theory that criminals were lodged on the lower rungs of the evolutionary ladder did not stand up to scientific scrutiny, the fact that Lombroso turned to empirical research, measuring thousands of live and dead prisoners, in his search for determinants of crime changed the nature of the questions asked by the generations of scholars who came after him. His influence continues in contemporary European research; American scientists, as the criminologist Marvin Wolfgang says, use him "as a straw man for attack on biological analyses of criminal behavior."[21] Thorsten Sellin has noted:

> Any scholar who succeeds in driving hundreds of fellow-students to search for the truth, and whose ideas after half a century possess vitality, merits an honorable place in the history of thought.[22]

At his death, true to his lifetime pursuits, Lombroso willed his body to the laboratory of legal medicine and his brain to the Institute of Anatomy at the University of Turin, where for so many years the father of modern criminology had espoused biological determinism.[23]

Enrico Ferri The best known of Lombroso's pupils was Enrico Ferri (1856–1929). Member of the Italian Parliament, accomplished public lecturer, brilliant lawyer, editor of a newspaper, and esteemed scholar, Ferri had published his first major book by the time he was 21. By age 25 he was a university professor. Although Ferri agreed with Lombroso on the biological bases of criminal behavior, his interest in socialism led him to recognize the importance of social, economic, and political determinants.

Ferri was a prolific writer on a vast number of criminological topics. His greatest contribution was his attack on the classical doctrine of free will, which argued that criminals should be held morally responsible for their crimes be-

CRIMINOLOGICAL FOCUS

The Mismeasure of Man

"Perhaps because its bold thesis [*Criminal Man* (1876)] seemed so clear, simple and impeccably scientific—criminals are ignorant apes with small brains as well as a brutish physical appearance—Lombroso's book won wide assent, despite its paltry data. At criminal trials for years afterward, a 'sinister look' signaled an incorrigible miscreant. 'Theoretical ethics,' declared Lombroso, 'passes over these diseased brains, as oil does over marble, without penetrating it.'"

In [a] study of biased science and its social abuse, Stephen Jay Gould marshals his many talents as a historian, biologist, and writer to debunk the work of men like Lombroso—scholars eager to bend any scrap of evidence to prove that some men are born inferior, whether by dint of apish physique, diminutive brain, or low IQ.

His story, which ends with Arthur Jensen's recent arguments for the inborn inferiority of blacks, begins in the mid-nineteenth century with Louis Agassiz, the great naturalist who believed Negroes to be a "degraded and degenerate race." In between, Gould brings back to life an astonishing rogues' gallery of once-eminent scientists, most of them committed to racial purity, a privileged elite, and the theory that class rule rests on immutable biological differences. Besides Lombroso, there is Francis Galton, a pioneer of modern statistics and the first apostle of "eugenics," a term he invented for the brave new science of breeding; Paul Broca, the French surgeon who spent a lifetime weighing brains and juggling figures to prove the superior heft of the European mind, and Samuel George Morton, a Philadelphia patrician who collected more than 1,000 skulls from all over the world, meticulously used BB's to measure the volume of each one, and then fudged the results to show that whites had bigger skulls than blacks.

Craniometry—the science of measuring skulls—seems the quaint vestige of a bygone era. Aptitude tests, by contrast, still determine educational opportunity in our own society. Ironically, Alfred Binet, the Frenchman who first devised such tests, viewed his own work with appropriate caution: since education could increase "the capacity to learn," he felt that his test scores should not be treated as if they recorded a fixed faculty. "Intellectual qualities," wrote Binet, "cannot be measured as linear surfaces are measured."

In America, psychologists obsessed with the idea of hereditary inferiority simply ignored Binet's own views. L. M. Terman, who developed the "Stanford-Binet scale," took for granted that IQ tests measured a real and unchanging thing, that his famous scale adequately rank-ordered variations in this thing, and that test scores could help public officials screen racial stocks and organize the division of labor, assigning "morons" to appropriately menial tasks. "It is safe to predict that in the near future intelligence tests will bring tens of thousands of these high-grade defectives under the surveillance and protection of society," exulted Terman in 1916. "This will ultimately result in curtailing the reproduction of feeblemindedness and in the elimination of an enormous amount of crime, pauperism, and industrial inefficiency."

Gould shows precisely how such scholars gathered data to suit their own assumptions. R. M. Yerkes, one of Terman's colleagues, tested immigrants for "innate" intelligence by asking them multiple-choice questions like, "Crisco is a: Patent medicine, disinfectant, toothpaste, food product." H. H. Goddard, another crusading advocate of IQ testing and scientific breeding, doctored photographs of "morons"—he coined the term—to make them look demented. And then there is the case of the late Sir Cyril Burt, the doyen of British mental testing, who palmed off faked data, "patent errors and specious claims," for more than 50 years.

Gould concedes that IQ testing can, in certain contexts, become a tool "for enhancing potential through proper education." But when prejudice passes for science and bigots wield IQ as a measure of innate human limits, the results are often tragic. Between 1924 and 1972, the state of Virginia secretly sterilized more than 7,500 people—simply because they scored low on one of Terman's dubious tests. Gould's eloquent book ends, appropriately enough, with the words of a victim: "My husband and me wanted children desperately. We were crazy about them. I never knew what they'd done to me."

Source: Jim Miller, review of *The Mismeasure of Man*, by Stephen Jay Gould, *Newsweek*, November 9, 1981, p. 106.

cause they must have made a rational decision to commit these acts. Ferri believed that criminals could not be held morally responsible because they did not choose to commit crimes, but rather were driven to commit them by conditions in their lives. He did, however, stress that society needed protection against criminal acts, and that it was the purpose of the criminal law and penal policy to provide that protection. Although he advocated conventional punishments and even the death penalty for those individuals who he assumed would never be fit to live in society, he was more interested in controlling crime through preventive measures—state control of the manufacture of weapons, inexpensive housing, better street lighting, and so forth.

Ferri claimed that strict adherence to preventive measures designed by scientific methods would eventually reduce crime and allow people to live together in society with less dependence on the penal system. Toward the end of his life he proudly admitted that he was an idealist, a statement with which generations of scholars have agreed. Though his prescription for crime reduction was overly optimistic, Ferri's importance to the development of modern criminology is undisputed. "When Enrico Ferri died on April 12, 1929," writes Thorsten Sellin, "one of the most colorful, influential figures in the history of criminology disappeared."[24]

Raffaele Garofalo Another follower of Lombroso was the Italian nobleman, magistrate, senator, and professor of law Raffaele Garofalo (1852–1934). Like Lombroso and Ferri, Garofalo was a positivist who rejected the doctrine of free will and supported the position that the only way to understand crime was to study it by scientific methods. Influenced by Lombroso's theory of atavistic stigmata, in which he found many shortcomings, Garofalo traced the roots of criminal behavior not to physical features but to their psychological equivalents, which he referred to as moral anomalies. According to this theory, natural crimes are found in all human societies, regardless of the views of lawmakers, and no civilized society can afford to disregard them.[25] Natural crimes, according to Garofalo, are those that offend the basic moral sentiments of probity (respect for the property of others) and piety (revulsion against the infliction of suffering on others). An individual who has an organic deficiency in these moral sentiments has no moral constraints against committing such crimes. Garofalo argued that these individuals could not be held responsible for their actions. But, like Ferri, he also emphasized that society needed protection and that penal policy should be designed to prevent criminals from inflicting harm.[26] Influenced by Darwinian theory, Garofalo suggested that the death penalty could rid society of its maladapted members, just as the natural selection process eliminated maladapted organisms. For less serious offenders, capable of adapting themselves to society in some measure, other types of punishments were preferable: transportation to remote lands, loss of privileges, institutionalization in farm colonies, or perhaps simply reparation. Clearly, Garofalo was much more interested in society's protection than in the individual rights of offenders.

Although Lombroso, Ferri, and Garofalo did not always agree on the causes of criminal behavior or on the way society should respond to it, their combined efforts marked a turning point in the development of the scientific study of crime. These three criminologists (one physician and two lawyers) were responsible for developing the positivist approach to criminality which influences criminology to the present day. Nevertheless, they had their critics. By introducing the scientific method for purposes of exploring crime causation, they paved the way for criminologists to support or refute the theories they themselves had created. The major challenge to Lombrosian theory resulted from the work of Charles Buckman Goring.

Challenges to Lombrosian theory From 1901 until 1913 Charles Buckman Goring (1870–1919), a medical officer at Parkhurst Prison in England, collected data on ninety-six traits of more than 3,000 convicts and a large control group of Oxford and Cambridge University stu-

Within 150 Miles of Milan: The Birth of Classical and Positivist Criminology

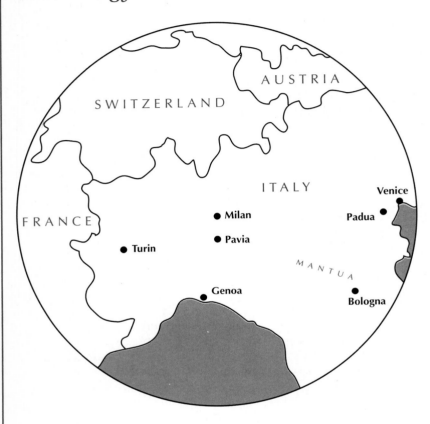

Cesare Beccaria, father of the classical school of criminology, was born in Milan, in northern Italy, and he worked there all his life. The Milanese are justly proud of their native son. So are the Austrians, who at that time—before the unification of Italy—had sovereignty over Milan, and whose imperial governor supported Beccaria's work and imported his ideas into Austria. Italy's French neighbors are equally proud of Beccaria, for their great Enlightenment thinkers, among them Montesquieu, Voltaire, and Jean-Jacques Rousseau, inspired Beccaria.

From Milan Beccaria's classical school made its world conquest. In England Jeremy Bentham, whose thoughts had developed along similar lines, promoted Beccaria's ideas. In the United States the founding fathers enshrined Beccaria's ideas in the Bill of Rights. Beccaria's work was swiftly translated into all major languages and affected criminal justice policies everywhere in Europe and the Americas.

The next major criminological school likewise emanated from northern Italy, about 150 miles east of Milan as the crow flies, in Venice, where another Cesare was born—Cesare Lombroso, father of the positivist school. He studied at the universities of Pavia, 25 miles south of Milan; Padua, 100 miles east of Milan; and Genoa, 75 miles south of Milan. His professorship was at the University of Turin, less than 100 miles southwest of Milan. His kindred in spirit, student, and fellow founder of the positivist school, Enrico Ferri, was born in the province of Mantua, less than 100 miles southeast of Milan. Ferri studied and worked in Bologna, 120 miles to the southeast of Milan. The third member of the positivist triumvirate, Raffaele Garofalo, was the only one of the four great pioneers of criminology not to originate within 150 miles of Milan. Born in Naples, where he became a professor, he also served as senator and minister of justice in Rome.

The traveler to these cities will find statues and commemorative plaques dedicated to these pioneers, some with fresh flowers and wreaths placed by visitors from all over the world. It may well have been sheer coincidence that cities within 150 miles of Milan, within a span of 150 years, would play such a monumental role in the creation of modern criminology. History might have favored other regions of Europe, where conditions were equally conducive to intellectual progress and the development of criminology. But history decided on Milan and its vicinity. It is not a coincidence, however, that Milan remains in the forefront of criminological progress, through its Center of Criminology, the Centro Nazionale di Prevenzione e Difesa Sociale.

dents, hospital patients, and soldiers. Among his research assistants was a famous statistician, Karl Pearson. When Goring had completed his examinations of physical and mental traits, he was armed with enough data to refute Lombroso's theory of the anthropological criminal type. Goring's report to the scientific community read:

> From a knowledge only of an undergraduate's cephalic [head] measurement, a better judgement could be given as to whether he were studying at an English or Scottish university than a prediction could be made as to whether he would eventually become a university professor or a convicted felon.[27]

This evaluation still stands as the most cogent critical analysis of Lombroso's theory of the born criminal. But though Goring rejected the claims that specific stigmata identify the criminal, he was convinced that poor physical condition plus a defective state of mind were determining factors in the criminal personality.

A return to biological determinism   After Goring's challenge, Lombrosian theory lost its academic popularity for about a quarter of a century. Then in 1939 Ernest Hooten (1887–1954), a physical anthropologist, reawakened an interest in biologically determined criminality with his publication of a massive study comparing American prisoners with a noncriminal control group. He concluded that

> in every population there are hereditary inferiors in mind and in body as well as physical and mental deficients.... Our information definitely proves that it is from the physically inferior element of the population that native born criminals from native parentage are mainly derived.[28]

Like his positivist predecessors, Hooten argued for the segregation of what he referred to as the "criminal stock," and he recommended their sterilization as well.[29]

In the search for the source of criminality, other scientists, too, looked for the elusive link between physical characteristics and crime. The **somatotype school of criminology,** which related body build to behavior, became popular during the first half of the twentieth century. It originated with the work of a German psychiatrist, Ernst Kretschmer (1888–1964), who distinguished three principal types of physiques: (1) the asthenic: lean, slightly built, narrow shoulders; (2) the athletic: medium to tall, strong, muscular, coarse bones; and (3) the pyknic: medium height, rounded figure, massive neck, broad face. He then related these physical types to various psychic disorders: pyknics to manic depression, asthenics and athletics to schizophrenia, and so on.[30]

Kretschmer's work was brought to the United States by William Sheldon (1898–1977), who formulated his own group of somatotypes: the endomorph, the mesomorph, and the ectomorph. Sheldon's father was a dog breeder who judged animals in competition, and Sheldon worked out a point system of his own for judging humans. Thus one could actually measure on a scale from 1 to 7 the relative dominance of each body type in any given individual. People with predominantly mesomorph traits (physically powerful, aggressive, athletic physiques), he argued, tend more than others to be involved in illegal behavior.[31] This finding was later supported by Sheldon Glueck (1896–1980) and Eleanor Glueck (1898–1972), who based their studies of delinquents on William Sheldon's somatotypes.[32]

By and large, studies based on somatotyping have been sharply criticized for their methodological flaws, including nonrepresentative selection of their samples (bias), failure to account for cultural stereotyping (our expectations of how muscular, physically active people should react), and poor statistical analyses. An anthropologist summed up the negative response of the scientific community by suggesting that somatotyping was "a New Phrenology in which the bumps on the buttocks take the place of the bumps on the skulls."[33] After World War II, somatotyping seemed too close to **eugenics** (the science of controlled reproduction to improve hereditary qualities), and the approach fell into disfavor. During the 1960s, however, the discovery of an extra sex chromosome in some criminal samples (as we shall see in Chapter 4) revived some interest in this theory.

Inherited criminality During the period when some researchers were measuring skulls and bodies of criminals in their search for the physical determinants of crime, others were arguing that criminality was an inherited trait passed on in the genes. To support the theory, they traced family histories through several generations. Richard Dugdale (1841–1883), for example, studied the lives of more than a thousand members of the family he called Jukes. His interest in the family began when he found six related people in a jail in upstate New York. Following one branch of the family, the descendants of Ada Jukes, whom he referred to as the "mother of criminals," Dugdale found among the thousand of them 280 paupers, 60 thieves, 7 murderers, 40 other criminals, 40 persons with venereal disease, and 50 prostitutes. His findings indicated, Dugdale claimed, that since some families produce generations of criminals, they must be transmitting a degenerate trait down the line.[34] A similar conclusion was reached by Henry Goddard (1866–1957). In a study of the family tree of a Revolutionary War soldier, Martin Kallikak, Goddard found many more criminals among the descendants of Kallikak's illegitimate son than among the descendants of his son by a later marriage with "a woman of his own quality."[35]

These early studies have been discredited primarily on the grounds that genetic and environmental influences could not be separated. But in the early twentieth century they were taken quite seriously. On the assumption that crime could be controlled if criminals could be prevented from transmitting their traits to the next generation, some states permitted the sterilization of habitual offenders. Sterilization laws were held constitutional by the U.S. Supreme Court in a 1927 opinion written by Justice Oliver Wendell Holmes, Jr., which included the well-known pronouncement that

> it is better for all the world, if instead of waiting to execute degenerate offspring for crime, or to let them starve for their imbecility, society can prevent those who are manifestly unfit from continuing their kind....Three generations of imbeciles are enough.[36]

Clearly the early positivists, with their focus on the physical characteristics of criminals, exerted great influence. They were destined to be overshadowed, though, by other investigators who focused on psychological characteristics.

Psychological Determinism

On the whole, scholars who investigated criminal behavior in the nineteenth and early twentieth centuries were far more interested in the human body than in the human mind. During that period, however, several contributions were made in the area of psychological explanations of crime. Some of the earliest contributions were made by physicians who were interested primarily in the legal responsibility of the criminally insane. Later on, psychologists entered the field applying their new testing techniques to the study of offenders (see Chapter 4).

Pioneers in psychocriminology Isaac Ray (1807–1881), acknowledged to be America's first forensic psychiatrist, was interested throughout his life in the application of psychiatric principles to the law. He is best known as the author of *The Medical Jurisprudence of Insanity*, a treatise on criminal responsibility which became widely quoted and influential.[37] In it he defended the concept of "moral insanity," a disorder that had first been described in 1806 by Philippe Pinel.[38] "Moral insanity" was a term used to describe persons who were normal in all respects except that something was wrong with the part of the brain that regulates affective responses. Ray questioned whether we could hold people legally responsible for their acts if they had such an impairment, because these people committed their crimes without an intent to do so.

Born in the same year as Lombroso, Henry Maudsley (1835–1918) shared Ray's concerns about criminal responsibility. According to Maudsley, some people may be considered either "insane or criminal according to the standpoint from which they are looked at." He believed that for many persons crime is an "outlet in which their unsound tendencies are discharged; they would go mad if they were not criminals."[39] Most of Maudsley's attention focused on the borderline between insanity and crime.

Psychological studies of criminals Around the turn of the twentieth century, psychologists used their new techniques of measurement to the study of offenders. The administering of intelligence tests to inmates of jails, prisons, and other public institutions was especially popular at that time, because it was a period of major controversy over the relation of mental deficiency to criminal behavior. The new technique seemed to provide an objective basis for differentiating criminals from noncriminals.

In 1914 Henry Goddard (1866–1957) examined some of the intelligence tests that had been given to inmates and concluded that 25 to 50 percent of the people in prison had intellectual defects that made them incapable of managing their own affairs.[40] These ideas remained dominant until they were challenged by the results of intelligence tests administered to World War I draftees, whose scores were found to be lower than those of prisoners in the federal penitentiary at Leavenworth. As a result of this study and others like it, intelligence quotient (IQ) measures largely disappeared as a basis for explaining criminal behavior.

Sociological Determinism

During the nineteenth and early twentieth centuries some scholars began to search for the social determinants of criminal behavior. The approach had its roots in Europe in the 1830s, between Beccaria's *On Crimes and Punishment* and Lombroso's *The Criminal Man*.

Adolphe Quételet and André Michel Guerry The Belgian mathematician Adolphe Quételet (1796–1874) and the French lawyer André Michel Guerry (1802–1866) were among the first scholars to repudiate the free-will doctrine of the classicists. Working independently on the relation of crime statistics to such factors as poverty, age, sex, race, and climate, both scholars concluded that society, not the decisions of individual offenders, was responsible for criminal behavior.

The first modern criminal statistics were published in France in 1827. Guerry used those statistics to demonstrate that crime rates varied with social factors. He found, for example, that the wealthiest region of France had the highest rate of property crime but only half the national rate of violent crime. He concluded that the main factor in property crime was opportunity: there was much more to steal in the richer provinces.

Quételet did an elaborate analysis of crime in France, Belgium, and Holland. After analyzing criminal statistics, which he called "moral statistics," he concluded that if we look at overall patterns of behavior of groups across a whole society, we find a startling regularity of rates of various behaviors. According to Quételet,

> we can enumerate in advance how many individuals will soil their hands in the blood of their fellows, how many will be frauds, how many prisoners; almost as one can enumerate in advance the births and deaths that will take place.[41]

By focusing on groups rather than individuals, he discovered that behavior is indeed predictable, regular, and understandable. Just as the physical world is governed by the laws of nature, human behavior is governed by forces external to the individual. The more we learn about those forces, the easier it becomes to predict behavior. A major goal of criminological research, according to Quételet, should be to identify factors related to crime and to assign to them their "proper degree of influence."[42] Though neither he nor Guerry offered a theory of criminal behavior, the fact that both of them studied social factors scientifically, using methods of quantitative research, made them key figures in the subsequent development of sociological theories of crime causation.

Gabriel Tarde One of the earliest sociological theories of criminal behavior was formulated by Gabriel Tarde (1843–1904), who served fifteen years as a provincial judge and was then placed in charge of France's national statistics. After an extensive analysis of these statistics, he came to the conclusion that the majority of murderers and notorious thieves began as children who had been abandoned, and the true seminary of crime must be sought for upon each public square or each crossroad of our towns, whether they be small or large, in those flocks of pillaging street urchins who, like bands of sparrows, associate together, at first for marauding, and then for theft, because of a lack of education and food in their homes.[43]

Tarde rejected the Lombrosian theory of biological abnormality, which was popular in his time, arguing that criminals were normal people who learned crime just as others learned legitimate trades. He formulated his theory in terms of **laws of imitation**—principles that governed the process by which people became criminals. According to Tarde's thesis, individuals emulate behavior patterns in much the same way that they copy styles of dress. Moreover, there is a pattern to the way such emulation takes place: (1) individuals imitate others in proportion to the intensity and frequency of their contacts; (2) inferiors imitate superiors; that is, trends flow from town to country and from upper to lower classes; and (3) when two behavior patterns clash, one may take the place of the other, as when guns largely replaced knives as murder weapons.[44] Tarde's work served as the basis for Edwin Sutherland's theory of differential association, which we shall examine in Chapter 5.

Emile Durkheim   Modern criminologists take two major approaches to the study of the social factors associated with crime. One of them we have discussed in relation to Tarde. This approach asks how individuals become criminal. What is the process? How are behavior patterns learned and transmitted? The second major approach looks at the social structure and its institutions. It asks how crime arises in the first place and how it is related to the functioning of a society. For answers to these questions, scholars begin with the work of Emile Durkheim (1858–1917).

Of all nineteenth-century writers on the relationship between crime and social factors, none has more powerfully influenced contemporary criminology than Durkheim, who is universally acknowledged as one of the founders of sociology. On October 12, 1870, when Durkheim was 12 years old, the German army invaded and occupied the city of his birth in eastern France. Thus at a very early age he witnessed social chaos and the effects of rapid change, topics with which he remained preoccupied throughout his life. At the age of 24 he became a professor of philosophy and at 29 he joined the faculty of the University of Bordeaux. There he taught the first course in sociology ever to be offered by a French university. By 1902 he had moved to the University of Paris, where he completed his doctoral studies. His *Division of Social Labor* became a landmark work on the organization of societies. According to Durkheim, crime is as normal a part of society as birth and death. Theoretically, crime could disappear altogether only if all members of society had the same values, and such a standardization of individuals is neither possible nor desirable. Furthermore, some crime is in fact necessary if a society is to progress.

> The opportunity for the genius to carry out his work affords the criminal his originality at a lower level.... According to Athenian law, Socrates was a criminal, and his condemnation was no more than just. However, his crime, namely, the independence of his thought, rendered a service not only to humanity but to his country.[45]

Durkheim pointed out further that all societies have not only crime but sanctions. The rationale for these sanctions varies in accordance with the structure of the society. In a strongly cohesive society, punishment of members who deviate is used to reinforce the value system—to remind people of what is right and what is wrong—thereby preserving the pool of common belief and thus the solidarity of the society. Punishment must be harsh to serve these ends. In a large, urbanized, heterogeneous society, on the other hand, punishment is used not to preserve solidarity but rather to right the wrong done to a victim. Punishment thus is evaluated in accordance with the harm done, with the goal of restitution and reinstatement of order as quickly as possible. The offense is not considered a threat to social cohesion, primarily because criminal events do not even come to the attention of most people in a large, complex society.

The contributions of Durkheim are many and profound, but the one that has been the most important to contemporary criminology is his concept of **anomie,** a breakdown of social order as a result of a loss of standards and values. In such a society (discussed in Chapter 5), disintegration and chaos replace social cohesion.

THE RELATION OF HISTORICAL AND CONTEMPORARY CRIMINOLOGY

Classical criminologists thought the problem of crime might be solved through limitations on governmental power, abolition of brutality, and creation of a more equitable system of justice. They argued that the punishment should fit the crime. For over a century this perspective dominated criminology. Later on, positivist criminologists influenced judges to give greater consideration to the offender than to the gravity of the crime when imposing sentences. The current era marks a return to the classical demand that the punishment must correspond to the se-

riousness of the crime and the guilt of the offender (as we shall see in Chapter 16).

As modern science discovered more and more about cause and effect in the physical and social universes, the theory that individuals commit crimes of their own free will began to lose favor. The positivists searched for determinants of crime in biological, psychological, and social factors. Biologically based theories were popular in the late nineteenth century, fell out of favor in the early part of the twentieth century, and emerged again in the 1970s (as we shall see in Chapter 4) with studies of hormone imbalances, diet, environmental contaminants, and so forth. Since the studies of criminal responsibility in the nineteenth century, centering on the insanity defense and of intelligence levels in the twentieth, psychiatrists and psychologists have continued to play their roles in the search for the causes of crime, especially after Sigmund Freud developed his well-known theory of human personality (Chapter 4). The sociological perspective became popular in the 1920s and has remained the predominant approach of criminological studies. We shall examine contemporary theories in Chapters 5 through 8.

REVIEW

In the history of criminology from ancient times to the early twentieth century, its many themes at times have clashed and at times have supported one another. There is no straight-line evolutionary track that we can follow from the inception of the first "criminological" thought to modern theories (see Table 3.1). Some scholars concentrated on criminal law and procedure, others on criminal behavior. Some took the biological route, others the psychological, still others the sociological, and the work of some investigators has encompassed a combination of factors. Toward the end of the nineteenth century a discipline began to emerge.

Tracing the major developments back in time helps us to understand how criminology grew

and blossomed into the discipline we know today. Many of the issues that appear on the intellectual battlefields as we approach the twenty-first century are the very same issues that our academic ancestors grappled with for hundreds, indeed thousands of years. With each new clash, some old concepts died, but most were incorporated within competing doctrinal boundaries, there to remain until the next challenge. Thus the controversies of one era become the foundations of knowledge for the next. As societies develop and are subjected to new technologies, the crime problem becomes ever more complex. So do the questions it raises. In Part II we shall see how twentieth-century theorists have dealt with them.

TABLE 3.1   PIONEERS IN CRIMINOLOGY: A CHRONOLOGY

| CLASSICAL CRIMINOLOGY | POSITIVIST CRIMINOLOGY | | |
FREE WILL	BIOLOGICAL DETERMINISM	PSYCHOLOGICAL DETERMINISM	SOCIAL DETERMINISM
Cesare Beccaria (1738–1794) Wrote first coherent comprehensive design for an enlightened criminal justice system based on law rather than arbitrary decisions.	Johann Kaspar Lavater (1741–1801) Early biological approach to crime causation. Developed phrenology, the study of the relationship between bumps on the brain's outer surface and psychological traits.		
Jeremy Bentham (1748–1832) Developed utilitarian principles of punishment based on the amount of happiness (pleasure) or unhappiness (pain) any given act will bring to the actor.	Franz Joseph Gall (1758–1828) Early biological approach to crime causation. Further developed phrenology.		
	Johann Kaspar Spurzheim (1776–1832) Early biological approach. Continued studies of phrenology.		
			Adolphe Quételet (1796–1874) Made early attempt to repudiate free-will doctrine of classicists. Studied social determinants of behavior.
			Auguste Comte (1798–1857) Brought modern scientific methods of the physical sciences into the social sciences.
		Isaac Ray (1807–1881) Questioned whether people who were "morally insane" could be held legally responsible for their acts.	André Michel Guerry (1802–1866) Made early attempt to repudiate free-will doctrine of classicists. Related crime statistics to social factors.

TABLE 3.1 **(Continued)**

CLASSICAL CRIMINOLOGY	POSITIVIST CRIMINOLOGY		
FREE WILL	BIOLOGICAL DETERMINISM	PSYCHOLOGICAL DETERMINISM	SOCIAL DETERMINISM
	Charles Darwin (1809–1882) Formulated theory of evolution, which challenged theological teaching and changed explanations of human behavior.		
	Cesare Lombroso (1835–1909) Replaced free will with determinism as the explanatory factor in criminal behavior. Posited the "born criminal." Shifted attention from act to actor. Father of modern criminology.	Henry Maudsley (1835–1918) Pioneered criteria for legal responsibility.	
	Richard Dugdale (1841–1883) Related criminal behavior to inherited traits (Jukes family).		Gabriel Tarde (1843–1904) Explained crime as learned behavior.
	Raffaele Garofalo (1852–1934) Traced roots of criminal behavior to "moral anomalies" rather than to physical stigmata.		
	Enrico Ferri (1856–1929) Produced first penal code based on principles of positivism. Replaced "moral responsibility" with social accountability.		Emile Durkheim (1858–1917) A founder of sociology. Developed theory of anomie, idea that crime is "normal" in all societies, relation between social change and behavior, etc.
		Henry Goddard (1866–1957) Related criminal behavior to intelligence levels (Kallikak family).	

TABLE 3.1   (Continued)

CLASSICAL CRIMINOLOGY	POSITIVIST CRIMINOLOGY		
FREE WILL	BIOLOGICAL DETERMINISM	PSYCHOLOGICAL DETERMINISM	SOCIAL DETERMINISM
			Charles Buckman Goring (1870–1919) Used empirical research to refute Lombroso's theory of criminal types.
	Ernest Hooten (1887–1954) Related criminality to hereditary inferiority.		
	Ernst Kretschmer (1888–1964) Introduced the somatotype (body build) school of criminology.		
	William Sheldon (1898–1977) Related body types to illegal behavior.		

KEY TERMS

anomie
atavistic stigmata
classical school of criminology
eugenics
laws of imitation

phrenology
physiognomy
positivist school of criminology
somatotype school of criminology
utilitarianism

NOTES

1. First quote: Attributed to Socrates by Plato, wording unconfirmed by researchers. See Suzy Platt (ed.), *Respectfully Quoted* (Washington, D.C.: Library of Congress, 1989), p. 42; second quote: Sophocles, *Antigone*, I, 720; third quote: Plato, *The Republic*, I, 343 d.

2. Leon Radzinowicz, *Ideology and Crime* (New York: Columbia University Press, 1966), p. 2; Marc Ancel, Introduction to *The French Penal Code*, ed. G. O. W. Mueller (South Hackensack, N.J.: Fred B. Rothman, 1960), pp. 1–2.

3. Thorsten Sellin, *Slavery and the Penal System* (New York: Elsevier, 1976); Torsten Eriksson, *The Reformers: An Historical Survey of Pioneer Experiments in the Treatment of Criminals* (New York: Elsevier, 1976).

4. Marcello T. Maestro, *Cesare Beccaria and the Origins of Penal Reform* (Philadelphia: Temple University Press, 1973), p. 16.

5. George Rude, *The Crowd in the French Revolution* (New York: Oxford University Press, 1959), appendix.

6. Harry Elmer Barnes, *The Story of Punishment: A Record of Man's Inhumanity to Man*, 2d ed. (Montclair, N.J.: Patterson Smith, 1972), p. 99.

7. Cesare Beccaria, *On Crimes and Punishment*, trans. Edward D. Ingraham, 2d ed. (Philadelphia: Philip H. Nicklin, 1819), pp. 15, 20, 22–23, 30–32, 60, 74–75, 80, 97–98, 149, 156. For a debate on the contribution of Beccaria to modern criminology, see G. O. W. Mueller, "Whose Prophet is Cesare Beccaria? An Essay on the Origins of Criminological Theory," *Advances in Criminological Theory* 2(1990): 1–14; and Graeme Newman and Pietro Marongiu, "Penological Reform and the Myth of Beccaria *Criminology* 28(1990): 325–346.

8. Marcello T. Maestro, *Voltaire and Beccaria as Reformers of Criminal Law* (New York: Columbia University Press, 1942), p. 73.

9. Jeremy Bentham, *A Fragment on Government and an Introduction to the Principles of Morals and Legislation*, ed. Wilfred Harrison (Oxford: Basil Blackwell, 1967), p. 21.

10. Barnes, *Story of Punishment*, p. 102.

11. Quoted in Leon Radzinowicz, *A History of English Criminal Law and Its Administration from 1750*, vol. 1 (New York: Macmillan, 1948), p. 330.

12. Charles Darwin, *Origin of Species* (1854; Cambridge: Harvard University Press, 1859), and *The Descent of Man and Selection in Relation to Sex* (1871; New York: A. L. Burt, 1874).

13. Havelock Ellis, *The Criminal*, 2d ed. (New York: Scribner's, 1900), p. 27.

14. Christopher Hibbert, *The Roots of Evil* (Boston: Little, Brown, 1963), p. 187.

15. Arthur E. Fink, *The Causes of Crime: Biological Theories in the United States, 1800–1915* (Philadelphia: University of Pennsylvania Press, 1938), p. 1.

16. Hermann Mannheim, *Comparative Criminology* (Boston: Houghton Mifflin, 1965), p. 213.

17. George B. Vold, *Theoretical Criminology* (New York: Oxford University Press, 1958), pp. 44–49.

18. Gina Lombroso Ferrero, *Criminal Man: According to the Classification of Cesare Lombroso, with an Introduction by Cesare Lombroso* (1911; Montclair, N.J.: Patterson Smith, 1972), pp. xxiv–xxv.

19. Cesare Lombroso and William Ferrero, *The Female Offender* (New York: D. Appleton, 1895), pp. 151–152.

20. Cesare Lombroso, *Crime, Its Causes and Remedies* (Boston: Little, Brown, 1918).

21. Marvin Wolfgang, "Cesare Lombroso," in *Pioneers in Criminology*, ed. Hermann Mannheim (London: Stevens, 1960), p. 168.

22. Thorsten Sellin, "The Lombrosian Myth in Criminology," *American Journal of Sociology* 42 (1937): 898–899.

23. Wolfgang, "Cesare Lombroso," p. 168.

24. Thorsten Sellin, "Enrico Ferri: Pioneer in Criminology, 1856–1929," in *The Positive School of Criminology: Three Lectures by Enrico Ferri*, ed. Stanley E. Grupp (Pittsburgh: University of Pittsburgh Press, 1968), p. 13.

25. Raffaele Garofalo, *Criminology*, trans. Robert Wyness Millar (Montclair, N.J.: Patterson Smith, 1968), pp. 4–5.

26. Marc Ancel, *Social Defense: The Future of Penal Reform* (Littleton, Colo.: Fred B. Rothman, 1987).

27. Charles B. Goring, *The English Convict: A Statistical Study* (London: His Majesty's Stationary Office, 1913), p. 145. For a critique of Goring's work, see Piers Beirne, "Heredity Versus Environment," *British Journal of Criminology* 28 (1988): 315–339.

28. E. A. Hooten, *The American Criminal* (Cambridge: Harvard University Press, 1939), p. 308.

29. E. A. Hooten, *Crime and the Man* (Cambridge: Harvard University Press, 1939), p. 13.

30. Ernst Kretschmer, *Physique and Character* (New York: Harcourt Brace, 1926).

31. William H. Sheldon, *Varieties of Delinquent Youth: An Introduction to Constitutional Psy-*

chiatry (New York: Harper, 1949). See also Emil M. Hartl, Edward P. Monnelly, and Ronald D. Elderkin, *Physique and Delinquent Behavior: A Thirty-Year Follow-up of William H. Sheldon's ''Varieties of Delinquent Youth''* (New York: Academic Press, 1982).

32. Eleanor Glueck and Sheldon Glueck, *Unraveling Juvenile Delinquency* (Cambridge: Harvard University Press, 1950). See also Sheldon Glueck and Eleanor Glueck, *Of Delinquency and Crime* (Springfield, Ill.: Charles C Thomas, 1974), p. 2. For a recent reanalysis of the Gluecks' data, see John H. Laub and Robert J. Sampson, ''Unravelling Families and Delinquency: A Reanalysis of the Gluecks' Data,'' *Criminology* 26 (1988): 355–380. For a study of constitutional variables, see Juan B. Cortes and Florence M. Gatti, *Delinquency and Crime: A Biopsychosocial Approach* (New York: Seminar Press, 1972).

33. S. L. Washburn, (Book Review) ''Varieties of Delinquent Youth, An Introduction to Constitutional Psychiatry,'' *American Anthropologist* 53 (1951): 561–563.

34. Richard L. Dugdale, *The Jukes: A Study in Crime, Pauperism, Disease, and Heredity*, 5th ed. (New York: Putnam, 1895), p. 8.

35. Henry H. Goddard, *The Kallikak Family: A Study in the Heredity of Feeble-mindedness* (New York: Macmillan, 1912), p. 50.

36. Buck v. Bell, 274 U.S. 200, 207 (1927).

37. Isaac Ray, *The Medical Jurisprudence of Insanity* (Boston: Little, Brown, 1838).

38. Philippe Pinel, *A Treatise on Insanity* (1806; New York: Hafner, 1962). See also Jean Etienne Dominique Esquirol, *Mental Maladies: A Treatise on Insanity*, facs. ed. (1845; New York: Hafner, 1965), pp. 320–321; James Cowles Prichard, *A Treatise on Insanity and Other Disorders Affecting the Mind* (New York: Arno, 1973).

39. Peter Scott, ''Henry Maudsley,'' in *Journal of Criminal Law, Criminology, and Police Science* 46 (March–April 1956): 753–769.

40. Henry H. Goddard, *The Criminal Imbecile* (New York: Macmillan, 1915), pp. 106–107.

41. Adolphe Quételet, *A Treatise on Man*, trans. Salomon Diamond, facs. ed. of 1842 ed. (1835; Gainesville, Fla.: Scholars Facsimiles and Reprints, 1969), p. 97. For a discussion of the historical significance of Quételet, see Piers Beirne, ''Adolphe Quételet and the Origins of Positivist Criminology,'' *American Journal of Sociology* 92 (1987): 1140–1169.

42. Quételet, *Treatise on Man*, p. 103. See also George von Mayr, as quoted in Gustav Aschaffenburg, *Crime and Its Repression* (Boston: Little, Brown, 1913), p. 106. For Quételet's influence on modern scholars, see Derral Cheatwood, ''Is There a Season for Homicide?'' *Criminology* 26 (May 1988): 287–306.

43. Gabriel Tarde, *Penal Philosophy*, trans. R. Howell (Boston: Little, Brown, 1912), p. 252. On the ancient and widespread practice of abandoning children, which still flourished in the nineteenth century, see John Boswell, *The Kindness of Strangers* (New York: Pantheon, 1988).

44. Gabriel Tarde, *Social Laws: An Outline of Sociology* (New York: Macmillan, 1907).

45. Emile Durkheim, *The Rules of Sociological Method*, ed. George E. G. Catlin (Chicago: University of Chicago Press, 1938), p. 71.

PART II

EXPLANATIONS OF CRIMINAL BEHAVIOR

Having explored the history of criminology, the early explanations of criminal behavior, and the scientific methods used by criminologists (Part I), we turn now to the theories and research of the twentieth century. Explanations of criminal behavior focus on biological, psychological, social, and economic factors. Biological and psychological theories assume that criminal behavior results from underlying physical or mental conditions that distinguish criminals from noncriminals (Chapter 4). These theories yield insight into individual cases, but they do not explain why crime rates vary from place to place and from one situation to another. Sociological theories seek to explain criminal behavior in terms of the social environment. Chapter 5 examines the strain and cultural deviance theories, which focus on the social forces that cause people to engage in criminal behavior. Both theories assume that social class and criminal behavior are related. Strain theorists argue that people commit crime because they are frustrated by not being able to achieve society's goals through legitimate means. Cultural deviance theorists claim that crime is learned in socially disorganized neighborhoods where criminal norms are transmitted from one generation to the next. In Chapter 6 we examine the subcultures in society which have their own norms, beliefs, and values that differ significantly from those of the dominant culture. Chapter 7 explains how people remain committed to conventional behavior in the face of frustration, poor living conditions, and other criminogenic factors. Finally, in Chapter 8 we discuss three theoretical perspectives which differ substantially from the foregoing in that they focus on society's role in creating criminals and defining them as such.

4

PSYCHO-LOGICAL AND BIOLOGICAL PERSPECTIVES

John W. Hinckley, Jr., began to withdraw from social relationships in his adolescence. He found it difficult to establish and maintain meaningful friendships with anyone other than his family. As a young adult, while attending Texas Tech, he spent most of his day listening to music, reading, watching television, and playing the guitar. After less than three years of college, John dropped out. He moved to Hollywood with the hope of becoming a songwriter. It was in Hollywood that John developed a fascination with the movie *Taxi Driver* and one of its characters, Iris—a fascination that led him to see the film about fifteen times. The movie had a complex plot, one that involved an alienated, lonely, and socially inept taxi driver who ends up planning to kill a presidential candidate over a failed relationship with one of the candidate's workers.

Early in 1979 John's outlook on life deteriorated. He was depressed over his parents' perceptions that he failed to achieve his goals. John did not sense a purpose in life or a reason to stay alive. In August 1979 he purchased a gun and later played "Russian roulette." John complained of sleeplessness, weakness, and headaches.

In the latter part of 1980, John went to New Haven, Connecticut, to visit Jodie Foster, the young actress who portrayed Iris in *Taxi Driver*. His goal was to establish a relationship with her. Over the next several months, John developed an obsession with Foster and considered the possibility of assassinating President Ronald Reagan. He wrote Foster love notes and also described his plan to assassinate the president. On March 30, 1981, as the nation watched television coverage of Reagan leaving a meeting, John made his attempt.

In the United States, explanations of criminal behavior have been dominated by sociological theories. These theories focus on lack of opportunities and the breakdown of the conventional value system in urban ghettos, the formation of subcultures whose norms deviate from those of the middle class, and the increasing inability of social institutions to exercise control over behavior (see Chapters 5, 6, and 7). Criminological texts treated psychological and biological theories as peripheral, perhaps because criminology held its disciplinary allegiance to sociology. Or perhaps when psychological theories were first advanced to explain criminal behavior, their emphasis was largely psychoanalytic, and so they may have seemed insufficiently quantitative to some criminologists. Others may have considered the early work of Lombroso, Goring, and Hooten too scientifically naive to take seriously.

Sociological theories focus on crime rates of groups that experience frustration in their efforts to achieve society's goals, not on the particular individual who becomes a criminal. Sociological theories cannot explain how a person can be born in a slum, be exposed to family discord and abuse, never attend school, have friends who are delinquents, and yet resist opportunities for crime, while another person who grows up in an affluent suburban neighborhood in a two-parent home can end up firing a gun at the president. In other words, sociologists do not address the individual differences between people.

Psychologists and biologists are interested in finding out what may account for these individual differences. Psychologists have considered a variety of possibilities—defective conscience, emotional immaturity, inadequate childhood socialization, maternal deprivation, poor moral development. They study how aggression is learned, which situations promote violent or delinquent reactions, how crime is related to personality factors, and the association between various mental disorders and criminality.

Within the last two decades biologists have followed in the tradition of Cesare Lombroso, Raffaele Garofalo, and Charles Goring in their search for answers to questions about human behavior. Geneticists, for example, have argued that the predisposition to act violently or aggressively in certain situations may be inherited. In other words, while criminals are not born criminal, the predisposition to commit crime may be present at birth. To demonstrate that certain traits are inherited, geneticists have studied children born of criminals but reared from birth by noncriminal adoptive parents. The geneticists wanted to know whether the behavior of the adoptive children was more similar to that of their biological parents than to that of their adoptive parents. The findings of genet-

icists play an important role in the debate on heredity versus environment. Other biologists, sometimes referred to as biocriminologists, take a different approach. Some question, for example, whether brain damage or inadequate nutrition results in criminal behavior. Others are interested in the influence of hormones, chromosomal abnormalities, and allergies. They investigate interactions between the brain and behavior and between diet and behavior.

PSYCHOLOGY AND CRIMINALITY

Psychological Development

Psychoanalytic theory   The **psychoanalytic theory** of criminality attributes delinquent and criminal behavior to a conscience that is either so overbearing that it arouses feelings of guilt or so weak that it cannot control the individual's impulses, and to a need for immediate gratification. Consider the case of Richard. Richard was 6 when he committed his first delinquent act: he stole a comic book from the corner drugstore. Three months before the incident, his father, an alcoholic, had been killed in an automobile accident, and his mother, unable to care for the family, had abandoned the children shortly thereafter. For the next ten years the county welfare agency moved Richard in and out of foster homes. During this time he actively pursued a life of crime, breaking into houses during daylight hours and stealing cars at night. By age 20, while serving a ten-year prison sentence for armed robbery, he voluntarily entered psychoanalysis. After two years Richard's analyst suggested three reasons for his criminality:

• Being caught and punished for stealing made him feel less guilty about hating his father and mother for abandoning him;
• Stealing did not violate his moral and ethical principles;
• Stealing resulted in immediate gratification and pleasure, both of which Richard had great difficulty resisting.

Sigmund Freud (1856–1939), the founder of

psychoanalysis, suggested that criminality may result from an overactive conscience that results in excessive guilt feelings. In treating patients, Freud noticed that those who were suffering from unbearable guilt committed crimes in order to be apprehended and punished.[1] Once they had been punished, their feelings of guilt were relieved. Thus Richard's psychoanalyst suggested that his anger over his father's death and his mother's abandonment created unconscious feelings of guilt, which he sought to relieve by committing a crime and being punished for it.

Richard's psychoanalyst offered an alternative explanation for his persistent criminal activities: his conscience was perhaps not too strong but too weak. The conscience, or **superego,** was so weak or defective that the **ego** (which acts as a moderator between the superego and id) was unable to control the impulses of the **id** (the part of the personality that contains powerful urges and drives for gratification and satisfaction). Because the superego is essentially an internalized parental image, developed when the child assumes the parents' attitudes and moral values, it follows that the absence of such an image may lead to an unrestrained id and thus to delinquency.[2]

Psychoanalytic theory also suggests another explanation for Richard's behavior: an insatiable need for immediate reward and gratification. A defect in the character formation of delinquents drives them to satisfy their desires at once, regardless of the consequences.[3] This urge, which psychoanalysts attribute to the id, is so strong that relationships with people are important only so long as they help to satisfy it. Most analysts view delinquents, then, as children unable to give up their desire for instant pleasure.

The psychoanalytic approach is still one of the most prominent explanations for both normal and asocial functioning. Despite criticism,[4] three basic principles still appeal to psychologists who study criminality:

- The actions and behavior of an adult are understood in terms of childhood development.
- Behavior and unconscious motives are intertwined, and their interaction must be unraveled if we are to understand criminality.

- Criminality is essentially a representation of psychological conflict.

Notwithstanding their appeal, psychoanalytic treatment techniques, devised to address these principles, have been controversial since their introduction by Sigmund Freud and his disciples. The controversy has involved questions concerning improvement following treatment and, perhaps more important, the very validity of the hypothetical conflicts that the treatment presupposes.

Moral development   Consider the following moral dilemma:

> In Europe, a woman is near death from a special kind of cancer. There is one drug that the doctors think might save her. It is a form of radium that a druggist in the same town has recently discovered. The drug is expensive to make, and the druggist is charging ten times that cost. He paid $200 for the radium and is charging $2,000 for a small dose of the drug. The sick woman's husband, Heinz, goes to everyone he knows to borrow the money, but he can get together only $1,000. He tells the druggist that his wife is dying and asks him to sell the drug more cheaply or to let him pay later. The druggist says, "No, I discovered the drug and I'm going to make money from it." Heinz is desperate and considers breaking into the man's store to steal the drug for his wife.[5]

This classic dilemma sets up complex moral issues. While you may know that it is wrong to steal, you may believe that this is a situation in which the written law should be circumvented. Or is it always wrong to steal, no matter what the circumstances? Regardless of what you decide, the way you reach the decision about whether or not to steal reveals much about your moral development. The psychologist Lawrence Kohlberg, who pioneered moral developmental theory, has found that moral reasoning develops in three stages.[6] In the first, preconventional stage, children's moral rules and moral values consist of the do's and don't's that avoid punishment. A desire to avoid punishment and a belief in the superior power of authorities are the two central reasons for doing what is right. According to this theory, children under the age of 9 to 11 usually reason at this preconventional level. They think, in effect, "If I steal, what are my chances of getting caught and punished?"

Adolescents typically reason at the conventional level. At this level, individuals believe in and have adopted the values and rules of society. Moreover, they seek to uphold these rules. They think, in effect, "It is illegal to steal and therefore I should not steal, under any circumstances."

Finally, at the postconventional level, individuals critically examine customs and social rules according to their own sense of universal human rights, moral principles, and duties. They think, in effect, "One must live within the law, but certain universal ethical principles, such as respect for human rights and for the dignity of human life, supersede the written law when the two conflict." This level of moral reasoning is generally seen in adults after the age of 20.

According to Kohlberg and his colleagues, most delinquents and criminals reason at the preconventional level. Low moral development or preconventional reasoning alone, however, does not result in criminality. Other factors, such as the situation or the absence of significant social bonds, may play a part.

Kohlberg has argued that basic moral principles and social norms are learned through social interaction and role playing. In essence, children learn how to be moral by reasoning with others who are at a higher level of moral development. Students of Kohlberg have looked at practical applications of his theory. What would happen, for instance, if delinquents who were poor moral reasoners were exposed to individuals who reasoned at a higher level? Joseph Hickey, William Jennings, and their associates designed programs for Connecticut and Florida prisons and applied them in school systems around the United States. The "just community intervention" approach involves a structured educational curriculum stressing democracy, fairness, and a sense of community. But above all the focus is on the growth and development of moral reasoning. A series of evaluations of just community programs have revealed significant increases in moral development.[7]

Maternal deprivation and attachment theory In a well-known psychological experiment, infant monkeys were provided with the choice between two wire "monkeys." One, made of uncovered cage wire, dispensed milk. The other, made of cage wire covered with soft fabric, did not give milk. The infant monkeys in the experiment gravitated to the warm cloth monkey, which provided comfort and security even though it did not provide food.

What does this have to do with criminality? Research has demonstrated that a phenomenon important to social development takes place shortly after the birth of any mammal: the construction of an emotional bond between the infant and its mother. The strength of this emotional bond, or **attachment,** will determine, or at least materially affect, a child's ability to form attachments in the future. In order to form a successful attachment, children need a warm, loving, and interactive caretaker.

The psychologist John Bowlby has studied both the need for warmth and affection from birth onward and the consequences of not having it. He has proposed a theory of attachment with seven important features:

• *Specificity.* Attachments are selective, usually directed to one or more individuals in some order of preference.

Infants develop attachment to mothers, or mother substitutes, for comfort, security, and warmth.

- *Duration.* Attachments endure and persist, sometimes throughout the life cycle.
- *Engagement of emotion.* Some of the most intense emotions are associated with attachment relationships.
- *Ontogeny* (course of development). Children form an attachment to one primary figure in the first nine months of life. That principal attachment figure is the person who supplies the most social interaction of a satisfying kind.
- *Learning.* Though learning plays a role in the development of attachment, Bowlby finds that attachments are the products not of rewards or reinforcements but of basic social interaction.
- *Organization.* Attachment behaviors follow a developmental organization from birth onward.
- *Biological function.* Attachment behavior has a biological function: survival. It is found in almost all species of mammals and in birds.[8]

Bowlby contends that children need to experience a warm, intimate, and continuous relationship with either a mother or a mother substitute in order to be securely attached. When a child is separated from its mother or is rejected by her, anxious attachment results, and the capacity to be affectionate and to develop intimate relationships with others is reduced. Habitual criminals, it is claimed, typically have an inability to form bonds of affection:

> More often than not the childhoods of such individuals are found to have been grossly disturbed by death, divorce, or separation of the parents, or by other events resulting in disruption of bonds, with an incidence of such disturbance far higher than is met with in any other comparable group, whether drawn from the general population or from psychiatric casualties of other sorts.[9]

Considerable research supports the relationship between anxious attachment and subsequent behavioral problems:

- In a study of 113 middle-class children observed at 1 year and again at 6 years, researchers noted a significant relationship between behavior at age 6 and attachment at age 1.[10]

- In a study of forty children seen when they were 1 year old and again at 18 months, it was noted that anxiously attached children were less empathetic, independent, compliant, and confident than securely attached children.[11]
- Researchers have noted that the quality of one's attachment correlates significantly with asocial preschool behavior—aggression, leaving the group, and the like.[12]

Criminologists also have examined the effects of the mother's absence, whether because of death, divorce, or abandonment. Does her absence *cause* delinquency? Empirical research is equivocal. Perhaps the most persuasive evidence comes from longitudinal research conducted by Joan McCord, who has investigated the relationship between family atmosphere (such as parental self-confidence, deviance, and affection) and delinquency. In one study, she collected data on the childhood homes of 201 men and their subsequent court records in order to identify family-related variables that would predict criminal activity. Such variables as inadequate maternal affection and supervision, parental conflict, the mother's lack of self-confidence, and the father's deviance were significantly related to the commission of crimes against persons and/or property. The father's absence was not by itself correlated with criminal behavior.[13] Other studies, such as those by Sheldon and Eleanor Glueck and the more recent studies by Lee N. Robins carried out in schools, juvenile courts, and psychiatric hospitals, suggest a moderate to strong relation between crime and childhood deprivation.[14] However, evidence that deprivation directly *causes* delinquency is lacking.[15]

So far we have considered psychological theories that attribute the causes of delinquency or criminality to unconscious problems and failures in moral development. Not all psychologists, however, agree with these explanations of criminal behavior. Some argue that human behavior develops through learning experiences. They say that we learn by observing others and by watching the responses to other people's behavior (on television or in the movies, for instance) and to our own. Social learning theorists reject the notion that internal functioning alone makes us prone to act aggressively or violently.

Learning Aggression and Violence

Social learning theory maintains that delinquent behavior is learned through the same psychological processes as all nondelinquent behavior. Behavior is learned when it is reinforced or rewarded, and not learned when it is not reinforced. Let us examine the various ways in which we learn behavior: through observation, direct exposure, and differential reinforcement.

Observational learning   Albert Bandura, a leading proponent of social learning theory, argues that individuals learn violence and aggression through **behavioral modeling:** children learn how to behave by fashioning their behavior after that of others. Thus behavior is socially transmitted through examples, which come primarily from the family, the subculture, and the mass media.[16]

Psychologists have been studying the effects of family violence (Chapter 10) on children. They have found that parents who try to resolve family controversies by violence teach their children to use similar tactics. Thus by observational learning a cycle of violence may be perpetuated through the generations. Of course, social learning theorists do not suggest that *only* violence and aggression can be learned in family situations. Observing a healthy and happy family environment tends to result in constructive and positive modeling.

To understand the influence of the social environment outside the home, social learning theorists have studied gangs, which often provide excellent models of observational learning of violence and aggression. They have found, in fact, that violence is very much a norm shared by some people in a community or gang. The highest incidence of aggressive behavior occurs where aggressiveness is a desired characteristic, as it is in some subcultures.

Observational learning takes place in front of the television set and at the movies, as well. Children who have seen others being rewarded

for violent acts often believe that violence and aggression are acceptable behaviors.[17] The psychologist Leonard Eron has argued that the "single best predictor of how aggressive a young man would be when he was 19 years old was the violence of the television programs he preferred when he was 8 years old."[18]

There is, of course, another side to the issue of television violence. Researchers conducted a longitudinal study to assess the association between children's aggressive behavior and exposure to violence on television. Questionnaire data were collected on 3,718 subjects in four time periods between 1970 and 1973. Responses were coded by exposure time and "violence weights" (Table 4.1). Responses were then compared with self-reports of violent behavior. The findings indicate that exposure to violence on television is statistically unrelated to self-reported violent behavior. The question remains open.[19]

Direct experience   What we learn by observation is determined by the behavior of others. What we learn from direct experience is determined by what we ourselves do and what happens to us. We remember the past and use its lessons to avoid future mistakes. Thus we learn through trial and error. According to social learning theorists, after engaging in a given behavior, most of us examine the responses to our

In some countries, television violence is strictly controlled because of a concern that children will learn aggressive behavior from watching it.

TABLE 4.1 VIOLENCE WEIGHTS ATTACHED TO POPULAR TELEVISION SHOWS, 1970–1973

TELEVISION SHOW	VIOLENCE WEIGHTS
FBI	7
Hawaii 5-0	7
Mannix	7
Mod Squad	7
Mission Impossible	6
Bonanza	5
Wrestling	5
Adam-12	4
Monday Night Football	4
Then Came Bronson	4
Laugh-in	1
Medical Center	1
Room 222	1
Andy Williams Show	0
Bewitched	0
Bill Cosby Show	0
Carol Burnett Show	0
The Odd Couple	0

actions and modify our behavior as necessary to obtain favorable responses. If we are praised or rewarded for our behavior, we are likely to repeat it. If we are subjected to verbal or physical punishment, we are likely to refrain from such behavior. Our behavior in the first instance and our restraint in the second are said to be "reinforced" by the rewards and punishments we receive.

The psychologist Gerald Patterson and his colleagues examined how aggression is learned by direct experience. They observed that some passive children at play were repeatedly victimized by other children but were occasionally successful in curbing the attacks by counteraggression. Over time these children learned defensive fighting, and eventually they initiated fights. Other passive children, who were rarely observed to be victimized, remained submissive.[20] Thus children, like adults, can learn to be aggressive and even violent by trial and error.

While violence and aggression are learned behaviors, they are not necessarily expressed until they are elicited in one of several ways. Albert Bandura describes the things that elicit behavioral responses as "instigators." Thus social learning theory describes not only how aggression is acquired but also how it is instigated. Consider the following instigators of aggression:

• Aversive instigators: physical assaults, verbal threats, and insults; adverse reductions in conditions of life (such as impoverishment) and the thwarting of goal-directed behavior.
• Incentive instigators: rewards, such as money and praise.
• Modeling instigators: violent or aggressive behaviors observed in others.
• Instructional instigators: observations of people carrying out instructions to engage in violence or aggression.
• Delusional instigators: unfounded or bizarre beliefs that violence is necessary or justified.[21]

Differential reinforcement In 1965 the criminologist C. Ray Jeffery suggested that learning theory could be used to explain criminality.[22] Within one year Ernest Burgess and Ronald Akers combined Bandura's psychologically based learning theory with Edwin Sutherland's sociologically based differential association theory (Chapter 5) to produce the theory of **differential association–reinforcement,** which states that the persistence of criminal behavior depends on whether or not it is rewarded or punished. The most meaningful rewards and punishments are those given by groups that are important in an individual's life—the peer group, the family, teachers in school, and so forth. In other words, people respond more readily to the reactions of the most significant people in their lives. If criminal behavior elicits more positive reinforcement or rewards than punishment, it will persist.[23]

Social learning theory helps us to understand why some, but not all, individuals who engage in violent and aggressive behavior do so: they learn to behave that way. But perhaps something within the personality of a criminal creates a susceptibility to aggressive or violent models in the first place. For example, perhaps

"Go right ahead. I realize you're bred to be violent, just as I'm bred to be passive."

criminals are more extraverted, irresponsible, or unsocialized than noncriminals. Or perhaps criminals are more intolerant and impulsive or have lower self-esteem.

Personality

Personality Characteristics   Four distinct lines of psychological research have examined the relation between personality and criminality. First, investigators have looked at the differences between the personality structures of criminals and noncriminals. Most of this work has been carried out in state and federal prisons, where psychologists have administered personality questionnaires such as the Minnesota Multiphasic Personality Inventory (MMPI) and the California Psychological Inventory (CPI) to inmates. The evidence from these studies shows that inmates are typically more impulsive, hostile, self-centered, and immature than noncriminals.[24]

Second, a vast amount of literature is devoted to the prediction of behavior. Criminologists want to know how to determine how a convict will respond to prison discipline and whether he or she will avoid crime after release from prison. The results are equivocal. At best, personality characteristics seem to be modest predictors of future criminality. Yet when they are combined with such variables as personal history, they tend to increase the power of prediction significantly.[25]

Third, many studies examine the degree to which normal personality dynamics operate in criminals. Findings from these studies suggest that the personality dynamics of criminals are often quite similar to those of noncriminals. Social criminals (those who act in concert with others), for example, are found to be more sociable, affiliative, outgoing, and self-confident than solitary criminals.[26]

Finally, some researchers have attempted to quantify individual differences between types and groups of offenders. Several studies have compared the personality characteristics of first-time offenders with those of repeat or habitual criminals. Other investigators have compared violent offenders with nonviolent offenders, and murderers with drug offenders. In addition, prison inmates have been classified according to their personality types.[27]

In general, research on criminals' personality characteristics has revealed some important associations. However, criminologists have been skeptical of the strength of the relationship of personality to criminality. A review of research on that relationship published in 1942 by Milton Metfessel and Constance Lovell dismissed personality as an important causal factor in criminal behavior.[28] In 1950 Karl Schuessler and Donald Cressey reached the same conclusion.[29] Twenty-seven years later, Daniel Tennenbaum's updated review was in agreement with earlier assessments. He found that "the data do not reveal any significant differences between criminal and noncriminal psychology.... Personality testing has not differentiated criminals from noncriminals."[30]

Despite these conclusions, whether or not criminals share personality characteristics continues to be debated. Are criminals in fact more aggressive, dominant, and manipulative than noncriminals? Are they more irresponsible? Clearly, many criminals are aggressive; many have manipulated a variety of situations; many assume no responsibility for their acts. But are such personality characteristics common to *all* criminals? Samuel Yochelson and Stanton Samenow addressed these questions. In *The Criminal Personality*, this psychiatrist-psychologist team described their growing disillusionment with traditional explanations of criminality. From their experience in treating criminals in the Forensic Division of St. Elizabeth's Hospital in Washington, D.C., they refuted the psychoanalysts' claims that crime is caused by inner conflict. Rather, they said, criminals share abnormal "thinking patterns" that lead to decisions to commit crimes. Yochelson and Samenow identified as many as fifty-two patterns of thinking common to the criminals they studied. They argued that criminals are "angry" people who feel a sense of superiority, expect not to be held accountable for their acts, and have a highly inflated self-image. Any perceived attack on their glorified self-image elicits a strong reaction, often a violent one.[31]

Other researchers have used different methods to study the association between criminality and personality. A review of the findings of a large sample of studies using the California Psychological Inventory was conducted by William Laufer and his colleagues. It revealed a common personality profile. The criminals tested showed remarkable similarity in their deficient self-control, intolerance, and lack of responsibility.[32]

Though studies dealing with personality correlates of crime are important, some psychologists are concerned that by focusing on the personalities of criminals in their search for explanations of criminal behavior, investigators may overlook other important factors. One such factor is the complex social environment in which a crime is committed.[33] A homicide that began as a barroom argument between two drunks who backed different teams to win the Super Bowl, for example, is very likely to hinge on factors other than just the patrons' personalities.

Personality and conditioning For over twenty years Hans J. Eysenck has been developing and refining a theory of the relationship between personality and criminality which considers more than just individual personality characteristics.[34] His theory has two parts. First, Eysenck claims that all human personality may be seen in three dimensions—psychoticism, extraversion, and neuroticism. Individuals who score high on measures of *psychoticism* are aggressive, egocentric, and impulsive. Those who score high on measures of *extraversion* are sensation-seeking, dominant, and assertive. High scorers on scales assessing *neuroticism* may be described as having low self-esteem, excessive anxiety, and wide mood swings. Eysenck has found that when criminals respond to items on the Eysenck Personality Questionnaire (EPQ), they uniformly score higher on each of these dimensions than do noncriminals.

The second part of Eysenck's theory suggests that humans develop a conscience through **conditioning.** From birth on, we are rewarded for social behavior and punished for asocial behavior. Eysenck likens this conditioning to the learning process of a dog. Puppies are not born house-trained. You have to teach a puppy that it is good to urinate and defecate outside your apartment or house by pairing kind words and perhaps some tangible reward (such as a dog

CRIMINOLOGICAL FOCUS

The Insanity Defense

John W. Hinckley, Jr., holds a pistol to his head in this self-portrait. One of Hinckley's letters to actress Jodie Foster was introduced as evidence to support his insanity defense.

When John W. Hinckley, Jr., was tried for the attempted assassination of President Ronald Reagan, he called upon an expert witness to testify that he was legally insane. To establish insanity, the psychiatrist for the defense described an earlier episode in the life of the defendant—an episode that involved the actress Jodie Foster, whose attention Hinckley had tried to get by

shooting the president. Dr. William T. Carpenter, Jr., the defense psychiatrist, is here being cross-examined by Assistant United States Attorney Roger Adelman:

Q. Now, Mr. Hinckley told you that he went up there because he admired Miss Foster, he was interested in her; right?

A. Well, those two things are true. That doesn't quite capture what was on his mind about Miss Foster, but it is true that part of what was on his mind included admiration and an interest.

Q. Right. And he was in a way obsessed with her?

A. He was more than obsessed. I mean he was obsessed with her.

Q. Was he delusional about her?

A. Yes, he had developed delusional expectations of that relationship by that time.... On the whole, the basis for being there, including making the telephone calls, was

treat) with successful outings. A loud, angry voice will convey disapproval and disappointment when mistakes are made inside. In time, most dogs learn and, according to Eysenck, develop a conscience. But as Eysenck also has noted, some dogs learn faster than others. German shepherds acquire good "bathroom habits" faster than basenjis, who are most difficult to train. It is argued that the same is true of humans. There are important individual differences in the conditionability of humans. Criminals become conditioned slowly and appear to care little whether or not their asocial actions bring them disapproval.

Eysenck has identified two additional aspects of a criminal's poor conditionability. First, he has found that extraverts are much more difficult to condition than introverts and thus have greater difficulty in developing a conscience. Youthful offenders tend to score highest on measures of extraversion. Second, Eysenck has observed that differences in conditionability are dependent on certain physiological factors, the most important of which is **cortical arousal,** or activation of the cerebral cortex. The cortex of the brain is responsible for higher intellectual functioning, information processing, and decision making. Eysenck found that those individ-

based on delusional information that he had in relationship to Jodie Foster....

He, by then, had come to believe that the only salvation that he had, the only way he could extricate himself from this life was through union with her. He had come to believe that a union with her was in some sense ordained, that he had taken it as a message to him that a number of her films had been shown on television during the time prior to that as the purpose— the purpose of that was a personal purpose, to spur him onward to activity in this regard.

He believed if he could make contact with her, that they could become an extraordinary couple.

He believed that he had some responsibilities toward her in terms of protecting her.

He believed that he could be made whole again in some sense in terms of the wretched existence and experiences that he was having.

[All] of these things...are called a delusion because there are many components of false beliefs upon which he is basing his activity, his plans, his actions.

In pursuing them he then makes telephone calls, and the delusions that are present during that whole period of time, including the telephone calls, are the type of thing I am saying.

This type of delusional formation would not [be expected] to interfere with ordinary activities like purchasing tickets or purchasing food or being able to make telephone calls.

Hinckley was found not guilty by reason of insanity. His behavior resulted from **psychosis,** a mental illness characterized by a loss of contact with reality. Gener-

ally psychoses are incompatible with criminality, since crime requires a criminal intent and psychoses often deprive the perpetrator of the capacity to form an intention. Acts committed by individuals who suffer from such mental illness are neither rational nor voluntary.

It is often difficult, however, to prove in court that a person's actions were caused by mental illness, so many mentally disordered offenders do end up in jails and prisons. According to a survey conducted by the New York State Department of Correctional Services in 1989, more than 24,000 inmates (6 percent of the total state correctional population) suffer some form of mental illness.

Source: P. W. Low, J. C. Jeffries, and R. J. Bonnie, *The Trial of John W. Hinckley, Jr.: A Case Study in the Insanity Defense* (New York: Foundation Press, 1986); New York State Department of Correctional Services, *Report on Prison Population* (Albany, 1989).

uals who are easily conditionable and develop a conscience have a high level of cortical arousal; they do not need intense external stimulation to become aroused. A low level of cortical arousal is associated with poor conditionability, difficulty in developing a conscience, and need for external stimulation.

Mental Disorders and Crime

It has been difficult for psychiatrists to derive criteria that would help them decide which offenders are mentally ill. According to the psychiatrist Seymour L. Halleck, the problem lies in the evolving conceptualization of mental illness. Traditionally the medical profession viewed mental illness as an absolute condition or status—you are either a psychotic or not a psychotic. Should such a view concern us? Halleck suggests that it should. "Although this kind of thinking is not compatible with current psychiatric knowledge," he writes, "it continues to exert considerable influence upon psychiatric practice.... As applied to the criminal, it also leads to rigid dichotomies between the 'sick criminal' and the 'normal criminal.'"[35] Halleck and other psychiatrists, such as Karl Menninger, conceptualize mental functioning as a process.[36] Thus mental illness may not be considered apart from mental health—the two exist on the same continuum. At various times in each of our lives we move along the continuum from mental health toward mental illness. For this reason, a diagnosis of "criminal" or "mentally ill" may overlook potentially important gradations in mental health and mental illness. This issue is perhaps no more apparent than in the insanity defense. Such a defense, discussed in Chapter 9, calls for a proof of sanity or insanity—rarely allowing for gradations in mental functioning.

Estimates vary, but between 20 and 60 percent of state correctional populations suffer from a type of mental disorder that in the nineteenth century was described by the French physician Philippe Pinel as *manie sans délire* (madness without confusion), by the English physician James C. Prichard as "moral insanity," and by Gina Lombroso-Ferrero as "irresistible atavistic impulses." Today such mental illness is called **psychopathy** or antisocial personality—a personality that is characterized by an inability to learn from experience, lack of warmth, and no sense of guilt.

The psychiatrist Hervey Cleckley views psychopathy as a serious illness even though patients may not appear to be ill. According to Cleckley, psychopaths appear to enjoy excellent mental health; but what we see is only a "mask of sanity." Initially they seem free of any kind of mental disorder, and appear to be reliable and honest. After some time, however, it becomes clear that true psychopaths have no sense of responsibility whatsoever. They show a disregard for truth, are insincere, and feel no sense of shame, guilt, or humiliation. Psychopaths lie and cheat without hesitation and engage in verbal as well as physical abuse without premeditation. Cleckley describes the following case:

> A sixteen-year-old boy was sent to jail for stealing a valuable watch. Though apparently... untouched by his situation, after a few questions were asked he began to seem more like a child who feels the unpleasantness of his position. He confessed that he had worried much about masturbation, saying he had been threatened and punished severely for it and told that it would cause him to become "insane."
>
> He admitted having broken into his moth-

er's jewelry box and stolen a watch valued at $150.00. He calmly related that he exchanged the watch for 15 cents' worth of ice cream and seemed entirely satisfied with what he had done. He readily admitted that his act was wrong, used the proper words to express his intention to cause no further trouble, and, when asked, said that he would like very much to get out of jail.

> He stated that he loved his mother devotedly. "I just kiss her and kiss her ten or twelve times when she comes to see me!" he exclaimed with shallow zeal. These manifestations of affection were so artificial, and, one would even say, unconsciously artificial, that few laymen would be convinced that any feeling, in the ordinary sense, lay in them. Nor was his mother convinced.
>
> A few weeks before this boy was sent to jail he displayed to his mother some rifle cartridges. When asked what he wanted with them he explained that they would fit the rifle in a nearby closet. "I've tried them," he announced. And in a lively tone added, "Why, I could put them in the gun and shoot you. You would fall right over!" He laughed and his eyes shone with a small but real impulse.[37]

Psychologists also have found that psychopaths, like Hans Eysenck's extraverts, have a low internal arousal level; thus psychopaths constantly seek external stimulation, are less susceptible to learning by direct experience (they do not modify their behavior after they are punished), are more impulsive, and experience far less anxiety than nonpsychopaths about any adverse consequences of their acts.[38]

Some psychiatrists consider "psychopathy" to be only an artificial label for an antisocial personality.[39] To Eysenck and others, it is a major behavioral category that presents significant challenges. Eysenck sums up this view by writing that the psychopath poses the riddle of delinquency. If we could solve the riddle, then we would have a powerful weapon to fight the problem of delinquency.[40]

BIOLOGY AND CRIMINALITY

Modern Biocriminology

Biocriminology investigates the physical aspects of psychological disorders. It has been known for some time that adults who suffer from depression show abnormalities in brain waves during sleep, experience disturbed nervous system functioning, and display biochemical abnormalities. Research on depressed children reveals the same physical problems; furthermore, their adult relatives show high rates of depression as well. In fact, children whose parents suffer from depression are more than four times more likely than the average child to experience a similar illness.[41] It thus appears that depression is an inherited condition that manifests itself in psychological *and* physical disturbances. But the more important point is that until only recently, physicians may have been missing the mark in their assessment and treatment of depressed children and adults, by ignoring the physiological aspects.

Criminologists who study sociology and psychology to the exclusion of the biological sciences may be missing the mark as well in their efforts to discover the causes of crime. Recent research has demonstrated that crime does indeed have psychobiological aspects that are similar to those found in studies of depression—biochemical abnormalities, abnormal brain waves, nervous system dysfunction. Investigators also have examined evidence that strongly suggests a genetic predisposition to criminality.

The resurgence of interest in integrating modern biological advances, theories, and principles into mainstream criminology began two decades ago. The sociobiological work of Edward Wilson on the interrelationship of biology, genetics, and social behavior was pivotal.[42] So were the contributions of C. Ray Jeffery, who argued that a biosocial interdisciplinary model should become the major theoretical framework for studying criminal behavior.[43] Criminologists once again began to consider the possibility that there are indeed traits that predispose a person to criminality and that these traits may be passed from parent to child through the genes. Other questions arose as well. Is it possible, for instance, that internal biochemical imbalances or deficiencies cause antisocial behavior? Could too much or too little sugar in the bloodstream increase the potential for aggression? Or could a vitamin de-

ficiency or some hormonal problem be responsible? Let us explore the evidence for a genetic predisposition to criminal behavior, the relationship between biochemical factors and criminality, and neurophysiological factors that result in criminal behavior.

Genetics and Criminality

The proposition that human beings are products of an interaction between environmental and genetic factors is all but universally accepted. We must stop asking, then, whether nature or nurture is more important in shaping us; we are the products of both nature and nurture. But what does the interaction between the two look like? And what concerns are raised by reliance on genetics to the exclusion of environmental factors? Consider the example of the XYY syndrome.

The XYY syndrome Chromosomes are the basic structures that contain our genes—the biological material that makes each of us unique. Each human being has twenty-three pairs of inherited chromosomes. One pair determines gender. A female receives an X chromosome from both mother and father; a male receives an X chromosome from his mother and a Y from his father. Sometimes a defect in the production of sperm or egg results in genetic abnormalities. One type of abnormality is the XYY chromosomal male. The XYY male receives two Y chromosomes rather than one from his father. Approximately 1 in 1,000 newborn males in the general population has this genetic composition.[44]

Initial studies done in the 1960s found the frequency of XYY chromosomes to be about twenty times greater than normal XY chromosomes among inmates in maximum security state hospitals.[45] Those inmates with XYY tended to be tall, physically aggressive, and frequently violent. Supporters of these data claimed to have uncovered the mystery of violent criminality. Critics voiced concern over the fact that these studies were done on small and unrepresentative samples.

The XYY syndrome, as this condition became known, received much public attention because of the case of Richard Speck. Speck, who in 1966 murdered eight nurses in Chicago, initially was diagnosed as an XYY chromosomal male. However, the diagnosis later turned out to be wrong. Nevertheless, public concern was aroused: were all XYY males potential killers? Studies undertaken since that time have discounted the relation between the extra Y chromosome and criminality.[46]

Although convincing evidence in support of the XYY hypothesis appears to be slight, it is nevertheless possible that aggressive and violent behavior is at least partly determined by genetic factors. The problem is how to investigate this possibility. One difficulty is to separate the external or environmental factors, such as family structure, culture, socioeconomic status, and peer influences, from the genetic predispositions with which they begin to interact at birth. One individual may have a genetic predisposition to be violent but be born into a wealthy, well-educated, loving, and calm familial environment. He may never commit a violent act. Another person may have a genetic predisposition to be rule-abiding and nonaggressive, yet be born into a poor, uneducated, physically abusive, and unloving family. He may commit violent criminal acts. How, then, can we determine the extent to which behavior is genetically influenced?

Twin studies   To discover whether or not crime is genetically predetermined, researchers have compared identical and fraternal twins. Identical or **monozygotic (MZ) twins** develop from a single fertilized egg that divides into two embryos. These twins share all of their genes. Fraternal or **dizygotic (DZ) twins** develop from two separate eggs, both fertilized at the same time. They share about half of their genes. Since the prenatal and postnatal family environments are, by and large, the same, greater behavioral similarity between identical twins than between fraternal twins would support an argument for genetic predisposition.

In the 1920s a German physician, Johannes Lange, found thirty pairs of same-sex twins—

"Separated at birth, the Mallifert twins meet accidentally."

thirteen identical and seventeen fraternal pairs. One of each pair was a known criminal. Lange found that in ten of the thirteen pairs of identical twins, both were criminal. In two of the seventeen pairs of fraternal twins, both were criminal.[47] The research techniques of the time were limited, but the results were nevertheless impressive.

Many similar studies have followed. The largest was a study by Karl Christiansen and Sarnoff A. Mednick, which included all twins born between 1881 and 1910 in a region of Denmark, a total of 3,586 pairs. Reviewing serious offenses only, Christiansen and Mednick found that the chance of finding a criminal twin when the other twin was a criminal was 50 percent for identical twins and 20 percent for same-sex fraternal twins. These findings lend support to the hypothesis that some genetic influences increase the risk of criminality.[48] A more recent American study conducted by David C. Rowe and D. Wayne Osgood reaches a similar conclusion.[49]

While the evidence from these and other twin studies looks persuasive, we should keep in mind the weakness of such research as well. One problem is that it may not be valid to assume a common environment for all twins who grow up in the same house at the same time. If the upbringing of identical twins is much more similar than that of fraternal twins, as it well may be, that circumstance could help explain their different rates of criminality.

Adoption studies   One way to separate the influence of inherited traits from that of environmental conditions would be to study infants separated at birth from their natural parents and placed randomly in foster homes. In such cases we could determine whether the behavior of the adopted child resembled that of the natural parents or that of the adoptive parents, and by how much. Children, however, are adopted at various ages and are not placed randomly in foster homes. Most such children are matched to their foster or adoptive parents by racial and religious criteria. And couples who adopt children may differ in some important ways from other couples. Despite such short-comings, adoption studies do help us to expand our knowledge of genetic influences on human variation.

The largest adoption study to have been conducted was based on a sample of 14,427 male and female adoptions in Denmark between 1924 and 1947. The hypothesis was that criminality in the biological parents would be associated with an increased risk of criminal behavior in the child. The parents were considered criminal if either the mother or father had been convicted of a felony. The researchers had sufficient information on more than 4,000 of the male children to assess whether or not both the biological and adoptive parents had criminal records. Mednick and his associates reported the following findings:

- Of boys whose adoptive and biological parents had no criminal record, 13.5 percent were convicted of crimes.
- Of boys who had criminal adoptive parents and noncriminal biological parents, 14.7 percent were convicted of crimes.
- Of boys who had noncriminal adoptive parents and criminal biological parents, 20 percent were convicted of crimes.
- Of boys who had both criminal adoptive parents and criminal biological parents, 24.5 percent were convicted of crimes.[50]

These findings support the claim that the criminality of the biological parents has more influence on the child than that of the adoptive parents. Other research on adopted children has reached similar conclusions. A major Swedish study examined 862 adopted males and 913 adopted females. The authors found a genetic predisposition to criminality in both sexes, but an even stronger one in females. An American study of children who were put up for adoption by a group of convicted mothers supports the Danish and Swedish findings on the significance of genetic factors.[51]

Results of adoption studies have been characterized as "highly suggestive" or "supportive" of a genetic link to criminality. But how solid is this link? There are significant problems with adoption studies. One problem is that little can be done to ensure the similarity of the adopted children's environment. Of even greater concern to criminologists, however, is the distinct possibility of mistaking correlation for causation. In other words, there appears to be a significant correlation between the criminality of biological parents and adopted children in the research we have reviewed, but this correlation does not prove that the genetic legacy passed on by a criminal parent *causes* an offspring to commit a crime.

So far research has failed to shed any light on the nature of the biological link that results in the association between the criminality of parents and that of their children. Furthermore, even if we could identify children with a higher than average probability of committing offenses as adults on the basis of their parents' criminal behavior, it is unclear what actions could be taken to avert the predicted criminality of these children.

A discussion of the association between genes and criminality would be incomplete without at least some attention to the debate over IQ and crime. Is an inferior intelligence inherited, and if so, how do we account for the strong relationship between IQ and criminality? Let us explore these questions.

The IQ Debate

Scientists began nearly a century ago to search for measures to determine people's intelligence, which they believed to be genetically determined. The first test to gain acceptance was developed by a French psychologist, Alfred Binet. The test measured the capacity of individual children to perform tasks or solve problems in relation to the average capacity of their peers.

Between 1888 and 1915 several physicians administered intelligence tests to incarcerated criminals and to boys in reform schools. Initial studies of the relationship between IQ and crime revealed some surprising results. Hugo Munsterberg estimated that 68 percent of the criminals that he tested were of low IQ. Using the Binet scale, Henry H. Goddard found that between 25 and 50 percent of criminals had low IQs.[52]

What could account for the divergence in results? Edwin Sutherland observed that the tests

were poor and there were too many variations among the many versions administered. He reasoned that social and environmental factors caused delinquency, not low IQ.[53]

In the 1950s Robert H. Gault added to Sutherland's criticism. He noted particularly that it was "strange that it did not occur immediately to the pioneers that they had examined only a small sample of caught and convicted offenders."[54]

For more than a generation the question about the relationship between IQ and criminal behavior was not studied, and the early inconsistencies remained unresolved. Then in the late 1970s the debate resumed.[55] Supporters of the view that inheritance determines intelligence once again began to present their arguments. Arthur Jensen suggested that race was a key factor in IQ differences; Richard J. Herrnstein, a geneticist, pointed to social class as a factor.[56] Both of these positions have spurred a heated debate, in which criminologists soon became involved. In 1977 Travis Hirschi and Michael Hindelang evaluated the existing literature on IQ and crime.[57] They cited the following three studies as especially important:

• Travis Hirschi, on the basis of a study of 3,600 California students, demonstrated that the effect of a low IQ on delinquent behavior is more significant than that of the father's education.[58]
• Marvin Wolfgang and associates, after studying 8,700 Philadelphia boys, found a strong relation between low IQ and delinquency, independent of social class.[59]
• Albert Reiss and Albert L. Rhodes, after an examination of the juvenile court records of 9,200 white Tennessee schoolboys, found IQ to be more closely related to delinquency than social class.[60]

Hirschi and Hindelang concluded that IQ is an even more important factor in predicting crime than is either race or social class. They found significant differences in intelligence between criminal and noncriminal populations within like racial and socioeconomic groups. A lower IQ increases the potential for crime within each group. Furthermore, they found that IQ is related to school performance. A low IQ ultimately results in association with similar nonperformers, dropping out of school, and delinquency. Hirschi and Hindelang's findings were confirmed by James Q. Wilson and Richard Herrnstein but rejected by Deborah Denno, who conducted a prospective investigation of 800 children from birth to age 17.[61] She failed to confirm a direct relationship between IQ and delinquency.

It is important to note that the debate over the relationship between IQ and crime has its roots in the controversy over whether intelligence is genetically or environmentally determined. IQ tests, many people believe, measure cultural factors rather than the innate biological makeup of an individual.[62] Studies by Sandra Scarr and Richard Weinberg of black and white adopted children confirmed that environment plays a significant role in IQ development. They found that black children adopted by white parents had IQs comparable to those of white adopted children and performed just as well.[63] With such evidence of cultural bias and environmental influence, why not abandon the use of intelligence tests? The answer is simple: they do predict performance in school and so have significant utility. Thus it appears that this debate will be with us for a long time.

Biochemical Factors

Biocriminologists have made significant contributions in areas other than the genetics of criminality. Their primary focus has been on biochemical and neurophysical factors. Research on biochemical factors relates food allergies, diet, hypoglycemia, and hormones to criminality. Neurophysical factors include brain lesions, brain wave abnormalities, and minimal brain dysfunction.

Food allergies Jerome was not a typical sixth-grader. He frequently engaged in fights with teenagers. His teachers found him to be disruptive, angry, moody, and rude. His mother complained that he had no friends and spent a good deal of time alone in his room crying. His father characterized him as irritable, unhappy, restless, aggressive, and hostile. Jerome had trouble falling asleep. He had other physical ailments as well.

Treatment with drugs and psychotherapy had failed. He was transferred to a private school, where the psychologist designed an individual study program for him. That, too, failed. Then the school nutritionist placed Jerome on a diet that contained no food dyes, milk, eggs, corn, cocoa, sugar, or wheat. Within a day he was a bit better. Within a week he was sleeping well, doing his homework, and making friends. And after six months, Jerome was a normal sixth-grader. But this is not the end of the story. After eight months, Jerome tested the waters. "What harm could a couple eggs do?" he reasoned. For lunch he ate one fried-egg sandwich on wheat bread with corn on the cob and a large glass of artificial lemonade. Within minutes Jerome's eyes became dilated and glassy, his face turned red, and he screamed without restraint. His violent and aggressive behavior returned more quickly than it had disappeared.[64]

Over the last decade researchers have investigated the relation between food allergies and antisocial behavior. In fact, since 1908 there have been numerous medical reports that various foods cause such reactions as irritability, hyperactivity, seizures, agitation, and behavior that is "out of character."[65] Investigators have identified the following food components that may result in severe allergic reactions:

- Phenylethylamine (found in chocolate).
- Tyramine (found in aged cheese and wine).
- Monosodium glutamate (used as a flavor enhancer in many foods).
- Aspartame (found in artificial sweeteners).
- Xanthines (found in caffeine).

Each of these food components has been associated with behavioral disorders, including criminality.

Diet Other investigations link criminality to diets high in sugar and carbohydrates, to vitamin deficiency or dependency, and to excessive food additives. Stephen Schoenthaler has con-

AT ISSUE

The Junk-Food Defense

Courts are often reluctant to accept any evidence on scientific questions until these have been so thoroughly established as to be no longer debatable. The "junk food defense" seems to be an exception. While scientists are still in the process of researching the links between diet and deviant behavior, several courts have allowed testimony on the diet-behavior relationship in defense or mitigation of criminal charges.

It began in 1979, when Dan White, a San Francisco city supervisor, was on trial for the murder of his fellow supervisor, Harvey Milk, and Mayor George Moscone. White defended himself with testimony on the impact of hypoglycemia on his behavior. The testimony showed that when White was depressed, he departed from his normal, healthy diet and resorted to high-sugar junk food, including Twinkies, Coca Cola, and chocolates. Thereafter, his behavior became less and less controlable. The jury found White guilty of manslaughter, rather than murder, due to diminished capacity.

(White served five years in prison and committed suicide after his release.) His defense was promptly dubbed the "Junk food defense," "Dan White's defense," or "Twinkie defense."

Most subsequent attempts to use the junk food defense have failed. Thus, in a 1989 Ohio case (Johnson), it was ruled that the defense may not be used to establish diminished capacity. In 1990, a Cape Cod man was unsuccessful when he defended himself on a charge of stealing (and eating) 300 candy bars (Callanan). Nor did the defense (Twinkie and soda pop) succeed in a feint effort to use it as a defense to a murder charge in Ohio (McDonald, 1988). But in a 1987 Florida case, a defendent (Rosenthal) was acquitted of drunk driving charges on evidence that consumption of chocolate mousse after half a glass of sherry caused an unusual hypoglycemia reaction.

On principle, there is no reason why courts should not admit evidence on the issue of behavior changes attributable to dietary problems, as long as such evidence pertains to the legally relevant question as to whether a defendant could and *did* act (normally and voluntarily) in committing the alleged crime. (See Chapter 9.)

---

ducted a series of studies on the relation between sugar and the behavior of institutionalized offenders. In these investigations inmates were placed on a modified diet that included very little sugar. They received fruit juice in place of soda and vegetables instead of candy. Schoenthaler found fewer disciplinary actions and a significant drop in aggressive behavior in the experimental group.[66] Some persons charged with crimes have used this finding to build a defense.

Other researchers have looked for the causes of crime in vitamin deficiencies. One such study found that 70 percent of criminals charged with serious offenses in one Canadian jurisdiction had a greater than normal need for vitamin B-6.[67] Other studies have noted deficiencies of vitamins B-3 and B-6 in criminal population samples.

Some investigators have examined the effects of food additives and food dyes on asocial behavior. Benjamin Feingold has argued that between 30 and 60 percent of all hyperactivity in children may be attributable to reactions to food coloring.[68] There is some additional support for this hypothesis.[69] And studies have suggested that a diet deficient in protein may be responsible for violent aggression.

Let us examine the association between the consumption of tryptophan, an amino acid (a protein building block), and crime rates. Tryptophan is a normal component of many foods. Low levels of it have been associated with aggression and, in criminal studies, an increased sensitivity to electric shock. Anthony R. Mawson and K. W. Jacobs reasoned that diets low in tryptophan would be likely to result in higher levels of violent crime, particularly aggressive violent offenses, such as homicide. They hypothesized that because corn-based diets are deficient in tryptophan, a cross-national comparison of countries should reveal a positive relationship between corn consumption and homicide rates. Mawson and Jacobs obtained homicide data from the United Nations and the mean per capita corn intake rates of fifty-three foreign countries from the U.S. Department of Agriculture. They discovered that countries whose per capita rates of corn consumption were above the median had significantly higher homicide rates than countries whose diets were based on wheat or rice.[70]

Hypoglycemia   Another biochemical factor related to criminality may be **hypoglycemia,** a condition that occurs when the level of sugar in the blood falls below an acceptable range. The brain is particularly vulnerable to hypoglycemia, and such a condition can impair its function. Symptoms of hypoglycemia include anxiety, headache, confusion, fatigue, and even aggressive behavior. As early as 1943 researchers linked the condition with violent crime, including murder, rape, and assault. Subsequent studies found that violent and impulsive male offenders had a higher rate of hypoglycemia than noncriminal controls. Consider the work of Matti Virkkunen, who has conducted a series of studies of habitually violent and psychopathic offenders. In one such study he examined the results of a glucose tolerance test (used to determine whether hypoglycemia is present) administered to thirty-seven habitually violent offenders with antisocial personalities, thirty-one habitually violent offenders with intermittent explosive disorders, and twenty controls. The offenders were found to be significantly more hypoglycemic than the controls.[71]

Hormones   Experiments have shown that male animals are typically more aggressive than females. Male aggression is directly linked to male hormones. If an aggressive male mouse is injected with female hormones, he will stop fighting.[72] Likewise, the administration of male hormones to pregnant monkeys results in female offspring who, even three years after

birth, are more aggressive than the daughters of noninjected mothers.[73]

While it would be misleading to equate male hormones with aggression and female hormones with nonaggression, there is some evidence that abnormal levels of male hormones in humans may prompt criminal behavior. Several investigators have found higher levels of testosterone (the male hormone) in the blood of individuals who have committed violent offenses.[74] Some studies also relate the premenstrual syndrome (PMS) to delinquency, concluding that women are at greater risk of aggressive and suicidal behavior before and during their menstrual period. After studying 156 newly admitted adult female prisoners, Katherina Dalton concluded that 49 percent of all their crimes were committed either in the premenstrual period or during menstruation.[75] Recently critics have challenged the association between menstrual distress and female crime.[76]

Neurophysiological Factors

In England in the mid-1950s a father hit his son with a mallet and then threw him out of a window, killing him instantly. Instead of pleading insanity, as many people expected him to do, he presented evidence of a brain tumor, which, he argued, resulted in uncontrollable rage and violence. A jury acquitted him on the grounds that the brain tumor had deprived him of any control over or knowledge of the act he was committing.[77] Brain lesions or brain tumors have led to violent outbursts in many similar cases. The focus of neurophysiological studies, however, has not been exclusively on brain tumors, but has included a wide range of investigations: brain wave studies, clinical reports of minimal brain dysfunction, and theoretical explorations into the relationship between the limbic system and criminality.

EEG abnormalities   The electroencephalogram (EEG) is a tracing made by an instrument that measures cerebral functioning by recording brain wave activity with electrodes that are placed on the scalp. Numerous studies that have examined the brain activity of violent prisoners reveal significant differences between the EEGs of criminals and those of noncriminals. Other findings relate significantly slow brain wave activity to young offenders and adult murderers.[78] When Sarnoff A. Mednick and his colleagues examined the criminal records and EEGs of 265 children in a birth cohort in Denmark, they found that certain types of brain wave activity, as measured by the EEG, enabled investigators to predict whether convicted thieves would steal again.[79] When Jan Volavka compared the EEGs of juvenile delinquents with those of comparable nondelinquents, he found a slowing of brain waves in the delinquent sample, most prominently in those children convicted of theft. He concluded that thievery "is more likely to develop in persons who have a slowing of alpha frequency than in persons who do not."[80]

Minimal brain dysfunction   Minimal brain dysfunction (MBD) is classified as "attention deficit hyperactivity disorder."[81] MBD produces such asocial behavioral patterns as impulsivity, hyperactivity, aggressiveness, low self-esteem, and temper outbursts. The syndrome is noteworthy for at least two reasons. First, MBD may explain criminality when social theories fail to do so; that is, when neighborhood, peer, and familial associations do not suggest a high risk of delinquency. Second, MBD is an easily overlooked diagnosis. Parents, teachers, and clinicians tend to focus more on the symptoms of a child's psychopathology than on the possibility of brain dysfunction, even though investigators have repeatedly found high rates of brain dysfunction in samples of suicidal adolescents and youthful offenders.[82]

Crime and Human Nature

The criminologist Edward Sagarin has written:

> In criminology, it appears that a number of views...have become increasingly delicate and sensitive, as if all those who espouse them were inherently evil, or at least stupidly insensitive to the consequences of their research.... In the study of crime, the examples of unpop-

ular orientations are many. Foremost is the link of crime to the factors of genes, biology, race, ethnicity, and religion.[83]

What is it about the linkage of biology and criminality that makes the subject delicate and sensitive? Why is it so offensive to so many people? One reason is that biocriminology denies the existence of individual free will. The idea of a predisposition to commit crimes engenders a sense of hopelessness. This criticism seems to have little merit. As Diana H. Fishbein has aptly noted, the idea of a "conditioned free will" is widely accepted.[84] This view suggests that individuals make choices in regard to a particular action within a range of possibilities that is "preset" yet flexible. Thus, when conditions permit rational thought, one is fully accountable and responsible for one's actions. It is only when conditions are somehow disturbed that free choice is constricted. The child of middle-class parents who has a low IQ might steer away from delinquent behavior. But if that child's circumstances changed so that he lived in a lower-class, single-parent environment, he might find the delinquent lifestyle of the children in the new neighborhood too tempting to resist.

Critics of biocriminology have other concerns as well. Some critics see a racist undertone to biocriminological research. If there is a genetic predisposition to commit crime and if minorities account for a disproportionate share of criminal activity, are minorities then predisposed to commit crime?

Other important questions have been raised. In Chapter 2 we learned that self-reports reveal that most people have engaged in delinquent or criminal behavior. How, then, do biocriminologists justify their claims that certain groups are more prone than others to criminal behavior? Could it be that the subjects of their investigations are only those criminals who have been caught and incarcerated? And is the attention of the police disproportionately drawn to members of minority groups?

How do biocriminologists account for the fact that most criminologists see the structure of our society, the decay of our neighborhoods, and the subcultures of certain areas as deter-

WINDOW TO THE WORLD

The Demise and Reincarnation of the Biological Theory

Benigno di Tullio was the last in the line of those who deserved "an honored place in the Hall of Fame of the 'Italian School' of criminology, in the select company of such pioneering thinkers on crime and correction as Lombroso, Ferri, and Garofalo," according to Sheldon Glueck.[1] In 1968, di Tullio was invited to a major colloquium in New York: Hundreds of criminologists and policy makers in criminal justice were invited to attend his lecture. Only ten did so. In this small company di Tullio made an impassioned plea for criminologists to consider genetic factors in crime causation. The social sciences, he expounded, can provide an explanation of criminality only if the biological, psychological, and the genetic aspects of the offender are taken into consideration. He presented the evidence of his own investigations and those of his many European contemporaries that biological causes of criminal behavior deserve the attention of criminology along with environmental factors. All inquiries, he claimed, aimed at obtaining a better understanding of the biological causes of criminality are meaningful, even when the results only allow us to formulate working hypotheses.

The ten people in attendance listened, but soon forgot. The "Italian School" had died; the biological and genetic approach to explaining crime and treating offenders had fallen out of favor. The attendance at di Tullio's colloquium seemed to prove it. But not entirely.

In Italy, Franco Ferracuti, best known for his work on the subculture of violence, pursued the investigation of psychological, biological, and sociological elements contributing to the explanation of crime. In the United States it was C. Ray Jeffery who prodded U.S. researchers to a reinvestigation of genetic and environmental elements that contribute to criminality. None of the researchers in the field, from di Tullio to Ferracuti to Jeffery, contend that genetics and biology offer the sole answer to the explanation of crime. But they do contend that we cannot explain crime without consideration of these elements. In 1987, David P. Farrington wrote, "The challenge to biological researchers is to disentangle the links between biological and nonbiological variables and build up an impressive corpus of knowledge about biology and crime."[2]

---

[1]Benigno di Tullio, *Horizons in Clinical Criminology,* Introduction by Sheldon Glueck. (New York: Criminal Law Education and Research Center, 1969).

---

[2]David P. Farrington, "Implications of Biological Findings for Criminological Research," in Sarnoff A. Mednick, Terrie E. Moffitt, and Susan A. Stack, *The Causes of Crime* (New York: Cambridge University Press, 1987), pp. 61–62.

---

minants of criminality? Are biocriminologists unfairly deemphasizing social and economic factors? (In Chapters 5 through 8 we review theories that attribute criminality to group and environmental forces.) These issues raise further questions that are at the core of all social and behavioral science: Is human behavior the product of nature (genetics) or nurture (environment)? The consensus among social and behavioral scientists today is that the interaction of nature and nurture is so pervasive that the two cannot be viewed in isolation.

Supporters of biocriminology also maintain that recognition of a predisposition to crime is not inconsistent with consideration of environmental factors. In fact, some believe that predispositions are triggered by environmental factors. Even if we agree that some people are predisposed to commit crime, we must recognize that the crime rate would be higher in those areas that provide more triggers. In sum, while some people may be predisposed to certain kinds of behavior, most scientists agree that both psychological and environmental factors shape the final forms of those behaviors.

In recent years the debate has found a new

forum in integrated biocriminological theories, such as the one proposed by James Q. Wilson and Richard Herrnstein. These scholars explain predatory street crime by showing how human nature develops from the interplay of psychological, biological, and social factors. It is the interaction of the genes with the environment that in some individuals forms the kind of personality likely to commit crimes. The argument takes into account such factors as IQ, body build, genetic makeup, impulsiveness, ability to delay gratification, aggressiveness, and even the drinking and smoking habits of pregnant mothers.

According to Wilson and Herrnstein, the choice between crime and conventional behavior is closely linked to individual biological and psychological traits and to such social factors as family and school experiences. Their conclusion is that "the offender offends not just because of immediate needs and circumstances, but also because of enduring personal characteristics, some of whose traces can be found in his behavior from early childhood on."[85] In essence, they argue that behavior results from a person's perception of the potential rewards and/or punishments that go along with a criminal act. If the potential rewards (such as money) are greater than the expected punishment (say, a small fine), the chance that a crime will be committed increases.

REVIEW

When psychologists have attempted to explain criminality, they have taken four general approaches. First, they have focused on failures in psychological development—an overbearing or weak conscience, inner conflict, insufficient moral development, and maternal deprivation with its concomitant failure of attachment. Second, they have investigated the ways in which aggression and violence are learned through modeling and direct experience. Third, they have investigated the personality characteristics of criminals and found that criminals do tend to be more impulsive, intolerant, and irresponsible than noncriminals. Fourth, psychologists have investigated the relation of criminality to such mental disorders as psychosis and psychopathy.

Biocriminologists investigate the biological correlates of criminality, including a genetic predisposition to commit crime. The XYY syndrome, though now generally discounted as a cause of criminality, suggests that aggressive and violent behavior may be at least partly determined by genetic factors. Studies of the behavior of identical and fraternal twins and of the rates of criminality among adopted children with both criminal and noncriminal biological and adoptive parents tend to support this hypothesis. Investigators have also found a strong correlation between a low IQ and delinquency. Biocriminologists' most recent and perhaps most important discovery is the relation of criminal behavior to biochemical factors (food allergies, dietary deficiencies, hormonal imbalances) and neurophysiological factors (EEG abnormalities and minimal brain dysfunction). Most scientists agree that if some people are biologically predisposed to certain behaviors, both psychological and environmental factors shape the forms of those behaviors.

It is clear that psychological, biological, and sociological explanations are not competing to answer the same specific questions. Rather, all three disciplines are searching for answers to different questions, albeit about the same act, status, or characteristic. We can understand crime in a society only if we view criminality from more than one level of analysis: why a certain individual commits a crime (psychological/biological explanations) and why some groups of individuals commit more or qualitatively different criminal acts than other groups (sociological explanations). Sociological theory and empirical research often ignore such factors as personality and human biology, almost as if they were irrelevant. And psychological theory is no less guilty, often focusing on the individual with little regard for the fact that while each one of us comes into the world with certain pre-

dispositions, from the moment we are born we interact with others in complex situations that influence our behavior.

KEY TERMS

attachment
behavioral modeling
biocriminology
chromosomes
conditioning
cortical arousal
differential association–reinforcement
dizygotic twins
ego
extraversion

hypoglycemia
id
minimal brain dysfunction
monozygotic twins
psychoanalytic theory
psychopathy
psychosis
psychoticism
social learning theory
superego

NOTES

1. See, e.g., Sigmund Freud, *A General Introduction to Psychoanalysis* (New York: Liveright, 1920) and *The Ego and the Id* (London: Hogarth, 1927).

2. August Aichhorn, *Wayward Youth* (New York: Viking, 1935).

3. Kate Friedlander, *The Psycho-Analytic Approach to Juvenile Delinquency* (New York: International Universities Press, 1947).

4. See Hans Eysenck, *The Rise and Fall of the Freudian Empire* (New York: Plenum, 1987).

5. Lawrence Kohlberg, "The Development of Modes of Moral Thinking and Choice in the Years Ten to Sixteen," Ph.D. dissertation, University of Chicago, 1958.

6. Lawrence Kohlberg, "Stage and Sequence: The Cognitive-Developmental Approach to Socialization," in *Handbook of Socialization Theory and Research*, ed. David A. Goslin (Chicago: Rand McNally, 1969).

7. William S. Jennings, Robert Kilkenny, and Lawrence Kohlberg, "Moral Development Theory and Practice for Youthful Offenders," in *Personality Theory, Moral Development, and Criminal Behavior*, ed. William S. Laufer and James M. Day (Lexington, Mass.: Lexington Books, 1983); see also Daniel D. Macphail, "The Moral Education Approach in Treating Adult Inmates,"

Criminal Justice and Behavior 16 (1989): 81–97; Jack Arbuthnot and Donald A. Gordon, "Crime and Cognition: Community Applications of Sociomoral Reasoning Development," *Criminal Justice and Behavior* 15 (1988): 379–393; J. E. LeCapitaine, "The Relationships Between Emotional Development and Moral Development and the Differential Impact of Three Psychological Interventions on Children," *Psychology in the Schools* 15 (1987): 379–393.

8. John Bowlby, *Attachment and Loss*, 2 vols. (New York: Basic Books, 1969, 1973); see also Bowlby's "Forty-four Juvenile Thieves: Their Characteristics and Home Life," *International Journal of Psychoanalysis* 25 (1944): 19–52.

9. John Bowlby, *The Making and Breaking of Affectional Bonds* (London: Tavistock, 1979); see also Michael Rutter, *Maternal Deprivation Reassessed* (Harmondsworth: Penguin, 1971).

10. Michael Lewis, Candice Feiring, Carolyn McGuffog, and John Jaskir, "Predicting Psychopathology in Six-Year-Olds from Early Social Relations," *Child Development* 55 (1984): 123–136.

11. L. Sroufe, "Infant Caregiver Attachment and Patterns of Adaptation in Preschool: The Roots of Maladaption and Competence," in *Minnesota Symposium on Child Psychology*, ed. Marion Perlmutter, vol. 16 (Hillsdale, N.J.: Erlbaum, 1982).

12. Alicia F. Lieberman, "Preschoolers' Competence with a Peer: Influence of Attachment and Social Experience," *Child Development* 48 (1977): 1277–1287.

13. Joan McCord, "Some Child-Rearing Antecedents of Criminal Behavior," *Journal of Personality and Social Psychology* 37 (1979): 1477–1486; "A Longitudinal View of the Relationship Between Paternal Absence and Crime," in *Abnormal Offenders, Delinquency, and the Criminal Justice System*, ed. John Gunn and David P. Farrington (London: Wiley, 1982). See also Scott W. Henggeler, Cindy L. Hanson, Charles M. Borduin, Sylvia M. Watson, and Molly A. Brunk, "Mother-Son Relationships of Juvenile Felons," *Journal of Consulting and Clinical Psychology* 53 (1985): 942–943; Francis I. Nye, *Family Relationships and Delinquent Behavior* (New York: Wiley, 1958).

14. Sheldon Glueck and Eleanor T. Glueck, *Unraveling Juvenile Delinquency* (New York: Commonwealth Fund, 1950); Lee N. Robins, "Aetiological Implications in Studies of Childhood Histories Relating to Antisocial Personality," in *Psychopathic Behaviour*, ed. Robert D. Hare and Daisy Schalling (Chichester: Wiley, 1970); Lee N. Robins, *Deviant Children Grow Up* (Baltimore: Williams & Wilkins, 1966).

15. Joan McCord, "Instigation and Insulation: How Families Affect Antisocial Aggression," in *Development of Antisocial and Prosocial Behavior: Research Theories and Issues*, ed. Dan Olweus, Jack Block, and M. Radke-Yarrow (London: Academic Press, 1986).

16. Albert Bandura, *Aggression: A Social Learning Analysis* (Englewood Cliffs, N.J.: Prentice-Hall, 1973), and "The Social Learning Perspective: Mechanism of Aggression," in *Psychology of Crime and Criminal Justice*, ed. Hans Toch (New York: Holt, Rinehart & Winston, 1979).

17. Leonard D. Eron and L. Rowell Huesmann, "Parent-Child Interaction, Television Violence, and Aggression of Children," *American Psychologist* 37 (1982): 197–211; Russell G. Geen, "Aggression and Television Violence," in *Aggression: Theoretical and Empirical Reviews*, ed. Russell G. Geen and Edward I. Donnerstein, vol. 2 (New York: Academic Press, 1983); Leonard D. Eron and L. Rowell Huesmann, "Adolescent Aggression and Television," *Annals of the New York Academy of Sciences* 347 (1980): 319–331.

18. Leonard D. Eron and L. Rowell Huesmann, "The Control of Aggressive Behavior by Changes in Attitudes, Values, and the Conditions of Learning," in *Advances in the Study of Aggression*, ed. Robert J. Blanchard and D. Caroline Blanchard, vol. 1 (Orlando, Fla: Academic Press, 1984).

19. J. Ronald Milavsky, H. H. Stipp, R. C. Kessler, and W. S. Rubens, *Television and Aggression: A Panel Study* (New York: Academic Press, 1982).

20. See Gerald R. Patterson, R. A. Littman, and W. Brickler, *Assertive Behavior in Children: A Step Toward a Theory of Aggression*, monograph of the Society for Research in Child Development no. 32 (1976).

21. Bandura, *Aggression*.

22. C. Ray Jeffery, "Criminal Behavior and Learning Theory," *Journal of Criminal Law, Criminology and Police Science* 56 (1965): 294–300.

23. Ernest L. Burgess and Ronald L. Akers, "A Differential Association-Reinforcement Theory of Criminal Behavior," *Social Problems* 14 (1966): 128–147. See also Adams, "Differential Association and Learning Principles Revisited," *Social Problems* 20 (1973): 458–470.

24. William S. Laufer, Dagna K. Skoog, and James M. Day, "Personality and Criminality: A Review of the California Psychological Inventory," *Journal of Clinical Psychology* 38 (1982): 562–573.

25. Michael L. Gearing, "The MMPI as a Primary Differentiator and Predictor of Behavior in Prison: A Methodological Critique and Review of the Recent Literature," *Psychological Bulletin* 36 (1979): 929–963.

26. Edwin I. Megargee and Martin J. Bohn, *Classifying Criminal Offenders* (Beverly Hills, Calif.: Sage, 1979); William S. Laufer, John A. Johnson, and Robert Hogan, "Ego Con-

trol and Criminal Behavior," *Journal of Personality and Social Psychology* 41 (1981): 179–184; Edwin I. Megargee, "Psychological Determinants and Correlates of Criminal Violence," in *Criminal Violence,* ed. Marvin E. Wolfgang and Neil A. Weiner (Beverly Hills, Calif.: Sage, 1982); Edwin I. Megargee, "The Role of Inhibition in the Assessment and Understanding of Violence," in *Current Topics in Clinical and Community Psychology,* ed. Charles Donald Spielberger (New York: Academic Press, 1971); Edwin I. Megargee, "Undercontrol and Overcontrol in Assaultive and Homicidal Adolescents," Ph.D. dissertation, University of California, Berkeley, 1964; Edwin I. Megargee, "Undercontrolled and Overcontrolled Personality Types in Extreme Antisocial Aggression," *Psychological Monographs* 80 (1966); Edwin I. Megargee and Gerald A. Mendelsohn, "A Cross-Validation of Twelve MMPI Indices of Hostility and Control," *Journal of Abnormal and Social Psychology* 65 (1962): 431–438.

27. See, e.g., William S. Laufer and James M. Day, eds., *Personality Theory, Moral Development, and Criminal Behavior* (Lexington, Mass.: Lexington Books, 1983).

28. Milton Metfessel and Constance Lovell, "Recent Literature on Individual Correlates of Crime," *Psychological Bulletin* 39 (1942): 133–164.

29. Karl E. Schuessler and Donald R. Cressey, "Personality Characteristics of Criminals," *American Journal of Sociology* 55 (1950): 476–484.

30. Daniel J. Tennenbaum, "Personality and Criminality: A Summary and Implications of the Literature," *Journal of Criminal Justice* 5 (1977): 225–235. See also G. P. Waldo and Simon Dinitz, "Personality Attributes of the Criminal: An Analysis of Research Studies, 1950–1965," *Journal of Research in Crime and Delinquency* 4 (1967): 185–202; R. D. Martin and D. G. Fischer, "Personality Factors in Juvenile Delinquency: A Review of the Literature," *Catalog of Selected Documents in Psychology,* vol. 8 (1978), Ms. 1759.

31. Samuel Yochelson and Stanton Samenow, *The Criminal Personality* (New York: Jason Aronson, 1976).

32. Laufer et al., "Personality and Criminality."

33. See Anne Campbell and John J. Gibbs, eds., *Violent Transactions: The Limits of Personality* (Oxford: Blackwell, 1986); Lawrence A. Pervin, "Personality: Current Controversies, Issues, and Direction," *Annual Review of Psychology* 36 (1985): 83–114; Lawrence A. Pervin, "Persons, Situations, Interactions: Perspectives on a Recurrent Issue," in *Violent Transactions: The Limits of Personality,* ed. Anne Campbell and John J. Gibbs (Oxford: Blackwell, 1986).

34. See Hans J. Eysenck, *Crime and Personality* (London: Routledge & Kegan Paul, 1977); Hans J. Eysenck, "Personality, Conditioning, and Antisocial Behavior," in Laufer and Day, *Personality Theory;* Hans J. Eysenck, "Personality and Criminality: A Dispositional Analysis," in *Advances in Criminological Theory,* ed. William S. Laufer and Freda Adler, vol. 1 (New Brunswick, N.J.: Transaction, 1989); Hans J. Eysenck and Gisli H. Gudjonsson, *The Causes and Cures of Crime* (New York: Plenum, 1990).

35. Seymour L. Halleck, *Psychiatry and the Dilemmas of Crime* (New York: Harper and Row, 1967); Nicholas N. Kittrie, *The Right to Be Different: Deviance and Enforced Therapy* (Baltimore, Md.: Johns Hopkins Press, 1971).

36. Karl Menninger, *The Crime of Punishment* (New York: Viking, 1968).

37. Hervey Cleckley, *The Mask of Sanity* (St. Louis: C. V. Mosby, 1980), pp. 56–57.

38. Ibid., p. 57; Robert D. Hare, *Psychopathy: Theory and Research* (New York: Wiley, 1970); M. Philip Feldman, *Criminal Behavior: A Psychological Analysis* (New York: Wiley, 1978); William McCord and Joan McCord, *Psychopathy and Delinquency* (New York: Wiley, 1956).

39. The American Psychiatric Association's *Diagnostic and Statistical Manual of Mental Disorders,* 3d rev. ed. (Washington, D.C., 1987) (*DSM III-R*), classifies psychopathy as "antisocial personality." See Benjamin Karpman, "On the Need of Separating Psychopathy into Two Distinct Clinical Types: The Symptomatic and the Ideopathic," *Journal of Criminal Psychopathology* 3 (1941): 112–137.

40. Eysenck and Gudjonnson, *The Causes and Cures of Crime*. See Robert D. Hare, "Research Scale for the Assessment of Psychopathology in Criminal Populations," *Personality and Individual Differences* 1 (1980): 111–119.

41. J. Puig-Antich, "Biological Factors in Prepubertal Major Depression," *Pediatric Annals* 12 (1986): 867–878.

42. Edward O. Wilson, *Sociobiology: The New Synthesis* (Cambridge: Harvard University Press, 1975).

43. C. Ray Jeffery, *Biology and Crime* (Beverly Hills, Calif.: Sage, 1979).

44. See Sarnoff A. Mednick, Terrie E. Moffitt, and Susan A. Stack, *The Causes of Crime: New Biological Approaches* (New York: Cambridge University Press, 1987).

45. A. A. Sandberg, G. F. Koepf, and T. Ishihara, "An XYY Human Male," *Lancet* (August 1961): 488–489.

46. Herman A. Witkin et al., "Criminality, Aggression, and Intelligence Among XYY and XXY Men," in *Biosocial Bases of Criminal Behavior*, ed. Sarnoff A. Mednick and Karl O. Christiansen (New York: Wiley, 1977).

47. Johannes Lange, *Verbrechen als Schicksal* (Leipzig: Georg Thieme, 1929).

48. See Karl O. Christiansen, "A Preliminary Study of Criminality Among Twins," in Mednick and Christiansen, *Biosocial Bases of Criminal Behavior*.

49. David C. Rowe and D. Wayne Osgood, "Heredity and Sociological Theories of Delinquency: A Reconsideration," *American Sociological Review* 49 (1986): 526–540; David C. Rowe, "Genetic and Environmental Components of Antisocial Behavior: A Study of 256 Twin Pairs," *Criminology* 24 (1986): 513–532.

50. Sarnoff A. Mednick, William Gabrielli, and Barry Hutchings, "Genetic Influences in Criminal Behavior: Evidence from an Adoption Court," in *Prospective Studies of Crime and Delinquency*, ed. K. Teilmann et al. (Boston: Kluver-Nijhoff, 1983).

51. These and other studies are reviewed in Mednick et al., *Causes of Crime*.

52. Hugo Munsterberg, *On the Witness Stand* (New York: Doubleday, 1908); Henry H. Goddard, *Feeble-Mindedness: Its Causes and Consequences* (New York: Macmillan, 1914).

53. Edwin H. Sutherland, "Mental Deficiency and Crime," in *Social Attitudes*, ed. K. Young (New York: Henry Holt, 1931).

54. Robert H. Gault, "Highlights of Forty Years in the Correctional Field—and Looking Ahead," *Federal Probation* 17 (1953): 3–4.

55. Arthur Jensen, *Bias in Mental Testing* (New York: Free Press, 1979).

56. Jensen, *Bias in Mental Testing*; Richard J. Herrnstein, *IQ in the Meritocracy* (Boston: Atlantic–Little, Brown, 1973).

57. Travis Hirschi and Michael J. Hindelang, "Intelligence and Delinquency: A Revisionist Review," *American Sociological Review* 42 (1977): 571–586.

58. Travis Hirschi, *Causes of Delinquency* (Berkeley: University of California Press, 1969).

59. Marvin E. Wolfgang, Robert F. Figlio, and Thorsten Sellin, *Delinquency in a Birth Cohort* (Chicago: University of Chicago Press, 1972).

60. Albert J. Reiss and Albert L. Rhodes, "The Distribution of Juvenile Delinquency in the Social Class Structure," *American Sociological Review* 26 (1961): 720–732.

61. James Q. Wilson and Richard Herrnstein, *Crime and Human Nature* (New York: Simon & Schuster, 1985); Deborah W. Denno, "Sociological and Human Developmental Explanations of Crime: Conflict or Consensus?" *Criminology* 23 (1985): 711–740. See also Deborah W. Denno, "Victim, Offender, and Situational Characteristics of Violent Crime," *Journal of Criminal Law and Criminology* 77 (1986): 1142–1158.

62. "Taking the Chitling Test," *Newsweek*, July 15, 1968.

63. Sandra Scarr and Richard Weinberg, "I.Q. Test Performance of Black Children Adopted by White Families," *American Psychologist* 31 (1976): 726–739.

64. See Doris J. Rapp, *Allergies and the Hyperactive Child* (New York: Simon & Schuster, 1981).

65. Diana H. Fishbein and Susan Pease, "The Effects of Diet on Behavior: Implications for Criminology and Corrections," *Research on Corrections* 1 (1988): 1–45.

66. Stephen Schoenthaler, "Diet and Crime: An Empirical Examination of the Value of Nutrition in the Control and Treatment of Incarcerated Juvenile Offenders," *International Journal of Biosocial Research* 4 (1982): 25–39.

67. Abram Hoffer, "The Relation of Crime to Nutrition," *Humanist in Canada* 8 (1975): 2–9.

68. Benjamin F. Feingold, *Why Is Your Child Hyperactive?* (New York: Random House, 1975).

69. James W. Swanson and Marcel Kinsbourne, "Food Dyes Impair Performance of Hyperactive Children on a Laboratory Test," *Science* 207 (1980): 1485–1487.

70. Anthony R. Mawson and K. W. Jacobs, "Corn Consumption, Tryptophan, and Cross-national Homicide Rates," *Journal of Orthomolecular Psychiatry* 7 (1978): 227–230.

71. Matti Virkkunen, "Insulin Secretion During the Glucose Tolerance Test Among Habitually Violent and Impulsive Offenders," *Aggressive Behavior* 12 (1986): 303–310.

72. E. A. Beeman, "The Effect of Male Hormones on Aggressive Behavior in Mice," *Physiological Zoology* 20 (1947): 373–405.

73. D. A. Hamburg and D. T. Lunde, "Sex Hormones in the Development of Sex Differences," in *The Development of Sex Differences*, ed. Eleanor E. Maccoby (Stanford, Calif.: Stanford University Press, 1966).

74. L. E. Kreuz and R. M. Rose, "Assessment of Aggressive Behavior and Plasma Testosterone of a Young Criminal Population," *Psychosomatic Medicine* 34 (1972): 321–332; R. T. Rada, D. R. Laws, and R. Kellner, "Plasma Testosterone Levels in the Rapist," *Psychosomatic Medicine* 38 (1976): 257–268.

75. Katharina Dalton, *The Premenstrual Syndrome* (Springfield, Ill.: Charles C Thomas, 1971).

76. Julie Horney, "Menstrual Cycles and Criminal Responsibility," *Law and Human Behavior* 2 (1978): 25–36.

77. Regina v. Charlson, 1 All. E. R. 859 (1955).

78. H. Forssman and T. S. Frey, "Electroencephalograms of Boys with Behavior Disorders," *Acta Psychologica et Neurologia Scandinavica* 28 (1953): 61–73; H. de Baudouin et al., "Study of a Population of 97 Confined Murderers," *Annales medico-psychologique* 119 (1961): 625–686.

79. Sarnoff A. Mednick, Jan Volavka, William F. Gabrielli, and Turan M. Itil, "EEG as a Predictor of Antisocial Behavior," *Criminology* 19 (1981): 219–229.

80. Jan Volavka, "Electroencephalogram Among Criminals," in Mednick et al., *Causes of Crime.*

81. *DSM III-R*, 314.01. See Michael Rutter, "Syndromes Attributed to 'Minimal Brain Dysfunction' in Children," *American Journal of Psychiatry* 139 (1980): 21–33.

82. Lorne T. Yeudall, D. Fromm-Auch, and P. Davies, "Neuropsychological Impairment of Persistent Delinquency," *Journal of Nervous and Mental Disorders* 170 (1982): 257–265; R. D. Robin et al., "Adolescents Who Attempt Suicide," *Journal of Pediatrics* 90 (1977): 636–638.

83. Edward Sagarin, "Taboo Subjects and Taboo Viewpoints in Criminology," in *Taboos in Criminology*, ed. Sagarin (Beverly Hills, Calif.: Sage, 1980), pp. 8–9.

84. Diana H. Fishbein, "Biological Perspectives in Criminology," *Criminology* 28 (1990): 27–40.

85. Wilson and Herrnstein, *Crime and Human Nature.*

5

STRAIN AND CULTURAL DEVIANCE THEORIES

The early decades of the twentieth century brought major changes to American society. One of the most significant was the change in the composition of the populations of cities. Between 1840 and 1924, forty-five million people—Irish, Swedes, Germans, Italians, Poles, Armenians, Bohemians, Russians—left the Old World; two-thirds of them were bound for the United States.[1] At the same time, increased mechanization in this country deprived many American farmworkers of their jobs and forced them to join the ranks of the foreign-born and the black laborers who had migrated from the South to northern and midwestern industrial centers. During the 1920s large American cities swelled with five million new arrivals.[2]

Chicago's expansion was particularly remarkable: its population doubled in twenty years. Many of the new arrivals brought nothing with them except what they could carry. The city offered them only meager wages, twelve-hour working days in conditions that jeopardized their health, and tenement housing in deteriorating areas of the city. Chicago had other problems as well: in the late 1920s and early 1930s it was the home of major organized crime groups, which fought over the profits from the illegal production and sale of liquor during Prohibition (as we shall see in Chapter 12).

The Chicago that was teeming with newcomers looking for work, corrupt politicians trying to buy their votes, and bootleggers growing more influential through sheer firepower and the political strength they controlled also had a rapidly increasing crime rate. Chicago soon became an inviting urban laboratory for criminologists, who began to challenge the then predominant theories of crime causation based on biological and psychological factors. Many of these criminologists were associated with the University of Chicago, which has the oldest sociology program in the United States (begun in 1892). By the 1920s these criminologists began to measure scientifically the amount of criminal behavior and its relation to the social turmoil Chicago was experiencing. Since that time sociological theories have remained at the forefront of the scientific investigation of crime causation.

THE INTERCONNECTEDNESS OF SOCIOLOGICAL THEORIES

The psychological and biological theories of criminal behavior (Chapter 4) share the assumption that such behavior is caused by some underlying physical or mental condition that separates the criminal from the noncriminal. They seek to identify the "kind of person" who becomes a criminal and to find the factors that caused the person to engage in criminal behavior. These theories yield insight into individual cases, but they do not explain why crime rates vary from one neighborhood to the next, from group to group, within large urban areas, or within groups of individuals. Sociological theories seek the reasons for differences in crime rates in the social environment. These theories can be grouped into three general categories: strain, cultural deviance, and social control.

The strain and cultural deviance perspectives, formulated between 1925 and 1940 and still popular today, laid the foundation for subcultural theories (Chapter 6). Strain and cultural deviance theories focus on the social forces that cause people to engage in criminal activity. Social control theories (Chapter 7) take a different approach: they are based on the assumption that the motivation to commit crime is part of human nature. Consequently, social control theories seek to discover why people do *not* commit crime. They examine the ability of social groups and institutions to make their rules effective.

Strain and cultural deviance theories both assume that social class and criminal behavior are related, but they differ as to the nature of the relationship. Strain theorists argue that all members of society subscribe to one set of cultural values—that of the middle class. One of the most important values is economic success. Since lower-class persons do not have legitimate means to reach this goal, they become frustrated and turn to illegitimate means in desperation. Cultural deviance theorists, by contrast, claim that lower-class people have a different set of values, which tends to conflict with the values of the middle class. Consequently, when lower-class persons conform to their own value system, they may be violating conventional norms.

THE ANOMIE THEORY OF EMILE DURKHEIM

The Structural-Functionalist Perspective

One way of studying a society is to look at its component parts in an effort to find out how they relate to each other. In other words, we look at the structure of a society to see how it functions. If the society is stable, its parts operating smoothly, the social arrangements are functional. Such a society is marked by cohesion, cooperation, and consensus. But if the component parts are arranged in such a way as to threaten the social order, the arrangements are said to be dysfunctional. In a class-oriented society, for example, the classes tend to be in conflict. Imagine a clock with all of its parts finely synchronized. It functions with precision. It keeps perfect time. But if one tiny weight or small spring breaks down, the whole mechanism fails to function properly.

This structural-functionalist perspective was developed by Emile Durkheim before the end of the nineteenth century.[3] To appreciate the impact of his work, remember that at that time the positivists had developed their biological theories, which relied on the search for individual differences between criminals and noncriminals, work that was carried out by Cesare Lombroso. Thus, at a time when science was searching for the abnormality of the criminal, Durkheim was writing about the normality of crime in society. To him the explanation of human conduct, and indeed human misconduct, lies not in the individual but in the group and the social organization. It is in this context that he introduced the term "anomie" (defined in Chapter 3 as the breakdown of social order as a result of the loss of standards and values).[4]

Durkheim, who throughout his career was preoccupied with the effects of social change, believed that when a simple society develops into a modern, urbanized one, the intimacy needed to sustain a common set of norms declines. Groups become fragmented, and in the absence of a common set of rules, the actions and expectations of people in one sector may clash with those in another. As behavior becomes unpredictable, the system gradually breaks down, and the society is in a state of anomie.[5]

Anomie and Suicide

Durkheim best illustrated his concept of anomie in a discussion not of crime but of suicide.[6] He suggested several reasons why suicide was more common in some groups than in others. For our purposes, we are interested in the particular form of suicide that he called **anomic suicide.** When he analyzed statistical data, he found that suicide rates increased during times of sudden economic change, whether that change was major depression or unexpected prosperity. In periods of rapid change people are abruptly thrown into an unfamiliar way of life. Rules that once guided behavior no longer hold.

Consider the events of the 1920s. Wealth came easily to many people in those heady, prosperous years. Toward the end, through July, August, and September of 1929, the stock market soared to new heights. Enormous profits were made from speculation in stocks. But on October 24, 1929, a day history records as Black Thursday, the stock market crashed. Thirteen million shares of stock were sold. As more and more shares were offered for sale, their value plummeted. In the wake of the crash, a severe depression overtook the country. Banks failed. Mortgages were foreclosed. Businesses went bankrupt. People lost their jobs. Lifestyles changed overnight. Many people were driven to sell apples on street corners to survive, and they had to stand in mile-long breadlines to feed their families. Suddenly the norms by which people lived were no longer relevant. People became disoriented and confused.

It is not difficult to understand rising suicide rates in such circumstances, but why would anyone fall into such despair at a time of sudden prosperity? According to Durkheim the same factors are at work in both situations. It is not the amount of money available that causes the problems, it's the sudden change. People who suddenly achieve more wealth than they ever dreamed of having tend to believe that nothing is impossible. Durkheim believed that human desires are boundless, an "insatiable and bottomless abyss."[7] Since nature does not set such strict biological limits to the capabilities of humans as it does to those of other animals, he argued, we have developed social rules that put a realistic cap on our aspirations. These regulations are incorporated into the individual conscience and thus make it possible for people to feel fulfilled. But with a sudden burst of prosperity, people's expectations change. When the old rules no longer determine how rewards are distributed among members of society, there is no longer any restraint on what people want. Once again the system breaks down. Thus, whether sudden change causes great prosperity or a great depression, the result is the same—anomie.

STRAIN THEORY

Disparity of Goals and Means

Like Durkheim, Robert Merton related the crime problem to anomie. But Merton's conception of anomie differs somewhat from Durkheim's. The real problem, he argued, is created not by sudden social change but by a social structure that holds out the same goals to all of its members without giving them equal means to achieve them. This lack of integration between what the culture calls for and what the structure permits, the former encouraging success and the latter preventing it, can cause norms to break down because they no longer are effective guides to behavior. Merton borrowed the term "anomie" from Durkheim to describe this breakdown of the normative system. According to Merton:

> It is only when a system of cultural values extols, virtually above all else, certain common symbols of success for the population at large while its social structure rigorously restricts or completely eliminates access to approved modes of acquiring these symbols for a considerable part of the same population, that antisocial behavior ensues on a considerable scale.[8]

WINDOW TO THE WORLD

A Social System Breaks Down

For centuries they lived undisturbed in the lush jungles of northern Brazil, carrying on traditions nearly as old as the forests that nurtured them. Today about 9,000 members of the Yanomami tribe survive. But now their way of life is threatened. Starting in 1987 as many as 45,000 gold prospectors—themselves mostly impoverished Brazilians hoping for quick riches—invaded the tribe's 35,000-square-mile habitat. Moving in small groups, the prospectors extracted ton after ton of gold and left behind the dubious gifts of the 20th century: disease, prostitution, weapons, alcohol, denuded forests and befouled rivers.

The plight of the Indians won sympathy from rock star Sting, who recently raised $2 million for their preservation. Now they have a champion closer to home. In only his second week in office, Brazilian President Fernando Collor de Mello moved against the miners, ordering 100 dirt landing strips destroyed to choke off access to Yanomami territory. "Dynamite them and be quick about it," the 40-year-old leader told Federal Police Chief Romeu Tuma. Some think the action may have come too late; almost 1,800 Yanomami have already died and unassimilated others suffer from diseases for which they have no natural immunity. Even Sting's millions and Collor's good intentions may not be enough to inoculate the Yanomami from the ills of modern civilization.

Source: *Newsweek*, April 9, 1990, p. 34.

Merton argued that in a class-oriented society, the opportunities to get to the top are not equally distributed. Very few members of the lower class ever get there. His anomie theory emphasizes the importance of two elements in any society: (1) cultural aspirations, or goals that people believe are worth striving for; and (2) institutionalized means or accepted ways to attain the desired ends. If a society is to be stable, these two elements must be reasonably well integrated; in other words, means should exist for individuals to reach the goals that are important to them. Disparity between goals and means fosters frustration, which leads to strain. Thus from this perspective the social structure is the root of the crime problem (hence the approach Merton takes is sometimes called a structural explanation). **Strain theory** assumes that people are law-abiding, but under great pressure they will resort to crime; disparity between goals and means provides that pressure.

Merton's theory explains crime in the United States in terms of the wide disparities in income among the various classes. Statistics clearly demonstrate that such disparities exist. The poorest fifth of American families received less than 5 percent of all income in 1985, while the highest fifth received 43.5 percent of all income—almost ten times as much.[9] A summary of Americans' income in the mid-1980s shows that the median income for whites was $24,700 and for blacks, Hispanics, and others $17,700.[10] It is not, however, solely wealth or income which determines people's position on a social ladder that ranges from the homeless on the streets to penthouse dwellers. Other attributes of social class are education, prestige, power, and even language.

Opportunities to move up the social ladder exist, but they are unequally distributed. It is clear that a child born to a single, uneducated, 13-year-old black girl living in a slum has practically no chance to move up, whereas the child of a middle-class white family has a better-than-average chance of reaching a professional or business position. Yet all people in the society share the same goals. Consider that those goals are shaped by billions of advertising dollars spent each year to spread the message that everyone can drive a sports car, take a well-deserved Caribbean vacation, and record the adventure on videotape—in short, can satisfy whatever material desires they may have. The mystique is reinforced by instant lottery millionaires, superstar athletes, the earnings of Wall Street traders, and rags-to-riches stories of such people as Ray Kroc. Kroc was a high school dropout whose idea that a 15-cent hamburger with a 10-cent bag of French fries could make dining out affordable for low-income families spread quickly through the United States—and to twenty-nine other countries that have opened convenience restaurants with the familiar golden arches outside. Though Merton argued that lack of legitimate means for everyone to reach the material goals exemplified by these success stories does create problems, he also made it clear that the high rate of deviant behavior cannot be explained solely on the basis of lack of means.

The world has produced more rigid class systems than our own and societies that limit people's ability to achieve their goals much more

strictly without causing the problems the United States faces. In the traditional society of India, for example, the untouchables at the bottom of the caste system are forbidden by custom (although no longer by law) even to enter the temples and schools used by those above them, while those at the top enjoy immense privileges. All Hindu castes fall within a hierarchy, each one imposing upon its members duties and prohibitions covering both public and private life. People of high status may give food to people of lower status, for example, but may not receive food from them. One may eat in the home of a person of lower status, but the food must be cooked and served by a person of equal or higher status. Members of such a rigid system clearly face many more restraints than we do. What, then, is the difference?

The answer lies in the fact that the Indians have learned from birth that people do not and cannot aspire to the same things. The egalitarian principle of the United States, however, denies the existence of limits to upward mobility within the social structure.[11] In reality, everyone in society experiences some pressures and strains, and the amounts are inversely related to one's position in the hierarchy: the lower the class, the higher the strain.

To be sure, not everyone who is denied access to the society's goals becomes deviant. Merton outlined five ways in which people adapt to society's goals and means. Their responses (modes of adaptation) depend on their attitudes toward the cultural goals and the institutional means to attain those goals. Their

TABLE 5.1   A TYPOLOGY OF MODES OF INDIVIDUAL ADAPTATION

MODES OF ADAPTATION	CULTURE GOALS	INSTITUTIONALIZED MEANS
Conformity	+	+
Innovation	+	−
Ritualism	−	+
Retreatism	−	−
Rebellion	±	±

+ = acceptance.
− = rejection.
± = rejection and substitution.

Source: Robert K. Merton, *Social Theory and Social Structure* (New York: Free Press, 1967), p. 140.

options are conformity, innovation, ritualism, retreatism, and rebellion (see Table 5.1).

Merton does not tell us the process by which any one individual chooses to become a drug pusher, for example, and another chooses to work on an assembly line. Instead he explains why crime rates are high in some groups and low in others.

Modes of Adaptation

Conformity is the most common mode of adjustment. Individuals accept both the culturally defined goals and the prescribed means for achieving those goals. They work, save, go to school, and follow the legitimate paths. Look around you in the classroom. You will see many children of decent, hard-working parents. After college they will find legitimate jobs. Some will excel. Some will walk the economic middle path. But all of those who are conformists will accept (though not necessarily achieve) the goals of our society and the means it approves for achieving them.

Individuals who choose the adaptation of innovation accept society's goals, but since they have few legitimate means to achieve them, they innovate, or design their own means to get ahead. Such means may be burglary, robbery, embezzlement, or a host of other crimes. Youngsters who have no parental attention, no encouragement in school, no way to the top, no future, may scrawl their signatures on subway

Inner city signatures on a subway car

cars and buildings and park benches in order to achieve recognition of a sort. Such illegitimate forms of innovation are certainly not restricted to the lower classes, as evidenced by such crimes as stock manipulation, sale of defective products, and income tax evasion.

People who adapt by ritualism abandon the goals they once believed to be within reach and resign themselves to their present lifestyles. They play by the rules, working on assembly lines, in middle-management jobs, or in some other safe routine.[12] Many workers have been catching a bus at the same street corner at the same hour every day for twenty years or more. They have long forgotten why, except that their jobs are where their paychecks come from. Their great relief is a two-week vacation in the summer.

Retreatism is the adaptation of people who give up both the goals (can't make it) and the means (why try?) and retreat into the world of drug addiction or alcoholism. They have internalized the value system and therefore are under internal pressure not to innovate. The retreatist mode allows for an escape into a nonproductive, nonstriving lifestyle. Some members of the antiwar movement of the 1960s opted to drop out entirely. The pressure was too great, the opportunities were unacceptable. They became addicts or followers of occult religions.

Rebellion occurs when both the cultural goals and the legitimate means are rejected. Many individuals substitute their own goals (get rid of the establishment) and their own means (by protest). They have an alternate scheme for a new social structure, however ill defined. In 1981, when the youth of conservative Zurich, Switzerland, grew frustrated over the establishment's rejection of their demands for a "youth house," they took to the streets, stripped naked, and threw eggs at the operagoers and at the opera house itself.

Merton's theory of how the social structure produces strain that may lead to deviant behavior is illustrated in Figure 5.1. His theory has challenged researchers for half a century.

Tests of strain theory   Merton and his followers (Chapter 6) predict that the greatest propor-

MODES OF DEVIANT BEHAVIOR

Common success goals (e.g., acquisition of wealth) of all members of society → Unequal distribution of means to achieve goals (limited jobs and education) → Disjunction of goals and means creates anomic condition → Lower class faced with strain → Pressure resolved by alternative solutions → Deviant behavior

Retain goals, reject means → **Innovation** → criminal behavior
Reject goals, reject means → **Retreatism** → drop out into drugs, alcohol, vagrancy
Create new goals, create new means → **Rebellion** → revolutionary activity

FIGURE 5.1

tion of crime will be found in the lower classes because lower-class people have the least opportunity to reach their goals legitimately. Many research studies designed to test the various propositions of the theory focus on the association between social class and delinquency (an association that evokes considerable controversy). Some studies report a strong inverse relationship: as class goes up, crime rates go down. Others find no association at all between the two variables (Chapter 2).

The controversy over the relationship between social class and crime began when researchers, using self-report questionnaires, found more serious and more frequent delinquency among lower-class boys.[13] In Chapter 2 we saw that other researchers seriously questioned those findings.[14] When Charles Tittle and his colleagues attempted to clarify the relationship by analyzing thirty-five empirical studies, they concluded that "class is not now and has not been related to criminality in the recent past."[15] Among the researchers who continued to question the association was Travis Hirschi, who commented that "if socioeconomic status is unrelated to delinquency, then consistency requires that 'socioeconomic status' be removed from the dictionary of delinquency theory and research."[16] Once again there was a critical reaction. A summary of more than one hundred

projects concluded that "lower-class people do commit those direct interpersonal types of crime which are normally handled by the police at a higher rate than middle-class people."[17]

If low social status creates frustration that pushes people to commit crime, why don't all the people in the lowest class commit crimes, or drop out into the drug world, or become revolutionaries? Since they clearly do not, there must be some limitations to the causal relationship between crime and social class. Terence Thornberry and Margaret Farnworth have tried to address this limitation by explaining that the problem arises with studies that make a simple connection between class and crime. The relationship, they say, is highly complex; it involves race, seriousness of the offense, education of family and offender, and many other factors.[18]

According to a number of researchers, we may be able to learn more about the relationship between social class and crime if we look closely at specific types of offenses rather than at aggregate crime (or delinquency) rates.[19] Take homicide. In two large cross-national studies, two teams of Canadian researchers explored the relationship between income inequality and national homicide rates.[20] Both teams reported results that support strain theory; when opportunities or means for success are not provided equally to all members of society (as indicated by crime rates), pressure is exerted on some members of that society to engage in deviant behavior (in this case, homicide). Further analyses by one of the teams showed that the effects of inequality on homicide may be even more pronounced in more democratic societies. The researchers commented: "Income inequality might be more likely to generate violent behavior in more democratic societies because of the coexistence of high material inequality and an egalitarian value system."[21]

David Brownfield also related social class to specific offenses, in this instance to fist fights and brawls among teenagers.[22] His information came from two sources: the Richmond Youth Study, conducted at the University of California at Berkeley, and the Community Tolerance Study, done by a team of researchers at the University of Arizona. Brownfield's analysis of questionnaires completed by 1,500 white male students in California and 1,300 white male students in Arizona suggests a very strong relation between poverty—as measured by unemployment and welfare assistance—and violent behavior. He concluded that the general public expresses much hostility against the "disreputable poor," a term used by David Matza to describe people who remain unemployed for a long time, even during periods of full employment.[23] In fact, Brownfield suggests, many people hold them in contempt. (He cites a *New York Times*/CBS poll that found over half of all the respondents believed that most people on welfare could get along without it if they only tried.) This hostility causes the "disreputable poor" to build up frustration, which is made worse by the lack of such fundamental necessities as food and shelter. Such a situation breeds discontent—and violence.

Yet another question that relates to strain theory concerns the relationship between racial inequality and violent crime. Judith and Peter Blau studied data from 125 metropolitan areas in the United States.[24] Their primary finding was that racial inequality—as measured by the difference in socioeconomic status between whites and nonwhites—is associated with the total rate of violent crime. The conclusion fits

well into Merton's theory. The Blaus argued that in a democratic society that stresses equal opportunities for individual achievement but in reality distributes resources on the basis of race, there is bound to be conflict. The most disadvantaged are precisely those who cannot make changes by political action. In such circumstances, frustrations created by racial inequalities tend to be expressed in various forms of aggression, such as violent crime. Several researchers have supported the Blaus' findings.[25]

Not all researchers have agreed with them, however. John Braithwaite examined Uniform Crime Report statistics for a sample of 175 American cities. He compared the rates of violent crime with racial inequality, as measured by the incomes of black families and the incomes of all other families in his sample cities. He concluded that racial inequality does not cause specific crime problems.[26] Other researchers confirm his finding.[27] Perhaps the crucial point is not whether one actually has an equal chance to be successful but rather how one *perceives* one's chances. According to this reasoning, people who feel the most strain are those who have not only high goals but also low expectations of reaching them. So far research has not supported this contention.[28]

Evaluation of strain theory   The strain perspective developed by Merton and his followers has influenced both research and theoretical developments in criminology. Yet as popular as this theory remains, it has been questioned on a variety of grounds. By concentrating on crime at the lower levels of the socioeconomic hierarchy, for example, it neglects crime committed by middle- and upper-class people. Radical criminologists (discussed in Chapter 8), in fact, claim that strain theory "stands accused of predicting too little *bourgeois* criminality and too much *proletarian* criminality."[29] Other critics believe that there is some question as to whether a society as heterogeneous as ours really does have goals on which everyone agrees. Some theorists argue that American subcultures have their own value systems (Chapter 6). If that is the case, we cannot account for deviant behavior on the basis of Merton's cultural goals.[30] Other questions are asked about the theory. If we have an agreed-upon set of goals, is material gain the dominant one? If crime is a means to an end, why is there so much useless, destructive behavior, especially among teenagers?

No matter how it is structured, each society defines goals for its members. The United States is far from being the only society in which people strive for wealth and prestige. Yet, while some people in other cultures have limited means to achieve these goals, not all of these societies have high crime rates. Two such societies are among the most developed and industrialized in the world—Japan and Switzerland. As Americans we have quite a bit in common with them. One thing we do not share is their very low crime rate.[31]

Despite the many critical assessments, strain theory, represented primarily by Merton's formulation of anomie, has had a major impact on contemporary criminology. For one thing, it appeals to common sense. Its propositions seem to be borne out by everyday observations. Generations of scholars have tried to figure out how crime is related to the problem created by inequities in a society that prides itself on its egalitarian principles. The theory has also had practical significance.

From theory to practice   Has strain theory helped us to develop a crime-prevention strategy? Yes, it has. If, as the theory tells us, frustration builds up in people who have few means to reach their goals, it makes sense to design programs that give lower-class people a bigger stake in society.

In the 1960s, Lyndon Johnson inaugurated the Head Start Program as part of a major antipoverty campaign. The goal of Head Start is to make children of low-income families more socially competent, better able to deal with their present environment and their later responsibilities.[32] The youngsters get a boost (or a head start) in a one-year preschool developmental program that is intended to prevent them from dropping out of society. Program components include community and parental involvement, an 8-to-1 child/staff ratio, and daily evaluation and involvement of all the children in the planning of and responsibility for their own activities.

Since a one-year program could not be expected to affect the remainder of a child's life, Project Follow Through was begun in an effort to provide the same opportunities for Head Start youngsters during elementary school. What started as a modest summer experience for half a million preschool children has expanded into a year-round program that provides educational and social services to millions of young people and their families. This, then, was a program clearly intended to remove stress from the group most likely to develop criminal behavior. Some research findings do indicate that the programs have had a certain measure of success.[33]

Another program that tried to ameliorate the disparity between goals and means in society was the Perry Preschool Project, begun in 1962 on the south side of Ypsilanti, Michigan. Its purpose was to develop skills that would give youngsters the means to get ahead at school and in the workplace, thereby reducing the amount and seriousness of delinquent behavior. One hundred and twenty-three black children 3 and 4 years old participated for two years, five days a week, two and a half hours a day. The program provided a teacher for every five children, weekly visits by a teacher to a child's home, and a follow-up of every child annually until age 11, and thereafter at ages 14, 15, and 19. There is little doubt about the effectiveness of the project. By age 19, the participants did better in several areas than a group that had not participated:

- Employment rates doubled.
- Rates of postsecondary education doubled.
- Teenage pregnancy was cut in half.
- The high school graduation rate was one-third higher.
- Arrest rates were 40 percent lower.[34]

Not all strain-reduction projects are as vast as Head Start or have as long a follow-up as the Perry Preschool Program. But there are smaller programs throughout the country. In 1975 the Marshall High School in Chicago had such se-

AT ISSUE

The College Options Program

In his first semester at Langston University in Oklahoma last year Peter Blackwell, a criminal justice major, struggled to a 2.4 grade point average, on a scale of 4. He raised his average to 2.7 in the second semester and to 3.5 last fall. Now he says with quiet confidence, "I'm ready to really do well this semester."

Mr. Blackwell's might be a typical story of a student sloughing off a tentative beginning and living up to his academic potential, except that his background is significantly different from that of most college students: He grew up a foster child in Washington, and an innovative municipal program is paying for his education.

Mr. Blackwell and 34 other young adults from Washington's foster-care program, all of whom are black, are beneficiaries of the College Options Program, under which the city pays for their college education and finds summer jobs for them with city agencies or private businesses.

The four-year-old program is still small. But city officials intend to expand it substantially next fall, a plan that has received enthusiastic support from the presidents of the nation's traditionally black colleges, which most of the College Options students attend....

While the youths in foster care get a paid college education, the city also gains because the annual cost is generally half of the $26,000 a year of foster care for one youth. And, he said, black colleges gain by increasing their student enrollments after years of struggling to recruit and retain students.

The Children's Defense Fund, a Washington advocacy group, estimates there are 276,000 foster children nationwide, one-third of whom are black....

Washington officials hope to send as many as 100 young people to college through the program next September.

Because the students apply through the schools' regular admissions process, their foster-care background is generally known only to a few college administrators and no special preference is given them....

Prospective collegians receive extensive counseling in choosing schools. In summer, they live together in a dormitory at Howard University in Washington "to keep them in a college environment and a more independent-living arrangement," said James Jones, who directs a foster-care group home and who conceived the college project idea.

The college project grew out of a program to prepare those in foster care to live on their own, Mr. Jones said. "One year of college works a great difference on them," he remarked. "They come back talking not about finding a job in a fast-food joint, but going to graduate school or going into business."

Source: Lee A. Daniels, "Youths Leave Foster Care for Campus," *New York Times*, April 6, 1988, p. B8.

---

vere problems that it was declared "out of control" by the Chicago Board of Education. Under the leadership of a strong principal, it turned around. He instituted discipline, effective teaching, high standards, and remedial education for poor students. By 1981 he had cut the rate of failure in major subjects from 40 to 17 percent of the students and had raised the proportion of graduates entering college from 40 to 60 percent, thereby reducing the number of delinquency-prone youngsters.[35] In 1978 several business groups in Seattle, Washington, established PIPE (Private Initiatives in Public Education) to get students involved with the workplace; banks, insurance firms, and hospitals participated.[36] The above special feature, At Issue, describes yet another program that tries to give low-income children—in this case those in foster care—legitimate means to reach their success goals. Such programs have been designed to reduce the amount of strain in society.

The programs that emanate from strain theory attempt to give lower-class children ways to achieve middle-class goals. Programs that are devised on the basis of cultural deviance theories concentrate on teaching middle-class values.

CULTURAL DEVIANCE THEORIES

The Interconnectedness of the Social Disorganization, Differential Association, and Culture Conflict Theories

Strain theory attributes criminal behavior in the United States to the striving of all its citizens to conform with the conventional values of the middle class, primarily financial success. **Cultural deviance theories**, on the other hand, attribute crime to a set of values peculiar to the lower class. Conformity with the lower-class value system, which determines behavior in slum areas, causes conflict with society's laws. Both strain and cultural deviance theories locate the causes of crime in the disadvantageous position of persons at the lowest stratum in a class-based society.

Scholars who view crime as resulting from cultural values that permit, or even demand, behavior in violation of the law are called cultural deviance theorists. The three major cultural deviance theories are social disorganization, differential association, and culture conflict. **Social disorganization theory** focuses on the development of high-crime areas associated with the disintegration of conventional values caused by rapid industrialization, increased immigration, and urbanization. **Differential association theory** maintains that people learn to commit crime as a result of contact with antisocial values, attitudes, and criminal behavior patterns. **Culture conflict theory** states that different groups learn different conduct norms (rules governing behavior), and that the conduct norms of some groups may clash with conventional middle-class rules. All three theories contend that criminals and delinquents in fact do conform—but to norms that deviate from those of the dominant middle class. Before we examine the specific theories that share the cultural deviance perspective, let us explore the nature of cultural deviance.

The Nature of Cultural Deviance

When you drive through rural Lancaster County, Pennsylvania; Holmes County, Ohio; or Elkhart and Lagrange counties, Indiana, in the midst of fertile fields and well-tended orchards, you will find isolated villages with prosperous and well-maintained farmhouses, but no electricity in many of them. You will see the farmers and their families traveling in horse-drawn buggies, dressed in homespun clothes and wearing brimmed hats. These people are Amish. Their ancestors came to this country as early as 1683 to escape persecution for their fundamentalist Christian beliefs. Shunning all use of motors, electricity, jewelry, and political parties, they are a nonconformist community within a highly materialistic culture.

Motorcycle gangs made their appearance shortly after World War II. The Hell's Angels were the first of many motorcycle gangs to be established in slum areas of cities across the country. To become a member of this gang, the initiates are subjected to grueling and revolting degradations. They are conditioned to have allegiance only to the gang. Their contacts with middle-class society are usually antagonistic and criminal. Motorcycle gangs finance their activities through illegal activities such as dealing drugs, running massage parlors and gambling operations, and selling stolen goods. Their codes of loyalty to one another and to their national and local groups make them extremely effective criminal organizations.

The normative systems of the Amish and the bikers are at odds with the conventional norms of the society in which they live. Both deviate from middle-class standards. Sociologists define **deviance** as any behavior that members of a social group define as violating their norms. As we can see, the concept of deviance can be applied to noncriminal acts that members of a group view as peculiar or unusual (the lifestyle of the Amish) or to criminal acts (behavior that society has made illegal). The Hell's Angels fit the expected stereotype of deviance as negative; the Amish culture demonstrates that deviance is not necessarily bad, just different.

Cultural deviance theorists argue that our society is made up of various groups and subgroups, each with its own standards of right and wrong. Behavior considered normal in one culture may be considered deviant by another. As a result, persons who conform to the standards of cultures that are considered deviant are behaving in accordance with their own norms, but by doing so may be breaking the law—the norms of the dominant culture.

You may wonder whether the Hell's Angels are outcasts in the slum neighborhoods where they live. They are not. They may even be looked up to by younger boys in an area where toughness and violence are not only acceptable but appropriate. Indeed, groups such as Hell's Angels may form to meet the needs of disadvantaged youngsters who are looking for a way to be important in a disorganized ghetto that offers few opportunities to gain status.

Social Disorganization Theory

As we have seen, scholars associated with the University of Chicago in the 1920s became interested in socially disorganized neighborhoods where criminal values and traditions replaced conventional ones and were transmitted from one generation to the next. They studied the neighborhoods and the people living in them. In their classic work *The Polish Peasant in Europe and America*, W. I. Thomas and Florian Znaniecki described the difficulties Polish peasants experienced when they left their rural Old World life to settle in an industrialized city in the New World.[37] The scholars compared the conditions the immigrants had left in Poland with those they found in Chicago. They also investigated the immigrants' assimilation. Older immigrants were not greatly affected by the move because they managed to continue living as they had lived as peasants, even within the urban slums. But the second generation did not grow up on Polish farms. They were city dwellers and they were American. They had few of the Old World traditions but were not yet assimilated into the new ones. The norms of the stable, homogeneous folk society were not transferable to the anonymous, materially oriented urban settings. Rates of crime and delinquency rose. Thomas and Znaniecki attributed this result to social disorganization—the breakdown of effective social bonds, family and neighborhood associations, and social controls in neighborhoods and communities. (See Figure 5.2.)

Thomas and Znaniecki's study greatly influenced other scholars at the University of Chicago. Among them were Robert Park and Ernest Burgess, who advanced the study of social disorganization by introducing an ecological analysis of human society.[38]

Ecology is the study of plants and animals in relation to each other and to their natural habitat, the place where they live and grow. Organisms exist in a complex web in which every part depends on other parts for its existence. Ecologists study these interrelationships, how the balance of nature continues and how organisms survive. Much the same approach is used by

| Rapid changes in industrialization or urbanization or increased immigration | → | Decline in the effectiveness of institutional and informal forces for social control in communities or neighborhoods; that is, social disorganization, which often occurs in gradient or concentric zones as a city grows and expands | → | Development of delinquency areas, as exemplified by high rates of delinquency and the existence of delinquent traditions and values in specific geographical areas or neighborhoods |

FIGURE 5.2 Social disorganization

Source: Donald J. Shoemaker, *Theories of Delinquency* (New York: Oxford University Press, 1984), p. 73.

scholars who study human ecology, the interrelationships of people and their environment.[39]

In their study of social disorganization, Park and Burgess examined area characteristics instead of criminals for explanations of high crime rates. They developed the idea of natural urban areas, consisting of concentric zones extending out from the downtown central business district to the commuter zone at the fringes of the city. Each zone had its own structure and organization, its cultural characteristics and unique inhabitants (Figure 5.3). Zone I, at the center, was called the Loop because the downtown business district of Chicago is demarcated by a loop of the elevated train system. It was occupied by commercial headquarters, law offices,

retail establishments, and some commercial recreation. Zone II was the zone in transition. The city's poor, unskilled, and disadvantaged lived in this zone, in dilapidated tenements next to old factories. Zone III housed the working class, people whose jobs enabled them to enjoy some of the comforts that the city had to offer at its fringes. The middle class—professionals, small business owners, and the managerial class—lived in Zone IV. Zone V was the commuter zone of satellite towns and suburbs.

Clifford Shaw and Henry McKay, two researchers at Chicago's Institute for Juvenile Research, had a close relationship with the University of Chicago's sociology department. They were particularly interested in the model

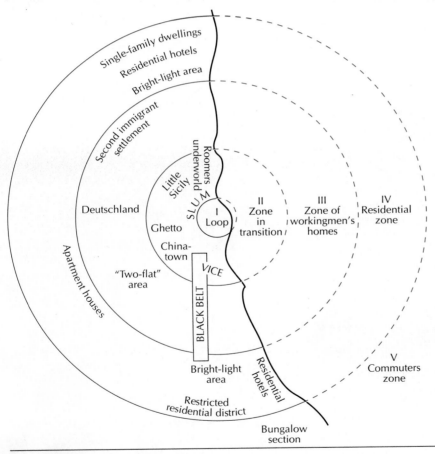

FIGURE 5.3 Park and Burgess's conception of the "natural urban areas" of Chicago

Source: Robert E. Park, Ernest W. Burgess, and R. D. McKenzie, *The City* (Chicago: University of Chicago Press, 1925), p. 55.

that Burgess had created to demonstrate how people were distributed spatially in the process of urban growth. They decided to use the model to investigate empirically the relationship between crime rates and the various zones of Chicago. Their data, found in 55,998 juvenile court records covering a period of thirty-three years, from 1900 to 1933, indicated the following:

- Crime rates were differentially distributed throughout the city, and areas of high crime rates had high rates of other community problems, such as truancy, mental disorders, and infant mortality.
- Most delinquency occurred in the areas nearest the central business district and decreased with distance from the center.
- Some areas consistently suffered high delinquency rates, regardless of the ethnic makeup of the population.
- High-delinquency areas were characterized by a high percentage of immigrants, non-whites, and low-income families, and a low percentage of homeownership.
- In high-delinquency areas there was a general acceptance of nonconventional norms, but these norms competed with conventional ones held by some of the inhabitants.[40]

Shaw and McKay demonstrated that the highest rates of delinquency persisted in the same areas of Chicago over an extended period from 1900 to 1933, even though the ethnic composition changed (Germans, Irish, and English at the turn of the century; Polish and Italian in the 1920s; increasing numbers of blacks in the 1930s). This finding led to the conclusion that the crucial factor was not ethnicity but rather the position of the group in the distribution of economic status and cultural values. Finally, through their study of three sets of Cook County Juvenile Court records—1900–1906, 1917–1923, and 1927–1933—they learned that older boys were associated with younger boys in various offenses and that the same techniques for committing delinquent acts had been passed on through the years. The evidence clearly indicated to them that delinquency was socially learned behavior, transmitted from one generation to the next in disorganized urban areas.[41] This is referred to as **cultural transmission**.

Tests of social disorganization theory More recent evidence supports the social disorganization and ecological approach of the Chicago school. Robert Sampson and W. Byron Groves analyzed data from two large national surveys of England and Wales in order to test Shaw and McKay's social disorganization theory. They found that communities characterized by unsupervised teenagers, low participation in organizations, and few friendship networks had high rates of reported criminal victimizations.[42]

Studies based on the approach have covered a wide range of topics. Douglas Smith looked at police behavior and characteristics of sixty neighborhoods in three large U.S. cities (Rochester, New York; St. Louis, Missouri; Tampa/St. Petersburg, Florida). His major findings suggest that police are less likely to file reports of crime incidents in high-crime areas than in low-crime areas, and that they are more likely to assist residents and initiate contacts with suspicious-looking people in low-crime neighborhoods.[43] Other researchers have compared gang delinquency in black and Hispanic communities, studied the correlation of delinquency with single-parent households, and investigated how neighborhood changes (such as urban renewal and increased homeownership) affect violence.[44]

An increasing amount of research has also been done on the relationship between social disorganization of neighborhoods and the fear of crime. Researchers are asking whether the belief that crime is a serious local problem makes people lose confidence in their neighborhood and trust in their neighbors. Do they become more fearful? According to recent studies, they usually do.[45]

Evaluation of social disorganization theory Though their influence has been great, the scholars who initiated the ecological approach to crime research have not been immune to challenges. Their work has been criticized for its dependence on official data, which may primarily reflect zealous police surveillance in disadvantaged neighborhoods, and for its focus

CRIMINOLOGICAL FOCUS

A Low-Crime Neighborhood in a High-Crime Area

A small area in New York City's South Bronx, surrounded on all sides by high-crime neighborhoods, has nevertheless managed to insulate itself from the pains of social disorganization. Criminologists have not yet conducted rigorous studies to find out why this little enclave has escaped. What we know is intuitive. *Crime in America,* an unusual documentary, was made in the neighborhood. It simply depicts members of the community going about their daily routines. The buildings are dilapidated. The people are poor. They are aware of the crime on their borders. The low-crime rate perhaps has something to do with the fact that residents know each other. The local grocers even call the youngsters by name. Young unmarried adults are expected to live at home and let the family know their whereabouts, especially at night. The local church is a focus of communal activities, supported by an active pastor who is very much involved with his parishioners. Despite the odds described by the early ecological/social disorganization literature, it appears that it is possible to create low-crime neighborhoods within high-crime areas.

only on how crime patterns are transmitted, not on how they start in the first place. The approach has also been faulted for failing to explain why delinquents desist from crime as they grow older, why most people in socially disorganized areas do not commit criminal acts, and why some deteriorated neighborhoods seem to be insulated from crime. Finally, critics have claimed that this approach does not come to grips with middle-class delinquency.

Clearly, modern criminology owes a debt to social disorganization theorists, particularly to Shaw and McKay, who in the 1920s began to look at the characteristics of people and places and to relate both to crime.[46] They have stimulated research not only in crime causation but also in crime prevention.

From theory to practice Theorists of the Chicago school were the first social scientists to suggest that most crime is committed by normal people responding in expected ways to their immediate surroundings, rather than by abnormal individuals acting out individual pathologies. If social disorganization is at the root of the problem, crime control must involve social organization. The community, not individuals, need treatment. Helping the community, then, should lower its crime rate.

Social disorganization theory was translated into practice in 1934 with the establishment of the Chicago Area Project (CAP), an experiment in neighborhood reorganization. The project was initiated by the Institute for Juvenile Research, at which Clifford Shaw and Henry McKay were working. The project coordinated the existing community support groups—local schools, churches, labor unions, clubs, and merchants. Special efforts were made to control delinquency through recreational facilities, summer camps, better law enforcement, and upgrading of neighborhood schools, sanitation, and general appearance.[47] In 1984 this first community-based delinquency-prevention program celebrated its fiftieth anniversary.[48] South Chicago, its largest area, physically remains very much the way it was over half a century ago. The pollution from the surrounding steel mills has been cleaned up, but the urban decay has not. Boarded-up buildings, trash-littered lots, and badly deteriorated housing still characterize the poverty area with which Shaw and McKay were originally concerned. CAP still works as a self-help group, committed mainly to community treatment of juvenile delinquency. Its motto is still "Concerned people striving to make South Chicago a better place to live." It has had modest success.

During the 1950s, Boston initiated the Mid-City Project, which was similar in many ways to CAP. But instead of waiting for gang members to come to community centers, workers went out into the streets to meet the gangs on their own turf. Good relationships were formed. Delinquency rates, however, stayed the same.[49] Local crime-prevention programs got a bigger boost in the 1960s, with John F. Kennedy's New Frontier and Lyndon Johnson's War on Poverty (Chapter 6). More recently another community action project has concentrated on revitalizing a Puerto Rican slum community. Sister Isolina Ferre worked for ten years in the violent Navy Yard section of Brooklyn, New York. In 1969 she returned to Ponce Plaza, a poverty-stricken area in Ponce, Puerto Rico, which was infested with disease, crime, and unemployment. The area's 16,000 people had no doctors, nurses, dentists, or social agencies. The project began with a handful of missionaries, university professors, dedicated citizens, and community members who were willing to become advocates for their neighborhood. Among the programs begun were a large community health center, Big Brother/Big Sister programs for juveniles sent from the courts, volunteer tutoring, and recreational activities to take young people off the streets. Young photographers of Ponce Plaza, supplied with a few cameras donated by friends at Kodak, mounted an exhibit at the Metropolitan Museum of Art in New York. Regular fiestas have given community members a chance to celebrate their own achievements as well.[50]

Programs based on social disorganization theory attempt to bring conventional social values to disorganized communities. They provide an opportunity for young people to learn norms other than those of delinquent peer groups. Let us see how such learning takes place.

Differential Association Theory

Many years ago hunters captured a young boy living with a flock of ostriches. He had grown up with them, ran with them as fast as they did, acted on their signals, and adopted their feeding habits. He could not speak like a human, but he communicated perfectly with his ostrich family, using their sounds. He had learned the ways of his group just as we learn the ways of ours. What we eat, what we say, what we believe—in fact, the way we respond to any situation—depend on the culture in which we have been reared. In other words, to a very large extent the social influences that people encounter determine their behavior. Whether a person becomes law-abiding or criminal, then, depends on his or her contacts with criminal values, attitudes, definitions, and behavior patterns. This proposition underlies one of the most important theories of crime causation in American criminology—differential association.

In 1939 Edwin Sutherland introduced differential association theory in his textbook *Principles of Criminology*. Since then scholars have read, tested, reexamined, and sometimes ridiculed this theory, which claimed to explain the development of all criminal behavior. The theory of differential association states that crime is learned through social interaction. People come into constant contact with "definitions favorable to violations of law" and "definitions unfavorable to violations of law." The ratio of these definitions—criminal to noncriminal—determines whether a person will engage in criminal behavior.[51] In formulating this theory, Sutherland relied heavily on Shaw and McKay's findings that delinquent values are transmitted within a community or group from one generation to the next. He explained the process by which this transmission of values takes place.

Differential association is based on nine propositions:

1. *Criminal behavior is learned.*

2. *Criminal behavior is learned in interaction with other persons in a process of communication.* A person does not become a criminal simply by living in a criminal environment. Crime is learned by participation with others in verbal and nonverbal communications.

3. *The principal part of the learning of criminal behavior occurs within intimate personal groups.* Families and friends have the most influence on the learning of deviant behavior. Their communications far outweigh those of the

mass media, such as movies, television, and newspapers.

4. *When criminal behavior is learned, the learning includes (a) techniques of committing the crime, which are sometimes very complicated, sometimes very simple and (b) the specific direction of motives, drives, rationalizations, and attitudes.* Young delinquents learn not only how to shoplift, crack a safe, pick a lock, or roll a joint but also how to rationalize and defend their actions. One safecracker accompanied another safecracker for one year before he cracked his first safe.[52] In other words, criminals, too, learn skills and gain experience.

5. *The specific direction of motives and drives is learned from definitions of the legal codes as favorable or unfavorable.* In some societies an individual is surrounded by persons who invariably define the legal codes as rules to be observed, while in others he is surrounded by persons whose definitions are favorable to the violation of the legal codes. Not everyone in our society agrees that the laws should be obeyed. Some people *define* them as unimportant. In American society, where definitions are mixed, we have a culture conflict in relation to legal codes.

6. *A person becomes delinquent because of an excess of definitions favorable to violation of law over definitions unfavorable to violation of law.* This is the key principle of differential association, the major thrust of the theory. In other words, learning criminal behavior is not simply a matter of associating with bad companions. Rather, learning criminal behavior depends on how many definitions we learn that are favorable to law violation as opposed to those that are unfavorable to law violation.

7. *Differential associations may vary in frequency, duration, priority, and intensity.* The extent to which one's associations/definitions will result in criminality is related to the frequency of contacts, the extent of their duration, and their meaning to the individual.

8. *The process of learning criminal behavior by association with criminal and anticriminal patterns involves all of the mechanisms that are involved in any other learning.* Learning criminal behavior patterns is very much like learning conventional behavior patterns and is not simply a matter of observation and imitation.

9. *While criminal behavior is an expression of general needs and values, it is not explained by those general needs and values, since noncriminal behavior is an expression of the same needs and values.* Shoplifters steal to get what they want. Others work to get money to buy what they want. The motives—frustration, desire to accumulate goods or social status, low self-concept, and the like—cannot logically be the same because they explain both lawful and criminal behavior.

Tests of differential association theory Since Sutherland presented his theory more than fifty years ago, researchers have tried to determine whether the principles of differential association lend themselves to empirical measurement. James Short tested a sample of 126 boys and 50 girls at a training school and reported a consistent relationship between delinquent behavior and frequency, duration, priority, and intensity of interactions with delinquent peers.[53] In another test Albert Reiss and A. Lewis Rhodes found that the chance of committing a delinquent act depends on whether friends commit the same act.[54] Similarly, Travis Hirschi demonstrated that boys with delinquent friends are more likely to become delinquent.[55] Adults have also been the subjects of differential association studies. Charles Tittle asked two thousand residents of New Jersey, Oregon, and Iowa such questions as how many people whom they knew personally had engaged in deviant acts and how many were frequently in trouble. He also asked the residents how often they attended church (assumed to be related to definitions unfavorable to the violation of law). His differential association scale correlated significantly with such crimes as illegal gambling, income tax cheating, and thefts.[56]

Evaluation of differential association theory Many researchers have attempted to validate Sutherland's differential association theory.

Others have criticized it. Much of the criticism stems from errors in interpretation. Perhaps this type of error is best demonstrated by the critics who ask why it is that not everyone in contact with an excess of criminal behavior patterns becomes a criminal. Take, for argument's sake, corrections officers, who come into constant contact with an excess of criminal associations over noncriminal ones. How do they escape from learning to be law violators themselves? The answer, of course, is that Sutherland does *not* tell us that individuals become criminal by associating with criminals, or even by association with criminal behavior patterns. He tells us rather that a person becomes delinquent because of an "excess of *definitions* favorable to violation of law over definitions unfavorable to violation of law." The key word is "definitions." Furthermore, unfavorable definitions may be communicated by persons who are not robbers or murderers or tax evaders. They may, for example, be law-abiding parents who, over time, define certain situations in such a way that their children may get verbal or nonverbal messages to the effect that antisocial behavior is acceptable.

Several scholars have asked whether the principles of differential association really explain all types of crime. They might explain theft, but what about homicide resulting from a jealous rage?[57] Why do some people who learn criminal behavior patterns not engage in criminal acts? Why is no account taken of nonsocial variables, such as a desperate need for money? Furthermore, while the principles may explain how criminal behavior is transmitted, they do not account for the origin of criminal techniques and definitions. In other words, the theory does not tell us how the first criminal became a criminal. There also seems to be an inevitability about the process of becoming a criminal. Once you reach the point where your definitions favorable to law violation exceed your definitions unfavorable to law violation, have you crossed an imaginary line into the criminal world? Even if we could add up the definitions encountered in a lifetime, could scientists measure the frequency, priority, duration, and intensity of differential associations?

Despite the many criticisms of differential association, the theory has had a profound influence on criminology.[58] Generations of scholars have tested it empirically, modified it to incorporate psychologically based learning theory (as we saw in Chapter 4), and used it as a foundation for their own theorizing (as we shall see in Chapter 6). The theory has also had many policy implications.

From theory to practice   If, according to differential association theory, a person can become criminal by learning definitions favorable to violating laws, it follows that programs that expose young people to definitions favorable to conventional behavior should reduce criminality. Such educational efforts as Head Start and the Perry Preschool Program have attempted to do just that. The same theory underlies many of the treatment programs for young offenders in facilities throughout the country, both residential (the Highfields Project in New Jersey) and nonresidential (the Provo Program in Utah). In group treatment sessions in these programs criminal behavior is attacked and conventional behavior is promoted.

Differential association theory is based on the learning of criminal (or deviant) norms or attitudes. Culture conflict theory focuses on the source of these criminal norms and attitudes.

Culture Conflict Theory

According to Thorsten Sellin, **conduct norms**—those norms that regulate our daily lives—are rules that reflect the attitudes of the groups to which each of us belongs.[59] Their purpose is to define what is considered appropriate or normal behavior and what is inappropriate or abnormal behavior. Sellin argues that different groups have different conduct norms and that the conduct norms of one group may conflict with those of another. Individuals may commit crimes by conforming to the norms of their own group if that group's norms conflict with those of the dominant society. According to this rationale, the main difference between a criminal and a noncriminal is that each is responding to different sets of conduct norms.

Sellin distinguishes between primary and secondary conflicts. Primary conflict occurs when norms of two cultures clash. A clash may occur at the border between neighboring cultural areas; when the law of one cultural group is extended to cover the territory of another; or when members of one group migrate to another culture. Secondary conflict arises when a single culture evolves into a variety of cultures, each having its own set of conduct norms. This type of conflict occurs when the homogeneous societies of simpler cultures become complex societies, such as our own, in which the number of social groupings multiplies constantly and norms are often at odds. Your college may make dormitory living mandatory for all freshmen, for example, but to follow the informal code of your peer group, you may seek the freedom of off-campus housing. Or you may have

to choose whether to violate work rules by leaving your job half an hour early to make a mandatory class or to violate school rules by walking into class half an hour late. Life situations are frequently controlled by conflicting norms, so that no matter how people act, they are violating a rule of one group or another, often without being aware that they are doing so.

In the next chapter, which deals with the formation and operation of subcultures, we will expand the discussion of the conflict of norms. We shall also examine the empirical research that seeks to discover whether there is indeed a multitude of value systems in our society, and if so, whether and how they conflict.

REVIEW

Contemporary criminologists tend to divide the sociological explanation of crime into three categories: strain, cultural deviance, and social control.[60] The strain and cultural deviance perspectives focus on the social forces that cause people to engage in deviant behavior. They assume that there is a relationship between social class and criminal behavior. Strain theorists argue that all people in society share one set of cultural values, and since lower-class persons often do not have legitimate means to attain society's goals, they may turn to illegitimate means instead. Cultural deviance theorists maintain that the lower class has a distinctive

set of values, and that these values often conflict with those of the middle class.

Cultural deviance theories—social disorganization, differential association, and culture conflict—relate criminal behavior to the learning of criminal values and norms. Social disorganization theory focuses on explaining the breakdown of social institutions as a precondition for the establishment of criminal norms. Differential association theory concentrates on the processes by which criminal behavior is taught and learned. And culture conflict theory focuses on the specifics of how the conduct norms of some groups may clash with those of the dominant culture.

KEY TERMS

anomic suicide
conduct norms
cultural deviance theories
cultural transmission
culture conflict theory

deviance
differential association theory
social disorganization theory
strain theory

NOTES

1. Ysabel Rennie, *The Search for Criminal Man* (Lexington, Mass.: Lexington Books, 1978), p. 125.

2. James T. Carey, *Sociology and Public Affairs:* *The Chicago School* (Beverly Hills, Calif.: Sage, 1975), pp. 19–20.

3. Emile Durkheim, *The Division of Labor in Society* (New York: Free Press, 1964).

4. Emile Durkheim, *Rules of Sociological Method* (New York: Free Press, 1966).

5. For a lengthy discussion of Durkheim's use of the term "anomie," see Stjepan G. Mestrovic and Helene M. Brown, "Durkheim's Concept of Anomie as Derèglement," *Social Problems* 33 (1985): 81–99.

6. Emile Durkheim, *Suicide* (Glencoe, Ill.: Free Press, 1951), pp. 241–276. For anomie-related research on suicide, see Andrew Henry and James F. Short, *Suicide and Homicide* (Glencoe, Ill.: Free Press, 1954); Ronald W. Maris, *Social Forces in Urban Suicide* (Homewood, Ill.: Dorsey, 1969); Jack P. Gibbs and Walter T. Martin, *Status Integration and Suicide* (Eugene: University of Oregon Press, 1964).

7. Durkheim, *Suicide,* p. 247.

8. Robert K. Merton, "Social Structure and Anomie," *American Sociological Review* 3 (1938): 672–682; several measures of anomie have been developed. Probably the best-known indicator of anomie at the social level was formulated by Bernard Lander in a study of 8,464 cases of juvenile delinquency in Baltimore between 1939 and 1942. Lander devised a measure that included the rate of delinquency, the percentage of nonwhite population in a given area, and the percentage of owner-occupied homes. According to Lander, those factors were indicative of the amount of normlessness (anomie) in a community. See Bernard Lander, *Towards an Understanding of Juvenile Delinquency* (New York: Columbia University Press, 1954), p. 65; also Roland J. Chilton, "Continuity in Delinquency Area Research: A Comparison of Studies of Baltimore, Detroit, and Indianapolis," *American Sociological Review* 29 (1964): 71–83.

9. U.S. Department of Commerce, Bureau of the Census, *Current Population Reports,* ser. no. 154 (Washington, D.C.: U.S. Government Printing Office, 1986).

10. U.S. Department of Commerce, Bureau of the Census, *Current Population Reports,* ser. no. 146 (Washington, D.C.: U.S. Government Printing Office, 1986), p. 60.

11. Robert K. Merton, *Social Theory and the Social Structure* (New York: Free Press of Glencoe, 1957), p. 187.

12. Ibid., p. 151.

13. John P. Clark and Eugene P. Wenninger, "Socioeconomic Class and Area as Correlates of Illegal Behavior Among Juveniles," *American Sociological Review* 27 (1962): 826–834; Albert J. Reiss, Jr., and Albert L. Rhodes, "The Distribution of Juvenile Delinquency in the Social Class Structure," *American Sociological Review* 26 (1961): 720–732.

14. F. Ivan Nye, James F. Short, and Virgil J. Olson, "Socioeconomic Status and Delinquent Behavior," *American Journal of Sociology* 63 (1958): 381–389; Robert A. Dentler and Lawrence J. Monroe, "Early Adolescent Theft," *American Sociological Review* 26 (1961): 733–743; Martin Gold, "Undetected Delinquent Behavior," *Journal of Research in Crime and Delinquency* 3 (1966): 27–46; Harwin L. Voss, "Socioeconomic Status and Reported Delinquent Behavior," *Social Problems* 13 (1966): 314–324.

15. Charles R. Tittle, Wayne J. Villemez, and Douglas A. Smith, "The Myth of Social Class and Criminality: An Empirical Assessment of the Empirical Evidence," *American Sociological Review* 43 (1978): 652.

16. Travis Hirschi, *Causes of Delinquency* (Berkeley: University of California Press, 1969), p. 67. See also Marvin D. Krohn, Ronald L. Akers, Marcia J. Radosevich, and Lonn Lanza-Kaduce, "Social Status and Deviance," *Criminology* 18 (1980): 303–318; Richard E. Johnson, "Social Class and Delinquent Behavior: A New Test," *Criminology* 18 (1980): 86–93.

17. John Braithwaite, "The Myth of Social Class and Criminality Reconsidered," *American Sociological Review* 46 (1981): 41. See also Delbert S. Elliott and Suzanne S. Ageton, "Reconciling Race and Class Differences in Self-reported and Official Estimates of Delinquency," *American Sociological Review* 45 (1980); 95–110; Donald Clelland and Timothy J. Carter, "The New Myth of Class and Crime," *Criminology* 18 (1980): 319–336.

18. Terence P. Thornberry and Margaret Farnworth, "Social Correlates of Criminal

Involvement: Further Evidence on the Relationship Between Social Status and Criminal Behavior," *American Sociological Review* 47 (1982): 505–518; Thomas J. Bernard, "Control Criticisms of Strain Theories: An Assessment of Theoretical and Empirical Adequacy," *Journal of Research in Crime and Delinquency* 21 (1984): 353–372; Delbert S. Elliott and David Huizinga, "Social Class and Delinquent Behavior in a National Youth Panel," *Criminology* 21 (1983): 149–177.

19. David Brownfield, "Social Class and Violent Behavior," *Criminology* 24 (1986): 421–438.

20. William R. Avison and Pamela L. Loring, "Population Diversity and Cross-National Homicide: The Effects of Inequality and Heterogeneity," *Criminology* 24 (1986): 733–749; Harvey Krahn, Timothy F. Hartnagel, and John W. Gartrell, "Income Inequality and Homicide Rates: Cross-National Data and Criminological Theories," *Criminology* 24 (1986): 269–295.

21. Krahn et al., "Income Inequality," p. 288. For a study that found no relationship between economic inequality and homicide, see Steven F. Messner and Kenneth Tardiff, "Economic Inequality and Levels of Homicide: An Analysis of Urban Neighborhoods," *Criminology* 24 (1986): 297–317.

22. Brownfield, "Social Class and Violent Behavior."

23. David Matza, "The Disreputable Poor," in *Class, Status, and Power,* ed. Reinhard Bendix and Seymour M. Lipset (New York: Free Press, 1966).

24. Judith R. Blau and Peter M. Blau, "The Cost of Inequality: Metropolitan Structure and Violent Crime," *American Sociological Review* 47 (1982): 114–129.

25. Peter M. Blau and Joseph E. Schwartz, *Crosscutting Social Circles* (Orlando, Fla.: Academic Press, 1984); Kirk R. Williams, "Economic Sources of Homicide: Reestimating the Effects of Poverty and Inequality," *American Sociological Review* 49 (1984): 283–289; Peter M. Blau and Reid M. Golden, "Metropolitan Structure and Criminal Violence," *Sociological Quarterly* 27 (1986): 15–26.

26. John Braithwaite, *Inequality, Crime, and Public Policy* (London: Routledge & Kegan Paul, 1979), p. 219.

27. Robert J. Sampson, "Race and Criminal Violence: A Demographically Disaggregated Analysis of Urban Homicide," *Crime and Delinquency* 31 (1985): 47–82; Reid M. Golden and Steven F. Messner, "Dimensions of Racial Inequality and Rates of Violent Crime" *Criminology* 25 (1987): 525–541. For a discussion of the influence of black power on black violence, see Roy Austin, "Progress Toward Racial Equality and Reduction of Black Criminal Violence," *Journal of Criminal Justice* 15 (1987): 437–459.

28. Delbert Elliott and Harwin L. Voss, *Delinquency and Dropout* (Lexington, Mass.: Lexington Books, 1974); Hirschi, *Causes of Delinquency;* William S. Laufer, "Vocational Interests of Homeless, Unemployed Men," *Journal of Vocational Behavior* 18 (1981): 196–201.

29. Ian Taylor, Paul Walton, and Jock Young, *The New Criminology* (New York: Harper & Row, 1973), p. 107.

30. Edwin M. Lemert, *Human Deviance, Social Problems, and Social Control,* 2d ed. (Englewood Cliffs, N.J.: Prentice-Hall, 1972), pp. 26–61. See also William S. Laufer, "Vocational Interests of Criminal Offenders: A Typological and Demographic Investigation," *Psychological Reports* 46 (1980): 315–324.

31. Freda Adler, *Nations Not Obsessed with Crime* (Littleton, Colo.: Fred B. Rothman, 1983).

32. M. Deutsch, "The Historical Context and the Challenge of Head Start," keynote presentation for the twentieth anniversary celebration of Head Start, New York University, Sept. 26, 1985; R. H. McKey, L. Condelle, H. Ganson, B. J. Barrett, C. McConkey, and M. C. Planty, *Executive Summary: The Impact of Head Start on Children, Families, and Communities: Final Report of the Head Start Evaluation, Synthesis, and Utilization Project,* for U.S. Department of Health and Human Services, Administration for Children, Youth, and Families (Washington, D.C.: U.S. Government Printing Office, 1985).

33. L. A. Meyer, "Long-Term Academic Effects

of the Direct Instruction Project Follow-Through," *Elementary School Journal* 84 (1984): 380–394.

34. John R. Berrueta-Clement, Lawrence J. Schweinhart, W. Steven Barnett, Ann S. Epstein, and David P. Weekart, *Changed Lives: The Effects of the Perry Preschool Program on Youths Through Age 19* (Ypsilanti, Mich.: High/Scope, 1984).

35. Anne Hallister, "Marshall High Shapes Up," in *American Renewal* (Chicago: Time Inc., 1981), pp. 78–87.

36. Jack Lule, "Making the Grades: Improving the Quality of U.S. Education," *DuPont Context* (1984), p. 26.

37. W. I. Thomas and Florian Znaniecki, *The Polish Peasant in Europe and America* (Boston: Gorham, 1920).

38. Robert E. Park, "Human Ecology," *American Journal of Sociology* 42 (1936): 1–15.

39. For a contemporary discussion of the human ecology approach to crime, see Rodney Stark, "Deviant Places: A Theory of the Ecology of Crime," *Criminology* 25 (1987): 893–909.

40. Clifford R. Shaw, Frederick M. Forbaugh, Henry D. McKay, and Leonard S. Cottrell, *Delinquency Areas* (Chicago: University of Chicago Press, 1929).

41. Clifford R. Shaw and Henry McKay, "Social Factors in Juvenile Delinquency," in *National Commission of Law Observance and Enforcement Report on the Causes of Crime*, vol. 2 (Washington, D.C., 1931); Clifford R. Shaw and Henry D. McKay, *Juvenile Delinquency and Urban Areas* (Chicago: University of Chicago Press, 1942); see also the revised and updated edition: Clifford Shaw and Henry D. McKay, *Juvenile Delinquency and Urban Areas: A Study of Delinquency in Relation to Differential Characteristics of Local Communities in American Cities* (Chicago: University of Chicago Press, 1969). Replication in other countries supports the idea of high-crime-rate areas, but not always decreasing rates from the center of the city outward. In Buenos Aires, Argentina, for example, the highest rate was found near the outskirts of the city, partly because the wealthy tend to live near the center. See Lois B. De Fleur,

"Ecological Variables in the Cross-Cultural Study of Delinquency," *Social Forces* 45 (1967): 556–570. Solomon Kobrin investigated further the process of cultural transmission and found both conventional and criminal value systems in high-crime areas. See Solomon Kobrin, "The Conflict of Values in Delinquency Areas," *American Sociological Review* 16 (1951): 653–661; Clifford Shaw, *The Jack-Roller* (Chicago: University of Chicago Press, 1930); Clifford Shaw, Henry D. McKay, and James McDonald, *Brothers in Crime* (Chicago: University of Chicago Press, 1938); and Frederick M. Thrasher, *The Gang* (Chicago: University of Chicago Press, 1927).

42. Robert J. Sampson and W. Byron Groves, "Community Structure and Crime: Testing Social Disorganization Theory," *American Journal of Sociology* 94 (1989): 774–802. Sampson concluded from another study that in neighborhoods where fewer people "watch over" the area, there were more opportunities for criminal acts: see Robert Sampson, "Neighborhood and Crime: The Structural Determinants of Personal Victimization," *Journal of Research in Crime and Delinquency* 22 (1985): 7–40; also Robert J. Sampson and John D. Wooldredge, "Linking the Micro- and Macro-Level Dimensions of Lifestyle—Routine Activity and Opportunity Models of Predatory Victimizations," *Journal of Quantitative Criminology* 3 (1987): 371–393.

43. Douglas A. Smith, "The Neighborhood Context of Police Behavior," in *Communities and Crime*, ed. Albert J. Reiss and Michael Tonry, pp. 313–341 (Chicago: University of Chicago Press, 1986); Douglas A. Smith and C. Roger Jarjoura, "Social Structure and Criminal Victimization," *Journal of Research in Crime and Delinquency* 25 (1988): 27–52.

44. G. David Curry and Irving A. Spergel, "Gang Homicide, Delinquency, and Community," *Criminology* 26 (1988): 381–405; Ora Simcha-Fagan and Joseph E. Schwartz, "Neighborhood and Delinquency: An Assessment of Contextual Effects," *Criminology* 24 (1986): 667–703; Ralph B. Taylor and Jeanette Covington, "Neighborhood Changes in Ecology and Violence," *Criminology* 26 (1988): 553–589. See also Leo A.

Schuerman and Solomon Kobrin, "Community Careers in Crime," in Reiss and Tonry, *Communities and Crime.*

45. Stephanie W. Greenberg, "Fear and Its Relationship to Crime, Neighborhood Deterioration, and Informed Social Control," in *The Social Ecology of Crime,* ed. James M. Byrne and Robert J. Sampson, pp. 47–62 (New York: Springer-Verlag, 1986).

46. James M. Byrne, "Cities, Citizens, and Crime: The Ecological/Nonecological Debate Reconsidered," in Byrne and Sampson, *Social Ecology of Crime,* pp. 77–101. See also Robert J. Bursik, Jr., "Social Disorganization and Theories of Crime and Delinquency: Problems and Prospects," *Criminology* 26 (1988): 519–551.

47. Solomon Kobrin, "The Chicago Area Project: 25 Years of Assessment," *Annals of the American Academy of Political and Social Science* 322 (1959): 20–29.

48. Steven Schlossman, Goul Zellman, and Richard Shavelson, "Delinquency Prevention in South Chicago: A Fifty-Year Assessment of the Chicago Area Project," prepared for the National Institute of Education by the Rand Corporation, May 1984, p. 1.

49. Walter Miller, "The Impact of a 'Total Community' Delinquency Control Project," *Social Problems* 10 (1962): 168–191.

50. M. Isolina Ferre, "Prevention and Control of Violence Through Community Revitalization, Individual Dignity, and Personal Self-confidence," *Annals of the American Academy of Political and Social Science* 494 (1987): 27–36.

51. Edwin H. Sutherland, *Principles of Criminology,* 3d ed. (Philadelphia: Lippincott, 1939).

52. William Chambliss, *Boxmen* (New York: Harper & Row, 1972).

53. James S. Short, "Differential Association as a Hypothesis: Problems of Empirical Testing," *Social Problems* 8 (1960): 14–15; Charles R. Tittle, Mary Jean Burke, and Elton F. Jackson, "Modeling Sutherland's Theory of Differential Association: Toward an Empirical Clarification," *Social Forces* 65 (1986): 405–432; R. Matsueda and K. Heimer, "Race, Family Structure, and Delinquency: A Test of Differential Association and Social Control Theories," *American Sociological Review* 52 (1987): 826–840.

54. Albert J. Reiss, Jr., and Albert L. Rhodes, "The Distribution of Juvenile Delinquency in the Social Class Structure," *American Sociological Review* 26 (1961): 720–732. For drug abuse studies that test differential association, see Susan M. Jaquith, "Adolescent Marijuana and Alcohol Use: An Empirical Test of Differential Association Theory," *Criminology* 19 (1981): 271–280; Brenda S. Griffin and Charles T. Griffin, "Marijuana Use Among Students and Peers," *Drug Forum* 7 (1978): 155–165; Ross L. Matsueda, "Testing Control Modeling Approach," *American Sociological Review* 47 (1982): 489–504.

55. Hirschi, *Causes of Delinquency,* p. 95.

56. Charles Tittle, *Sanctions and Social Deviance* (New York: Praeger, 1980). See also James D. Orcutt, "Differential Association and Marijuana Use: A Closer Look at Sutherland (With a Little Help from Becker)," *Criminology* 25 (1987): 341–358; Tittle et al., "Modeling Sutherland's Theory"; Matsueda and Heimer, "Race, Family Structure, and Delinquency."

57. Clayton A. Hartjen, *Crime and Criminalization* (New York: Praeger, 1974), p. 51.

58. Ross L. Matsueda, "The Current State of Differential Association," *Crime and Delinquency* 34 (1988): 277–306; Gary F. Jenson, "Parents, Peers, and Delinquent Action: A Test of the Differential Association Perspective," *American Journal of Sociology* 78 (1972): 562–575, in which he finds no support for differential association theory; Ronald L. Simons, Martin G. Miller, and Stephen M. Aigner, "Contemporary Theories of Deviance and Female Delinquency: An Empirical Test," *Journal of Research in Crime and Delinquency* 17 (1980): 42–57, which uses differential association theory to look at the relationship between values of friends and self-reported delinquency (result: girls tended more than boys to be influenced by their friends); D. A. Andrews, "Some Experimental Investigations of the Principles of Differential Association Through Deliberate Manipulations of the Structure of Ser-

vice Systems," *American Sociological Review*
45 (1980): 448–462; Ivor D. Shorts, "Delinquency by Association?" *British Journal of
Criminology* 26 (1986): 156–163; Craig Reinar-
man and Jeffrey Fagan, "Social Organization and Differential Association: A Research Note from a Longitudinal Study of
Violent Juvenile Offenders," *Crime and Delinquency* 34 (1988): 307–327.

59. Thorsten Sellin, *Culture Conflict and Crime*,
bulletin 41 (New York: Social Science Research Council, 1938). For an empirical test
of the relation between homicide rates and
conflicting norms, see Avison and Loring,
"Population Diversity and Cross-National
Homicide."

60. See the discussion of sociological theory in
Frank P. Williams III and Marilyn D.
McShane, *Criminological Theory* (Englewood
Cliffs, N.J.: Prentice-Hall, 1988).

6

THE FORMATION OF SUBCULTURES

It was a warm Southern California evening, just after sunset. Suddenly there was a burst of gunfire. It came from the automatic assault rifle and shotguns that protruded from the windows of a car that had been cruising down West 46th Street in the center of Los Angeles' urban war zone. A group of young people were hanging out on the corner. One of them, 20-year-old Stacey Childress, was killed instantly. Eleven more, including a 4-year-old boy, lay wounded on the sidewalks.[1]

Los Angeles has close to 70,000 gang members. Among them are the "wannabes" and the "gonnabes," the younger boys waiting to go through initiation rules that sometimes demand a drive-by murder. Two of the most violent gangs are the Crisps and the Bloods. Crisps wear blue; Bloods wear red. Their rivalry pervades all aspects of day-to-day living. A Blood will ask you for a "bigarette" to avoid using the letter C (as in Crisp). Mothers in the neighborhood dress their children in any color except blue or red, in order to keep them "neutral," not aligned with either gang.

Gangs like the Crisps and the Bloods inhabit the streets and back alleys of most large cities. They fill the files of police reports, of juvenile courts, and of adult courts as well. How did these groups get started in American society? What keeps them going?

THE FUNCTION OF SUBCULTURES

We saw in Chapter 5 that strain theorists explain criminal behavior as a result of the frustrations suffered by lower-class people deprived of legitimate means to reach their goals, and that cultural deviance theories assume that people become criminal by learning the criminal values of the groups to which they belong. In conforming to their own group standards, these people break the laws of the dominant culture. These two perspectives laid the foundation for the development of subcultural theory, which emerged in the mid-1950s and held criminologists' attention for over a decade.

A **subculture** is a subdivision within the dominant culture that has its own norms, beliefs, and values. Subcultures typically emerge when people in similar circumstances find themselves isolated from the mainstream and band together for mutual support. Subcultures may form among members of racial and ethnic minorities, among prisoners, among occupational groups, among ghetto dwellers. Subcultures exist within a larger society, not apart from it. They therefore share some of its values. Nevertheless, the lifestyles of their members are significantly different from those of the dominant culture.

Subcultural theories in criminology were developed to account for delinquency among lower-class males, especially for one of its most important expressions—the teenage gang. According to subcultural theorists, delinquent subcultures, like all subcultures, emerge in response to special problems that members of the dominant culture do not face. Theories developed by Albert Cohen and by Richard Cloward and Lloyd Ohlin are extensions of the strain, social disorganization, and differential association theories. They explain why delinquent subcultures emerge in the first place (strain), why they take a particular form (social disorganization), and how they are passed on from one generation to the next (differential association). The explanations of delinquency developed by Marvin Wolfgang and Franco Ferracuti and by Walter Miller are somewhat different. They do not suggest that delinquency begins with failure to reach middle-class goals. Their explanations are rooted in culture conflict theory. The **subculture of violence** thesis argues that the value systems of some subcultures demand the overt use of violence in certain social situations. This norm, which affects daily behavior, is in conflict with the conventional norms of the middle class. Along the same lines, Miller suggests that the characteristics of lower-class delinquency reflect the value system of the lower-class culture, and that the lower-class values and norms conflict with those of the dominant culture.

Although Miller contends that the lower-class culture as a whole—not a subculture within it—is responsible for criminal behavior in urban slums, his theory is appropriate to our discussion because it demonstrates how the needs of young urban males are met by mem-

bership in a street gang. Miller's street gangs, like those of Cohen and of Cloward and Ohlin, condone violent criminal activity as one of the few means of attaining status in a slum.

SUBCULTURAL THEORIES OF DELINQUENCY AND CRIME

The Middle-Class Measuring Rod

Albert Cohen was a student of Robert Merton and of Edwin Sutherland, both of whom had made convincing arguments about the causes of delinquency. Sutherland persuaded Cohen that differential association and the cultural transmission of criminal norms led to criminal behavior. From Merton he learned about structurally induced strain. Cohen combined and expanded these perspectives to explain how the delinquent subculture arises, where it is found within the social structure, and why it has the particular characteristics that it does.[2]

According to Cohen, delinquent subcultures—subcultures whose values are in opposition to those of the dominant culture—emerge in the slum areas of larger American cities. They are rooted in class differentials in parental aspirations, child-rearing practices, and classroom standards. Cohen contends that the relative position of a youngster's family in the social structure determines the problems the child will have to face throughout life. Lower-class families who have never known a middle-class lifestyle, for example, cannot socialize their children in a way that prepares them to enter the middle class. The children grow up with poor communication skills, lack of commitment to education, and an inability to delay gratification. Schools present a particular problem. There, lower-class children are evaluated by middle-class teachers on the basis of a middle-class measuring rod. These measures are based on such middle-class values as self-reliance, good manners, respect for property, and long-range planning. By such measures, lower-class children fall far short of the standards they must meet if they are to compete successfully with middle-class children. Cohen argues that they experience status frustration and strain, to

Subcultures flourish in socially disorganized neighborhoods.

which they respond by adopting one of three roles: corner boy, college boy, or delinquent boy.

Corner boys try to make the best of a bad situation. The corner boy hangs out in the neighborhood with his peer group, spending the day in some group activity such as gambling or athletic competition. He receives support from his peers and is very loyal to them. Most lower-class boys become corner boys. Eventually they get menial jobs and live a conventional lifestyle.

There are very few college boys. These boys continually strive to live up to middle-class standards, but their chances for success are limited because of academic and social handicaps.

Delinquent boys band together to form a subculture in which they can define status in ways that to them seem attainable. Cohen claims that even though these lower-class youths set up their own norms by which they *can* be successful, they have internalized the norms of the dominant class, and they feel anxious when they go against these norms. To deal with this conflict they resort to **reaction forma-tion,** a mechanism that relieves anxiety through a process of rejecting with abnormal intensity what one wants but cannot obtain. These boys turn the middle-class norms upside down, thereby making conduct *right* in their subculture precisely because it is *wrong* by the norms of the larger culture (Figure 6.1). Consequently, their delinquent acts serve no useful purpose and are merely malicious and negative. These boys don't steal things to eat them, wear them, or sell them. In fact, they often discard or destroy what they have stolen. They appear to delight in the discomfort of others and in breaking taboos. Their delinquent acts are directed against people and property at random, unlike the goal-oriented activities of many adult criminal groups. The subculture is typically characterized by short-run hedonism, pure pleasure-seeking, with no planning or deliberation about what to do, where, or when. The delinquents hang out on the street corner until someone gets an idea; then they act impulsively, without considering the consequences. The group's autonomy is all-important. Its members are loyal to each other and resist any attempts on the

FIGURE 6.1   The process of reaction formation among delinquent boys

Working-class
socialization   →   Lower-class failure   →   Loss of self-esteem   →
+   in the school system   and increased
Middle-class values   (among many)   feelings of rejection
of success

School dropout and   Increased hostility   Improved self-image
association with   and resentment   in a gang context
delinquent peers   →   toward middle-class   →   and through
(among some)   standards and   negative and
                             symbols, thus   malicious delin-
                             reaction formation   quent behavior

Source: Donald J. Shoemaker, *Theories of Delinquency: An Examination of Explanations of Delinquent Behavior* (New York: Oxford University Press, 1984), p. 105.

part of families, school, or community to restrain their behavior.

Tests of Cohen's theory   Criminological researchers generally agree that Cohen's theory is responsible for major advances in research on delinquency. Many support Cohen's thesis.[3] Among them are researchers who have found a relationship between delinquency and social status in our society (Chapter 5). Much evidence also supports Cohen's assumption that lower-class children perform more poorly in school than middle-class children.[4] Teachers often expect them to perform less ably than their middle-class students, and this expectation is one of the components of poor performance.

Researchers have demonstrated that poor performance in school is related to delinquency. When Travis Hirschi studied more than 4,000 California schoolchildren, he found that youths who were academically incompetent and performed poorly in school came to dislike school; disliking it, they rejected its authority; rejecting its authority, they committed delinquent acts[5] (Chapter 7). Delbert Elliott and Harwin Voss also investigated the relationship between school and delinquency. They analyzed annual school performance and delinquency records of 2,000 students in California from ninth grade to one year after the expected graduation date. Their findings indicated that those who dropped out of school had higher rates of delinquency than those who graduated. They also found that academic achievement and alienation from school were closely related to dropping out of school.[6] All of these findings support Cohen's theory. Other findings, however, do not.

In a study of 12,524 students in Davidson County, Tennessee, Albert Reiss and Albert Rhodes found only a slight relationship between delinquency and status deprivation.[7] This conclusion was supported by the research of Marvin Krohn and his associates.[8] Furthermore, several criminologists have challenged Cohen's claim that delinquent behavior is purposeless and nonutilitarian. They contend that much of delinquent behavior is serious and calculated, and often engaged in for profit.[9] John Kitsuse and David Dietrick have also questioned the consistency of the theory: Cohen argues that the behavior of delinquent boys is a deliberate response to middle-class opinion, yet he also argues that the boys do not care about the opinions of middle-class people.[10]

Evaluation of Cohen's theory   Researchers have praised and criticized Cohen's work. Cohen's theory answers a number of questions left unresolved by the strain and cultural deviance theories. It explains the origin of delinquent behavior and why some youths raised in

MASS-MEDIA STEREOTYPING OF CRIME AND CRIMINALS

Wronged by the lawless system around him, Josey Wales becomes an outlaw in the post–Civil War era. His violent exploits, portrayed by Clint Eastwood in *The Outlaw Josey Wales*, fill moviegoers with admiration. In *Butch Cassidy and the Sundance Kid*, the title characters (played by Katherine Ross, Paul Newman, and Robert Redford) led a happy-go-lucky life robbing trains and banks, seemingly fighting "capitalistic exploiters" in North and South America. Moviegoers periodically experience the resurrection of the classic film *Robin Hood*.

The Prohibition era spawned additional "heroes," often admired for their daring, arrogance, and resourcefulness in fighting against unpopular laws: In *Bonnie and Clyde* (the title roles of which were portrayed by Faye Dunaway and Warren Beatty), it was the banking and bankruptcy laws; in *The Untouchables* (with Robert De Niro as Al Capone), it was the Prohibition laws. The main character in *The Godfather*, played by Marlon Brando, epitomizes the successful, ruthless, and opulent gangster boss whose defiance of the law makes him a folk "hero."

Modern times have created a new set of romanticized outlaws. In *The Death Wish*, Charles Bronson portrays a ruthless vigilante who, dissatisfied with the criminal justice system, takes the law into his own hands. Sylvester Stallone, in *Rambo*, plays another character who fights a lonely cause, living by his own moral code as avenger.

The "heroes" of the eight motion pictures mentioned here could be called mass murderers, serial murderers, chronic offenders, and career criminals. Instead, the mass media has glorified them for their bravado, seeming invulnerability, charisma, resourcefulness, loyalty to friends, and sheer arrogance in defying the laws. The question relevant to this book is: Has Hollywood's exploitation and manipulation of our cultural values—competition, success, individualism, courage, prestige—been detrimental to society?

Clint Eastwood in The Outlaw Josey Wales.

*Katherine Ross, Paul New-
man, and Robert Redford in*
Butch Cassidy and the Sundance Kid.

Robert De Niro in The Untouchables.

Faye Dunaway and Warren Beatty in Bonnie and Clyde.

Marlon Brando in The Godfather.

Charles Bronson in Death Wish 3.

Sylvester Stallone in Rambo II.

the same neighborhoods and attending the same schools do not become involved in delinquent subcultures. His concepts of status deprivation and the middle-class measuring rod have been useful to researchers. Yet his theory does not explain why most delinquents eventually become law-abiding even though their position in the class structure remains relatively fixed. Some criminologists also question whether youths are driven by some serious motivating force or whether they are simply out on the streets looking for fun.[11] Moreover, if delinquent subcultures result from the practice of measuring lower-class boys by a middle-class measuring rod, how does one account for middle-class delinquents? Other questions concern the difficulties of trying to test the concepts of reaction formation, internalization of middle-class values, and status deprivation, among others. To answer some of his critics, Cohen, with his colleague James Short, expanded the idea of delinquent subcultures to include not only lower-class delinquent behavior but also such variants as middle-class delinquent subcultures and female delinquents.[12]

Criminological researchers generally agree that Cohen's theory is responsible for major advances in delinquency research. Cohen took Merton's strain theory a step forward by elaborating on the development of delinquent behavior. He described how strain actually creates frustration and status deprivation, which in turn fosters the development of an alternative set of values that afford lower-class boys a chance to achieve recognition, albeit in a deviant subculture. Since the mid-1950s Cohen's theory has stimulated not only research but the formulation of new theories.

Delinquency and Opportunity

Like Cohen's theory, the theory of differential opportunity developed by Richard Cloward and Lloyd Ohlin combines strain, differential association, and social disorganization theory.[13] Both theories begin with the assumption that conventional means to conventional success are inequitably distributed among the socioeconomic classes; that lack of means causes frustration for lower-class youths; and that criminal behavior is learned and culturally transmitted.

Both theories also agree that the common solution to shared problems leads to the formation of delinquent subcultures. They disagree, however, on the content of these subcultures. As we have noted, norms in Cohen's delinquent subcultures are right precisely because they are wrong in the dominant culture. Delinquent acts, therefore, are negative and nonutilitarian. Cloward and Ohlin disagree; they suggest that lower-class delinquents remain goal-oriented. The types of delinquent behavior they engage in depends on the illegitimate opportunities available to them.

According to Cloward and Ohlin's **differential opportunity theory,** delinquent subcultures flourish in lower-class areas and take the particular forms that they do because opportunities for illegitimate success are no more equitably distributed than those for conventional success. Just as means—opportunities—are unequally distributed in the conventional world, opportunities to reach one's goals are unequally distributed in the criminal world. A person cannot simply decide to join a theft-oriented gang or, for that matter, a violence-oriented one. Cloward and Ohlin maintain that the types of subcultures and of the juvenile gangs that flourish within them depend on the types of neighborhoods in which they develop (Figure 6.2). In areas where conventional and illegitimate values and behavior are integrated by a close connection of illegitimate and legitimate businesses, *criminal gangs* emerge. Older criminals serve as role models. They teach youngsters whom to exploit, the necessary criminal skills, the importance of loyal relationships with criminal associates, and how to make the right connections with shady lawyers, bail bondsmen, crooked politicians, and corrupt police officers. Adolescent members of criminal gangs, like adult criminals in the neighborhood, are involved in extortion, fraud, theft, and other activities that yield illegal income. This type of neighborhood was described by one of its members in the following way:

> Stealing in the neighborhood was a common practice among the children and approved by the parents. Whenever the boys got together they talked about robbing and made more plans for stealing. I hardly knew any boys who did not go robbing. The little fellows went in

FIGURE 6.2 Factors leading to development of three types of delinquent gangs

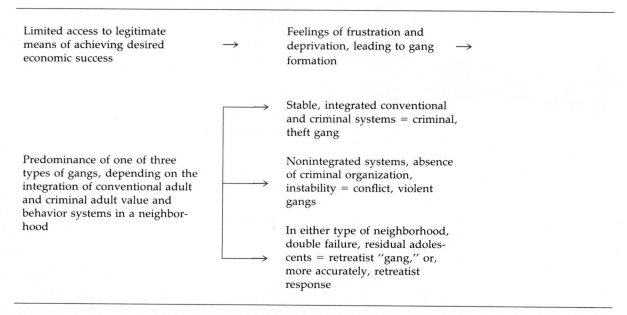

Source: Donald J. Shoemaker, *Theories of Delinquency: An Examination of Explanations of Delinquent Behavior* (New York: Oxford University Press, 1984), p. 114.

for petty stealing, breaking into freight cars, and stealing junk. The older guys did big jobs like stick-ups, burglary, and stealing autos. The little fellows admired the "big shots" and longed for the day when they could get into the big racket. Fellows who had "done time" were the big shots and looked up to and gave the little fellows tips on how to get by and pull off big jobs.[14]

Neighborhoods characterized by transiency and instability, Cloward and Ohlin argue, offer few opportunities to get ahead in organized criminal activities. This world gives rise to fighting gangs whose goal is to gain a reputation for toughness and destructive violence. Thus "one particular biker would catch a bird and then bite off its head, allowing the blood to trickle from his mouth as he yelled 'all right!'"[15] It is the world of the warrior: fight, show courage against all odds, defend, and maintain the honor of the group. Above all, never show fear.

Such are the means used to gain status in the *conflict gangs*. Conventional society's recognition of the "worst" gangs becomes a mark of

prestige, perpetuating the high standards of their members. Conflict gangs emerge in lower-class areas where neither criminal nor conventional adult role models exercise appreciable control over youngsters.

A third subcultural response to differential opportunities is the formation of *retreatist gangs*. Cloward and Ohlin describe members of retreatist gangs as double failures because they have not been successful in the legitimate world and have been equally unsuccessful in the illegitimate worlds of organized criminal activity and violence-oriented gangs. This subculture is characterized by a continuous search for getting high through alcohol, atypical sexual experiences, marijuana, hard drugs, or a combination of all of these.

The retreatist hides in a world of sensual adventure, borrowing, begging, or stealing to support his habit, whatever it may be. He may peddle drugs or work as a pimp or look for some other deviant income-producing activity. But the income is not his primary concern; he is interested only in the next high. Belonging to a

retreatist gang offers a sense of superiority and well-being that is otherwise beyond the reach of these least successful dropouts.

Not all lower-class youngsters who are unable to reach society's goals become members of criminal, conflict, or retreatist gangs. Many choose to accept their situation and to live within its constraints. These law-abiding youngsters are Cohen's corner boys.

Cloward and Ohlin's differential opportunity theory presented many new ideas to criminologists. A variety of studies emerged to test it empirically.

Tests of opportunity theory   The first of Cloward and Ohlin's assumptions—that blocked opportunities are related to delinquency—has mixed support. Travis Hirschi, for example, demonstrated that "the greater one's acceptance of conventional (or even quasi-conventional) success goals, the less likely one is to be delinquent, regardless of the likelihood these goals will someday be attained."[16] Delbert Elliott and Harwin Voss, too, have found no relationship between actual or anticipated failure to reach occupational success and self-reported delinquency. In other words, the youngsters who stick to hard work and education to get ahead in society are the least likely to become delinquent, no matter what their real chances of reaching their goals.[17] Judson

Landis and Frank Scarpitti disagree. When they compared a group of incarcerated youths and a high school control group, they found that the delinquent boys perceived opportunities to be much more limited than the nondelinquent boys did.[18] There is also evidence that both gang *and* nongang boys believe the middle-class values of hard work and scholastic achievement to be important. Gang boys, however, are more ready than nongang boys to approve of a wide range of behaviors, including aggressive acts and drug use.[19]

The second assumption of differential opportunity theory—that the type of lower-class gangs that exist depends on the type of neighborhoods in which they emerge—has also drawn the attention of criminologists. Empirical evidence suggests that gang behavior is more versatile and involves a wider range of criminal and noncriminal acts than the specific patterns outlined by Cloward and Ohlin.[20] A new subculture that emerged in the 1980s combined violence, which had become much more vicious than in earlier years, with big business in cocaine and crack trafficking. Rival gangs killed for more than simply turf. In cities around the world teenagers began to drive BMWs with concealed Uzi submachine guns under the driver's seat and thousands of dollars in their pockets so that they could make bail at any moment.

WINDOW TO THE WORLD

Bosozoku Gangs of Japan

The bosozoku make their nefarious rounds by night on huge unmuffled motorcycles, scorning the police as they terrorize motorists on the highways or indulge in orgies of noise in sleepy neighborhoods.

Young, violent and in love with speed, the bosozoku ride in gangs of about 30 on bikes and in cars with oversized engines.

The national police recently published unsettling figures showing that this scourge of Japanese city-dwellers is growing every year.

More than 107,000 bosozokus were arrested last year, 21 percent more than in 1988, and 24,000 vehicles, more than half of them motorcycles, were temporarily confiscated for failing to conform to legal standards.

Some 3,600 bosozoku were arrested in 1989 and charged with beatings and robberies.

Police recorded more than 114,000 telephone calls last year, up 34.7 percent over 1988, from citizens outraged by the bosozoku shattering the quiet outside their homes.

But the police seem powerless to control the rising menace, with measures such as suspending driving licenses for 90 days proving ineffective.

In April, two bosozoku murdered a reporter for the Mainichi Newspapers in Fujisawa, 50 kilometers (31 miles) south of here.

The reporter, Masahiro Yoshino, 56, died of injuries after the pair beat him up for complaining about their noise.

The two young killers, factory workers aged 25 and 26, showed faint remorse at their trial last week, when they were convicted and sentenced to only two and a half years in prison.

The court justified the light sentence, widely denounced in Japan, by arguing that the bosozoku felt threatened when the reporter brandished a metal pipe.

The bosozoku phenomenon has emerged alongside Japan's rapid motorization since the 1960s, when superhighways began crisscrossing Tokyo and other major cities.

The precursors of the bosozoku, the kaminari-zoku—or thunder tribes—and the sahkittozoku—the circuit tribes—were tame by comparison, contenting themselves with noisy track races.

But they evolved over the last 20 years into the bosozoku, organized gangs bent on violence.

Wearing World War II kamikaze pilot suits and military boots, the bosozoku gangs give themselves menacing names like Black Emperor or Killer Alliance.

Accompanied by their "ladies," the bosozoku love to drink, and love to fight.

They travel with a maximum of noise, their stereos blasting at full volume.

Most bosozoku are under 20, but more than 16—the minimum age for a motorcycle license—and of modest means, many of them gas station attendants or mechanics.

"Their existence reflects such social problems as education, family relations, living space and being dissatisfied with school or jobs," a report by the National Research Institute of Police Science said.

Source: *Mainichi Daily News*, Tokyo, February 7, 1990, p. 12.

Evaluation of differential opportunity theory For three decades criminologists have reviewed, examined, and revised the work of Cloward and Ohlin. One of the main criticisms of their theory is that it is class-oriented. If, as Cloward and Ohlin claim, delinquency is a response to blocked opportunities, how can middle-class delinquency be explained? Another question arises from the contradictory statements of Cohen and of Cloward and

Ohlin. How can delinquent groups be non-utilitarian, negativistic, and malicious (Cohen) and also be goal-oriented and utilitarian? Despite its shortcomings, however, differential opportunity theory has identified some of the reasons why lower-class youngsters may become alienated from conventional norms. Cloward and Ohlin's work has also challenged researchers to study further the nature of the subcultures in our society. Marvin Wolfgang and Franco Ferracuti concentrate on one of them—the subculture of violence.

The Subculture of Violence

Like Cohen, and like Cloward and Ohlin, Marvin Wolfgang and Franco Ferracuti turned to subcultural theory to explain criminal behavior among urban, lower-class young males. All three theories assume the existence of subcultures made up of people who share a value system that differs from that of the dominant culture. And they assume that each subculture has its own rules or conduct norms that dictate how individuals should act under varying circumstances. The three theories also agree that these values and norms persist over time because they are learned by successive generations. The theories differ, however, in their focus. Cohen and Cloward and Ohlin focus on the origin of the subculture, specifically culturally induced strain, whereas the major thrust of Wolfgang and Ferracuti is on culture conflict. Furthermore, the earlier theories encompass all types of delinquency and crime, whereas Wolfgang and Ferracuti concentrate on violent crime. They argue that in some subcultures the norms of behavior are dictated by a value system that demands the overt use of force or violence.[21] Subcultures that adhere to conduct norms conducive to violence are referred to as subcultures of violence. Violence is not used in all situations, but it is frequently an expected response. The appearance of a weapon, a slight shove or push, a derogatory remark, or the opportunity to wield power undetected may very well evoke in subculture members an aggressive reaction that seems uncalled for to middle-class people. Fists rather than words settle disputes. Knives or guns are readily available. Thus, confrontations can quickly escalate. Violence is a pervasive part of everyday life. Child-rearing practices (hitting), gang activities (street wars), domestic quarrels (battering), and social events (drunken brawls) are all permeated by violence. Violence is not considered antisocial. Thus, members of this subculture feel no guilt about their aggression. In fact, individuals who do not resort to violence may be reprimanded. The value system is transmitted from generation to generation, long after the original reason for the violence has disappeared. The pattern is very hard to eradicate.

When Wolfgang and Ferracuti described population groups that are likely to respond violently to stress, they posed a powerful question to the criminal justice system. How does one go about changing a subcultural norm? This question becomes increasingly significant with the merging of the drug subculture and the subculture of violence.

Tests of the subculture of violence   Howard Erlanger, using nationwide data collected for the President's Commission on the Causes and Prevention of Violence, found an absence of major differences in attitudes toward violence by class or race. Erlanger concluded that though members of the lower class evince no greater approval of violence than middle-class persons do, they lack the sophistication necessary to settle grievances by other means.[22]

The subculture of violence thesis has also generated a line of empirical research that looks at regional differences in levels of violent crime. The South (as you will see in Chapter 10) has the highest homicide rate in the country. Some researchers have attributed this high rate to subcultural values.[23] They argue that a southern subculture of violence has its historical roots in an exaggerated defense of honor by southern gentlemen, mob violence (especially lynching), a military tradition, the acceptance of personal vengeance, and the widespread availability and use of handguns.[24] The problem with many of these studies is that it is difficult to separate the effects of economic and social factors from those of cultural values. Several researchers have sought to solve this prob-

Colors and patches denote membership and rank in motorcycle gangs, which represent the subculture of violence in its most visible form.

lem. Colin Loftin and Robert Hill, for example, using a sophisticated measure of poverty, found that economic factors, not cultural ones, explained regional variation in homicide rates.[25] Others suggest that high homicide rates and gun ownership may have little to do with a subculture of violence, but may have a great deal to do with socioeconomic conditions, especially racial inequality in the South.[26]

Other researchers support the subculture of violence thesis with statistics on characteristics of homicide offenders and victims:

• Lower-class, inner-city black males are disproportionately represented in the FBI's Uniform Crime Reports.
• The majority of the offenders are young, most in their twenties, but many in their late teens.
• Typically the offender and the victim know each other.
• The offender and the victim are usually in the same age group and of the same race.[27]

Furthermore, in a study of 556 males interviewed at age 26, 19 percent of the respondents, all inner-city males, reported having been shot or stabbed. These victimizations were found to be highly correlated with both self-reported offenses and official arrest statistics. In fact, the best single predictor of committing a violent act was found to be whether or not he had been a victim of a violent crime. Though most people in the dominant society who are shot or stabbed do not commit a criminal act in response, it appears that many inner-city males alternate the roles of victim and offender in a way that fosters the maintenance of the values and attitudes of a violent subculture.[28]

Evaluation of the subculture of violence thesis   Though empirical evidence concerning the subculture of violence thesis remains inconclusive, the thesis is supported by the distribution of violent crime in American society.[29] Gang warfare, which takes the lives of innocent bystanders in ghetto areas, is a part of life in most of the impoverished densely populated neighborhoods in such major cities as Los Angeles, New York, Chicago, Miami, Washington, D.C., and Atlanta, and in smaller disintegrating urban centers as well. For example, over the three years between 1985 and 1988, Jamaican "bosses"—gangs transplanted from Kingston, Jamaica, to the United States—have been involved in 1,400 homicides.[30] Though not all persons in these subcultures adhere to the norm of violence, it appears that a dismaying number of them attach less and less importance to the value of human life and turn increasingly to violence to resolve immediate problems and frustrations.

The Focal Concerns of the Lower Class

All the theorists that we have examined thus far explain criminal and delinquent behavior in terms of subcultural values that emerge and are perpetuated from one generation to the next in lower-class urban slums. Walter Miller reasons differently. According to Miller,

> In the case of "gang" delinquency, the cultural system which exerts the most direct influence on behavior is that of the lower-class community itself—a long-established, distinctively patterned tradition with an integrity of its own—rather than a so-called "delinquent subculture" which has arisen through conflict with middle-class culture and is oriented to the deliberate violation of middle-class norms.[31]

To Miller, juvenile delinquency is not rooted in the rejection of middle-class values; it stems rather from lower-class culture, which has its own value system. This value system has evolved as a response to living in slums. Gang norms are simply the adolescent expression of the lower-class culture in which the boys have grown up. This lower-class culture exists apart from the middle-class culture, and has done so for generations. The value system, not the gang norms, generates delinquent acts.

Miller has identified six focal concerns, or areas to which lower-class males give persistent attention. Concern over *trouble* is a major fea-

ture of lower-class life. Staying out of trouble and getting into trouble are daily preoccupations. Trouble can get a person into the hands of the authorities or it can result in prestige. Lower-class persons are often evaluated by their involvement in troublemaking activities, such as fighting, drinking, and sexual misbehavior.

These young men are almost obsessively concerned with *toughness*, which requires a show of masculinity, a denial of sentimentality, and a display of physical strength. Miller argues that this concern over toughness is related to the fact that a large proportion of lower-class males grow up in female-dominated households and have no male figure from whom to learn the male role. They join street gangs in order to find males with whom they can identify. Claude Brown's autobiography, *Manchild in the Promised Land*, illustrates the concerns about trouble and toughness among adolescents growing up in an urban slum:

> My friends were all daring like me, tough like me, dirty like me, ragged like me, cursed like me, and had a great love for trouble like me. We took pride in being able to hitch rides on trolleys, buses, taxicabs and in knowing how to steal and fight. We knew that we were the only kids in the neighborhood who usually had more than ten dollars in their pockets.... Somebody was always trying to shake us down or rob us. This was usually done by the older hustlers in the neighborhood or by storekeepers or cops.... We accepted this as a way of life.[32]

Another focal concern is *smartness*—the ability to gain something by outsmarting, outwitting, or conning another person. In lower-class neighborhoods youngsters practice outsmarting each other in card games, exchanges of insults, and so forth. Prestige is awarded to those who demonstrate such skills.

Many aspects of lower-class life are related to a search for *excitement*, another focal concern. Youngsters alternate between hanging out with peers and looking for excitement, which can be found in fighting, getting drunk, and using drugs. Risks, danger, and thrills break up the monotony of their existence.

Fate plays an important role in lower-class life. Many individuals believe that their lives are subject to forces over which they have little control. If they get lucky, their rather drab life could change quickly. Common discussions center on whether lucky numbers come up, cards are right, or dice are good. Brown recalls:

> After a while [Mama] settled down, and we stopped talking about her feelings, then somebody came upstairs and told her she had hit the numbers.
>
> We just forgot all about her feelings. I forgot about her feelings. Mama forgot about her feelings. Everybody did. She started concentrating on the number. This was the first time she'd had a hit in a long time. They bought some liquor. Mama and Dad started drinking: everyone started making a lot of noise and playing records.[33]

Miller's last focal concern, *autonomy*, stems from the lower-class person's resentment of external controls, whether parents, teachers, or the police. This desire for personal freedom is expressed often in such terms as "No one can push me around" and "I don't need nobody."[34]

According to Miller, in every class status is associated with the possession of qualities that are valued. In the lower class the six focal concerns define one's status. It is apparent that by engaging in behavior that affords status by these criteria, many people will be breaking the laws of the dominant society (Figure 6.3).

Tests of Miller's theory   An obvious question is whether in our urban, heterogeneous, secular, technologically based society any isolated pockets of culture are still to be found. The pervasiveness of mass advertising, mass transit, and mass communication makes it seem unlikely that an entire class of people could be unaware of the dominant value system that surrounds them. Empirical research on opportunity theory has found that lower-class boys share the conventional success goals of the dominant culture. This finding suggests that the idea of culture isolation from the dominant value system does not accord with reality. Empirical research has also found, however, that while gang boys may support middle-class values, they are willing to deviate from these. Thus, if an opportunity arises to gain prestige in a fight, gang boys are willing to take a chance that their act will not result in punishment.

Most empirical tests of values question young people on their attachment to middle-class values. Stephen Cernovich expanded this type of research by investigating attachment to lower-class focal concerns.[35] He found that toughness, excitement, trouble, and pleasure-seeking were related to self-reported delinquency in all classes. His findings also showed that boys of all classes were committed to delayed gratification, hard work, and education. Cernovich concluded that values rather than class are associated with delinquency.

FIGURE 6.3   The relationship between delinquency and lower-class focal concerns

Lower-class focal concerns
+
Female-dominated households
→
Desire of lower-class male adolescents to seek male identity and status in "one-sex peer unit" street-corner gangs
→

Behavior in accordance with lower-class focal concerns
→
Behavior that is often delinquent and criminal

Source: Donald J. Shoemaker, *Theories of Delinquency: An Examination of Explanations of Delinquent Behavior* (New York: Oxford University Press, 1984), p. 122.

Evaluation of Miller's theory   Criminologists have been disturbed by Miller's assumption that the lower-class lifestyle is generally in contravention of the law. In making such an assumption, they say, Miller disregards the fact that most people in the lower class do conform to conventional norms. Moreover, some criminologists ask, if lower-class boys are conforming to their own value system, why would they suffer guilt or shame when they commit delinquent acts?[36]

Perhaps the best support for Miller's ideas is found in qualitative rather than quantitative accounts of life in a lower-class slum. Oscar Lewis used the term **culture of poverty** to describe cultures that are characterized by helplessness, cynicism, and mistrust of authority as represented by schools and the police.[37] Ken Auletta refers to members of these cultures as the "underclass."[38] They have little in the way of education or skills to enable them to keep up with the demands of a modern society. These cultures have also been the subject of television documentaries, movies, plays, newspaper stories, and autobiographical accounts, such as Brown's *Manchild in the Promised Land*. In our discussion of cultural deviance and subcultural theories we noted that the values and norms that define behavior in the slums do not change much over time. Successive generations have to deal with the same problems. They typically share similar responses. By and large, descriptions of life in poverty-stricken areas, whether written by people who have lived in them or people who have studied them, demonstrate the dreary routine, the boredom, the constant trouble, and the problems with drugs, alcohol, and crime of the lower class. As the father tells his son in Eugene O'Neill's autobiographical play *Long Day's Journey into Night*, "There was no damned romance in our poverty."[39]

Female Delinquent Subcultures

Despite the large number of theoretical and empirical studies on male delinquent subcultures, little was known about female delinquent subcultures until recently. In 1958 Albert Cohen and James Short suggested that female delinquent subcultures, like their male counterparts, were composed of members who had been frustrated in their efforts to achieve conventional goals (respectability, marriage, status). They thus had drifted into a subculture that offered them substitute status, albeit outside legitimate society. Drug use and prostitution became all but inevitable. Since the research that led to this finding was conducted among mostly lower-class black females, Cohen and Short admitted that their findings probably could not be generalized to all female delinquent subcultures.[40]

Twenty-six years after Cohen and Short's tentative findings, Anne Campbell published the first major work on the lifestyle of female gang members in New York. She spent two years with three gangs: one Hispanic (the Sex Girls), one black (the Five Percent Nation), and one racially mixed (the Sandman Ladies). Campbell's findings demonstrate that girls, like boys, join gangs for mutual support, protection, and a sense of belonging. They, too, gain status by living up to the value system of their gang. Campbell also noted that these youngsters will probably end up, as their mothers have done, living on welfare assistance in a ghetto apartment. Men will come and go in their lives, but after their gang days the women are constantly threatened by feelings of isolation.[41] (See Criminological Focus.)

About 10 percent of the gang members nationwide are female. Many of the female gangs are affiliates of male gangs, often offering support for the young men they refer to as their homeboys. They do, however, have their own initiation rites (which mimic male ceremonies, but the beating of the initiate is much less violent), their own gang colors, and a strong allegiance to their own gang members. For many of these youngsters the gang takes the place of a family. Shorty, a member of the Tiny Diablas, a female gang in Los Angeles, had no family except a grandmother, who had given up on trying to control her. Shorty's mother was a gang member who abandoned her at an early age. Her father overdosed on heroin and was identified by a tattoo of Shorty's name. Her aunt had a teardrop tattoo next to her eye, to signify

CRIMINOLOGICAL FOCUS

The Girls in the Gang

All the girls in the gang come from families that are poor. Many have never known their fathers. Most are immigrants from Puerto Rico. As children the girls moved from apartment to apartment as they were evicted or burned out by arsonists. Unable to keep any friends they managed to make and alienated from their mothers, whose lack of English restricted their ability to control or understand their daughters' lives, the girls dropped out of school early and grew up on the streets. In the company of older kids and street-corner men, they graduated early into the adult world. They began to use drugs and by puberty had been initiated into sexual activity. By fifteen many were pregnant. Shocked, their mothers tried to pull them off the streets. Some sent their daughters back to relatives in Puerto Rico while they had their babies. Abortion was out of the question in this Catholic world.

Those who stayed had "spoiled their identity" as good girls. Their reputations were marred before they ever reached adulthood. On the streets, among the gang members, the girls found a convenient identity in the female gang. Often they had friends or distant relatives who introduced them as "prospects." After a trial period, they could undertake the initiation rite: they had to fight an established member nominated by the godmother. What was at issue was not winning or losing but demonstrating "heart," or courage. Gangs do not welcome members who join only to gain protection. The loyalty of other gang members has to be won by a clear demonstration of willingness to "get down," or fight.

Paradoxically, the female gang goes to considerable lengths to control the sexual behavior of its members. Although the neighborhood may believe they are fast women, the girls themselves do not tolerate members who sleep around. A promiscuous girl is a threat to the other members' relationships with their boyfriends. Members can take a boyfriend from among the male gang members (indeed, they are forbidden to take one from any other gang) but they are required to be monogamous. A shout of "Whore!" is the most frequent cause of fistfights among the female members.

On the positive side, the gang provides a strong sense of belonging and sisterhood. After the terrible isolation of their lives, the girls acquire a ready-made circle of friends who have shared many of their experiences and who are always willing to support them against hostile words or deeds by outsiders. Fighting together generates a strong sense of camaraderie and as a bonus earns them the reputation of being "crazy." This reputation is extremely useful in the tough neighborhoods where they live. Their reputation for carrying knives and for solidarity effectively deters outsiders from challenging them. They work hard at fostering their tough "rep" not only in their deeds but in their social talk. They spend hours recounting and embroidering stories of fights they have been in. Behind all this bravado it is easy to sense the fear they work so hard to deny. Terrified of being victims (as many of them have already been in their families and as newcomers in their schools), they make much of their own "craziness"—the violent unpredictability that frightens away anyone who might try to harm them.

Source: Written by Anne Campbell. Adapted from Anne Campbell, *The Girls in the Gang* (New York and Oxford: Basil Blackwell, 1984).

one year in jail; her uncle had two teardrops. These scenarios of family ties are not unusual among gang members.[42]

Despite the various interpretations of the origins of delinquency, theorists describe the norms of the delinquent subcultures in much the same way. Let us see now whether the values, norms, and behavior of middle-class delinquents differ from those of lower-class delinquents.

Middle-Class Delinquency

Most explanations of middle-class delinquency are extensions of subcultural explanations of lower-class delinquency. Albert Cohen, for example, suggested that changes in the social structure have weakened the value traditionally associated with delay of gratification. Some criminologists say that growing numbers of middle-class youngsters no longer believe that the way to reach their goals is through hard work and delayed pleasure. Rather, behavior has become more hedonistic and more peer-oriented. While most of this youth subculture exhibits nondelinquent behavior, sometimes the pleasure-seeking activities have led to delinquent acts.[43] Bored and restless, these youngsters seek to break the monotony with artificial excitement and conspicuous consumption of cars, clothes, alcohol, drugs, and sexual activity.[44]

American middle-class youths, according to Ralph England, have been gradually removed from the economic life of the community by protective labor laws, the loss of apprenticeship roles in a high-technology society, and the like. Conflicting demands are made. Teenagers cannot work, but they should not loaf; they should delay marriage but are not to be sexually promiscuous; they cannot vote but they can join the army. Conflict produces tensions; tensions are relieved by creation of a new value system: the middle-class teen culture, in which their needs can be met.[45]

Herbert Bloch and Arthur Niederhoffer have suggested that perhaps delinquency is a general problem of adolescence, not of a particular class, culture, or race.[46] In America today there is no official point at which one passes from childhood to adulthood. Rather, there is a vague, floundering, in-between stage during which young people have one foot in childhood and the other in adulthood. We have no rites of passage comparable to those in more primitive societies. Margaret Mead describes one such ritual:

> The essentials of the initiation remain the same: there is a ritual segregation from the company of women, during which time the novice observes certain special food taboos, is incised, eats a sacrificial meal of the blood of the older men, and is shown various marvelous things...that he has never seen before, such as masks and other carvings....
>
> His childhood is ended. From one who has been grown by the daily carefulness and hard work of others, he now passes into the class of those whose care is for others' growth.[47]

Perhaps adolescents try to develop their own rites and symbols. Perhaps tattoos, leather jackets, motorcycles, hand signals, fast cars, and drugs are all aspects of the informal rituals of the contemporary American rites of passage.

From Theory to Practice

Subcultural theory assumes that individuals engage in delinquent or criminal behavior because (1) legitimate opportunities for success are blocked and (2) criminal values and norms are learned in lower-class slums.

The theory was translated into action programs during the 1960s. Both John F. Kennedy and Lyndon Johnson directed that huge sums of money be spent on programs to help move lower-class youths into the social mainstream.

The best-known, Mobilization for Youth (MOBY), was based on opportunity theory.[48] It provided employment, social services, teacher training, legal aid, and other crime-prevention services to an area on New York's Lower East Side. The cost was over $12 million. MOBY ultimately became highly controversial. Many people accused it of being too radical, especially when neighborhood participants became involved in rent strikes, lawsuits charging discrimination, and public demonstrations. News of the conflict between its supporters and its opponents, and between the staff and the neighborhood it served, reached Congress, which made it clear that the point of the project was to reduce delinquency, not to reform society. Little was done to evaluate the program's success. The project was eventually abandoned, and the commission that had established it ceased to exist. The political climate had changed, and federal money was no longer available for sweeping social programs. How-

AT ISSUE

The Emergence of Middle-Class Gangs

In suburban Hawthorne, social workers tell of the police officers who responded to a report of gang violence, only to let the instigators drive away in expensive cars, thinking they were a group of teen-agers on their way to the beach.

In Tucson, Ariz., a white middle-class teen-ager wearing gang colors died, a victim of a drive-by shooting, as he stood with black and Hispanic members of the Bloods gang.

At Antelope Valley High School in Lancaster, Calif., about 50 miles north of Los Angeles, 200 students threw stones at a policeman who had been called to help enforce a ban on the gang outfits that have become a fad on some campuses.

Around the country, a growing number of well-to-do youths have begun flirting with gangs in a dalliance that can be as innocent as a fashion statement or as deadly as hard-core drug dealing and violence.

The phenomenon is emerging in a variety of forms. Some affluent white youths are joining established black or Hispanic gangs like the Crips and Bloods; others are forming what are sometimes called copycat or mutant or yuppie gangs.

The development seems to defy the usual socioeconomic explanations for the growth of gangs in inner cities, and it appears to have caught parents, teachers and law-enforcement officers off guard.

Police experts and social workers offer an array of reasons: a misguided sense of the romance of gangs; pursuit of the easy money of drugs; self-defense against the spread of established hard-core gangs. And they note that well-to-do families in the suburbs can be as empty and loveless as poor families in the inner city, leaving young people searching for a sense of group identity.

Furthermore, "kids have always tried to shock their parents," said Marianne Diaz-Parton, a social worker who works with young gang members in the Los Angeles suburb of Lawndale, "and these days becoming a gang member is one way to do it."

A member of the South Bay Family gang in Hermosa Beach, a 21-year-old surfer called Road Dog who said his family owned a chain of pharmacies, put it this way: "This is the 90's, man. We're the type of people who don't take no for an

answer. If your mom says no to a kid in the 90's, the kid's just going to laugh." He and his friends shouted in appreciation as another gang member lifted his long hair to reveal a tattoo on a bare shoulder: "Mama tried."

Separating their gang identities from their home lives, the South Bay Family members give themselves nicknames that they carry in elaborate tattoos around the backs of their necks. They consented to interviews on the condition that only these gang names be used.

The gang's leader, who said he was the son of a bank vice president, flexed a bicep so the tattooed figure of a nearly naked woman moved suggestively. Voicing his own version of the basic street philosophy of gang solidarity, the leader, who is called Thumper, said, "If you want to be able to walk the mall, you have to know you've got your boys behind you."

Source: Excerpted from Seth Mydans, "Not Just the Inner City: Well-to-Do Join Gangs," *New York Times*, April 10, 1990, p. A10.

ever, MOBY's failure does not detract from the opportunity theory on which it was based.

Many other programs based on subcultural theory have attempted to change the attitudes and behavior of ghetto youngsters who have spent most of their lives learning unconven-

tional street norms. Change is accomplished through the setting up of an extended family environment for high-risk youths, one that provides positive role models, academic and vocational training, strict rules for behavior, drug treatment, health care, and other services. For many youths these programs provide the first warm, caring living arrangement they have ever had. One such program is the House of Umoja (a Swahili word for "unity") in Philadelphia. At any given time about twenty-five black male teenage offenders live together as "sons" of the founder, Sister Fattah. Each resident signs a contract with Umoja obligating himself to help in the household, become an active part of the family group, study, and work either in one of the program's businesses (a restaurant, a moving company, a painting shop) or elsewhere. By many measures this program is successful. In 1972 a newly elected mayor threatened, "All gang members have ten days to turn their guns in to the nearest firehouse, after which time we [the police] will kick your door in and take them."[49] Umoja responded by calling a meeting of representatives of all gangs. More than 5,000 youths from 75 gangs showed up. The result of the meeting was a sixty-day truce. During those sixty days no one died in gang warfare.

Programs similar to Umoja exist throughout the country; they include Argus in New York's South Bronx; Violent Juvenile Offender Research and Development Programs in Chicago, Dallas, New Orleans, Los Angeles, and San Diego; and Neighborhood Anticrime Self-Help Programs in Baltimore, Newark, Cleveland, Boston, Miami, and Washington, D.C. All of these programs have the same mission: to provide a bridge from a delinquent subcultural value system to a conventional one.[50]

Other means have been used to break up delinquent subcultures. Street workers, many of them former gang members (called OGs, for "original gangsters"), serve as a "street-smart diplomatic corps" in many of the poorest ghettos in the country.[51] In Los Angeles, where some 70,000 gang members control the streets, the OGs work for the Community Youth Gang Service (a government-funded agency). Five nights a week more than fifty of these street workers cover the city, trying to settle disputes between rival gangs and to discourage nonmembers from joining them. They look for alternatives to violence, in baseball matches, fairs, and written peace treaties. During a typical evening the street workers may try to head off a gang fight:

Parton [street worker]: Hey, you guys, Lennox is going to be rollin' by here. . . .

Ms. Diaz [street worker]: You with your back to the street, homeboy. They goin' to be lookin' for this car, some burgundy car.

Boy: If they want to find me, they know where I'm at.

Ms. Diaz: I'm tellin' you to be afraid of them. There are some girls here. You better tell them to move down the street. . . . We are goin' back over there to try to keep them there. Don't get lazy or drunk and not know what you're doin'. I know you don't think it's serious, but if one of your friends gets killed tonight, you will.

Boy: It's serious, I know.

Ms. Diaz: We're goin' to keep them in their 'hood, you just stay in yours for a while.

Boy: All right.[52]

After two hours of negotiation, the fight was called off. There was plenty of work left for the team. They would continue the next day to help the gang members find jobs.

REVIEW

In the decade between the mid-1950s and mid-1960s, criminologists began to theorize about the development and content of youth subcultures and the gangs that flourish within them. Some suggested that lower-class males, frustrated by their inability to meet middle-class standards, set up their own norms by which they can find status. Often these norms clash with those of the dominant culture. Other investigators have refuted the idea that delinquent behavior stems from a rejection of middle-class values. They have claimed that lower-class values are separate and distinct from middle-class values, and it is this value system that generates delinquent behavior. The explanations of female delinquent subcultures and middle-class delinquency are an extension of subcultural explanations of lower-class delinquency. While the theories of reaction formation, the subculture of violence, and differential opportunity differ in some respects, they all share one basic assumption—that delinquent and criminal behavior are linked to the values and norms of the areas where youngsters grow up.

KEY TERMS

culture of poverty
differential opportunity theory
reaction formation

subculture
subculture of violence

NOTES

1. Robert Reinhold, "In the Middle of L.A.'s Gang Warfare," *New York Times Magazine*, May 22, 1988, pp. 30, 33.

2. Albert K. Cohen, *Delinquent Boys: The Culture of the Gang* (Glencoe, Ill.: Free Press, 1955).

3. E.g., James F. Short, Jr., and Fred L. Strodtbeck, *Group Process and Gang Delinquency* (Chicago: University of Chicago Press, 1965).

4. Kenneth Polk and Walter B. Schafer, eds., *School and Delinquency* (Englewood Cliffs, N.J.: Prentice-Hall, 1972); Alexander Liazos, "School, Alienation, and Delinquency," *Crime and Delinquency* 24 (1978): 355–370.

5. Travis Hirschi, *Causes of Delinquency* (Berkeley: University of California Press, 1969).

6. Delbert S. Elliott and Harwin L. Voss, *Delinquency and Dropout* (Lexington, Mass.: Lexington Books, 1974).

7. Albert J. Reiss and Albert L. Rhodes, "Deprivation and Delinquent Behavior," *Sociological Quarterly* 4 (1963): 135–149.

8. Marvin Krohn, R. L. Akers, M. J. Radosevich, and L. Lanza-Kaduce, "Social Status and Deviance," *Criminology* 18 (1980): 303–318. For a discussion of being a have-not in a community of haves, see John W. C. Johnstone, "Social Class, Social Areas, and Delinquency," *Sociological and Social Research* 63 (1978): 49–72.

9. David F. Greenberg, "Delinquency and the Age Structure of Society," *Contemporary Crisis* 1 (1977): 189–223.

10. John I. Kitsuse and David C. Dietrick, "Delinquent Boys: A Critique," *American Sociological Review* 24 (1959): 208–215.

11. David J. Bordua, "Delinquent Subcultures: Sociological Interpretations of Gang Delinquency," *Annals of the American Academy of Political and Social Science* 338 (1961): 119–136.

12. Albert K. Cohen and James F. Short, Jr., "Research in Delinquent Subcultures," *Journal of Social Issues* 14 (1958): 20–37.

13. Richard A. Cloward and Lloyd E. Ohlin, *Delinquency and Opportunity* (Glencoe, Ill.: Free Press, 1960).

14. Clifford R. Shaw, *The Jack-Roller* (Chicago, Ill.: University of Chicago Press, 1930), p. 54.

15. James R. David, *Street Gangs* (Dubuque, Ia.: Kendall/Hunt, 1982).

16. Travis Hirschi, *Causes of Delinquency* (Berkeley: University of California Press, 1969), p. 227.

17. Elliott and Voss, *Delinquency and Dropout.*

18. Judson Landis and Frank Scarpitti, "Perceptions Regarding Value Orientation and Legitimate Opportunity: Delinquency and Non-Delinquents," *Social Forces* 84 (1965): 57–61.

19. James Short, Ramon Rivera, and Ray Tennyson, "Perceived Opportunities, Gang Membership, and Delinquency," *American Sociological Review* 30 (1965): 56–57. For a discussion of adolescent goals, see Robert Agnew, "Goal Achievement and Delin-

quency," *Sociology and Social Research* 68 (1984): 435–451.

20. Irving Spergel, *Racketville, Slumtown, and Haulberg* (Chicago, Ill.: University of Chicago Press, 1964); see also Dean G. Rojek and Maynard L. Erickson, "Delinquent Careers: A Test of the Career Escalation Model," *Criminology* 20 (1982): 5–28; Robert J. Bursik, Jr., "The Dynamics of Specialization in Juvenile Offenses," *Social Forces* 58 (1980): 851–864; and Gerald D. Robin, "Gang Member Delinquency: Its Extent, Sequence, and Typology," *Journal of Criminal Law, Criminology, and Police Science* 55 (1964): 59–69.

21. Marvin E. Wolfgang and Franco Ferracuti, *The Subculture of Violence* (London: Tavistock, 1967).

22. Howard S. Erlanger, "The Empirical Status of the Subcultures of Violence Thesis," *Social Problems* 22 (1974): 280–292. See also Sandra Ball-Rokeach, "Values and Violence: A Test of the Subculture of Violence Thesis," *American Sociological Review* 38 (1973): 736–749; for an interesting test of the subculture of violence theory, see Marvin E. Wolfgang and Franco Ferracuti.

23. William G. Doerner, "A Regional Analysis of Homicide Rates in the United States," *Criminology* 13 (1975): 90–101; Raymond D. Gastel, "Homicide and a Regional Culture of Violence," *American Sociological Review* 36 (1971): 412–427. See also Sheldon Hackney, "Southern Violence," *American Historical Review* 74 (1969): 906–925; John S. Reed, *The Enduring South: Subcultural Persistence in Mass Society* (Lexington, Mass.: Lexington Books, 1972), and *One South: An Ethnic Approach to Regional Culture* (Baton Rouge: Louisiana State University Press, 1982).

24. Jo Dixon and Alan J. Lizotte, "Gun Ownership and the Southern Subculture of Violence," *American Journal of Sociology* 93 (1987): 383–405.

25. Colin Loftin and Robert Hill, "Regional Subculture of Violence: An Examination of the Gastril-Hackney Thesis," *American Sociological Review* 39 (1974): 714–724.

26. Judith Blau and Peter Blau, "Metropolitan Structure and Violent Crime," *American So-ciological Review* 47 (1982): 114–129. For a study that examines the subculture of violence thesis as it relates to three ethnic groups—blacks, Hispanics, and American Indians—see Donald J. Shoemaker and J. Sherwood Williams, "The Subculture of Violence and Ethnicity," *Journal of Criminal Justice* 15 (1987): 461–472.

27. Wolfgang and Ferracuti, *Subculture of Violence*, pp. 258–265. See also Marvin E. Wolfgang, *Patterns in Criminal Homicide* (Philadelphia: University of Pennsylvania Press, 1958); Franco Ferracuti, "La personalità dell' omicida," *Quaderni di Criminologia Clinica* 4 (1961): 419–456.

28. Marvin E. Wolfgang, Robert M. Figlio, and Thorsten Sellin, *Delinquency in a Birth Cohort* (Chicago: University of Chicago Press, 1972); Simon I. Singer, "Victims of Serious Violence and Their Criminal Behavior: Subcultural Theory and Beyond," *Violence and Victims* 1 (1986): 61–70. See also Neil Alan Weiner and Marvin E. Wolfgang, "The Extent and Character of Violent Crime in America, 1969–1982," in *American Violence and Public Policy*, ed. Lynn Curtis, pp. 17–39 (New Haven, Conn.: Yale University Press, 1985).

29. Steven Messner, "Regional and Racial Effects on the Urban Homicide Rate: The Subculture of Violence Revisited," *American Journal of Sociology* 88 (1983): 997–1007.

30. Joseph B. Treaster, "Jamaica's Gangs Take Root in U.S.," *New York Times*, Nov. 13, 1988, p. 15. For a comparison of the seriousness of the gang problem in Hispanic and black communities, see G. David Curry and Irving A. Spergel, "Gang Homicide, Delinquency, and Community," *Criminology* 26 (1988): 381–405.

31. Walter B. Miller, "Lower-Class Culture as a Generating Milieu of Gang Delinquency," *Journal of Social Issues* 14 (1958): 5–19.

32. Claude Brown, *Manchild in the Promised Land: A Modern Classic of the Black Experience* (New York: New American Library, 1965), p. 22.

33. Ibid., p. 129.

34. Miller, "Lower-Class Culture."

35. Stephen A. Cernovich, "Value Orientations and Delinquency Involvement," *Criminology* 15 (1978): 443–458.

36. Gresham Sykes and David Matza, "Techniques of Neutralization: A Theory of Delinquency," *American Sociological Review* 22 (1957): 664–673.

37. Oscar Lewis, "The Culture of Poverty," *Scientific American* 215 (1966): 19–25.

38. Ken Auletta, *The Under Class* (New York: Random House, 1982).

39. Eugene O'Neill, *Long Day's Journey into Night,* in *Great Scenes from the World Theater,* ed. James L. Steffenson, Jr. (New York: Avon, 1965), p. 199.

40. Albert K. Cohen and James F. Short, Jr., "Research in Delinquent Subcultures," *Journal of Social Issues* 14 (1958): 20–37.

41. Anne Campbell, *The Girls in the Gang* (New York and Oxford: Basil Blackwell, 1984), p. 267.

42. Seth Mydans, "Life in Girl's Gang: Colors and Bloody Noses," *New York Times,* Jan. 29, 1990, pp. 1, 20.

43. Albert K. Cohen, "Middle-Class Delinquency and the Social Structure," in *Middle-Class Delinquency,* ed. E. W. Vaz, pp. 207–221 (New York: Harper & Row, 1967). See also Fred J. Shanley, "Middle-Class Delinquency as a Social Problem," *Sociology and Social Research* 51 (1967): 185–198.

44. Pamela Richards, Richard A. Berk, and Brenda Forster, *Crime as Play: Delinquency in a Middle-Class Suburb* (Cambridge, Mass.: Ballinger, 1979), p. 11.

45. Ralph England, "A Theory of Middle-Class Delinquency," *Journal of Criminal Law, Criminology, and Police Science* 50 (1960): 535–540.

46. Herbert Bloch and Arthur Niederhoffer, *The Gang: A Study of Adolescent Behavior* (New York: Philosophical Library, 1958).

47. Margaret Mead, *Sex and Temperament in Three Primitive Societies* (1935; New York: New American Library, 1950), pp. 66, 68, 69. See also G. O. W. Mueller, *Puberty and Delinquency: Examination of a Juvenile Delinquency Fad* (South Hackensack, N.J.: Fred B. Rothman, 1971).

48. J. Robert Lilly, Francis T. Cullen, and Richard A. Ball, *Criminological Theory: Context and Consequences* (Newbury Park, Calif.: Sage, 1989), pp. 78–80.

49. Quoted in David Fattah, "The House of Umoja as a Case Study for Social Change," *Annals of the American Academy of Political and Social Science* 494 (1987): 37–41.

50. Lynn A. Curtis, "Preface," in "Policies to Prevent Crime: Neighborhood, Family, and Employment Strategies," ed. Curtis, *Annals of the American Academy of Political and Social Science* 494 (1987).

51. Reinhold, "In the Middle of L.A.'s Gang Warfare," p. 31.

52. Ibid., p. 70.

7

SOCIAL CONTROL THEORY

In William Golding's novel *Lord of the Flies*, a group of boys is stranded on an island far from civilization. Deprived of any superior authority—all the grown-ups, their parents, their teachers, their government that have until now determined their lives—they begin to decide on a structure of government for themselves. Ralph declares:

> "We can't have everybody talking at once. We'll have to have 'Hands up' like at school.... Then I'll give him the conch."
> "Conch?"
> "That's what this shell is called. I'll give the conch to the next person to speak. He can hold it when he's speaking!"...
> Jack was on his feet.
> "We'll have rules!" he cried excitedly. "Lots of rules!"[1]

But does the existence of rules alone guarantee the peaceful existence of the group? Who and what ensure compliance with the rules? Social control theorists are studying these questions.

Strain theorists, as we noted, study the question why some people violate norms, for example, by committing crimes. Social control theorists, on the other hand, are interested in learning why people conform to norms. Control theorists take it for granted that drugs can tempt even the youngest schoolchildren; that truancy can lure otherwise good children onto a path of academic failure and subsequent unemployment; that petty fighting, petty theft, and recreational drinking are attractive features of adolescence and young adulthood. They ask why people conform in the face of so much inducement, temptation, and peer pressure. The answer is that juveniles and adults conform to the law in response to certain controlling forces in their lives. They become criminals when the controlling forces are defective or absent.

What are those controlling forces? Think about the time and energy you have invested in your school, your job, your extracurricular activities. Think about how your academic or vocational ambition would be jeopardized by persistent delinquency. Think about how the responsibility of homework has weighed you down, setting limits on your free time. Reflect

Boys cast away on an uninhabited island, devoid of the social controls of their pasts, search for a new set of norms to control their new society (Lord of the Flies).

on the quality of your relationships with your family, friends, and acquaintances, and how your attachment to them has encouraged you to do right and discouraged you from doing wrong.

WHAT IS SOCIAL CONTROL?

Social control theory focuses on techniques and strategies that regulate human behavior and lead to conformity, or obedience to society's rules—the influences of family and school, religious beliefs, moral values, friends, and even beliefs about government. The more involved and committed a person is to conventional activities and values and the greater the attachment to parents, loved ones, and friends, the less likely that person is to violate society's rules, thereby jeopardizing relationships and aspirations.

The concept of social control emerged around the turn of the century in a volume by E. A. Ross, one of the founders of American sociology. According to Ross, belief systems rather than specific laws guide what people do and universally serve to control behavior, no matter what form the beliefs take. Since that time, the concept has taken on a wide variety of meanings. Social control has been conceptualized as all-encompassing, representing practically any phenomenon that leads to conformity to norms. The term is found in studies of laws, customs, mores, ideologies, and folkways describing a host of controlling forces.[2]

Is there danger in defining social control so broadly? It depends on one's orientation. To some sociologists, the vagueness of the term—its tendency to encompass almost the entire field of sociology—has significantly decreased its value as a concept.[3] To others, the value of "social control" lies in its broad representation of a mechanism by which society regulates its members. According to this view, "social control" defines what is considered deviant behavior, what is right or wrong, and what is a violation of the law. Theorists who have adopted this orientation consider law, norms, customs, mores, ethics, and etiquette to be forms of social control. Donald Black, a sociologist of law, noted, "Social control is found whenever people hold each other to standards, explicitly or implicitly, consciously or not: on the street, in prison, at home, at a party."[4]

SOCIAL CONTROL THEORY

Macrosociological Views of Control

Why is social control conceptualized in such different ways? Perhaps because social control has been examined from both a macro- and microsociological perspective. **Macrosociological studies** explore formal systems for the control of groups:

- The legal system, laws, and particularly law enforcement.
- Powerful groups in society.
- Social and economic directives of governmental or private groups.

These types of control can be either positive— that is, inhibiting rule-breaking behavior by a type of social guidance—or negative—that is, fostering oppressive, restrictive, or corrupt practices by those in power.[5]

Microsociological Views of Control

The microsociological perspective of social control is similar to the macrosociological approach in that it, too, explains why people conform, and considers the source of control to be external (outside the person). **Microsociological studies,** however, focus on informal control systems. Researchers collect data from individuals (usually by self-report methods), often are guided by hypotheses that apply to individuals as well as groups, and frequently make reference to or examine a person's internal control system.

Travis Hirschi has been the spokesperson of the microsociological perspective since the publication of his *Causes of Delinquency* in 1969. He is not, however, the first scholar to examine the extent of individual social control and its relationship to delinquency. In 1957 Jackson Toby introduced the notion of individual "commit-

ment" as a powerful determining force in the social control of behavior.[6] Eight years later Scott Briar and Irving Piliavin extended Toby's thesis by advancing the view that the extent of individual commitment and conformity plays a role in decreasing the likelihood of deviance. They noted that the degree of an adolescent's commitment is reflected in his or her relationships with adult authority figures and with friends, and is determined in part by "belief in God, affection for conventionally behaving peers, occupational aspirations, ties to parents, desire to perform well at school, and fear of material deprivations and punishments associated with arrest."[7]

Briar and Piliavin were not entirely satisfied with control dimensions alone, however, and added another factor: individual motivation to be delinquent. This motivation may stem from a person's wish to "obtain valued goods, to portray courage in the presence of, or to belong to, peers, to strike out at someone who is disliked, or simply to get his kicks."[8]

Hirschi was less interested in the source of an individual's motivation to commit delinquent acts than in the reasons why people do not commit delinquent acts. He claimed that social control theory explains conformity and adherence to rules, not deviance. It is thus not a crime causation theory in a strict sense, but a theory of prosocial behavior used by criminologists to explain deviance.

Social Bonds

Hirschi posited four social bonds that promote socialization and conformity: attachment, commitment, involvement, and belief. The stronger these bonds, he claimed, the less likelihood of delinquency.[9] In order to test this hypothesis, he administered to 4,077 junior and senior high school students in California a self-report questionnaire (see Figure 7.1) that measured both involvement in delinquency and the strength of the four social bonds. Hirschi found that weakness in any of the bonds was associated with delinquent behavior.

Attachment   The first bond, **attachment,** takes three forms: attachment to parents, to school

CRIMINOLOGICAL FOCUS

Social Control in 1941: Just Say No to Pinball

A bonfire, supervised by police, raged at the city dump in South Philadelphia. "We are determined," announced Captain Craig Ellis of the vice squad, "to break up the practice of storekeepers permitting boys to gamble on these machines." The blaze consumed $20,000 worth of confiscated pinball machines that night.

Ellis had been seizing machines since early 1941, acting on a court ruling that a pinball game could be hauled off if its owner was observed paying a winner in cash or other prizes. Captain Ellis and his crew of 25 took to their task with a vengeance, making hundreds of busts and using a giant van to haul the offending games out of bars and drugstores. Assistant City Solicitor James F. Ryan announced his hope to ban all pinball machines "except those with foolproof guarantees against gambling."

However, an earlier state Supreme Court ruling held that pinball machines were games of skill, not gambling devices, and so could not be banned outright. That precedent was challenged in court...in March of 1941. Police argued that pinball had become the most heavily patronized form of gambling in the city, earning three times as much as the numbers racket. During one session, a pair of pinball machines was brought into the courtroom and played by both Ryan and Captain Ellis while Judge Levinthal watched. "It's a sucker's game," stated Ellis, who did not win any free games.

Counsel for the machine owners disputed the charge. "This is amusement. The police have no more right to seize these than they would to pounce on a pack of cards in a store," said one lawyer.

After hearing the arguments and watching the game played, Judge Levinthal decided that not only could pinball machines be confiscated if gambling was witnessed, but also if a machine had a device for canceling free games (machine owners who awarded cash prizes usually allowed no free games to the winners). This ruling made it much easier for police, since witnesses were no longer necessary.

Ryan hailed the decision for sounding "the death-knell of the pinball business in Philadelphia," and before long police had seized more than 400 machines. In February of 1942, the Superior Court of Pennsylvania expanded the ban to include even pinball machines that paid winners in free games *only*—essentially outlawing pinball in Philadelphia.

The death of pinball, however, was only temporary. Early in 1943, the state Superior Court changed its mind, allowing pinball to start anew its wicked seduction of teenage boys with too much time (and change) to spare.

Source: Lou Harry, *Philadelphia Magazine,* July 1988, p. 15.

(teachers), and to peers. According to Hirschi, youths who have formed a significant attachment to a parent refrain from delinquency because the consequences of such an act would be likely to place that relationship in jeopardy. The bond of affection between a parent and child thus becomes a primary deterrent to criminal activities.[10] The strength of this deterrent depends on the

FIGURE 7.1   Items from Travis Hirschi's Measure of Social Control

1. In general, do you like or dislike school?
   A. Like it
   B. Like it and dislike it about equally
   C. Dislike it

2. How important is getting good grades to you personally?
   A. Very important
   B. Somewhat important
   C. Fairly important
   D. Completely unimportant

3. Do you care what teachers think of you?
   A. I care a lot
   B. I care some
   C. I don't care much

4. Would you like to be the kind of person your father is?
   A. In every way
   B. In most ways
   C. In some ways
   D. In just a few ways
   E. Not at all

5. Did your mother read to you when you were little?
   A. No
   B. Once or twice
   C. Several times
   D. Many times, but not regularly
   E. Many times, and regularly
   F. I don't remember

6. Do you ever feel that "there's nothing to do"?
   A. Often
   B. Sometimes
   C. Rarely
   D. Never

Source: Travis Hirschi, *Causes of Delinquency* (Berkeley: University of California Press, 1969).

depth and quality of parent-child interaction. The bond between the parent and child forms a path through which conventional ideals and expectations can pass. This bond is bolstered by:

• The amount of time the child spends with parents, particularly the presence of a parent at times when the child is tempted to engage in criminal activity.
• The intimacy of communication between parent and child.
• The affectional identification between parent and child.[11]

Next Hirschi considered the importance of the school. As we saw in Chapter 6, Hirschi linked inability to function well in school to delinquency through the following chain of events: academic incompetence leads to poor school performance; poor school performance results in a dislike of school, which leads to rejection of the teachers and administrators as authorities. The result is delinquent acts. Thus attachment to school depends on one's appreciation for the institution, one's perception of how he or she is received by teachers and peers, and how well one does in class.

Hirschi found that one's attachment to parents and school overshadows the bond formed with one's peers:

As was true for parents and teachers, those most closely attached to or respectful of their friends are least likely to have committed delinquent acts. The relation does not appear to be as strong as was the case for parents and teachers, but the ideas that delinquents are unusually dependent upon their peers, that loyalty and solidarity are characteristic of delinquent groups, that attachment to adolescent peers fosters nonconventional behavior, and that the delinquent is unusually likely to sacrifice his personal advantage to the "requirements of the group" are simply not supported by the data.[12]

Commitment   Hirschi's second group of bonds consists of **commitment** to or investment in conventional lines of action; that is, support of and participation in social activities that tie the individual to the society's moral or ethical code. Hirschi identified a number of stakes in conformity or commitments: vocational aspirations, educational expectations, educational aspirations. Though Hirschi's theory is at odds with the competing theories of Albert Cohen and Richard Cloward and Lloyd Ohlin (Chapter 6), Hirschi provided empirical support for the

AT ISSUE

Social Control in Japan

When the game was won, the employees rose to sing the company song. They took off the blue plastic cowboy hats the company had given them and raised their fists. They sang of Nissan, the automaker: "Looking at Mount Fuji, surrounded with white clouds in the morning."

Men peeked at the lyrics on the song card, and the children fell a half-beat behind. But the voice was a single voice, the voice of 4,000 employees of the Nissan Motor Company and their families, chosen by lottery and by exemplary job performance to spend half the workday at the ball park, rooting for the company team in the 56th annual National Intercity Amateur Baseball Tournament.

It is an event that might be better named the Corporate Baseball Championship.

On Tuesday, the 32 survivors of a 320-team field began play in the championship round. Nippon Steel will play Nippon Life Insurance, Mitsubishi will play Honda, and so on. The two finalists will play in Tokyo's Korakuen Stadium before 50,000 people on Aug. 2.

"Not only the company employees, but the residents of the city where they work, they come to Korakuen and root for the team, too," Eiichiro Yamamoto, executive vice president of the Japanese Amateur Baseball Association, said of the championship game, which in the United States would be akin to I.B.M. playing General Motors before a full house at Yankee Stadium.

"The Japanese are very loyal," Mr. Yamamoto said. "For a normal Japanese, everything revolves round his work and work place. Private life is more often a sacrifice for the company."...

Nissan won last year's championship before 10,000 of the company's 60,000 employees. The players wept as their co-workers sang the company song. It is that sense of closeness that the company wants to sustain each summer by sending busloads of employees to Korakuen, with box lunches, company hats and plastic cards inscribed with the lyrics of the company song.

"The company sends a ratio of employees from each section to cheer," Mr. Makino said. "Employees can get the feeling of togetherness with the team. They can feel, 'We are part of the family.'"...

At the final out, the teams lined up, facing each other. They took off their hats and bowed. Then they ran over to their boosters and bowed to them too. The next two teams and company boosters began filing into the stadium.

Outside, as the players milled with their friends and families, the employees were led back to the buses. Because it was only 2:30 P.M. and because the Nissan plant was only a 45-minute drive away, the buses took their passengers back to the office where, after three hours off, they went back to work.

Source: Michael Shapiro, "In Japan, The Corporate Pastime Is Baseball," *New York Times*, July 25, 1985, p. A1.

notion that the greater the aspiration and expectation, the more unlikely delinquency becomes. Also "students who smoke, those who drink, and those who date are more likely to commit delinquent acts;...the more the boy is involved in adult activities, the greater his involvement in delinquency."[13]

Involvement   Hirschi's third bond is **involvement,** or preoccupation with activities that promote the interests of society. This bond is derived from involvement in school-related activities (such as homework) rather than in working-class adult activities (such as smoking and drinking). A person who is busy doing conventional things has little time for involvement in deviant activities.

Belief   The last of the bonds—**belief**—consists of assent to the society's value system. Essentially, the value system of any society entails respect for its laws and for the people and institutions that enforce them. The results of Hirschi's survey lead to the conclusion that if young people no longer believe that the laws are fair, their bond to society weakens, and the probability that they will commit delinquent acts increases.[14]

Empirical Tests of Hirschi's Theory

Hirschi's work has inspired a vast number of studies. We can examine only a small selection of some of the more significant research efforts. Michael Hindelang studied rural boys and girls in grades 6 through 12 on the East Coast. His self-report delinquency measure and questionnaire items were very similar to those devised by Hirschi. Hindelang found few differences between his results and those of Hirschi. Two of those differences, however, were significant. First, he found no relationship between attachment to mother and attachment to peers. Hirschi had observed a positive relationship (the stronger the attachment to the mother, the stronger the attachment to peers). Second, involvement in delinquency was positively related to attachment to peers.[15] Hirschi had found an inverse relationship (the stronger the attachment to peers, the less the involvement in delinquency).

Marvin Krohn and James Massey administered a self-report questionnaire to 3,056 male and female students in three midwestern states. These researchers were critical of Hirschi's conceptualization of both commitment and involvement, finding it difficult to understand how he separated the two. Meaningful involvement, they argued, is quite unlikely without commitment. Thus they combined commitment and involvement items and ended up with only three bonds: attachment, commitment, and belief.[16]

The study related these bonds to alcohol and marijuana use, use of strong drugs, minor de-

linquent behavior, and serious delinquent behavior. The results suggested that strong social bonds were more highly correlated with less serious deviance than with such delinquent acts as motor vehicle theft and assault. Also, the social bonds were more predictive of deviance in girls than in boys. Moreover, Krohn and Massey noticed that the commitment bond (now joined with involvement) was more significantly correlated with delinquent behavior than were the remaining two bonds (attachment and belief).

Michael Wiatrowski, David Griswold, and Mary Roberts, using the results of questionnaires administered to 2,213 tenth-grade boys at 86 schools, sought to answer three questions: First, are Hirschi's four bonds distinct entities? Second, why did Hirschi name only four bonds? Third, why were some factors related to educational and occupational aspiration (such as ability and family socioeconomic status) omitted from his questionnaire? To answer these questions, the authors constructed new scales for measuring attachment, commitment, involvement, and belief. They used a self-report measure to assess delinquency. They found little that is independent or distinctive about any of the bonds.[17]

Robert Agnew provided the first longitudinal test of Hirschi's theory by using data on 1,886 boys in the tenth and eleventh grades. Eight social control scales (parental attachment, grades, dating index, school attachment, involvement, commitment, peer attachment, and belief) were examined at two periods in relation to two self-report scales (one measuring total delinquency and the other measuring seriousness of delinquency). Agnew found the eight control scales to be strongly correlated with the self-reported delinquency, but the social control measures did little to predict the extent of future delinquency reported at the second administration. Agnew concluded that the importance of Hirschi's control theory has probably been exaggerated.[18]

Evaluation of Hirschi's Social Control Theory

While social control theory has held a position of prominence in criminology for several decades, it is not without weaknesses. For example, social control theory seeks to explain delinquency, not adult crime. It concerns attitudes, beliefs, desires, and behaviors that, though deviant, are often characteristic of adolescents. This is unfortunate because there is evidence that social bonds are significant explanatory factors in the analysis of postadolescent behavior also.[19] But Hirschi's social control theory is silent on this issue.

Questions also have been raised about the bonds in Hirschi's theory. Hirschi claims that antisocial acts result from a lack of affective values, beliefs, norms, and attitudes that inhibit delinquency. But these terms are never clearly defined.[20] Critics have also faulted Hirschi's work for

- The use of too few questionnaire items that measure social bonds.
- Failure to describe the chain of events that results in defective or inadequate social bonds.
- The creation of an artificial division of socialized versus unsocialized youths.
- The suggestion that social control theory explains why delinquency occurs when in fact it typically explains no more than 50 percent of delinquent behavior and only 1 to 2 percent of the variance in future delinquency.[21]

Despite the criticisms, Hirschi's work has made a major contribution to criminology. The mere fact that two decades of scholars have tried to validate and replicate it testifies to its importance.

SOCIAL CONTROL AND DRIFT

In the 1960s David Matza developed a significantly different perspective on social control that explains why some adolescents drift in and out of delinquency. According to Matza, juveniles sense a moral obligation to be bound by the law. A "bind" between a person and the law, something that creates responsibility and control, remains in place most of the time. When it is not in place, the youth may enter into a state of **drift**, or a period when

> the delinquent *transiently* exists in limbo between convention and crime, responding in

turn to the demands of each, flirting now with one, now the other, but postponing commitment, evading decision. Thus, he drifts between criminal and conventional action.[22]

If adolescents are indeed bound by the social order, how do they justify their delinquent acts? The answer is that they develop **techniques of neutralization** to rationalize their actions. These techniques are defense mechanisms that release the youth from the constraints of the moral order:

- Denial of responsibility. ("It wasn't my fault, I was a victim of circumstances.")
- Denial of injury. ("No one was hurt, and they have insurance, so what's the problem?")
- Denial of the victim. ("Anybody would have done the same thing in my position—I did what I had to do given the situation.")
- Condemnation of the condemner. ("I bet the judge and everyone on the jury has done much worse than what I was arrested for.")
- Appeal to higher loyalties. ("My friends were depending on me and I see them every day—what was I supposed to do?")[23]

Empirical support for drift theory has not been clear. Some studies show that delinquents consider such rationalizations valid,[24] while other research suggests that they do not. Further investigations also demonstrate that delinquents do not share the moral code or values of nondelinquents.[25]

PERSONAL AND SOCIAL CONTROL

Over the last forty years support has increased for the notion that both social (external) and personal (internal) control systems are important forces in keeping people from committing crimes. In other words, Hirschi's social bonds and Matza's drift paradigm may be inadequate by themselves to explain why people do not commit crimes.

Albert J. Reiss, a sociologist, was one of the first researchers to isolate a group of personal and social control factors. According to Reiss, delinquency is the result of (1) a failure to internalize socially accepted and prescribed norms

LEO CULLUM

*"Attention, please. At 8:45 A.M. on Tuesday, July 29, 2008, you are
all scheduled to take the New York State bar exam."*

of behavior; (2) a breakdown of internal controls; and (3) a lack of social rules that prescribe behavior in the family, the school, and other important social groups. To test these notions Reiss collected control-related data on 1,110 juvenile delinquents placed on probation in Cook County (Chicago), Illinois. He examined three sources of information: (1) a diverse set of data on such variables as family economic status and moral ideals and/or techniques of control by parents during childhood; (2) community/institutional information bearing on control, such as residence in a delinquency area and homeownership; and (3) personal control information, such as ego or superego controls, gleaned from clinical judgments of social workers and written psychiatric reports. Reiss concluded that measures of both personal and social control seem "to yield more efficient prediction of delinquent recidivism than items which are measures of the strength of social control."[26]

Six years after the publication of Reiss's study, Jackson Toby proposed a different personal/social control model. Toby discussed the complementary role of the social disorganization of a neighborhood and an individual's own stake in conformity. He agreed that the so-

cial disorganization of the slums explains why some communities have high crime rates while others do not—in the slums both the community and the family are powerless to control their members' behavior. Thieves and hoodlums usually come from such neighborhoods. But a great many law-abiding youngsters come from slums as well. Toby questioned how a theory that turned so much on group behavior could account for individual differences in response to a poor environment. In other words, how can the theory of social disorganization explain why only a few among so many slum youths actually commit crimes?[27]

According to Toby, the social disorganization approach can explain why one neighborhood has a much higher crime rate than another, but not why one particular individual becomes a hoodlum while another does not. What accounts for the difference is a differing stake in **conformity,** or correspondence of behavior to society's patterns, norms, or standards. One person may respond to conditions in a "bad" neighborhood by becoming hostile to conventional values, perhaps because he or she knows that the chances for success within a legitimate lifestyle are poor. Another person in the same neighborhood may still maintain his or her stake in conformity, and a commitment to abiding by the law. Toby reminds us that when we try to account for crime in general, we should look at both group-level explanations (social disorganization) and individual-level explanations (stake in conformity).

The idea that both internal and external factors are involved in controlling behavior has interested a number of scholars. Ivan Nye, for example, developed the notion that multiple control factors operate at the same time to determine human behavior. He argued that **internalized control**, or self-regulation, was a product of guilt aroused in the conscience when norms have been internalized. **Indirect control** comes from an individual's identification with noncriminals and a desire not to embarrass parents and well-socialized friends by acting against their expectations. Nye believes that social control involves "needs satisfaction," by which he means that control depends on how well a family can prepare the child for success at school, with peers, and in the workplace. Finally, **direct control**, a purely external control, depends on rules, restrictions, and punishments.[28]

Other researchers have looked at direct controls in different ways. Parental control, for example, may depend on such factors as a broken home, the mother's employment, and a large number of children in the family; such factors indicate some loss of direct control. Once again we find mixed results. Some studies indicate that there is very little relationship between a broken home and delinquency, except for minor offenses such as truancy and running away.[29] The same can be said about the consequences of a mother's employment and family size.[30] A national study of 1,886 males concluded, however, that direct parental control as measured by strictness and punitiveness is indeed correlated with delinquent behavior, and warned us not to dismiss this fact lightly. The question remains open, however.[31]

CONTAINMENT THEORY

The broadest extension of the relationship between personal and social controls is found in Walter Reckless's presentation of containment theory.[32] **Containment theory** assumes that there exists for every individual a containing external structure and a protective internal structure, both of which provide defense, protection, or insulation against delinquency. According to Reckless, outer containment, or the structural buffer that holds the person in bounds, can be found in the following components:

- A role that provides a guide for a person's activities;
- A set of reasonable limits and responsibilities;
- An opportunity for the individual to achieve status;
- Cohesion among members of a group, including joint activity and togetherness;
- A sense of belongingness (identification with the group);
- Identification with one or more persons within the group; and
- Provisions for supplying alternative ways and means of satisfaction (when one or more ways are closed).[33]

Inner containment or personal control is ensured by

- A good self-concept;
- Self-control;
- A strong ego;
- A well-developed conscience;
- A high frustration tolerance; and
- A high sense of responsibility.

Reckless suggests that the probability of deviance is directly related to the extent to which internal pushes (such as a need for immediate gratification, restlessness, and hostility), external pressures (such as poverty, unemployment, and blocked opportunities), and external pulls are controlled by one's inner and outer containment. The primary containment factor is found in one's self-concept, or the way one views oneself in relation to others, and to the world as well. A strong self-concept, coupled with some additional inner controls (such as a strong conscience and sense of responsibility) and outer controls, makes delinquency highly unlikely.

Table 7.1 shows how the probability of deviance changes as an individual's inner and outer containment weakens. But why is it important to examine inner and outer controls simultaneously? Consider John, a college freshman, who had extensive community ties and strong family attachments and was valedictorian of his high school class. He also was a dealer in cocaine. All efforts to explain John's drug selling would prove disappointing if measures of social control were used alone. In other words, according to Hirschi's social control theory, John should be a conformist—he should focus his efforts on becoming a pharmacist or teacher! Containment theory, on the other hand, would be sensitive to the fact that John, while socially controlled and bonded by external forces, had a poorly developed self-concept, had an immature or undeveloped conscience, and was extremely impulsive. In short, he was driven to drugs as a result of a poor set of inner controls.

Empirical Tests of Containment Theory

To test containment theory, Reckless and his associates asked how boys living in bad neighborhoods can grow up to be good, law-abiding citizens. How are these boys protected from crime-producing influences? To answer the question the researchers had high school teach-

ers in a high-crime neighborhood nominate boys whom they believed would neither commit delinquent acts nor come into contact with police and juvenile court. The 125 "good boys" scored high on a social responsibility test and low on a delinquency-proneness test. These boys avoided trouble, had good relations with parents and teachers, and had a good self-concept. They thought of themselves as obedient. Reckless concluded that nondelinquent boys adhere to conventional values even in bad neighborhoods if they maintain their positive self-image. It is this positive self-image that protects them from involvement in delinquent acts. In a follow-up study the research team compared "good boys" with those nominated by teachers as "bad boys" (those they believed were headed for trouble). The "good boys" scored better on parental relation, self-image, and social responsibility tests. Far more of the "bad boys" had indeed acquired police and juvenile court records.[34]

Evaluation of Containment Theory

Containment theory, like Hirschi's social control theory, has drawn significant criticism.[35] The most damaging has come from Clarence Schrag, who contends that the terminology used is vague and poorly defined; the theory is difficult to test empirically; and the theory fails to consider why certain poorly contained

TABLE 7.1 THE PROBABILITY OF DEVIANCE AS INDICATED BY INNER AND OUTER CONTAINMENT

OUTER CONTAINMENT (SOCIAL CONTROL)	INNER CONTAINMENT (PERSONAL CONTROL)	
	STRONG	WEAK
STRONG	+ +	+ −
WEAK	+ −	− −

+ + = very low
+ − = average
− − = very high

Source: Adapted from Walter C. Reckless, "A Non-causal Explanation: Containment Theory," *Excerpta Criminologia* 2 (1962): 131–132.

youths commit violent crimes while others commit property crimes.[36]

These criticisms are not easily dismissed. Moreover, because little empirical research has been done to validate the findings of Reckless and his colleagues over the intervening thirty years, evidence of the validity of containment theory is minimal.

THE INTEGRATION OF SOCIAL CONTROL THEORIES

Interest in social control theory stimulated a series of attempts to merge or integrate its premises with those of other prominent theories.[37] While the attraction of a "better" or "more powerful" integrated theory is understandable, the process of integration has some problems. First, the theories that are to be integrated must explain the same phenomenon. It would be difficult, for example, to merge a theory of burglary with a general theory of juvenile delinquency. Second, there are problems in selecting which theories to integrate. Should one choose the theory that appears to explain more criminality? Or perhaps the one that appears to be more valid? All too often the choice of theories to be integrated depends on the theories with which the researcher is most familiar or the one to which the researcher has developed an allegiance. Despite the inherent problems, important attempts have been made.

When we discussed the concept of anomie and its relation to strain theory (Chapter 5), we focused on the fact that a society's institutions often fail to provide the means to attain the society's goals. Initially it may seem that social control would be a strange fit with strain theory. What does lack of opportunity to get ahead have to do with attachment to parents or school? But the ways in which we are socialized, the values that are instilled in us, and the bonds that we develop are very closely related to social class. It is social class that helps to form our vision of cultural goals and the means to attain them.

In 1979 Delbert Elliott and his colleagues proposed a theory that integrated social control and strain theories. They suggested that limited or blocked opportunities and a subsequent failure to achieve cultural goals would weaken or even destroy a bond to the social order. In other words, even if a person establishes strong bonds in childhood, a series of bad experiences in school, in the community, and at home, coupled with blocked access to opportunities to advancement, would most likely lead to a weakening of those social bonds. As strain weakens social bonds, the chance of delinquency increases.[38]

Another integrated theory combines control with learning theory (Chapter 4). Terence Thornberry argues that the potential for delinquency begins with the weakening of a person's bonds to the conventional world (parents, school, and accepted values). But if the potential is to become a reality, one needs a social setting in which to learn delinquent values. It is quite clear that social position is also important. It is the poorest youngsters who are typically the least bonded and the most exposed to influences that can teach them criminal behavior.[39]

FROM THEORY TO PRACTICE

Social control theory tells us that people commit crimes when they have not adequately developed attachments, have not become involved in and committed to conventional lines of activity, and have not internalized the rules of society (or do not care about them). Given these assumptions, it follows that efforts to prevent crime must include the teaching of values. It is also necessary to devise ways to enhance individual bonds to society, commitment to the conventional order, and involvement in conventional activities. One way is to strengthen the informal institutions that socialize people and continue to regulate their behavior throughout life—the family, the school, and the workplace.

Findings from a study of sixty-six countries lend support to this premise (see Window to the World). The purpose of the study was to identify the ten countries in the world with the lowest crime rates and to try to determine what those countries had in common that helped them to keep their crime rates low. The countries seemed to have little in common. Some were very rich (Japan), others very poor (Peru). Their economic systems ranged from capitalist (Costa Rica) to socialist (Bulgaria). Some were urbanized (German Democratic Republic), others rural and underdeveloped (Nepal). In some countries unemployment was high (Republic of Ireland), in others low (Saudi Arabia); some had homogeneous populations (Algeria), others fairly heterogeneous populations (Switzerland). One common denominator, however, was found: all ten countries had a very strong informal social control system. Most countries had very strong, intact family structures. In some, especially the Moslem countries, religion dominated all aspects of daily life. And in most of the ten countries the citizens participated in creating their destiny; they were involved in taking care of the young, maintaining social cohesion, making their laws, running their towns, and in general creating a sense of community, which was passed on from one generation to the next.[40] (See Window to the World.)

Family   In the early 1980s an experimental school-based parent training program opened in Seattle, Washington, as part of a delinquency prevention project. First-graders in six schools were assigned to either an experimental classroom or a control classroom. The parents of those in the experimental group were given training and the parents of the children in the control group were not. The major premise of the experiment was that a child's bond to a family is crucial. To develop this bond, parents learned to provide an opportunity for the child to participate and succeed in a social unit such as the school (by demonstrating good study habits, for example) and to reinforce conformity or punish violations of the group's norms. Preliminary results suggest that such a training program decreases child aggressiveness and increases parental skills.[41]

School   A program called PATHE (Positive Action Through Holistic Education) operated in four middle schools and three high schools of Charleston County, South Carolina, between 1980 and 1983. The object was to reduce delinquency by strengthening students' commitment to school and attachment to conforming members; in other words, to bond young people to the conventional system. PATHE brought together students, school staff, and community to plan and implement a program that was designed to make a better school climate (encourage more open discussion), improve academic skills, and prepare students for careers. The results of the program were higher grades, better attendance, fewer dropouts, and increased commitment to education.[42]

Neighborhood   Historically the church and the family have helped to protect and maintain the social order in neighborhoods, to instill a sense of pride and comfort in their residents. This is no longer the case in many areas. The neighborhood as an institution of informal social control has become weak. Various agencies have tried to reverse this trend. Between 1981 and 1986 programs to prevent juvenile crime were implemented through neighborhood-based organizations in Chicago, Dallas, Los Angeles, New York, New Orleans, and San Diego. These federally funded programs sought to reduce crime by strengthening neighborhood cohesion. Each program assessed the needs of its residents and then set up crisis intervention centers, mediation (between youngsters and school, family, or police or between warring gangs), youth training, supervision programs, and family support systems. Within the first three years, serious juvenile crime decreased in three of the target areas (in comparison with their respective cities).[43] Hundreds of such community crime-prevention projects around the country have been organized by government agencies, private persons, and religious groups.[44] They have made a local impact, but they have not been able to change the national crime rate. The most successful models, however, may offer a plan for crime prevention on a broader, perhaps even a national scale.

WINDOW TO THE WORLD

Low Crime Rates—And Why

In each of five major regions of the world the two countries with the lowest crime rates were identified. What did those ten countries have in common that kept the crime rates low? An analysis of a vast amount of quantitative data (for example, income, population density, and numbers in the work force) yielded no answers; an analysis of qualitative information did. Here are the results:

The major findings of the qualitative part of the study suggest that all ten countries appear to have developed some form of strong social control, outside and apart from the criminal justice system. The social control systems... do not aim to control by formal restraint. Rather, they transmit and maintain values by providing for a sharing of norms and by ensuring cohesiveness.

Among those social control systems, there is, above all, the family. Most of the countries under study have seen little disruption of their strong family system. For Nepal, where no rural-to-urban flight has yet occurred, the clans, as extended families, remain as a formidably effective system serving the preservation of harmony and the transmission of values.

Extended families form the basis of the social structure by serving as the social, economic, and, often, the political unit. Thus, Peruvian kinship groups provide the mainstay of stability among both Indians (where tribal values are more important than individual needs) and Hispanics (with their overriding commitment to family loyalty). Costa Rican families are characterized as tightly-knit units with defined membership roles and rigid

discipline, and that is true for Swiss families. Saudi Arabian and Algerian societies expect family loyalties to supersede all others, as dictated by the Moslem tradition. In Bulgaria, young people stay home and close to the family where they receive a solid grounding in social and moral duties. The Japanese system is patriarchal in structure, highly indulgent and highly restrictive. Any disgrace which befalls the individual shames the entire family.

It is noteworthy that among our sample of ten countries, family controls have been maintained even in the wake of modernization, i.e., mechanization of agriculture and dwindling agricultural employment opportunities and industrialization with new employment opportunities at distant industrial sites, usually urban areas. Bulgaria, the

REVIEW

The term "social control" has taken on a wide variety of meanings. In general, it encompasses any mechanism that leads to conformity to social norms. Mainstream studies of social control take one of two approaches. Macrosociological studies focus on formal systems of social control. Most contemporary criminological research takes the microsociological approach, focusing on informal control systems. Travis

Hirschi's social control theory has had a long-lasting impact on the scholarly community. Hirschi posited four social bonds that promote adherence to society's values: attachment, commitment, involvement, and belief. The stronger these bonds, Hirschi claimed, the less likelihood of delinquency.

Most investigators today believe that personal (inner) controls are as important as social

German Democratic Republic, Japan, Saudi Arabia, and Switzerland are among the countries which were faced with that challenge. Each has responded with imagination and within the context of its own cultural traditions and ideological commitments. Each has made a deliberate and costly governmental effort to keep the family intact as a strong social control organ. Just as one can plan for and work toward crime control, one can plan for and work toward preservation of the viability of the family and, secondarily, thereby to plan for crime control.

Nevertheless, the research noted that in some countries extended families were losing control, and in some the nuclear family was endangered. These countries were challenged to find substitutes for the social control of the clan.

Japan, perhaps, has been most fortunate in the discovery of a "surrogate family" to supplement the dwindling natural family. There emerged, in Japanese society, the concept of the industrial community, which young workers enter pretty much as they would have entered the clan of an in-law in times past. Just as the production unit of Socialist countries serves as a surrogate or additional family, the industrial community of a capitalist Japanese enterprise provides many of the protections, services, and controls which the clan once had available, ranging virtually from birth to death, and including child rearing services, leisure time activities, vacations, pensions, and burial. While the Japanese industrial community was probably organized as a means of ensuring efficient industrial productivity, it nevertheless turned out to be a culturally harmonious agency of social service and control.

From the Japanese factory to the Bulgarian commune to the Nepalese village Panchayat to the Swiss Gemeinde and Canton to the Algerian assemblies, there appears to be a steady effort on the part of most of the ten countries to maintain the involvement of the citizens in the affairs which concern their own destiny. The sharing of activities "for the common good" accounts for an apparently strong social solidarity.

The researcher called this state of social solidarity achieved through sharing of values **synnomie** to denote the opposite of anomie. The term, like anomie, is derived from the Greek: *syn* meaning *with* and *nomos* meaning *norms* or *values*. Anomie appears to mark societies with high crime rates; synnomie appears to mark societies with low crime rates.

Source: Freda Adler, *Nations Not Obsessed with Crime* (Littleton, Colo.: Fred B. Rothman & Co., 1983), pp. 130–132.

---

controls in keeping people from committing crimes. Albert Reiss found that personal controls reinforce social controls. Jackson Toby stressed the importance of a stake in conformity as a factor that keeps a person from responding to social disorganization with delinquent behavior. Ivan Nye argued that multiple control factors operate simultaneously to determine human behavior: internalized, indirect, and direct controls.

The containment theory of Walter Reckless assumes that every person has a containing external structure (a role in a social group with reasonable limits and responsibilities and alternative means of attaining satisfaction) and a protective internal structure that depends on a good self-concept, self-control, a well-developed conscience, a tolerance for frustration, and a strong sense of responsibility.

In efforts to reduce delinquency, a variety of programs have been instituted to help parents, schools, and neighborhood groups develop social controls.

KEY TERMS

attachment
belief
commitment
conformity
containment theory
direct control
drift
indirect control

internalized control
involvement
macrosociological studies
microsociological studies
social control theory
synnomie
techniques of neutralization

NOTES

1. William Golding, *Lord of the Flies* (New York: Coward McCann, 1954), p. 31.

2. Jack P. Gibbs, *Social Control,* Warner module no. 1. See also Freda Adler, *Nations Not Obsessed with Crime* (Littleton, Colo.: Fred B. Rothman, 1983).

3. Travis Hirschi, *Causes of Delinquency* (Berkeley: University of California Press, 1969).

4. Donald J. Black, *The Behavior of Law* (New York: Academic Press, 1976), p. 105.

5. Nanette J. Davis and Bo Anderson, *Social Control: The Production of Deviance in the Modern State* (New York: Irvington, 1983); S. Cohen and A. Scull, eds., *Social Control and the State* (New York: St. Martin's Press, 1983).

6. Jackson Toby, "Social Disorganization and Stake in Conformity: Complementary Factors in the Predatory Behavior of Hoodlums," *Journal of Criminal Law, Criminology, and Police Science* 48 (1957): 12–17.

7. Scott Briar and Irving Piliavin, "Delinquency, Situational Inducements, and Commitment to Conformity," *Social Problems* 13 (1965): 41.

8. Ibid., p. 36.

9. Hirschi, *Causes of Delinquency.*

10. See John Bowlby, *Attachment and Loss,* 2 vols. (New York: Basic Books, 1969, 1973); "Forty-four Juvenile Thieves: Their Characteristics and Home Life," *International Journal of Psychoanalysis* 25 (1944): 19–25; and *The Making and Breaking of Affectional Bonds* (London: Tavistock, 1979).

11. Hirschi, *Causes of Delinquency.*

12. Ibid., p. 145.

13. Ibid., p. 169.

14. Hirschi, *Causes of Delinquency.*

15. Michael J. Hindelang, "Causes of Delinquency: A Partial Replication and Extension," *Social Problems* 20 (1973): 471–487.

16. Marvin D. Krohn and James L. Massey, "Social Control and Delinquent Behavior: An Examination of the Elements of the Social Bond," *Sociological Quarterly* 21 (1980): 529–544. For a critique of this study see Richard L. Amdur, "Testing Causal Models of Delinquency: A Methodological Critique," *Criminal Justice and Behavior* 16 (1989): 35–62.

17. Michael D. Wiatrowski, David Griswold, and Mary K. Roberts, "Social Control Theory and Delinquency," *American Sociological Review* 46 (1985): 525–541.

18. Robert Agnew, "Social Control Theory and Delinquency: A Longitudinal Test," *Criminology* 23 (1985): 47–61. See also Michael D. Wiatrowski and Kristine L. Anderson, "The Dimensionality of the Bond," *Journal of Quantitative Criminology* 3 (1987): 65–81; Jennifer Friedman and Dennis P. Rosenbaum, "Social Control Theory: The Salience of Components by Age, Gender, and Type of Crime," *Journal of Quantitative Criminology* 4 (1988): 363–381; James R. Lasley, "Toward a Control Theory of White-Collar Offending," *Journal of Quantitative Criminology* 4 (1988): 347–362.

19. Karen S. Rook, "Promoting Social Bonding: Strategies for Helping the Lonely and Socially Isolated," *American Psychologist* 39 (1984): 1389–1407.

20. Milton Rokeach, *The Nature of Human Values* (New York: Free Press, 1973).

21. See Donald J. Shoemaker, *Theories of Delinquency: An Examination of Explanations of De-*

linquent Behavior (New York: Oxford University Press, 1984), pp. 112–175, for an evaluation of social control theory.

22. David Matza, *Delinquency and Drift* (New York: Wiley, 1964), p. 21.

23. Gresham Sykes and David Matza, "Techniques of Neutralization: A Theory of Delinquency," *American Sociological Review* 22 (1957): 664–670. For a more recent look at techniques of neutralization, see John Hamlin, "The Misplaced Role of Rational Choice in Neutralization Theory," *Criminology* 26 (1988): 425–438.

24. Richard A. Ball, "An Empirical Exploration of Neutralization Theory," *Criminologica* 4 (1966): 103–120. See also N. William Minor, "The Neutralization of Criminal Offense," *Criminology* 18 (1980): 103–120.

25. Robert Gordon, James F. Short, Jr., D. Cartwright, and Fred L. Strodtbeck, "Values and Gang Delinquency: A Study of Street Corner Groups," *American Journal of Sociology* 69 (1963): 109–128.

26. Albert J. Reiss, "Delinquency as the Failure of Personal and Social Controls," *American Sociological Review* 16 (1951): 206. See also William S. Laufer, "The Development of a Measure of Psychosocial Control," *Journal of Clinical Psychology*, in press.

27. Toby, "Social Disorganization," p. 137.

28. Francis Ivan Nye, *Family Relationships and Delinquent Behavior* (New York: Wiley, 1958).

29. L. Edward Wells and Joseph H. Rankin, "Broken Homes and Juvenile Delinquency: An Empirical Review," *Criminal Justice Abstracts* 17 (1985): 249–272; Lawrence Rosen and Kathleen Neilson, "Broken Homes," in *Contemporary Criminology*, ed. Leonard Savitz and Norman Johnston (New York: Wiley, 1982).

30. Mary Reige, "Parental Affection and Juvenile Delinquency in Girls," *British Journal of Criminology* 12 (1972): 55–73; Hirschi, *Causes of Delinquency*, p. 237; Lawrence Rosen, "Family and Delinquency: Structure or Function?" *Criminology* 23 (1985): 553–573.

31. L. Edward Wells and Joseph H. Rankin, "Direct Parental Controls and Delinquency," *Criminology* 26 (1988): 263–285. See also Douglas Smith and Raymond Pa-ternoster, "The Gender Gap in Theories of Deviance: Issues and Evidence," *Journal of Research in Crime and Delinquency* 24 (1987): 140–172; John Hagan, A. R. Gillis, and John Simpson, "The Class Structure of Gender and Delinquency: Toward a Power-Control Theory of Common Delinquent Behavior," *American Journal of Sociology* 90 (1985): 1151–1178. For a discussion of paternal and maternal patterns of control on male and female children, see Gary D. Hill and Maxine P. Atkinson, "Gender, Familial Control, and Delinquency," *Criminology* 26 (1988): 127–149. In a thirty-year follow-up of 250 boys treated in the Cambridge-Somerville Youth Study, Joan McCord found that poor parental supervision was the best predictor of property and personal crime later in life: "Some Child-Rearing Antecedents of Criminal Behavior in Adult Men," *Journal of Personality and Social Psychology* 36 (1979): 1477–1486. Lee Robins reports similar results in "Sturdy Childhood Predictors of Adult Outcomes: Republications from Longitudinal Studies," in *Stress and Mental Disorders*, ed. J. E. Barrett, R. M. Rose, and G. L. Kleerman, pp. 219–235 (New York: Raven, 1979). London studies by D. J. West and David P. Farrington found that cruel parents, poor supervision, passive parental attitudes, and parental conflict predicted juvenile delinquency. See their *Who Becomes Delinquent?* (London: Heinemann, 1973). For an examination of the family backgrounds of female offenders, see Jill Leslie Rosenbaum, "Family Dysfunction and Female Delinquency," *Crime and Delinquency* 35 (1989): 31–44.

32. Walter C. Reckless, "A New Theory of Delinquency and Crime," *Federal Probation* 25 (1961): 42–46; Walter C. Reckless, Simon Dinitz, and Barbara Kay, "The Self Component in Potential Delinquency and Potential Non-delinquency," *American Sociological Review* 22 (1957): 556–570; Walter C. Reckless, Simon Dinitz, and E. Murray, "Self-concept as an Insulator Against Delinquency," *American Sociological Review* 21 (1956): 744–746; Frank R. Scarpitti, Ellen Murray, Simon Dinitz, and Walter C. Reckless, "The Good Boy in a High Delinquency Area: Four Years Later," *American Sociological Review* 25 (1960): 555–558; Simon Dinitz, Barbara Kay, and Walter C. Reckless, "Delinquency Proneness and School Achieve-

ment," *Educational Research Bulletin* 36 (1957): 131–136; Simon Dinitz, Walter C. Reckless, and Barbara Kay, "A Self-Gradient Among Potential Delinquents," *Journal of Criminal Law, Criminology, and Police Science* 49 (1958): 230–233; S. Dinitz, Frank R. Scarpitti, and Walter C. Reckless, "Delinquency Vulnerability: A Cross Group and Longitudinal Analysis," *American Sociological Review* 27 (1962): 515–517; E. P. Donald and Simon Dinitz, "Self-concept and Delinquency Proneness," in *Interdisciplinary Problems in Criminology*, ed. Walter C. Reckless and C. Newman (Columbus: Ohio State University Press, 1964).

33. Walter C. Reckless, "A Non-causal Explanation: Containment Theory," *Excerpta Criminologia* 2 (1962): 131–132.

34. Reckless et al., "Self-concept as an Insulator"; Scarpitti et al., "Good Boy in a High Delinquency Area."

35. Gary F. Jensen, "Delinquency and Adolescent Self-conceptions: A Study of the Personal Relevance of Infraction," *Social Problems* 20 (1972): 84–103; S. S. Tangri and M. Schwartz, "Delinquency and the Self-concept Variable," *Journal of Criminal Law and Criminology* 58 (1967): 182–190.

36. Clarence Schrag, *Crime and Justice American Style* (Washington, D.C.: U.S. Government Printing Office, 1971), pp. 82–89.

37. R. J. Hepburn, "Testing Alternative Models of Delinquency Causation," *Journal of Criminal Law and Criminology* 67 (1977): 450–460; T. Ross Matsueda, "Testing Control Theory and Differential Association: A Causal Modeling Approach," *American Sociological Review* 47 (1982): 489–497; W. E. Thompson, J. Mitchell, and R. A. Dodder, "An Empirical Test of Hirschi's Control Theory of Delinquency," *Deviant Behavior* 5 (1984): 11–22; Frank S. Pearson and Neil A. Weiner, "Toward an Integration of Criminological Theories," *Journal of Criminal Law and Criminology* 76 (1985): 116–150.

38. Delbert S. Elliott, Suzanne S. Ageton, and R. J. Canter, "An Integrated Theoretical Perspective on Delinquent Behavior," *Journal of Research in Crime and Delinquency* 16 (1979): 3–27.

39. Terence P. Thornberry, "Toward an Inter-actional Theory of Delinquency," *Criminology* 25 (1987): 863–891. See also Madeline G. Aultman and Charles F. Wellford, "Toward an Integrated Model of Delinquency Causation: An Empirical Analysis," *Sociology and Social Research* 63 (1979): 316–317.

40. Adler, *Nations Not Obsessed with Crime*. See also W. Timothy Austin, "Crime and Custom in an Orderly Society: The Singapore Prototype," *Criminology* 25 (1987): 279–294; Charles Fenwick, "Culture, Philosophy and Crime: The Japanese Experience," *International Journal of Comparative and Applied Criminal Justice* 9 (1985): 76–81; J. M. Day and William S. Laufer, eds., *Crime, Values, and Religion* (Norwood, N.J.: Ablex, 1987); Freda Adler and William S. Laufer, "Social Control and the Workplace," in *US-USSR Approaches to Urban Crime Prevention*, eds. James Finckenauer and Alexander Yakovlev (Moscow: Soviet Academy of State and Law, 1987).

41. J. David Hawkins, Richard F. Catalano, Gwen Jones, and David Fine, "Delinquency Prevention Through Parent-Training: Results and Issues from Work in Progress," in *From Children to Citizens*, vol. 3, *Families, Schools, and Delinquency Prevention*, ed. James Q. Wilson and Glenn C. Loury, pp. 186–204 (New York: Springer-Verlag, 1987).

42. Denise C. Gottfredson, "An Empirical Test of School-Based Environmental and Individual Interventions to Reduce the Risk of Delinquent Behavior," *Criminology* 24 (1986): 705–731.

43. Jeffrey Fagan, "Neighborhood Education, Mobilization, and Organization for Juvenile Crime Prevention," *Annals of the American Academy for the Advancement of Political and Social Sciences* 494 (1987): 54–70.

44. For an interesting examination of community social control, see David Weisburd, "Vigilantism as Community Social Control: Developing a Quantitative Criminological Model," *Journal of Quantitative Criminology* 4 (1988): 137–153. For a discussion of how interventions must make sure that labeling a child or family as a problem does not affect the child's self-concept or social involvement, see Charles E. Wellford, "Delinquency Prevention and Labeling," in Wilson and Loury, *Families, Schools, and Delinquency Prevention*, pp. 257–267.

8

ALTERNATIVE EXPLANATIONS OF CRIME: LABELING, CONFLICT, AND RADICAL THEORIES

History is punctuated by eras of social and political turmoil, and each one has produced profound changes in people's lives. Perhaps no such era was so significant for criminology as the 1960s. A society with conservative values was shaken out of its complacency when young people, blacks, women, and other disadvantaged groups demanded a part in the shaping of national policies. They saw the gaps between philosophical political demands and reality: blacks had little opportunity to advance, women were kept in an inferior status, old politicians made wars in which the young had to die. Rebellion broke out, and some criminologists joined it.

These criminologists turned away from theories that explained crime by reference to characteristics of the offender or of the social structure. They set out to demonstrate that people become criminals not because of some internal flaw but because of what others with power, especially those in the criminal justice system, do. The alternative explanations largely reject the consensus model of crime, on which all earlier theories rested, whether of the classical or the positivist school. The new theories not only question the traditional explanations of the creation and enforcement of the criminal law but blame that law for the making of criminals. (See Table 8.1.) It may not sound so radical to assert that unless an act is made criminal by law, no person who performs that act can be adjudicated a criminal. The exponents of the contemporary alternative explanations of crime grant that much. But they also ask: Who makes these laws in the first place? And why? Is breaking such laws the most important criterion for being a criminal? Are all people who break these laws criminals? Do all members of society agree that those singled out by the criminal law to be called criminals are criminals, and not others?

LABELING THEORY

The 1950s was a period of general prosperity and pride for Americans. Yet some social scientists became uneasy about the complacency they saw. They turned their attention to the social order. They noted that some of the ideals

TABLE 8.1   EXPLANATIONS OF CRIMINAL LAWS AND OF CRIMINAL BEHAVIOR AND FOCUS OF STUDY OF FOUR CRIMINOLOGICAL PERSPECTIVES

PERSPECTIVE	ORIGIN OF CRIMINAL LAW	CAUSES OF CRIMINAL BEHAVIOR	FOCUS OF STUDY
Traditional/ consensus	Laws reflect values shared by the community.	Psychological, biological, or sociological factors.	Psychological and biological factors (Chap. 4). Unequal distribution of means to reach society's established goals (Chap. 5) Learning of criminal behavior in disorganized neighborhoods (Chap. 5). Criminal behavior considered acceptable or even "right" by some subcultures (Chap. 6). Social control by society's institutions (family, school, others) (Chap. 7).
Labeling	Persons or groups in power create the laws, decide who will be rule breakers.	The process that defines (or labels) certain persons as criminals.	Effects of stigmatizing a person by the label "criminal"; sociopolitical factors behind reform legislation (e.g., juvenile court, sentencing, laws, imprisonment); origin of laws (e.g., vagrancy, theft); deviant behavior (prostitution, public drunkenness, and drug addiction) (Chap. 8).
Conflict	Powerful groups make laws that support their interests by making illegal any behavior that might be a threat.	Interests of one group do not coincide with needs of another. Behaviors common among society's disadvantaged have greater likelihood of being called "crime" than those activities in which the powerful participate.	Bias and discrimination in criminal justice system; differential crime rates of powerful and powerless; development of criminal laws (e.g., theft, vagrancy) by those in power; relationship between rulers and ruled (Chap. 8).
Critical (Marxist)	Laws serve interests of the wealthy ruling class by protecting its property and making criminal any behavior that threatens it.	Struggle between classes, which relates to distribution of resources in a capitalist system.	Relationship between crime and economics; ways in which state serves interests of capitalists; solution to crime problem based on collapse of capitalism; how traditional criminologists serve state's interests in controlling lower class (Chap. 8).

the United States had fought for in World War II had not been achieved at home. Human rights existed on paper but were often lacking in practice. It was clear, for example, that blacks continued to live as second-class citizens. Even though the Fourteenth Amendment to the Constitution guaranteed blacks equal rights, neither the law of the country nor the socioeconomic system provided them with equal opportunities. Nowhere was this fact more apparent than in the criminal justice system. Social scientists and liberal lawyers pressed for change, and the Supreme Court, under Chief Justice Earl Warren, responded. In case after case the Court found a pervasive influence of rules and customs that violated the concepts of **due process,** under which a person cannot be deprived of life, liberty, or property without lawful procedures, and **equal protection,** under which no one can be denied the safeguards of the law. The result of hundreds of Supreme Court decisions was that both black and white citizens now were guaranteed the right to counsel in all criminal cases, freedom from self-incrimination, and other rights enumerated in the first ten amendments to the Constitution.[1] Nevertheless, a great deal of social injustice remained.

In this social climate, a small group of social scientists, referred to as labeling theorists, began to explore how and why certain acts were defined as criminal or, more broadly, deviant behavior, and others were not, and how and why certain people were defined as criminal or deviant. These theorists viewed criminals not as inherently evil persons engaged in inherently wrong acts but rather as individuals who had had criminal status conferred upon them by both the criminal justice system and the community at large. Viewed from this perspective, the criminal acts themselves are not particularly significant; the social reaction to them, however, is. Thus deviance and its control involve a process of social definition in which the response of others to an individual's behavior is the key influence on subsequent behavior and on individuals' view of themselves. The sociologist Howard S. Becker has written:

> Deviance is not a quality of the act the person commits, but rather a consequence of the application by others of rules and sanctions to an "offender." The deviant is one to whom that label has successfully been applied; deviant behavior is behavior that people so label.[2]

In focusing on the ways in which social interactions create deviance, **labeling theory** declares that the reaction of other people and the subsequent effects of those reactions create deviance. Once it becomes known that a person has engaged in deviant acts, he or she is segregated from conventional society, and a label such as "thief," "whore," or "junkie" is attached to the transgressor. This process of segregation creates "outsiders" (as Becker called them), or outcasts from society, who begin to associate with others who also have been cast out. As more people begin to think of these people as deviants and to respond to them accordingly, the deviants react to the response by continuing to engage in the behavior society now expects of them. Through this process their self-images gradually change as well. In sum, the key factor is the label that is attached to an individual: "If men define situations as real, they are real in their consequences."[3]

The Origins of Labeling Theory

The intellectual roots of labeling theory can be traced to the post–World War I work of Charles Horton Cooley, William I. Thomas, and George Herbert Mead. These scholars, who viewed the human self as formed through a process of social interaction, were called **social interactionists.** In 1918 Mead likened the impact of social labeling to "the angel with the fiery sword at the gate who can cut one off from the world to which he belongs."[4] Labeling, then, separates the good from the bad, the conventional from the deviant. Mead's interest in deviance focused not on the consequences of the act but on the social interactions by which one becomes a deviant. The person is not just a fixed structure whose action is the result of certain factors acting upon it. Rather, social behavior develops in a continuous process of action and reaction.[5] The way we perceive ourselves, our self-concept, is built not only on what we think of ourselves but also on what others think of us.

Somewhat later, the historian Frank Tannenbaum (1893–1969) used the same argument in his study of the causes of criminal behavior. He described a process for the creation of a criminal. Breaking windows, climbing onto roofs, and playing truant are all normal parts of the adolescent search for excitement and adventure. Local merchants and others who experience these activities may consider them a nuisance or perhaps even evil. This conflict is the beginning of the process by which the evil act transforms the transgressor into an evil individual. From that point on, the evil individuals are separated from those in the conventional society. Given a criminal label, they gradually begin to think of themselves as they have been officially defined. Tannenbaum maintained that it is the process of labeling, or the "dramatization of evil," that locks a mischievous boy into a delinquent role ("the person becomes the thing he is described as being"). Accordingly, "the entire process of dealing with young delinquents is mischievous insofar as it identifies him to himself and to the environment as a delinquent person."[6] Thus the system starts with a child in trouble and ends up with a juvenile delinquent.

Basic Assumptions of Labeling Theory

In the 1940s the sociologist Edwin Lemert elaborated on Tannenbaum's discussion by formulating the basic assumptions of labeling theory.[7] He reminded us that people are constantly involved in behavior that runs the risk of being labeled delinquent or criminal. Although many run that risk only a few are labeled. The reason for this disparity, Lemert contended, is that there are two kinds of deviant acts: primary and secondary.[8] Primary deviations are those initial deviant acts that bring on the first social response. These acts do not affect the individual's self-concept. It is the secondary deviations, the acts that follow the societal response to the primary deviation, that are of major concern. These are the acts that result from the change in self-concept brought about by the labeling process.[9] The scenario goes something like this:

1. An individual commits a simple deviant act (primary deviation), such as throwing a stone at a neighbor's car.

2. There is an informal social reaction; the neighbor gets angry.

3. The individual continues to break rules (primary deviations)—lets the neighbor's dog out of the yard.

4. There is increased but still primary social reaction; the neighbor tells the youth's parents.

5. The individual commits a more serious deviant act; he is caught shoplifting (still primary deviation).

6. There is a formal reaction; the youth is adjudicated a "juvenile delinquent" in juvenile court.

7. The youth is now labeled "delinquent" by the court and "bad" by the neighborhood, by his conventional peers, and by others.

8. The youth begins to think of himself as "delinquent"; he joins other unconventional youths.

9. The individual commits another, yet more serious deviant act (secondary deviation)—robs a local grocery store with members of a gang.

10. The individual is returned to juvenile court, has more offenses added to his record, is cast out further from conventional society, and takes on a completely deviant lifestyle.

According to Lemert's theory, secondary deviance sets in after the community has become aware of an individual's primary deviance. Individuals experience "a continuing sense of injustice, which [is] reinforced by job rejections, police cognizance, and strained interaction with normals."[10] In short, deviant individuals have to bear the stigma of the delinquent label, just as English and American convicts, as late as the eighteenth century, bore stigmas in the form of an *M* for murder or a *T* for thief, burned or cut into their bodies to designate them as persons to be shunned.[11] Once such a label is attached to a person, a deviant or criminal career has been set in motion. Yet the full significance of labeling theory was not recognized, either in Europe or in the United States, until political events provided the opportunity.[12]

Labeling in the 1960s

The 1960s witnessed a movement among students and professors to join advocacy groups and become activists in the social causes that rapidly were gaining popularity on college campuses across the nation, such as equal rights for minorities, liberation for women, and peace for humankind. The generation of the 1960s had become disenchanted with an establishment that seemed to have given only lip service to social change. The protests took many forms—demonstrations and rallies, sit-ins and teach-ins, beards and long hair, rock music and marijuana, dropping out of school, burning draft cards. Arrests of middle-class youth increased rapidly. Crime was no longer confined to the ghettos. People asked whether arrests were being made for behavior that was not really criminal. Were the real criminals the legislators and policy makers who pursued a criminal war in Vietnam while creating the artificial crime of draft-card burning at home? Were the real criminals the National Guardsmen who shot and killed campus demonstrators at Kent State University? Labeling theorists made their appearance and provided answers. The sociologist Kai Erickson has put it well:

> Deviance is not a property inherent in certain forms of behavior; it is a property conferred upon these forms by audiences which directly or indirectly witness them. The critical variable in the study of deviance, then, is the social audience rather than the individual actor, since it is the audience which eventually determines whether or not any episode or behavior or any class of episodes is labeled deviant.[13]

Edwin Schur, one of the leading labeling theorists of the 1960s, elaborated Erickson's explanation:

> Human behavior is deviant to the extent that it comes to be viewed as involving a personally discreditable departure from a group's normative expectation, and it elicits interpersonal and collective reactions that serve to "isolate," "treat," "correct," or "punish" individuals engaged in such behavior.[14]

Schur also expanded on Lemert's "secondary deviance" with his own concept of "secondary elaboration," by which he meant that the effects of the labeling process become so significant that individuals who want to escape from their deviant groups and return to the conventional world find it difficult to do so. Schur points to members of the gay and drug cultures.[15] The strength of the label, once acquired, tends to exclude such people permanently from the mainstream culture.[16] Schur found that involvement in activities that are disapproved of may very well lead to more participation in deviance than one had originally planned, and so increase the social distance between the person labeled deviant and the conventional world.[17]

The labeling theorists then asked: Who makes up the rules that define deviant behavior, including crime? According to Howard Becker, it is the "moral entrepreneurs"—the people whose high social position gives them the power to make and enforce the social rules by which members of society have to live. By making the rules that define the criminal, Becker argues, certain members of society create outsiders. The whole process thus becomes a political one, pitting the rule makers against the rule breakers. (See Window to the World.) Becker goes even further, suggesting that people can be labeled without actually committing a deviant act, by being falsely accused. As long as others believe that someone has participated in a given deviant behavior, that individual will experience society's negative social reaction. People can also suffer the effects of labeling when they have committed a deviant act that has not been discovered. Since most people know how they would be labeled if they were apprehended, these secret deviants may experience the same labeling effects as those who have been caught.[18]

WINDOW TO THE WORLD

Jomo Kenyatta, Who Reversed the Labels

As a youth Jomo Kenyatta was trained in the virtues of his East African tribal culture. Alert, bright, and inquisitive, he moved to the big city, Nairobi. There he learned European ways swiftly. While working at menial and clerical jobs, he obtained a superior education. He even earned a degree in England. In 1922 he joined a group of fellow Africans who yearned for independence from colonial rule. He soon became a leader in the movement. Several times he visited Europe, working, studying, taking leading roles at conferences of labor unionists and liberals intent on ending colonial rule. He visited Moscow twice.

In 1952, seven years after the end of World War II, a rebellion broke out against colonial rule in East Africa—the Mau Mau uprising. The East Africans wanted self-determination, which had long been proclaimed by the United Nations. Yet the white settlers and the colonial power resisted. The Mau Maus were declared to be terrorists by the British authorities. The struggle was bloody on both sides. Because Kenyatta had visited Moscow, the British labeled him a Marxist terrorist and arrested him. In 1953 he was convicted of terrorist crimes; he was found to have managed the Mau Mau uprising—a charge he steadfastly denied. They called him "leader of darkness and death."

In 1960 he was still in prison, though he had already served his full sentence. All the same, the Kenyans elected him president of the Kenya National Union. Finally released from prison in 1961, he made his triumphant entry into London in 1962 to negotiate the constitutional terms for Kenya's independence. In 1963 he won the preindependence election and became prime minister of the newly independent state of Kenya. He held this post until his death on August 22, 1978. During his premiership, Kenyatta turned Kenya into the most prosperous and democratic country in Africa. He always was the most pro-British of African leaders.

In an instant Kenyatta's labels had been switched. The Marxist terrorist, the violator of (colonial) laws became a national—indeed, an international—leader and statesman. It was not Kenyatta who changed. It was the law that changed his status and his label, overnight. But the Kenyatta story raises many more questions for labeling, conflict, and radical criminologists. Foremost among them is the justness of a cause (determined by whom?) to overturn an unjust (as determined by whom?) order. Does the new order necessarily guarantee justness (as perceived by whom?). In virtually no country on earth has nationhood been achieved without violent struggle. Everywhere yesterday's criminal rebel is tomorrow's heroic patriot.

Empirical Evidence for Labeling Theory

Empirical investigations of labeling theory have been carried out by researchers in many disciplines by a variety of methodologies. One group of investigators arranged to have eight sane volunteers apply for admission to various mental hospitals. In order to get themselves admitted, the subjects claimed to be hearing voices, a symptom of schizophrenia. Once admitted to the hospital, however, they behaved normally. The experiences of these pseudopatients clearly reveal the effects of labeling (see Criminological Focus). Doctors, nurses, and assistants treated them as schizophrenic patients. They interpreted the normal everyday behavior of the pseudopatients as manifestations of illness. An early arrival at the lunchroom, for example, was described as exhibiting "oral aggressive" behavior; a patient seen writing something was referred to as a "compulsive note-taker." Interestingly enough, none of the other patients believed that the pseudopatients were mad; they assumed that they were researchers or journalists. When at length the subjects were discharged from

CRIMINOLOGICAL FOCUS

On Being Sane in Insane Places

As far as I can determine, diagnoses were in no way affected by the relative health of the circumstances of a pseudopatient's life. Rather, the reverse occurred: the perception of his circumstances was shaped entirely by the diagnosis. A clear example of such translation is found in the case of a pseudopatient who had had a close relationship with his mother but was rather remote from his father during his early childhood. During adolescence and beyond, however, his father became a close friend, while his relationship with his mother cooled. His present relationship with his wife was characteristically close and warm. Apart from occasional angry exchanges, friction was minimal. The children had rarely been spanked. Surely there is nothing especially pathological about such a history. Indeed, many readers may see a similar pattern in their own experiences, with no markedly deleterious

consequences. Observe, however, how such a history was translated in the psychopathological context, this from the case summary prepared after the patient was discharged.

This white 39-year-old male...manifests a long history of considerable ambivalence in close relationships, which begins in early childhood. A warm relationship with his mother cools during his adolescence. A distant relationship to his father is described as becoming very intense. Affective stability is absent. His attempts to control emotionality with his wife and children are punctuated by angry outbursts and, in the case of the children, spankings. And while he says that he has several good friends, one senses considerable ambivalence embedded in those relationships also....

A psychiatric label has a life and an influence of its own. Once the impression has been formed that the

patient is schizophrenic, the expectation is that he will continue to be schizophrenic. When a sufficient amount of time has passed, during which the patient has done nothing bizarre, he is considered to be in remission and available for discharge. But the label endures beyond discharge, with the unconfirmed expectation that he will behave as a schizophrenic again. Such labels, conferred by mental health professionals, are as influential on the patient as they are on his relatives and friends, and it should not surprise anyone that the diagnosis acts on all of them as a self-fulfilling prophecy. Eventually, the patient himself accepts the diagnosis, with all of its surplus meanings and expectations, and behaves accordingly.

Source: D. L. Rosenhan, "On Being Sane in Insane Places," *Science* 179 (January 19, 1973): 253–254.

---

the hospital, it was as schizophrenics "in remission."

The findings support criminological labeling theory. Once the sane individuals were labeled schizophrenic, they were unable to eliminate the label by acting normally. Even when they supposedly had recovered, the label stayed with them in the form of "schizophrenia in remission," which implied that future episodes of the illness could be expected.[19]

Researchers also have looked at the way labels affect people and groups who have unconventional lifestyles, whether prohibited by law or not—such labels as "gays," "public drunks," "junkies," "strippers," and "streetwalkers."[20] The results of research, no matter what the group, were largely in conformity: "Once a ..., always a ...." Labeling by adjudication may have lifelong consequences. Richard Schwartz and Jerome Skolnick, for example, found that employers were reluctant to hire anyone with a court record even though the person had been found not guilty.[21]

The criminologist Anthony Platt has investigated how particular kinds of individuals are singled out to receive labels. Focusing on the label "juvenile delinquent," he explains how the social reformers of the late nineteenth century helped to create delinquency by establishing a special institution, the juvenile court, for the processing of troubled youths. The Chicago society women who lobbied for the establishment of juvenile courts may have had the most praiseworthy motives in turning their charitable attention to the plight of immigrants' children, who were out of control by their standards. But according to Platt, by getting the juvenile court established, they simply widened the net of state agencies empowered to label, officially, some children as deviant. The state thus aggravated the official problem of juvenile delinquency, which until then had been a neighborhood nuisance, to be handled by parents, neighbors, priests, the local grocer, or the police officer on the street. Juvenile delinquency, according to Platt, was invented. Through its labeling effect it contributed to its own growth.[22]

The criminologist William Chambliss also studied the question of the way labels are distributed. Consider the following description:

> Eight promising young men [the Saints]—children of good, stable, white upper-middle-class families, active in school affairs, good pre-college students—were some of the most delinquent boys at Hanibal High School.... The Saints were constantly occupied with truancy, drinking, wild driving, petty theft and vandalism. Yet not one was officially arrested for any misdeed during the *two* years I observed them.
>
> This record was particularly surprising in light of my observations during the same two years of another gang of Hanibal High School students, six lower-class white boys known as the Roughnecks. The Roughnecks were constantly in trouble with police and community even though their rate of delinquency was about equal with that of the Saints.[23]

What accounts for the different responses to these two groups of boys? According to

Chambliss, the crucial factor is that the social class of the boys determined the community's judgment of their activities. The Roughnecks were poor, outspoken, openly hostile to authority, and highly visible, because they could not afford cars to get out of town. Their behavior was discovered, processed, and punished. The Saints, on the other hand, had reputations for being bright, they acted apologetic when authorities confronted them, they held school offices, they played on athletic teams, and they had cars to get them out of town so that their delinquent acts would not be noticed. Their behavior went undiscovered, unprocessed, and unpunished.

Up to this point, the arguments of labeling theorists and the evidence they present provide a persuasive argument for the validity of labeling theory. Despite the scientific evidence in support of labeling theory, it has been heavily criticized.

Evaluation of Labeling Theory

Critics of labeling theory ask: Why is it that individuals, knowing they might be labeled, get involved in socially disapproved behavior to begin with? Most of the labeled persons, some argue, have indeed engaged in some act that is considered morally or legally wrong.[24] According to the sociologist Ronald Akers, the impression sometimes is given that people are passive actors in the process by which the bad system bestows a derogatory label, thereby declaring them unacceptable, or different, or untouchable.[25] Critics suggest that possibly the labels identify real behavior rather than create it. After all, many delinquents have in fact had a long history of deviant behavior, even though they have never been apprehended and consequently stigmatized. These critics question the overly active role that labeling theory has assigned to the community and its criminal justice system, and the overly passive role it has assigned to offenders.

Some criminologists also question how labeling theory accounts for those individuals who have gone through formal processing but do not continue their deviant lifestyles. They suggest that punishment really does work as a deterrent.[26] The argument is that labeling theorists are so intent on the reaction to behavior that they completely neglect the fact that someone has defied the conventions of society.[27] The criminologist Charles Wellford reminds us that, by and large, offenders get into the hands of authorities because they have broken the law, and furthermore, the decisions made about them are heavily influenced by the seriousness of their offenses. He concludes:

> The assumption that labels are differentially distributed, and that differential labelling affects behavior is not supported by the existing criminological research. In sum, one should conclude that to the degree that these assumptions can be taken to be basic to the labelling perspective, the perspective must be seriously questioned; and criminologists should be encouraged to explore other ways to conceptualize the causal process of the creation, perpetuation, and intensification of criminal and delinquent behavior.[28]

While most critics believe that labeling theorists put too much emphasis on the system, others, of a more radical or Marxist persuasion, believe that labeling theorists have not gone far enough in their censure of the system. They claim that the labeling approach concentrates too heavily on "nuts, sluts, and perverts," the exotic varieties of deviants who capture public imagination, rather than on "the unethical, illegal and destructive actions of powerful individuals, groups, and institutions of our society."[29] We shall look at this argument more closely in a moment.

The empirical evidence that substantiates the claims of labeling theory has been modest. All the same, the theory has been instrumental in calling attention to some important questions, particularly about the way defendants are processed through the criminal justice system. Labeling theorists have carried out important scientific investigations of that system, which complement the search of mainstream criminologists for the causes of crime and delinquency.

Some of the criticism of labeling theory can best be countered by one of its own proponents. Howard Becker explains that labeling is intended not as a theory of causation but rather as a perspective, "a way of looking at a general area of human activity, which expands the traditional research to include the process of social control."[30] Labeling theory not only has provided this perspective; it also has spawned further incisive inquiry into the causes of crime, as we shall see.

CONFLICT THEORY

Labeling theorists are as well aware as mainstream criminologists that some people make rules and some break them. Their primary concern is the consequences of making and enforcing rules. One group of scholars has carried this thought further by questioning the rulemaking process itself. They claim that a struggle for power is a basic feature of human existence. It is by means of such power struggles that various interest groups manage to control lawmaking and law enforcement. To understand the theoretical approach of these scholars, called conflict theorists, we must go back to the traditional approach, which views crime and criminal justice as arising from communal consensus.

The Consensus Model

Sometimes (as we saw in Chapter 1) members of a society consider certain acts so threatening to the community's survival that they designate these acts as crimes. If the vast majority of the group members share this view, the group has acted by consensus. This is the **consensus model** of criminal-law making. The consensus model assumes that members of society by and large agree on what is right and wrong, and that in essence law is the codification of these agreed-upon social values. The law is a mechanism to settle disputes that arise when individuals stray too far from what the community considers acceptable behavior. In Durkheim's words, "We can...say that an act is criminal when it offends strong and defined states of the collective conscience."[31]

Consensus theorists view society as a stable entity in which laws are created for the general good. The laws' function is to reconcile and to harmonize most of the interests that most members of a community cherish, with the least amount of sacrifice.[32] Deviant acts are not only regarded as part of the normal functioning of society but in fact are considered necessary, because when the members of society unite against a deviant, they reaffirm their commitment to shared values. Durkheim captured this view:

> We have only to notice what happens, particularly in a small town, when some moral scandal has been committed. They stop each other on the street, they visit each other, they seek to come together to talk of the event and to wax indignant in common. From all the similar impressions which are exchanged, for all the temper that gets itself expressed, there emerges a unique temper, more or less determinate according to the circumstances, which is everybody's without being anybody's in particular. That is the public temper.[33]

Such a society, its citizens agreeing on right and wrong and its occasional deviant serving the useful purpose of reminding people how not to behave, is not prevalent today. It could be found among primitive peoples at the very beginning of social evolution. By and large, consensus theory recognizes that not everyone can agree on what is best for society. Yet consensus theory holds that conflicting interests can be reconciled by means of law, as Roscoe Pound, legal philosopher and educator, maintained.[34]

The Conflict Model

With this view of the consensus model, we can understand and evaluate the arguments of the conflict theorists. In the 1960s, while labeling theorists were questioning why some people were designated criminals, another group of scholars began to ask questions not just about the process by which one becomes criminal but about who in society has the power to make and enforce the laws. Conflict theory, already well established in the field of sociology, thus became popular as an explanation of crime and justice as well.

Like labeling theory, **conflict theory** has its roots in rebellion and the questioning of values. But while labeling theorists and traditional criminologists focused on the crime and the criminal, including the labeling of the criminal as such by the system, conflict theorists questioned the existence of the system itself. The clash between traditional and labeling theorists on the one hand and conflict theorists on the other became ideological. Conflict theorists challenged the consensus view of the origin of criminal law and its enforcement.

Conflict theorists asked: If people agree on the value system, as consensus theorists suggest, why are so many people in rebellion, why are there so many crimes, so many punitive threats, so many people in prison? Clearly conflict is to be found everywhere in the world, between one country and another, between gay rights and antigay groups, between people who view abortion as a right and others who view it as murder, between suspects and police, between family members, between neighbor and neighbor. If the criminal law supports the collective communal interest, why do so many people deviate from it? Conflict theorists answered that, contrary to consensus theory, laws do not exist for the collective good; they represent the interests of specific groups that have the power to get them enacted.[35]

The key concept in conflict theory is power.

Pro-choice and anti-abortion demonstrations in front of the U.S. Supreme Court, while the court was hearing arguments on this issue.

"Power" is derived from the Latin *potis*, "able." The people who have political control in any given society are the ones who are *able* to make things happen. They have power. Conflict theory holds that the people who possess the power work to keep the powerless at a disadvantage. The laws thus have their origin in the interests of the few; these few shape the values, and the values, in turn, shape the laws.[36] It follows that the person who is defined as criminal and the behavior that is defined as crime at any given time and place mirror the society's power relationships, and the definitions are subject to change as other interests gain power. The changing of definitions can be seen in those acts we now designate as "victimless" crimes. Possession of marijuana, prostitution, gambling, refusing to join the armed forces when one is called to do so—all have been legal at some times, illegal at others. We may ask whether any of these acts is inherently evil. The conflict theorist would answer that none is inherently wrong, but that all are made evil when they are so designated by the people in power and thus defined as crimes in the legal codes.

The legal status of victimless crimes is subject to change. But what about murder, a crime that is considered evil in all contemporary societies? Many conflict theorists would respond that the definition of murder as a criminal offense is likewise rooted in the effort of some groups to guard its power. A political terrorist may very well become a national hero. Conflict theorists further emphasize the relativity of norms to time and place: capital punishment is legal in some states, outlawed in others; alcohol consumption is illegal in Saudi Arabia but not in the United States. In sum, powerful groups maintain their interests by making illegal any behavior that might be a threat to them. Laws thus become a mechanism of control, or "a weapon in social conflict."[37]

Conflict Theory and Criminology

The sociologist George Vold (1896–1967) was the first theorist to relate conflict theory to criminology. He argued that individuals band together in groups because they are social animals with needs that are best served through collective action. If the group serves its members, it survives; if not, new groups form to take its place. Individuals constantly clash as they try to advance the interests of their particular group over those of all the others. The result is that society is in a constant state of conflict, "one of the principal and essential social processes upon which the continuing ongoing of society depends." Vold contended that the entire process of lawmaking and crime control is a direct reflection of conflict between interest groups, all trying to get laws passed in their favor and to gain control of the state's police power.[38]

The sociologist Ralf Dahrendorf and the criminologist Austin Turk are major contemporary contributors to the application of conflict theory to criminology. To Dahrendorf, the consensus model of society is utopian. He believes that enforced constraint rather than cooperation binds people together. Whether society is capitalist, socialist, feudal, or whatever, some people have the authority and others are subjected to it. Society is made up of a large number of interest groups. The interests of one group do not always coincide with the needs of another—unions and management, for instance. Dahrendorf argues that social change is constant, social conflicts are ever present, disintegration and change are ongoing, and all societies are characterized by coercion of some people by others. The most important characteristics of class, he contends, are power and authority. The inequities remain for him the lasting determinant of social conflict. Conflict can be either destructive or constructive, depending on whether it leads to a breakdown of the social structure or to positive change in the social order.[39]

Austin Turk has continued and expanded this theoretical approach to conflict theory. "Criminality is not a biological, psychological, or even behavioral phenomenon," he says, "but a social status defined by the way in which an individual is perceived, evaluated, and treated by legal authorities." Criminal status is defined by those whom he calls the "authorities," the dominant class of decisionmakers. Criminal status is imposed on the "subjects," the subordinate class. Turk explains that this process works in such a way that both authorities and subjects learn to interact with each other as performers in their dominant and submissive roles. There are "social norms of dominance" and "social norms of deference." Conflict arises when some people refuse to go along with the lesson, and challenge the authorities. "Law breaking, then, becomes a measure of the stability of the ruler/ruled relationship."[40] The people who make the laws struggle to hold on to their power, while those who do not make laws struggle to do so. Thus every society has its "ins" and its "outs," and those who are the ins at any given time control the means of force to protect their interests.

People with authority use several forms of power to control society's goods and services: police or war power, economic power, political power, and ideological power (beliefs, values).[41] The laws made by the ins to condemn or condone various behaviors help to shape all of society's institutions—indeed, much of the entire culture. Where education is mandatory, for example, the people in power are able to maintain the status quo by passing on their own value system from one generation to the next.[42]

History seems to demonstrate that primitive societies, in their earliest phases of development, tend to be homogeneous and to make laws by consensus. The more a society develops economically and politically, the more difficult it becomes to resolve conflict situations by consensus.

For an early instance of criminal lawmaking by the conflict model, we can go back to 1530, when King Henry VIII of England broke away from the Roman Catholic church because the pope refused to annul his marriage to Catherine of Aragon so that he could marry Anne Boleyn. He then confiscated the church's property and closed all the monasteries. Virtually overnight tens of thousands of people who had been dependent on the monasteries for support were cast out, to roam the countryside in search of a living. Most ended up as beggars. This huge army of vagrants posed a burden on and danger to the establishment. To cope with the problem, Parliament revived the vagrancy laws of 1349, which prohibited the giving of aid to vagrants and beggars. Thus the powerful, by controlling the laws, gained control over the powerless.[43]

(a)

(b)

(c)

a) Police power was used to control crowds at a neo-Nazi rally in Evanston, Illinois. b) Financial power as wielded by the New York Stock Exchange. c) Political power as exercised by the Congress of the United States.

Empirical Evidence for the Conflict Model

Researchers have tested several of the hypotheses of conflict theory, such as those pertaining to bias and discrimination in the criminal justice system, differential crime rates of powerful and powerless groups, and the intent behind the development of the criminal law. The findings of this research offer mixed support for the theory. Alan Lizotte studied 816 criminal cases in the Chicago courts over one year to test the assumption that the powerless get prejudicial sentences. His analysis relating legal factors (such as the offense committed) and extralegal factors (such as the race and job of the defendant) to the lengths of prison sentences pointed to significant inequalities of sentencing related to race and occupation.[44] When Freda Adler studied the importance of nonlegal factors in the decision making of juries, she found that the socioeconomic level of the defendants significantly influenced their judgment.[45] While these and similar studies tend to support conflict theory by demonstrating class or racial bias in the administration of criminal justice, others, unexpectedly, show an opposite bias. [46]

When we evaluate the contribution of conflict theory to criminological thought, we must keep in mind Austin Turk's warning that conflict theory is often misunderstood. The theory does not, he points out, suggest that most criminals are innocent or that powerful persons engage in the same amount of deviant behavior or that law enforcers typically discriminate against people with little power. It does acknowledge, however, that behaviors common among society's more disadvantaged members have a greater likelihood of being called ''crime'' than those activities in which the more powerful typically participate.[47] Conflict theory does not attempt to explain crime, it simply identifies social conflict as a basic fact of life and as a source of discriminatory treatment by the criminal justice system of groups and classes that lack the power and status of those who make and enforce the laws. Once we have come to this recognition, we may then find it possible to change the process of criminalizing people, so as to provide greater justice. Conflict theorists anticipate a guided evolution, not a revolution, to improve the existing criminal justice system.

RADICAL THEORY

While labeling and conflict theorists were developing their perspectives, social and political conditions in the United States and Europe were changing rapidly and drastically. The youth of America were deeply disillusioned about the political and social structure that had brought about the assassinations of John F. Kennedy, Robert Kennedy, and Martin Luther King, Jr., the bloody war in Vietnam, and the Watergate debacle. Many looked for radical solutions to society's social problems, and a number of young criminologists searched for radical answers to the nation's questions about crime and criminal justice. They found their answers in Marxism, a philosophy born in similar social turmoil a century earlier.

The Intellectual Heritage of Marxist Criminology

The great industrial centers of Europe suffered grave hardships during the nineteenth century. The mechanization of industry and of agriculture, heavy population increases, and high rates of urbanization had created a massive labor surplus, high unemployment, and a burgeoning class of young urban migrants forced into the streets by poverty. London is said to have had at least 20,000 individuals who ''rose every morning without knowing how they were to be supported through the day or where they were to lodge on the succeeding night, and cases of death from starvation appeared in the coroner's lists daily.''[48] In other cities conditions were even worse.

Friedrich Engels It was against this background that Friedrich Engels (1820–1895) addressed the effects of the Industrial Revolution. A partner in his father's industrial empire, Engels was himself a member of the class he so vehemently attacked as ''brutally selfish.'' After a two-year stay in England, he documented the despicable social conditions, the suffering, and the great increases in crime and arrests. All of these problems he blamed on one factor—competition. In *The Condition of the Working Class in England,* published in 1845, he spelled out the association between crime and poverty as a political problem:

> The earliest, crudest, and least fruitful form of this rebellion was that of crime. The working man lived in poverty and want, and saw that others were better off than he.... Want conquered his inherited respect for the sacredness of property, and he stole.[49]

Karl Marx   Though Karl Marx (1818–1883) paid little attention to crime specifically, he argued that all aspects of social life, including the laws, are determined by economic organization. His philosophy reflects the economic despair that followed the Industrial Revolution.

In his *Communist Manifesto* (1848) Marx viewed the history of all societies as a documentation of class struggles: "Freeman and slave, patrician and plebeian, lord and serf, guildmaster and journeyman, in a word, oppressor and oppressed, stood in constant opposition to one another."[50] Marx went on to describe the most important relationship in industrial society as that between the capitalist bourgeoisie, who own the means of production, and the proletariat, or workers, who labor for them. Society, according to Marx, has always been organized in such a hierarchical fashion, with the state representing not the common interest but the interests of those who own the means of production. Capitalism breeds egocentricity, greed, and predatory behavior; but the worst crime of all is the owners' exploitation of workers. Revolution, Marx concluded, is the only means to bring about change, and for that reason it is morally justifiable.

Many philosophers before Marx had noted the linkage between economic conditions and social problems, including crime. Among them were Plato, Aristotle, Virgil, Horace, Sir Thomas More, Cesare Beccaria, Jeremy Bentham, André Guerry, Adolphe Quételet, and Gabriel Tarde (several of whom we met in Chapter 3). But none of them had advocated revolutionary change. And none had constructed a coherent criminological theory in conformity with *economic determinism*, the cornerstone of the Marxist explanation that people who are kept in a state of poverty will rebel by committing crimes. Not until 1905 can we speak of Marxist criminology.

Willem Adriaan Bonger   As a student at the University of Amsterdam, Willem Adriaan Bonger (1876–1940) entered a paper in a competition on the influence of economic factors on crime. His entry did not win; but its expanded version, *Criminality and Economic Conditions,* which appeared in French in 1905, was selected for translation by the American Institute of Criminal Law and Criminology. Bonger wrote in his preface that he was "convinced that my ideas about the etiology of crime will not be shared by a great many readers of the American edition."[51] He was right. Nevertheless, the book is considered a classic and is invaluable to students doing research on crime and economics.

Bonger explained that the social environment of primitive people was interwoven with the means of production. People helped each other. They used what they produced. When food was plentiful, everyone ate. When food was scarce, everyone was hungry. Whatever they had, they shared with each other. People were subordinate to nature. In a modern capitalist society, people are much less altruistic, concentrating on production for profit rather than for the needs of their community. Capitalism, therefore, encourages criminal behavior by creating a climate that is less conducive to social responsibility. "We have a right," argued Bonger, "to say that the part played by economic conditions in criminality is predominant, even decisive."[52]

Willem Bonger died as he had lived, a fervent antagonist of the evils of the social order. An archenemy of Nazism and a prominent name on Hitler's list of people to be eliminated, he refused to emigrate even when the German army was at the border. On May 10, 1940, as the German invasion of Holland began, he wrote to his son: "I don't see any future for myself and I cannot bow to this scum which will now overmaster us."[53] He then took his own life. He left a powerful political and criminological legacy. Foremost among his followers were German socialist philosophers of the progressive school of Frankfurt.

Georg Rusche and Otto Kirchheimer   Georg Rusche and Otto Kirchheimer began to write their classic work at the University of Frankfurt, where they were strongly influenced by the work of Willem Bonger. Driven out of Germany by Nazi persecution, they continued their research in exile in Paris and completed it at Columbia University in 1939. In *Punishment and the Social Structure* they wrote that punishments had always been related to the modes of production and the availability of labor, rather than to the nature of the crimes themselves. Consider galley slavery. Before the development of modern sailing techniques, oarsmen were needed to power merchant ships; the result was galley slavery as a punishment in the Middle Ages. As sailing techniques were perfected, galley slavery was no longer necessary, and it lost favor as a sanction. By documenting the real purposes of punishments through the ages, Rusche and Kirchheimer made **penologists,** who study the penal system, aware that severe and cruel treatment of offenders had more to do with the value of human life and the needs of the economy than with preventing people from committing crimes.

Marx, Engels, Bonger, and Rusche and Kirchheimer provided the intellectual basis for radical criminology, yet their names were all but forgotten by the mainstream criminologists of the 1940s and 1950s, perhaps because of Americans' relative prosperity and conservatism during those years. But when tranquility turned to turmoil in the mid-1960s, the forgotten names found new prominence with American and European radical criminologists, who explicitly stated their commitment to Marxism.

Radical Criminology of the 1970s and 1980s

Radical (also called critical, new, and Marxist) criminology made its first public appearance in 1968, when a group of British sociologists organized the National Deviancy Conference (NDC), a group of more than three hundred intellectuals, social critics, deviants, and activists of various persuasions. What the group members had in common was a basic disillusionment with the criminological studies being done by the British Home Office, which they believed was system-serving and "practical." They were concerned with the way the system controlled people rather than with traditional sociological and psychological explanations of crime. They shared respect for the interactionist and labeling theorists but believed that these theorists had become too traditional. Their answer was to form a new criminology based on Marxist principles.

The conference was followed by the publication in 1973 of *The New Criminology*, the first textual formulation of the new **radical criminology.** According to its authors, Ian Taylor, Paul Walton, and Jock Young, it is the underclass, the "labor forces of the industrial society," that is controlled through the criminal law and its enforcement, while "the owners of labor will be bound only by a civil law which regulates their competition between each other." The economic institution, then, is the source of all conflicts; struggles between classes always relate to the distribution of resources and power, and only when capitalism is abolished will crime disappear.[54]

About the time that Marxist criminology was being formulated in England, it was also developing in the United States, particularly at the School of Criminology of the University of California at Berkeley, where Richard Quinney, Anthony Platt, Herman and Julia Schwendinger, William Chambliss, and Paul Takagi were at the forefront of the movement. These researchers were also influenced by interactionist and labeling theorists, and by the conflict theories of Vold, Dahrendorf, and Turk.

Though the radical criminologists share the central tenet of conflict theory, that laws are created by the powerful to protect their own interests, they disagree on the quantity of the forces competing in the power struggle. For Marxist criminologists, there is only one dominating segment, the capitalist ruling class, which uses the criminal law to impose its morality on the rest of the people in order to protect its property and to define as criminal any behavior that threatens the status quo.[55]

The leading American spokesman for radical criminology is Richard Quinney. His earliest Marxist publications appeared in 1973: "Crime Control in Capitalist Society" and "There's a Lot of Us Folks Grateful to the Lone Ranger."[56] The second of these essays describes how Quinney drifted away from capitalism with its folklore myths embodied in individual heroes, such as the Lone Ranger. He asserts that

> the state is organized to serve the interests of the dominant economic class, the capitalist ruling class; that criminal law is an instrument the state and dominant ruling class use to maintain and perpetuate the social and economic order; that the contradictions of advanced capitalism ...require that the subordinate classes remain oppressed by whatever means necessary, especially by the legal system's coercion and violence; and that only with the collapse of capitalist society, based on socialist principles, will there be a solution to the crime problem.[57]

In *Class, State, and Crime* Quinney proclaims that "the criminal justice movement is...a state-initiated and state-supported effort to rationalize mechanisms of social control. The larger purpose is to secure a capitalist order that is in grave crisis, likely in its final stage of development."[58] Quinney implores criminologists to discard their traditional ways of thinking about causation, to study what *could be* rather than what is, to question the assumptions of the social order, and to "ultimately develop a Marxist perspective."[59]

Marxist theory also can be found in the writings of other scholars who have adopted the radical approach to criminology. William Chambliss and Robert Seidman present their version in *Law, Order, and Power:*

> Society is composed of groups that are in conflict with one another and...the law represents an institutionalized tool of those in power (ruling class) which functions to provide them with superior moral as well as coercive power in conflict.

They comment that if, in the operation of the criminal justice system by the powerful, "justice or fairness happen to be served, it is sheer coincidence."[60]

To Barry Krisberg, crime is a function of privilege. The rich create crimes to deflect attention from the injustices they inflict on the masses. Enforcement power determines which group holds the privilege, which Krisberg defines as that which is valued by a given social group in a given historical time.[61] Herman and Julia Schwendinger warn that because of

> the inherent antagonisms built into the capitalist system, all laws generally contradict their stated purpose of producing justice. Legal relations maintain patterns of individualism and selfishness and in so doing perpetuate a class system characterized by anarchy, oppression, and crime.[62]

Anthony Platt, in a forceful attack on traditional criminology, has even suggested that it would not be "too farfetched to characterize many criminologists as domestic war criminals" because of the way they have "serviced domestic repression in the same way that economics, political science, and anthropology have greased the wheels and even manufactured some of the important parts of modern imperialism."[63] He suggested that traditional criminology serves the state through its many research studies that purport to "investigate" the conditions of the lower class but in reality only prove, with their probes of family life, education, jobs, and so on, that the members of the lower class are in fact less intelligent and more criminal than the rest of us. Platt claims that these inquiries, based as they are on biased and inaccurate data, are merely tools of the middle-class oppressors.

A number of other areas have come under the scrutiny of Marxist criminologists. They have studied how informal means of settling disputes outside of courts actually extend the control of the criminal justice system by adjudicating cases that are not serious enough for the courts; how juvenile court dispositions are unfairly based on social class; the failure of sentencing reform to benefit the lower class; police practices during the latter half of the nineteenth century which were geared to control labor rather than crime; how rape victims are made to feel guilty; how penitentiary reform has benefited the ruling class by giving them more control over the lower class; and how capitalist interests are strengthened by private policing.[64]

Evaluation of Marxist Criminological Theory

Critiques of Marxist criminology range from support for the attention the approach calls to the crimes of the powerful to accusations that the approach is nothing more than a revival of the Robin Hood myth, in which the poor steal from the rich in order to survive.[65] By far the most incisive criticism is that of the sociologist Carl Klockars, who points out that the division of society into social classes may have a beneficial effect, contrary to Marxist thought. Standards, he argues, are created by some people to inspire the remainder of society. In present-day America, he claims, poverty has lost some of its meaning because luxuries and benefits are spread out over classes. To him, ownership and control of industry are two different things. Anyone who buys a share of stock, for example, can be an owner, while control is handled by bureaucrats who may or may not be owners. Klockars attacks Marxists for focusing exclusively on class interests and ignoring the fact that society is made up of many interest groups. This Marxist bias has yielded results that are untrustworthy and predictable, ignore reality, explain issues that are self-evident (some business people are greedy and corrupt), and do not explain issues that are relevant (why socialist states have crime).[66] Not without a note of sympathy, Richard Sparks summed up the criticism when he said, "Marxist criminologists tend to be committed to praxis and the desire for radical social reform; but this commitment is not entailed by the scientific claims which Marxists make, and it has sometimes led to those claims being improperly suspect."[67]

Opposition to the new criminology follows many paths, but the most popular, in one way or another, is concerned with its oversimplification of crime causation by its exclusive focus on capitalism.[68] Critics also attack Marxist criminologists for their assertion that even by studying crime empirically, criminologists are legitimating the status quo. That puts Marxist criminologists on the defensive, because if they are not ideologically in a position or willing to expose their theories to empirical research, their assertions will remain just that—assertions with no proof.[69]

Even sharper criticism of Marxist theory can be anticipated in the wake of the collapse of the Marxist economic order in the Soviet Union, Poland, Czechoslovakia, Hungary, the German Democratic Republic, Bulgaria, and Romania, as well as in countries in Africa and Latin America. Many East European criminologists are no longer quoting Marx in their publications, which tend increasingly to focus on the classical rule-of-law concept. But Quinney has never seen the conditions in those countries as representative of Marxism. According to him, a true Marxist state has not yet been attained, but the ideal is worth pursuing.[70]

To the credit of radical criminologists, it must be said that they have encouraged their more traditional colleagues to look with a critical eye at all aspects of the criminal justice system, which includes the response of the system to both poor and rich offenders. Their concern is the exercise of power. They ask: Whose power? On whose behalf? For whose benefit? What is the legitimacy of that power? And who is excluded from the exercise of power, by whom, and why? Criminologists have had to address all of these questions. Many may not have changed their answers, but the fact that such questions have been raised has ensured clearer answers than had been offered before.

Despite the decline of Marxist criminology in Marxist countries around the world, the voices of radical criminology in the United States will continue to be heard as long as there are substantial population groups who have no share in the making of laws and in the response to the breaking of laws. Such groups include the growing number of homeless and the increasing proportion of the population whom radical Marxists call the working poor, but some of whom, in fact, are not working at all, because the social system has not equipped them with working skills.

AT ISSUE

The Rights of the Poorest

The poorest and least powerful have had little influence on the making of laws and on society's reaction to the breaking of laws. Somehow, the poorest have to survive in a society on which they have no apparent impact.

Do the poor have a constitutional right to beg? Yes, says New York federal district-court judge Leonard Sand. In a novel ruling, Sand found that panhandling is a form of free speech protected by the First Amendment. "A true test of one's commitment to constitutional principles," he wrote, "is the extent to which recognition is given to the rights of those in our midst who are the least affluent, least powerful and least welcome."

The case grew out of attempts by the Metropolitan Transit Authority to crack down on panhandling in New York City subway cars and stations, but the ruling has nationwide implications. Seeking to stem the proliferation of needy and homeless in a system that serves 1 billion passengers a year, the MTA last October launched its so-called Operation Enforcement. Within weeks, two homeless panhandlers—Papa Joe Walley, 50, and William Young, Jr., 40—complained to the Legal Action Center for the Homeless that they were being harassed by the police while begging in the subway. The center filed a class action against the MTA on behalf of Walley, Young and others like them.

In his ruling, handed down two weeks ago, Judge Sand indicated that the MTA had gone too far by imposing a total ban instead of specifying the times, places and types of begging that it considered out

REVIEW

Labeling theory, conflict theory, and radical theory offer alternative explanations of crime, in the sense that they do not restrict their inquiry to the criminal's characteristics or to the social or communal processes, which all the other theories associate with crime. These three theories examine the impact of the processes of lawmaking and law enforcement on the creation of offenders. The labeling and conflict theories, as critical as they are of the existing sys-

of bounds. "While the government has an interest in preserving the quality of urban life," wrote Sand, "this interest must be discounted where the regulation has the principal effect of keeping a public problem involving human beings out of sight and therefore out of mind."

Advocates for the needy applauded the decision, which has continued to reverberate nationally. "If you silence a beggar, you cut off one of his or her most effective means of communication and advocacy," said Douglas Lasdon, executive director of the Legal Action Center for the Homeless. "If the homeless have received any assistance, it is because their pleas have been seen and heard." Burt Neuborne, a law professor at New York University, concurred, arguing that "to the extent subways are simply extensions of the streets, the same freedoms should apply in both places." But the MTA denounced the judge's action and said it would appeal. "The subway is there for one purpose and one purpose alone: to move people from one place to another," said Chairman Robert Kiley. "We are not the same as an auditorium or an arena or even a street."

Judge Sand's opinion runs contrary to the traditional American legal view of begging. Although panhandling involves speaking, the activity has not generally been viewed as a First Amendment issue. Throughout history, begging has been regulated, monitored and sometimes prohibited; half the states in the U.S. currently have statutes that limit or ban begging. Yet Sand's reasoning could prove persuasive to other courts in search of answers to the problem of panhandling by the homeless. Moreover, his ruling is in line with three cases in the past decade in which the U.S. Supreme Court has held that professional fund raisers have a First Amendment right to seek donations.

Judge Sand's ruling created a spate of mostly virulent comments focusing on the judiciary's right to rule on the conduct of those dispossessed of power. One critic responded to these attacks:

Judges as the ultimate guardians and interpreters of the constitution have been charged with the duty of insuring that its fundamental guarantees such as freedom of speech and assembly are not abridged by the government. In this capacity they may sometimes be required to make unpopular decisions.

It is at least arguable that panhandling or begging is a form of symbolic speech—if only because it may be the only avenue of expression open to those society has shunned. Time, place, and manner restrictions, while undoubtedly an important protection for the community, can also be a convenient means of ignoring constitutional guarantees. They will not, however, make the homeless disappear.

In May 1990, the U.S. Court of Appeals reversed the decision of the District Court. A decision by the U.S. Supreme Court is to be expected.

Source: Andrea Sachs, *Time*, February 12, 1990, p. 55; Jill Adler, *International Herald Tribune*, February 15, 1990, p. 9.

tem of criminal justice, envisage a system made more just and equitable by reform and democratic processes; radical theory demands revolutionary change. With long historical antecedents, all three theories gained prominence during the era of rebellion against the social, political, and economic inequities of the 1960s and early 1970s.

Labeling theory does not presume to explain all crime, but it does demonstrate that the criminal justice system is selective in determining who is to be labeled a criminal. It explains how this labeling process occurs, and it blames the criminal justice system for contributing to the labeling process, and therefore to the crime problem.

Conflict theory goes a step beyond labeling theory in identifying the forces that selectively decide in the first place what conduct should be singled out for condemnation—usually, so it is claimed, to the detriment of the powerless and for the benefit of the powerful.

Radical theory singles out the relationship between the owners of the means of production and the workers under capitalism as the root cause of crime and of all social inequities. Radical theory demands the overthrow of the existing order, which is said to perpetuate criminal-ity by keeping the oppressed classes under the domination of the capitalist oppressors. Only true socialism can reduce the crime rate.

All three theories have their adherents and their opponents. Research to demonstrate their validity has produced mixed results. More important, all of these theories have challenged conventional criminologists to rethink their approaches and to provide answers to questions that had not been asked before.

KEY TERMS

conflict theory
consensus model
due process
equal protection

labeling theory
penologists
radical criminology
social interactionists

NOTES

1. The Supreme Court decisions are covered in Pt. IV, especially Chap. 16.

2. Howard S. Becker, *Outsiders: Studies in the Sociology of Deviance* (New York: Macmillan, 1963), p. 9. For an excellent discussion of how society controls deviance, see Nicholas N. Kittrie, *The Right to Be Different* (Baltimore: Johns Hopkins University Press, 1972).

3. William I. Thomas, *The Unadjusted Girl* (1923; New York: Harper & Row, 1967).

4. George Herbert Mead, "The Psychology of Punitive Justice," *American Journal of Sociology* 23 (1918): 577–602. See also Charles Horton Cooley, "The Roots of Social Knowledge," *American Journal of Sociology* 32 (1926): 59–79.

5. Herbert Blumer, "Sociological Implications of the Thought of George Herbert Mead," in *Symbolic Interactionism*, ed. Herbert Blumer (Englewood Cliffs, N.J.: Prentice-Hall, 1969), pp. 62, 65, 66.

6. Frank Tannenbaum, *Crime and the Community* (Boston: Ginn, 1938), p. 27.

7. Edwin M. Lemert, *Social Pathology* (New York: McGraw-Hill, 1951).

8. Edwin M. Lemert, *Human Deviance, Social Problems, and Social Control* (Englewood Cliffs, N.J.: Prentice-Hall, 1967), Chap. 3.

9. Lemert, *Social Pathology*, pp. 75–76.

10. Lemert, *Human Deviance*, p. 46. See also Albert K. Cohen, *Deviance and Control* (Englewood Cliffs, N.J.: Prentice-Hall, 1966), pp. 24–25.

11. Erving Goffman, *Stigma: Notes on the Management of Spoiled Identity* (Englewood Cliffs, N.J.: Prentice-Hall, 1963).

12. Gerhard O. W. Mueller, "Resocialization of the Young Adult Offender in Switzerland," *Journal of Criminal Law and Criminology* 43 (1953): 578–591, at p. 584. At the time that Lemert was developing the principles of labeling theory in the United States, Swiss correctional administrators already fully comprehended the significance of labeling. Convicts were "considered as being afflicted with the self conception of being criminal or wayward by either their own imagination...or the acceptance of the repeated judgment of others tendered on them."

13. Kai T. Erikson, "Notes on the Sociology of Deviance," in *The Other Side: Perspectives on Deviance*, ed. Howard S. Becker (New York: Free Press, 1964), p. 11.

14. Edwin Schur, *Labeling Deviant Behavior* (New York: Harper & Row, 1971), p. 21.

15. Edwin M. Schur, *Crimes Without Victims* (Englewood Cliffs, N.J.: Prentice-Hall, 1965).

16. M. Ray, "The Cycle of Abstinence and Relapse Among Heroin Addicts," *Social Problems* 9 (1961): 132–140.

17. David Matza, *Becoming Deviant* (Englewood Cliffs, N.J.: Prentice-Hall, 1969), pp. 44–53.

18. Becker, *Outsiders*, pp. 18, 20.

19. D. L. Rosenhan, "On Being Sane in Insane Places," *Science* 179 (1973): 250–258. See also Bruce G. Link, "Understanding Labeling Effects in the Area of Mental Disorders: An Assessment of the Effects of Expectations of Rejection," *American Sociological Review* 52 (February 1987): 96–112.

20. Carol Warren and John Johnson, "A Critique of Labeling Theory from the Phenomenological Perspective," in *Theoretical Perspectives on Deviance*, ed. J. D. Douglas and R. Scott (New York: Basic Books, 1973), p. 77; James P. Spradley, *You Owe Yourself a Drunk: An Ethnography of Urban Nomads* (Boston: Little, Brown, 1979), p. 254; M. Ray, "Cycle of Abstinence"; M. Salutin, "Stripper Morality," *Trans-action* 9 (June 1971): 12–27; Bernard Cohen, *Deviant Street Networks: Prostitution in New York City* (Lexington, Mass.: Lexington Books, 1980).

21. Richard D. Schwartz and Jerome H. Skolnick, "Two Studies of Legal Stigma," *Social Problems* 10 (1962): 133–138.

22. Anthony Platt, *The Child Savers* (Chicago: University of Chicago Press, 1969). For a further discussion of the effects of stigmatization by the criminal justice system, see Charles W. Thomas and Donna M. Bishop, "The Effect of Formal and Informal Sanctions on Delinquency: A Longitudinal Comparison of Labeling and Deterrence Theories," *Journal of Criminal Law and Criminology* 75 (1984): 1222–1245. See also Anne Rankin Maloney, "The Effect of Labeling upon Youths in the Juvenile Justice System: A Review of the Evidence," *Law and Society Review* 8 (Summer 1974): 583–614; Dennis B. Anderson and Donald F. Schoen, "Diversion Programs: Effects of Stigmatization on Juvenile/Status Offenders," *Juvenile and Family Court Journal* 36 (Summer 1985): 13–25; Gordon Bazemore, "Delinquent Reform and the Labeling Perspective," *Criminal Justice and Behavior* 12 (June 1985): 131–169.

23. William J. Chambliss, "The Saints and the Roughnecks," *Society* 11 (1973): 24–31.

24. Walter R. Gove, "Deviant Behavior, Social Intervention, and Labeling Theory," in *The Uses of Controversy in Sociology*, ed. Lewis A. Coser and Otto N. Larsen (New York: Free Press, 1976), pp. 219–227.

25. Ronald L. Akers, "Problems in the Sociology of Deviance," *Social Forces* 46 (1968): 455–465.

26. Ronald L. Akers, *Deviant Behavior: A Social Learning Approach*, 2d ed. (Belmont, Calif.: Wadsworth, 1977).

27. Jack P. Gibbs, "Conceptions of Deviant Behavior: The Old and the New," *Pacific Sociological Review* 9 (Spring 1966): 9–14.

28. Charles Wellford, "Labelling Theory and Criminology: An Assessment," *Social Problems* 22 (February 1975): 343.

29. Alexander Liazos, "The Poverty of the Sociology of Deviance: Nuts, Sluts, and Perverts," *Social Problems* 20 (Summer 1972): 103–120.

30. Howard S. Becker, "Labelling Theory Reconsidered," in *Outsiders: Studies in the Sociology of Deviance*, ed. Becker, rev. ed. (New York: Free Press, 1973), pp. 177–208. See also Schur, *Labeling Deviant Behavior*, for an excellent review of labeling theory.

31. Emile Durkheim, *The Division of Labor in Society* (New York: Free Press, 1947), p. 80.

32. Roscoe Pound, "A Survey of Social Interests," *Harvard Law Review* 57 (1943): 1–39, at 39.

33. Durkheim, *Division of Labor*, p. 102.

34. Roscoe Pound, *An Introduction to the Philosophy of Law* (Boston: Little, Brown, 1922), p. 98.

35. Richard Quinney, *Crime and Justice in Society* (Boston: Little, Brown, 1969), pp. 26–30.

36. William Chambliss, "The State, the Law, and the Definition of Behavior as Criminal or Delinquent," in *Handbook of Criminology,* ed. Daniel Glaser (Chicago: Rand McNally, 1974), pp. 7–44.

37. Austin Turk, "Law as a Weapon in Social Conflict," *Social Problems* 23 (1976): 276–291.

38. George Vold, *Theoretical Criminology* (New York: Oxford University Press, 1958), pp. 204, 209.

39. Ralf Dahrendorf, *Class and Class Conflict in Industrial Society* (Stanford, Calif.: Stanford University Press, 1959). See also Ralf Dahrendorf, "Out of Utopia: Toward a Reorientation of Sociological Analysis," *American Journal of Sociology* 64 (September 1958): 127.

40. Austin Turk, *Criminality and Legal Order* (Chicago: Rand McNally, 1969), pp. 25, 33, 41–42, 48.

41. Austin Turk, *Political Criminality: The Defiance and Defense of Authority* (Beverly Hills, Calif.: Sage, 1982), p. 15.

42. Turk, "Law as a Weapon."

43. William J. Chambliss, "A Sociological Analysis of the Law of Vagrancy," *Social Problems* 12 (1966): 67–77. For an opposing view on the historical development of criminal law, see Jeffrey S. Adler, "A Historical Analysis of the Law of Vagrancy," *Criminology* 27 (1989): 209–229; and a rejoinder to Adler: William J. Chambliss, "On Trashing Criminology," ibid., pp. 231–238.

44. Alan Lizotte, "Extra-legal Factors in Chicago's Criminal Courts: Testing the Conflict Model of Criminal Justice," *Social Problems* 25 (1978): 564–580. See also Kathleen Daly, "Neither Conflict nor Labeling nor Paternalism Will Suffice: Intersections of Race, Ethnicity, Gender, and Family in Criminal Court Decisions," *Crime and Delinquency* 35 (January 1989): 136–168.

45. Freda Adler, "Socioeconomic Variables Influencing Jury Verdicts," *New York University Review of Law on Social Change* 3 (1973): 16–36. See also Martha A. Myers, "Social Background and the Sentencing Behavior of Judges," *Criminology* 26 (November 1988): 649–675.

46. Celesta A. Albonetti, Robert M. Hauser, John Hagan, and Ilene H. Nagel, "Criminal Justice Decision-Making as a Stratification Process: The Role of Race and Stratification Resources in Pretrial Release," *Journal of Quantitative Criminology* 5 (March 1989): 57–82. See also Theodore Chiricos and Gordon Waldo, "Socioeconomic Status and Criminal Sentencing: An Empirical Assessment of a Conflict Proposition," *American Sociological Review* 40 (1975): 753–772. For a compilation of recent tests of the conflict model, see John Hagan, *Structural Criminology* (New Brunswick, N.J.: Rutgers University Press, 1989).

47. Austin Turk, "Law, Conflict, and Order: From Theorizing Toward Theories," *Canadian Review of Sociology and Anthropology* 13 (1976): 282–294.

48. Georg Rusche and Otto Kirchheimer, *Punishment and Social Structure* (New York: Columbia University Press, 1939), p. 93.

49. Friedrich Engels, "To the Working Class of Great Britain," introduction to *The Condition of the Working Class in England* (1845), in Karl Marx and Friedrich Engels, *Collected Works* (New York: International Publishers, 1974), vol. 4, pp. 213–214, 298.

50. Karl Marx and Friedrich Engels, *The Communist Manifesto* (1848; New York: International Publishers, 1979), p. 9.

51. Willem Adriaan Bonger, *Criminality and Economic Conditions*, trans. Henry P. Horton (Boston: Little, Brown, 1916).

52. Ibid., p. 669.

53. J. M. Van Bemmelen, "Willem Adriaan Bonger," in *Pioneers in Criminology*, ed. Hermann Mannheim (London: Stevens, 1960), p. 361.

54. Ian Taylor, Paul Walton, and Jock Young, *The New Criminology: For a Social Theory of Deviance* (London: Routledge & Kegan Paul, 1973), pp. 264, 281. See also Jock Young, "Radical Criminology in Britain: The Emergence of a Competing Paradigm," *British Journal of Criminology* 28 (1988): 159–183.

55. Gresham Sykes, "The Rise of Critical Criminology," *Journal of Criminal Law and Criminology* 65 (1974): 206–213.

56. Richard Quinney, "Crime Control in Capitalist Society: A Critical Philosophy of Legal Order," *Issues in Criminology* 8 (1973): 75–95, and "There's a Lot of Us Folks Grateful to the Lone Ranger: Some Notes on the Rise and Fall of American Criminology," *Insurgent Sociologist* 4 (1973): 56–64.

57. Quinney, "Crime Control in Capitalist Society," in *Critical Criminology*, ed. Ian Taylor, Paul Walton, and Jock Young (London: Routledge & Kegan Paul, 1975), p. 199.

58. Richard Quinney, *Class, State, and Crime: On the Theory and Practice of Criminal Justice*, 2d ed. (New York: David McKay, 1977), p. 10.

59. Richard Quinney, *Critique of Legal Order: Crime Control in a Capitalist Society* (Boston: Little, Brown, 1974), pp. 11–13.

60. William Chambliss and Robert Seidman, *Law, Order, and Power* (Reading, Mass.: Addison-Wesley, 1971), pp. 503, 504.

61. Barry Krisberg, *Crime and Privilege: Toward a New Criminology* (Englewood Cliffs, N.J.: Prentice-Hall, 1975).

62. Herman Schwendinger and Julia Schwendinger, "Delinquency and Social Reform: A Radical Perspective," in *Juvenile Justice*, ed. Lamar Empey (Charlottesville: University of Virginia Press, 1979), pp. 246–290.

63. Elliot Currie, "A Dialogue with Anthony M. Platt," *Issues in Criminology* 8 (1973): 28.

64. Lance H. Selva and Robert M. Bohm, "A Critical Examination of the Informalism Experiment in the Administration of Justice," *Crime and Social Justice* 29 (1987): 43–57; Timothy Carter and Donald Clelland, "A Neo-Marxian Critique, Formulation, and Test of Juvenile Dispositions as a Function of Social Class," *Social Problems* 27 (1979): 96–108;

David Greenberg and Drew Humphries, "The Co-optation of Fixed Sentencing Reform," *Crime and Delinquency* 26 (1980): 216–225; Sidney L. Harring and Lorraine M. McMullen, "The Buffalo Police, 1897–1900: Labor Unrest, Political Power, and the Creation of the Police Institution," *Crime and Social Justice* 4 (1975): 5–14; Herman Schwendinger and Julia Schwendinger, "Rape Victims and the False Sense of Guilt," *Crime and Social Justice* 13 (1980): 4–17; Paul Takagi, "The Walnut Street Jail: A Penal Reform to Centralize the Powers of the State," *Federal Probation* 39 (1975): 18–26; Steven Spitzer and Andrew T. Scull, "Privatization and Capitalist Development: The Case of the Private Police," *Social Problems* 25 (1977): 18–29.

65. Jackson Toby, "The New Criminology Is the Old Sentimentality," *Criminology* 16 (1979): 516–526.

66. Carl B. Klockars, "The Contemporary Crises of Marxist Criminology," *Criminology* 16 (1979): 477–515.

67. Richard F. Sparks, "A Critique of Marxist Criminology," *Crime and Justice: An Annual Review of Research*, ed. Norval Morris and Michael Tonry (Chicago: University of Chicago Press, 1980), p. 159.

68. Milton Mankoff, "On the Responsibility of Marxist Criminology: A Reply to Quinney," *Contemporary Crisis* 2 (1978): 293–301.

69. Austin T. Turk, "Analyzing Official Deviance: For Nonpartisan Conflict Analysis in Criminology," in *Radical Criminology: The Coming Crisis*, ed. James A. Inciardi (Beverly Hills, Calif.: Sage, 1980), pp. 78–91. See also Sykes, "Rise of Critical Criminology," p. 212.

70. Quinney, *Class, State, and Crime*, p. 40.

PART III

TYPES OF CRIME

The word "crime" conjures up many images, of mugging and murder, of cheating on taxes and selling crack. The penal codes define thousands of crimes, differing from each other but with certain common elements. They all are human acts in violation of law, committed by an actor who acted with a criminal intent to cause a specified harm. The law has developed a variety of defenses to crime by which, in effect, the defendant alleges that one of the required elements was missing.

After analyzing the common ingredients of all crimes, we shall examine the occurrence of criminal events from two criminological perspectives (Chapter 9). The rational choice perspective explains the criminal event in terms of the criminal, the motivation, and the situational factors surrounding the crime. The routine activities perspective explains the criminal event in terms of motivated offenders, suitable targets, and the absence of guardians. Violent crime (Chapter 10); a broad range of crimes against property (Chapter 11); white-collar, corporate, and organized crime (Chapter 12); and a variety of crimes related to drug and alcohol trafficking and consumption and to sexual mores (Chapter 13) are explained in terms of legal and criminological perspectives. Their occurrence, frequency, and pervasiveness are also discussed in comparison with the occurrence of crime in other parts of the world.

9

THE CONCEPT OF CRIME

There is hardly a subject on which the public holds stronger views than that of crime. Perhaps this is as it should be, since crime concerns the entire community much more than most other subjects. Then, of course, most other subjects seem to be more technical than crime, and most people lack the information to debate topics involving astrophysics or electronmicroscopy. Yet, crime is not just an emotional issue capable of being discussed by everybody. It, too, is a highly technical subject, a legal construct developed by high courts and legal scholars over the centuries, and a concept (or concepts) developed and being further refined by social and behavioral scientists.

In this chapter we shall explore crime as a legal construct, and we shall discuss its theoretical and practical implications affecting criminal liability. We shall place our discussion (in this and the following chapters in this part) into the context of the situational aspects of its occurrence, such as the opportunities for crimes to be committed, the motivation of the perpetrator, the role the victim plays, the socioeconomic environment that favors the event, and any other factors that may have anything to do with the occurrence of crime.

THEORIES OF CRIME

Rational Choice

In recent years, some criminologists have focused attention on why offenders choose to commit one offense rather than another at a given time and place. They stress the important distinction between theories of crime and theories of criminality. Theories of criminality, Michael Gottfredson and Travis Hirschi point out, explain why some people are more likely than others to commit crimes; theories of crime identify conditions under which those persons who are prone to commit crime will in fact do so.[1] Crimes are events. They take place at a specific time in a specific place. The presence of an offender is only one of the necessary components of a crime. Crimes require many conditions that are independent of the offender, such as the availability of goods to be stolen or persons to be assaulted. Some experts have argued that if crimes are to be prevented and crime control policies developed, the study of criminal behavior must be closely tied to the decision-making process of offenders and to the criminal acts themselves. The **rational choice** perspective, developed by Derek Cornish and Ronald Clarke, takes into account the entire criminal event, which includes the criminal, the motivation, and the situational factors surrounding the crime.[2] "Rational" refers to the fact that criminals process information and evaluate alternatives. "Choice" suggests that they make decisions. According to Cornish and Clarke, an individual commits a crime after he or she has made a rational decision to do so—has weighed the risks and benefits of the act and selected a particular offense according to various criteria.[3] Before committing a theft, for example, an offender may consider

- the number of targets and their accessibility;
- his or her familiarity with the chosen method (for example, fraud by credit card);
- the monetary yield per crime;
- the expertise needed;
- the time required to commit the act;
- the physical danger involved; and
- the risk of apprehension.

Consider the following scenario: A young man is unemployed. He has no savings. Most of the money he makes doing odd jobs go into his car, which the bank is about to repossess. He feels desperate. He needs money just to tide him over. Some of his peers have suggested that he work in the local crack house. He knows that though the rewards are good, the risks are high. The neighborhood is under surveillance. Instead, he decides to commit a robbery. Where can he find the best target? The local bank? No, it's too well protected. The gasoline station? No, it has guard dogs—and besides, he knows a couple of guys who work there. The Burger Queen in the next town is perfect. Only two people work behind the counter after midnight, a side street offers a quick getaway, police seldom put in an appearance, and no one over there knows him.

Let us analyze this scenario in terms of the rational choice approach. The young man is desperate for money and he needs it fast (the motive). He weighs the risks. The probability of a raid on the crack house is too high. He looks for suitable targets that are not well protected and are likely to have quite a bit of cash on hand. Two distinct sets of characteristics, then, are involved in law-violating behavior—those of the offender and those of the offense. The offender's characteristics include specific needs, values, learning experiences, and so on. The characteristics of the offense include the location of the target and the potential monetary yield. According to rational choice theory, involvement in crime depends on a personal decision made after one has weighed available information.

What will happen if the young man is frustrated in his holdup attempt? Suppose he arrives at the Burger Queen only to find police officers having dinner there. Will he then automatically look for another place to rob? Cornish and Clarke argue that displacement—the commission of a qualitatively similar crime at a different time or place—does not always follow. Of course, some offenders will try again, but the rational choice approach suggests that others will quit for some time—or, indeed, forever. We shall consider the choices made by offenders further when we discuss specific types of crimes in later chapters.

Routine Activities

Another new approach, **routine activities,** is closely linked to the rational choice perspective. It, too, focuses on the characteristics of the crime rather than on those of the offender. According to Lawrence Cohen and Marcus Felson, there will always be an ample supply of motivated offenders.[4] What we need to understand is the range of options among which offenders choose when they decide to commit a crime. "Just as lions look for deer near their watering hole," Felson says, "criminal offenders disproportionately find victims in certain settings."[5] This approach focuses on the circumstances in which crimes are committed. Each criminal act requires the convergence of three elements

- likely and motivated offenders (e.g., unemployed teenagers);
- suitable targets (e.g., easily transportable goods);
- an absence of capable guardians to prevent the would-be offender from committing the crime (e.g., friends or neighbors).

Cohen and Felson point out that crime rates rise in tandem with the number of suitable targets and the absence of people to protect those targets. Over the last few decades the number and variety of suitable targets—goods easily transported and sold, such as videocassette recorders and compact disc players—have increased steadily. At the same time, changes in the routine activities of everyday life have left most of those targets unguarded a good part of the day. In the past, American neighborhoods were smaller than they are now; when people left home, they walked. They shopped at neighborhood stores, visited movie houses and restaurants and clubs and friends close to home. Few places they went to regularly were more than a couple of blocks away. Since World War II, the territory of routine activities has expanded outward. The development of suburbs and expressways, the ease of air travel, the proliferation of day-care centers and nursery schools, and the increasing participation of women in the labor force have left homes empty and unguarded.

The logic of the argument is straightforward: the routine patterns of work, play, and leisure time affect the convergence in time and place of motivated offenders, suitable targets, and the absence of guardians. Cohen and Felson argue that if one component is missing, the crime is unlikely to be committed. Conversely, if all components are in place and one of them is strengthened, crime is likely to increase. If the proportions of motivated offenders and targets stay the same, for example, changes in routine activities of the sort we have experienced since World War II will alone increase the crime rate by multiplying the opportunities for crime. This approach has helped to explain, among other things, rates of victimization for specific crimes, rates of urban homicide, and "hot spots"—areas that produce a disproportionate number of calls to police.[6] We shall be returning to the routine activities approach in the following chapters.

Both the rational choice and the routine activity perspectives demonstrate that the commission of crime is not related solely to the biological and psychological characteristics of individuals or to social and economic factors. Accordingly, rather than focus attention solely on the people who commit crimes, we should concentrate also on the situational factors that influence the commission of crimes. This approach is particularly important for the development of crime-control policy and of "situational" crime prevention, which consists of changing the conditions and circumstances under which crime is committed. Situational crime prevention includes such measures as **target hardening** (steps taken to make it more difficult for offenders to carry out crimes against specific targets, such as the installation of better locks); organizing neighborhood watch groups, whose members are alert to any nonroutine activity at neighboring homes; and changing environmental designs of buildings and streets to afford more protection (as by installing more street lights). Theories of crime, according to Gottfredson and Hirschi, "acknowledge the ability of society to control crime without fundamental reconstruction of itself or the individuals within it."[7]

In the remaining chapters of Part Three we shall examine what criminologists have discovered about the characteristics of violent crimes, property crimes, organizational crimes, and crimes related to drugs, alcohol, and sex. Before we do so, it is important to review that part of criminal law which deals with the common legal ingredients, or elements, found in all crimes. With few exceptions, if any one of these elements is not present, no crime has been committed.[8] All of the defenses available to a person charged with a crime allege that at least one of these elements is not present.

INGREDIENTS OF CRIME

The American criminal law scholar Jerome Hall has developed the theory that a human event, in order to qualify as a crime, must meet seven basic requirements. These are

1. The Act Requirement;
2. The Legality Requirement;
3. The Harm Requirement;
4. The Causation Requirement;
5. The Mens Rea Requirement;
6. The Concurrence Requirement; and
7. The Punishment Requirement.[9]

The Act Requirement

Law scholars have long agreed that one of the most fundamental ingredients of every crime is a human act. And what is an "act"?

Suppose a sleepwalker, in a trance, grabs a stone and hurls it at a passerby, with lethal consequences. The law does not consider this event to be an act, as it is commonly understood that before any human behavior can qualify as an act, there must be a conscious interaction between mind and body, a physical movement that results from the determination or effort of the actor. Thus the Model Penal Code (MPC), which the American Law Institute proposed to legislatures in 1962, says that the following behavior forms are not voluntary acts

• a reflex or convulsion;
• a bodily movement during unconsciousness or sleep;
• conduct during hypnosis or resulting from hypnotic suggestion; and
• a bodily movement that is not determined by the actor, as when somebody is pushed by another person.[10]

This formulation gives the impression that the law is based on the premise of "free will," the idea that people are accountable only if they freely choose to do a thing and then consciously do it. Yet scientists and lawyers alike have yet to discover an individual who is free in his or her choices. All of us have been molded by factors beyond our control, and our choices

are to some extent conditioned by such factors and forces. It is only when our choices are overpoweringly influenced by forces beyond our control, such as those of the sleepwalking stone thrower, that the law will exempt us and consider our behavior irrational and beyond its reach.

Opposed to the advocates of the free will theory stand the determinists, who argue (as we saw in Chapter 3) that all human behavior is determined by forces beyond the control of human actors. Rational choice/routine activities scholars take no position in this debate. Rational choice theory neither demands nor presupposes the existence of free will. To choose one moment rather than another, or one target rather than another, does not require the existence of free will. Even a mouse learns quickly that it cannot get at the cheese by gnawing at the refrigerator door. But cheese on an open tray is fair game. Obviously the mouse prefers the tray to be in the room without the cat. Rational choice theorists are above all interested in preventing a crime (once something is recognized to be a crime). Thus they would recommend putting a glass dome over the cheese tray.

There is more to the "act" requirement than the issue of a voluntary, rational act: there is the problem of distinguishing between act and status. A California law made it a criminal offense, subject to a jail term, to "be" a drug addict. In *Robinson* v. *California* the U.S. Supreme Court held that statute to be unconstitutional. By making a status or condition a crime, without requiring an act, the Court ruled, the statute violated the Eighth Amendment to the U.S. Constitution, which prohibits "cruel and unusual punishments." Addiction, the Court noted, is a condition, an illness, much like leprosy or venereal disease. Even babies born of addict mothers are addicts. Said the Court: "Even one day in prison would be cruel and unusual punishment for the 'crime' of having a common cold."[11]

In a subsequent case, *Powell* v. *Texas*, the Supreme Court backed away from its recognition of the act requirement.[12] A Texas statute had made it a crime to be drunk in public. Powell was a chronic alcoholic, prosecuted for *being* in a public place while inebriated. It was contended in his behalf that chronic alcoholics cannot refrain from drinking. If they are homeless, they cannot help being in public places. The Supreme Court, however, upheld Powell's conviction, in essence saying that he had not been punished just for *being* a chronic alcoholic, but for doing something—for going to a public place. This ruling is considered by many to be inconsistent with the *Robinson* decision.

In sum, the criminal law, in principle, does not penalize anyone for a status or condition. Suppose the law made it a crime to be more than six feet tall, or to have red hair. Or suppose the law made it a crime to be a member of the family of an army deserter or to be of a given religion or ethnic background. That was exactly the situation in the Soviet Union under Stalin's penal code, which made it a crime to be related to a deserter from the Red Army, and in Hitler's Germany, where, in effect, it was a crime to be Jewish, punishable by death.

The act requirement has yet another aspect. As we have seen, an act requires the interaction of mind and body. If only the mind is active and the body does not move, we do not have an act. Just thinking about punching someone in the nose is not a crime. We are free to think. But if we carry a thought into physical action, we commit an act, which may be a crime.

Finally, there is the problem of omission, or failure to act. If the law requires young men to register for the draft, and if you are a young man with the form before you and you decide not to fill it out, you are guilty of a crime by omission. But haven't you really *acted*? You told your hand not to pick up that pen, not to fill out the form. So, inaction may be action when the law clearly spells out what you have to do and you decide not to do it. The law in most American states imposes no duty to be a Good Samaritan, to offer help to another person in distress. The Kitty Genovese case is one well-known example. Not one of her thirty-eight neighbors was a Good Samaritan (see Criminological Focus). The law requires action only if one has a legally imposed duty to act. Lifeguards, for example, are contractually obligated to save bathers from drowning; parents are obligated by law to protect their children; law enforcement officers and firefighters are required to rescue people in distress; and babysitters must protect babies in their care from harm. In addition, the law imposes a duty to continue rescue operations on anybody who, though not required to do so, has voluntarily come to the aid of a person in need of assistance.

The Kitty Genovese incident occurred in 1964. Later the same year the New York Legislature adopted a new penal code. After much debate, the legislators voted not to include a "Good Samaritan provision," which would have made it criminal not to come to the rescue of a fellow human being in distress, if it was possible to do so without undue risk. But then, the Biblical Good Samaritan was not compelled to act by any penal code. To him it was a matter of heart and conscience (Luke 10:33–35).

The Legality Requirement

Marion Palendrano was charged with, among other things, being a "common scold." She moved that the charge be dismissed, and the Superior Court of New Jersey agreed with her, reasoning:

1. Such a crime cannot be found anywhere in the New Jersey statute books. Hence there is no such crime.

2. "Being a common scold" is so vague a concept that to punish somebody for it would violate constitutional due process: "We insist that laws give the person of ordinary intelligence a reasonable opportunity to know what is prohibited, so that he may act accordingly," ruled the court.[13]

If we want a person to adhere to a standard, the person has to know what that standard is. Thus we have the ancient proposition that the only conduct that can be a crime is that which has been made criminal by law before an act is committed; in Latin, *nullum crimen sine lege:* no crime without law. It is obviously impossible to require people to abide by a law that does not yet exist. The law is interested only in an act

CRIMINOLOGICAL FOCUS

The Kitty Genovese Case

(1) *Where she parked her car.*
(2) *Place of initial attack.*
(3) *Place of second attack.*
(4) *Place of third attack.*

At 3:20 A.M., twenty-eight-year-old Kitty Genovese had returned from work, parked her car on a lot only 100 feet away from the entrance to her apartment building in the staid, middle-class Kew Gardens section of Queens, New York, and headed for home. At that moment she saw a man lurking at the far end of the lot. She knew of a nearby police call box and headed for it. But the man caught up with her, grabbed her, and stabbed her. Kitty screamed: "Oh, my God, he stabbed me! Please help me! Please help me!" Windows opened and a neighbor's voice was heard: "Let that girl alone." The attacker withdrew, but only momentarily; then he returned and stabbed Kitty again. With all the power she could summon Kitty screamed: "I'm dying! I'm dying!"

The attacker left. Kitty, bleeding profusely, staggered toward the apartment house door. A city bus passed. Lights went on in some windows. Kitty reached the entrance at 3:35 A.M. and slumped to the floor. The attacker returned and stabbed her again. Kitty was dead.

Not until 3:50 A.M. did the police receive a call from a reluctant neighbor. Thirty-eight people had witnessed the attack—respectable, law-abiding neighbors, in a part of town where few crimes were committed. A swift call to the police could have saved Kitty's life, with no danger to the caller.

Source: Based on A. M. Rosenthal, *Thirty-Eight Witnesses* (New York: McGraw-Hill, 1964).

(*actus*) that is *reus*, in the sense of guilty, evil, and prohibited.

Police, prosecutors, and courts are not interested in the billions of acts that human beings engage in, unless such acts have previously been defined by law as criminal. Additionally, as Marion Palendrano's case demonstrates, when the law has made some behavior a crime, the language defining it must be clear enough to be understood.

The Harm Requirement

Every crime has been created to prevent something bad from happening: that is, a given harm. Murder is prohibited because we don't want people to inflict death. Theft is prohibited because we don't want people to be deprived of their property. This detrimental consequence that we are trying to avoid is called harm. If the specified harm has not been created by the defendant's act, the crime is not complete. Just think of the would-be assassin John W. Hinckley, Jr., who wanted to kill President Reagan. He shot Reagan, but the president did not die. The harm envisioned by the law against murder had not been accomplished. (Hinckley could have been found guilty of attempted murder—but then, after all, he was acquitted by reason of insanity.)

Every crime has been created with a harm in mind. Pooper-scooper laws (you must clean up after your dog) are designed to prevent the harm of dirty streets and sidewalks. Arson laws seek to avoid the burning of houses, and so on. Sometimes the harm is less drastic than a dead body or a burned house, as in the case of drunk-driving statutes. Here the harm is not of a physical nature. (If the drunk driver kills someone, a more serious charge is brought.) The harm consists of the grave danger to the public which driving while intoxicated constitutes.

From a criminological perspective, most crimes are grouped in accordance with the harm that each entails. Offenses against the person involve harm to a person, and offenses against property involve damages to property or loss of its possession. (These crimes are discussed in Chapters 10 and 11.) The notion of harm is of singular significance to the rational choice/routine activities theory. After all, criminal law is meant to prevent the harm envisaged by penal statutes. Consequently, the interests threatened by criminal harm, the values of life and property, need protection from people who have a motivation and an opportunity to inflict such harm.

The Causation Requirement

What is the act of hitting a home run? Of course it is a hit that allows a batter to run to first, second, and third base and then back to home plate. Actually it is much more complicated than that. It starts with the decision to swing a bat, at a certain angle, with a particular intensity, in a specific direction, in order to cause a home run. Now suppose that at a San Diego Padres home game, the batter hits a ball unusually high in the air. A passing pelican picks it up, flies off with it, and then drops it into the bleachers. Has the batter hit a home run? We doubt it. It's the same in crime. The requirement is that the actor must achieve the result (the harm) through his or her own effort. If *A*, in an effort to kill *B*, wounds him, but *B* actually dies when the ambulance carrying him to the hospital collides with another vehicle, then *A* did not succeed in killing *B*. He may be guilty of an attempt to kill. The causation requirement, then, is that a crime is not complete unless the actor's conduct necessarily caused the harm without interference by somebody else.[14]

Mens Rea: The "Guilty Mind" Requirement

Every crime, according to tradition, requires **mens rea,** a "guilty mind." Let us examine the case of Ms. Lambert. She was convicted in Los Angeles of an offense created by city ordinance: having lived in the city without registering with the police as a person previously convicted of a crime. Ms. Lambert had no idea that Los Angeles had such a registration requirement. Nor could she possibly have known that she was required to register. She appealed all the way to the U.S. Supreme Court, and she won. Said the Court: "Where a person did not know [of the prohibition] (s)he may not be convicted consistent with due process."[15]

Of course, to blame Ms. Lambert for violating the Los Angeles city ordinance would make no sense. Ms. Lambert had no notion that she was doing something wrong by living in Los Angeles and not registering herself as a convicted person. The potential of blame which follows a choice to commit a crime is meant to be a powerful incentive to do the right thing and avoid doing the wrong thing. That is the function of mens rea. (We shall return to Ms. Lambert later on.)

With Ms. Lambert's case we have reached a fundamental point: the all-important principle that no one can be guilty of a crime unless he or she acted with the knowledge of doing something wrong. That is not a very difficult proposition. Anyone who violently attacks another person or takes another's property, or invades another's home, or forces intercourse, or forges a signature on someone else's check knows rather well that he or she is doing something wrong. This principle always has existed. It is implicit in the concept of crime that the perpetrator knows the wrongfulness of the act. It is not required that the perpetrator know the penal code or have personal feelings of guilt. It suffices that the perpetrator knows that he or she had no right to do what he or she did—and decided to do it anyway.[16]

All of the examples of mens rea which we have provided so far entail an intention to achieve harm, or a knowledge that the prohibited harm will result. For some crimes, however, less than a definite intention suffices; namely, reckless action by which the actor consciously risks producing a prohibited harm (for example, the driver who races down a rain-slick highway, or the employer who sends his employees to work without safety equipment, knowing full well that lives are thereby being endangered).

Strict liability is an exception to the mens rea requirement. There is a class of offenses for which legislatures or courts require no showing of criminal intent or mens rea. With respect to such offenses, the fact that the actor makes an innocent mistake and proceeds in good faith will not affect the criminal liability. Such offenses are called **strict liability** offenses, and they crept into our law with the Industrial Revolution. Most of them involve conduct subject to regulation, conduct that seemingly threatens public welfare as a whole. Such offenses range all the way from distributing adulterated food to passing a red light. Typically only small penalties are threatened for such offenses, but in a few cases very substantial punishments can be and have been imposed.[17]

The Concurrence Requirement

The concurrence requirement posits that the criminal act must concur with an equally criminal mind. Suppose a striker throws a stone at an office window in order to shatter it, and a broken piece of glass pierces the throat of a secretary, who bleeds to death. Wanting to do property damage deserves condemnation, but of a far lesser degree than wanting to kill. Act and intent did not concur in this case. The striker should not be found guilty of murder. The law has created many exceptions to the concurrence requirement, one of which, the felony murder rule, we shall discuss in Chapter 10.

The Punishment Requirement

The seventh and last of the ingredients needed to constitute a crime is that of punishment. An illegal act coupled with an evil mind (criminal intent or mens rea) still does not constitute a crime unless the law subjects it to a punishment. If a sign is posted in the park which says, "Do not step on the grass," and you do it anyway, have you committed a criminal offense? Not unless there is a law that subjects that act to punishment. Otherwise it is simply an improper or inconsiderate act, no more. The punishment requirement, more than any of the others, also helps us differentiate between crimes (which are subject to punishments) and **torts**, civil wrongs for which the law does not prescribe punishment but merely grants the injured party the right to recover damages.

The nature and severity of punishments also help us to differentiate between grades of crime. Most penal codes recognize three degrees of severity: **felonies** are severe crimes subject to punishments of a year or more in prison or to capital punishment; **misdemeanors** are less severe crimes, subject to a maximum of one year in jail. For crimes of both grades, fines can also

©1962 *The Saturday Evening Post*

Has a crime been committed? Is walking on the grass prohibited by law, subject to punishment? Did the actor commit the act by actually walking on the grass, or did he merely have a criminal intent to do so? Perhaps the actor is incapable of forming a legally relevant intent because he is too young to do so!

The arrest of Hinckley after he shot President Reagan and others. Hinckley was ultimately acquitted by reason of insanity.

be imposed as punishments. There are also infractions of the law called **violations**, for which, normally, only fines can be imposed. The types and forms of punishment to which a convict may be sentenced are discussed in Chapter 16, and the execution of sentences within the correctional system in Chapter 17.

THE DEFENSES

As we noted earlier, before an act can be considered a crime, all seven basic ingredients must be present. When we turn to the various defenses recognized by law, we discover that each defense simply claims that one or more of the seven basic constituent elements of the crime does not exist. In other words, what at first glance may indicate that a crime was committed—a dead body or a burned building—may turn out not to be a crime after all because, for example, the perpetrator lacked criminal intent or the law granted the actor the right to do what he or she did.

The Insanity Defense

On March 30, 1981, a young man stood in front of the Hilton Hotel in Washington, D.C., and mixed with the crowd that had assembled to greet President Reagan. As the president and his entourage left the hotel, the young man drew a revolver and fired several shots, wounding the president, White House Press Secretary John Brady, a Secret Service agent, and a District of Columbia police officer.[18] All survived, but Brady was permanently disabled.

The young man, as we discussed in Chapter 4, turned out to be John W. Hinckley, Jr., who had formed a fascination for the movie actress Jodie Foster. She had appeared in a movie that featured a deranged taxi driver who armed himself and killed a political candidate. Hinckley seemed to follow the movie script, believing that his only hope of winning Miss Foster's admiration lay in killing the president. Hinckley pleaded not guilty by reason of insanity. That plea amounts to saying: "Whatever happened, I am not guilty because I suffered from a mental illness that made me incapable of committing the crime you have charged me with."

In its modern form, the insanity defense was formulated by the House of Lords, following a case that was not very different from Hinckley's. Daniel M'Naghten was obsessed by the idea that the prime minister, Sir Robert Peel, wanted to destroy the liberties of English subjects. In 1829, when Peel was home secretary, with responsibility for security and internal affairs, he created a police force, and in the 1830s and 1840s he used the police to suppress public dissent. M'Naghten joined a campaign against Sir Robert. As a consequence of these activities, he became convinced that Sir Robert was spying on and persecuting him. When M'Naghten could no longer stand the pressure of his obsession, he traveled to London and loitered around 10 Downing Street, the prime minister's official residence. M'Naghten's opportunity came on Friday, January 20, 1843. He shot into the back of the person whom he thought to be Sir Robert, but the victim was in fact the prime minister's private secretary, Edward Drummond. A few days later Mr. Drummond died of the gunshot wounds. The trial of Daniel M'Naghten became a *cause célèbre* (a notorious case), and the ladies and gentlemen of the court were frequently in attendance.[19] M'Naghten was acquitted by reason of insanity. (Queen Victoria is rumored to have quipped: "A person who would want to shoot my Prime Minister must be sane!")

The M'Naghten test   After M'Naghten's acquittal the question of insanity was debated in the House of Lords, the upper house of Parliament (as well as England's highest court), which formulated the now famous M'Naghten rules:

> The jurors ought to be told in all cases that every man is to be presumed to be sane, and to possess a sufficient degree of reason to be responsible for his crimes, until the contrary is proved to their satisfaction; and that, to establish a defense on the ground of insanity, it must be clearly proved that, at the time of the committing of the act, the party accused was labouring under such a defect of reason, from disease of the mind, as not to know the nature and quality of the act he was doing; or, if he did know it, that he did not know he was doing what was wrong.[20]

This test of insanity can be reduced to the following formula: As a result of mental illness, the accused either

1. Did not know the nature and quality of his act; that is, the voluntary act requirement was not fulfilled; or

2. Did not know that the act was wrong; that is, the mens rea requirement was not fulfilled.

In either case there can be no crime.[21]

The debate about the M'Naghten test has raged for nearly a century and a half. Some courts have misunderstood the test, believing that the only criterion for insanity was whether the defendant knew the difference between right and wrong. Hence they called it the "right-wrong test." Others thought that a test that focuses only on what a person knows failed to capture the complexity of the human mind and its processes.

The irresistible impulse test   Imagine a case in which the defendant "knows" perfectly well what he is doing, and that what he is doing is wrong. But the defendant contends that somehow he lost control over his actions; that is, he lost the power to choose between right and wrong. Some process in his mind compelled him to do what he did. To deal with that kind of situation, some American courts in the second half of the nineteenth century added another component to the M'Naghten rules: If as a result of mental illness the accused was unable to control his or her actions, then he or she must be acquitted. Such loss of self-control has been termed an "irresistible impulse."[22]

The Durham rule or "product test"   Judge David Bazelon's opinion in *Durham* v. *United States* in 1954 developed a new insanity test, partially based on an old New Hampshire case:[23] The defendant was to be acquitted if the crime was the product of mental disease or defect. As soon as the defendant introduced some evidence of disease or defect, the prosecution had to prove the contrary beyond a reasonable doubt. Of all the tests, *Durham* has met with the most criticism and resistance from the legal community. In order to be acquitted by reason of insanity under the *Durham* formulation, a defendant simply had to introduce "some" evidence that the crime charged was a "product of" mental illness; that is, a mental disease or defect had the effect of producing the crime.

The *Durham* test allowed the medical profession to determine exclusively what was included among mental diseases or defects. The list of diseases and defects grew longer and longer. Ultimately the Court of Appeals for the District of Columbia, in *United States* v. *Brawner*, abolished the *Durham* test in favor of the American Law Institute (A.L.I.) test.[24] Today the *Durham* test is used in only one jurisdiction: Maine.

The A.L.I. test   The Model Penal Code of the American Law Institute (1962) formulated an insanity test that incorporated features of the M'Naghten rules and the irresistible impulse test. Under this test,

> a person is not responsible for criminal conduct if at the time of such conduct as a result of mental disease or defect he lacks substantial capacity either to appreciate the criminality [wrongfulness] of his conduct or to conform his conduct to the requirements of law.[25]

The special feature of this compromise test is that it leads to an acquittal when the defendant lacks "substantial capacity," whereas the M'Naghten test was frequently understood to require a total lack of capacity. This test is now in use in about half of the American states.

The new federal test   Let us return to the Hinckley case. The acquittal of Hinckley by reason of insanity caused the same kind of public outcry that M'Naghten's acquittal had caused nearly a century and a half earlier. At the time of the Hinckley case, the District of Columbia was using the A.L.I. test. But in reaction to Hinckley's acquittal, Congress for the first time debated what the insanity defense should be for the federal courts, just as the House of Lords in 1843 had discussed the same question following M'Naghten's acquittal. Congress came to the conclusion that the defendant should be acquitted by reason of insanity if "at the time of the commission of the act the defendant, as a result of a severe mental disease or defect, was unable to appreciate the nature and quality or wrongfulness of his act."[26] This new test added the requirement that the mental disease or defect must be *severe*.

The insanity defense is actually so rare that the debate on it is of more academic interest than practical significance. Defendants evaluated for insanity at the Colorado State Hospital in the early 1980s, for example, represented only 0.03 percent of all persons arrested in Colorado, and those ultimately acquitted by reason of insanity amounted to only 0.007 percent of all persons arrested.[27] Despite the statistical infrequency of the insanity defense, some legislatures have abolished it and others are planning to do so, out of fear that no matter how few such defendants may be, a "guilty" one might go free.

Guilty but Mentally Ill

Ten states have found yet another way to deal with troublesome insanity cases. They have added to the three available verdicts—guilty, not guilty, not guilty by reason of insanity—a fourth one: guilty but mentally ill; in some states, guilty but insane. This verdict is considered appropriate when a defendant suffers from a mental disease that is not severe enough to warrant acquittal by reason of insanity. In essence, it acknowledges the defendant's guilt and at the same time it recognizes as a mitigating factor the presence of a significant but not disabling mental disorder.

The Intoxication Defense

As we have just learned, mental illness can affect the mind to such an extent that the accused does not have the required guilty mind or could not fulfill the act requirement. Can anything other than mental illness disable the mind? The most prominent example is intoxication, whether by alcohol or by drugs.

It can readily be imagined that the Puritans were extremely averse to excusing the actions of people who drank to excess. In fact, drunkenness itself was an offense. But over the centuries American law made some concessions. The clearest case is that of "involuntary" intoxication. Suppose that, after taking a prescription drug, a person becomes so disoriented and confused as to lose the capacity to act rationally or to form a criminal intent. Suppose that person commits a crime. All courts would acquit an involuntarily intoxicated defendant who lacked the capacity to form the required guilty mind. Such cases are extremely rare.

Let us now look at situations in which a perpetrator is voluntarily intoxicated. This is a common problem (as we shall see in Chapter 13). According to a 1986 study of state prison inmates, 53.8 percent of all convicts had been under the influence of drugs or alcohol at the time they committed their offenses.[28] As these figures indicate, alcohol and drugs play an important role in crime. The figures do not tell us much about the nature of the role an intoxicant may have played in any given case. Among the persons who acted while under the influence of drugs, we find addicts who have committed offenses to pay for their habits. We also know that most persons who have committed crimes after drinking alcohol are likely to have experienced a lowering of inhibitions induced by the alcohol they drank. These perpetrators might not have acted violently had they not been under the influence of alcohol.

Voluntary intoxication is available in most states as a defense, which may at best exonerate a defendant if it negates mens rea, but most often reduces the degree of crime charged— from murder in the first degree to murder in the second degree, for example. It is as if the law has retained its original Puritan imprint: drunkenness is bad, and people who drink and violate the law do not deserve much leniency.

Mistake of Fact

This sort of thing can happen to anyone: A restaurant patron goes to the coat rack to retrieve his raincoat. He verifies the manufacturer's label, takes the coat, and departs. Another patron, obviously agitated, jumps up and grabs the coat-taker. "You stole my coat!" The first man is greatly embarrassed. It turns out that the coat is not his. But is he a thief?

To be a thief, as we shall see in Chapter 11, one has to intend to deprive someone else of his or her property. That is the mens rea re-

quirement. In this instance, did the first patron intend to deprive the owner of his property? No. He is *not* a thief, because he had no mens rea, no awareness of wrongdoing. That is the essence of the defense of mistake of fact. If there is no mens rea, there is no crime. When an honest mistake of fact negates the mens rea requirement, no crime is committed.[29]

Mistake or Ignorance of Law

At this point let us return to Ms. Lambert. Recall that Ms. Lambert had no idea that she was doing something wrong when she failed to register as an ex-felon in Los Angeles. Yet a jury had convicted her, and the court fined her $250. But does it make any sense to punish Ms. Lambert for what she did, or rather for what she didn't do? Nobody ever told her of the existence of the registration ordinance. What conceivable end could Ms. Lambert's punishment possibly serve under these circumstances? It is clear that she had no mens rea—no guilty mind—and thus did not commit a crime. But her mistake was not one of fact. Rather, she acted under ignorance of law, and ignorance of the law is no defense, according to an ancient maxim of the common law. It will be recalled that in the extreme circumstances of Ms. Lambert's case, the Supreme Court ultimately granted her a defense of ignorance of law. But, in about all other situations where mistake or ignorance of law is established, the defendant is not exonerated. Obviously the maxim that ignorance or mistake of law is no defense made good sense in the old days when the criminal law was restricted to such crimes as clubbing somebody over the head or slaughtering somebody else's cow. In such cases people could not claim that they did not know that it was forbidden to do what they had done. But times have changed, and who now can know all the laws? Even attorneys often have to do extensive research to find out if and how something is covered by criminal law. And if we all were to refrain from doing anything and everything until after we had gotten legal advice, life would come to a standstill. Yet most courts perpetuate the fiction that "everybody is presumed to know the law." Charles Dickens's Mr. Bumble, the beadle (clerk) in *Oliver Twist*, has an answer to that sort of presumption: "If the law supposes that, the law is a ass, a idiot!"

All of the defenses discussed so far have one common ingredient: they simply negate the existence of the crime charged because the defendant, in effect, alleges that as a result of some internal or external condition, his mind did not participate in his behavior, so that he did not commit the required act or form the guilty mind. In the next group of defenses the defendant fulfills all the act and intent requirements, and still the law does not impose criminal liability.

Duress

A robber approaches a bank teller with the following demand: "Your money or you're dead!" Not a fun choice, but a simple one. The teller probably reaches into the drawer and hands over the cash. Is the teller guilty of larceny or embezzlement? It is not her money. Her job as a teller does not give her the right to steal, or to embezzle funds entrusted to her.

To deal with such situations, the law has established the defense of duress:

> It is . . . [a] defense that the actor engaged in the conduct charged to constitute an offense because he was coerced to do so by the use of, or a threat to use, unlawful force against his person or the person of another, which a person of reasonable firmness in his situation would have been unable to resist.[30]

This defense applies when the actor has done something the law prohibits. The bank teller has taken money entrusted to her and given it to someone else. She has not been authorized to do so. All the elements of the crime of embezzlement are there. But the teller had no choice. And that is precisely the point. The law recognizes that we cannot be expected to yield our lives, our limbs, the safety of our relatives, our houses, or our property when we are confronted by a criminal threat that forces us to violate a law. But there is a general requirement that the evil that threatens the actor ("Your money or you're dead") and the evil created by the actor (handing over cash out of the till) be commensurate, that is, not out of proportion.

Necessity

As a general rule, necessity is a defense to a criminal charge when one has violated a law in the reasonable belief that this act was necessary to avoid an imminent and greater harm than the one that would be caused by commission of the crime. If the necessity defense is to apply, the paramount threat must emanate from a force other than a human aggressor. The cause is, as it has been called, an "act of God"—a storm, a fire, a shipwreck. (If the source of the threat is a human aggressor, the defense is duress.)[31] Suppose two hikers are surprised by a snowstorm. They stumble upon a vacation cottage. Under the rule of necessity, they may break into and enter the cottage and use its provisions to stay alive.

The question that has plagued the courts most is whether the defense of necessity ever permits the taking of an innocent life. Courts in England and the United States have reached contrasting solutions. English law does not permit the taking of an innocent life, even under the most dire necessity. American law permits the taking of innocent lives under certain conditions. A person who has fulfilled all legal obligations may sacrifice innocent human life, by random lot selection, in order to save more lives (see Window to the World).

Public Duty

The term "justification" is nowhere applied more appropriately than in conjunction with the defense of public duty, particularly when force has been used by an officer of the law. _Jus_ is the Latin term for law. Thus _jus_tifications are instances in which the law itself has created a counterlaw. Law prohibits an act, the counterlaw commands or authorizes it nevertheless (see Table 9.1).

By far the most frequent justification defense is use of force in law enforcement. In brief, law enforcement officers may use such force as is necessary to effect an arrest, but no more force than necessary. The use of deadly force is subject to severe restrictions (as we shall see in Chapter 15). Law enforcement officers who use more force than necessary are likely to be com-

WINDOW TO THE WORLD

Necessity at Sea

THE AMERICAN CASE

The American packet [passenger vessel] *William Brown* was en route from Liverpool to Philadelphia with a shipload of 65 Scottish and Irish immigrants when she struck an iceberg on April 19, 1841, 250 miles southeast of Race, Newfoundland. She sank rapidly in a howling nor'easter. The captain and some sailors manned the jolly boat [lifeboat], with one passenger aboard. The first mate and eight sailors manned the longboat. Even while the longboat was shoving off, they saw the *William Brown* go down, with the remaining passengers screaming, praying, and disappearing in the waves. The jolly boat, under the command of the captain, was never seen again. The first mate managed to keep the longboat afloat, but the seas and wind grew worse. The sea cock plug was lost, and the boat took on more and more water. The crew bailed as much as they could. The first mate shouted to his fellow sailors, "This work won't do. Help me, God. Men, go to work." Finally, the sailors obeyed, throwing a number of passengers overboard, being careful not to separate husband from wife, or mother from child. By such action the longboat was saved, and all still aboard were rescued by a passing vessel.

Holmes, one of the sailors, was tried on a murder charge and found guilty of manslaughter, but only because, as the court said, he had failed to exercise his duties toward passengers by throwing some of them overboard indiscriminately rather than by casting lots. This ruling has been much debated by lawyers and sailors alike.... Unlike English law, American law recognizes the defense of necessity in taking of innocent lives on the high seas under extreme conditions and subject to certain limitations, particularly the paramount duty of masters and mariners toward their passengers, to whom they are bound by a contract of safe carriage at sea.*

THE ENGLISH CASE

[T]hree shipwrecked sailors had been adrift in an open boat in the doldrums of the equatorial Atlantic. Their predicament had lasted for weeks. They had neither food nor water. They were delirious and the end appeared near, especially for the cabin boy, who was about to expire. In phantasmagoric exasperation, Dudley and Stephens killed the cabin boy and ate his flesh. This enabled them to survive for another few days until they were rescued by a passing vessel. The Court of Kings Bench convicted them of manslaughter: Innocent human life must never be taken even to save one's own life, and even under the most dire necessity. Yet, the manslaughter conviction was justified because, in their psychological and emotional condition, the two sailors were in fact incapable of harboring the malignity of heart that common law requires as malice aforethought for murder.†

The crew of the yacht Mignonette *in an open boat at sea, from sketches by Mr. Stephens, mate of the* Mignonette *and co-defendant in this famous case.*

United States v. *Holmes*, 1 Wall—Jr. 1, 26 Fed. Cas. 360 (U.S. Cir.Ct., E.D. Pa., 1842).
†*Regina* v. *Dudley and Stephens*, 14 Q.B.D. 273 (1884).

Source: G. O. W. Mueller and Freda Adler, *Outlaws of the Ocean: The Complete Book of Contemporary Crime on the High Seas* (New York: Hearst Marine Books [William Morrow], 1985), pp. 217–218.

TABLE 9.1   LAW PROHIBITIONS AND COUNTERLAW JUSTIFICATIONS

LAW PROHIBITIONS	COUNTERLAW JUSTIFICATIONS
The law prohibits the taking of life (criminal homicide).	The counterlaw requires execution of a convict sentenced to capital punishment.
	The counterlaw permits the shooting of a fleeing felon who is armed and constitutes a threat to life.
The law prohibits the taking of property (as in larceny).	The counterlaw allows impoundment of an illegally parked car.
The law prohibits the seizure of a person (as in false imprisonment or kidnapping).	The counterlaw requires the arrest of a person on probable cause.

mitting a criminal offense, such as assault and battery.

Self-Defense, Defense of Others, and Defense of Property

On the Saturday before Christmas in 1984 Bernhard H. Goetz entered a subway car at the IRT station at Seventh Avenue and 14th Street in Manhattan. He sat down close to four young men in their late teens. One of them offered a "How are ya," then approached Goetz and asked for $5. At that point Goetz pulled out a .38-caliber revolver and shot all four youths (one in the back).[32]

Few cases have ignited so much controversy as the Goetz case. Some people saw Goetz as the avenger of the city dweller, who constantly suffers from crime and the fear of crime. Others labeled him a vigilante. Or was he simply the meek underdog, as his appearance suggested, trying to defend himself against yet another attack on the subway? He could have been any one of those things. Goetz was charged with attempted murder, assault, and illegal possession of a weapon. In legal terms, the case simply raised the question of the right to use force, even deadly force, in self-defense, and the extent to which the defense still exists if the actor is mistaken about the actual threat that confronts him.

It is safe to say that in most states a person can use as much force as is reasonably necessary to defend himself or herself against what appears to be an immediate threat of violence

by another as long as the following four elements are present:

- The person must have an "honest and reasonable belief" that the force is necessary.
- The person must believe that the harm threatened will be immediately forthcoming.
- The harm threatened must be unlawful.
- The force used must be reasonable—only so much as appears necessary under the circumstances.

Let us return to the Goetz case. Did Goetz find himself in a life-threatening situation? We shall never know. As it turned out, some of the victims of his shooting had criminal records. They carried no firearms, only screwdrivers, which they said they used to pilfer vending machines. Objectively, it appears that Goetz was in no immediate physical danger. What, then, went on in his mind? He had experienced a brutal mugging preceded by similar circumstances. Like many other subway riders, he feared the predators who seemed to be ever present beneath the streets. The defense made a strong case that Goetz was in fear of his life. The legal question was whether he should be judged by a subjective standard—whether *he* felt in fear of his life—or by an objective standard: whether a reasonable person in his situation would have been in fear of his or her life. The jury resolved this issue by acquitting him of all charges except one: illegal possession of a handgun.

The right to use reasonable force, and if necessary deadly force, extends to the defense of

TABLE 9.2   CIRCUMSTANCES IN WHICH USE OF DEADLY FORCE IS JUSTIFIED, BY STATE

STATE	EVEN IF LIFE IS NOT THREATENED, DEADLY FORCE MAY BE JUSTIFIED TO PROTECT:		SPECIFIC CRIME AGAINST WHICH DEADLY FORCE MAY BE JUSTIFIED
	DWELLING	PROPERTY	
Alabama	Yes	No	Arson, burglary, rape, kidnapping, or robbery in "any degree"
Alaska	Yes	No	Actual commission of felony
Arizona	Yes	No	Arson, burglary, kidnapping, aggravated assaults
Arkansas	Yes	No	Felonies as defined by statute
California	Yes	No	Unlawful or forcible entry
Colorado	Yes	No	Felonies, including assault, robbery, rape, arson, kidnapping
Connecticut	Yes	No	Any violent crime
Delaware	Yes	No	Felonious activity
District of Columbia	Yes	No	Felony
Florida	Yes	No	Forcible felony
Georgia	Yes	Yes	Actual commission of a forcible felony
Hawaii	Yes	Yes	Felonious property damage, burglary, robbery, etc.
Idaho	Yes	Yes	Felonious breaking and entering
Illinois	Yes	Yes	Forcible felony
Indiana	Yes	No	Unlawful entry
Iowa	Yes	Yes	Breaking and entering
Kansas	Yes	No	Breaking and entering, including attempts
Kentucky	No	No	—
Louisiana	Yes	No	Unlawful entry, including attempts
Maine	Yes	No	Criminal trespass, kidnapping, rape, arson
Maryland	No	No	—
Massachusetts	No	No	—
Michigan	Yes	No	Circumstances on a case-by-case basis

others. In most jurisdictions, a defender can use as much force on behalf of another as he or she could have used in self-defense. Of course, such defenders must reasonably believe that if they were in the other person's position, they would have the right to defend themselves, and the amount of force used must be necessary. But some states require in addition that the person

TABLE 9.2   (Cont.)

STATE	EVEN IF LIFE IS NOT THREATENED, DEADLY FORCE MAY BE JUSTIFIED TO PROTECT:		SPECIFIC CRIME AGAINST WHICH DEADLY FORCE MAY BE JUSTIFIED
	DWELLING	PROPERTY	
Minnesota	Yes	No	Felony
Mississippi	Yes	—	Felony, including attempts
Missouri	No	No	—
Montana	Yes	Yes	Any forcible felony
Nebraska	Yes	No	Unlawful entry, kidnapping, and rape
Nevada	Yes	—	Actual commission of felony
New Hampshire	Yes	—	Felony
New Jersey	Yes	No	Burglary, arson, and robbery
New Mexico	Yes	Yes	Any felony
New York	Yes	No	Burglary, arson, kidnapping, and robbery, including attempts
North Carolina	Yes	No	Intending to commit a felony
North Dakota	Yes	No	Any violent felony
Ohio	—	—	—
Oklahoma	Yes	No	Felony within a dwelling
Oregon	Yes	—	Burglary in a dwelling, including attempts
Pennsylvania	Yes	—	Burglary or criminal trespass
Rhode Island	Yes	—	Breaking or entering
South Carolina	No	No	—
South Dakota	Yes	—	Burglary, including attempts
Tennessee	Yes	No	Felony
Texas	Yes	No	Burglary, robbery, or theft during the night
Utah	Yes	—	Felony
Vermont	Yes	—	Forcible felony
Virginia	No	No	—
Washington	No	No	—
West Virginia	Yes	No	Any felony
Wisconsin	No	No	—
Wyoming	No	No	—

Note: All states allow ultimate recourse to deadly force when life is in immediate danger.

Source: U.S. Department of Justice, *Report to the Nation on Crime and Justice*, 2d ed. (Washington, D.C.: U.S. Government Printing Office, 1988).

being assisted must also have the right to use force, regardless of the defender's perception.

The law views the protection of property and human life differently (Table 9.2). With few exceptions, the right of self-defense is far more extensive than the right of defense of property. The general rule in this area is that nondeadly force may be used, typically after some request

AT ISSUE

The Battered Woman—Self-Defense and the Penal Codes

The law is very strict when it comes to the application of force in self-defense. The Model Penal Code decrees "the use of force upon or toward another person is justifiable when the actor believes that such force is immediately necessary for the purpose of protecting himself against the use of unlawful force by such other person on the present occasion" [M.P.C. Sec. 3.04]. In recent years an increasing number of women abused by their mates have resorted to deadly force. The law has treated such women leniently in some respects, harshly in others. To begin with, the standard of law is phrased in terms of "protecting himself." How will courts translate the himself standard, based on centuries of experience with male self-defense, into a herself standard? Do women think and react differently from men in assessing the danger that derives from physical abuse? Do women "believe" differently from men? Do women have a different view of the "immediacy" of the warranted self-protective action? How do women view "the present occasion" when they are being victimized constantly? Where is the tolerance limit? Lenore E. Walker's study of the Battered Woman Syndrome permitted her to conclude:

Occasionally (less than 15 percent of all homicides) a woman will kill her abuser while trying to defend herself or her children. Sometimes, she strikes back during a calm period, knowing that the tension is building towards another acute battering incident, where this time she may die. When examining the statistics, we find that more women than men are charged with first or second degree murder. There seems to be a sexist bias operating in which the courts find it more difficult to see justifiable or mitigating circumstances for women who kill. The now classic Broverman et al. (1970) studies demonstrated that the kinds of behaviors and emotions expressed when committing an aggressive act will be viewed as normal for men but not for women. On the other hand, women's violence is more likely to be found excusable, if her insanity under the law can be demonstrated. Any changes in the insanity laws will probably have the greatest impact on women and other assault victims who reach a breaking point and no longer know the difference between right and wrong and/or can no longer refrain from an irresistible impulse to survive.

In most states' criminal codes, self-defense is defined as the justifiable commission of a criminal act by using the least amount of force necessary to prevent imminent bodily harm which needs only to be reasonably perceived as about to happen. The perception of how much force is necessary must also be reasonable. Such a definition works against women because they are not socialized to use physical force, are rarely equal to a man in size, strength, or physical training, and may have learned to expect more injury with inadequate attempts to repel a man's attack. Thus, some courts have ruled it would be reasonable for a woman to defend herself with a deadly weapon against a man armed only with the parts of his body he learned to use as a deadly weapon. Courts also have been allowing evidence to account for the cumulative effects of repeated violence in self-defense and diminished-capacity assertions. Expert witness testimony has been admitted in many states to help explain the reasonableness of such perceptions.

It would be rash to conclude that the penal codes need immediate reform to protect women who kill in perceived self-defense. But it is reasonable to expect that penal code reformers review the entirety of penal codes so as to accommodate the fact that men and women are covered and protected equally, under particular consideration of contemporary life situations. [See also Jacqueline Walus-Wigle and J. Reid Meloy, "Battered Woman Syndrome as a Criminal Defense," *The Journal of Psychiatry and the Law*, 1988 (Fall): 389–401.]

Source: Lenore E. Walker, *The Battered Woman Syndrome* (New York: Springer Publishing Co., 1984), pp. 142–143.

has been made to desist, when it is necessary to thwart an intrusion. When there is some indication that the intruder intends to commit a felony on the premises, and a warning to desist has been issued and ignored, then deadly force may be used.

ATTEMPT AND ACCESSORYSHIP

The doctrines pertaining to defenses are not the only doctrines of criminal law used to assess criminal charges. Foremost among the remaining doctrines is the one pertaining to attempted crimes. What should the law do to someone who tries to commit a crime but does not succeed? Under early common law, attempts to commit crimes were not considered crimes, because the actus reus was not completed. But a person who tries to complete a crime surely has the same mens rea and thus the same culpability as one who succeeds in creating harm. Should the would-be perpetrator be treated differently just because he or she did not succeed?

In 1784, it was decided in England that an attempt to commit a felony was indeed a crime.[33] That case laid the foundation for our present conceptualization of **criminal attempt:** "an act or omission constituting a substantial step in a course of conduct planned to culminate in the commission of a crime."[34]

The common law also created a sophisticated system for determining the liability of all persons involved in the commission of a crime. When, where, and how the various parties could be prosecuted, and the use of evidence at trial, depended on the type of participation. Today most states recognize only **principals** (all persons who commit an offense by their own conduct) and **accomplices** (all those who aid the perpetrator). That system has not solved all problems, because the line between committing a crime and aiding in its commission is a fine one. Though principals and accomplices are usually considered equally culpable, in practice judges often impose lighter sentences on accomplices.

REVIEW

Unlike theories of criminality (discussed in Part Two), which explain why people commit crimes, recent approaches, such as the theories of rational choice and routine activities, concentrate on the crimes themselves and try to explain why specific crimes are committed. As the emphasis of these new crime-specific theories is on the crime rather than on the perpetrator, it becomes necessary to focus on the meaning of crime. In exploring the legal meaning of crime, we have found that in order for a crime to exist, seven basic elements must be present: (1) an act (actus) that (2) is in violation of law (reus), that (3) causes (4) the harm identified by the law and which is committed with (5) criminal intent (mens rea, or a guilty mind). In addition, (6) the criminal act must concur with the guilty mind and (7) the act must be subject to punishment.

The various defenses to a criminal charge work rather logically. A defense simply negates the existence of one of the seven basic elements of crime, usually the mens rea (as in mistake of fact and insanity), sometimes even the act itself (as in some insanity defenses), and sometimes the unlawfulness of the act (as in justification defenses). Now that we have examined the legal elements common to all crimes, in the next chapter we turn to an analysis of specific types of crime.

KEY TERMS

accomplices
criminal attempt

felonies
mens rea

misdemeanors
principals
rational choice
routine activities

strict liability
target hardening
torts
violations

NOTES

1. Michael Gottfredson and Travis Hirschi, "A Propensity-Event Theory of Crime," in *Advances in Criminological Theory,* ed. William S. Laufer and Freda Adler, pp. 57–67 (New Brunswick, N.J.: Transaction, 1989).

2. Derek B. Cornish and Ronald V. Clarke, eds., *The Reasoning Criminal* (New York: Springer-Verlag, 1986), p. vi.

3. Derek B. Cornish and Ronald V. Clarke, "Understanding Crime Displacement: An Application of Rational Choice Theory," *Criminology* 25 (November 1987): 933–947, at 940.

4. Lawrence E. Cohen and Marcus Felson, "Social Changes and Crime Rate Trends: A Routine Activity Approach," *American Sociological Review* 44 (1979): 588–608.

5. Marcus Felson, "Routine Activities and Crime Prevention in the Developing Metropolis," *Criminology* 25 (November 1987): 911–931, at 914.

6. Lawrence W. Sherman, Patrick R. Gartin, and Michael E. Buerger, "Hot Spots of Predatory Crime: Routine Activities and the Criminology of Place," *Criminology* 27 (February 1989): 27–55.

7. Gottfredson and Hirschi, "Propensity Event Theory," p. 58.

8. The Anglo-American concept of crime was developed by a long line of distinguished legal scholars. Works that have contributed to this concept include Sir James Fitzjames Stephen, *A Digest of the Criminal Law of England* (London: Macmillan, 1877) and *History of the Criminal Law of England,* 3 vols. (London: Macmillan, 1883) (a revision of *A General View of the Criminal Law,* 1869); Glanville L. Williams, *Criminal Law—The General Part,* 2d ed. (London: Stevens, 1961); Joel Prentice Bishop, *Commentaries on the Criminal Law,* 2 vols. (Boston: Little, Brown, 1856, 1858); Francis W. Wharton, *A Treatise on the Criminal Law of the United States* (Philadelphia: J. Key, 1852); George Fletcher, *Rethinking Criminal Law* (Boston: Little, Brown, 1978); Paul H. Robinson, *Fundamentals of Criminal Law* (Boston: Little, Brown, 1988) and *Criminal Law Defenses* (St. Paul, Minn.: West, 1984). For a general assessment of criminal law scholarship, see G. O. W. Mueller, *Crime, Law, and the Scholars* (London: Heinemann; Seattle: University of Washington Press, 1969).

9. Jerome Hall, *General Principles of Criminal Law,* 2d ed. (Indianapolis: Bobbs-Merrill, 1960).

10. American Law Institute, Model Penal Code, sec. 2.01(1). The American Law Institute, dedicated to law reform, is an association of some of the most prestigious American lawyers. Between 1954 and 1962 this group sought to codify the best features of the penal codes of the various states. The resultant Model Penal Code (MPC) has had considerable influence on law reform in many states, and has been adopted nearly in full by New Jersey and Pennsylvania. We shall have frequent occasion to refer to the MPC as "typical" American criminal law.

11. Robinson v. California, 370 U.S. 660 (1962).

12. Powell v. Texas, 392 U.S. 514 (1968).

13. State v. Palendrano, 120 N.J. Super. 336, 293 A.2d 747 (1972).

14. G. O. W. Mueller, "Causing Criminal Harm," in *Essays in Criminal Science,* ed. Mueller, pp. 167–214 (South Hackensack, N.J.: Fred B. Rothman; London: Sweet & Maxwell, Ltd., 1961).

15. Lambert v. California, 355 U.S. 225 (1957). This decision must be approached with care: it does not stand for the proposition that ignorance of the law is an excuse. The Supreme Court was very careful to limit the scope of its decision to offenses by omission of adherence to regulations not commonly known, when the defendant in fact did not know—and had no means of knowing—of the prohibition.

16. G. O. W. Mueller, "On Common Law Mens Rea," *Minnesota Law Review* 42 (1958): 1043–1104, at 1060.

17. Wayne R. LaFave and Austin W. Scott, Jr., *Criminal Law* (St. Paul, Minn.: West, 1983), p. 222.

18. Peter W. Low, John Calvin Jeffries, Jr., and Richard J. Bonnie, *The Trial of John W. Hinckley, Jr.* (Mineola, N.Y.: Foundation Press, 1986).

19. Richard Moran, *Knowing Right from Wrong: The Insanity Defense of Daniel McNaughten* (New York: Free Press, 1981), is a fascinating discussion of the M'Naghten case. See also Bernard L. Diamond, "Isaac Ray and the Trial of Daniel M'Naghten," *American Journal of Psychiatry* 112 (February 1956): 651–656.

20. Daniel M'Naghten Case, 10 C.F. 200, 210–211, 8 Eng. Rep. 718, 722–723 (1843).

21. G. O. W. Mueller, "M'Naghten Remains Irreplaceable: Recent Events in the Law of Incapacity," *Georgetown Law Journal* 50 (1961): 105–119. The literature on the law of insanity is extensive. Among more recent works are Abraham S. Goldstein, *The Insanity Defense* (New Haven, Conn.: Yale University Press, 1967); Joel Feinberg, *Doing and Deserving: Essays in the Theory of Responsibility* (Princeton, N.J.: Princeton University Press, 1970); Herbert Fingarette and Ann Fingarette Hasse, *Mental Disabilities and Criminal Responsibility* (Berkeley: University of California Press, 1979); Norval Morris, *Madness and the Criminal Law* (Chicago: University of Chicago Press, 1982); Donald H. J. Herfmann, *The Insanity Defense: Philosophical, Historical, and Legal Perspectives* (Springfield, Ill.: Charles C Thomas, 1983); Michael S. Moore, *Law and Psychiatry: Rethinking the Relationship* (New York: Cambridge University Press, 1984).

22. See Parsons v. State, 81 Ala. 577, 2 So. 854 (1887).

23. Durham v. United States, 214 F.2d 862 (D.C. Cir. 1954); State v. Pike, 49 N.H. 399 (1869).

24. United States v. Brawner, 471 F.2d 696 (D.C. Cir. 1972).

25. MPC, sec. 4.01.

26. 18 U.S.C. § 17.

27. Richard A. Pasewark, Richard, Jeffrey and Stephen Bieber, "Differentiating Successful and Unsuccessful Insanity Plea Defendants in Colorado," *Journal of Psychiatry and Law* 15 (1987): 55–82, at 65, covering the period July 1, 1980, to June 30, 1983.

28. U.S. Department of Justice, Bureau of Justice Statistics, *Profile of State Prison Inmates, 1986*, Special Report NCJ-109926 (Washington, D.C.: U.S. Government Printing Office, January 1988), p. 6, Table 12.

29. Paul H. Robinson, *Fundamentals of Criminal Law* (Boston: Little, Brown, 1988), pp. 287ff.

30. Basically, the defense is not available if the actor was at fault by placing himself in the situation: MPC, sec. 2.09(1).

31. American Law Institute, *Model Penal Code, Tentative Draft No. 8* (Philadelphia, 1958), pp. 5–10.

32. For a fascinating legal and factual analysis of the case, see George P. Fletcher, *A Crime of Self-Defense: Bernhard Goetz and the Law on Trial* (New York: Free Press, 1988).

33. Rex v. Scofield (1784 Cald. 402).

34. MPC, sec. 5.01(1)(c).

10

VIOLENT CRIMES

To millions of Americans few things are more pervasive, more frightening, more real today than violent crime and the fear of being assaulted, mugged, robbed, or raped. The fear of being victimized by criminal attack has touched us all in some way. People are fleeing their residences in cities to the expected safety of suburban living. Residents of many areas will not go out on the street at night. Others have added bars and extra locks to windows and doors in their homes. Bus drivers in major cities do not carry cash because incidents of robbery have been so frequent. In some areas local citizens patrol the streets at night to attain the safety they feel has not been provided....

There are numerous conflicting definitions of criminal violence as a class of behavior. Police, prosecutors, jurists, federal agents, local detention officials, and behavioral scientists all hold somewhat different viewpoints as to what constitute acts of violence. All would probably agree, however, as the police reports make abundantly clear, that criminal violence involves the use of or the threat of force on a victim by an offender.[1]

Having explored the ingredients of crime in general, let us now focus on specific crimes of violence. The penal law defines types of violent crime, and each is distinguished by a particular set of characteristics. We will explore the frequency with which each type of violent crime is committed, the methods used in its commission, and its distribution through time and place. We will also examine the people who commit the offense and those who are its victims. As we indicated earlier, if we can ascertain when, where, and how a specific type of crime is likely to be committed, we will be in a better position to reduce the incidence of that crime by devising appropriate strategies to prevent it.

The taking of life is the most serious harm one can inflict on another human being. Consequently, we begin with homicide. Serious attacks that fall short of homicide are assaults of various kinds, including serious sexual assault (rape) and the forceful taking of property from another person (robbery). Other patterns of violence are not defined as such in the penal codes but are so important in practice as to require separate discussion. Family-related violence and terrorism, both of which encompass a variety of crimes, fall into this category.

HOMICIDE

Homicide is the killing of one human being by another. Some homicides are sanctioned by law. In this category of **justifiable homicide,** we find homicides committed by law enforcement officers in the course of carrying out duties imposed on them by law (see the Public Duty defense, Chapter 9). Here we also find the homicides committed by soldiers in combat. Other killings are considered excusable, as when a homeowner has no recourse other than to kill an intruder who threatens lives of family members. Criminologists are most interested in criminal homicides—unlawful killings, without justification or excuse. Criminal homicides are subdivided into three categories: murder, manslaughter, and negligent homicide.

Murder

At common law, **murder** was defined as the intentional killing of another person with **malice aforethought.** Courts have struggled with an exact definition of malice. To describe it they have used such terms as "evil mind" and "abandoned and malignant heart." Actually, malice is a very simple concept. It is the defendant's awareness that he or she had no right to kill but intended to kill anyway.[2] Originally the malice had to be "aforethought": the defendant had to have killed after some contemplation, rather than on the spur of the moment. But the concept of "aforethought" became meaningless because some courts considered even a few seconds of contemplation sufficient to establish forethought. The dividing line between contemplated and spur-of-the-moment killings disappeared. But many legislators believed that contemplation was an appropriate concept, as it permitted differentiation between the more and the less heinous types of murder. They reintroduced it, calling it "premeditation and deliberation." A premeditated, deliberate, intentional killing became **murder in the first degree,** while an intentional killing without premeditation

and deliberation became **murder in the second degree.** States that had the death penalty reserved it for murder in the first degree. Some state statutes listed particular means of committing a murder as indicative of premeditation and deliberation, such as killing by poison or by lying in wait. More recently the charge of murder in the first degree has been reserved for the killing of a law enforcement officer or of a corrections officer, and for the killing of any person by a prisoner serving a life sentence. Also among the most heinous forms of murder is **assassination,** the killing of a head of state or government, or of an otherwise highly visible figure (see Window to the World).

A special form of murder, **felony murder,** requires no intention to kill. It requires instead the intention to commit some other felony, such as robbery or rape, and the death of a person during the commission of, or flight from, that felony. Even accomplices are guilty of felony murder when one of their associates has caused a death. For example, *A* and *B* are holding up a gas station attendant, *A* fires a warning shot, and the bullet ricochets and kills a passerby. Both *A* and *B* are guilty of felony murder. The rule originated in England centuries ago, when death sentences were imposed for all felonies. Thus it made no difference whether a perpetrator actually intended to kill or intended merely to rob. Most states today apply the felony murder rule only when the underlying felony is a life-endangering one, such as arson, rape, or robbery.

Manslaughter

Manslaughter is the unlawful killing of another person without malice. Manslaughter may be either voluntary or involuntary.

Voluntary manslaughter   Voluntary manslaughter is a killing committed intentionally but without malice, as in the heat of passion or in response to strong provocation. Persons who kill under extreme provocation cannot make rational decisions as to whether they have a right to kill or not. They therefore act without the necessary malice.[3]

WINDOW TO THE WORLD

Assassinations around the Globe

Since earliest times the fate of nations and world history have been affected by assassinations. Assassinations were so common in ancient Rome that it became forbidden to carry daggers into the Senate. That did not keep Gaius Julius Caesar's assassins from stabbing him to death on the Ides of March (March 15), 44 B.C. Their weapons were stilichos, pencil-like tools used to write on wax tablets.

The United States has had more than its share of assassinations. Abraham Lincoln was killed by John Wilkes Booth in 1865. American presidents and political leaders have remained favorite targets: James A. Garfield, 1881; William McKinley, 1901; John F. Kennedy, 1963; Senator Robert F. Kennedy, 1968; Dr. Martin Luther King, Jr., 1968. Attempted assassinations have been directed once or repeatedly at Presidents Theodore Roosevelt, Franklin Delano Roosevelt, Harry S Truman, Richard Nixon, Gerald Ford, and Ronald Reagan and at Governor George C. Wallace of Alabama. The penal codes treat the assassination of a head of state or government as a category of homicide distinct from, or higher than, ordinary murder. The Federal Criminal Code, Title 18 U.S. Code ¶ 1751, imposes the death penalty for the assassination of the president of the United States, the president-elect, other potential successors, and specially appointed executive staff members. However, this legislation has not discouraged would-be assassins.

In the last fifteen years the number of assassinations around the world appears to have increased. In 1975 President Richard Ratsimandraua of Madagascar, King Faisal of Saudi Arabia, and President Sheik Mujibur Rahman of Bangladesh were assassinated; in 1976 the Nigerian head of state, General Murtala Ramat Mohammed; in 1977 President Marien Ngouabi of the Congo; in 1978 former Iraqi premier Abdul Razak Al-Naif and former Italian premier Aldo Moro; in 1979 Lord Mountbatten and South Korean president Park Chung Hee; in 1980 Liberian president William R. Tolbert and former Nicaraguan president Anastasio Somoza Debayle; in 1981 Egyptian president Anwar El-Sadat; in 1982 Lebanese president-elect Bashir Gemayel; in 1983 Philippine opposition leader Benigno Acquino; in 1984 Indian prime minister Indira Gandhi; in 1986 Swedish prime minister Olof Palme; and in 1988 Lebanese premier Rashid Karami. Many more assassinations of political leaders occurred around the world. Hundreds more were attempted but did not succeed. Assassinations are just as likely to occur in politically stable countries as in countries with turmoil, in developed and developing countries.

What prompts people to kill a national leader? Obviously some assassins are psychologically disturbed. For example, Daniel M'Naghten, who wanted to kill Sir Robert Peel, the prime minister, was acquitted by reason of insanity. Several recent assassins may also fall into this category: Lee Harvey Oswald, who has been identified as the killer of President Kennedy; President Ford's two would-be assassins, Lynette "Squeaky" Fromme and Sarah Jane Moore; and John Hinckley, who tried to kill President Reagan. But some assassins act for political, idealistic reasons, such as the Puerto Rican nationalists Oscar Collazo and Griselio Torresola, who tried to kill President Truman.

Are all political assassins bad? The citizens of the Federal Republic of Germany commemorate July 20, the day on which, in 1944, Colonel Count Klaus von Stauffenberg, acting on behalf of hundreds of conspirators, detonated a bomb in Adolf Hitler's bunker which almost killed him. That was to be the last of 43 attempted assassinations of Hitler, who committed suicide less than a year later, but not until after Colonel von Stauffenberg and more than 200 officers had been summarily tried by Nazi courts and hanged.

Just as passion, fright, fear, or consternation may affect a person's capacity to act rationally, so may drugs or alcohol. In some states a charge of murder may be reduced to voluntary manslaughter when the defendant was so grossly intoxicated as not to be fully aware of the implications of his or her actions. All voluntary manslaughter cases have one thing in common: the defendant's awareness of the unlawfulness of the act was dulled or grossly reduced by shock, fright, consternation, or intoxication.

Involuntary manslaughter   A crime is designated as **involuntary manslaughter** when a person has caused the death of another unintentionally but recklessly by consciously taking a grave risk that endangered the other person's life. Many states have created an additional homicide category, negligent homicide, for purposes of establishing criminal liability for grossly negligent killing, even when the offender was not aware of the risk but should have been. The crime of involuntary manslaughter plays an increasingly prominent role in our society, with its high concentrations of population, high-tech risks, and chemical and even nuclear dangers. No case casts a clearer light on the crime of involuntary manslaughter than the 1942 Coconut Grove disaster, in which 491 people perished because of the nightclub owner's unconscious negligence in creating fire hazards.[4] The nightclub was overcrowded, it was furnished and decorated with highly flammable materials, and exits were blocked.

The Extent of Homicide

When social scientists look at homicides, their perspective differs from that of the legislators who define these crimes. Social scientists are concerned with the rates and patterns of criminal activities.

The American murder rate always has been high. It reached a peak in 1980 and has been declining erratically since then. In 1988, our population of 245.8 million experienced 20,675 murders and nonnegligent homicides (as reported to the police), or 8.4 per 100,000 of the population. This rate is not equally distributed over

the whole country. The murder rates are higher in the southern and western states (10.3 and 8.5 per 100,000, respectively) than in the northeastern and midwestern states (7.5 and 6.4 per 100,000, respectively). Your chance of becoming a murder victim is much higher if you are male than if you are female: of all murder victims, 74 percent are male, 26 percent female. Age plays a role—nearly half of all murder victims are between the ages of 20 and 34—and so does race: 53 percent of all murder victims are white, 45 percent are black, and the remaining 2 percent are of other ethnic origins.[5] Ninety-four percent of the black murder victims were slain by black offenders and 88 percent of the white murder victims were killed by white offenders. Intentional criminal homicide apparently is an intraracial crime. But it is not an intragender crime. The data show that a majority of both males and females are murdered by males. Among each 100,000 of our population, 8 white males and 3 white females were murdered, compared to 40 black males and 11 black females. The population at the highest risk consists of black men between 25 and 35 years of age.[6]

Researchers have asked what happens to homicide rates over time when the composition of the population changes. What is the effect, for example, of a change in the racial composition of a city? Roland Chilton, using data on offenses committed in Chicago between 1960 and 1980 and census data for those years, found that about 20 percent of the total increase in homicide rates could be explained by increases in the nonwhite male population. The same correlation is found in most major cities in the United States. Chilton argues that the problem will remain because of the poverty and demoralization of the groups involved, and we can even expect that it will get worse if city governments are unable to improve the schools, lessen unemployment, and extend social services.[7] Until conditions change, what has been poignantly referred to as "the subculture of exasperation" will continue to produce a high homicide rate among nonwhite inner-city males.[8] Coramae Mann has found that although black women make up about 11 percent of the female population in the United States, they are arrested for three-fourths of all homicides committed by females. She argues that given such a disproportionate involvement in violent crime, one has to question whether the "subculture of exasperation" alone is entirely responsible.[9] But so few studies have been done on the subject that we cannot reach any definitive conclusion. Other investigators agree that homicide rates cannot be explained solely by such factors as poverty; they are significantly associated also with cultural approval of a resort to violence.[10]

The Nature of Homicide

Let us take a closer look at killers and their victims and see how they are related to each other. In the 1950s Marvin Wolfgang studied homicide situations, perpetrators, and victims in the Philadelphia area. The victims and offenders were predominantly young black adults of low socioeconomic status. The offenses were committed in the inner city; they occurred primarily in the home of the victim or offender, on weekends, in the evening hours, and among friends or acquaintances. Building on the pioneering work of Hans von Hentig,[11] Wolfgang found that many of the victims had actually initiated the social interaction that led to the homicidal response, in a direct or subliminal way. He coined the term **victim precipitation** for such instances, which may account for as many as a quarter to a half of all intentional homicides. In such cases it is the victim who, by insinuation, bodily movement, verbal incitement, or the actual use of physical force, initiates a series of events that results in his or her own death. For example:

> During an argument in which a male called a female many vile names, she tried to telephone the police. He grabbed the phone from her hands, knocked her down, kicked her, and hit her with a tire gauge. She ran to the kitchen, grabbed a butcher knife, and stabbed him in the stomach.[12]

Recent studies have provided additional insight into the patterns of homicide. Robert Silverman and Leslie Kennedy demonstrated that gender relationships, age, means of commission of the act, and location vary with relational distance, from closest relatives (lovers, spouses) to total strangers.[13] Margaret Zahn and Philip Sagi have developed a model that distinguishes among homicides on the basis of characteristics of victims, offenders, location, method of attack, and presence of witnesses. They conclude that all these characteristics and variables serve to differentiate four categories of homicides: (1) those within the family, (2) those among friends and acquaintances, (3) stranger homicides associated with felonies, and (4) stranger homicides not associated with felonies.[14]

Stranger homicides   According to the Supplementary Homicide Reports (SHR) of the Uniform Crime Reporting Program, the rate of **stranger homicide**—a killing in which killer and victim have had no known previous contact—varied only slightly between 1977 (13.4 percent) and 1985 (14.5 percent). Marc Riedel, however, found these stranger homicide rates to be considerably understated. The true figures, according to Riedel, ranged from 14 percent to 29 percent. Furthermore, the impact of these stranger homicides on the quality of urban life—especially the fear of crime they engender—is far greater than their relatively small numbers would suggest.[15]

Relatives and acquaintances   Homicides among acquaintances and friends remained fairly stable between 1976 and 1985: around 40 percent of all homicides.[16] Intrafamily homicides dropped slightly, from 19.4 percent in 1976 to 17.3 percent of all homicides in 1985. Of these homicides, killings by women of their mates have received particular attention. Researchers take special interest in the factors behind such crimes. Angela Browne found that there was a high incidence of long-term abuse suffered by women who subsequently killed their mates.[17] And a recent study by two psychologists suggests that mate homicides are the result of a husband's efforts to control his wife and the wife's efforts to retain her independence.[18] Some recent trends are also noteworthy: an increase in women who kill in domestic encounters, more planned killings, and less acceptance of self-defense as a motive in such cases.[19]

Children are also at risk of death at the hands of family members. One investigator found that in the 5- to 9-year age group, black boys had the highest homicide fatality rate: 25 per 100,000, 3.7 times higher than the rate for white boys. High rates of child homicide persist in low-income areas.[20] Once again, many observers blame the "subculture of exasperation."[21]

Young and old perpetrators   Not surprisingly, the very young and the elderly have very low homicide rates. Children under 15 rarely kill.[22] In 1988, 201 homicide charges were placed against youngsters under 15. This figure does not include the number of homicides in which the young killers were dealt with by juvenile courts or welfare agencies. Homicides in the juvenile age group (up to age 18) are infrequent (though property offenses are very frequent). Of the 16,326 persons of all ages arrested for homicide in 1988, 1,765 were under 18. The elderly, too, are underrepresented among killers. People aged 55 and older accounted for only 2.8 percent of all murders in 1988.[23]

Homicide without apparent motive   In nearly all the homicides we have discussed, the killer has a motive or a reason for killing the victim. Indeed, the vast majority of homicides are committed for a reason. Popular fiction tells us that detectives tend to consider a case solved if they can establish the motive. But research shows that in a substantial number of murders the motive remains unclear. These "unmotivated" murderers are the puzzle—and they constitute 25 percent of all homicide offenders. Though in most respects the killers without motive are similar to those who kill for a reason, they are more likely to have "(1) no history of alcohol abuse; (2) a recent release from prison; (3) claims of amnesia for the crime; (4) denial of the crime; and (5) a tendency to exhibit psychotic behavior following the crime and to be assessed not guilty of the crime due to mental illness."[24]

Mass and serial murders   Criminological researchers have accorded special attention to

WANTED BY THE FBI
INTERSTATE FLIGHT - MURDER

THEODORE ROBERT BUNDY
DESCRIPTION
Born November 24, 1946, Burlington, Vermont (not supported by birth records); Height, 5'11" to 6'; Weight, 145 to 175 pounds; Build, slender, athletic; Hair, dark brown, collar length; Eyes, blue; Complexion, pale / sallow; Race, white; Nationality, American; Occupations, bellboy, busboy, cook's helper, dishwasher, janitor, law school student, office worker, political campaign worker, psychiatric social worker, salesman, security guard; Scars and Marks, mole on neck, scar on scalp; Social Security Number used, 533-44-4655; Remarks, occasionally stammers when upset; has worn glasses, false mustache and beard as disguise in past; left-handed; can imitate British accent; reportedly physical fitness and health enthusiast.

CRIMINAL RECORD
Bundy has been convicted of aggravated kidnaping.

CAUTION
BUNDY, A COLLEGE-EDUCATED PHYSICAL FITNESS ENTHUSIAST WITH A PRIOR HISTORY OF ESCAPE, IS BEING SOUGHT AS A PRISON ESCAPEE AFTER BEING CONVICTED OF KIDNAPING AND WHILE AWAITING TRIAL INVOLVING A BRUTAL SEX SLAYING OF A WOMAN AT A SKI RESORT.

The FBI placed convicted Utah kidnapper Theodore Bundy on its list of the 10 Most Wanted Fugitives. Bundy escaped from jail in Colorado, while awaiting trial for the murder of a Michigan nurse. Her body was found in Aspen. The FBI said that Bundy is a suspect in thirty-six sex-related killings in the West.

two types of murders that are particularly disturbing to the community: **mass murders,** killings of multiple victims in one event or in very quick succession; and **serial murders,** killings of several victims over a period of time. Between 1970 and 1987 U.S. police knew of approximately 120 cases of multiple homicides. The literature on the subject is voluminous.[25] Some recent multiple murderers have become infamous. Theodore "Ted" Bundy, law student and former crime commission staff member, killed between nineteen and thirty-six young women in the northwestern states and Florida; David Berkowitz, the "Son of Sam," killed six young women in New York; Douglas Clark, the "Sunset Strip killer," killed between seven and fifty prostitutes in Hollywood; the "Green River killer" of Seattle may have killed more than forty-five victims; and James Huberty walked into a McDonald's in California and killed twenty people.

It is popularly believed that multiple murderers are mentally ill; their offenses, after all, are often quite bizarre. In many such cases psychiatrists have indeed found severe psychopathology.[26] Yet juries are reluctant to find these offenders not guilty by reason of insanity. Albert Fish, who cooked and ate the children he murdered, died in the electric chair.[27] Edmund Kemper, who killed hitchhikers as well as his own mother—he used her head as a dart board—received a life term.[28]

The criminologists Jack Levin and James Fox do not support the hypothesis that all mass and serial murderers are mentally diseased (e.g., psychotic) and therefore legally insane or incompetent. On the contrary, they say, serial killers are **sociopaths**, persons who lack internal controls, completely disregard common values, and have an intense desire to dominate others. Psychological characteristics alone cannot explain the actions of these people. They are also influenced by the social environment in which they function: the openness of our society, the ease of travel, the lack of external controls and supervision, and the general friendliness and trust of Americans in dealing with each other and with strangers.[29]

Levin and Fox suggest that the recent increase in mass and serial murders, despite a general decline in the murder rate, is to some extent attributable to the publicity accorded to mass murders and the resulting copy-cat phenomenon, the repetition of a crime as a result of the publicity it receives. Thus when one person killed at random by poisoning Tylenol capsules with arsenic, others copied the idea. This phenomenon has prompted Ronald Holmes and James de Burger to recommend that the media cooperate with the criminal justice system when the circumstances demand discretion.[30] Yet cooperation may be hard to achieve precisely in situations in which the media's help is needed to alert the public to a health hazard (as in the Tylenol cases). In any event, the First Amendment's guarantee of freedom of the press does not permit controls.

Gang murder Up to this point we have dealt largely with homicides committed by single offenders. But what about homicides by gangs of offenders? Are there any differences between the two types? On the basis of an analysis of the data contained in 700 homicide investigation files, researchers found that "gang homicides differ both qualitatively and quantitatively from nongang homicides. Most distinctly, they differ with respect to ethnicity [more likely to be intraethnic], age [gang killers are five years younger], number of participants [2.5 times as many participants], and relationship between the participants [gang killers are twice as likely not to know their victims]."[31] But similarities can also be seen. The causes of gang homicides are attributable to social disorganization, economic inequality, and deprivation.[32]

Over the past forty years the nature of gang murder has changed dramatically.

> Week by week and year by year, the ominous statistics mount up: in 1987, when gang homicides rose to 387 in Los Angeles County, the cops made more than 12,000 gang-related arrests and countless thousands of curb-side rousts in south-central L.A.[33]

Compare those 387 murders with the number of gang killings in the 1950s and 1960s, when such cities as Philadelphia and Los Angeles reported 30 or 40 a year. Even as recently as 1982, Chicago figures peaked at 84. Motives also have changed through the years. Once gang wars, with their few related homicides, took place over "turf," territory that members protected, using knives, rocks, or metal chains as weapons. Now the wars are over drugs, and the weapons are assault rifles or semiautomatic guns.

A Cross-National Comparison of Homicide Rates

The criminal homicides we have been discussing are those that are committed in the United States. By comparing homicide rates in this country with those of other countries, we gain a broader understanding of that crime. In 1977 the United Nations published its first World Crime Survey, covering the period 1970 to 1975. It was based on statistical questionnaires to which sixty-four countries responded. The survey revealed that the average worldwide homicide rate stood at 4 for each 100,000 of the world's population. But in the developing countries (the "Third World") the homicide rate was higher, 5 per 100,000, than the rate in developed (industrialized Western) countries, 3 per 100,000. Murder rates were 4 times higher in Latin America (8 per 100,000) than in Western European countries (2 per 100,000).[34] These figures demonstrated that by comparison with the rest of the world, the United States was not doing well: its homicide rate was then (1975) 10 per 100,000 population, the highest rate among industrialized Western countries. In 1988 the rate was 8.4 per 100,000. Figures 10.1 and 10.2 illustrate that the United States is the leader in homicide rates.

A cross-national study found a moderate association between inequality of income and rate of homicide. It likewise revealed a relationship between a youthful population and the homicide rate. The analysis, the study concluded, "suggests that homicide rates are higher in poorer countries, more culturally diverse countries, in countries which spend less on defense, in less democratic societies, and in countries where fewer young people are enrolled in school."[35]

Another researcher who compared the homicide rates in seventy-six countries with that in the United States found that when he took into consideration the differences in the age and sex distributions of the various populations, the United States had a higher rate than all but fifteen countries,[36] most of which were experiencing civil war or internal strife.

Dane Archer and Rosemary Gartner collected their own crime statistics—the Comparative Crime Data File (CCDF)—from 110 nations over a five-year period. A comparison of their homicide rates with historical and socioeconomic data led them to the following conclusions:

• Combatant nations experience an increase in homicides following cessation of hostilities (violence has come to be seen as a legitimate means of settling disputes).
• The largest cities have the highest homicide

rates; the smallest have the lowest homicide rates; but, paradoxically, as a city grows, its homicide rate per capita does not.
• The availability of capital punishment does not result in fewer homicides and in fact often results in more; abolition of capital punishment decreases the homicide rate.[37]

Most international comparative studies find some linkage between economic development and the homicide rate.[38]

These, then, are the characteristics of criminal homicide on which social scientists focus: the extent of homicide in the societies under consideration, its spatial and temporal features, the demographic characteristics of killers and of their victims, and the relationship between killers and victims. We have seen that murder rates are not distributed equally among countries, not even within a single country. In the United States a greater proportion of males, young people, and blacks are perpetrators and victims of this offense, which tends to be committed against someone the killer knows, at or near the home of at least one of the persons involved, in the evening or on a weekend. These patterns of homicide have recently been interpreted in accordance with the rational choice and routine activity framework (discussed in Chapter 9). Advocates of this approach hold that when the wide variety of findings concerning homicide are related to the normal, everyday patterns of interactions, the resultant information can serve in the development of various preventive measures.[39]

ASSAULT

The crimes of homicide and serious assault share many characteristics. Both are typically committed by young males, and a disproportionate number of arrestees are members of minority groups. Assault victims, too, often know their attackers. Spatial and temporal distributions are also quite comparable. Assault rates, like those of homicide, are highest in urban areas, during the summer months, in the evening hours, and in the South. Though the patterns are the same, the legal definitions are not. A

FIGURE 10.1   Number of homicides in U.S. cities and in cities of comparable size in four other industrialized nations, 1988

Population	City	Number of homicides
		U.S.A./Denmark
470,000	Atlanta	186
	Copenhagen	18
290,000	Tampa	79
	Aarhus	1
235,000	Santa Ana, Calif.	32
	Odensen	3
200,000	Mobile	47
	Aalborg	0
		U.S.A./France
2 million	Houston	408
	Paris	156
800,000	Baltimore	240
	Lyon	66
375,000	Tulsa	40
	Toulouse	10
350,000	Charlotte, N.C.	53
	Nice	21
320,000	Newark, N.J.	113
	Nantes	12
		U.S.A./Great Britain
7 million	New York	1,582
	London	67
863,000	San Antonio	162
	Birmingham	31
730,000	San Francisco	114
	Leeds	22
540,000	Cleveland	124
	Liverpool	14
400,000	Miami	148
	Manchester	16
380,000	Tucson	41
	Bristol	11
282,000	Birmingham	88
	New Castle	8
229,000	Anchorage	17
	Barsley	3
		U.S.A./Japan
7 million	New York	1,582
	Tokyo	111
1 million	Dallas	347
	Hiroshima	14
725,000	San Jose	39
	Chiba	9
500,000	Indianapolis	63
	Amagasaki	11
450,000	Kansas City	116
	Funabashi	5

Source: *The Police Chief*, March 1988, pp. 36–37.

FIGURE 10.2   Homicide and Young Males

Homicides per 100,000 population for males 15 through 24 years of age in 1986 or 1987.

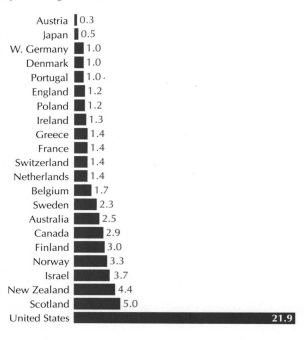

Austria	0.3
Japan	0.5
W. Germany	1.0
Denmark	1.0
Portugal	1.0
England	1.2
Poland	1.2
Ireland	1.3
Greece	1.4
France	1.4
Switzerland	1.4
Netherlands	1.4
Belgium	1.7
Sweden	2.3
Australia	2.5
Canada	2.9
Finland	3.0
Norway	3.3
Israel	3.7
New Zealand	4.4
Scotland	5.0
United States	21.9

Source: National Center for Health Statistics, World Health Organization, and country reports.

murder, as we have seen, is an act that causes the death of another person and that is intended to cause death. An **assault** is an attack on another person with apparent ability to inflict injury and the intent to frighten. (An attack that results in touching or striking the victim is called a **battery**.) Modern statutes usually recognize two types of assault: a **simple assault** is one that inflicts little or no physical hurt; a felonious or **aggravated assault** is one in which the perpetrator inflicts serious harm on the victim or uses a deadly weapon.

Criminologists have looked closely at situations in which assaults are committed. David Luckenbill has identified six stages of a confrontational situation that leads to an assault:

1. One person insults another.

2. The insulted person perceives the signifi-

cance of the insult, often by noting the reactions of others present, and becomes angry.

3. The insulted person contemplates a response: fight, flight, or conciliation. If the response chosen is a fight, the insultee assaults the insulter then and there. If another response is chosen, the situation advances to stage 4.

4. The original insulter, now reprimanded, shamed, or embarrassed, makes a countermove: fight or flight.

5. If the choice is a fight, the insulter assaults (and possibly kills) the insultee.

6. The "triumphant" party either flees or awaits the consequences (e.g., police response).[40]

We can see that crucial decisions are made at all stages, and that the nature of the decisions depends on the context in which they are made. At stage 1, nobody is likely to offer an insult in a peaceful group or situation. At stage 2, the witnesses to the scene could respond in a conciliatory manner. (Let us call this a conflict-resolution situation.) At stage 3, the insulted person could leave the scene with dignity. (A confrontational person would call it flight; a conflict-resolution-minded person would call it a dignified end to a confrontational situation.) Stage 4 is a critical stage, since it calls for a counterresponse. The original aggressor could see this as the last chance to avoid violence and withdraw with apologies. That would be the end of the matter. In a confrontational situation, however, the blows will be delivered now, if none have been dealt already.

The National Crime Survey estimates that 3,142,170 simple assaults were committed in 1988.[41] Assault is the most common of all violent crimes reported to the police. The number of aggravated assaults has risen steadily in recent years, until it reached 1,735,820 in 1988. These figures, however, grossly underestimate the real incidence of assaults. Many people involved in an assault consider the event to be a private matter, not to be revealed to outsiders—particularly if the assault took place within the family or household. Consequently, until quite

recently little was known about family-related violence. But the focus of recent research is changing that situation rapidly.

FAMILY-RELATED CRIMES

In 1962 five physicians exposed the gravity of the "battered child syndrome" in the *Journal of the American Medical Association*.[42] When they reviewed X-ray photographs of patients in the emergency rooms of seventy-one hospitals across the country over the course of a year, they found three hundred cases of child abuse, of which 11 percent resulted in death and over 28 percent in permanent brain damage. Shortly thereafter the women's movement rallied to the plight of the battered wife and, somewhat later, to the personal and legal problems of wives who were raped by their husbands.[43] It was in the 1960s and 1970s that various organizations, fighting for the rights of women and children, exposed the harm that results from physical and psychological abuse in the home. They demanded public action. They created public awareness of the extensiveness of the problem. Psychologists, physicians, anthropologists, and social scientists, among others, increasingly focused attention on the various factors that enter into episodes of domestic violence. Such factors include the sources of conflict, arguments, physical attacks, injuries, and temporal and spatial elements. Within three decades family violence, the "well-kept secret," has come to be recognized as a major social problem. Family violence shares some of the characteristics of other forms of violence, yet the intimacy of the marital, cohabitational, or parent-child relationships sets family violence apart. The physical and emotional harm inflicted in such violent episodes tends to be spread over longer periods of time and to have more lasting impact on all members of the living unit. Moreover, such events tend to be self-perpetuating.

Spouse Abuse

The extent of spouse abuse   In a national sample of 6,002 households, Murray A. Straus and Richard J. Gelles found that

Question 92 + 93

• One of every six couples experienced a physical assault in 1985. That figure indicates that 8.7 million of the 54 million couples who then lived in the United States experienced at least one physical assault during the year.[44]

• Both husbands and wives perpetrated acts of violence, but the consequences of their acts differed. Men, who more often used guns, knives, or fists, inflicted more pain and injury.[45]

• About 60 percent of the assaults consisted of minor shoving, slapping, pushing; the other 40 percent were considered severe violence: punching, kicking, stabbing, choking.[46]

Researchers agree that assaultive behavior within the family is a highly underreported crime.[47] Data from the National Crime Survey indicate that

• One-half of the incidents of domestic assault are not reported.

• The most common reason given for failure to report a domestic assault to the police was that the victim considered the incident a private matter.

• Victims who reported such incidents to the police did so to prevent future assaults.

• Though the police classified two-thirds of the reported incidents of domestic violence as simple assaults, half of them inflicted bodily injury as serious as or more serious than the injuries inflicted during rapes, robberies, and aggravated assaults.[48]

The nature of spouse abuse   Before we can understand spouse abuse we first need information about abusers. Some experts have found that interpersonal violence is learned at home and transmitted from one generation to the next. Studies demonstrate that children who are raised by aggressive parents tend to grow up to be aggressive adults.[49] Other researchers have demonstrated how stress, frustration, and severe psychopathology take their toll on family relationships.[50] A few researchers have also explored the role of body chemistry; one investigation ties abuse to the tendency of males to secrete adrenaline when they feel sexually threatened.[51] The relationship between domestic violence and the use of alcohol and drugs has also been explored; abusive men with severe drug and alcohol problems are more likely to abuse their wives or girlfriends when they are drunk or high, and to inflict more injury.[52]

The study of spouse abuse also focuses on environmental factors. Cultural support for the abuse of women is well documented in a study of 160 battered women in Morocco. According to Mohammed Ayat, about 25 percent of these women believed that if a man does not beat his wife, he must be under some magic spell; 8 percent believed that such a man has a weak personality and is afraid of his wife; 2 percent believed that he must be abnormal; and another 2 percent believed that he doesn't love her or has little interest in her.[53] Wife beating, then, appears to be accepted as a norm by over one-third of the women studied—women who are themselves beaten. It even appears to be an expected behavior. In fact, in only 15 of 90 cultures studied by David Levinson was spouse beating rare or nonexistent.[54]

Some members of our own society take such a relaxed attitude toward violence that it is very much a part of their routine activities, within and outside of the family.[55] And the imbalance of power between male and female partners has not been overlooked. The historical view of wives as possessions of their husbands persists even today.[56]

Until recently spousal abuse was perceived as a problem more of social service than of criminal justice.[57] Police responding to domestic disturbance calls typically do not make an arrest unless the assailant is drunk, has caused serious injury, or has assaulted the officers.[58] When they do make an arrest, they tend to classify the offense as a misdemeanor—again, unless the offender has inflicted a serious injury.[59] By and large, the victims of family violence—those who are willing to look for help—have turned to crisis telephone lines and to shelters for battered women (safe havens that first appeared in the early 1970s to provide legal, social, and psychological services).[60] Whether those informal interventions are as effective as the criminal justice system, however, is a matter of controversy. Should violence between cohabiting partners be treated any differently from violence between strangers on the street?[61] A study conducted some years ago provides insight. In the Minneapolis Domestic Violence Experiment three types of action were taken: (1) the batterer was arrested, (2) the partners were required to separate for a designated period of time, and (3) a mediator intervened between the partners. Over a six-month period the offenders who were arrested had the lowest recidivism rate (10 percent), those who were required to separate had the highest (24 percent), and those who submitted to mediation fell in between (19 percent).[62] Questions on the subject of spouse abuse still far outnumber answers. And personal, ethical, and moral concerns make the issue highly sensitive.[63]

Child Abuse

The extent of child abuse   It is very difficult to measure the extent of child abuse. Battering usually takes place in the home, and the child victims rarely notify the police. Edna Erez reported that in only 1 percent of domestic disturbance calls did police encounter abused children.[64] Most of the available data come from the National Incidence Study (NIS), sponsored by the National Center on Child Abuse and Neglect, and from official reports compiled by the American Humane Association (AHA). The NIS collected information on child maltreatment (abuse and neglect) from hospitals, police, courts, schools, and child protective agencies in a randomly selected sample of twenty-six counties in ten states during 1979–1980. These data—which covered reported cases only—yielded the following nationwide estimates:

- 5.7 children per 1,000 under age 18 are physically, sexually, or emotionally abused annually (physically abused children make up the largest category: 3.4).
- 5.3 children per 1,000 under age 18 are neglected annually.[65]

The mid-1980 AHA National Study of Child Abuse and Neglect Reporting estimated, from cases reported to official child protective agen-

An expert witness holds a photo of Lisa Steinberg during a session of the second-degree murder trial of her foster father, Joel Steinberg, age 47, a disbarred lawyer. The evidence showed that Joel Steinberg severely beat Lisa and then left her.

cies across the country, that 30.6 children per 1,000 are maltreated (physically abused, emotionally abused, sexually abused, or neglected) annually.[66]

The estimates yielded by these two large surveys are obviously far apart. Part of the increase that occurred in the five-year period may be due to better reporting, part to greater public awareness, and part to differences in the surveys themselves. Nevertheless, even the figure of 30.6 per 1,000 is considered a low estimate of the actual number of battered children in our society.[67] Moreover, we know very little about these children, except that most of them are between 12 and 17 years old, that girls are more likely to be abused than boys, and that low-income families are disproportionately represented in the official statistics.[68]

The nature of child abuse   When child abuse first began to be investigated in the early 1960s, the investigators were predominantly physicians, who looked to the psychopathology of the abusers. In doing so they discovered that a high proportion of abusers suffered from alcoholism, drug abuse, mental retardation, poor attachment, low self-esteem, or sadistic psychosis. Later the search for causes moved in other directions. Some researchers pointed out that abusive parents did not know how to discipline children or, for that matter, even how to provide their basic needs, such as nutrition and medical attention. Claims have been made that abusers have themselves been abused; to date, however, the evidence in regard to this hypothesis is mixed.[69] The list of environmental factors related to child abuse is long. We know, for example, that the rate of child abuse in lower-class families is high. This finding is probably related to the fact that low-income parents have few resources to deal with the environmental stress to which they are subjected, such as poor housing and financial problems. When they cannot cope with their responsibilities, they may become overwhelmed. The rate of child abuse may also be related to the acceptance of physical responses to conflict situations in what has been termed the subculture of violence (Chapter 6). Moreover, since child abuse among poor families is likely to be handled by a public agency, these cases tend to appear in official statistics.

Recall from our discussion of battered wives that many researchers have found that formal action—arrest and prosecution—is the most effective means to limit repeat offenses. The situation seems to be otherwise when children are involved. Several advocates for children oppose any involvement of the criminal justice system. They believe that the parent-child attachment remains crucial to the child's development, and they fear that punishment of parents can only go against the child's need for a stable family environment. Only in the most extreme cases would they separate children from parents and place them in shelters or in foster homes. The preference is to prevent child abuse by other means, such as self-help groups (Parents Anonymous), baby-sitting assistance, and crisis

phone lines. The results of various types of interventions are characterized by the title of a 1986 report on child maltreatment: "Half Full and Half Empty."[70] Rates of repeated abuse are high, yet some families have had positive results, and advances have been made in identifying the best treatment for various types of clients. Though our understanding of the problem has indeed increased, we need to know a great deal more about the offense before we can reduce its occurrence.[71]

Abuse of the Elderly

Abuse of the elderly has become an area of special concern to social scientists. The population group that is considered to be elderly is variously defined. The majority of researchers consider 65 the age at which one falls into the category of the elderly. As health care in the United States has improved, longevity has increased. The population of elderly people has grown larger over the decades: from 4 percent of the total population in 1900 to 11 percent in the 1980s. Every day 1,000 people join these ranks. It is estimated that by the year 2020, 20 percent of the population will be elderly.[72]

Elderly persons who are being cared for by their adult children are at a certain risk of abuse. The extent of the problem, however, is still largely unknown. The abused elderly frequently do not talk about their abuse for fear of the embarrassment of public exposure and possible retaliation by the abuser. Congressional hearings on domestic abuse estimate that between 500,000 and 2.5 million elderly people are abused annually.[73] Among the causes of such abuse are caregivers who themselves have grown up in homes where violence was a way of life, the stress of caregiving in a private home rather than an institution, generational conflicts, and frustration with gerontological (old age) problems of the care receiver, such as illness and senility.[74]

We can see that criminologists share a growing concern about family-related violence. Child abuse has received the attention of scholars for three decades. Spousal abuse has been studied for two decades. The abuse of the elderly has begun to receive attention much more recently. Family abuse is not new; our awareness of the size and seriousness of the problem is. The same could be said about yet another offense. It was not until the 1960s that women's advocates launched a national campaign on behalf of victims of rape. Since then rape has become a major topic in criminological literature.

RAPE AND SEXUAL ASSAULT

The common law defined **rape** as an act of enforced intercourse by a man of a woman (other than the attacker's wife) without her consent. Intercourse includes any sexual penetration, however slight. The exclusion of wives from the crime of rape rested on several outdated legal fictions, among them the propositions that the marriage vows grant implicit permanent rights of sexual access and that spouses cannot testify against each other. Older laws universally classify rape as a sex crime. But rape has always been much more than that. It is inherently a crime of violence, an exercise of power.

Oddly, as Susan Brownmiller forcefully argues, it really started as a property crime. Men as archetypal aggressors (the penis as a weapon) subjugated women by the persistent threat of rape. That threat forced each woman to submit to a man for protection and thus to become a wife, the property of a man. Rape then was made a crime to protect one man's property—his wife—from the sexual aggressions of other men.[75] But even that view regards rape as a violent crime against the person, one that destroys the freedom of a woman (and nowadays of a man as well) to decide whether, when, and with whom to enter a sexually oriented relationship.

Few criminological topics have commanded more scholarly attention in recent years than rape. Well over a thousand books, scholarly articles, and papers have been produced on the topic of rape and sexual assault since the 1960s. Much that was obscure and ill understood has now been clarified by research generated largely by the initiatives of the feminist movement, the National Center for the Prevention and Control of Rape (NCPCR), and other governmental and private funding agencies. While most of the crimes in our penal codes have more or less retained their original form, the law on rape has changed rapidly and drastically. The name of the crime, its definition, the rules of evidence and procedure, society's reaction to it—all have changed.[76]

Americans regard rape as one of the most serious crimes. Respondents to the 1985 National Survey of Crime Severity rated the severity of forcible rape that resulted in injury requiring hospitalization as the fourteenth most serious of 204 offenses. Among the crimes considered more serious were stabbing that results in death, planting bombs in public places when life is lost, and armed robbery that results in death.[77]

Characteristics of the Rape Event

According to the Uniform Crime Reports, there were 92,486 forcible rapes in 1988. This figure represents 6 percent of the total number of violent crimes.[78] The incidence of rape rose 10 percent between 1984 and 1988. Of all the men arrested for forcible rape, 43 percent were under age 25; 53 percent were white, 46 percent were black, and 1 percent were of other racial groups. Most rapes are committed in the summer, particularly in July. Several decades ago, Menachem Amir demonstrated that close to half of all rapes in Philadelphia from 1958 to 1965 were committed by a person known or even friendly to the victim.[79] Recent victimization data show that the situation has not changed: 51.4 percent of rapes are committed by men who know their victims.[80] The offender may even be the husband, who in some states can now qualify as a rapist. Research in this area thus far has not been extensive. One report estimates that 12 percent of wives are raped by their husbands.[81]

Recent studies have focused attention on yet another form of rape in relational situations: date rape.[82] One study indicated that as many as 25 percent of all female students may have experienced rape.[83] Criminologists have difficulty estimating the frequency of date rape. But, in all likelihood date rape has increased significantly.[84] Despite the frequency of date rapes, it is estimated that only one-tenth of those committed are reported to the police. A recent study demonstrated that prosecutions for date rape are particularly susceptible to long-held prejudices against victims.[85]

The clearance rate for all types of forcible rape cases is about 52 percent. James L. LeBeau, who studied rapes in San Diego, made the point that many "stranger rapists" remain at large because they commit their acts in ways that produce little tangible evidence as to their identities. They maintain a distance from the victim by not interacting with her before the attack. The serial rapist also attacks strangers, but because he finds his victims repeatedly in the same places, his behavior is more predictable and so leads to a better clearance rate.[86]

Who Are the Rapists?

Psychological factors   Several experts view rapists as suffering from mental illness or personality disorders. Richard Rada argues that some are psychotic, sociopathic, or sadistic, or feel deficient in masculinity.[87] Paul Gebhard and his associates have found that most rapists show hostile feelings toward women, have histories of violence, and tend to attack strangers.[88] Other rapists view women as sex objects whose role is to satisfy them. Nicholas Groth claims that all forcible rapes are committed because of anger, a drive for power (expressed as sexual conquest), or the enjoyment of maltreating a victim (sadism).[89]

Sociocultural factors   Psychological explanations assume that men who rape are maladjusted in some way. But several studies done in the 1980s demonstrate that rapists are indistinguishable from other groups of offenders.[90] These studies generally conclude that rape is culturally related to societal norms that approve of aggression as a demonstration of masculinity[91] (as we saw in Chapter 6), or that rape is the mechanism by which men maintain their power over women.

The social significance of rape has long been a part of anthropological literature. A cross-cultural study of 95 tribal societies found that 47 percent were rapefree, 35 percent intermediate, and 18 percent rape-prone. In the rape-prone societies women had low status and little decision-making power, and they lived apart from men. The author of this study concluded, "Violence is socially, not biologically programmed."[92]

Despite anthropologists' traditional interest in gender relationships, it was not until the feminist movement and radical criminology focused on the subject that the relationship of rape, gender inequality, and socioeconomic status was fully articulated.[93] Writing from the Marxist perspective, which we explored in Chapter 8, Julia and Herman Schwendinger posited that "the impoverishment of the working class and the widening gap between rich and poor" create conditions for the prevalence of sexual violence.[94] A test of this hypothesis showed that while the incidence of sexual violence was not related to ethnic inequality, it was significantly related to general income inequality.[95] A more recent study analyzed these findings and concluded that economic inequality was not the sole determinant of violent crime in our society. Forcible rape was found to be an added "cost" of many factors, including social disorganization.[96]

In sum, many factors have been associated with the crime of rape: psychological problems, social factors, and even sociopolitical factors. Some experts suggest that boys are socialized to be aggressive and dominating, that the innate male sex drive leads to rape, and that pornography encourages men to rape by making sex objects of women, degrading them and glamorizing violence against them. Rape has been explained in such a wide variety of ways that it is extremely difficult to plan preventive strategies and to formulate crime-control policy. Moreover, it has created major difficulties in the criminal justice system.

Rape and the Legal System

Difficulties of prosecution   The difficulties of rape prosecutions have their roots in the English common law. Sir Matthew Hale, a seventeenth-century jurist, explained in *Pleas of the Crown* (1736) how a jury was to be cautious in viewing evidence of rape: "[It] must be remembered...that it is an accusation easily to be made and hard to be proved, and harder to be defended by the party accused, tho never so innocent."[97] This instruction, which so definitively protects the defendant, has until recently been a mandatory instruction to juries in the United States, but many jurisdictions have now cast it aside. An extension of the issue of proof has been that of corroboration. The victim's testimony alone does not suffice for conviction; some additional supporting evidence of the rape—semen, torn clothes, scratches—must be offered. The requirement of particularly stringent proof in rape cases had always been justified by the seriousness of the offense and the heavy penalties associated with it, plus the stigma attached to such a conviction.

Another major issue has been that of consent. Did the victim encourage, entice, or maybe even agree to the act? Was the attack forced? Did the victim resist? Martin Schwartz and Todd Clear sum up the reasons for such questions: "There is a widespread belief in our culture that women 'ask for it,' either individually or as a group." They compared rape victims to victims of other offenses: "Curiously, society does not censure the robbery victim for walking around with $10, or the burglary victim for keeping all of those nice things in his house, or the car theft victim for showing off his flashy new machine, just asking for someone to covet it."[98] Because defendants in rape cases so often claim that the victim was in some way responsible for the attack, rape victims in the courtroom tend to become the "accused," required to prove their good reputations, their propriety, and their mental soundness. In sum, so many burdens are placed on the victim that no one seriously wonders why only a fraction of rapes are reported and why so few men accused of rape are convicted (see At Issue).

Legislative changes   The feminist movement has had a considerable impact on laws and attitudes concerning rape in our country. The state of Michigan was a leader in the movement to reform such laws by creating, in 1975, the new crime of "criminal sexual conduct" to replace the traditional rape laws. It distinguishes four degrees of assaultive sexual acts, differentiated by the amount of force used, the infliction of injury, and the age and mental condition of the victim.[99] The new law is gender neutral, in that it makes illegal any type of forcible sex, including homosexual rape. Other states have followed Michigan's lead. Schwartz and Clear have suggested that the law reform should go one step further. They argue that if rape were covered by the general assault laws rather than by a separate sex-crime statute, the emphasis would be on the assault (the action of the offender) and not on the resistance (the action of the victim).[100]

Recent legislation has also removed many of the barriers women encountered as witnesses in the courtroom. Thus in states with rape shield laws women are no longer required to disclose their prior sexual activity, and corroboration requirements have been reduced or eliminated; as noted earlier, some states have reversed two centuries of legal tradition by striking down the "marital rape exemption" so that a wife may now charge her husband with rape.[101]

But law reform has limits. Unfortunately, prejudices die hard. One study concludes that "forcible rape cases are more likely to be dropped than other kinds of cases and that the reasons for this pattern do not necessarily conform to prior expectations that reluctant victims are responsible for much of the case attrition."[102]

Community Response

Women's advocates have taken an interest not only in legislative reform but also in the community's response to the victims of rape. In 1970 the first rape-specific support project, the Bay Area Women Against Rape—a volunteer-staffed emergency phone information service—was established in Berkeley, California.[103] By 1973, similar projects had spread throughout the country. Run by small, unaffiliated groups, they handled crises, monitored agencies (hospitals, police, courts) that came in contact with victims, educated the public about the problems of victims, and even provided lessons in

AT ISSUE

Rape Victims Speak Out

"If I had it to do again, I would never have gone through with the prosecution. I wouldn't even have reported it," said one twenty-seven-year-old woman who suffered through months of legal proceedings and publicity only to see her rapist found innocent because she was unable to prove that she did not consent to the act. Despite extensive body bruises and a wound in her forehead that took six stitches to close, the defense attorney argued that "vigorous love play" did not necessarily indicate nonconsent and, in fact, could even indicate enthusiastic approval and passionate involvement in the act.

"From the beginning I had this feeling that I was the one who was on trial rather than the guy they picked up and charged," said the woman, raped by an intruder who entered her apartment through a window, from an adjacent rooftop. She was at the time sleeping in the nude...a fact that is frequently alleged in rape cases to prove "willingness to have intercourse."

"Right after it happened. ...I mean here I was lying on the floor, my face was streaming with blood, I was damned near hysterical when I called the police. They arrived and the very first question this one guy asked me was, 'Did you enjoy it? Did you *really* try to resist the guy?'

"Then the questions really started. I couldn't believe what they asked me. About five officers were crowded into my bedroom. They said things to me like 'Lay on the bed exactly as you were when the guy came in. Why did you spread your legs if you didn't want to be raped? Did you see his penis? Describe it. Did you touch his penis? Did you put it in your mouth? Did you have an orgasm?'

"Then there was the hospital they took me to. There were maybe three dozen people sitting around in this large ward. This one guy in a white coat takes my name and he yells down the ward, at the top of his lungs, 'Hey, Pete, I got a rape case here. Check her out, will you?' It was just incredible. The guy checking me out left me sitting on this table for like an hour. One of his questions was, 'Did you give the guy a blow job or what?'

"Later at the police station. They caught the guy from my description. He was sitting there and one of the cops went out to get him a cup of coffee and gave him a cigarette. They told me, 'Sit over there, lady, we'll get to you in a minute.'

"Over and over again, the police, the district attorney, the defense attorneys, even my own goddamned private lawyer asked me the same thing: 'Are you sure you really resisted? Did you *really* want to get raped subconsciously?'

"In the end the guy who did it got off. They even brought in this one boy—a man now—that I knew in high school. That was ten years ago. He testified he had intercourse with me, after a prom. The defense attorney said, 'She was pretty easy, wasn't she?' The guy just grinned and shook his head.

"I learned. I still live alone, but now I have a gun. I have a permit and everything like that for it. I keep it right on the night table, loaded."

The ordeal of this anonymous rape victim has been experienced by thousands of other women. Only recently have rape victims decided to go public. One of them, Nancy Ziegenmeyer, was urged to do so by a courageous newspaper editor, Geneva Overholser. The story of Ziegenmeyer's rape, and the experiences that followed it, appeared on the front page of five consecutive issues of *The Desmoines Register*. The favorable response to the story, according to Overholser, demonstrates "how dramatically attitudes towards rape have changed. 'Americans are ready to look at this crime, not in a way that judges a victim. Indeed, if they're looking at her, they're judging her as a hero.'"

Source: Freda Adler, *Sisters in Crime* (New York: McGraw-Hill, 1975), pp. 214–215; and David Margolick, "A Name, a Face and a Rape: Iowa Victim Tells Her Story," *The New York Times*, March 25, 1990, pp. 1, 28.

self-defense. By the late 1970s the number of these centers and their activities had increased dramatically. The mass media reported on their successes. Federal and later state and local support for such services rose. As the centers became more professional, they formed boards of directors, prepared detailed budgets to comply with the requirements of funding agencies, hired social workers and mental health personnel, and developed their political action component.

Thus the very concept of rape has undergone rapid change. But legal and public response to another crime of violence that also involves a temporary and complete domination of the victim has not changed at all. It is defined as it always has been: robbery.

ROBBERY

Violence is the basic ingredient of all crimes discussed in this chapter. **Robbery** is no exception. It is the taking of property from a victim by force and violence or by the threat of violence. [104]

The MPC (sec. 222.1) grades robbery as a felony of the second degree, commanding a prison term of up to ten years. If the robber has intentionally inflicted serious physical injury or attempted to kill, the sentence may be as long as life. In reality, however, the average sentence upon conviction for one charge of robbery is 6.4 years. It increases to 17.6 years if the charges number four or more. [105] In almost half of all robberies, the offenders display weapons, mostly guns and knives. Since 44 percent of all robberies net the perpetrator less than $50, the overall reporting rate for robbery is only slightly higher than 50 percent. Robberies of individuals occur most frequently on the street (54.0 percent). The remaining robberies are of commercial houses (11.9 percent), residences (10.5 percent), service stations (2.9 percent), convenience stores (6.4 percent), banks (1.4 percent), and miscellaneous establishments (12.9 percent). [106]

Characteristics of Robberies and Robbers

Criminologists have classified the characteristics of robberies as well as the characteristics of robbers. According to Frederick McClintock and Evelyn Gibson, there are five distinct varieties of robbery, each with a different frequency of commission. In their sample of London robberies, robberies of commercial establishments and street robberies seem to have been most prevalent. [107] André Normandeau found a similar distribution in Philadelphia, but with a disproportionate number of street robberies. [108]

Robbery attracts a variety of perpetrators. John Conklin detected four types:

- *The professional robber* carefully plans and executes a robbery, often with many accomplices; steals large sums of money; and has a long-term, deep commitment to robbery as a means of supporting a hedonistic lifestyle.
- *The opportunistic robber* (the most common) has no long-term commitment to robbery, targets victims for small amounts of money ($20 or less), victimizes old ladies, drunks, cab drivers, and other people who seem to be in no position to resist, and is young and generally inexperienced.
- *The addict robber* is addicted to drugs, has a low level of commitment to robbery but a high level of commitment to theft, plans less than professional robbers but more than opportunistic robbers, wants just enough money for a fix, and may or may not carry a weapon.
- *The alcoholic robber* has no commitment to robbery as a way of life, has no commitment to theft, does not plan his robberies, usually robs people he has first assaulted, takes few precautions, and is apprehended more often than other robbers. [109]

In a classification system restricted to bank robbers, Terry Baumer and Michael Carrington identified three types. First is the unarmed lone bandit who passes a note to the teller demanding money, and often leaves without ever raising the suspicions of patrons or other employees. The second type is the armed lone bandit who usually shows a handgun and makes an oral demand. Two-thirds of Baumer and Carrington's sample fell into this category. Third, armed teams present themselves as robbers, order employees and customers to "get down on the floor," and proceed with a well-formulated plan. They usually take large sums of money. Of all bank robbers, tellers most fear these armed teams.[110]

The Consequences of Robbery

Robbery is a property crime as well as a violent crime. It is the combination of the motive for economic gain and the violent nature of robbery that makes it so serious. An estimated $343 million was lost as a result of robbery in 1988 alone. The value of stolen property per incident averaged $631, and the average amount of money stolen ranged from $344 (from convenience stores) to $2,885 (from banks).[111]

Loss of money, however, is certainly not the only consequence of robbery. The million-odd robberies that take place each year leave psychological and physical traumas in their wake, not to mention the pervasive fear and anxiety over robbery which lead to the decay of our inner cities. Not all criminologists agree, however, that the high level of fear is warranted. After examining trends in robbery-homicide data from fifty-two of the largest cities in the United States, Philip Cook found "little support for the fears that there is a new breed of street criminals who cause more serious injuries and deaths in robberies. Very recent trends point in the other direction. Killing a robbery victim appears to be going out of fashion."[112] Franklin E. Zimring and James Zuehl agree. They found that injuries were inflicted in a moderate number of Chicago robberies (28 percent) and that about 11 percent of robberies ended in death.[113]

Opportunities for Robbery

What determines the attractiveness of an opportunity for robbery? Cook's research on commercial robbery suggests that some offenders carefully examine the location of the potential robbery, the potential gain, the capability of security personnel, the possibility of intervention by bystanders, and the presence of guards, cameras, and alarms.[114] Criminologists have found that potential victims and establishments can do quite a bit to decrease the likelihood of being robbed. Following a series of convenience store robberies in Gainesville, Florida, in 1985, a city ordinance required store owners to clear their windows of signs that obstructed the view of the interior, to position cash registers where they would be visible from the street, and to install approved electronic cameras. Within little over a year, convenience store robberies had decreased 64 percent.[115] This is a perfect example of crime control through target hardening (see Chapter 9).

Individual victims of robbery also play a role in the success or failure of a robbery in progress. Some criminologists have suggested that forceful resistance decreases the chance of the robbery's success but increases the risk of physical injury to the victim. Nonforceful resistance also decreases the risk of losing one's property and tends to reduce the risk of injury.[116] But such preliminary findings should not be taken as a guide for future robbery victims. Robberies, for the most part, are potentially lethal events.

KIDNAPPING AND TERRORISM

Kidnapping

Seizing and holding a person for ransom or reward is akin to robbery, in that it involves the use or threat of violence for the purpose of acquiring property illegally.

The term "kidnapping" is a composite of two old English slang words: "kid" = child and "nap" (or "nab"), to snatch. Kidnapping as such was not recognized as a felony under common law, but some forms of kidnapping were criminalized by statute, such as "sending any person under the government into parts beyond the seas out of the King's obedience, to be educated in the Romish religion." The most frequent form of kidnapping, according to the great legal scholar Sir William Blackstone, was the stealing of children and sending them to servitude in the American colonies. This offense was regarded as a misdemeanor under common law. Other forms of kidnapping were the "crimping" or shanghaiing of persons for involuntary service aboard ships and the ab-

CRIMINOLOGICAL FOCUS

The Lindbergh Kidnapping Case

Hopewell is a little town ten miles from Princeton, New Jersey. Colonel and Mrs. Lindbergh had built a new home at a wild and somewhat isolated spot called Somiland Mountain. The colonel was basking in the glory of his international acclaim as the first person to fly alone across the Atlantic in a single-engine plane. After dinner on the evening of March 1, 1932, the colonel rested in the living room, just underneath the nursery. The Lindberghs' baby, little Charles Augustus Lindbergh, Jr., who had a nasty cold, had been tucked into his crib at 8:30 P.M. At 10:00 P.M.

the child's nurse, Betty Gow, went upstairs to check on him. The crib was empty. She ran downstairs and notified the parents. All searched frantically for little Charles. They found no trace of him, but they saw muddy footprints in the nursery and an opened window screen. A ladder was propped against the side of the house beneath the window. A note lay on the sill. Nobody ever revealed what the note said.

The Hopewell police were alerted and arrived within twenty minutes. Then the teletype messages went through the state of New Jersey and out to the world.

The baby of America's foremost hero had been kidnapped. The person arrested for the abduction, Bruno Richard Hauptmann, never confessed to kidnapping the Lindberghs' child, but the evidence against him was solid: the wood of the homemade ladder was proved to have come from the attic of Hauptmann's house. He was convicted, sentenced to death, and executed. The baby was never found.

Source: L. M. Seidman, "The Trial and Execution of Bruno Richard Hauptmann: Still Another Case That Will Not Die," *Georgetown Law Journal* 66 (1977): 1–48.

---

duction of women for purposes of prostitution abroad. All of these offenses have elements in common, and together they define the crime of **kidnapping:** abduction and detention by force or fraud and transportation beyond the authority of the place where the crime was committed. It was not until the kidnapping of the infant son of Charles Lindbergh in 1932 that comprehensive kidnapping legislation was enacted in the United States. In passing the federal kidnapping statute—the so-called Lindbergh Act (now 18 U.S. Code § 1201)—Congress made it a felony to kidnap and transport a victim across a state or national border. The crime was subject to the death penalty, unless the victim was released unharmed; the death penalty has since been dropped.

Kidnapping in the form of hostage taking is frequently an element of a larger scheme that encompasses several distinct crimes of violence. The totality of such violence is called terrorism, but that term is not found in the lawbooks.

Terrorism

Terrorism is a resort to violence or a threat of violence on the part of a group seeking to accomplish a purpose against the opposition of constituted authority. Crucial in the terrorists' scheme is the exploitation of the media to attract attention to their cause. Many clandestine organizations around the world have sought to draw attention to their causes—the Irish Republican Army (IRA), committed to the cause of uniting the British counties of Northern Ireland with the Republic of Ireland; various Palestinian factions seeking an independent state of Palestine; radical groups over the world seeking an end to capitalism or colonialism or the imposition of one or another form of totalitarian rule.

From the outset the member states of the United Nations have been concerned about international terrorism because it endangers or takes innocent human lives and jeopardizes fundamental freedoms, such as the freedom to travel and to congregate for public events. The U.N. effort to control international terrorism concentrates on removal of the underlying grievances that provoke people to sacrifice human lives, including their own, in an attempt to effect radical changes.[117] This approach to control of terrorism is not concerned with the individual motivations of terrorists. Some of them may be highly motivated idealists; others are recruited for substantial rewards. The control effort is directed rather at the situational conditions that give rise to terrorism, and at the removal of such conditions.

To the extent that some grievances have been reduced by political action, such as the granting of independence to colonies, terrorism has declined. But other problems remain, especially in Northern Ireland, India, Central America, Africa, and the West Bank and Gaza Strip occupied by Israel. Crimes of a terrorist nature occur virtually every day and will continue for the foreseeable future. Terrorist activities include but are not restricted to assassinations, hostage taking, and interference with or destruction of ships, aircraft, or means of land transport (see Table 10.1). When funding by clandestine supporters is not forthcoming, terrorists have carried out robberies to finance their operations.

The extent of terrorism The incidence of terrorism may seem slight in the light of overall national crime statistics, especially those of the United States. But the worldwide destructive impact of such acts is considerable. So too are the costs of increased security to combat terrorism. The airline industry alone is spending $500 million a year for security.[118] After the bombing of the U.S. embassy in Beirut, Lebanon, with the loss of the lives of 241 marines, the strengthening of U.S. embassy security all over the world cost well over $3 billion.

In 1985 terrorists were responsible for

- 4 letter bombs;
- 5 barricade-hostage incidents;
- 9 hijackings;
- 17 specific threats;
- 54 kidnappings;

- 70 attempted attacks;
- 84 armed assaults; and
- 165 bombings and arsons.

Twelve of these crimes were committed in Belgium, 14 in Chile, 29 in Colombia, 12 in Cyprus, 35 in West Germany, 12 in France, 29 in Greece, 17 in Italy, 47 in Lebanon, 10 in Peru, 18 in Portugal, 15 in Spain, 10 in the United Kingdom, and 148 in other countries (that experienced fewer than 10 incidents each). Regionally, Western Europe was hardest hit (182), followed by the Middle East (70) and South America (62). The remaining incidents are spread all over the other regions, with Asia and the Far East suffering the fewest terrorist incidents. Of the targets, 151 were political, 80 were diplomatic, 79 were economic, and 54 were various random public places, specific persons, and facilities.[119] It is noteworthy that 31 of the 408 terrorist acts were committed on behalf of governments.

Among the most active terrorist groups were the Islamic Jihad (35 acts), the Fatah Revolutionary Council (24), the West German Red Army Faction (19), the Portuguese Popular Forces of 25 April (15), and the Chilean Manuel Rodríguez Popular Front (14). In the course of these acts of terrorism, 265 persons were killed, among them 46 Americans, 16 French, 15 British, 11 Germans, 11 Italians, 10 Israelis, and 9 staff members of international organizations. The terrorists suffered fewer deaths.

International efforts to control terrorism Governments have greatly increased their security measures in recent years, and the world community has agreed on three international conventions to combat terrorism:

- Convention on Offenses and Certain Other Acts Committed on Board Aircraft, signed at Tokyo on September 14, 1963.
- Convention for the Suppression of Unlawful Seizure of Aircraft, signed at The Hague on December 16, 1970.
- Convention for the Suppression of Unlawful Acts Against the Safety of Civil Aviation, signed at Montreal on September 23, 1971.

TABLE 10.1   TERRORIST EVENTS AROUND THE WORLD, 1986

DATE	COUNTRY	EVENT
February 18	Portugal	Bomb explodes in car being inspected at gate of U.S. embassy, Lisbon. No casualties. Portuguese terrorist group Popular Forces of 25 April claims responsibility.
April 2	Greece	Bomb explodes aboard TWA flight 840 approaching Athens airport, killing four Americans. Device similar to bombs used earlier by Palestinian 15 May Organization found to have been carried aboard by a Lebanese woman who left the plane at an earlier stop.
April 4	West Germany	Bomb explodes in crowded West Berlin discotheque, killing three, wounding more than 200 others. Evidence of Libyan complicity leads to U.S. bombing raids on Tripoli and Benghazi, April 15.
April 17	England	Irish woman boarding El Al jet in London found to have bomb in carry-on luggage. Her Jordanian boyfriend, convicted, implicates Syrian ambassador and his staff. Britain breaks diplomatic relations with Syria.
May 3	Sri Lanka	Explosion blows tail off Air Lanka jet preparing to leave Colombo airport for Maldives, killing 16. Tamil separatist guerrillas claim responsibility.
June 25	Peru	Maoist group plants bomb aboard tourist train bound for Inca ruins of Machu Picchu, killing seven, wounding scores.
June 26	Spain	Bomb placed in suitcase partially detonates at Madrid's Barajas Airport, wounding 11. Device intended to explode on El Al flight to Tel Aviv. Suitcase traced to a Palestinian.
September 5	Pakistan	Four Palestinian gunmen, members of Abu Nidal, attempt to hijack Pan Am 747 in Karachi, hold plane on runway overnight till overpowered by security personnel; 21 passengers killed.
November 16	West Germany	Palestinian Terrorist Group Hind Alamed bombs IBM scientific center at Heidelberg, damages amounting to millions of marks.
December 25	Saudi Arabia	Iraqi airliner crashes in Saudi Arabia following hijacking attempt, killing 62, including two hijackers. Several groups claim credit, but Iranian-backed terrorists probably responsible.

Selected from a 1986 chronology of significant terrorist events. *Source*: Adapted from United States Department of State, *Patterns of Global Terrorism: 1986* (Washington, D.C.: Office of the Ambassador at Large for Counter-Terrorism, January 1988), pp. 33–39; and Edward F. Mickolus, Todd Sandler, and Jean M. Murdock, *International Terrorism in the 1980s*, vol. II, 1984–1987 (Ames, Iowa: Iowa State University Press, 1989), p. 498.

These conventions, which provide for widespread international cooperation in the prevention of airplane hijacking and the pursuit and *extradition* (surrender to a requesting country) of offenders, produced a dramatic drop in the number of such incidents. Subsequently, the international diplomatic community agreed on two further conventions to protect diplomats, their families, and their installations:

• Convention on the Prevention and Punishment of Crimes Against Internationally Protected Persons, Including Diplomatic Agents, adopted by the General Assembly of the United Nations on December 14, 1973.
• International Convention Against the Taking of Hostages, adopted by the General Assembly of the United Nations on December 17, 1979.[120]

Above all, it appears that by 1989 several governments that had been financially supporting certain ''freedom fighters'' (elsewhere called terrorist groups) had grown disenchanted with their exercise of arbitrary violence against uninvolved civilian targets, such as airplane passengers, and had ceased support for such groups.[121] Nevertheless, terrorist groups proliferate. Several international directories list well over a thousand terrorist groups, many of them well financed. Until all grievances are removed—and some of them have been built up over centuries—such groups will continue to resort to violent crime in order to use the world media as leverage to advance their causes.

VIOLENCE AND GUN CONTROL

Clearly, violence is a massive problem throughout the world. Researchers have suggested a variety of causes for violence. Violence in the United States is frequently attributed to historical conditioning (the need of frontier people to survive in a hostile environment), social factors (poverty, inequities, and other inner-city problems), and the laxity of the criminal justice system (failure to apprehend and convict enough criminals and to imprison long enough those who are convicted). Some researchers have focused on one common element in a large pro-

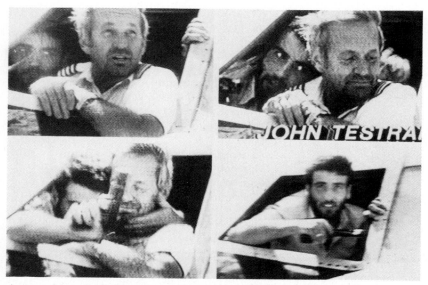

An armed terrorist holds a gun on Trans World Airlines pilot John Testrake during an interview from the hijacked plane at the Beirut airport. Top row: left, gunman stands behind the pilot; right, gunman ends the interview. Bottom row: left, gunman waves a gun in front of the pilot and grabs the pilot; right, gunman later tells the ABC news crew to leave.

portion of violent crime: the availability of fire-arms in the United States. This has been one of the hottest and longest political and scholarly debates in our history. Should and can Americans drastically restrict the availability of firearms, and would such controls substantially reduce the rate and severity of violent crime?

The Extent of Firearm-Related Offenses

Though exact figures are not known, it is estimated that about 100 million firearms are privately owned in the United States: 37 percent rifles, 33 percent shotguns, and 30 percent handguns.[122] Half of the handguns are so-called Saturday-night specials (defined by the Bureau of Alcohol, Tobacco, and Firearms as a small weapon of .32 caliber or less with a barrel length of less than three inches and costing $50 or less). The supply of handguns increases by about 1.5 million each year.[123] Approximately 13,500 of every 100,000 Americans own handguns. Compare this figure with the rates of other Western industrialized nations: Canada, 3,000 in every 100,000; Austria, 3,000; the Netherlands, under 500; and Great Britain, also under 500.[124]

Time magazine devoted its issue of July 17, 1989, to "Death by Gun." Reporting on "America's toll in one typical week," a twenty-eight-page portfolio described the deaths and provided photographs of most of the victims: 464 Americans who died violently by gun during the first week of May 1989. Two hundred sixteen (47 percent) had shot themselves to death. Nine of the suicides killed someone else before taking their own lives. Twenty-two deaths were preventable accidents. Only 14 people were killed in self-defense. The rest of the deaths were criminal homicides.

The Federal Bureau of Investigation has reported that a handgun is used in about half of all murders and one-third of the rapes and robberies. Two-thirds of police deaths in the line of duty are attributed to the use of handguns.[125] Rates of crime involving guns are far lower in most other developed Western nations than in the United States.[126] According to the Task Force on Firearms of the National Commission on the Causes and Prevention of Violence, the

rate of homicide by gun is forty times higher in the United States than in England and Wales, and our rate of robbery by gun is sixty times higher.

Gun-Control Legislation

While most people agree that gun-related crime is a particularly serious part of our crime problem, there is little agreement as to what to do about it. Civic organizations and police associations are calling for more laws prescribing mandatory sentences for the illegal purchase, possession, or use of firearms. The local, state, and federal laws currently in force cover a broad range of prohibitions and sanctions. The Federal Gun Control Act of 1968, for example, prohibited minors, felons, and other designated groups to own firearms; curtailed the importation of Saturday-night specials; outlawed private ownership of bazookas, submachine guns, and similar devices; and subjected gun dealers to various controls. The new Federal Gun Control Act of 1986 is very similar but has fewer regulations. A 1977 District of Columbia law is more stringent: the sale, transfer, and possession of handguns by residents of the District of Columbia are prohibited.[127]

Some states have passed what are referred to as sentencing-enhancement statutes: the punishment for an offense is more severe if a person commits it under certain conditions, such as by using a gun. The Massachusetts law (1975) mandates a minimum sentence of one year's incarceration upon conviction for the illegal carrying of a firearm.[128] Michigan created a new offense—commission of a felony while possessing a firearm—and added a mandatory two-year prison sentence to the sentence received for the commission of the felony itself. The state mounted a widespread publicity campaign: "One with a gun gets you two," read the billboards and bumper stickers.[129]

States continue to pass stringent gun-control laws. At the same time, researchers continue to reach conflicting conclusions as to their effectiveness in controlling gun-related crimes. A study of the deterrent effects of the Massachusetts legislation, for example, found a significant decline in the use of firearms in homicides and assaults, but not in robberies.[130] A Michigan study concluded that the "gun law did not significantly alter the number or type of violent offenses committed in Detroit."[131] No agreement seems to be in sight.

The Gun-Control Debate

The battle line on gun control appears to be clearly drawn between the opponents of regulation (including the 3 million members of the National Rifle Association [NRA] and their supporters) on the one hand and the advocates of control (including the twelve major law enforcement groups, the private organization Handgun Control, and three-quarters of the American public) on the other. The gun lobby likes to say that it is people who kill, not guns, so it is the people who use guns illegally who should be punished. To deter these people, the gun enthusiasts say, we need to have stiffer penalties, including mandatory sentences that take these offenders off the streets. Gun-control opponents often have bumper stickers that read, "When guns are outlawed, only outlaws will have guns." Moreover, most gun owners claim that it is their right to own firearms to protect their homes, especially when they lose confidence in the police and courts.[132] And by controlling guns, they say, the government intrudes in their private affairs. They interpret the Second Amendment to the Constitution as giving them their individual right "to keep and bear arms." Furthermore, the gun lobby maintains, people may wish to enjoy their guns as collectors or for sport and hunting. Another argument concerns what is called the displacement effect: people who are deterred by gun-control legislation from using guns to commit their offenses will use some other weapon to achieve their goals. Or perhaps even more violent offenses will be committed if offenders can rely on the fact that the consequences of a non-firearm offense are less serious.[133]

Gun-control advocates point to our gun-related crime statistics for support of their argument. Many compare our extremely high homicide rate to the much lower rates of other countries with tighter gun-control laws, including our neighbor Canada. They also argue that the availability of a gun makes homicide and suicide much more probable, because it is easier to produce death with a gun than with any other weapon. Moreover, they claim, better regulation or prohibition of gun ownership is a much faster way to lessen gun-related criminality than such long-term approaches as finding remedies for social problems. Researchers are testing the claims, but thus far no definitive conclusions have been reached.

The gun-control controversy is a prime example of the difference between the offender-specific and crime-specific approaches to crime. The offender-specific approach ("Guns don't kill people, people do") suggests that we look into the reasons why people kill. The offense-specific approach focuses on changing the situation by subjecting firearms to strict control in the expectation that fewer firearms will result in fewer deaths.

REVIEW

Murder, assaults of various kinds, rape, robbery, kidnapping—all share the bond of violence, though they differ in many ways: in the harm they cause, the intention of the perpetrator, the punishment they warrant, and other legal criteria. Social scientists have been exploring the frequency with which these crimes are committed in our society and elsewhere, their distributions through time and place, and the role played by situational circumstances, including the environment and people's behavior patterns (routine activities), in facilitating or preventing them. Such categories as mass murder, serial murder, gang murder, and date rape are shorthand designations for frequently occurring modalities of crime which have no legal standing. Two other patterns of crime that are not defined as such in the penal codes have become so important that they may be considered in conjunction with the other crimes of violence: family-related crime and terrorism. Both of these patterns encompass a variety of violent crimes. The gun-control controversy demonstrates that both the definitions of crimes and the social and environmental characteristics associated with them must be studied in order to develop strategies to control and prevent them. Our violence-prone society will have to make serious choices if it is to reach that level of peaceful living achieved by many other modern societies.

KEY TERMS

aggravated assault
assassination
assault
battery
felony murder
homicide
involuntary manslaughter
justifiable homicide
kidnapping
malice aforethought
manslaughter
mass murders
murder

murder in the first degree
murder in the second degree
rape
robbery
serial murders
simple assault
sociopaths
stranger homicide
terrorism
victim precipitation
voluntary manslaughter

NOTES

1. *Crimes of Violence: A Staff Report Submitted to the National Commission on the Causes and Prevention of Violence* (Washington, D.C.: Government Printing Office, December 1969), vol. 12, p. xxvii; vol. 11, p. 4.

2. G. O. W. Mueller, "Where Murder Begins," *New Hampshire Bar Journal* 2 (1960): 214–224, and "On Common Law Mens Rea," *Minnesota Law Review* 42 (1958): 1043–1104.

3. Wayne R. LaFave and Austin W. Scott, *Handbook on Criminal Law* (St. Paul, Minn.: West, 1972), pp. 572–577. The provocation is judged by an objective standard; in other words, the provocation must be the kind that would have prompted a reasonable person to act similarly in that situation.

4. Commonwealth v. Welansky, 316 Mass. 383, N.E. 2d 902 (1944), at 906–907. See G. O. W. Mueller, "The Devil May Care—Or Should We? A Reexamination of Criminal Negligence," *Kentucky Law Journal* 55 (1966–1967): 29–49.

5. U.S. Department of Justice, Federal Bureau of Investigation, *Crime in the United States, 1988* (Washington, D.C.: U.S. Government Printing Office, 1989), pp. 8–14; hereafter cited as Uniform Crime Reports.

6. Ibid.

7. Roland Chilton, "Twenty Years of Homicide and Robbery in Chicago: The Impact of the City's Changing Racial and Age Composition," *Journal of Quantitative Criminology* 3 (1987): 195–213. See also Carolyn Rebecca Block, *Homicide in Chicago* (Chicago: Loyola University of Chicago, 1986), p. 7; William Wilbanks, *Murder in Miami* (Lanham, Md.: University Press of America, 1984).

8. William B. Harvey, "Homicide Among Young Black Adults: Life in the Subculture of Exasperation," in *Homicide Among Black Americans*, ed. Darnell F. Hawkins (Lanham, Md.: University Press of America, 1986), pp. 153–171. On this issue, all of the articles in Hawkins's volume are worthy of attention. See also Robert L. Hamp-

ton, "Family Violence and Homicide in the Black Community: Are They Linked?" in *Violence in the Black Family*, ed. Robert L. Hampton (Lexington, Mass.: Lexington Books, 1987), pp. 135–156.

9. Coramae Richey Mann, "Black Women Who Kill," in Hawkins, *Homicide Among Black Americans*, pp. 157–186.

10. Larry Baron and Murray A. Straus, "Cultural and Economic Sources of Homicide in the United States," *Sociological Quarterly* 29 (1988): 371–390.

11. Hans von Hentig, *The Criminal and His Victim* (New Haven, Conn.: Yale University Press, 1948).

12. Marvin E. Wolfgang, *Patterns in Criminal Homicide* (Philadelphia: University of Pennsylvania Press, 1958), p. 253. See also Marvin E. Wolfgang, "A Sociological Analysis of Criminal Homicide," in *Studies in Homicide*, ed. Wolfgang (New York: Harper & Row, 1967), pp. 15–28.

13. Robert A. Silverman and Leslie W. Kennedy, "Relational Distance and Homicide: The Role of the Stranger," *Journal of Criminal Law and Criminology* 78 (1987): 272–308.

14. Margaret A. Zahn and Philip C. Sagi, "Stranger Homicides in Nine American Cities," *Journal of Criminal Law and Criminology* 78 (1987): 377–397.

15. Marc Riedel, "Stranger Violence: Perspectives, Issues, and Problems," *Journal of Criminal Law and Criminology* 78 (1987): 223–258. For a discussion of the *Supplementary Homicide Report* (SHR), see Colin Loftin, "The Validity of Robbery-Murder Classifications in Baltimore," *Violence and Victims* 1 (1986): 191–204.

16. See, for example, Colin Loftin, Karen Kindley, Sandra L. Norris, and Brian Wiersema, "An Attribute Approach to Relationships Between Offenders and Victims in Homicide," *Journal of Criminal Law and Criminology* 78 (1987): 259–271.

17. Angela Browne, "Assault and Homicide at Home: When Battered Women Kill," *Advances in Applied Social Psychology* 3 (1986): 57–79.

18. Martin Daly and Margo Wilson, *Homicide* (New York: Aldine–de Gruyter, 1988), pp. 294–295.

19. Coramae Richey Mann, "Getting Even?: Women Who Kill in Domestic Encounters," *Justice Quarterly* 5 (1988): 33–51.

20. Joshua E. Muscat, "Characteristics of Childhood Homicide in Ohio, 1974–1984," *American Journal of Public Health* 78 (1988): 822–824.

21. This theory is not necessarily inconsistent with the sociobiological explanation offered by Martin Daly and Margo Wilson, "Children as Homicide Victims," in *Child Abuse and Neglect: Biosocial Dimension*, ed. Richard J. Gelles and Jane B. Lancaster (New York: Aldine–de Gruyter, 1987), pp. 201–214.

22. For one of the first efforts to deal with juvenile homicide from clinical and theoretical perspectives, see Elissa P. Benedek and Dewey G. Cornell, eds., *Juvenile Homicide* (Washington, D.C.: American Psychiatric Press, 1989).

23. Uniform Crime Reports, 1988, pp. 178–184.

24. William R. Holcomb and Anasseril E. Daniel, "Homicide Without an Apparent Motive," *Behavioral Sciences and the Law* 6 (1988): 429–439.

25. See especially Michael Newton, *Mass Murder: An Annotated Bibliography* (New York: Garland, 1988).

26. Psychoanalysts are more likely to find such murderers to be psychotic. See, e.g., three works by David Abrahamsen: *The Murdering Mind* (New York: Harper & Row, 1973); *The Psychology of Crime* (New York: Columbia University Press, 1960); and *Crime and the Human Mind* (New York: Columbia University Press, 1944).

27. Mel Heimer, *The Cannibal: The Case of Albert Fish* (New York: Lyle Stuart, 1971).

28. Margaret Cheney, *The Co-ed Killer* (New York: Walker, 1976).

29. Jack Levin and James Alan Fox, *Mass Murder: America's Growing Menace* (New York: Plenum, 1985).

30. Ronald M. Holmes and James de Burger, *Serial Murder* (Newbury Park, Calif.: Sage, 1988), p. 155. For a criminal justice response to serial murder, see Pierce R. Brooks, Michael J. Devine, Terence J. Green, Barbara L. Hart, and Merlyn D. Moore, "Serial Murder: A Criminal Justice Response," *Police Chief* 54 (1987): 37–43.

31. Cheryl L. Maxson, Margaret A. Gordon, and Malcolm W. Klein, "Differences Between Gang and Nongang Homicides," *Criminology* 23 (1985): 209–222.

32. G. David Curry and Irving A. Spergel, "Gang Homicide, Delinquency, and Community," *Criminology* 26 (1988): 381–405.

33. *Newsweek*, March 25, 1988, p. 20.

34. Data from United Nations General Assembly, *Crime Prevention and Control: Report of the Secretary General*, A/32/199, Sept. 22, 1977, generally known as the First World Crime Survey. The data contained in this survey must be interpreted with great caution. These are crude data, unadjusted for such factors as the age structures of the populations. For a more reliable method of comparing international homicide statistics, see Glenn D. Deane, "Cross-National Comparison of Homicide: Age/Sex-Adjusted Rates Using the 1980 U.S. Homicide Experience as a Standard," *Journal of Quantitative Criminology* 3 (1987): 215–227.

35. Harvey Krahn, Timothy F. Hartnagel, and John W. Gartrell, "Income Inequality and Homicide Rates: Cross-National Data and Criminological Theories," *Criminology* 24 (1986): 269–295.

36. Deane, "Cross-National Comparison of Homicide." This study was conducted on the basis of the statistics of the International Criminal Police Organization (Interpol).

37. Dane Archer and Rosemary Gartner, *Violence and Crime in Cross-National Perspective* (New Haven, Conn.: Yale University Press, 1984).

38. M. Harvey Brenner, "Time-Series Analysis: Effects of the Economy on Criminal Behavior and the Administration of Criminal Justice in the United States, Canada, England and Wales, and Scotland," in United Nations Social Defense Research Institute, *Economic Crises and Crime: Correlations Between the State of the Economy, Deviance, and the Control of Deviance*, publication no. 15 (Rome, 1976), pp. 25–65. See also Philip J. Cook and Gary A. Zarkin, "Homicide and Economic Conditions: A Replication and Critique of M. Harvey Brenner's New Report to the U.S. Congress," *Journal of Quantitative Criminology* 2 (1986): 69–103.

39. Steven F. Messner and Kenneth Tardiff, "The Social Ecology of Urban Homicide: An Application of the Routine Activities Approach," *Criminology* 23 (1985): 241–267.

40. David F. Luckenbill, "Criminal Homicide as a Situated Transaction," *Social Problems* 25 (1977): 176–186. Although Luckenbill focused on homicides, the stages he identified are identical in assaults.

41. U.S. Department of Justice, Bureau of Justice Statistics, *Criminal Victimization in the United States, 1988: A National Survey Report (Preliminary Findings)* (Washington, D.C.: U.S. Government Printing Office, 1989).

42. C. H. Kempe, F. N. Silverman, B. F. Steele, W. Droegemueller, and H. K. Silver, "The Battered-Child Syndrome," *Journal of the American Medical Association* 181 (1962): 17–24.

43. Elizabeth Pleck, "Criminal Approaches to Family Violence, 1640–1980," in *Family Violence*, ed. Lloyd Ohlin and Michael Tonry, 2: 19–57 (Chicago: University of Chicago Press, 1989).

44. Murray A. Straus and Richard J. Gelles, "How Violent Are American Families?: Estimates from the National Family Violence Resurvey and Other Studies," in *Family Abuse and Its Consequences*, ed. Gerald T. Hotaling, David Finkelhor, John T. Kirkpatrick, and Murray A. Straus (Newbury Park, Calif.: Sage, 1988). The Conflict Tactics Scales used to measure violence are described in Murray A. Straus, *Measuring Physical and Emotional Abuse of Children with the Conflict Tactics Scales* (Durham: Family Research Laboratory, University of New Hampshire, 1988).

45. Murray A. Straus, Richard J. Gelles, and S.

K. Steinmetz, *Behind Closed Doors: Violence in the American Family* (Garden City, N.Y.: Doubleday, 1980); Murray A. Straus, "Victims and Aggressors in Marital Violence," *American Behavioral Scientist* 23 (1980): 681–704. See also M. D. Pagelow, *Family Violence* (New York: Praeger, 1984), p. 274; S. F. Berk and D. R. Loseke, "'Handling' Family Violence: Situational Determinants of Police Arrest in Domestic Disturbances," *Law and Society Review* 15 (1981): 317–346.

46. Straus and Gelles, "How Violent Are American Families?" p. 17; see also Scott L. Feld and Murray A. Straus, "Escalation and Desistance of Wife Assault in Marriage," *Criminology* 27 (1989): 141–161.

47. R. E. Dobash and R. P. Dobash, "Wives: The 'Appropriate' Victims of Marital Violence," *Victimology* 2 (1977–1978): 426–442; J. P. Deschner, *The Hitting Habit* (New York: Free Press, 1984); D. J. Sonkin, *Learning to Live Without Violence: A Handbook for Men*, 2d ed. (San Francisco: Volcano, 1985); P. A. Klaus and M. R. Rand, *Family Violence*, U.S. Department of Justice (Washington, D.C.: U.S. Government Printing Office, 1984); D. E. H. Russell, *Rape in Marriage* (New York: Macmillan, 1982); L. W. Kennedy and D. G. Dutton, *The Incidence of Wife Assault in Alberta*, Edmonton Area Series Report no. 53 (Edmonton: University of Alberta, Population Research Laboratory, 1987); W. H. Meredith, D. A. Abbott, and S. L. Adams, "Family Violence: Its Relation to Marital and Parental Satisfaction and Family Strengths," *Journal of Family Violence* 1 (1986): 299–305.

48. Patrick A. Langan and Christopher A. Innes, *Preventing Domestic Violence Against Women*, for U.S. Department of Justice, Bureau of Justice Statistics (Washington, D.C.: U.S. Government Printing Office, 1986).

49. Joan McCord, "Parental Aggressiveness and Physical Punishment in Long-Term Perspective," in Hotaling et al., *Family Abuse*, pp. 91–98; also D. J. Sonkin, D. Martin, and L. E. Walker, eds., *The Male Batterer: A Treatment Approach* (New York: Springer, 1985).

50. See Robert L. Burgess and Patricia Draper, "The Explanation of Family Violence: The Role of Biological, Behavioral, and Cultural Selection," in Ohlin and Tonry, *Family Violence*, 2: 59–116. See also Phyllis D. Coontz and Judith A. Martin, "Understanding Violent Mothers and Fathers: Assessing Explanations Offered by Mothers and Fathers for Their Use of Control Punishment," in Hotaling et al., *Family Abuse*, pp. 77–90; Nancy Hutchings, ed., *The Violent Family* (New York: Human Science Press, 1988).

51. Donald G. Dutton, *The Domestic Assault of Women* (Boston: Allyn & Bacon, 1988), p. 15.

52. Lenore E. Walker, *The Battered Woman Syndrome* (New York: Springer, 1984); Angela Browne, *When Battered Women Kill* (New York: Free Press, 1987); G. T. Hotaling and D. B. Sugarman, "An Analysis of Risk Markers in Husband to Wife Violence: The Current State of Knowledge," *Violence and Victims* 1 (1986): 101–124.

53. Study conducted by Mohammed Ayat, Atiqui Abdelaziz, Najat Kfita, and El Khazouni Zineb, at the request of UNESCO and the Union of Arab Lawyers, Fez, Morocco, 1989.

54. David Levinson, *Family Violence in Cross-Cultural Perspective* (Newbury Park, Calif.: Sage, 1989).

55. Ibid., pp. 14–20; Marvin E. Wolfgang and Franco Ferracuti, *The Subculture of Violence: Toward an Integrated Theory in Criminology* (London: Tavistock, 1967).

56. Carolyn F. Swift, "Surviving: Women's Strength Through Connections," in *Abuse and Victimization Across the Life Span*, ed. Martha Straus (Baltimore: Johns Hopkins University Press, 1988), pp. 153–169. See also Dobash and Dobash, "Wives."

57. For an account of public policy and family privacy, see Frank E. Zimring, "Toward a Jurisprudence of Family Violence," in Ohlin and Tonry, *Family Violence*, 2: 547–569.

58. R. A. Berk, S. F. Berk, and P. J. Newton, "An Empirical Analysis of Police Responses to Incidents of Wife Battery," paper presented at the Second National Conference of Family Violence Researchers, University of New Hampshire, Durham, July 1984; R. E. Worden and A. A. Pollitz, "Police Arrests in Domestic Disturbances: A Further Look," *Law and Society Review* 18 (1984): 105–119; R. Tong, *Women, Sex, and the Law* (Totowa, N.J.: Rowman & Allanheld, 1984). On prosecution of cases, see Lisa G. Lerman, "Prosecution of Wife Beaters: Institutional Obstacles and Innovations," in *Violence in the Home: Interdisciplinary Perspectives,* ed. Mary Lystad (New York: Brunner/Mazel, 1986).

59. G. A. Goolkasian, *Confronting Domestic Violence: A Guide for Criminal Justice Agencies,* for U.S. Department of Justice (Washington, D.C.: U.S. Government Printing Office, 1986).

60. Lee H. Bowker, *Ending the Violence* (Holmes Beach, Fla.: Learning Publications, 1986); Daniel G. Saunders and Sandra T. Azar, "Treatment Programs for Family Violence," in Ohlin and Tonry, *Family Violence,* 2: 481–546; Anna F. Kuhl and Linda E. Saltzman, "Battered Women and the Criminal Justice System," in *The Changing Roles of Women in the Criminal Justice System,* ed. Imogene L. Moyer (Prospect Heights, Ill.: Waveland, 1985).

61. Jeffrey Fagan and Sandra Wexler, "Crime at Home and in the Streets: The Relationship Between Family and Stranger Violence," *Violence and Victims* 2 (1987): 5–23; Jeffrey Fagan, Douglas K. Stewart, and Karen V. Hansen, "Violent Men or Violent Husbands?: Background Factors and Situational Correlates," in *The Dark Side of Families,* ed. David Finkelhor, Murray A. Straus, Gerald T. Hotaling, and Richard J. Gelles (Beverly Hills, Calif.: Sage, 1983), pp. 49–67. See also N. M. Shields and C. R. Hanneke, "Battered Wives' Reactions to Marital Rape," in Finkelhor et al., *Dark Side of Families;* Jeffrey Fagan, "Cessation of Family Violence: Deterrence and Dissuasion," in Ohlin and Tonry, *Family Violence,* 2: 377–425.

62. Lawrence W. Sherman and Richard A. Berk, "The Minneapolis Domestic Violence Experiment," *Police Foundation Reports* 1 (1984): 1–8; Lawrence W. Sherman, and Richard A. Berk, "The Specific Deterrent Effects of Arrest for Domestic Assault," *American Sociological Review* 49 (1984): 261–272. See also Delbert S. Elliott, "Criminal Justice Procedures in Family Violence Cases," in Ohlin and Tonry, *Family Violence,* 2: 427–480.

63. For evidence that many people are unsympathetic to battered women, see C. S. Greenblat, "Don't Hit Your Wife... Unless...": Preliminary Findings on Normative Support for the Use of Physical Force by Husbands," *Victimology* 10 (1985): 221–241; D. G. Saunders, A. B. Lynch, M. Grayson, and D. Linz, "The Inventory of Beliefs About Wife Beating: The Construction and Initial Validation of a Measure of Beliefs and Attitudes," *Violence and Victims* 2 (1986): 39–57; D. G. Saunders, "When Battered Women Use Violence: Husband-Abuse or Self-Defense?" *Victims and Violence* 1 (1986): 47–60. For an article on methodological problems in family violence research, see Joseph G. Weis, "Family Violence Research Methodology and Design," in Ohlin and Tonry, *Family Violence,* 2: 117–162. For a general survey and critique of the literature, see Irene Hanson Frieze and Angela Browne, "Violence in Marriage," in Ohlin and Tonry, *Family Violence,* 2: 163–218.

64. Edna Erez, "Intimacy, Violence, and the Police," *Human Relations* 39 (1986): 265–281.

65. K. Burgdorf, "Recognition and Reporting of Child Maltreatment," in *Findings from the National Study of the Incidence and Severity of Child Abuse and Neglect* (Washington, D.C.: National Center on Child Abuse and Neglect, 1980), p. 370. For a discussion of the underestimates of the NIS, see also S. D. Petgers, G. E. Wyatt, and D. Finkelhor, "Prevalence," in *A Sourcebook on Child Sexual Abuse,* ed. D. Finkelhor, S. Araji, L. Baron, A Browne, S. D. Peters, and G. E. Wyatt (Newbury Park, Calif.: Sage, 1986).

66. American Association for Protecting Children, *Highlights of Official Child Neglect and Abuse Reporting, 1984* (Denver: American Humane Society, 1986).

67. For a comprehensive discussion of the es-

timates of child maltreatment, see James Garbarino, "The Incidence and Prevalence of Child Maltreatment," in Ohlin and Tonry, *Family Violence,* 2: 219–261.

68. Mildred Daley Pagelow, "The Incidence and Prevalence of Criminal Abuse of Other Family Members," in Ohlin and Tonry, *Family Violence,* 2: 263–311.

69. Cathy Spatz Widom, "The Cycle of Violence," *Science* 244 (1989): 160–166; E. C. Herrenkohl, R. C. Herrenkohl, and L. J. Toedter, "Perspectives on the Intergenerational Transmission of Abuse," in Finkelhor et al., *Dark Side of Families;* Joan McCord, "A Forty Year Perspective on the Effects of Child Abuse and Neglect," *Child Abuse and Neglect* 7 (1983): 265–270. For a discussion of the higher arrest rates of adults who were abused or neglected as children, see also Cathy Spatz Widom, "Criminal Abuse, Neglect, and Violent Criminal Behavior," *Criminology* 27 (1989): 251–271.

70. Deborah Daro, "Half Full and Half Empty: The Evaluation of Results of Nineteen Clinical Research and Demonstration Projects," *Summary of Nineteen Clinical Demonstration Projects Funded by the National Center on Child Abuse and Neglect, 1978–81* (Berkeley: University of California, School of Social Welfare, 1986).

71. Richard J. Gelles, "What to Learn from Cross-Cultural and Historical Research on Child Abuse and Neglect: An Overview," in *Child Abuse and Neglect,* ed. Richard J. Gelles and Jane B. Lancaster, pp. 15–30 (New York: Aldine–de Gruyter, 1987).

72. Craig J. Forsyth and Robert Gramling, "Elderly Crime: Fact and Artifact," in *Older Offenders,* ed. Belinda McCarthy and Robert Langworthy, pp. 3–13 (New York: Praeger, 1988); Terry Fulmer, "Elder Abuse," in Straus, *Abuse and Victimization,* pp. 188–199.

73. Pagelow, "Incidence and Prevalence of Criminal Abuse," p. 267.

74. Mary Joy Quinn and Susan K. Tomita, *Elder Abuse and Neglect* (New York: Springer, 1986), chap. 4. See also Rachel Filinson and Stanley R. Ingman, eds., *Elder Abuse:*

Practice and Policy (New York: Human Sciences Press, 1989); Alan A. Malinchak, *Crime and Gerontology* (Englewood Cliffs, N.J.: Prentice-Hall, 1980).

75. Susan Brownmiller, *Against Our Will: Men, Women, and Rape* (New York: Simon & Schuster, 1975), pp. 1–9.

76. Duncan Chappell, "Sexual Criminal Violence," in *Pathways to Criminal Violence,* ed. Neil Alan Weiner and Marvin E. Wolfgang, pp. 68–108 (Newbury Park, Calif.: Sage, 1989).

77. Marvin E. Wolfgang, Robert M. Figlio, Paul E. Tracy, and Simon I. Singer, *The National Survey of Crime Severity* (Washington, D.C.: U.S. Government Printing Office, 1985).

78. Uniform Crime Reports, 1988, p. 16.

79. Menachem Amir, *Patterns in Forcible Rape* (Chicago: University of Chicago Press, 1977), pp. 233–234.

80. National Crime Survey, 1987, p. 56.

81. David Finkelhor and Kersti Yllo, "Forced Sex in Marriage: A Preliminary Research Report," *Crime and Delinquency* 28 (1982): 459–478. See also the report presented by Diana Russel to the American Sociological Association and quoted in the *New York Times,* Nov. 29, 1982, p. 20.

82. Andrea Parrot, *Coping with Date Rape and Acquaintance Rape* (New York: Rosen, 1988). See also John E. Murphy, "Date Abuse and Forced Intercourse Among College Students," in Hotaling et al., *Family Abuse,* pp. 285–296.

83. M. P. Koss, C. A. Gidycz, and N. Wisniewski, "The Scope of Rape: Incidence and Prevalence of Sexual Aggression and Victimization in a National Sample of Higher Education Students," *Journal of Consulting and Clinical Psychology* 55 (1987): 162–170.

84. On this subject see R. Thomas Dull and David J. Giacopassi, "Demographic Correlates of Sexual and Dating Attitudes: A Study of Date Rape, "*Criminal Justice and Behavior* 14 (1987): 175–193.

85. Joanne Belknap and Sandra Evans Skov-

ron, "Public Perceptions of Date Rape" (1988), report on file with National Council on Crime and Delinquency, School of Criminal Justice Library, Rutgers University.

86. James L. LeBeau, "Patterns of Stranger and Serial Rape Offending: Factors Distinguishing Apprehended and At Large Offenders," *Journal of Criminal Law and Criminology* 78 (1987): 309–326.

87. Richard Rada, *Clinical Aspects of the Report* (New York: Grune & Stratton, 1978), pp. 123–130.

88. Paul H. Gebhard, John H. Gagman, Wardell B. Pomeroy, and Cornelia V. Christenson, *Sex Offenders: An Analysis of Types* (New York: Harper & Row, 1965), pp. 198–204.

89. Nicholas A. Groth, *Men Who Rape: The Psychology of the Offender* (New York: Plenum, 1979), pp. 14–58.

90. J. Marolla and D. Scully, *Attitudes Toward Women, Violence, and Rape: A Comparison of Convicted Rapists and Other Felons* (Rockville, Md.: National Institute of Mental Health, 1982); M. P. Koss and K. E. Leonard, "Sexually Aggressive Men: Empirical Findings and Theoretical Implications," in *Pornography and Sexual Aggression,* ed. N. Malamuth and E. Donnerstein, pp. 213–232 (New York: Academic Press, 1984); Ilsa L. Lottes, "Sexual Socialization and Attitudes Toward Rape," in *Rape and Sexual Assault,* ed. Ann Wolbert Burgess, pp. 193–220 (New York: Garland, 1988).

91. Christine Alder, "An Exploration of Self-Reported Sexually Aggressive Behavior," *Crime and Delinquency* 31 (1985): 306–331.

92. P. R. Sanday, "The Socio-cultural Context of Rape: A Cross-Cultural Study," *Journal of Social Issues* 37 (1981): 5–27.

93. Susan Estrich, *Real Rape* (Cambridge, Mass.: Harvard University Press, 1987); S. Griffin, "Rape: The All-American Crime," *Ramparts* 10 (1971): 26–35.

94. Julia R. Schwendinger and Herman Schwendinger, *Rape and Inequality* (Beverly Hills, Calif.: Sage, 1983), p. 220.

95. M. Dwayne Smith and Nathan Bennett, "Poverty, Inequality, and Theories of Forc-

ible Rape," *Crime and Delinquency* 31 (1985): 295–305.

96. Ruth D. Peterson and William C. Bailey, "Forcible Rape, Poverty, and Economic Inequality in U.S. Metropolitan Communities," *Journal of Quantitative Criminology* 4 (1988): 99–119.

97. Matthew Hale, *History of the Pleas of the Crown* (London, 1736), 1: 635.

98. Martin D. Schwartz and Todd R. Clear, "Toward a New Law on Rape," *Crime and Delinquency* 26 (1980): 129–151.

99. Chappell, "Sexual Criminal Violence," p. 76.

100. Schwartz and Clear, "Toward a New Law."

101. Andrew Z. Soshnick, "The Rape Shield Paradox: Complainant Protection Amidst Oscillating Trends of State Judicial Interpretation," Comment, *Journal of Criminal Law and Criminology* 78 (1987): 644–698; Ken Polk, "Rape Reform and Criminal Justice Processing," *Crime and Delinquency* 31 (1985): 191–205; Gilbert Geis, "Rape-in-Marriage: Law and Law Reform in England, the United States, and Sweden," *Adelaide Law Review* 6 (1978): 284–303.

102. Kristen M. Williams, *The Prosecution of Sexual Assaults* (Washington, D.C.: Institute of Law and Social Research, 1978), p. 30. See also Gary LaFree, *Rape and Criminal Justice: The Social Construction of Sexual Assault* (Belmont, Calif.: Wadsworth, 1989).

103. Janet Gornick, Martha R. Burt, and Karen J. Pittman, "Structures and Activities of Rape Crisis Centers in the Early 1980's," *Crime and Delinquency* 31 (1985): 247–268.

104. Philip J. Cook, "Robbery Violence," *Journal of Criminal Law and Criminology* 78 (1987): 357–376; Colin Loftin, "The Validity of Robber-Murder Classifications in Baltimore," *Violence and Victims* 1 (1986): 191–204.

105. U.S. Department of Justice, *Report to the Nation on Crime and Justice,* 2d ed. (Washington, D.C.: U.S. Government Printing Office, 1988), p. 97.

106. Uniform Crime Reports, 1988, p. 19.

107. Frederick H. McClintock and Evelyn Gibson, *Robbery in London* (London: Macmillan, 1961).

108. André Normandeau, "Trends and Patterns in Crimes of Robbery" (Ph.D. dissertation, University of Pennsylvania, 1968).

109. John Conklin, *Robbery and the Criminal Justice System* (Philadelphia: Lippincott, 1972), pp. 59–78.

110. Terry L. Baumer and Michael D. Carrington, *The Robbery of Financial Institutions,* for U.S. Department of Justice (Washington, D.C.: U.S. Government Printing Office, 1986).

111. Uniform Crime Reports, 1988, p. 19.

112. Philip J. Cook, "Is Robbery Becoming More Violent?: An Analysis of Robbery Murder Trends Since 1968," *Journal of Criminal Law and Criminology* 76 (1985): 480–489.

113. Franklin E. Zimring and James Zuehl, "Victim Injury and Death in Urban Robbery: A Chicago Study," *Journal of Legal Studies* 15 (1986): 1–40.

114. Philip J. Cook, *Robbery in the United States: An Analysis of Recent Trends and Patterns,* for U.S. Department of Justice (Washington, D.C.: U.S. Government Printing Office, 1983).

115. Wayland Clifton, Jr., *Convenience Store Robberies in Gainesville, Florida* (Gainesville, Fla.: Gainesville Police Department, 1987), p. 15.

116. Richard Block and Wesley G. Skogan, "Resistance and Non-fatal Outcomes in Stranger-to-Stranger Predatory Crime," *Violence and Victims* 1 (1986): 241–253.

117. United Nations General Assembly Resolution 40/61, Dec. 9, 1985. For a discussion of violence and terrorism see also Paul Wilkinson, *Terrorism and the Liberal State,* 2d ed. (New York: New York University Press, 1986), pp. 23–68; Beau Grosscup, *The Explosion of Terrorism* (Far Hills, N.J.: New Horizon, 1987).

118. Harvey J. Iglarsh, "Terrorism and Corporate Costs," *Terrorism* 10 (1987): 227–230.

119. Ariel Merari, Tamer Prat, Sophia Kotzer, Anat Kurz, and Yoram Schweitzer, *Inter 85: A Review of International Terrorism in 1985* (Boulder, Colo.: Westview, 1986), p. 106.

120. Noemi Gal-Or, *International Cooperation to Suppress Terrorism* (New York: St. Martin's, 1985), pp. 90–96.

121. United Nations General Assembly Resolution 40/61.

122. James D. Wright, Peter H. Rossi, and Kathleen Daly, *Under the Gun: Weapons, Crime, and Violence in America* (New York: Aldine, 1983), p. 42.

123. Samuel Walker, *Sense and Nonsense About Crime* (Monterey, Calif.: Brooks/Cole, 1985), pp. 149–150.

124. George D. Newton, Jr., and Frank E. Zimring, *Firearms and Violence in American Life: A Staff Report Submitted to the National Commission on the Causes and Prevention of Violence* (Washington, D.C.: National Commission on the Causes and Prevention of Violence, 1969), p. 121.

125. Walker, *Sense and Nonsense About Crime,* pp. 149–150.

126. Franklin E. Zimring and Gordon Hawkins, *The Citizen's Guide to Gun Control* (New York: Macmillan, 1987), p. 5.

127. Anne D. Garner, *Firearm Statutes in the United States: Federal, State, and Local* (Washington, D.C.: United States Conference of Mayors, 1981).

128. James A. Beha II, "And Nobody Can Get You Out: The Impact of a Mandatory Prison Sentence for the Illegal Carrying of a Firearm on the Administration of Criminal Justice in Boston," *Boston University Law Review* 57 (1977): 96–146, 289–333.

129. Colin Loftin, Milton Heumann, and David McDowall, "Mandatory Sentencing and Firearms Violence: Evaluating an Alternative to Gun Control," *Law and Society Review* 17 (1983): 288–318.

130. Beha, "And Nobody Can Get You Out." See also Stuart Jay Deutsch and Francis B. Alt, "The Effect of the Massachusetts Gun

Control Law on Gun-Related Crimes in the City of Boston," *Evaluation Quarterly* 1 (1977): 543–568.

131. Colin Loftin and David McDowall, "One With a Gun Gets You Two: Mandatory Sentencing and Firearms Violence in Detroit," *Annals of the American Academy of Political and Social Science* 455 (1981): 150–167. See also Edward D. Jones III, "The District of Columbia's Firearms Control Regulations Act of 1975: The Toughest Handgun Control Law in the United States: Or Is It?" ibid., pp. 138–149; Mona Margarita *The 1980 New York Gun Law: An Evaluation of Its Implementation and Impact* (Washington, D.C.: Police Foundation, 1987); Richard S. Morelli, *The Deterrent Effects of Pennsylvania's Five-Year Mandatory Sentencing Law in Robbery and Assaults with Firearms* (Harrisburg: Pennsylvania Commission on Crime and Delinquency, 1984); and Bruce B. Stout, "An Empirical Assessment of the Impact of the Graves Act on the Weapons Involvement Character of Violent Crime in New Jersey" (Ph.D. dissertation, Rutgers University, 1989).

132. Robert L. Young, David McDowall, and Colin Loftin, "Collective Security and the Ownership of Firearms for Protection," *Criminology* 25 (1987): 47–62.

133. Glenn L. Pierce and William J. Bowers, *The Impact of the Massachusetts Gun Law on Gun and Non-Gun-Related Crime* (Boston: Northeastern University Press, 1979). For a discussion of the deterrent effect of gun ownership by citizens, see Gary S. Green, "Citizen Gun Ownership and Criminal Deterrence: Theory, Research, and Policy," *Criminology* 25 (1987): 63–81.

11

CRIMES AGAINST PROPERTY

The motion picture *The Gods Must Be Crazy* introduces us to a society of happy aborigines, remote from the hustle and bustle of modern life. Such tools as they have are shared and can easily be replaced from an abundance of sticks and stones.

High up, a "noisy bird" passes over the camp of these happy people. The pilot of the noisy bird casually throws an empty Coke bottle out of the cockpit. It lands in the middle of the camp. The aborigines stare at this foreign object. They handle it delicately and then discover what a useful object it is—it holds water, it can be used for rolling dough, for hammering, for many things. Everybody needs it and wants it. Fights ensue over who can have it. The peace and tranquility of this little society are shattered. These people have discovered the concept of property, and they are experiencing all the troubles that go with the possession of property, including property crime.

The film has a happy ending. The aborigines finally get rid of the bottle, and life returns to normal.

We have explored some of the patterns of social interaction and the routine activities of daily life that set the stage for offenders to commit violent crimes and for other people—family members, acquaintances, strangers, airplane passengers—to become victims. We know that if effective policies are to be developed to prevent and control violent crime, we must have a thorough understanding of the characteristics of specific offenses; we need to know where, when, and how they are committed, and which individuals are most likely to commit them. The same is true for property offenses. To develop crime prevention strategies, we need to study the characteristics that differentiate the various types of offenses that deprive people of their property.

Do such offenses as pocket-picking, shoplifting, check forgery, theft by use of stolen credit cards, car theft, and burglary have different payoffs and risks? What kinds of resources are needed (weapons, places to sell stolen property)? Are there any specific skills needed to carry out these offenses? The opportunities to commit property crime are all but unlimited. Studies demonstrate that if these opportunities are reduced, the incidence of crime is reduced as well.

The traditional property crimes are larceny (theft, stealing); obtaining property by fraud of various sorts, including false pretenses, confidence games, forgery, and unauthorized use of credit cards; burglary, which does not necessarily involve theft; and arson, which not only deprives the owner of property but also endangers the lives of the occupants. We shall defer until Chapter 12 discussion of the crimes by which criminals deprive people of their property through organizational manipulations—individual white-collar crimes, corporate crimes, and activities related to organized crime.

LARCENY

The Definition and Extent of Larceny

Larceny (theft, stealing) is the prototype of all property offenses. It is also the most prevalent crime in our society. Yet in the thirteenth century, when Henry de Bracton set out to collect from all parts of England what was common in law—and thus common law—he learned to his surprise that there was no agreement on any concept of larceny. He found a confusing variety of ancient Germanic laws. So he did what he always did in such circumstances: he remembered what he had learned about Roman law from Professor Azo in Bologna, and simply inserted it into his text of English law in 1250. Thus our "common law" definition of larceny is virtually identical with the concept in Roman law.[1] These, then, are the constituent elements of **larceny** (or theft, or stealing):

- A "trespassory"
- Taking and
- Carrying away of
- Personal property
- Belonging to another
- With the intent to deprive the owner of the property
- Permanently.

None of these elements of the crime of larceny is self-explanatory; each has a long history that gives it its meaning. The first element is per-

haps the easiest. There must be a trespass. *Trespass,* a Norman-French term, has a variety of meanings. In the law of larceny, however, it simply means any absence of authority or permission for the taking. Second, the property must be taken: the perpetrator must exert authority over the property, as by putting a hand on a piece of merchandise or getting into the driver's seat of the targeted car. Third, the property must be carried away. The slightest removal suffices to fulfill this element: moving merchandise from a counter, however slightly; loosening the brakes of a car so that it starts rolling, even an inch. Fourth, the property in question, at common law, has to be personal property. (Real estate is not subject to larceny.) Fifth, the property has to belong to another, in the sense that the person has the right to possess that property. Sixth, the taker must intend to deprive the rightful owner permanently of the property. This element is present when the taker (thief) intends to deprive the rightful owner of the property forever. In many states, however, the law no longer requires proof that the thief intended to deprive the owner "permanently" of the property.

Larceny, except for the most petty varieties, was a capital offense in old England.[2] Courts interpreted all of its elements quite strictly—that is, in favor of defendants—so as to limit the use of capital punishment. Only once did the courts expand the reach of larceny, when they ruled that a transporter who surreptitiously opens a box entrusted to him and takes out some items has committed larceny by "breaking bulk." For the other forms of deceptive acquisition of property, such as embezzlement and obtaining property by false pretenses, Parliament had to enact legislation.

In the United States the rate of larceny is extraordinarily high. Figure 11.1 shows the increase over the last five years. The UCR reported 7.7 million thefts in 1988, or a rate of 3,135 for each 100,000 of the population. If we add unreported thefts—as estimated by victimization surveys—the figure nearly doubles, to 13.5 million, or 6,810 per 100,000 population, and that figure does not include automobile thefts.[3] The vast majority of thefts are and always have been furtive and without personal contact with the victims. Thefts involving per-

FIGURE 11.1 Number of larcenies known and rate per 100,000 population, 1984–1988

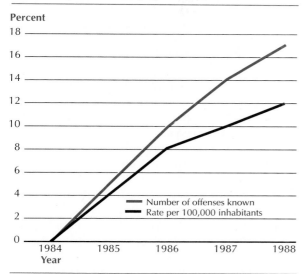

Source: Uniform Crime Reports, 1988, p. 34.

sonal contact—pocket-picking, purse-snatching, and other varieties of larceny—lag behind. Figure 11.2 shows the distribution of all larcenies known to the police in 1988.

Who Are the Thieves?

Nobody knows exactly how many of the overall number of thefts are committed by amateurs who lead rather conventional lives and how many are the work of professionals. According to some criminologists, the two types differ considerably.[4]

The amateur thief Amateur thieves are occasional offenders. They tend to be opportunists who take advantage of a chance to steal when little risk is involved. Typically their acts are carried out with little skill, are unplanned, and result from some pressing situation, such as the need to pay the rent or a gambling debt.[5] In other words, amateurs resolve some immediate crisis by stealing. Most occasional offenders commit crimes infrequently; some commit only one crime. Many are juveniles who do not go on to commit crimes in adulthood. Amateur thieves neither think of themselves as professional criminals nor are recognized as such by thieves who do think of themselves as professionals. In other words, the lives of amateur thieves are quite conventional: they work, go to school, have conventional friends, and find little support or approval for their criminal behavior.

The professional thief Professional thieves make a regular business of stealing. Crime is a way of life. They take pride in their profession. They are imaginative and creative in their work and accept its risks (see Criminological Focus, Chapter 2, p. 27). The most common types of crime committed by professional thieves are "pickpocketing," shoplifting, forgery, confidence swindling, and burglary (which we shall discuss shortly). Professional thieves also are involved in art theft, auto vehicle theft, and fraud or theft by use of stolen or forged credit cards, among other crimes.

Thomas Bartholomew Moran, a professional thief who died in a Miami rescue mission in 1971, has been considered the best of American pickpockets. His career began in 1906, when as a teenager he started to pick women's purses. Under the careful guidance of Mary Kelly, a well-known pickpocket, he soon sharpened his skills until he could take wallets from pants, jeweled pins from clothing, and watches from vests without alerting the victims. He devoted his life to shoplifting, forgery, and other forms

FIGURE 11.2 Percentage distribution of larcenies known to police, 1988

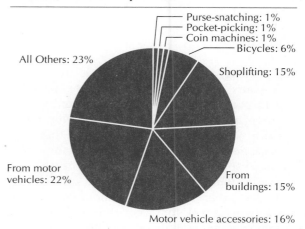

Source: Uniform Crime Reports, 1988, p. 37.

of theft. In 1912 he boarded the *Titanic*, James Inciardi tells, with the intention of profiting handsomely from proximity to

> the more than 300 first-class passengers whose collective wealth exceeded $250 million. His immediate ambitions were dimmed, however, when the *Titanic* brushed an iceberg in the North Atlantic [and sank] only two hours and forty minutes later. But Moran was among the 705 passengers who managed to find space in one of the ship's twenty lifeboats, and his career in crime continued to flourish for the better part of the 59 remaining years of his life.[6]

The most influential study of professional thieves was conducted by Edwin Sutherland in 1937. Sutherland found that professional thieves share five characteristics:

1. They have well-developed technical skills for their particular mode of operation.

2. They enjoy status, accorded to them by their own subculture and by law enforcement.

3. They are bound by consensus, a sharing of values with their own peers.

4. Not only do they learn from each other, but they also protect each other.

5. They are organized, however loosely.[7]

Subsequent studies tend to confirm Sutherland's findings. Researchers have been concerned about many different types of larceny that are committed by both amateurs and professionals.

Shoplifting

Shoplifting, the stealing of goods from retail merchants, is a very common crime, constituting 15 percent of all larcenies. A recent survey in Spokane, Washington, revealed that every twelfth shopper is a shoplifter, and that men and women are equally likely to be offenders.[8] Perhaps shoplifting is so frequent because it is a low-risk offense, with a detection rate of perhaps less than 1 percent.[9] Shoppers are extremely reluctant to report shoplifters to the store management.[10] Mary Owen Cameron

found that professional shoplifters largely conform to Sutherland's five characteristics but that amateurs do not. She estimates that of all shoplifters, only 10 percent are professionals—people who derive most of their income from the sale of stolen goods.[11] A broad range of motivations may lead to shoplifting. Among amateurs, need and greed as well as opportunity may precipitate the event.[12] Other researchers point to depression and other emotional disturbances and to use of various prescription drugs.[13] To most people, shoplifting is a rather insignificant offense. After all, how much can be stolen? On an individual basis, usually not very much: each shoplifter in a supermarket or grocery store takes only one item, with an average value of $11.19. All those thefts in all those stores, however, add up to more than $2.2 billion a year.[14]

As shoplifters decrease the profits of stores, the price of goods goes up; and stepped-up security further adds to the cost. Stores typically hire more and more security personnel, though

it has been demonstrated that physical or electronic methods of securing merchandise are more cost-effective than the deployment of guards.[15] It is only the amateur shoplifter who is deterred by the presence of guards or store personnel, not the professional shoplifter.[16]

Art Theft

Shoplifting ranks at the low end of the larceny scale in terms of the value of each victimization; at the high end we find art theft. The public knows and seems to care little about art theft, yet it is as old as art itself. Marauders have stolen priceless treasures from Egyptian tombs ever since they were built. As prices for antiques and for modern art soar, the demand for stolen art objects soars. Mexico and other countries with a precious cultural heritage are in danger of losing their treasures to gangs of thieves who destroy what they cannot take with them from historic and archaeological sites.

The International Foundation for Art Research in New York began reporting art thefts in 1976. In 1979 it had a record of 1,300 stolen works. By May 1989 the number of cases on file stood at 30,000, most of them representing priceless and irreplaceable works by great masters. One of the most grandiose art thefts occurred on May 21, 1986, when a gang of Irish thieves invaded an estate in Ireland with commando precision and made off with eleven paintings, among them a Goya, two Rubenses, a Gainsborough, and a Vermeer.

Italy has produced some of the greatest art of Western culture. It therefore has offered the greatest opportunity for art thieves. The Italian government consequently established an art theft office within the Carabinieri (the national police force) to deal with the problem of art theft in Italy. Every day this office receives reports on twenty to thirty art thefts, most of them committed by professionals. Most works stolen by professionals are not recovered. Many wind up in private collections. Works stolen for ransom are recovered more frequently, and the thieves are likely to be arrested. Nobody knows the overall cost of art theft. Some paintings are worth $50, others $5,000, others $50 million.

INTERNATIONAL FOUNDATION FOR ART RESEARCH

STOLEN ART ALERT

14TH CENTURY BLUE AND WHITE WARE VASE	SCARAB VASE BY ADELAIDE ALSOP ROBINEAU
Stolen from the Museum of Fine Arts, Boston, MA February 21, 1989	Stolen from the Everson Museum of Art, Syracuse, NY February 13-14, 1989

Mei-p'ing-type porcelain with floral design in underglaze blue (dark cobalt). Ching-te-chen ware. Yuan dynasty. Height 15 in. (38.2 cm). Diameter 8 5/8 in. (22.0 cm). Accession no. 1974.480

Carved and glazed porcelain. Executed 1910. Height 16 1/8 in. (41.0 cm) with stand. "AR" monogram on the base and stand, 1910 on the base. Inscribed "Apotheosis of the Toiler 1910", and marked "Made for the American Woman's League U.C."

REWARD of $100,000
For information leading to safe recovery.
Call: Museum (617) 247-4000 or
F.B.I. (617) 742-5533

REWARD of $25,000
For information leading to safe recovery.
Call: Museum (315) 474-6064 or
F.B.I. (315) 422-0141 or
Syracuse P.D. (315) 425-6631

Or contact IFAR, 46 East 70th Street, New York, NY 10021. (212) 879-1780
IFAR is a non-profit organization dedicated to curtailing the circulation of stolen art in the marketplace.

Tens of thousands of paintings and other art objects are missing.[17]

People who commit larceny aim for places and objects that seem to offer the highest and most secure rewards. Our open mercantile society affords an abundance of opportunities. While shoplifters need little expertise and a low level of professional connection, art thieves must have sophisticated knowledge of art and its value and good connections in the art world if they are to dispose of the art they steal. Other types of larceny, such as theft of automobiles and boats, require a moderate degree of skill—but more and more members of the general public are acquiring such skills.

Motor Vehicle Theft

Nearly 1.5 million automobiles were stolen in the United States in 1988, according to the UCR, for a total loss of over $7 billion. Between 1973 and 1985, the overall loss from motor vehicle theft was $52 billion to owners, before insurance compensation and recovery of vehicles. After insurance and recovery, the loss was $16.1 billion, but even the difference of $35.9 billion ultimately is paid by the public, largely in high insurance rates.

Motor vehicle thefts have increased steadily from 440.1 per 100,000 population in 1973 to 582.9 in 1988.[18] In 1988, 77 percent of the vehicles stolen were passenger cars. The clearance rate (by arrest), as distinguished from the recovery rate (of vehicles), is low—about 15 percent. Many cars are stolen during July and August, when schools are not in session (see Figure 11.3). Forty percent of the thieves are youngsters under 19. Most of their acts amount to "joyriding," a type of larceny in which the element of "intent to deprive the owner permanently" of property is absent. The thieves simply take the vehicle for momentary pleasure, status, or transportation. At the other end of the spectrum are professional auto thieves who steal designated cars on consignment for resale in an altered condition (with identifying numbers changed) or for disposition in "chop shops," which strip the cars for the resale value of their parts.[19]

Manufacturers of automobiles have tried to make cars more theftproof. The invention of the ignition key made it harder to steal cars. In recent years, steering shaft locks, better door-locks, and alarm systems have increased the security of protected cars. Such efforts (as we saw in Chapter 9) are examples of target hardening—that is, designing the target (the car) in such a way that it is harder to steal. Other means of providing for greater car protection include the improvement of the safety of parking facilities. For example, Ronald Clarke has demonstrated that parking lots with attendants experience far fewer motor vehicle thefts than unattended lots.[20]

Vehicle theft protection can also come as an unforeseen by-product of a totally unrelated development. When German legislation in 1980 mandated that motorcyclists wear crash helmets, motorcycle thefts dropped 60 percent. Perhaps most motorcycle thefts had been spur-of-the-moment affairs. Obviously, spur-of-the-moment thieves do not carry crash helmets about on the off chance that they may see an unattended motorcycle and feel like taking it. But perhaps also motorcyclists may have chained their helmets with their motorcycles, thus doubling the effort required by potential thieves. Surprisingly, researchers noted no displacement effect: frustrated motorcycle thieves did not switch to stealing bikes or cars.[21]

FIGURE 11.3   Monthly variation in motor vehicle thefts from annual average, 1988

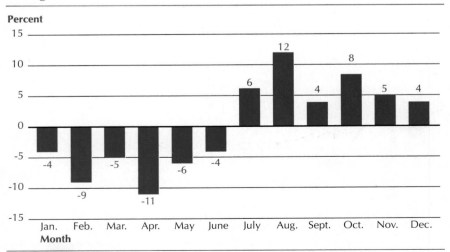

Source: Uniform Crime Reports, 1988, p. 40.

AT ISSUE

"Follow This Car! I'm Being Stolen!"

Manufacturers are introducing radio-equipped car alarms that could allow stolen vehicles to be recovered quickly, perhaps in minutes. Some can sense a theft in progress and give the car's location at all times.

So far only one product, Lojack, is available in only one state, Massachusetts, and its signal does not begin until the police learn of the theft and take action to trigger the device. Several companies plan to introduce products starting next year. All need the participation of state police agencies.

Lojack has been used in Massachusetts for three years.

Lojack's trackers and the ones that its competitors will offer carry a price tag of $500 to $700. They are purchased from car dealers, alarm installers or representatives of the manufacturer. Some manufacturers plan to charge $10 to $20 a month to listen for their signals.

An inconspicuous device about the size of a blackboard eraser is installed, usually in the trunk or under the dashboard. When the police or the thief trigger the device—the thief does so inadvertently, by failing to shut it off when entering the car—the signal lets the monitoring agency determine the vehicle's location.

So far, the police in Massachusetts and other states are enthusiastic about the potential of alarm tracking devices, and insurers are offering some reductions in premiums for vehicles that have the gadgets.

Auto theft has increased rapidly since 1983, the Federal Bureau of Investigation says, because it carries such low risks and high profits. Last year 1.4 million vehicles were stolen, 11.2 percent more than in 1987, for a loss of $7 billion.

Despite Lojack's success, many experts say it is too early to endorse tracking devices. They want to see what technical problems develop, how many people want to use them and how the police react to them.

Since a motor vehicle is stolen every 22 seconds in the United States, on average, urban police departments could become overwhelmed with electronic reports of stolen cars. Another concern is that the police could become so busy with electronic reports that they would have less time to investigate thefts of cars whose owners cannot afford the devices.

Four systems now exist for tracking stolen vehicles. One, to be marketed by Mobile Electronic Tracking Systems in Indianapolis,

is similar to Lojack in that it relies on the police to use the manufacturer's tracking equipment and computer in patrol cars. Another, by Prevent-a-Theft International of Irvine, Calif., does not require a report to the police to set it off; it is set off by the thief, and it will use satellites to track the signal and will report the location to the police by facsimile machine.

A third system, which would also require no report to the police to begin tracking, is to be marketed by International Teletrac Systems of Inglewood, Calif. It would use radio towers in 200 metropolitan regions to track vehicles.

All three manufacturers are seeking state police participation around the country.

With Lojack, if the thief manages to get out of Massachusetts, neither the police nor the company can track the vehicle. But Gordon M. Tucker, Lojack's executive vice president, said the company has agreements with police agencies to make the system available next year in New Jersey, Michigan, Miami and Los Angeles.

Source: Michael deCourcy Hinds, "'Follow This Car! I'm Being Stolen!'" *C. J. the Americas* 3 (February–March 1990): 21.

Boat Theft

It is not our purpose to classify all larceny by the type of property stolen. We have singled out automobile theft and art theft to demonstrate the socioeconomic significance of these types of larceny, their dependence on the economic situation, and the challenge of changing the situational conditions that encourage people to commit them. Another type of larceny, the theft of working and pleasure boats, of little fishing skiffs and rowboats, is similarly tied to socioeconomic conditions.

No statistics were kept on boat theft in the United States before 1970. Obviously boat thefts have occurred ever since there have been boats. But such thefts attained high proportions only in the 1970s and 1980s. The FBI's National Crime Information Center started a stolen boat file in 1969. During the first few years this service was little known, so that the number of boats listed as stolen was initially small. But by the mid-1970s, law enforcement agencies all over the country had become very familiar with this service and had begun reporting the number of stolen boats in their jurisdictions.

Figure 11.4 shows the number of boats stolen and not recovered from 1970 to 1990. Boat theft cases on file peaked by January 1988 and have dropped somewhat since then.

Most boat thefts, both in the water and on land, are linked to the vast increase in the number of boats in the United States. Increased boat ownership among all population groups goes hand in hand with a proliferation of skills in handling boats and outboard motors. The number of automobile thefts rose during the days when automobile ownership and driving skills

FIGURE 11.4   Boats stolen and not recovered as of January 1, 1970–January 1, 1990

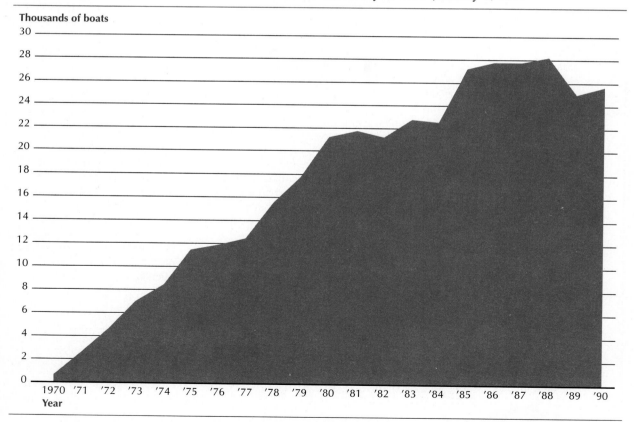

Source: G. O. W. Mueller and Freda Adler, *Outlaws of the Ocean—The Complete Book of Contemporary Crime on the High Seas* (New York: Hearst Marine Books, 1985), p. 223. Updated by personal communication with the FBI.

increased rapidly. Now we are witnessing the same phenomenon with boats. Some of the same crime-specific approaches developed to render cars more and more theftproof are currently being tried to protect boats and boating equipment—registration, secret and indelible identification numbers, locking devices, alarm systems, marina guards, protection campaigns for boat owners. Already we have some indication that the choices for boat thieves are becoming more limited, and that they are choosing their targets with increasing care.

With the exception of some brazen pickpockets, people who commit larcenies tend to avoid personal contact with their victims. Other criminals seek such contact in order to deprive victims of their property by deception.

FRAUD

Fraud is the acquisition of the property of another person through cheating or deception. In England these crimes owed their existence to the interaction of five circumstances: the advancement of trade and commerce, the inventiveness of swindlers in exploiting these economic advances, the demand of merchants for better protection, the unwillingness of the royal courts to expand the old concept of larceny, and the willingness of Parliament to designate new crimes in order to protect mercantile interests. In brief, medieval England developed a market economy that required the transport of goods by wagon trains across the country, from producer or importer to consumer. Later on, when the crown sought to encourage settlement of colonies in America, stock companies were created to raise money for such ventures. People with money to invest acquired part ownership in these companies in the expectation of profit. Just as some dishonest transporters withheld some of the property entrusted to them for transport, some dishonest investment clerks used funds entrusted to them for their own purposes. Merchants suffered greatly from such losses, yet the royal courts refused to extend the definition of larceny to cover the novel means of depriving owners of their property. But merchants demanded protection, and from time to time, as need arose, Parliament desig-

nated new, noncapital offenses so that the swindlers could be punished.

Obtaining Property by False Pretenses

The essence of the crime of **obtaining property by false pretenses** is that the victim is made to part with property voluntarily, as a result of the perpetrator's untrue statement regarding a supposedly existing fact. Suppose the doorbell rings. A gentleman greets you politely and identifies himself as a representative of a charitable organization, collecting money for disaster victims. On a typed list are the names of all the households in your building, with a dollar amount next to each name. Each household has supposedly contributed an average of $20. Not wanting to be considered cheap, you hand the gentleman a $20 bill. He promptly writes "$20" next to your name and thanks you. Of course, the gentleman does not represent the charitable organization, there may not even be such a charity, there may not have been a disaster, and you may have been the first victim on his list. The man has obtained property from you by false pretenses. He has not committed a common law larceny because he did not engage in any "trespassory taking" of property.

Cheating was made a crime relatively late in history (in 1757 in England). Until that time the attitude was that people should look out for their own interests and beware of cheaters. Today the obtaining of property by false pretenses is a crime in all states, and some have included it in their general larceny statutes.

Confidence Games and Frauds

In an attempt to protect people from their own greed, a few fraud statutes have included a statutory offense called **confidence game.** In an effort to cover the enormous variety of confidence swindles, legislators have worded the statutory definitions somewhat vaguely. The essence of the offense is that the offender gains the confidence of the victim, induces in the victim the expectation of a future gain, and by abusing the trust thus created makes the victim part with some property. In a sense, confidence games are an aggravated form of obtaining property

WINDOW TO THE WORLD

International Fraud at Sea

On a warm January day in 1980, the supertanker *Salem* (214,000 tons), off the coast of Senegal, was ripped apart by a series of mysterious explosions. She sank swiftly, carrying her cargo of 193,000 tons of crude oil with her. Or did she?

Fortunately, no lives were lost. Officers and crew soon after arrived healthy and with all their suitcases packed, at their preregistered hotel rooms in Senegal, whence they dispersed to the four corners of the earth. This sinking could have caused a major environmental disaster. Indeed, it should have created the oil slick of the century! But no oil slick ever floated off the West African shores and questions began to arise. Barbara Conway, author of *The Piracy Business,* found the answers: The *Salem*'s name had been

painted over. Under a false name she deviated from her course, unloaded her crude at Shell Oil's own Durban, South Africa, facilities, and there sold her cargo for $43.5 million to Sasol, a South African oil company. The proceeds vanished smoothly in Swiss and Italian bank accounts. Sasol had been happy to get the cargo and asked no questions, since OPEC had placed an oil embargo on South Africa for its apartheid policies. The aging *Salem,* then called the *South Sun,* had been purchased for close to $12 million. Mr. Soudan, her Lebanese-American owner, residing in Texas, and his Dutch and German business associates had insured her hull for $24 million, her cargo for $60 million. The ship, built in Sweden, had been flying the Liberian flag of

convenience. Her unlicensed captain was Greek (at the time under investigation for another alleged fraud), the crew Tunisian and Greek. She carried Kuwaiti oil for Pontoil, an Italian firm, which sold it in transit to Shell International. The conclusion of this nightmarish entanglement was that Sasol agreed to pay Shell $30.5 million in compensation for the oil it had purchased from the swindlers. Mr. Soudan has changed his phone number four times, has not been available for comment, and has not pressed a claim with Lloyd's of London for the insurance on his vessel. But presumably he is some $40 million richer.

Source: G. O. W. Mueller and Freda Adler, *Outlaws of the Ocean—The Complete Book of Contemporary Crime on the High Seas* (New York: Hearst Marine Books, 1985), p. 209.

---

by false pretenses. To illustrate, *A* sees a shiny object lying on the sidewalk. As he stoops to pick it up, *B* grabs it. A dispute ensues over who should have the "lost diamond ring." A third person (*C*) comes by and offers to mediate. He happens to be a jeweler, he says. *C* takes a jeweler's loupe out of his pocket, examines the diamond ring, and pronounces it worth $500. At this point, *B* generously offers his share in the ring to *A* for a mere $100. *A* pays and gets what turns out to be a worthless object. By the time he discovers this fact, *B* and *C* are long gone.

Frauds of this sort have been with us for cen-

turies. But frauds change with commercial developments. Some of the more prevalent fraud schemes of today would have been unimaginable a few decades ago, simply because the commercial opportunities for their occurrence had not yet been invented (see Window to the World).

Check Forgery

Persons motivated to deprive others of their property have always exploited new opportunities to do so. The invention of "instant cash," or credit, by means of a check issued by a creditable, trustworthy person provided new opportunities. Ever since checks were invented, they have been forged and abused. All jurisdictions make it a criminal offense to use a counterfeit or stolen check or to pass a check on a nonexisting account, or even on one with insufficient funds, with intent to defraud. The intent may be demonstrated by the defendant's inability or unwillingness to reimburse the payee within a specified time period. Another fraud, called **check forging,** consists of altering a check with intent to defraud. The criminologist Edwin Lemert found that most check forgers—or "hot check artists," as they are frequently called—are amateurs who act in times of financial need or stress, do not consider themselves criminals, and often believe that nobody really gets hurt.[22]

Just as the introduction of checks for payment for goods and services opened up opportunities for fraudsters to gain illegitimate financial advantages, so did the introduction of "plastic money," the credit card. Nor will the invention of the credit card offer the last opportunity to swindlers to deprive others of their property. Opportunities always challenge the imagination of legitimate and illegitimate entrepreneurs. As for the illegitimate entrepreneurs, the problem always is whether they are in violation of existing criminal laws or whether new legislation will have to be drawn up to cover their fraudulent schemes.

Credit and Cash Card Crimes

Electronic cash transfer by automated teller machines has become routine in the United States and is spreading rapidly throughout the Western world. In 1983 2.7 billion such transfers were made, involving $262 billion, and the volume has been increasing since then. Around $100 million was lost to fraudulent transactions:

- Unauthorized use of a lost or stolen card.
- Overdrafts.
- "Bad deposits."
- Use of counterfeit cards.

The loss involved in each fraudulent transaction averaged $200. While these figures do not indicate a crisis, they do show a potential for ever greater abuse.[23] The banking industry has studied the schemes of credit card abuse and has improved the electronic system with target-hardening responses. In 1971 Congress enacted legislation that limited the financial liability of owners of stolen credit cards to $50. Many states have enacted legislation making it a distinct offense to obtain property or services by means of a stolen or forged credit card, while others include this type of fraud under their broadly conceived larceny statutes.

Originally the users of stolen credit cards had the inconvenience of selling the merchandise they fraudulently obtained with the cards. But when banks introduced the practice of cashing the checks of strangers as long as the transactions were guaranteed by a credit card, the perpetrator gained direct access to cash and no longer had to resort to a dealer in stolen goods.[24]

BURGLARY

A "burg," in Anglo-Saxon terminology, was a secure place for the protection of oneself, one's family, and one's property. If the burg protects a person from larceny and assault, what protects the burg? The burghers, perhaps. But there had to be a law behind the burghers. And that was the law of burglary, which made it a crime to break and enter the dwelling of another person at night with the intention of committing a crime therein. (Of course it had to be at night, for during the day the inhabitants could defend themselves, or so it was thought.) The common law defined **burglary** as

- the breaking
- and entering
- of the dwelling house
- of another person
- at night
- with the intention to commit a felony or larceny inside.

By "breaking," the law meant any trespass (unauthorized entry), but usually one accompanied by a forceful act, such as cracking the lock,

"If we pull this off, we've made burglary history!"

breaking a windowpane, or scaling the roof and entering through the chimney. The "entry" was complete as soon as the perpetrator extended any part of his body into the house—in pursuit of the objective of committing a crime in the house. The house had to be a "dwelling," but that definition was extended to cover the "curtilage," the attached servants' quarters, carriage houses, and barns. The dwelling also had to be that of "another." And, as we mentioned, the event had to occur at night, between sundown and sunup. The most troublesome element has always been the "intention to commit a crime" (a felony or a larceny, even a petty or misdemeanor larceny) inside the premises. How can we know what a burglar intends to do? The best evidence of intent is what the burglar actually does inside the premises: steal jewelry? rape someone? set the house afire? Any crime the burglar commits inside is considered as evidence of criminal intention at the moment the burglar broke and entered the dwelling.[25]

Today burglary is no longer limited to night attacks, although by statute the crime may be usually considered more serious if it is committed at night. Statutes have also added buildings other than dwellings to the definition. The UCR defines burglary simply as the unlawful entry of a structure (criminal trespass) to commit a felony or theft. The use of force to gain entry is not a required element of burglary under the UCR.

In 1988 more than 3.2 million burglaries were reported to the police, with an overall loss of $3.3 billion. These crimes account for nearly a quarter of all Index offenses. Most burglaries (87 percent) are not cleared by arrests. Burglary rates have declined modestly since 1986 (see Figure 11.5). Could the decline be due to greater awareness on the part of homeowners of the risks in leaving doors and windows open? Or might it be caused by the increased use of burglar alarms?[26] Until recently, criminologists were not interested in examining such questions; they focused rather on classifying burglars. Neal Shover described the "good burglar" as having competence, personal integrity, a specialty in burglary, financial success, and an ability to avoid prison.[27] Criminologists were also interested in the difference between professional and casual burglars.[28] Research on burglary now has changed considerably. Instead of asking who is likely to commit a burglary or what distinguishes one burglar from another, criminologists now ask:

• What is the process that leads to the burglary of a particular house in a specific neighborhood?

FIGURE 11.5   Number of burglaries known and rate per 100,000 population, 1984–1988

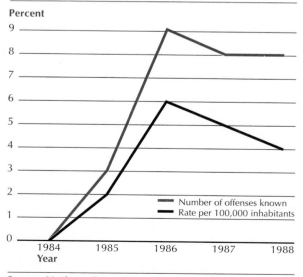

Source: Uniform Crime Reports, 1988, p. 29.

- How does a burglar discriminate between individual areas and targets when there are so many alternatives to accept or reject?
- How can we make the process of burglary more difficult for any burglar?

In short, criminologists are now more interested in the factors that go into a decision to burglarize: the location or setting of a building, the presence of guards, dogs, the type of burglar alarms and external lighting, and so forth. Does the presence of a car in the driveway or a radio playing music in a house have a significant impact on the choice of home to burglarize? Such are the questions being asked and studied today.

The criminologist-geographer George Rengert has conducted extensive interviews with burglars in an effort to understand their techniques. He found significant differences in (a) the amount of planning that precedes a burglary (professional burglars plan more than amateur criminals); (b) the extent to which a burglar will engage in systematic selection of a home (some burglars examine the obvious clues, such as presence of burglar alarms, watchdog, mail piled up in a mailbox, newspapers on a doorstep; more experienced burglars look for subtle clues, for example, closed windows coupled with air conditioners that are turned off); and (c) the extent to which a burglar will pay attention to situational cues (some burglars routinely choose a corner property because it offers more avenues of escape, has fewer adjoining properties, and offers better visibility).[29]

Rengert and his colleagues have also examined the use of time and place in burglaries. Time is a critical factor to burglars, for three reasons:

- They must minimize the time spent in targeted places so as not to reveal their intention to burglarize.
- Opportunities for burglary occur only when a dwelling is unguarded (see Figure 11.6).
- Burglars have "working hours"; that is, they have time available only during a limited number of hours (if they have a legitimate job, for example). (See Criminological Focus.)

Finally, burglars commit their offenses in certain areas for important reasons—familiarity

FIGURE 11.6 Home guardianship and residential burglary

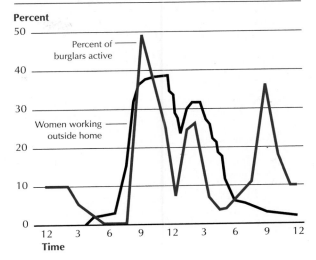

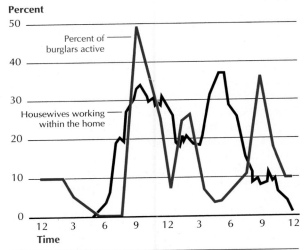

Source: George Rengert and John Wasilchick, *Suburban Burglary: A Time and a Place for Everything* (Springfield, Ill.: Charles C Thomas, 1985), p. 128.

with the area, fear of recognition, concern over "standing out" as someone who does not belong, or the perception (following some successful burglaries) that a particular area is no longer cost-beneficial. Researchers have also compared burglary target choices of experienced burglars (aged 18–33) with those of a control group of students and householders. As one might expect, the burglars' responses were far more alike in their assessment of the vulnerability of a house (e.g., a corner location, lack of

CRIMINOLOGICAL FOCUS

The Use of Time in Burglary: The Crime Day of Burglar #28

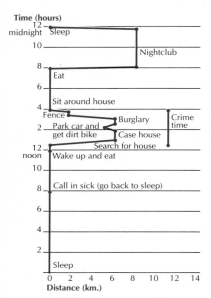

Time (hours)

Distance (km.)

Individual #28 is an afternoon burglar. He worked while active as a burglar. He simply called in sick toward the end of the week and took a day off for crime. He was not a drug user, although he acquired an addiction to gambling in Atlantic City casinos.... Individual #28 reasoned that the only means of collecting enough money to gamble over a weekend was to burglarize at least one day a week. This day was during the latter part of the week, usually a Thursday afternoon.

Trace through a typical crime day for burglar #28 on the graph. During a burglary day, individual #28 would call in sick at 8:30 in the morning and go back to sleep. He would wake up at noon, eat, and leave the house by 1:00. His method of operation was somewhat more complex than [that of] other burglars, and it required a little more time. After he found a likely house to burglarize, he would spend 30 minutes to case it. Then he would drive his car around to the area immediately behind the house. He would open his trunk and remove a "dirt bike," a small motorcycle built to run over unpaved areas. He would ride his bike to the victim's street and park it three or four houses away. He reasoned that if anything went wrong, he could ride the dirt bike across the expansive yards and woods of this suburban area. On the dirt bike, he could easily outdistance anyone chasing him by foot or auto. He could always retrieve his car later. This technique added about 30 minutes to his "crime time" and he did not return home until about 4:00 P.M. The total time required for this crime block was three hours.

This individual could meet a work schedule and commit burglaries because he restricted himself to one or two burglary days a week. His job was janitorial work for a house and office cleaning firm. Individual #28 reasoned that the firm was accustomed to high job turnover and frequent no shows because of the relatively low pay scale and menial tasks. He was not sure how much longer the frequency of his sick days would be tolerated. He felt that sooner or later they would catch on to his regular pattern of absences and either force him to work more regularly or fire him. If that time of reckoning ever arrived, individual #28 had no doubt about the course he would follow. As he stated, "I could make more burglarizing in one day than for a week's work as a janitor." Traditional employment could not compete with crime economically or socially. Burglary paid better and was a lot more fun than janitorial work.

Source: George Rengert and John Wasilchick, *Suburban Burglary: A Time and a Place for Everything* (Springfield, Ill.: Charles C Thomas, 1985), pp. 36–38.

security devices).[30] Similarly, young English burglars aged 15–17 largely agreed on their target selections (e.g., presence of bushes or other cover, absence of the family car, no dog, no alarm).[31]

Burglaries tend to be concentrated in certain "hot spot" areas. In a study of 323,979 calls to the Minneapolis police from December 1985 to December 1986, Lawrence Sherman, Patrick Garten, and Michael Buerger found that these calls came from 155,000 addresses and intersections, but that the 15,901 burglary calls among them came from only 11 percent of these addresses and intersections.[32] It thus becomes possible to target these hot spots for special prevention strategies and substantially reduce opportunities for burglary.

Irvin Waller and Norman Okihiro suggest that householders can make their homes less attractive to burglars by being careful to keep their doors locked, increasing surveillance, and ensuring that someone is in the house much of the time.[33] Burglars seek to avoid contact with occupants; their trade is one of stealth.

We are viewing burglary as a property crime. An occasional burglar enters with the intention of committing rape, arson, or some other felony inside the building. But most burglars are thieves; they are looking for cash and for other property that can be turned into cash. Burglars and thieves thus depend on a network of "fences" to turn their stolen property into cash.

"FENCING": RECEIVING STOLEN PROPERTY

Jonathan Wild controlled the London underworld from about 1714 till his hanging in 1725. For over two and a half centuries he has captured the imagination of historians, social scientists, and writers. Henry Fielding wrote *The Life of Mr. Jonathan Wild, the Great,* and Mack the Knife in John Gay's *Beggar's Opera* was modeled on Wild. Wild was known as a "thief-taker." Thief-takers made an occupation of capturing thieves and claiming the rewards offered for their arrest. By law, thief-takers were allowed to keep the possessions of the thieves they caught, except objects that had been stolen, which were returned to their owners. But Wild added a devious twist to his trade: he bought stolen goods from thieves and sold them back to their rightful owners. The owners paid much more than the thief could get from other fences, so both Wild and the thief made a considerable profit. To thieves, he was a fellow thief; to honest people, he was a legitimate citizen helping to get back their property. Playing both roles well, he ran competing fencing operations out of business, employed about 7,000 thieves, and became the most famous fence of all time.[34]

A **fence** is a person who buys stolen property on a regular basis, for resale. Fences, or dealers in stolen property, operate much like legitimate businesses: they buy and sell for profit. Their activity thrives on an understanding of the law governing the receiving of stolen property, on cooperation with the law when necessary, and on networking. The difference between a legitimate business and a fencing operation is that the channeling of stolen goods takes place in a clandestine environment (created by law enforcement and deviant associates) with high risks and with a need to justify one's activities in the eyes of conventional society.

Carl Klockars' *Professional Fence* and Darrell Steffensmeier's *Fence,* each focusing on the life of a particular fence, present us with fascinating accounts of the criminal business of fencing. The proprietors of such businesses deal in almost any commodity. "Oh, I done lots a business with him," said Klockars' fence, Vincent Swazzi. "One time I got teeth, maybe five thousand teeth in one action. You know, the kind they use for making false teeth—you see, you never know what a thief's gonna come up with." And many fences are quite proud of their positions in the community. Said Swazzi, "The way I look at it, this is actually my street. I mean I am the mayor. I walk down the street an' people come out the doors to say hello."[35]

Until recently it was believed that professional thieves and fences were totally interdependent and that their respective illegal activities were mutually reinforcing. Recent research, however, demonstrates a change in the market for stolen goods. D'Aunn Wester Avery, Paul F. Cromwell, and James N. Olson conducted extensive interviews with thirty-eight active burglars, shoplifters, and their fences and concluded that it is no longer the professional fence who takes care of stolen goods, but rather occasional and lay receivers, otherwise honest citizens, who buy from thieves directly or at flea markets.[36] This willingness to buy merchandise that the buyers must at least suspect has been stolen may indicate that the general public is more tolerant of stealing than previous generations were.

ARSON

The crimes against property that we have discussed so far involve the illegitimate transfer of possession. The property in question is "personal property" rather than real property, or real estate. Only two types of property crime are concerned not simply with personal property but with real property. Burglary is one; the other is arson.

The common law defined **arson** as the malicious burning or setting fire to the dwelling of another person. Modern statutes have distinguished degrees of severity of the offense and have increased its scope to include other structures and even personal property, such as automobiles. The most severe punishments are reserved for arson of dwellings, because of the likelihood that persons in the building may be injured or die. Arson always has been viewed as a more violent crime than burglary. In comparison with burglary, however, arson is a fairly infrequent offense. A total of 101,097 arson offenses were reported in 1988. A national survey of fire departments, however, indicates that the actual number of arson incidents is likely to be far higher than the reported figure.[37] Buildings were the most frequent targets (55 percent); 28 percent of the targets were mobile property (motor vehicles, trailers, etc.). UCR figures for 1988 put the national property loss due to arson at over $1 billion, but the National Fire Protection Association estimates property loss at close to $6 billion, and adds 4,985 civilian lives lost.[38]

The seriousness of this crime is also demonstrated by a series of spectacular fires set in resort hotels in such cities as San Juan, Puerto Rico (in conjunction with a labor dispute), and Las Vegas, Nevada. Although these fires were not set with the intent to kill any of the people in the buildings, many lives were lost. The inferno created by arsonists in the Du Pont Plaza Hotel in San Juan in 1987 killed 97 people. The arson at the Las Vegas Hilton caused no deaths but $14 million in damages, not including the loss of business.

While insurance fraudsters and organized

Police and fire officials mill about the Happyland Social club in the Bronx following a fire that killed 87 people. Most of them died from smoke inhalation.

crime torches may be responsible for some of the more spectacular arsons, it is juveniles who account for the single, most significant share. Consider the following statistics:

- In 1988 juveniles under age 18 accounted for about 40 percent of the arson arrests nationwide.
- One of every sixteen persons arrested for arson is under age 10, and one of every four is under age 15.
- Juveniles are responsible for approximately 50 percent of the arson fires in Seattle.
- 38 percent of children in grades 1 to 8 in Rochester, New York, admitted playing with fire.[39]

Why do children set fires? [40] Recent research suggests that the motive may be psychological pain, anger, revenge, the need for attention, malicious mischief, or excitement.[41] Juvenile firesetters have been classified in three groups: the playing-with-matches firesetter, the crying-for-help firesetter, and the severely disturbed firesetter.[42] Many juvenile firesetters are in urgent need of help. In response to these needs, juvenile arson intervention programs have been established in recent years.[43] An interesting English study found that while arsonists were in many respects comparable to offenders classified as violent, they had a lower incidence of interpersonal aggression and rated themselves as less assertive than violent offenders, perhaps because, as the study showed, arsonists were taken into care at an earlier age.[44]

The motives of adult arsonists are somewhat different from those of juveniles. Though here, too, we find disturbed offenders (pyromaniacs) and people who set fires out of spite, we are much more likely to encounter insurance fraudsters and organized crime figures who force compliance or impose revenge by burning establishments (the "torches").[45]

John M. Macdonald, a psychiatrist, classifies all firesetters by their motives:

- Revenge, jealousy, and hatred.
- Financial gain (mostly insurance fraud).

FIGURE 11.7 World crime: proportions of total crime according to crime categories

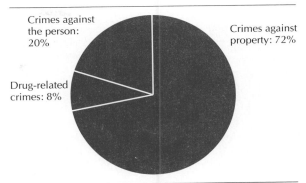

Source: *Crime Prevention and Control, Report of the Secretary-General,* A/32/199, 22 September 1977 (known as the first United Nations World Crime Survey), p. 10.

- Intimidation and/or extortion (often involving organized crime).
- Need for attention.
- Social protest.
- Arson to conceal other crimes.
- Arson to facilitate other crimes.
- Vandalism and accidental firesetting.[46]

As arson continues to be a serious national problem, policy makers have been developing two distinct approaches for dealing with it. An offender-specific approach focuses on educational outreach in schools and the early identification of troubled children, for purposes of counseling and other assistance.[47] The other, an offense-specific (geographic) approach, focuses on places. It seeks to identify areas with a record of or a high potential for arson. The aim, then, is to deploy arson specialists to correct problems and to stabilize endangered buildings and neighborhoods.[48]

The rates of property crimes are much higher than those of the violent crimes we discussed in Chapter 10. It is interesting to compare these rates in various regions of the world.

COMPARATIVE CRIME RATES

The first United Nations World Crime Survey reported that 72 percent of all major crimes

FIGURE 11.8   Crime in developed countries: proportions of total crime according to broad crime categories, 1970–1975

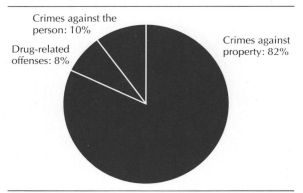

Source: *Crime Prevention and Control, Report of the Secretary-General*, A/32/199, 22 September 1977 (known as the first United Nations World Crime Survey), p. 15.

FIGURE 11.9   Crime in developing countries: proportions of total crime according to broad crime categories, 1970–1975

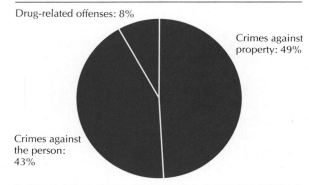

Source: *Crime Prevention and Control, Report of the Secretary-General*, A/32/199, 22 September 1977 (known as the first United Nations World Crime Survey), p. 12.

committed throughout the world from 1970 through 1975 were crimes against property (Figure 11.7). That in itself is not startling. But if we compare the property-owning, consumer-oriented countries of the industrialized Western world with the still largely agricultural but rapidly urbanizing countries of the Third World, we note a significant discrepancy: 82 percent of all crimes in the developed countries were crimes against property (Figure 11.8), while only 49 percent of all crimes in developing countries were crimes against property (Figure

11.9). Recall the Coca-Cola bottle that disrupted the lives of the aborigines in *The Gods Must Be Crazy*. We just may have discovered the secret of that Coca-Cola bottle: if there is no Coke bottle, no one is going to steal it. The more property people have, especially portable property, the more opportunity other people have to make off with it. Europeans have an old saying: Opportunity makes thieves. The foremost opportunity for theft may simply be an abundance of property.

REVIEW

Not all crimes against property are aimed at acquiring such property. A burglar invades a dwelling or other structure usually—but not necessarily—to commit a larceny inside. An arsonist endangers the existence of the structure and its occupants. Both amateurs and professionals commit property crimes of all sorts. Each new routine activity of legitimate trade, such as the development of credit cards, offers criminals new opportunities to exploit the situation for gain. In this perpetual struggle between the developers of legitimate pursuits and

the exploiters, scientists have begun—but just begun—to play a positive new role. By studying opportunities for crime and by analyzing the way criminals choose their targets, social scientists are helping to reduce crime by devising strategies that make crimes harder to commit.

Some property-oriented crimes, as we shall see in Chapter 12, depend not only on the cunning and daring of the perpetrator who targets a lone victim but on the normal business operations of legitimate enterprises—and of illegitimate ones as well.

KEY TERMS

arson
burglary
check forging
confidence game
false pretense, obtaining property by

fence
fraud
larceny
shoplifting

NOTES

1. J. W. Cecil Turner, *Kenny's Outlines of Criminal Law*, 2d ed. (Cambridge: Cambridge University Press, 1958), p. 238.

2. Jerome Hall, *Theft, Law, and Society* (Indianapolis: Bobbs-Merrill, 1935).

3. U.S. Department of Justice, Bureau of Justice Statistics, *Criminal Victimization in the United States, 1988: A National Crime Survey Report* (Washington, D.C.: U.S. Government Printing Office, 1989) (preliminary statistics).

4. See Abraham S. Blumberg, "Typologies of Criminal Behavior," in *Current Perspectives on Criminal Behavior*, 2d ed., ed. Blumberg (New York: Knopf, 1981).

5. See John Hepburn, "Occasional Criminals," in *Major Forms of Crime*, ed. Robert Meier, pp. 73–94 (Beverly Hills, Calif.: Sage, 1984); John Gibbs and Peggy Shelly, "Life in the Fast Lane: A Retrospective View by Commercial Thieves," *Journal of Research in Crime and Delinquency* 19 (1982): 299–330, at 327.

6. James Inciardi, "Professional Thief," in *Major Forms of Crime*, p. 224. See also Harry King and William Chambliss, *Box Man—A Professional Thief's Journal* (New York: Harper & Row, 1972).

7. *The Professional Thief*, annotated and interpreted by Edwin H. Sutherland (Chicago: University of Chicago Press, 1937).

8. Jo-Ann Ray, "Every Twelfth Shopper: Who Shoplifts and Why?" *Social Casework* 68 (1987): 234–239.

9. Abigail Buckle and David P. Farrington, "An Observational Study of Shoplifting," *British Journal of Criminology* 24 (1984): 63–73.

10. Donald Hartmann, Donna Gelfand, Brent Page, and Patrice Walder, "Rates of Bystander Observation and Reporting of Contrived Shoplifting Incidents," *Criminology* 10 (1972): 247–267.

11. Mary Owen Cameron, *The Booster and the Snitch* (New York: Free Press, 1964); see also John Rosecrance, "The Stooper: A Professional Thief in the Sutherland Manner," *Criminology* 24 (February 1986): 29–40.

12. Richard Moore, "Shoplifting in Middle America: Patterns and Motivational Correlates," *International Journal of Offender Therapy and Comparative Criminology* 28 (1984): 53–64; Hepburn, "Occasional Criminals."

13. Trevor N. Gibbens, C. Palmer, and Joyce Prince, "Mental Health Aspects of Shoplifting," *British Medical Journal* 3 (1971): 612–615; Richard Williams and J. Thomas Dalby, "Benzodiazepines and Shoplifting," *International Journal of Offender Therapy and Comparative Criminology* 30 (1986): 35–39.

14. Roger Griffin, *Shoplifting in Supermarkets* (San Diego: Commercial Service Systems, 1988).

15. Barry Poyner and Ruth Woodall, *Preventing Shoplifting: A Study in Oxford Street* (London: Police Foundation, 1987). For a general "ethnography" of English shoplifting, see Daniel J. I. Murphy, *Customers and Thieves* (Brookfield, Vt.: Gower, 1986).

16. John Carroll and Frances Weaver, "Shoplifters' Perceptions of Crime Opportunities: A Process-Tracing Study," in *The Reasoning Criminal*, ed. Derek Cornish and Ronald V. Clarke, pp. 19–38 (New York: Springer-Verlag, 1986).

17. See Christopher Dickey, "Missing Masterpieces," *Newsweek*, May 29, 1989, pp. 65–68;

Milton Esterow, "Confessions of an Art Cop," *Art News*, May 1988, pp. 134–137.

18. Uniform Crime Reports, 1973, p. 50; 1988, p. 38.

19. See Charles McCaghy, Peggy Giordano, and Trudy Knicely Henson, "Auto Theft," *Criminology* 15 (1977): 367–385.

20. Ronald V. Clarke, "Situational Crime Prevention: Theoretical Basis and Practical Scope," in *Crime and Justice: An Annual Review of Research*, ed. Michael Tonry and Norval Morris, vol. 4 (Chicago: University of Chicago Press, 1983).

21. Pat Mayhew, Ronald V. Clarke, and David Elliott, "Motorcycle Theft, Helmet Legislation and Displacement," *Howard Journal of Criminal Justice* 28 (1989): 1–8.

22. Edwin Lemert, "An Isolation and Closure Theory of Naive Check Forgery," *Journal of Criminal Law, Criminology, and Police Science* 44 (1953–1954): 296–307.

23. James M. Tien, Thomas F. Rich, and Michael F. Cahn, *Electronic Fund Transfer Systems Fraud*, for U.S. Department of Justice, Bureau of Justice Statistics (Washington, D.C.: U.S. Government Printing Office, 1986). For the variety of credit card frauds, see State of Hawaii, Department of the Attorney General, Hawaii Criminal Justice Data Center, *Credit Card Fraud in Hawaii* (Honolulu, 1986).

24. Pierre Tremblay, "Designing Crime," *British Journal of Criminology* 26 (1986): 234–253.

25. Kenneth C. Sears and Henry Weihofen, *May's Law of Crimes*, 4th ed. (Boston: Little, Brown, 1938), pp. 307–317.

26. George Rengert and John Wasilchick, *Suburban Burglary: A Time and a Place for Everything* (Springfield, Ill.: Charles C Thomas, 1985).

27. Neal Shover, "Structures and Careers in Burglary," *Journal of Criminal Law and Criminology* 63 (1972): 540–549.

28. H. A. Scarr, *Patterns of Burglary* (Washington, D.C.: U.S. Government Printing Office, 1973). For a discussion of "commercial burglars," see Gibbs and Shelly, "Life in the Fast Lane."

29. Rengert and Wasilchick, *Suburban Burglary*.

30. M. Taylor and C. Nee, "The Role and Cues in Simulated Residential Burglary," *British Journal of Criminology* 28 (1988): 396–401.

31. Richard Wright and Robert H. Logie, "How Young House Burglars Choose Targets," *Howard Journal of Criminal Justice* 27 (1988): 92–104.

32. Lawrence W. Sherman, Patrick R. Garten, and Michael E. Buerger, "Hot Spots of Predatory Crime: Routine Activities and the Criminology of Place," *Criminology* 27 (February 1989): 27–55.

33. Irvin Waller and Norman Okihiro, *Burglary: The Victim and the Public* (Toronto: University of Toronto Press, 1978); see also Ronald Clarke and Tim Hope, eds., *Coping with Burglary* (Boston: Kluwer-Nijhoff, 1984).

34. Darrell Steffensmeier, *The Fence: In the Shadow of Two Worlds* (Totowa, N.J.: Rowman & Littlefield, 1986), p. 7.

35. Carl Klockars, *The Professional Fence* (New York: Free Press, 1976), pp. 110, 113.

36. D'Aunn Wester Avery, Paul F. Cromwell, and James N. Olson, "Marketing Stolen Property: Burglars and Their Fences," paper presented at the 1988 Annual Meeting of the American Society of Criminology, Reno, Nev.

37. Patrick G. Jackson, "Assessing the Validity of Official Data on Arson," *Criminology* 26 (1988): 181–195; see also Frederick Mercilliott, "The Effectiveness of Alternative Approaches to Investigating Arson: A Study of 155 Cities" (Ph.D. dissertation, City University of New York, 1988).

38. Michael J. Kartes, Jr., "A Look at Fire Loss During 1986," *Fire Journal*, September/October 1987, p. 40.

39. Uniform Crime Reports, 1988, p. 178; also see Rebecca K. Hersch, *A Look at Juvenile Firesetter Programs*, for U.S. Department of Justice, Office of Justice Programs, Office of Juvenile Justice and Delinquency Prevention (Washington, D.C.: U.S. Government Printing Office, May 1989), p. 1.

40. Irving Kaufman and Lora W. Heims, "A Re-evaluation of the Dynamics of Fire-

setting," *American Journal of Orthopsychiatry* 31 (1961): 123–136.

41. Hersch, *A Look at Juvenile Firesetter Programs.*

42. Wayne S. Wooden and Martha Lou Berkey, *Children and Arson* (New York: Plenum, 1984), p. 3.

43. See Jessica Gaynor and Chris Hatcher, *The Psychology of Child Firesetting* (New York: Brunner/Mazel, 1987).

44. Howard F. Jackson, Susan Hope, and Clive Glass, "Why Are Arsonists Not Violent Offenders?" *International Journal of Offender Therapy and Comparative Criminology* 31 (1987): 143–151.

45. See Wayne W. Bennett and Karen Matison Hess, *Investigating Arson* (Springfield, Ill.: Charles C Thomas, 1984), pp. 34–38.

46. John M. Macdonald, *Bombers and Firesetters* (Springfield, Ill.: Charles C Thomas, 1977), pp. 198–204.

47. See Federal Emergency Management Agency, U.S. Fire Administration, *Interviewing and Counselling Juvenile Firesetters* (Washington, D.C.: U.S. Government Printing Office, 1979).

48. Clifford L. Karchmer, *Preventing Arson Epidemics: The Role of Early Warning Strategies,* Aetna Arson Prevention Series (Hartford, Conn.: Aetna Life & Casualty, 1981).

12

ORGANIZA-
TIONAL
CRIMINALITY

The Department of Justice today [May 2, 1985] filed a criminal information charging E. F. Hutton & Company Inc., one of the nation's largest securities dealers, with 2,000 counts of mail and wire fraud.

The essence of the charges was that Hutton obtained the interest-free use of millions of dollars by intentionally writing checks in excess of the funds it had on deposit in various banks.

Attorney General Edwin Meese III said the filing of the criminal information with the federal district court in Scranton, Pennsylvania, was followed immediately by the entry of a guilty plea to all 2,000 counts of wire and mail fraud by the firm.

In accordance with a plea agreement between Hutton and the government, Judge William Nealon, Jr., imposed the maximum criminal fine, $2 million, and assessed costs of the investigation of $750,000. The agreement also calls for payment of restitution to the banks, the Attorney General said. More than 400 banks throughout the United States are believed to have been affected.

The information charged that during the course of the scheme, which it said began about July 1980 and continued through February 1982, Hutton's drawings against uncollected funds totaled more than $1 billion, with daily overdrafts sometimes exceeding $250 million.

The purpose of the scheme, according to the information, was to obtain the daily, interest-free use of millions of dollars in bank funds, thereby avoiding the necessity to borrow funds at interest rates which, during the course of the scheme, reached an annual rate of 20 percent.[1]

* * *

General Electric has been charged with price fixing and other monopolistic practices not only for its light bulbs, but for turbines, generators, transformers, motors, relays, radio tubes, heavy metals, and lightning arresters. At least 67 suits have been brought against General Electric by the Antitrust Division of the Justice Department since 1911, and 180 antitrust suits were brought against General Electric by private companies in the early 1960's alone. General Electric's many trips to court hardly seem to have "reformed" the company: In 1962, after 50 years' experience with General Electric, even the Justice Department was moved to comment on General Electric's proclivity for frequent and persistent involvement in antitrust violations.[2]

* * *

In 1963, Attorney General Robert F. Kennedy testified before the McClellan Committee on the matter of organized crime. He spoke of a "private government" of organized crime. This government has a yearly income of billions of dollars and is organized around a commission which is responsible for decisions concerning policy. The commission also settles disputes and problems between families and organizations. At this hearing, a member of La Cosa Nostra (Joseph Valachi) disclosed for the first time, confidential information on the organization and operations of the Mafia.[3]

What do the crimes of E. F. Hutton, General Electric, and the Cosa Nostra, or Mafia, have in common? According to the criminologist Dwight Smith, white-collar, corporate, and organized crimes all involve business enterprises.[4] An offender, whether a corporation employee, the corporation itself, or a lieutenant in a Mafia family, uses a business enterprise (perhaps an insurance company, a garbage collection company, or a prostitution ring) to profit illegally. It is the use of a legitimate or illegitimate business enterprise for illegal profit that distinguishes organizational crimes from other types of offenses. These offenses are also different in another important respect. Unlike violent crimes and property offenses, which the Model Penal Code classifies quite neatly, organizational offenses are a heterogeneous mix of crimes, from homicide, fraud, and conspiracy to racketeering, gambling, and the violation of a host of federal environmental statutes.

How much white-collar crime is committed each year? What are the attributes of organized crimes? How much crime is committed by major U.S. corporations? Answers to such questions, no matter how preliminary, may provide valuable information to guide efforts to control and prevent white-collar, corporate, and organized crime.

WHITE-COLLAR CRIME

White-collar crime is not a new phenomenon. In ancient Greece public officials reportedly violated the law by purchasing land slated for government acquisition.[5] But much of what we today define as white-collar crime is the result of laws passed within the last century. For example, the **Sherman Antitrust Act,** passed by Congress in 1890, authorized the criminal prosecution of corporations engaged in monopolistic practices. Federal laws regulating the issuance and sale of stocks and other securities were passed in 1933 and 1934, and in 1940 Edwin H. Sutherland provided criminologists with the first scholarly account of **white-collar crime.** He defined it as crime "committed by a person of respectability and high social status in the course of his occupation."[6]

The E. F. Hutton and General Electric cases demonstrate that Sutherland's definition is not entirely satisfactory: white-collar crime can be committed by a corporation as well as by an individual. As Gilbert Geis has noted, Sutherland's work is limited by his own definition. He has a "striking inability to differentiate between the corporations themselves and their executive management personnel."[7] Other criminologists have suggested that the term "white-collar crime" not be used at all; we should speak instead of "corporate crime" and "occupational crime."[8]

The victims of white-collar offenders range from the savvy investor to the unsuspecting consumer. No one person or group is immune. The Vatican lost millions of dollars in a fraudulent stock scheme, fraudulent charities have swindled fortunes from unsuspecting investors, and many banks have been forced into bankruptcy by losses due to deception and fraud.[9]

White-Collar Crimes Committed by Individuals

As we have noted, white-collar crime is a violation of the law committed by a person or group of persons in the course of an otherwise respected and legitimate occupation or business enterprise.[10] Over time socioeconomic developments have increasingly changed the dimensions of such crimes. Historically, people have needed but few types of business relationships to make their way through life. One had to deal with one's employer or employees. One dealt on a basis of trust and confidence with the local shoemaker and grocer. One had virtually no dealings with government. This way of life has changed significantly and very rapidly during the last few decades. People have become dependent on large bureaucratic structures; they are manipulated by agents and officials with whom they have no personal relationship. This situation creates a basis for potential abuses in four sets of relations:

- Employees of large entities may abuse their authority for private gain, by making their services to members of the public contingent on a bribe, a kickback, or some other favor. A corrupt employee of an insurance company, for example, may write a favorable claim assessment in exchange for half of the insurance payment.
- Taking advantage of the complexity and anonymity of a large organization, such as a corporation, employees may abuse the systems available to them or the power they hold within the structure for purposes of unlawful gain, as by embezzlement.
- Members of the public who have to deal with a large organization do not have the faith and trust they had when they dealt with individual merchants. If they see an opportunity to defraud a large organization, they may seize it in the belief that the large organization can easily absorb the loss and nobody will be hurt.
- Since the relation of buyer to seller (or of service provider to client) has become increasingly less personal in an age of medical group practice, large law firms, and drugstore chains, opportunities for **occupational crimes**—crimes committed by individuals for themselves in the course of rendering a service—have correspondingly increased. Medicare fraud, misuse of clients' funds by lawyers and brokers, substitution of inferior goods—all such offenses are occupational crimes.[11]

White-collar crimes are as difficult to detect as they are easy to induce.[12] The crime-detection mechanisms on which the police traditionally rely seem singularly inadequate for this vast new body of crimes. Moreover, though people have learned through the ages to be wary of strangers on the street, they have not yet learned to protect themselves against these newer forms of crime. The available data have not yet permitted us to develop workable prevention strategies. Much more scientific study has to be undertaken on the causes, extent, and characteristics of these offenses.[13]

Types of White-Collar Crimes

The lawyer August Bequai suggests nine categories of white-collar offenses committed by individuals:

- Securities-related crimes.
- Bankruptcy frauds.
- Fraud against the government.
- Consumer fraud.
- Computer crimes.
- Insurance fraud.
- Tax fraud.
- Bribery, corruption, and political fraud.
- Insider-related fraud.[14]

Let us briefly examine each type of crime.

Securities-related crimes   State and federal securities laws seek to regulate both the registration and issuance of a security and the employment of personnel in the securities industries. Following the precipitous plunge of the stock market on October 26, 1929, the federal government responded to public pressure by enacting a series of regulatory laws, including the Securities Act of 1933 and the Securities Exchange Act of 1934, aimed at prohibiting manipulation and deceptive practices. The 1934 act provided for the establishment of the Securities and Exchange Commission (SEC), an organization with broad regulatory and enforcement powers. The SEC is empowered to initiate civil suits and administrative actions and to refer criminal cases to the U.S. Department of Justice.

Even so, crime in the securities field remains commonplace. Four kinds of offenses are prevalent: churning, trading on insider information, stock manipulation, and boiler-room operations. **Churning,** a violation of federal securities laws, is the practice of trading a client's shares of stock frequently in order to generate large

CRIMINOLOGICAL FOCUS

A Penny Scam That Adds Up to Millions

How do penny stock promoters ply their trade? Take a look at Hughes Capital Corp. The Securities and Exchange Commission charged that Hughes, F. D. Roberts—the firm that brought it public—and twelve individuals associated with both companies had violated securities laws. It's a textbook case in penny stock scams. Here's how it worked, according to the SEC documents:

Corp. for $10,000 in December 1985 from the estate of Richard L. Chatham. Hughes Capital is a shell company without revenues or operations. They pay with checks drawn on others' accounts to hide their ownership. They also recruit John L. Knoblauch to serve as Hughes chairman and nominal owner. Working with Reifler and Beall is Frederic E. Mascolo, a lawyer and business associate.

share. Hughes Capital hires F. D. Roberts Securities Inc. to underwrite the offering. Consultant Dominick Fiorese meets with Roberts' brokers to drum up support for Hughes. He tells the brokers they will not get shares from the IPO but will be able to trade them in the aftermarket.

PLACE THE STOCK IN FRIENDLY HANDS

In mid-August, 1986, two F. D. Roberts directors, Frederick E. Galiardo and John Perfetti, open 33 brokerage accounts to which they distribute the 90,000 units of the Hughes IPO. Among the names on the accounts is Lionel Lachance, an alias used by Reifler. Other accounts are under the aliases

FIND A SHELL AND HIDE THE OWNERSHIP

Lionel M. Reifler and Gilbert E. Beall acquire Hughes Capital

PLAN AN INITIAL PUBLIC OFFERING

Hughes Capital files a registration statement with the SEC to sell 90,000 units at $2 each. Each unit consists of one share of stock plus 21 five-year warrants to purchase stock at prices from $2.50 to $4.50 per

commissions. A broker earns a commission on every trade, so whether the stock traded increases or decreases in value, the broker makes

money. Churning is difficult to prove, because some discretion is typically afforded brokers. Therefore, unless the client has given the broof Reifler's wife and daughter. Some belong to corporations controlled by Reifler and Beall. Checks are drawn to give the appearance that the owner of each account is paying for his units.

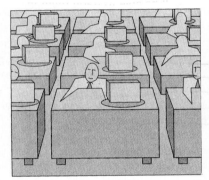

START TRADING THE SHARES

On Aug. 25 the Hughes units are split into stocks and warrants. F. D. Roberts then purchases all 90,000 shares of stock from the accounts at $2.25 each. Roberts' brokers begin to sell the shares at prices as high as $6.50 by the end of the first day, $8 by the end of the first week. The sales effort has been so successful that Roberts has actually sold 30,000 more shares than have

been issued. Roberts then covers the "short sales" by exercising the warrants.

HYPE!

Knoblauch hires a public relations firm to promote Hughes Capital's acquisitions: Conserdyne, Insuranshares of America, Susan Lachance Interior Design, and Flat Rock Developers. Press releases fail to disclose that Knoblauch has a controlling interest in Conserdyne. The Conserdyne release claims the company has "received letters of intent representing more than $200 million in potential business." The other three are controlled all or in part by Reifler, Beall, and Mascolo.

RAKE IN THE PROFITS

In early 1987 the stock runs up to $15. Insiders sell nearly 200,000 warrants for at least $1.15 million. The SEC suspends trading in Hughes Capital on Feb. 13, 1987. When it resumes, the stock collapses and is now worthless. In December 1988 the SEC brings charges. Galiardo, Perfetti, and two others sign consent orders and agree to leave the securities business. Knoblauch denies fraud charges. Others have not yet responded. Estimated loss to the public: $1.5 million.

Source: "A Penny Scam That Adds Up to Millions," *Business Week*, Jan. 23, 1989, p. 75.

ker specific instructions in writing, a claim of churning often amounts to no more than the client's word against the broker's.

Insider trading is the use of material, nonpublic, financial information to obtain an unfair advantage in trading securities. A person who has access to confidential corporate information may make significant profits by buying or selling stock on the strength of that information. Dennis Levine, a 34-year-old managing director of the securities firm Drexel Burnham Lambert, used insider information to guide the purchase of stock for himself and others in such corporations as International Telephone and Telegraph (ITT), Sperry Corporation, Coastal Corporation, American National Resources, and McGraw Edison. After the SEC found out, Levine implicated other Wall Street executives—including Ivan Boesky, who had made millions of dollars in profit.

Stock manipulation is common in the penny stock market—the over-the-counter market, in which some stocks are traded at very low prices—but it is by no means limited to such stocks. Brokers who have a stake in a particular security may make misleading or even false statements to clients in an effort to foster the impression that the price of the stock is about to rise and thus to create an artificial demand for it. (See Criminological Focus.)

Boiler rooms are operations run by stock manipulators who, through deception and misleading sales techniques, seduce the unsuspecting and uninformed public into buying stocks in obscure and often poorly financed corporations.

Bankruptcy frauds   The filing of a bankruptcy petition results in proceedings in which the property and financial obligations of an insolvent person or corporation are disposed of. Bankruptcy proceedings are governed by laws enacted to protect insolvent debtors. Unscrupulous persons have devised numerous means to commit **bankruptcy frauds**—scams designed to take advantage of loopholes in the bankruptcy laws. The most common are the "similar-name" scam, the "old-company" scam, the "new-company" technique, and the "successful-business" scam.

The similar-name scam involves the creation of a corporation that has a name similar to that of an established firm. The objective of this scam is to create the erroneous impression that this new company is actually the older one. If the ruse is successful, the swindlers place large orders with established suppliers and quickly resell any merchandise they receive, often to fences. At the same time the swindlers remove all money and assets of the corporation and either file for bankruptcy or wait until their creditors sue. Either way, they leave the jurisdiction or adeptly erase their tracks.

The old-company scam involves employees of an already established firm who, motivated by a desire for quick profits, bilk the company of its money and assets and file for bankruptcy. Such a scam is typically used when the company is losing money or has lost its hold on a market.

The new-company scam is much like the similar-name scam: a new corporation is formed, credit is obtained, and orders are placed. Once merchandise is received, it is converted into cash with the assistance of a fence. By the time the company is forced into bankruptcy, the architects of this scheme have liquidated the corporation's assets.

The successful-business scam involves a profitable corporation that is well positioned in a market but experiences a change in ownership. After the new owners have bilked the corporation of all its money and assets, the firm is forced into bankruptcy.

Fraud against the government   The government, as well as corporations, is the victim of a vast amount of fraud, which includes collusion in bidding, payoffs and kickbacks to government officials, expenditures by a government official that exceed the budget, the filing of false claims, the hiring of friends or associates formerly employed by the government, and offers of inducements to government officials. Consider, for example, the fall of the Wedtech Corporation. At one time the Wedtech Corporation was hailed as the first major hirer of unemployed blacks and Hispanics in the slums of New York City's South Bronx. Before its fall from grace, Wedtech was a high-flier on the New York Stock Exchange. What fueled the company? As a minority-controlled business, it won defense contracts without the need to bid. But in early 1986 Wedtech lost its status as a minority business, and by the end of that year the company was in ruins. Wedtech officials had used fraudulent accounting methods, issued false financial reports, and counted profits before they were received. Caught in the crossfire of charges was Congressman Mario Biaggi, who was later convicted of soliciting bribes in order to obtain special governmental support for Wedtech. Other company and government officials either pleaded guilty or were convicted.[15]

Is the Wedtech scandal an isolated case? Clearly not. In fiscal year 1987 alone, the Department of Defense reported fraud amounting to $53.8 million (see At Issue). And this may be a conservative estimate. In response to a tip from a former navy employee, the Federal Bureau of Investigation and the Naval Intelligence Service initiated a secret two-year investigation of bribery, fraud, illegal exchanges of information, and collusion at the Pentagon. This investigation has already resulted in the issuance of 200 grand jury subpoenas, as well as the execution of thirty-eight search warrants in twelve states and Washington, D.C.[16] It is hoped that this investigation will reveal an accurate estimate of government contract fraud.

An important step to curb government contract fraud was taken with the passage of the Major Fraud Act, signed by President Ronald Reagan in November 1988. This act creates a separate offense of government contract fraud in excess of $1 million. What kinds of activities does this act cover? Federal prosecutors can seek indictments against contractors who engage in deceptive pricing or overcharging by submitting inaccurate cost and pricing data; mischarging of billing the government for improper or nonallowable charges; collusion in bidding (a conspiracy between presumed competitors to inflate bids); product substitution or the delivery or inferior, nonconforming, or untested goods; or who use bribes, gratuities, conflicts of interest, and a whole gamut of techniques designed to influence procurement officials.

Clearly there is more to government-related fraud than the manipulation of contractors and consultants. The Inspector General's Office in the Department of Health and Human Services indicates that about $2 billion may be lost annually to fraud in the Medicare program alone.[17]

Welfare fraud may amount to as much as 9 percent of the total welfare budget. Fortunately, recent studies suggest that computer programs matching welfare benefits with other information (motor vehicle licenses, voter registrations, income tax returns) may significantly reduce such fraud.

Consumer fraud Consumer fraud is the act of causing a consumer to surrender money through deceit or a misrepresentation of a material fact. Consumer frauds often appear as confidence games and may take some of the following forms:

- *Home-improvement fraud.* Consumers have been defrauded through the promise of low-cost home renovation. The homeowners give sizable down payments to the contractors, who have no plans to complete the job. In fact, contractors often leave the jurisdiction or declare bankruptcy.
- *Deceptive advertising.* Consumers are often baited by misleading advertising—lured into a store by an announcement that a product is priced low for a limited period of time. Once in the store, the customer is told that the product is sold out and is offered a substitute, typically of inferior quality or at a much higher price. These schemes are known as "bait-and-switch advertising."
- *Land fraud.* Consumers are easy prey for land-fraud swindlers. Here the pitch is that a certain piece of vacation or retirement property is a worthy investment, that many improvements to the property will be made and many facilities will be made available in the area. Consumers often make purchases of worthless or overvalued land.
- *Business opportunity fraud.* The objective of business opportunity fraud is to persuade a consumer to invest money in a business concern through misrepresentation of its actual worth. Work-at-home frauds are common: victims are told they can make big money by addressing envelopes at home or performing some other simple task. Consumers lose large sums of money investing in these business ventures.

Computer crimes Computer crime has increased considerably since the mid-1960s, but

AT ISSUE

Government Procurement Fraud

Defense-contract procurement fraud...against the federal government undermines our national defense at the same time it subverts our national values; it simultaneously attacks our sense of justice and our hard-earned tax dollars. It is wrongdoing of an especially offensive kind, and it, too, may be widespread.

The inspector general of the Defense Department recently informed Congress that forty-five defense-contracting firms were under investigation. The allegations read like a catalog of possible offenses: mischarging costs, mischarging labor, taking kickbacks from subcontractors, substituting products, compromising security, defectively pricing, duplicating costs, making false claims, failing to account accurately for supplies, offering gratuities, rigging bids, and giving bribes. Apparently, not many opportunities for gouging Uncle Sam, and breaking the law, have been

overlooked. And some of these investigations have already resulted in convictions. General Electric, for example, guilty of price-fixing in 1961, recently pleaded guilty to defrauding the Pentagon on its Minuteman missile contract.

But more than any other, the company that makes my point is General Dynamics. Last year, General Dynamics had about $8 billion in sales of which all but $1 billion was from government contracts. General Dynamics has now been indicted for mischarging the government, between 1978 and 1981, to the tune of $7.5 million—all of this, by the way, in connection with the ill-fated Sergeant York Anti-Aircraft Gun, now canceled as unusable, for which the government paid $1.8 *billion* and received only sixty-five guns. In cancelling the Sergeant York program, Defense Secretary Caspar Weinberger said, "The system didn't work well enough."

He might just as easily have made the same comment about our system of legal accountability.

General Dynamics is contesting the recent indictments. According to the company, "the issue is a highly sophisticated regulatory and accounting matter which should be resolved in a civil forum, not a criminal case." Nothing we say here should be understood as prejudging the corporation or its officers. They are entitled to a fair trial to assess their responsibility. These recent indictments, however, are only the latest in a series of problems for the nation's third largest military contractor. Last May, after pointing to what he called a pervasive attitude at General Dynamics "that we find inappropriate to the public trust," Navy Secretary John Lehman suspended its major divisions in Groton, Connecticut, and Los Angeles.

its true extent remains unknown. Quite apart from the difficulty of defining computer criminality, and apart from the absence of clearly applicable legislation in many jurisdictions, computer criminality shares with other forms of economic crime the difficulty of detecting it. Most such crimes—some investigators claim as many as 99 percent—are not reported because publicity about a company's economic problems may undermine the public's trust and confidence in that institution. Claims filed with insurance companies for losses through computer fraud indicate that such claims are filed in less

than 20 percent of known cases.[18] In 1976 the General Accounting Office found sixty-nine cases of computer criminality known to federal law enforcement agencies; in 1984 the Federal Bureau of Investigation had fewer than fifty such cases pending.[19]

Research in a number of Western countries indicates that computer criminality has not yet become the menace it was predicted to become in the early 1970s. A survey of 2,000 institutional computer users in Australia indicated that fifty-three cases of computer crime had become known there by 1980. A similar survey

Three months later, the Navy said it was lifting that ban, but as part of the original censure, the Navy canceled two missile contracts worth $22.5 million and put them up for competitive bidding. It also fined the company nearly $700,000 for giving more than $67,000 in gratuities to Admiral Hyman Rickover, head of the Navy's nuclear submarine program until 1981. On December 4, front-page headlines announced that General Dynamics had been suspended from *any* future work with the Defense Department because of the fraud indictments. The next day, however, the Navy sheepishly declared that bidding on four Los Angeles class attack submarines would be indefinitely postponed so that General Dynamics could be kept in the competition. But then the day after that, Secretary Weinberger hinted that the company might be kept out of the bidding after all.

These flip-flops in policy have been portrayed as a way of protecting taxpayer interests. Obviously, the taxpayers would be better served if there were competitive bidding between General Dynamics and Newport News on the construction of these submarines. But the impression created by making these announcements and then immediately backpedaling has been extremely harmful. Most people already believe that most corporate offenses go unpunished and that government contracts have become a license to steal. Indecision and ambiguity among our highest officials should not encourage them to even greater cynicism. The trouble is, of course, that big defense contractors like General Dynamics can take advantage of their unique, if not indispensable, relationship to the government. General Dynamics is the primary contractor for nuclear submarines. Obviously, therefore, the Defense Department cannot simply "debar" the company from future contracts with the government. And even if debarment were realistic, it would be the thousands of laid-off, lower-level, wage-role workers who would be hurt the most, not those higher up who are in fact responsible for whatever offenses have occurred. Government contract rules are so complex, and corporate structure and accountability so convoluted, that in many cases holding top executives criminally liable for fraud is difficult, if not constitutionally impossible. So prosecutors settle for fining the corporation or, as we have seen, for the illusion of suspension from future contracting.

Source: Joseph R. Biden, "Foreword," *American Criminal Law Review* 23 (1986): 243, 248–249.

among 648 computer users in Canada revealed thirteen cases. In Finland, seventeen cases were known to the police. The government of Japan reported that thirty computer crimes had been committed by 1982. There were twenty-two cases in Sweden and twenty-two in Austria by 1983. Research conducted by the Max Planck Institute at Freiburg revealed thirty-eight prosecutions for computer crimes in the Federal Republic of Germany, and that country's Federal Criminal Police Office reported fifty-three such cases by the mid-1980s.[20]

The number of reported computer crimes may seem to be insignificant, but many of those that have been successful have netted huge profits. Even as early as 1974, it was estimated that the "average" loss in computer fraud cases amounted to $450,000.[21] The Equity Funding Corporation gained $1.8 million through computer manipulation; the employees involved netted another $144,000.[22] Some investigators have estimated the total annual losses through computer fraud to be as high as $5 billion.[23]

Let us look at the various types of computer crimes to see what they have in common and how they differ. The rebellious students who briefly held New York University's Argonne National Laboratory computer for $100,000 ransom in the turbulent 1960s obviously committed a computer crime, but investigators of computer crime generally ignore such acts focusing instead on activities that entail access to the computer's hardware and software. Most such acts have in common a loss to the rightful owner of data, and often the perpetrator gains financially. But this need not be the case. Some computer crimes may even pose a threat to the national security. Such was the case when the data base of the Los Alamos National Laboratory was entered.

Computer crimes show little uniformity as to either motive or harm. But computer crimes can be viewed in the context of existing crime categories, outside the computer sphere. We therefore propose the following five basic categories as a framework:

- **Computer fraud** involves the falsification of stored data or deception in legitimate transactions by manipulation of data or programming, including the unlawful acquisition of data or programs for purposes of financial gain of the perpetrator or of a third party.
- **Computer espionage** consists of activities by which unauthorized computer access yields information for purposes of exploitation from data bases belonging to government or private parties.
- **Computer sabotage** consists of the tampering with, destruction of, or scrambling of data or software by means of gaining surreptitious access to data banks.
- **Computer hacking** is the act of gaining unlawful access to data banks for malicious though not necessarily destructive purposes, and for neither financial gain nor purposes of espionage.
- **Theft of computer time, software, and hardware** includes not only the unauthorized use of computer time and software services but also the unauthorized copying of software programs, and the outright theft of computer equipment.

These categories, descriptive of the perpetrator's activities and motives, could well serve federal and state legislators in their efforts to develop legislation encompassing a comprehensive set of prohibitions to protect society against computer abuses. During the 1980s the federal government and forty-seven states passed computer crime legislation of various sorts and of various degrees of effectiveness.[24] So far, most known computer crimes seem to involve manipulations for purposes of fraud or industrial espionage. But the number of computer nuisance crimes, including sabotage and hacking, has been increasing, and thefts of computer time and software are predicted to rise rapidly.[25]

Insurance fraud   There are many varieties of insurance fraud: policyholders defraud insurers, insurers defraud the public, management defrauds the public, and third parties defraud insurers. Policyholder fraud is most often accomplished by the filing of false claims for life, fire, marine, or casualty insurance. Sometimes an employee of the insurance company is part of the fraud, assisting in the preparation of the claim. The fraud may be simple—a false death claim—or it may become complex when multiple policies are purchased.

A different type of insurance fraud is committed when a small group of people create a shell insurance firm without true assets for the purpose of defrauding policyholders. Policies are sold with no intent to pay legitimate claims. In fact, when large claims are presented to these shell insurance companies, they disband, leaving a trail of victims. In yet another form of insurance fraud, mid- and upper-level managers of an insurance company loot the firm's assets by removing funds and debiting them as payments of claims to legitimate or bogus policyholders.[26]

Criminologists Paul Tracy and James Fox conducted a field experiment to find out how many auto body repair shops in Massachusetts inflate repair estimates to insurance companies, and by how much. These researchers rented two Buick Skylarks with moderate damage, a Volvo 740 GLE with superficial damage, and a Ford Tempo with substantial damage. Then they obtained 191 repair estimates, some with a clear understanding that the car was insured, others with the understanding that there was no insurance coverage. The results were un-equivocal: repair estimates for insured vehicles were significantly higher than those for noncovered cars. This finding is highly sugges-tive of fraud.[27]

Tax fraud   The Internal Revenue Code makes willful failure to file a tax return a misde-meanor. An attempt to evade or defeat a tax, nonpayment of a tax, or willful filing of a fraud-ulent tax return is a felony. What must the gov-ernment prove? In order to sustain a convic-tion, the government must present evidence of income tax due and owing, willful avoidance of payment, and an affirmative act toward tax evasion.[28]

How are tax frauds accomplished? Consider the following techniques:

• *Keeping two sets of books.* A person may keep one set of books reflecting actual profits and losses and another set for the purpose of mis-leading the Internal Revenue Service.

"Hotel Queen" Leona Helmsley holds her lawyer's hand as they leave the courthouse after she was found guilty of tax evasion.

• *Shifting funds.* In order to avoid detection, tax evaders often shift funds continually from account to account, from bank to bank.
• *Faking forms.* Tax evaders often use faked in-voices, create fictitious expenses, conceal as-sets, and destroy books and records.

The IRS lacks the resources to investigate all suspicious tax forms. When the difficulty of dis-tinguishing between careless mistakes and will-ful evasion is taken into account, the taxes that go uncollected each year are estimated to ex-ceed $100 billion.[29]

Bribery, corruption, and political fraud   Judges who fix traffic tickets in exchange for political favors, municipal employees who speculate with city funds, businesspeople who bribe local politicians to obtain favorable treatment—all are part of the corruption in our municipal, state, and federal governments. The objectives of such offenses vary—favors, special privileges, services, business. The actors may include officers of cor-porations as well as of government; indeed, they may belong to the police or the courts.

Bribery and other forms of corruption are in-grained in the political machinery of local and state governments. Examples abound: mayors of large cities attempt to obtain favors through bribes, manufacturers pay off political figures for favors, municipal officials demand kick-backs from contractors.[30] In response to the se-riousness of political corruption and bribery, Congress only recently established two new crimes: it is now a felony to accept a bribe or to provide a bribe.[31] Of course, political bribery and other forms of corruption do not stop at the nation's borders. Kickbacks to foreign officials are common practice.[32]

Corruption can be found in private industry as well. One firm pays another to induce it to use a product or service; a firm pays its own board of directors or officers to dispense special favors; two or more firms, presumably compet-itors, secretly agree to charge the same prices for their products or services.

Insider-related fraud   Insider-related fraud in-volves the use and misuse of one's position for pecuniary gain or privilege. This category of offenses includes embezzlement, employee-related thefts, and sale of confidential information.

Embezzlement is the conversion of property or money with which one is entrusted or for which one has a fiduciary responsibility. Yearly losses attributable to embezzlement are estimated at over \$1 billion.[33] Employee-related thefts of company property are responsible for a significant share of industry losses. Estimates place such losses between \$4 billion and \$13 billion each year. Criminologists John Clark and Richard Hollinger have estimated that the 35 percent rate of employee pilferage in some corporations results primarily from vocational dissatisfaction and a perception of exploitation.[34] And not only goods and services are taken; time and money are at risk as well. Phony payrolls, fictitious overtime charges, false claims for business-related travel, and the like are common.

Finally, in a free marketplace where a premium is placed on competition, corporations must guard confidential information and trade secrets. The best insurance policy is employee loyalty. Where there is no loyalty, or where loyalty is compromised, abuse of confidential information is possible. The purchase of confidential information from employees willing to commit industrial espionage is estimated to be a multimillion-dollar business.[35]

CORPORATE CRIME

Crimes Committed by Corporations

During the Great Depression thousands of unemployed people heard that there was work to be had in the little West Virginia town of Hawk's Nest, where a huge tunnel was to be dug. Thousands of people came in rickety cars or pickup trucks piled high with their belongings to work for a pittance. The company set the men up in crude camps and put them to work right away drilling rock for the tunnel project—without masks or other safety equipment. The silicon dust that filled the air was breathed in and settled in the workers' lungs. Many contracted silicosis, a chronic disease that

leads to certain death. The men died by the dozens. Security guards dragged the bodies away and buried them secretly. No one was to know. The work went on. The deaths multiplied. Who was to blame? The corporation?[36]

A corporation is an artificial person created by state charter. The charter provides such an entity with the right to engage in certain activities—to buy and sell certain goods or to run a railroad. The charter limits the liability of the persons who own the corporation (the shareholders) to the extent of the value of their investment (their shares). The corporation thus is an entity separate from the people who either own or manage it. This convenient form of pooling resources for commercial purposes, with a view toward profiting from one's investment, has had a significant impact on the development of the United States as a commercial and industrial power. At the same time, millions of wage earners whose savings or union funds are invested in corporate stocks and bonds reap the benefit of such investments in the form of income or retirement benefits.

But what if a corporation engages in unlawful activity? Can a corporation commit crimes? If so, what can be done about it? What is the extent of corporate wrongdoing?[37] Initially corporations were deemed incapable of committing crimes. After all, crimes require *mens rea,* an awareness of wrongdoing. Since corporations are bodies without souls, they were deemed to be incapable of forming that requisite sense of wrongdoing. For that matter, a corporation could not be imprisoned for its crimes. Further, corporations were not *authorized* to commit crimes; they were authorized only to engage in the business for which they had been chartered.

A different theory of corporate criminal liability eventually emerged when courts and legislators began to ask why, if a corporation is chartered to run a railroad, it should not be held accountable for manslaughter if the negligent action of its operatives causes the death of a human being. After all, the actions of its employees are part of running a railroad. And so it was decided in 1917.[38] Thereafter, the theory that a corporation can be held accountable for criminal acts was widened, until the Model Penal Code broadly subjected corporations to liability for most criminal offenses, especially those that were "authorized, requested, commanded, performed or recklessly tolerated by the board of directors or by a high managerial agent acting in behalf of the corporation within the scope of his office or employment."[39]

Corporate misconduct is covered by a broad range of federal and state statutes, including the federal conspiracy laws; the **Racketeer Influenced and Corrupt Organizations Act (RICO)**; federal securities laws; mail-fraud statutes; the **Federal Corrupt Practices Act**; the **Federal Election Campaign Act**; legislation on lobbying, bribery, and corruption; the Internal Revenue Code (especially as regards major tax crimes, slush funds, and improper payments); the **Bank Secrecy Act**; and federal provisions on obstruction of justice, perjury, and false statements. The underlying theory is that if the brain of the artificial person (usually the board of directors of the corporation) authorizes or condones the act in question, the body (the corporation, meaning its shareholders) must suffer criminal penalty. That seems fair enough, except for the fact that if the corporation gets punished—usually by a substantial fine—the penalty falls on the shareholders, few of whom had any vote in the corporate decision. And the financial loss resulting from the fine may be passed on to the consumer.

Early Governmental Control of Corporations

Beginning in the nineteenth century, corporations were suspected of wielding monopolistic power to the detriment of consumers. The theory behind monopoly is simple: if you buy out all your competitors or drive them out of business, then you are the only one from whom people can buy the product you sell. So you can set the price, and you set it very high, for your profit and to the detriment of the consumers. The Sugar Trust was one such monopoly. A few powerful businessmen eliminated all competitors and then drove the price of sugar up, to the detriment of the public. Theodore Roosevelt fought and broke up the Sugar Trust. As mentioned earlier, in 1890 Congress passed the Sherman Antitrust Act, which effectively limited the exercise of monopolies.[40] This legislation was followed by the Clayton Antitrust Act, which further curbed the ability of corporations to enrich their shareholders at the expense of the public by prohibiting such acts as price-fixing.[41] But the remedies that this act provided consisted largely of either splitting up monopolistic enterprises or imposing damages, sometimes even triple damages, for the harm caused. In a strict sense, this was not a use of the criminal law to govern corporate misconduct.

Recent Governmental Control of Corporations

A movement away from exclusive reliance on civil litigation was apparent in the 1960s, when it was discovered that either corporate mismanagement or negligence on the part of officers or employees could inflict vast harm on identifiable groups of victims. Negligent management at a nuclear power plant can result in the release of radiation and injury to thousands or millions of people. The marketing of an unsafe drug can cause crippling deformities in tens of thousands of bodies.[42] Violation of environmental standards can cause injury and suffering to generations of people who will be exposed to unsafe drinking water, harmful air, or eroded soil. The manufacture of hazardous products can result in multiple deaths.[43]

The problem of corporate criminal liability since the 1960s, then, goes far beyond an individual death or injury. Ultimately it concerns the health and even the survival of humankind. Nor is the problem confined to the United States. It is a global problem. It thus becomes necessary to look at the variety of criminal activities attributable to corporations which in recent years have been recognized as particularly harmful to society.

When it comes to proving corporate criminal liability, prosecutors face formidable problems: Day-to-day corporate activity has a low level of visibility. Regulatory agencies that monitor corporate conduct have various recording systems. Offending corporations operate in a multitude of jurisdictions, some of which regard a given activity as criminal, others not. Frequently the facts of a case are not adjudicated at a trial. Instead, the parties may simply agree on a settlement approved by the court. The accused corporation may be permitted to plead *nolo contendere* (no contest) in return for an agreed-upon fine or settlement.

In sum, we know very little about the extent of this form of economic criminality in the United States. There is no national statistical base for the assessment of corporate criminality, and corporations are not likely to release information about their wrongdoing voluntarily. The situation is worse in other countries, and worst in the forty-some developing countries of Africa south of the Sahara, where few national crime statistics are kept and where corporations are least subject to governmental control. Yet the evidence in regard to corporate crime is gradually coming in.[44]

Investigating Corporate Crime

The first American criminologist who was alert to the potential for harm in corporate conduct was Edwin Sutherland. He detailed the criminal behavior of 70 of the 200 largest production corporations in his *White Collar Crime*.[45] An even more ambitious study was completed by Marshall B. Clinard and Peter C. Yeager, who investigated corporations within the jurisdiction of twenty-five federal agencies during 1975 and 1976. Sixty percent of 477 major American corporations whose conduct was regulated by these agencies had violated the law. Of the 300 violating corporations, 38 (or 13 percent) accounted for 52 percent of all violations charged in 1975 to 1976, an average of 23.5 violations per firm.[46] Large corporations were found to be the chief violators, and a few particular industries (pharmaceutical, automotive) were the most likely to violate the law. According to Clinard and Yeager, what makes it so difficult to curb corporate crime is the enormous political power that corporations can exert in the shaping and administration of the laws that govern their conduct. This is particularly the case in regard to multinational corporations that wish to operate in developing countries. The promise of jobs and development held forth by a giant cor-

poration is a temptation too great for the governments of many such countries to resist. They would rather have employment opportunities with harmful air and polluted water than unemployment in a clean environment. Above all, government officials in some Third World countries can be bribed to create or maintain a legal climate favorable to the business interests of the corporation, even though it may be detrimental to the people of the host country.

The work of Sutherland, Clinard and Yeager, and other traditional scholars, as well as that of a group of radical criminologists;[47] hearings on white-collar and corporate crime held by the Subcommittee on Crime of the House Judiciary Committee, under the leadership of Congressman John Conyers, Jr., in 1978; the consumer protection movement, spearheaded by Ralph Nader; and recent investigative reporting by the press have all contributed to public awareness of large corporations' power to inflict harm on large population groups. In 1975 James Q. Wilson still considered such crime to be insignificant,[48] but more recent studies show that the public considers this sort of criminality more serious than street crime. For example, Marvin Wolfgang and his associates found in a national survey that Americans regard illegal retail price-fixing (the artificial setting of prices at a high level, without regard for the demand for the product) as a more serious crime than robbery committed with a lead pipe.[49]

Within the sphere of corporate criminality perhaps no other group of offenses has had so great an impact on public consciousness as crimes against the environment. As we shall see, however, enforcement of major environmental statutes has been inadequate.

Environmental Crimes

The world's legal systems include few effective laws and mechanisms to curb destruction of the environment. The emission of noxious fumes into the air and of pollutants into the water have until recently been regarded as common law nuisances at the level of misdemeanors, commanding usually no more than a small fine. Industrial polluters could easily absorb such a fine and regard it merely as a kind of business tax. Only in 1969 did Congress pass the National Environmental Policy Act (NEPA). Among other things, the act created the Environmental Protection Agency (EPA). It requires environmental impact studies to prevent any new development that significantly affects the environment. The EPA is charged with enforcing federal statutes and assisting in the enforcement of state laws enacted to protect the environment. The agency monitors plant discharges all over the country and may take action against private industry or municipal governments. Yet during the first five years of its existence the EPA had referred only 130 cases to the U.S. Department of Justice for criminal prosecution. Only six of the cases involved major corporate offenders. The government actually charged only one of these corporations, Allied Chemical, which admitted responsibility for 940 misdemeanor counts of discharging toxic chemicals into the Charles River in Virginia, thereby causing 80 people to become ill.[50]

A 1979 report of the General Accounting Office stated that the EPA inadequately monitored, inaccurately reported, and ineffectively enforced the nation's basic law on air pollution, although the agency's then chief contended that corrective action had been taken during the past year.[51] The situation improved during the 1980s, but the environment is far from safe. Catastrophic releases of toxic and even nuclear substances, usually attributable to inadequate safeguards and human negligence, pose a particularly grave hazard, as the disasters at Bhopal in India and at Chernobyl in the Soviet Union have demonstrated.

The difficulties of enforcing legislation designed to protect the environment are seen in the 250,000 barrels of oil spilled when the tanker *Exxon Valdez* went aground in Prince William Sound, Alaska, in 1989. Developing effective laws to protect the environment is a complex problem. It is far easier to define the crimes of murder and theft than to define acts of pollution, which are infinitely varied. A particular challenge is to separate harmful activities from socially useful ones. Moreover, pollution is hard to quantify. For instance, how much of a chemical must be discharged into water before the discharge is considered noxious and sub-

"So that's where it goes! Well, I'd like to thank you fellows for bringing it to my attention."

jects the polluter to punishment? Discharge of a gallon by one polluter may not warrant punishment, and a small quantity may not even be detectable, but what do we do with one hundred polluters, each of whom discharges a gallon? Many other issues must be addressed as well. For instance, should accidental pollution warrant the same punishment as intentional or negligent pollution? Since many polluters are corporations, what are the implications of penalties that force the plant to install costly anti-pollution devices? To cover the costs, the corporation may have to increase the price of its product, sometimes to the point where it becomes prohibitive. Should the plant be allowed to lower the wages of its workers instead? Should the plant be forced or permitted to shut down, thereby increasing unemployment in the community? The plant may choose to move to another country that is more hospitable.

These issues are increasingly being addressed. Fines imposed on intentional polluters

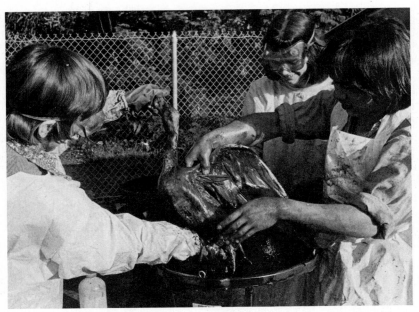

An oil-covered duck, one of the many victims of an oil spill, is being cleaned by volunteers at a bird rescue center.

have been increased so that they can no longer be shrugged off as an ordinary cost of doing business. The General Electric Company was fined $7 million and the Allied Chemical Corporation $13.2 million for their pollutions. Fines of such magnitude are powerful incentives to corporations to limit their pollutions. But since many of the enterprises that are likely to pollute are in the public sector, or produce for the public sector, the public ultimately will have to pay the fine in the form of increased gas or electricity bills.[52]

The problems of punishing and preventing pollution are enormous in the Third World. Industries preparing to locate there have the power to influence governments and officials, surreptitiously and officially, into passing pollution legislation favorable to the industry. The desire to industrialize outweighs the desire to preserve the environment. Some countries find ways to address the problem, only to relinquish controls when they prove irksome. While Japan was trying to establish its industrial dominance, for example, it observed a constitutional provision stating, "The conservation of life environment shall be balanced against the needs of eco-

nomic development."[53] This provision was deleted in 1970, when Japan had achieved economic strength.

U.S. legislators have several options in developing legislation to protect the environment:

• The independent use of the criminal sanction: direct prohibition of polluting activities. This is the way American legislators have typically tried to cope with the problem in the past. They simply made it a criminal offense to maintain a "nuisance"; that is, an ongoing activity that pollutes the water, the soil, or the air.

• The dependent-direct use of the criminal sanction: prohibition of certain polluting activities that exceed specified limits. This is a more sophisticated legislative method. If pollution is to be kept at a low level, no one person or company can be allowed to emit more than an insignificant amount of noxious waste into the environment. This amount is fixed by administrative regulation. Anyone who exceeds the limit commits a criminal offense.

• The dependent-indirect approach: the criminal sanction is reserved for firms that fail to comply with specific rulings rendered by ad-

THE INTERNATIONAL DRUG CYCLE

High in the Andes, in Bolivia and Peru, peasants cultivate coca plants. The coca is transported to clandestine refineries in Colombia where, increasingly, police and the military have been conducting raids, destroying the raw materials, the product (cocaine) and the refineries themselves. Drug lords are pitted against the governments of the affected countries in a cocaine war that has claimed many victims, including presidential candidates, cabinet officers, judges of all courts, and hundreds of law enforcement officers and civilians.

The cocaine is shipped from Colombian ports to consumer countries in North America and Europe. Police dogs assist customs officers and other law enforcement agents in detecting drug cargoes. Though many drug loads are intercepted, far more are coming in undetected. The U.S. Coast Guard plays a significant role in patrolling the sea-lanes leading to American shores, in an effort to intercept drugs en route. The success rate has been modest, as attested to by the vast amounts of narcotic drugs available on American streets, feeding the habit of hundreds of thousands of addicts who snort coke, shoot heroin, and consume hundreds of other illicit drugs in a variety of ways. Drug busts have become a daily occurrence in cities across America, netting mostly street vendors.

Most of the enormous profits of the illicit trade in narcotics (only a small proportion of which are seized in police action) are taken abroad and deposited in secret accounts in countries that permit such practices. The resultant "clean" ("laundered") money is transferred into open accounts throughout the Western world. Much of this laundered money buys property and shares of the economy in America and Europe. Some of it flows back to the producer countries, financing extravagant life-styles for the drug lords and underwriting the drug war against legitimate governments. Thus the cycle is completed.

In Colombia, a soldier stands guard over a drug bonfire.   *Farmers weed around coca plants in Bolivia.*

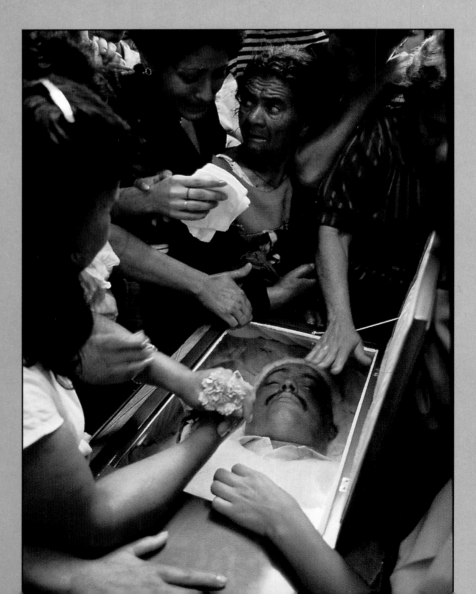

In Colombia, mourners surround the casket of assassinated Jairo Signero Gomez.

Drug agent with drug-sniffing dog at the Houston Ship
Channel.

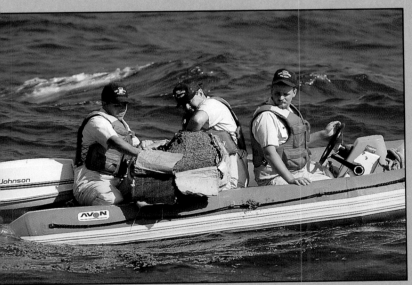

U.S. Coast Guard emptying bales of marijuana they
found at sea.

Crack, and other drugs, have become common on the
streets.

Snorting cocaine is not uncommon in offices as well as in homes.

Suspects being lined up after a bust.

Money on display after a drug bust in Miami.

ministrative organs against violators of standards. Under this option, polluters have already been identified by regulatory agencies, and are now under order to comply with the agencies' requirements. If they violate these orders, a criminal punishment can be imposed.

• The preventive use of the criminal sanction: penalties are imposed for failure to install or maintain prescribed antipollution equipment. This is the newest and most sophisticated means of regulating polluting industries. The law determines what preventive and protective measures must be taken (to filter industrial waste water, to put chemical screens on smokestacks, etc.). Any firm that fails to take the prescribed measures is guilty of a violation.[54]

In the past, legal systems have relied primarily on the independent use of the criminal sanction. More recent legislation has concentrated on heavy administrative orders and technological prevention.

Curbing Corporate Crime

Laws and regulations prescribing criminal sanctions have been passed and continue to be passed to guard the public against the dangers that are rooted in the power of corporate enterprise.[55] Often, however, these laws simply increase the complexity of the situation, as in the case of environmental crimes. That is not to say that society should not continue to try to prevent powerful entities, public and private, from doing harm to the public, though the effectiveness of such legislation may be limited. We cannot dispense with minimum wage laws designed to protect the public from exploitation by unscrupulous entrepreneurs, or with health and sanitation statutes designed to safeguard the water we drink and the air we breathe.[56] Such laws do help to curb the ability of corporations to inflict harm on the general public.

Many governments recognize that criminal justice systems are not yet prepared to deal with these economic crimes. They also recognize the importance of attacking this problem at the international level, perhaps by designing strategies, standards, and guidelines that may be helpful to all governments.[57] But a disturbing thought remains: Is the imposition of criminal liability for the conduct of corporations on the corporations themselves really the proper means to curb corporate misconduct? If corporations act on the decisions of their principal officers, might it not be appropriate to subject these corporate officers to criminal liability for their criminal decisions, rather than to subject innocent and uninformed shareholders to financial loss? The idea of penalizing corporate officials, together with their corporations, has, indeed, been gaining in popularity since business crimes began to proliferate in the 1980s.

ORGANIZED CRIME

Earlier we noted that all forms of organizational criminality have in common the use of business enterprises for illegal profit. So they do; yet we have recognized some significant problems not only with existing definitions and conceptualizations of white-collar and corporate crime but with the criminal justice response to such offenses. Analogous problems arise in efforts to deal with organized crime. These crimes, too, depend on business enterprises. And like corporate crime, organized crime comes in so many varieties that attempts to define it precisely lead to frustration. The difficulty of gaining access to information on organized crime also has hindered attempts to conceptualize the problems posed by this kind of law violation. Finally, law enforcement efforts have been inadequate to control the influence of organized crime. As will be evident, a greater effort must be made to uncover the nature, pattern, and extent of organized crime.

The History of Organized Crime

Organized crime had its origin in the great wave of immigrants from southern Italy (especially from Sicily) to the United States between 1875 and 1920. The immigrants came from an environment that historically had been hostile to them. Suppressed by successive waves of invaders and alien rulers (Roman, Byzantine, Arab, Norman, Spanish) and exploited by mostly absentee landlords with their armies, Sicilians had learned to survive by relying on the strength of their own families. Indeed, these families had undergone little change since the Greco-Roman period, two millennia before. A traditional Sicilian family has been described as an extended family, or clan; it includes lineal relations (grandparents, parents, children, grandchildren) and lateral relations through the paternal line—uncles, aunts, and cousins as far as the bloodline can be traced. This *famiglia* is hierarchically organized and administered by the head of the family, the *capo di famiglia* (the Romans called him *pater familias*), to whom obedience and loyalty are owed. Strangers, especially those in positions of power in state or church, are not to be trusted. All problems are resolved within the family, which must be kept strong. Its prestige, honor, wealth, and power have to be defended and strengthened, sometimes through alliances with more distant kin.[58]

Throughout history these strong families have served each other and Sicily as a whole. Upon migration to America, members of Sicilian families soon found that the social environment in their new country was as hostile as that of the old. Aspirations were encouraged, yet legitimate means to realize them were not available to most immigrants. And the new country seemed already to have an established pattern for achieving wealth and power by unethical means. Many of America's great fortunes—those of the Astors, the Vanderbilts, the Goulds, the Sages, the Stanfords, the Rockefellers, the Carnegies, the Lords, the Harrimans, and many others—had been made by cunning, greed, and exploitation. These methods violated some existing criminal laws. As time passed, new laws were enacted to address conspiracies in restraint of trade and other economic offenses. Yet by the time the last wave of Sicilian immigrants reached America, the names of these great **robber barons** were connected with great universities, foundations, and charitable institutions.[59]

At the local level, the Sicilian immigrants found themselves involved in a system of politics in which patronage and protection were dispensed by corrupt politicians and petty hoodlums from earlier immigrant groups—German, Irish, and Jewish. The Sicilian family structure helped its members to survive in this hostile environment. It also created the organizational basis that permitted them to respond to the opportunity created when, on January 16, 1920, the Eighteenth Amendment to the Constitution outlawed the manufacture, sale, and transportation of alcoholic beverages. Howard Abadinsky explains what happened:

> Prohibition acted as a catalyst for the mobilization of criminal elements in an unprecedented manner. Pre-prohibition crime, insofar as it was organized, centered around corrupt political machines, vice entrepreneurs, and, at the bottom, gangs. Prohibition unleashed an unparalleled level of competitive criminal violence and changed the order—the gang leaders emerged on top.[60]

During the early years of Prohibition, the names of the most notorious bootleggers, mobsters, and gangsters sounded Germanic, Irish, and Jewish: Arthur Fiegenheimer (better known as Dutch Schultz), Otto Gass, Bo and George Weinberg, Arnold Rothstein, John T. Nolen (Legs Diamond), Vincent "Mad Dog" Coll, Joe Rock. By the time Prohibition was repealed, Al Capone, Lucky Luciano, Frank Costello, Johnny Torrio, and many other Sicilians were preeminent in the underworld. They had become folk heroes and role models for the kids in the Italian ghettos, many of whom were to seek their own places in this new society. Sicilian families were every bit as ruthless in establishing their crime empires as the earlier immigrant groups had been. They were so successful in their domination of organized crime that, especially after World War II, organized crime became virtually synonymous with the Sicilian **Mafia**.

The term "Mafia" appears to derive from an Arabic word denoting "place of refuge." The concept, which was adopted in Sicily during the era of Arab rule, gradually came to describe a mode of life and survival. The Mafia provided "protection against the arrogance of the powerful, remedy to any damage, sturdiness of body, strength and security of spirit, and the best and most exquisite part of life."[61] Ultimately, "Mafia" represented the entirety of those Sicilian families that were loosely associated with one another in operating organized crime, both in America and in Sicily.[62] Ever since the testimony of the *mafioso* Joseph Valachi before the Senate's McClellan Committee in 1963, the Mafia has also been referred to as "La Cosa Nostra," "our thing."[63]

Despite Valachi's testimony and later revelations, some scholars still doubt the existence of a Sicilian-based American crime syndicate. To the criminologist Jay Albanese, for instance,

> it is clear...that despite popular opinion which has for many years insisted on the existence of a secret criminal society called "the Mafia," which somehow evolved from Italy, many separate historical investigations have found no evidence to support such a belief.[64]

Research on the issue continues.

The Structure and Impact of Organized Crime

Americans have felt the impact of organized crime, and they have followed the media coverage of the mob wars and their victims with fascination. But little was known about the Mafia's actual structure in the United States until a succession of government investigations began to unravel its mysteries. The major investigations were conducted by the Committee on Mercenary Crimes, in 1932; the Special Senate Committee to Investigate Organized Crime in Interstate Commerce (the Kefauver Crime Committee), from 1950 to 1951; the Senate Permanent Subcommittee on Investigations (the McClellan Committee), from 1956 to 1963; President Lyndon Johnson's Commission on Law Enforcement and Administration of Justice (the Task Force on Organized Crime), from 1964 to 1967; and the President's Commission on Organized Crime, which reported to President Reagan in 1986 and 1987.[65] The findings of these investigations established the magnitude of organized crime in the United States. It had become an empire almost beyond the reach of government, with vast resources derived from a virtual monopoly on gambling and loansharking, drug trafficking, pornography and prostitution, labor racketeering, murder for hire, the control of local crime activities, and the theft and fencing of securities, cars, jewels, and consumer goods of all sorts.[66] Above all, it was found that organized crime had infiltrated a

vast variety of legitimate types of business, such as stevedoring (the loading and unloading of ships), the fish and meat industries, the wholesale and retail liquor industry (including bars and taverns), the vending machine business, the securities and investment business, the waste disposal business, and the construction industry.[67]

Specific legislation and law enforcement programs have allowed governmental agencies to assert some measure of control over organized crime. Cases have been successfully prosecuted under the Racketeer Influenced and Corrupt Organizations Act (RICO) of 1970. This statute attacks racketeering activities by prohibiting the investment of any funds derived from racketeering in any enterprise that is engaged in interstate commerce. In addition, the **Federal Witness Protection Program,** established under the Organized Crime Control Act of 1970, has made it easier for witnesses to testify in court by guaranteeing them a new identity, thus protecting them against revenge. Fourteen thousand witnesses are currently in the program.[68]

The information provided by the governmental commissions, in combination with scholarly research, has established that the structure of an organized crime group is similar to that of a Sicilian family. Family members are joined by "adopted" members; the family is then aided at the functional level by nonmember auxiliaries.[69] The use of military designations such as *caporegima* (lieutenant) and "soldier" does not alter the fact that a criminal organization is rather more like a closely knit family business enterprise than like an army.[70] On the basis of testimony presented by Joseph Valachi to the President's Commission on Law Enforcement and Criminal Justice in 1963, the commission's Task Force on Organized Crime was able to construct an organization chart of the typical Mafia, or Cosa Nostra, family (Figure 12.1).

Relations among the various families which were formerly determined in ruthlessly fought gang wars have more recently been facilitated by a loosely formed coordinating body called "the Commission." By agreement, the country has been divided into territorial areas of jurisdiction, influence, and operation. These arrangements are subject to revision from time to

FIGURE 12.1   Organization chart of the typical Mafia family

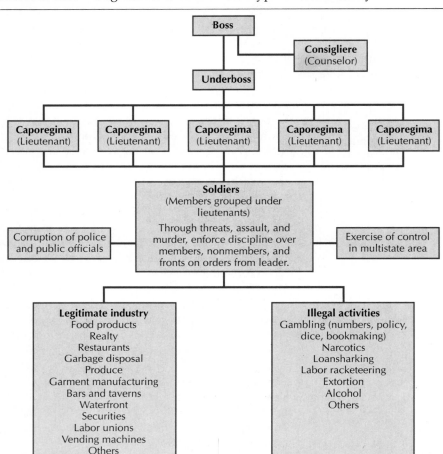

Source: *President's Commission on Law Enforcement and Administration of Justice*, Task Force on Organized Crime (Washington, D.C.: U.S. Government Printing Office, 1967), p. 9.

time, by mutual agreement. Likewise, rules of conduct have become subject to control or regulation by the heads of the various crime families. They consider, for example, to what extent each family should enter the hard drug market, how much violence should be used, and how each will deal with public officials and the police.[71] Informants at the "convention" of the so-called Apalachin conspirators provided a rare opportunity to learn about the way crime families reach agreement on their operations. On November 14, 1957, sixty-three of the country's most notorious underworld figures were arrested in Apalachin, New York, at or near the home of Joseph M. Barbara, a well-known organized crime figure. Apparently they had congregated at Barbara's home to settle a dispute among the families, which had earlier resulted in the assassination of mobster Albert Anastasio and the attempted murder of Frank Costello. None of the conspirators, however, publicly revealed the true nature of their meeting. Some suggested that, quite by coincidence, all had simply come to visit their sick friend Joe Barbara. All were indicted and convicted for refusing to answer the grand jury's questions about the true purpose of the meeting. The convictions were subsequently reversed.[72]

The activities of the Mafia appear to have shifted from the once extremely violent bootlegging and street crime operations to a far more sophisticated level of criminal activity.[73] Modern organized crime has assumed international dimensions.[74] It extends not only to international drug traffic but also to such legitimate enterprises as real estate and trade in securities, and indeed to many other lucrative business enterprises. This transition has been accomplished both by extortion and by entry with laundered money derived from illegitimate activity. It is tempting to wonder whether we may be witnessing the same kind of metamorphosis that occurred a century ago, when the robber barons became legitimate business tycoons and, ultimately, philanthropists.

The New Diversity of Ethnic Backgrounds in Organized Crime Activities

Organized crime is not necessarily synonymous with the Mafia. Other organized crime groups also operate in the United States. Foremost among them are the Colombian, Bolivian, Peruvian, and Jamaican crime families, which since the 1970s have organized the production, transportation, and distribution within the United States of cocaine and marijuana.

Another form of organized crime, initiated by disillusioned veterans of the Korean War and reinforced by veterans of Vietnam, is seen in the outlaw motorcycle gangs. Among them are the Hell's Angels, the Pagans, the Outlaws, and the Bandidos. All of them are organized along hierarchical military lines; all are devoted to violence; all are involved in the production and distribution of narcotics and other drugs. Many members are also involved in other criminal activities, including extortion and prostitution, trafficking in stolen motorcycles and parts, and dealing in automatic weapons and explosives.

Among other organized groups engaged in various criminal activities are Chinese gangs (see Window to the World), the so-called Israeli Mafia, the recently emerging Russian-Jewish Mafia, and the Japanese Yakuza. All of these groups have demonstrated the potential for great social disruption.[75]

REVIEW

Organizational crimes are characterized by the use of a legitimate or illegitimate business enterprise for illegal profit. As corporations grew in the nineteenth and twentieth centuries, they amassed much of the nation's wealth. Many corporations abused their economic power. Government stepped in to curb such abuses of power by legislation.

Edwin Sutherland, who provided the first scholarly insight into the wrongdoing of corporations, originated the concept of white-collar crime. Subsequent scholars have distinguished white-collar crime, committed by individuals, from corporate crime, committed by business organizations. Corporate or individual white-collar offenses include securities-related crimes, such as misrepresentation and churning; bankruptcy frauds and scams of various kinds; fraud against the government, in particular contract and procurement fraud; consumer fraud, computer fraud, insurance fraud, tax fraud, bribery and political fraud, and insider-related fraud. In the twentieth century, corporations have been subjected to criminal liability for an increasing number of offenses, including common law crimes and environmental as well as other statutory offenses.

Organized crime got its start in this country when Sicilian immigrants replicated their traditional family structure in organizing criminal activities. These families and their associates were so successful in controlling bootlegging, gambling, prostitution, loansharking, labor racketeering, drug trafficking, and other illegal enterprises that they were able to assume control of many legitimate businesses. In recent years members of other ethnic groups—Latin Americans, Jamaicans, Israelis, Russian Jews, Japanese, Chinese—have challenged the Sicilian Mafia for supremacy in organized crime.

WINDOW TO THE WORLD

Chinese Triads Develop International Ties

A huge international heroin ring broken up by federal agents recently is part of a network of Chinese criminal societies that increasingly are worrying state and federal law enforcement agents, authorities say.

The societies—known as triads, are close-knit criminal organizations that originally were formed to resist the Ching Dynasty in China. They flourished in Hong Kong and the Republic of China on Taiwan in the 1950s and 1960s and since have become active in the United States.

A report from the President's Commission on Organized Crime...issued in 1986 documented the growing menace of the triads: "Now members of triads (in the U.S.) are...active in drug trafficking, illegal gambling and loan-sharking.

"They operate through youth gangs, under the direction of established Chinese businessmen and community leaders. They cooperate with La Cosa Nostra (Mafia)

families and maintain close ties to criminal associates in Hong Kong, Taiwan, Thailand and The People's Republic of China."

State organized crime experts say four major Hong Kong–based triads are active in California: the Wo Group, the San Yee On Triad, the Luen Group and the 14K Triad. They are joined by two major criminal syndicates based in Taiwan—United Bamboo and the Four Seas Triad.

All are suspected of involvement in narcotics dealing, money laundering, extortion and a host of other criminal activities.

"We have been noticing a marked increase in the amount of heroin traffic in California, and we suspect that the heroin is being trafficked by Hong Kong triads," said one state law-enforcement expert on gangs who asked not to be quoted by name.

"The big problem has been finding the evidence that we could take into court against them," the source said.

This recent big heroin bust involved suspects whom authorities believe are associated with the 14K Triad, which has become increasingly active in California in recent years, experts said.

According to the most recent report from the Attorney General's Bureau of Organized Crime and Criminal Intelligence, in 1987, two California members of the 14K Triad were indicted in an alleged attempt to bilk New Jersey casinos out of $2.7 million. Federal agents in Orange County arrested six suspected members of the 14K Triad with 18 pounds of high-grade heroin in 1986.

Because China will take over Hong Kong in 1997, law enforcement authorities have predicted an exodus of gang members into the United States from the British colony in the near future.

Source: *C. J. International* 5 (July–August 1989): 17.

KEY TERMS

Bank Secrecy Act
bankruptcy frauds
boiler rooms
churning
computer espionage
computer fraud
computer hacking
computer sabotage

consumer fraud
embezzlement
Federal Corrupt Practices Act
Federal Election Campaign Act
Federal Witness Protection Program
insider trading
Mafia
occupational crimes

Racketeer Influenced and Corrupt
  Organizations Act (RICO)
robber barons
Sherman Antitrust Act

stock manipulation
theft of computer time, software, and
  hardware
white-collar crime

NOTES

1. United States Department of Justice Press Release, "United States v. E. F. Hutton and Co., Inc.," ed. Leonard Orland and Harold R. Tyler, Jr., in New Developments and Perspectives on Corporate Crime Law Enforcement in America (New York: Practicing Law Institute, 1987), pp. 731–732.

2. Marshall B. Clinard and Peter C. Yeager, Corporate Crime (New York: Free Press, 1980), pp. 59–60.

3. Gordon Hawkins, "God and the Mafia," Public Interest 14 (1969): 32–46.

4. Dwight Smith, "White-Collar Crime, Organized Crime, and the Business Establishment: Resolving a Crisis in Criminological Theory," in White Collar and Economic Crime, ed. Peter Whickman and Timothy Dailey (Lexington, Mass.: Lexington Books, 1982).

5. P. Renfrew, "Introduction to Symposium on White Collar Crime," Memphis State University Law Review 10 (1980): 416.

6. Edwin H. Sutherland, "White Collar Criminality," American Sociological Review 5 (1940): 1–20.

7. Gilbert Geis, On White Collar Crime (Lexington, Mass.: Lexington Books, 1982), p. 9.

8. Marshall B. Clinard and Richard Quinney, Criminal Behavior Systems, 2d ed. (New York: Holt, Rinehart & Winston, 1982).

9. August Bequai, White Collar Crime: A 20th-Century Crisis (Lexington, Mass.: Lexington Books, 1978), p. 3.

10. See also James W. Coleman, The Criminal Elite: The Sociological White-Collar Crime, 2d ed. (New York: St. Martin's Press, 1989).

11. Gilbert Geis, Henry N. Pontell, and Paul Jesilow, "Medicaid Fraud," in Controversial Issues in Criminology and Criminal Justice, ed. Joseph E. Scott and Travis Hirschi (Beverly Hills, Calif.: Sage, 1987).

12. For an outline of a general theory of crime causation applicable to both street crime and white-collar crime, see Travis Hirschi and Michael Gottfredson, "Causes of White-Collar Crime," Criminology 25 (1987): 949–974; James W. Coleman, "Toward an Integrated Theory of White Collar Crime," American Journal of Sociology 93 (1987): 406–439; James R. Lasley, "Toward a Control Theory of White Collar Offending," Journal of Quantitative Criminology 4 (1988): 347–362.

13. Donald R. Cressey, "The Poverty of Theory in Corporate Crime Research," ed. William Laufer and Freda Adler, Advances in Criminological Theory vol. 1 (New Brunswick: Transaction, 1988); for a response see John Braithwaite and Brent Fisse, "On the Plausibility of Corporate Crime Theory," ed. William Laufer and Freda Adler, Advances in Criminological Theory, vol. 2 (New Brunswick: Transaction, 1990). See also Travis Hirschi and Michael Gottfredson, "The Significance of White-Collar Crime for a General Theory of Crime," Criminology 27 (1989): 359–371; Darrell Steffensmeir, "On the Causes of 'White Collar' Crime: An Assessment of Hirschi and Gottfredson's Claims," Criminology 27 (1989): 345–358.

14. Bequai, White Collar Crime. Bequai also includes antitrust and environmental offenses, which are corporate crimes, discussed in the next section.

15. William Power, "New York Rep. Biaggi and Six Others Indicted as WedTech Scandal Greatly Expands," Wall Street Journal, June 4, 1987, p. 9

16. "Annual Survey of White Collar Crime," American Criminal Law Review 25 (1988): 560.

17. Bequai, White Collar Crime, pp. 70–71.

18. Peter Poerting and Ernst G. Pott, Computer Kriminalität (Wiesbaden: Bundeskriminalamt, 1986), p. 44.

19. General Accounting Office, Computer-Related Crime in Federal Programs (Washington, D.C.: U.S. Government Printing Office, 1976).

20. Poerting and Pott, *Computer Kriminalität*, pp. 24–25.

21. W. Thomas Porter, Jr., "Computer Raped by Telephone," *New York Times Magazine*, September 8, 1974, p. 40.

22. Raymond L. Dirks and Leonard Gross, *The Great Wall Street Scandal* (New York: McGraw-Hill, 1974).

23. Gina Kolata, "When Criminals Turn To Computers: Is Anything Safe?" *Smithsonian* 13 (1982): 1176–1206.

24. Richard C. Hollinger and Lonn Lanza Kaduce, "The Process of Criminalization: The Case of Computer Crime Laws," *Criminology* (1988): 101–127.

25. Poerting and Pott, *Computer Kriminalität*.

26. Andrew Tobias, *The Invisible Banker* (New York: Washington Square Press, 1982).

27. Paul E. Tracy and James A. Fox, "A Field Experiment on Insurance Fraud in Auto Body Repair," *Criminology* 27 (1989): 589–603.

28. Kathleen I. Brickey, *Corporate Criminal Liability* (Wilmette, Ill.: Callaghan, 1984), vol. 2.

29. Alan Murray, "IRS Is Losing Battle Against Tax Evaders Despite Its New Gain," *Wall Street Journal*, April 10, 1984, p. 1.

30. Ralph Salerno and John S. Tompkins, "Protecting Organized Crime," in *Theft of the City*, ed. John A. Gardiner and David Olson (Bloomington: Indiana University Press, 1984); Edwin Sutherland, *The Professional Thief* (Chicago: University of Chicago Press, 1937).

31. 18 U.S.C. § 166(b) and (c).

32. Bequai, *White Collar Crime*, p. 45.

33. Ibid., p. 87.

34. John Clark and Richard Hollinger, *Theft by Employees in Work Organization* (Washington, D.C.: U.S. Government Printing Office, 1983).

35. Bequai, *White Collar Crime*, p. 89.

36. For a general overview of the corporate crime problem, see Francis T. Cullen, William J. Maakestad, and Gray Cavender, *Corporate Crime Under Attack: The Ford Pinto Case and Beyond* (Cincinnati: Anderson, 1987), pp. 37–99.

37. Gerhard O. W. Mueller, "Mens Rea and the Corporation: A Study of the Model Penal Code Position on Corporate Criminal Liability," *University of Pittsburgh Law Review* 19 (1957): 21–50.

38. State v. Lehigh Valley R. Co., 90 N.J. Law 372, 103 A. 685 (1917).

39. Model Penal Code, 1962, sec. 2.07(1)(c).

40. Sherman Antitrust Act, Act of July 2, 1890, c. 647, 26 Stat. 209, 15 U.S.C. § 1–7 (1976).

41. Clayton Antitrust Act, Act of October 15, 1914, c. 322, 38 Stat. 730, 15 U.S.C. § 12–27 (1976); Robinson-Patman Act, Act of June 19, 1936, c. 592, § 1, 49 Stat. 1526, 15 U.S.C. § 13(a) (1973). See also Kathleen F. Brickey, *Corporate Criminal Law Liability: A Treatise on the Criminal Liability of Corporations, Their Officers and Agents* (Wilmette, Ill.: Callaghan, 1984).

42. Phillip Knightly, Harold Evans, Elaine Potter, and Marjorie Wallace, *Suffer the Children: The Story of Thalidomide* (New York: Viking Press, 1979).

43. The Ford Pinto case is fully described in Cullen et al., *Corporate Crime Under Attack*. For more information on crimes against consumer safety, see Raymond J. Michalowski, *Order, Law, and Crime* (New York: Random House, 1985), pp. 334–340.

44. See Russell Mokhiber, *Corporate Crime and Violence: Big Business Power and the Abuse of the Public Trust* (San Francisco: Sierra Club, 1988); Susan P. Shapiro, *Wayward Capitalists: Target of the Securities and Exchange Commission* (New Haven: Yale University Press, 1984); M. David Ermen and Richard J. Lundman, *Corporate and Governmental Deviance: Problems of Organizational Behavior in Contemporary Society*, 2d ed. (New York: Oxford University Press, 1982); Cullen et al., *Corporate Crime Under Attack*; Knightly et al., *Suffer the Children*; W. Byron Groves and Graeme Newman, *Punishment and Privilege* (New York: Harrow & Heston, 1986).

45. Sutherland had earlier published articles on

the topic, including "White Collar Criminality," *American Sociological Review* 5 (1940): 1–12, and "Is White Collar Crime 'Crime'?" *American Sociological Review* 10 (1945): 132–139.

46. Marshall B. Clinard and Peter C. Yeager, *Corporate Crime* (New York: Free Press, 1980), p. 116. See also Peter C. Yeager, "Analysing Corporate Offences: Progress and Prospects," ed. Lee E. Preston, *Research in Corporate Social Performance and Policy* 8 (1986): 93–120. For similar findings in Canada, see Colin H. Goff and Charles E. Reasons, *Corporate Crime in Canada* (Scarborough, Ont.: Prentice-Hall, 1978).

47. Richard Quinney, *Critique of Legal Order: Crime Control in Capitalist Society* (Boston: Little, Brown, 1974), and *Class, State, and Crime: On the Theory and Practice of Criminal Justice* (New York: David McKay, 1977); Ian Taylor, Paul Walton, and Jock Young, *The New Criminology: For a Social Theory of Deviance* (London: Routledge & Kegan Paul, 1973); William Chambliss and Robert Seidman, *Law, Order, and Power,* 2d ed. (Reading, Mass.: Addison-Wesley, 1982).

48. James Q. Wilson, *Thinking About Crime* (New York: Basic Books, 1975).

49. Patsy Klaus and Carol Kalish, *The Severity of Crime,* Bureau of Justice Statistics Bulletin NCJ-92326 (Washington, D.C.: U.S. Government Printing Office, 1984). See also L. Schrager and James Short, "How Serious a Crime? Perceptions of Organizational and Common Crimes," in Gilbert Geis and E. Stotland, *White Collar Crime: Theory and Research* (Beverly Hills: Sage, 1980); Francis Cullen, B. Link, and C. Polanzi, "The Seriousness of Crime Revisited," *Criminology* 20 (1982): 83–102; Francis Cullen, R. Mathers, G. Clark, and J. Cullen, "Public Support for Punishing White Collar Crime: Blaming the Victim Revisited," *Journal of Criminal Justice* 11 (1983): 481–493; David Dodd, Richard Sparks, H. Genn, and D. Dodd, *Surveying Victims* (New York: Wiley, 1977).

50. Clinard and Yeager, *Corporate Crime,* p. 92, citing *New York Times* survey of July 15, 1979.

51. Gerhard O. W. Mueller, "Offenses Against the Environment and Their Prevention: An International Appraisal," *Annals of the American Academy of Political and Social Science* 444 (1979): 56–66.

52. Ibid., p. 60.

53. Ryuichi Hirano, *The Criminal Law Protection of Environment: General Report,* Tenth International Congress of Comparative Law, Budapest, 1978. For a discussion of the problems of multinational corporations operating in developing countries, see Richard Schaffer, Beverly Earle, and Filberto Aguste, *International Business Law and Its Environment* (St. Paul, Minn.: West, 1990).

54. Ibid.

55. John Braithwaite, "Challenging Just Deserts: Punishing White-Collar Criminals," *Journal of Criminal Law and Criminology* 73 (1982): 723–763; Stanton Wheeler, David Weisburd, and Nancy Boden, "Sentencing the White-Collar Offender," *American Sociological Review* 47 (1982): 641–659. For a thoughtful analysis of corporate illegality, see Nancy Frank and Michael Lombness, *Corporate Illegality and Regulatory Justice* (Cincinnati: Anderson, 1988).

56. Susan Shapiro, "Detecting Illegalities: A Perspective on the Control of Securities Violations" (Ph.D. dissertation, Yale University [University Microfilms], 1980); Albert J. Reiss and Albert D. Biderman, *Data Sources on White-Collar Law-Breaking* (Washington, D.C.: National Institute of Justice, 1980); Genevra Richardson, *Policing Pollution: A Study of Regulation and Enforcement* (Oxford: Clarendon, 1982). See also Frank and Lombness, *Corporate Illegality.*

57. See, for example, Dan Magnuson, ed., *Economic Crime: Programs for Future Research* (Stockholm: National Council for Crime Prevention, 1985).

58. Richard Gambino, *Blood of My Blood: The Dilemma of the Italian American* (Garden City, N.Y.: Doubleday, 1974), p. 3; Luigi Barzini, "Italians in New York: The Way We Were in 1929," *New York Magazine,* April 4, 1977, p. 36; Howard Abadinsky, *Organized Crime,* 2d ed. (Chicago: Nelson Hall, 1985).

59. Abadinsky, *Organized Crime,* pp. 43–53.

60. Ibid., p. 91.

61. James Inciardi, *Careers in Crime* (Chicago: Rand McNally, 1975), p. 113; Norman Lewis, *The Honored Society: A Searching Look at the Mafia* (New York: Putnam, 1964), p. 25.

62. Abadinsky, *Organized Crime*, pp. 56–62.

63. Annelise Graebner Anderson, *The Business of Organized Crime: A Cosa Nostra Family* (Stanford, Calif.: Hoover Institution Press, 1979); Peter Maas, *The Valachi Papers* (New York: Putnam, 1968).

64. Jay Albanese, *Organized Crime in America* (Cincinnati: Anderson, 1985), p. 25. See also Francis A. J. Ianni, *A Family Business: Kinship and Social Control in Organized Crime* (New York: Russell Sage, 1972); Joseph Albini, *The American Mafia: Genesis of a Legend* (New York: Irvington, 1971); Merry Morash, "Organized Crime," in *Major Forms of Crime*, ed. Robert F. Meier, pp. 191–220 (Beverly Hills, Calif.: Sage, 1984).

65. For a perceptive analysis of the changing focus of the two most recent commission reports, see Jay S. Albanese, "Government Perceptions of Organized Crime: The Presidential Commissions, 1967 and 1987," *Federal Probation* 52 (1988): 58–63.

66. Abadinsky, *Organized Crime*. See also Dwight Smith, *The Mafia Mystique* (New York: Basic Books, 1975).

67. For a discussion of predicting which legitimate businesses will be infiltrated by organized crime, see Jay S. Albanese, "Predicting the Incidence of Organized Crime: A Preliminary Model," in *Organized Crime in America: Concepts and Controversies*, ed. Timothy S. Bynum, pp. 103–114 (Monsey, N.Y.: Willow Tree Press, 1987). See especially President's Commission on Law Enforcement and Administration of Justice, *Task Force Report: Organized Crime* (Washington, D.C.: U.S. Government Printing Office, 1967), p. 9.

68. Fred Montanino, "Protecting the Federal Witness," *American Behavioral Scientist* 27 (4): 501–529.

69. Donald Cressey, *Theft of the Nation* (New York: Harper & Row, 1969).

70. Abadinsky, *Organized Crime*, pp. 8–23; Donald Cressey, in President's Commission, *Task Force Report*, pp. 7–8; Gay Talese, *Honor Thy Father* (New York: World, 1971).

71. For a discussion of violence in organized crime, see Kip Schlegel, "Violence in Organized Crime: A Content Analysis of the DeCavalcante and DeCarlo Transcripts," in Bynum, *Organized Crime in America*, pp. 55–70.

72. United States v. Bonanno, 180 F. Supp. 71 (S.D.N.Y. 1960), upholding the Apalachin roundup as constitutional; United States v. Bonanno, 177 F. Supp. 106 (S.D.N.Y. 1959), sustaining the validity of the conspiracy indictment; United States v. Bufalino, 285 F.2d 408 (2nd Cir. 1960), reversing the conspiracy conviction.

73. James Walston, "Mafia in the Eighties," *Violence, Aggression, and Terrorism* 1 (1987): 13–39.

74. "New Dimensions of Criminality and Crime Prevention in the Context of Development," working paper prepared by the United Nations Secretariat, A/CONF. 121 (1985), p. 20. For a global perspective, see Robert J. Kelley, ed., *Organized Crime: A Global Perspective* (Totowa, N.J.: Rowman & Littlefield, 1986).

75. Gerald L. Posner, *Warlords of Crime: Chinese Secret Societies: The New Mafia* (New York: McGraw-Hill, 1988); Richard W. Slatta, *Bandidos: The Varieties of Latin American Banditry* (New York: Greenwood, 1987); Francis A. J. Ianni, "New Mafia: Black, Hispanic, and Italian Styles," *Society* 11 (1974): 26–39, and *Black Mafia: Ethnic Succession in Organized Crime* (New York: Simon & Schuster, 1974).

13

DRUG-, ALCOHOL-, AND SEX-RELATED CRIME

In cities across the country and around the world, people buying and selling illicit goods and services congregate in certain areas—Times Square in New York, The Ramblas district in Barcelona (see Window to the World), St. Pauli in Hamburg—that are easily identifiable by their theater marquees advertising live sex shows. Shops feature everything from child pornography to sadomasochistic slide shows; prostitutes openly solicit clients; drunks propped up in doorways clutch brown bags; drug addicts deal small amounts of whatever they can get to sell to support their habits. The friendly locals will deliver virtually any service to visitors, for a price.

The activities involved—prostitution, drunkenness, sex acts between consenting adults, drug use—were commonly called victimless crimes. Perhaps that is because it was assumed that people who engage in them rationally choose to do so and do not view themselves as victims. Often no one complains to the police about being victimized by such consensual activity. But contemporary forms of such activities and their ramifications may entail massive victimizations: How many murders are committed during drug-gang wars? How many thefts are committed by addicts seeking to support their habits? How much damage is done to persons and property by drunken drivers? Does pornography encourage rape by making sexual objects of women?

DRUG ABUSE AND CRIME

A woman arrives at the airport in Los Angeles with very few belongings, no hotel reservations, no family or friends in the United States, and a passport showing eight recent trips from Bogotá, Colombia. A patdown and strip search reveals a firm, distended abdomen, which is discovered to hold eighty-eight balloons filled with cocaine.[1] In New York City a heroin addict admits that "the only livin' thing that counts is the fix...: Like I would steal off anybody—anybody, at all, my own mother gladly included."[2] In Chicago, crack cocaine is now transforming some of the country's toughest gangs into ghetto-based drug-trafficking organizations that

311

guard their turf with machine guns and assault rifles.[3] On a college campus in the Northeast a crowd sits in the basement of a fraternity house drinking beer and smoking pot through the night. At a beachfront house in Miami three young professional couples gather for a barbecue. After dinner they sit down at a card table in the playroom and line up a white powdery substance into rows about one-eighth of an inch wide and an inch long. Through rolled-up paper they breathe the powder into their nostrils and await the "rush" of the coke.

These incidents demonstrate that when we speak of the "drug problem," we are talking not about a single problem but about a wide variety of problems that stretch beyond the U.S. borders, that involve all social classes, and that in one way or another touch most people's lives. These incidents involve only a few of the actors in the drug drama. We could have included the manufacturers, importers, primary distributors (for large geographical areas), smugglers (who transport large quantities of drugs from their place of origin), dealers (who sell drugs on the street and in crack houses), corrupt criminal justice officials, users who endanger other people's lives through negligence (train engineers, pilots, physicians), and even unborn children. The drug problem is further complicated by the wide diversity of substances abused, their varying effects on the mind and body, and the kinds of dependencies that users develop. Then, too, there is the much-debated issue of the connection between drug use and crime—an issue infinitely more complex than the stereotype of a dope fiend committing heinous acts under the influence of drugs or to get the money to support a habit. Many of the crimes we have discussed in earlier chapters are part of what has been called the nation's (or the world's) drug problem. Let us examine this problem in detail.

The History of Drug Abuse

The use of chemical substances that alter physiological and psychological functioning dates back to the Old Stone Age, some two million years ago.[4] Egyptian relics dating back to 3500 B.C. depict the use of opium in religious rituals.

By 1600 B.C. an Egyptian reference work listed opium as an analgesic, or painkiller. The Incas are known to have used cocaine at least 5,000 years ago. Cannabis, the hemp plant from which marijuana and hashish are derived, also has a 5,000-year history.[5]

Since antiquity people have cultivated a variety of drugs for religious, medicinal, and social purposes. The modern era of drug abuse in the United States began with the use of drugs for medicinal purposes. By the nineteenth century the two components of opium, which is derived from the juice of the opium poppy, were identified and given the names morphine and codeine. Ignorant of the addictive properties of these drugs, physicians used them to treat a wide variety of human illnesses. So great was their popularity that they found their way into almost all patent medicines used for pain relief and were even incorporated in soothing syrups for babies (Mother Barley's Quieting Syrup and Mumm's Elixir were very popular). During the Civil War the use of injectable morphine to ease the pain of battle casualties was so extensive that morphine addiction among veterans came to be known as "the soldier's disease."[6] By the time the medical profession and the public recognized just how addictive morphine was, its use had reached epidemic proportions. Then in 1898 the Bayer company in Germany introduced a new opiate, supposedly a nonaddictive substitute for morphine and codeine. It came out under the trade name Heroin, and proved to be even more addictive than morphine.[7]

When cocaine, which was isolated from the coca leaf in 1860, appeared on the national drug scene, it, too, was used for medicinal purposes. (Its use to unblock the sinuses initiated the "snorting" of cocaine into the nostrils.) Its popularity spread, and soon it was used in other products: Peruvian Wine of Coca ($1 a bottle in the Sears, Roebuck catalog), a variety of tonics, and, the most famous of all, Coca-Cola, which was made with coca until 1903.[8]

As the consumption of opium products (narcotics) and cocaine spread, the states passed a variety of laws to restrict the sale of these substances. Federal authorities estimated that there were 200,000 addicts in the early 1900s. Growing concern over the increase in addiction led in

WINDOW TO THE WORLD

Deviance on the Ramblas

Sociologist Bernard Cohen, a nonparticipant observer of Barcelona's "red light" district, recorded a typical day:

The Ramblas in Barcelona is a tree-lined promenade stretching from the Placa de Catalunya south to the Mediterranean port, an area about a mile in length and several dozen yards wide. It is Barcelona's chief tourist attraction. The Ramblas bustles with sailors, tourists, sightseers, browsers, and businesspeople who patronize the district's taverns, hotels, snack bars, bookshops, flower stalls, and retail shops. Dozens of narrow, winding streets jut out from the main thoroughfare creating a mazelike structure.

The Ramblas is crime ridden and dangerous. Large numbers of gaunt, unshaven, and poorly dressed young men perambulate the promenade and its ancillary arteries at all hours of day and night constantly eyeballing bulging pockets and pocketbooks. In one incident an unsavory tough approached one of the few visible American tourists and asked, "Are you enjoying your holiday?" The tough was obviously less interested in the status of the tourist's vacation than in the contents of his wallet. Beggars, men and women, of all ages with hands outstretched are encountered everywhere. Youngsters not more than five or six years of age ramble back and forth among tables at the outdoor cafes coaxed by their mothers to obtain a few pesetas

from every customer. Men estimated in their 30s and 40s roam the Ramblas confronting patrons relaxing in outdoor cafes, demanding cigarettes. In another incident a man asked a patron for the remainder of his beverage and receiving no answer lifted the half-empty glass and sipped what was left of the drink. A woman who appeared in her thirties used similar techniques and finished off the remaining lemonade of another startled patron.

A pair of local toughs entered a partitioned outdoor cafe and harassed two young women seated at a table. The waiter observed the encounter from afar, fearful to become involved and possibly get hurt himself. Drug addicts wandered up and down the Ramblas and several were seated in public areas until the municipal custodian asked for the few pesetas required to rent the chairs. An argument ensued and only then did the addicts depart. One woman obviously doing drugs sat down next to a young man and caressed and kissed him for a few pesetas.

One afternoon, a man attempted to steal the shoulder bag of an elderly gentleman who was relaxing on a chair. An altercation broke out between the two men while friends of the victim rushed to his aid. A police officer was summoned and broke up the fight, sending the perpetrator on his way. The overall visible police

presence on the Ramblas especially during evenings was negligible. Only three two-officer teams, including one female officer, were spotted patrolling on foot the entire Ramblas over a six-hour period.

Twenty to thirty prostitutes were visible on the Ramblas near the Calle Escudellers. Many leaned against buildings, solicited customers, and accompanied them to a nearby rooming house. Several prostitutes were quite hostile, accosting potential patrons and holding their arms hoping to induce them to do their bidding. Two prostitutes visible to passersby attempted to steal the wallet of an intoxicated youth. No one dared or perhaps cared to intervene. One evening around 10 P.M., while strolling on the Ramblas, a transvestite prostitute among a group of six or seven solicited a gentleman and on refusal struck him on the back. Only his rapid escape from the area saved the tourist from a more serious fate.

Many of the hotels lining the Ramblas offer safe deposit boxes consisting of a steel or iron box riveted to a wall in the closet of the hotel room. One safe deposit box had a wood bottom that could be penetrated by a drill and another that could easily be torn from the wall.

Source: Personal communication from Bernard Cohen.

1914 to the passage of the Harrison Act, designed to regulate the domestic use, sale, and transfer of opium and coca products. Though this legislation decreased the number of addicts, it was a double-edged sword: by restricting the importation and distribution of drugs, it initiated the drug smuggling and black-market operations that are so deeply entrenched today.

It was not until the 1930s that the abuse of marijuana began to arouse public concern. Because marijuana use was associated with groups outside the social mainstream—petty criminals, jazz musicians, Bohemians, and, in the Southwest, Mexicans—a public outcry for its regulation arose.[9] Congress responded with the Marijuana Tax Act of 1937, which placed a prohibitive tax of $100 an ounce on the drug. With the passage of the Boggs Act in 1951, penalties for possession of and trafficking in marijuana (and other controlled substances) increased. Despite all the legislation, the popularity of marijuana continued.

As the drugs being used proliferated to include glue, tranquilizers (such as Valium and Librium), LSD, and many others, the public became increasingly aware of the dangers of drug abuse. In 1970 another major drug law, the Comprehensive Drug Abuse Prevention and Control Act (the Controlled Substances Act), updated all federal drug laws since the Harrison Act.[10] This act placed marijuana in the category of the most serious substances. The 1970 federal legislation made it necessary to bring state legislation into conformity with federal law. Consequently a Uniform Controlled Substances Act was drafted and now is the law in forty-eight states, the District of Columbia, Puerto Rico, the Virgin Islands, and Guam.

Most of the basic federal antidrug legislation has been drawn together in Title 21 of the United States Code, the collection of all federal laws. It includes many amendments passed since 1970, especially the Anti–Drug Abuse Amendments Act of 1988, which states a forceful purpose: "It is the declared policy of the United States Government to create a drug-free America by 1995."[11] Title 21, as amended, has elaborate provisions for the funding of national and international drug programs, establishes an Office of National Drug Control Policy headed by the so-called drug czar, and provides for a

set of stiff penalties for drug offenses. The manufacture, distribution, and dispensing of listed substances in stated (large) quantities are each subject to a prison sentence of from ten years to life and a fine (for individuals) of from $4 to $10 million. Even simple possession now carries a punishment of up to one year in prison and a $100,000 fine. Title 21 defines many other drug crimes as well and provides for the forfeiture of any property constituting or derived from the proceeds of drug trading.

The Extent of Drug Abuse

Historically, the substance (other than alcohol) most frequently abused in the United States has been marijuana. In annual surveys, high school seniors were asked whether they ever used marijuana. Between 1975 and 1986, the proportion answering yes ranged from a high of 51 percent in 1979 to a low of 39 percent in 1986. Of the young adults (high school graduates one to nine years beyond high school) who were asked whether they had used the drug within the last twelve months, 37 percent answered yes—approximately the same proportion as among high school seniors.[12] A national household survey that measured drug use among the American population aged 12 and older in 1985 estimated that 32 percent had used marijuana, 7 percent inhalants, 7 percent hallucinogens, and 9 percent stimulants.[13] Although marijuana use has declined in recent years, the drug still remains popular. Among other frequently used psychoactive drugs are amphetamines, barbiturates, LSD, cocaine, hashish, tranquilizers, codeine, methadone, and heroin (see Table 13.1). In the 1980s cocaine created the country's major drug problem. An estimated 22 million people had tried the substance and another 4 million were using it regularly.[14] The use of heroin is much less pervasive; the number of users is estimated to be about 250,000.[15]

Newer drugs on the market are crack, a derivative of cocaine, and the so-called designer drugs (such as Ecstasy)—substances that have been chemically altered in such a way that they no longer fall within the legal definition of controlled substances.[16] It is difficult to esti-

Los Angeles police officers search one of seven people arrested for investigation of narcotics for sale. Shots were fired after a police battering ram was used on the front door. No one was hurt in the gang-related arrest. On this night, April 9, 1988, more than 1,000 police officers raided strongholds in the biggest attack on drug dealing and street violence in the nation's second largest city.

mate how many people are abusing these new drugs.[17]

Patterns of Drug Abuse

The increasing number of addicts, new and more potent varieties of substances, and the amount of property and violent crime associated with drug abuse have led researchers to ask many questions about the phenomenon. Is drug abuse a symptom of an underlying mental or psychological disorder that makes some people more vulnerable than others? Some investigators argue that the addict is characterized by strong dependency needs, feelings of inadequacy, a need for immediate gratification, and lack of internal controls.[18] Or is it possible that addicts lack certain body chemicals, and that drugs make them feel better by compensating for this deficit? Perhaps the causes are neither psychological nor physiological but environmental. Is drug abuse a norm in our deteriorated inner cities, where youngsters are learn-

ing how to behave from older addicted role models? Do people escape from the realities of slum life by retreating into drug abuse?[19] If so, how do we explain drug abuse among the upper classes?

Just as there are many causes of drug abuse, there are many addict lifestyles—and the lifestyles may be linked to the use of particular substances. During the 1950s, heroin abuse began to increase markedly in the inner cities, particularly among young black and Hispanic males.[20] In fact, it was their drug of choice throughout the 1960s and early 1970s. Heroin addicts spend their days buying heroin, finding a safe place to "shoot" the substance into a vein with a needle attached to a hypodermic syringe, waiting for the euphoric feeling or "rush" that follows the injection, and ultimately reaching a feeling of overall well-being known as a "high," which lasts about four hours.[21] The heroin abuser's lifestyle is typically characterized by ill health, crime, arrest, imprisonment, and temporary stays in drug treatment programs.[22] Today AIDS,

TABLE 13.1   USES AND EFFECTS OF CONTROLLED SUBSTANCES

DRUGS	TRADE OR OTHER NAMES	MEDICAL USES	PHYSICAL DEPENDENCE	PSYCHO-LOGICAL DEPENDENCE
Narcotics				
Opium	Dover's Powder, paregoric, Parepectolin	Analgesic, antidiarrheal	High	High
Morphine	Morphine, pectoral syrup	Analgesic, antitussive		
Codeine	Codeine, Empirin compound with codeine, Robitussin A–C	Analgesic, antitussive	Moderate	Moderate
Heroin	Diacetylmorphine, horse, smack	Under investigation		
Hydromorphone	Dilaudid	Analgesic		
Meperidine (pethidine)	Demerol, Pethadol	Analgesic	High	High
Methadone	Dolophine, methadone, methadose	Analgesic, heroin substitute		
Other narcotics	LAAM, Leritine, Levo-Dromoran, Percodan, Tussionex, Fentanyl, Darvon,* Talwin,* Lomotil	Analgesic, antidiarrheal, antitussive	High–low	High–low
Depressants				
Chloral hydrate	Noctec, Somnos	Hypnotic	Moderate	Moderate
Barbiturates	Amobarbital, phenobarbital, Butisol, Phenoxbarbital, Secobarbital, Tuinal	Anesthetic, anticonvulsant, sedative, hypnotic	High–moderate	High–moderate
Glutethimide	Doriden			
Methaqualone	Optimil, Parest, Quaalude, Somnafac, Sopor	Sedative, hypnotic	High	High
Benzodiazepines	Ativan, Azene, Clonopin, Dalmane, Diazepam, Librium, Serax, Tranxene, Valium, Verstran	Anti-anxiety, anticonvulsant, sedative, hypnotic	Low	Low
Other depressants	Equanil, Miltown, Noludar, Placidyl, Valmid	Anti-anxiety, sedative, hypnotic	Moderate	Moderate
Stimulants				
Cocaine†	Coke, flake, snow	Local anesthetic		
Amphetamines	Biphetamine, Delcobese, Desoxyn, Dexedrine, Mediatric			
Phenmetrazine	Preludin	Hyperkinesis, narcolepsy, weight control	Possible	High
Methylphenidate	Ritalin			
Other stimulants	Adipex, Bacarate, Cylert, Didrex, Ionamin, Plegine, Pre-Sate, Sanorex, Tenuate, Tepanil, Voranil			
Hallucinogens				
LSD	Acid, microdot		None	Degree unknown
Mescaline and peyote	Mesc, buttons, cactus	None		
Amphetamine variants	2,5-DMA, PMA, STP, MDA, MMDA, TMA, DOM, DOB		Unknown	
Phencyclidine	PCP, angel dust, hog	Veterinary anesthetic	Degree unknown	High
Phencyclidine analogs	PCE, PCPy, TCP			
Other hallucinogens	Bufotenine, Ibogaine, DMT, DET, psilocybin, psilocyn	None	None	Degree unknown
Cannabis				
Marijuana	Pot, Acapulco gold, grass, reefer, sinsemilla, Thai sticks	Under investigation	Degree unknown	Moderate
Tetrahydrocannabinol	THC			
Hashish	Hash	None		
Hashish oil	Hash Oil			

*Not designated a narcotic under the Controlled Substances Act.

†Designated a narcotic under the Controlled Substances Act.

Source: U.S. Department of Justice, 1979.

TABLE 13.1   USES AND EFFECTS OF CONTROLLED SUBSTANCES (*continued*)

TOLERANCE	DURATION OF EFFECTS (in hours)	USUAL METHODS OF ADMINISTRATION	POSSIBLE EFFECTS	EFFECTS OF OVERDOSE	WITHDRAWAL SYNDROME
Yes	3–6	Oral, smoked	Euphoria, drowsiness, respiratory depression, constricted pupils, nausea	Slow and shallow breathing, clammy skin, convulsions, coma, possible death	Watery eyes, runny nose, yawning, loss of appetite, irritability, tremors, panic, chills and sweating, cramps, nausea
		Oral, injected, smoked			
		Oral, injected			
		Injected, sniffed, smoked			
	12–24	Oral, injected			
	Variable				
Possible	5–8	Oral	Slurred speech, disorientation, drunken behavior without odor of alcohol	Shallow respiration, cold and clammy skin, dilated pupils, weak and rapid pulse, coma, possible death	Anxiety, insomnia, tremors, delirium, convulsions, possible death
Yes	1–16	Oral, injected			
	4–8				
Possible	1–2	Sniffed, injected	Increased alertness, excitation, euphoria, increased pulse rate and blood pressure, insomnia, loss of appetite	Agitation, increase in body temperature, hallucinations, convulsions, possible death	Apathy, long periods of sleep, irritability, depression, disorientation
Yes	2–4	Oral, injected			
		Oral			
Yes	8–12	Oral	Illusions and hallucinations, poor perception of time and distance	Longer, more intense "trip" episodes, psychosis, possible death	Withdrawal syndrome not reported
	Up to days	Oral, injected			
	Variable	Smoked, oral, injected			
Possible		Oral, injected, smoked, sniffed			
Yes	2–4	Smoked, oral	Euphoria, relaxed inhibitions, increased appetite, disoriented behavior	Fatigue, paranoia, possible psychosis	Insomnia, hyperactivity, and decreased appetite occasionally reported

which is spread, among other ways, by the shared use of needles, has become the most serious health problem among heroin addicts.

During the 1960s marijuana became one of the major drugs of choice in the United States, particularly among white, middle-class young people who identified themselves as antiestablishment. Their lifestyles were distinct from those of the inner-city heroin addicts. What began as a hippie drug culture in the Haight-Ashbury area of San Francisco spread quickly through the country's college campuses.[23] In fact, a Harvard psychologist, Timothy Leary, traveled across the country in the 1960s telling students to "turn on, tune in, and drop out." Young marijuana users tended to live for the moment, not planning for the future. Disillusioned by what they perceived as a rigid and hypocritical society, they challenged its norms through deviant behavior. Drugs—first marijuana, then hallucinogens (principally LSD), amphetamines, and barbiturates—came to symbolize the counterculture.[24] In the 1960s and 1970s, attitudes toward recreational drug use had become quite lax, perhaps as a result of the wide acceptance of marijuana.[25]

By the 1980s, cocaine, once associated only with deviants, had become the drug of choice among the privileged, who watched (and copied) the well-publicized drug-oriented lifestyles of some celebrities and athletes. Typical cocaine users are well-educated, prosperous, upwardly mobile professionals in their twenties and thirties. They are lawyers and architects, editors and stockbrokers. They earn enough money to spend at least $100 an evening on their illegal recreational activities. By and large they are otherwise law-abiding, even though they know well that their behavior is against the law. The majority of cocaine users are men, but the number of women users is increasing. Teenagers, too, are increasingly drawn to cocaine.[26] In some areas, such as the coastal communities of southern California, whole subcultures of users, dealers, and smugglers have developed a lifestyle characterized by extravagant spending, drug abuse, uninhibited sexual mores, and indeed any behavior that brings instant gratification.[27] Although most cocaine use is recreational, many users retreat from nondrug-related activities into a singleminded pursuit of pleasure through drugs.

During the 1980s, crack, often referred to as the "poor man's cocaine," spread to the inner-city population that traditionally had abused heroin.[28] Crack is cheaper than powdered cocaine, fast-acting, and powerful. Though individual doses are inexpensive, once a person is hooked on crack a daily supply can run between $100 and $250. Aspects of life in this subculture are described in the Criminological Focus. The information comes from a new program sponsored by the National Institute of Justice called Drug Use Forecasting (DUF). To follow emerging trends in drug use and the link between drug use and crime, investigators asked a sample of newly arrested individuals in twenty-two cities to submit to a voluntary and confidential interview.

Drug addicts continually search for a new way to extend their high. In 1989 a mixture of crack and heroin, called "crank," began to be used. Crank is smoked in a pipe.[29] It is potentially very dangerous, first, because it prolongs the brief high of crack alone, and second, because it appeals to younger drug addicts who are concerned about the link between AIDS and the sharing of hypodermic needles. It is not clear whether crank will retain its popularity. But the history of drug abuse suggests that in all probability it will soon be replaced by yet another substance that promises a better and faster high.

Crime-Related Activities

Many researchers have examined the criminal implications of addiction to heroin and, more recently, cocaine. James Inciardi found that 356 addicts in Miami, according to self-reports, committed 118,134 offenses (27,464 Index crimes) over a one-year period.[30] In another study of incarcerated offenders, 75 percent of inmates in jails and 78 percent of prison inmates reported that they had used drugs (see Table 13.2). Thirty-five percent of state prison inmates reported that they had been under the influence of drugs when they committed the offense for which they were incarcerated, and 43 percent said they had used drugs every day in

TABLE 13.2   PERCENTAGE OF OFFENDERS AND NONOFFENDERS WHO REPORTED USE OF DRUGS, 1979–1985

	JAIL INMATES	PRISON INMATES	GENERAL POPULATION
Any drug	75%	78%	37%
Marijuana	72	75	33
Cocaine	38	37	25
Amphetamines	32	37	9
Barbiturates	27	35	6
Heroin	22	30	2

Source: U.S. Department of Justice, *Report to the Nation on Crime and Justice*, 2d ed. (Washington, D.C.: U.S. Government Printing Office, 1988), p. 50.

the month before they were convicted.[31] Though no separate official statistics called "drug-related offenses" are kept, these investigations and others make it quite clear that street crime is significantly related to drug abuse.

The nature of that relationship is less clear. Is the addict typically an adolescent who never committed a crime before he or she became hooked, but thereafter was forced to commit crimes to get money to support the drug habit? In other words, does drug abuse lead to crime?[32] Or does criminal behavior precede drug abuse? Another possibility is that both drug abuse and criminal behavior stem from the same factors (biological, psychological, or sociological).[33] The debate continues, and many questions are still unanswered. But on one point most researchers agree: Whatever the temporal or causal sequence of drug abuse and crime, the frequency and seriousness of criminality increase as addiction increases. Thus drug abuse may not "cause" criminal behavior, but it does enhance it.[34]

Until the late 1970s most investigators of the drug-crime relationship reported that drug abusers were arrested primarily for property offenses. Recent scholarly literature, however, presents us with a different perspective. There appears to be an increasing amount of violence among drug abusers, and it may be attributable largely to the appearance of crack.

There is, of course, another side to drug-related criminality: drug wars. Cities across the country have been divided into distinct turfs. Rival drug dealers settle territorial disputes with guns, power struggles within a single drug enterprise lead to assaults and homicides, one dealer robs another, informers are killed, their associates retaliate, and bystanders, some of them children, get caught in the crossfire.[35]

The International Drug Economy

The drug problem is a worldwide phenomenon and as such is beyond the power of any one government to deal with.[36] Nor are drugs simply a concern of law enforcement agencies. Drugs influence politics, international relations, peace and war, and the economies of individual countries and of the entire world. Let us take a brief look at the political and economic impact of the international drug trade, specifically as it concerns cocaine, heroin, and marijuana.

Cocaine   Today the largest cocaine producer is Peru. In 1987 a harvest of 56,000 to 84,000 metric tons of coca leaves yielded from 178 to 366 tons of pure cocaine. Bolivia is not far behind with a yield of 92 to 148 tons.[37] Colombia, which produces only 20 tons of pure cocaine, exports more than any other country—80 percent of the world supply. The "cocaine cartel," which controls production and distribution, is said to be composed of no more than twelve families, located principally in Colombia and Bolivia. However, organized crime interests in other South American countries are establish-

CRIMINOLOGICAL FOCUS

The Crack Culture

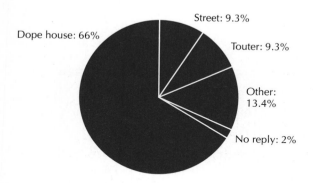

Dope house: 66%
Street: 9.3%
Touter: 9.3%
Other: 13.4%
No reply: 2%

THE MARKETPLACE

In Detroit, distribution of crack ordinarily takes place indoors; very few sales occur on the street. As [the pie chart] shows, the "dope house" or "crack house" is, by a wide margin, the primary retailing mechanism.

Anecdotal information from [our] interviews showed contrasting descriptions of sale places. Some were of the "buy, get high, and party" variety, but others were strictly (and literally) "holes in the wall." A house would have a small aperture into which the customer puts his money. A few moments pass, and then a hand materializes and deposits the crack. At that point the customer's departure is imperative, since "hanging out" is not tolerated. One goal of the Detroit DUF [Drug Use Forecasting] is to learn more details about the operation and organization of the crack house.

"Touters" are circulating salespeople who generally are also users. The "other" category in [the pie chart] generally meant, to survey respondents, users who gratuitously shared their drugs with friends. "Street" sales are generally made by "runners," "rollers," or "beepermen"— low-level retail dealers who may or may not also use the drugs they sell.

THE TYPES OF CRACK DEALERS

We asked the 30 respondents who admitted to dealing to characterize their own "style" of selling. Did they sell to support their own use, or mostly for profit? Were they largely "go-betweens" (touters), often accepting drugs as payment, or a combination of touter and profit-dealer? Two-thirds of those who had sold crack most frequently chose the "user-dealer" description. Twenty percent said they sold mainly for profit, and the remainder acted as touters.

It is unlikely that any of the 30 respondents are importers or wholesalers. Those respondents who admitted to selling crack seem mostly to be what researchers of drug distributing systems call "hustlers." A hustler's market is a market operated and dominated by users who sell drugs in order to fund their own use.

Of the 116 respondents who admitted they were crack users, 89 denied *any* crack-dealing activity. A comparison of these users to the 30 self-admitted sellers failed to reveal any major distinctions. Fifty-four percent of the 89 who denied selling crack were urine positive for cocaine, compared with 63.3 percent of the dealers. The rates for both groups are quite similar to that of the total sample, which was 58.2 percent.

MANUFACTURING DISPENSERS

Ten of the informants discussed in some detail the process of preparing crack from granular cocaine. Some said they processed as much as 1 or 2 ounces, or as little as half a gram; those who processed larger quantities tended to work toward selling enough "rock" to cover their own use costs. Some entertained ideas of profitable returns on their investment. A popular unit of transaction reported was the "eightball, " which is equivalent to between 2.5 and 3.5 grams of powder cocaine. It retailed from $125 to $250 and was expected to yield 45 to 55 "rocks," which could be retailed at prices from $10 to $15.

An additional motive for manufacturing crack was the desire to control the quality of the product. Many said that "street crack" was so variable that they felt more secure by producing their own from "powder" (cocaine hydrochloride, the granular salt). Some exhibited a sense of accomplishment as "good chemists" or "good cookers." Informants reported a wide range of recipes and formulas. This information is valuable for determining what substances typically go into the final composition of retail crack.

Street crack is often alleged to be heavily laced with amphetamine (although DUF urine screens do not support this belief in Detroit, where amphetamine use within the DUF sample is almost zero). It is also believed that street crack is adulterated with compounds like "B12," "benzoyl," "high cocaine," and other fillers used to "swell up" the rock. So both considerations of quality as well as profitability are relevant to manufacturing processes.

BRAND NAME OR GENERIC?

Currently we have compiled, from the interviews, a list of more than 100 street terms for crack. These terms reflect both generic names (rock, boulder) and brand names ("Schoolcraft," "Troop," etc.). [The table lists] some of these terms.

In addition to these descriptive terms, a series of number designations is also used to characterize certain methods of crack consumption. Crack crushed and sprinkled into a tobacco cigarette is referred to as a "51" or "501" or sometimes a "151." This may also refer to crack used with marijuana, although some informants have stated that used in this fashion, crack users would be smoking a "38."

Descriptive terms and the lexicon of drug and crack use themselves constitute an important phenomenon. Clearly, criminal justice professionals would be served by having a clearer understanding of drug terminology (it is interesting to note that the most recently published drug lexicographies...do not even list the term "crack"). It may be critical to establishing the meaning of information obtained from wiretaps or interrogation. Physicians, in taking medical histories, have an important need to know such referents.

Furthermore, the popularization of certain terms tells us something of the world view of the drug users and sellers themselves. For instance, the terms may reflect technologies used or believed to be used in processing. Informants have used the terms "ether-based," "synthetic," and "chemical" in describing crack types. A small number of "brand name" designations have been developed and used by particular distribution organizations. Examples of such terms include "eye-opener," "swell up," "speed," "Pony," "Eastside Player," and "Wrecking Crew."

FREQUENCY OF NAMES REPORTED FOR CRACK

Rock	60
Rox	21
Boulder	44
Yeaho	15
Stone	11
Roxanne	4
Eightball	4
Dime	4
Caine	4
Bump	3

Source: Tom Miecykowski, "Understanding Life in the Crack Culture: The Investigative Utility of the Drug Use Forecasting System," *NIJ Reports*, December 1989, pp. 7–9.

ing themselves in the market. Figure 13.1 shows the sources of the cocaine available in the United States.

Figures on the tonnage of drugs seized by law enforcement agents give us an indication of the mode of transport of cocaine into the United States (see Figure 13.2). Nearly half of all cocaine seized was being shipped to the United States on private planes. Small planes evade controls and land on little-used airstrips or drop their cargos offshore to waiting speedboats.[38] Boats carrying drugs mingle with the local pleasure craft and bring the cargo to shore. Wholesalers who work for the Colombian cartels take care of the nationwide distribution. Some of the estimated 100,000 Colombians living illegally in the United States are thought to belong to the distribution apparatus.

Heroin   According to intelligence estimates, nearly half of all heroin available on American streets comes from southwest Asian countries, the so-called Golden Crescent of Iran, Afghanistan, and Pakistan. In 1987 Afghanistan produced between 400 and 800 metric tons of opium; Iran, 200 to 900 tons; and Pakistan, 80 to 135 tons. Far less heroin comes from the so-called Golden Triangle countries of Southeast Asia—Myanmar (formerly Burma), Thailand,

FIGURE 13.1   Probable sources of cocaine available in the United States, 1985 (estimated percent of total supply)

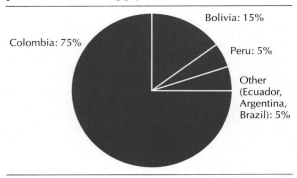

Note: Percentages are general estimates because it is difficult to trace drugs to their original source.
Source: Royal Canadian Mounted Police, *The Illicit Drug Situation in the United States and Canada* (Ottawa, 1984–1986), p. 10.

FIGURE 13.2   Cocaine seizures from various smuggling conveyances destined for the United States, January–October 1986 (percent of total volume)

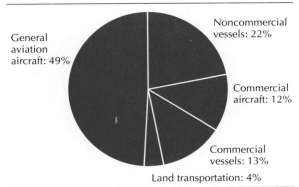

Source: Royal Canadian Mounted Police, *The Illicit Drug Situation in the United States and Canada* (Ottawa, 1984–1986), p. 12.

Laos, Kampuchea (formerly Cambodia), and Vietnam. Production in these countries is organized by local warlords, illegitimate traders, and corrupt administrators; it is tending to come increasingly under the control of triads—organized crime families of Chinese origin, based in Hong Kong and Taiwan. Increasingly, heroin in the United States is of Mexican origin—39 percent in 1985 (see Figure 13.3). Most of the heroin from the Golden Crescent and Golden Triangle enters the United States on commercial aircraft, whereas Mexican heroin comes overland. In Europe and in the United States the traditional Sicilian Mafia families have assumed significant roles in the refining and distribution of heroin.

Marijuana   Because marijuana is bulky, smugglers prefer to transport it on oceangoing vessels. From January through October 1986, 87 percent of the total volume of marijuana seized was taken from privately owned pleasure craft or charter vessels not engaged in commercial trade (see Figure 13.4). Most of the Colombian marijuana—about one-third of all marijuana imported into the United States—is shipped by sea. Mexican marijuana, trucked overland, constitutes another third, and the remainder comes in by private plane from such countries as

FIGURE 13.3   Sources of heroin encountered in the United States, 1985 (estimated percent of total supply)

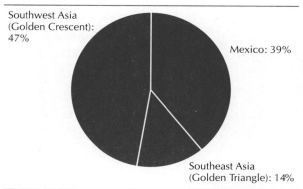

Southwest Asia
(Golden Crescent):
47%

Mexico: 39%

Southeast Asia
(Golden Triangle): 14%

These estimates were derived from heroin signature analysis, an intelligence program in which a special chemical analysis identifies and quantifies selected heroin characteristics and secondary ingredients. From the resultant data, heroin exhibits are classified according to the process by which they were manufactured, which in turn enables the association of exhibits with geographic regions.
Source: Royal Canadian Mounted Police, *The Illicit Drug Situation in the United States and Canada* (Ottawa, 1984–1986), p. 19.

FIGURE 13.4   Marijuana seizures from various smuggling conveyances destined for the United States, January–October 1986 (percent of total volume)

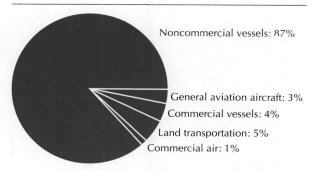

Noncommercial vessels: 87%

General aviation aircraft: 3%
Commercial vessels: 4%
Land transportation: 5%
Commercial air: 1%

Source: Royal Canadian Mounted Police, *The Illicit Drug Situation in the United States and Canada* (Ottawa, 1984–1986), p. 6.

Belize and Jamaica. Hashish, a concentrated form of marijuana, which comes predominantly from Pakistan (60–65 percent) and Lebanon (25–30 percent), is imported by noncommercial ships.

Money laundering   The illegal drug economy is vast. Its annual sales are estimated to be between $300 and $500 billion. The American drug economy alone may account for almost half of the sales. Profits are enormous, and no taxes are paid on them. Because they are "dirty money," they must undergo a **money laundering** process. Typically, the cash obtained from drug sales in the United States is physically smuggled out of the country, as it cannot be legally exported without disclosure. Smuggling cash is not easy—$1 million in $20 bills weighs 100 pounds—yet billions of dollars are exported, in false-bottomed suitcases and smugglers' vests, to countries that allow numbered bank accounts without identification of names (the Cayman Islands, Panama, Switzerland, and Liechtenstein, among others). Once deposited in foreign accounts, the funds are "clean" and can be returned to legitimate businesses and investments. They may also be used for illegal purposes, such as the purchase of arms for export to terrorist groups.

The political impact   The political impact of the drug trade on producer countries is devastating. In the late 1970s and early 1980s, the government of Bolivia became completely corrupt. The minister of justice was referred to as the "minister of cocaine." In Colombia, drug lords and terrorists combined their resources to wrest power from the democratically elected government. Thirteen Supreme Court judges and 167 police officers were killed; the minister of justice and the ambassador to Hungary were assassinated. The message being sent was that death was the price for refusal to succumb to drug corruption. In 1989 a highly respected presidential candidate who had come out against the cocaine cartel was assassinated. The government of that country is unstable. Colombia is not alone. Before General Manuel Noriega was persuaded to surrender to the United States to face charges of drug smuggling, he had made himself military dictator of Panama.

Corruption and crime are rife in all drug-producing countries. Government instability is the necessary consequence. Coups replace elections. The populations of these countries are

Sailors from the U.S. Coast Guard are removing four tons of marijuana from a vessel engaged in smuggling.

not immune to addiction themselves. Several Andean countries, including Colombia, Bolivia, and Peru, are now experiencing major addiction problems; Peru alone has some 60,000 addicts. The Asian narcotics-producing countries, which had thought themselves immune to the addiction problem, likewise became victims of their own production. Pakistan now counts about 200,000 addicts.[39] Indeed, one of the more remarkable aspects of the expansion of the drug trade has been the spread of addiction and the drug economy to the Third World and to the socialist countries. Of all political problems, however, the most vicious is the alliance that drug dealers have forged with terrorist groups in the Near East, in Latin America, and in Europe.[40]

Drug Control

In September 1989 President Bush unveiled his antidrug strategy. On the international level, the president emphasized two plans. First, he sought modest funding for the United Nations effort to combat the international narcotic drug traffic. Second, he called for far greater expenditures for bilateral cooperation with other countries in efforts to deal with drug producers and traffickers. This effort extends to crop eradication programs.[41] He singled out Colombia, Bolivia, and Peru for such efforts and immediately sent U.S. Army assistance, including helicopters and crews, to Colombia for use in that country's very difficult battle with the Medellín cartel.

On the national level the president proposed federal aid to state and local police for street-level attacks on drug users and small dealers, for whom he proposed alternative punishments such as house arrest (confinement in one's home rather than in a jail cell) and boot camps (short but harsh incarceration with military drill). He also called for rigorous enforcement of forfeiture laws, under which money is confiscated from offenders if it can be established that it derived from the drug trade; property purchased with such money is also forfeited. While the president's plan continues America's emphasis on law enforcement options for drug control, it also provides for some treatment and education. Treatment and prevention, however, received only a fraction of the money allocated to traditional law enforcement efforts throughout the 1980s (see Figure 13.5).

Treatment   The treatment approach to drug control is not new. During the late 1960s and into the 1970s some hope for the country's drug problem centered on treatment programs. These programs took a variety of forms, among them self-help groups (Narcotics Anonymous, Cocaine Anonymous), psychotherapy, detoxification ("drying out" in a hospital for less than two weeks), "rap" houses (neighborhood centers where addicts can come for group therapy sessions), various community social-action efforts (addicts clean up neighborhoods, plant trees, etc.), and—the two most popular—residential therapeutic communities and methadone maintenance programs.[42] The therapeutic community is a twenty-four-hour, total-care facility where former addicts and professionals work together to help addicts become drugfree. In methadone maintenance programs, narcotics addicts are given a synthetic narcotic, methadone, which prevents withdrawal symptoms (physical and psychological pain associated with giving up drugs), while addicts reduce their drug intake slowly over a period of time. Throughout the program addicts receive counseling designed to help them return to a normal life. It is difficult to assess the success of drug-abuse treatment programs. Even if individuals appear to be drugfree within a program, it is hard to find out what happens to them once they leave it (or even during a week when they don't show up). In addition, it may well be that the addicts who succeed in drug treatment programs are only those who have already resolved to stop abusing drugs before they voluntarily come in for treatment, and that the real hard-core users do not even make an effort to become drugfree.[43]

FIGURE 13.5   Percentage of federal antidrug funds allocated to law enforcement and to treatment and prevention, 1970–1987

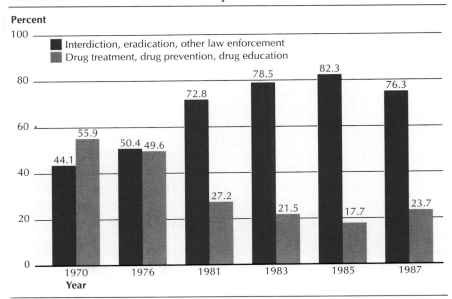

Source: Marsha Rosenbaum, *Just Say What? An Alternative View on Solving America's Drug Problem,* for National Council on Crime and Delinquency (Washington, D.C.: U.S. Government Printing Office, 1989), p. 17.

Education   While drug treatment deals with the problem of addiction after the fact, education tries to prevent people from taking illegal drugs in the first place. The idea behind educational programs is straightforward: People who have information about the harmful effects of illegal drugs are likely to stay away from them. Sometimes the presentation of the facts concerning the dangers of drugs has been coupled with scare techniques. Some well-known athletes and entertainers have joined the crusade with public service messages ("a questionable approach," says Howard Abadinsky, "given the level of substance abuse reported in these groups").[44]

The educational approach has several drawbacks. Critics maintain that most drug addicts are quite knowledgeable about the potential consequences of taking drugs, but they think of them as just a part of the "game."[45] Most people who begin to use drugs believe they will never become addicted, even when they have information about addiction.[46] Inner-city youngsters do not lack information about the harmful effects of drugs. They learn about the dangers from daily exposure to addicts desperately searching for drugs, sleeping on the streets, going through withdrawal, and stealing family belongings to get money.[47]

Legalization of drugs   Despite the recent increases in government funding for an expanded war on drugs, many observers see little hope for a drugfree society by 1995. There is much evidence that all of the approaches, even the "new" ones, have been tried before with little or no effect. In the light of this disillusionment, some experts are beginning to advocate a very different approach—legalization of drugs. Their reasoning is that since our drug problem seems to elude all control efforts, why not deal with heroin and cocaine the same way we deal with alcohol and tobacco? In other words, why not subject these drugs to some government control and restrictions, but make them freely available to all adults?[48] They argue that current drug-control policies impose tremendous costs on taxpayers without demonstrating effective results. In addition to spending less money on crime control, the government would make money on tax revenue from the sale of legalized drugs. This is, of course, a hotly debated issue. Given the dangers of drug abuse and the morality issues at stake, it surely has no easy solution.

ALCOHOL AND CRIME

Alcohol is yet another substance that contributes to social problems. One of the major differences between alcohol and the other drugs we have been discussing is that the sale and purchase of alcohol are legal in most jurisdictions of the United States. The average annual consumption of alcoholic beverages by each individual 14 years of age and over is equivalent to 591 cans of beer, 115 bottles of wine, and 35 fifths of liquor; this is more than the average individual consumption of coffee and milk.[49] Alcohol is consumed at recreational events, business meetings, lunches and dinners at home, and celebrations; in short, drinking alcohol has become the expected behavior in many social situations.

Drinking is widespread among young people. Lloyd D. Johnston, Patrick M. O'Malley, and Jerald G. Bachman asked students at seventy-five high schools in seven states how many times during the last month (excluding religious services) they had consumed any beer, wine, or liquor. The responses showed that by age 15 the majority of boys and girls drank on at least one occasion in any given month. Of the male students aged 17 or older, one-quarter drank ten or more times a month. And a significant proportion reported that intoxication was a necessary part of their lives. Yet the authors also reported that alcohol consumption has declined during recent years.[50]

The History of Legalization

Alcohol consumption is not new to our culture. In colonial days alcohol was even considered safer and healthier than water. Notwithstanding its popularity, the history of alcohol consumption is filled with controversy. Many people through the years have viewed it as the sinful behavior of the wicked and degenerate. By the turn of the twentieth century, social reformers linked liquor to prostitution, poverty, the immigrant culture, and corrupt politics. Various lobbying groups, such as the Women's Christian Temperance Union and the American Anti-Saloon League, bombarded politicians with demands for the prohibition of alcohol.[51] On January 16, 1920, the Eighteenth Amendment to the Constitution went into force, prohibiting the manufacture, sale, and transportation of alcoholic beverages. The Volstead Act of 1919 had already defined as intoxicating liquor any beverage that contained more than one-half of 1 percent alcohol.

Historians generally agree that no law in America has ever been more widely violated or more unpopular. Vast numbers of people continued to consume alcohol. It was easy to manufacture and to import. It brought tremendous profits to suppliers, and it could not be controlled by enforcement officers, who were too inefficient, too few, or too corrupt. The unlawful sale of alcohol was called "bootlegging." The term originated in the early practice of concealing liquor in one's boot to avoid payment of liquor taxes. Bootlegging created empires for such gangsters as Al Capone and Dutch Schultz, as we saw in Chapter 12. Private saloons, or "speakeasies," prospered. Unpopular and unenforceable, the Eighteenth Amendment was repealed thirteen years after its birth—on December 5, 1933. Except for a few places, the manufacture and sale of alcohol have been legal in the United States since that time.

Crime-Related Activities

The alcohol-related activities that have become serious problems to the criminal justice system are violent crime, drunken driving, and public intoxication.

Violence   National surveys of inmates in jails and prisons show that

• Almost half of the convicted offenders incarcerated for violent crimes (particularly assaults) used alcohol immediately before the crimes.

• Almost 50 percent of the inmates drank an average of one ounce or more each day (compared to 10 percent of all persons aged 18 and older in the general population).
• Over one-third of the inmates drank alcoholic beverages every day during the year before they committed their crimes.
• 34 to 45 percent of inmates convicted of homicide, assault, rape, and robbery described themselves as heavy drinkers.[52]

For many decades criminologists have probed the relationship between alcohol and violence. Marvin Wolfgang, in a study of 588 homicides in Philadelphia, found alcohol present in two-thirds of all homicide cases (both victim and offender, 44 percent; victim only, 9 percent; offender only, 11 percent).[53] Similar findings were reported from northern Sweden: Two-thirds of the offenders who committed homicide between 1970 and 1981 and almost half of their victims were intoxicated when the crime was committed.[54] Many other offenses show a significant relationship between alcohol and violence: In the United States 58 percent of those convicted for assault and 64 percent of offenders who assaulted police officers had been drinking.[55] In about one-third of rapes, the offender, the victim, or both had been drinking immediately before the attack.[56] The role of alcohol in violent family disputes has been increasingly recognized. Among 2,413 American couples, the rate of severe violence by the husband was 2.10 per 100 couples in homes where the husbands were never drunk and 30.89 per 100 couples in homes where husbands were drunk "very often."[57]

Many explanations have been offered for the relationship between alcohol and violence.[58] Some of these explanations focus on the individual. When people are provoked, for example, alcohol can reduce restraints on aggression.[59] Alcohol also escalates aggression by reducing people's awareness of what will happen to them if they act on their urges.[60] Other studies analyze the particular social situation in which drinking takes place. Experts argue that in some situations aggressive behavior is considered appropriate or is even expected when people drink together.[61]

Drunk driving   The effect of alcohol on driving is causing increasing concern. The incidence of drunk driving, referred to in statutes as "driving under the influence" and "driving while intoxicated" (depending on the level of alcohol found in the blood), has been steadily rising. Statistics show that:

- Driving under the influence (DUI) arrests increased nearly 223 percent between 1970 and 1986, while the number of licensed drivers increased only 42 percent.
- Before arrest for driving while intoxicated (DWI), convicted offenders drink at least six ounces of pure alcohol within four hours.
- A recent national survey showed that about 7 percent of all persons confined in jails were charged with or convicted of DWI; 13 percent had a current charge or prior conviction for DWI; and almost half of those in jail for DWI had a previous sentence of probation, jail, or prison for the same offense.
- Over 650,000 persons are injured in alcohol-related crashes each year.
- The annual cost of drunk driving (property damage, medical bills, etc.) is estimated at $24 billion.
- In 1986 there were 23,990 alcohol-related traffic deaths.
- There were 1.8 million arrests for driving under the influence in 1988.[62]

Cari Lightner, aged 13, was killed in May 1980 by a drunken driver while she was walking on a sidewalk.[63] The driver had been arrested only a few days before on a DUI charge. The victim's mother, Candy, took action almost immediately to push for new legislation that would mandate much stiffer penalties for drunk driving. It was difficult at first to stimulate a government response, but she did get the attention of journalists. By the end of the year in which Cari died, Mrs. Lightner had organized the Governor's Task Force on Drinking and Driving in California. And her own advocacy group, MADD (Mothers Against Drunk Driving), was in the national spotlight. MADD's members were people who themselves had been injured or whose family members had been injured or killed in an accident involving an intoxicated driver. The organization has grown to more than three hundred chapters.[64] RID (Remove Intoxicated Drivers) and SADD (Students Against Drunk Drivers) have joined the campaign.

The citizens' groups called public attention to a major health and social problem, demanded action, and got it. Congress proclaimed one week each December to be Drunk and Drugged Awareness Week, and a Presidential Commission on Drunk Driving was formed. Candy Lightner was appointed a commissioner. The federal government attached the distribution of state highway funds to various anti-drunk-driving measures, thereby pressuring the states into putting recommendations into action. Old laws have been changed and new laws have been passed. After the ratification in 1971 of the 26th Amendment to the U.S. Constitution, which lowered the voting age to 18 years, many states lowered their minimum age requirement for the purchase and sale of alcoholic beverages. By 1983 thirty-three states had done so, but by 1987 all but one state had raised the minimum drinking age back to 21. Under New York's Civil Forfeiture Law, the government can take any car involved in a felony drunk-driving case, sell it, and give the money to the victims. Texas has a similar law.[65] Tuscarawas County in Ohio places brightly colored orange plates on cars of drivers whose licenses have been suspended for drunken driving.[66]

Other objectives of legislation have been to limit the "happy hours" during which bars serve drinks at reduced prices, to shorten hours when alcoholic beverages can be sold, to make hosts and bartenders liable for damages if their guests or patrons drink too much and become involved in an accident, to limit advertisements, and to put health warnings on bottles. Most states have increased their penalties for drunk driving to include automatic license suspension, higher minimum fines, and even mandatory jail sentences. Thus far the results of such legislation are mixed: a study carried out in Seattle, Minneapolis, and Cincinnati found that such measures did indeed lower the number of traffic deaths, while other investigations did not show positive results.[67] Nevertheless, drunken driving has achieved national attention, and even modern technology is being used in the effort to find solutions: Japanese and American technicians have come up with a device that locks the ignition system and can be unlocked only when the attached breathalyzer (which registers alcohol in the blood) indicates that the driver is sober.[68] California, Washington, Texas, Michigan, and Oregon have passed legislation authorizing its use.

SEXUAL MORALITY OFFENSES

All societies have endeavored to regulate sexual behavior. What specifically has been deemed impermissible sexual behavior has varied from society to society and from time to time. The legal regulation of sexual conduct in Anglo-American law has been greatly influenced by both the Old and the New Testament. In the Middle Ages the enforcement of laws pertaining to sexual morality was the province of clerical (church) courts. Today, to the extent that immorality is still illegal, it is the regular criminal courts that enforce such laws. Morality laws have always been controversial, whether they seek to prevent alcohol abuse or to prohibit certain forms of sexual behavior or its public display or depiction.

Sexual activity other than intercourse between spouses for the purpose of procreation has been severely penalized in many societies, and until only recently in the United States. Sexual intercourse between unmarried persons ("lewd cohabitation"), seduction of a female by promise of marriage, and all forms of "unnatural" sexual relations were serious crimes, some carrying capital sentences, as late as the nineteenth century. In 1962 the Model Penal Code proposed some important changes. Fornication and lewd cohabitation were dropped from the list of offenses, as was homosexual intercourse between consenting adults. The idea behind these changes is that the sexual relations of consenting adults should be beyond the control of the law, not only because throughout history such efforts have proved ineffective but also because the harm to society, if any, is too slight to deserve the condemnation of law. "The state's power to regulate sexual conduct ought to stop at the bedroom door or at the barn door," said the sex researcher Alfred Kinsey nearly four decades ago.[69]

Although the MPC has removed or limited sanctions for conduct among consenting adults, whenever children are subjected to sexual activities, the code retains strong prohibitions. Penalties are severe for **statutory rape** (intercourse by an adult male with an underaged female regardless of consent), deviate sexual intercourse with a child, corruption of a minor, sexual assault, and endangering the welfare of a child. Of course the recommendations of the American Law Institute are not always accepted by state legislatures. A sizable number of states have retained large portions of the old common law.

Let us now take a close look at three still existing offenses involving sexual morality: "deviate sexual intercourse by force or imposition," prostitution, and pornography.

"Deviate Sexual Intercourse by Force or Imposition"

The Model Penal Code defines "deviate sexual intercourse" as "sexual intercourse per os or per anum [by mouth or by anus] between human beings who are not husband and wife, and any form of sexual intercourse with an animal" (sec. 213.2[1]). The common law had called such sexual acts **sodomy,** after the Biblical city of Sodom, which the Lord destroyed for its wickedness, presumably because its citizens had engaged in such "deviate sexual intercourse." The common law had dealt harshly with sodomy, making it a capital offense and referring to it as *crimen innominatum*—a crime without a name. Yet other cultures, including ancient Greece, did not frown on homosexual activities. And Alfred Kinsey reminded us that homosexual (from the Greek "same") relations are common among all mammals, of which humans are but one species.[70]

The Model Penal Code subjects "deviate sexual intercourse" between two human beings to punishment only if it is accomplished by severe compulsion, or if the other person is incapable of granting consent or is a child less than ten years old. To conservatives, this model legislation is far too liberal; to liberals, it does not go far enough. Generally, liberals prefer the law not to interfere with the sexual practices of consenting adults at all. The gay and lesbian rights movements have done much to destigmatize consensual, private adult sexual relationships. Yet legislatures have been slow to respond, and the U.S. Supreme Court has taken a conservative stance as well. In 1986 it sustained a Georgia statute that criminalizes consensual sexual acts between adults of the same gender, even if they are performed in the privacy of one's home.[71]

Prostitution

Not so long ago it was a crime to be a prostitute. The law punished women for a status acquired on the basis of sexual intercourse with more than one man. Under some statutes it was not even necessary to prove that money was paid for the sexual act. As we saw in Chapter 9, the Supreme Court ruled in 1962—in a case involving the status of being a drug addict—that criminal liability can be based only on conduct, that is, on *doing* something in violation of law.[72] This decision would seem to apply to **prostitution**. Therefore, one can no longer be penalized for being a prostitute, but soliciting for sex is an act, not a status, and nearly all states make solicitation of sex for money a misdemeanor.

The Uniform Crime Reports recorded 104,100 arrests for prostitution and commercialized vice during 1988—only half as many arrests as for motor vehicle theft (which stood at 208,400).[73] A quarter of the arrested prostitutes were from 25 to 29 years old. Yet prostitution and commercialized vice reach into all age brackets, from under 15 to over 65 years of age. The number of recorded arrests for prostitution bears no relation to the actual number of prostitution events. The number would be extremely high if we were to include all acts of sexual favor granted in return for some gratuity. Even if the number were limited to straightforward cash transactions (including, nowadays, credit card transactions), there is no way of arriving at a figure. Many persons may act as prostitutes for a while and then return to legitimate lifestyles. There are part-time and full-time prostitutes, male and female prostitutes, itinerant and resident prostitutes, street hookers, and high-priced escorts who do not consider themselves to be prostitutes. Many law enforcement agencies do not relish the task of suppressing prostitution. In some jurisdictions the police have little time to spend on vice control, given the extent of violent and property crimes. Thus, when prostitutes are arrested, it is likely to be in response to demands by neighborhood groups, business establishments, or church leaders to "clean up the neighborhood." Occasionally the police find it expedient to arrest prostitutes because they may divulge information about unsolved crimes, such as narcotics distribution, theft, receiving stolen property, or organized crime.

Prostitution encompasses a variety of both acts and actors. The prostitute, female or male, is not alone in the business of prostitution. A **pimp** provides access to prostitutes and protects and exploits them, living off their proceeds. There are still some "madams" who maintain houses of prostitution, but many such places have been replaced by massage parlors and sex clubs.

And finally, there are the patrons of prostitutes, popularly called "johns." Ordinarily it is not a criminal offense to patronize a prostitute. Yet the MPC proposed to criminalize this act. This section was hotly debated before the American Law Institute. A final vote of the members favored retention of the prohibition.

Researchers have found that many prostitutes come from broken homes and poor neighborhoods and are school dropouts. Yet all social classes contribute to the prostitution hierarchy. High-priced call girls, many of them well-educated women, may operate singly or out of agencies. The television "blue channels" that broadcast after midnight in most metropolitan areas carry commercials advertising the availability of call girls, their phone numbers, and sometimes their specialties. At the next level of the prostitution hierarchy are the massage parlor prostitutes. When Shirley, a masseuse, was asked, "Do you consider yourself a prostitute?" she answered: "Yes, as well as a masseuse, and a healer, and a couple of other things."[74] One rung lower on the prostitution ladder are the "inmates" (a term used by the MPC) of the houses of prostitution, locally called bordellos, cathouses, or red-light houses.

According to people "in the life" (prostitution), the streetwalkers are the least respected class in the hierarchy. They are the "working girls" or "hookers." They are found clustered on their accustomed street corners, on thoroughfares, or in truck and bus depots, dressed in bright attire, ready to negotiate a price with any passerby. The sexual services are performed in vehicles or in nearby "hot sheet" hotel rooms. Life for these prostitutes—some of whom are transvestite males—is dangerous and grim. Self-reports suggest that many are drug addicts. Other varieties of prostitution range from the legal houses that a few counties permit to operate in Nevada to troupes of prostitutes who travel from one place of opportunity to another (work projects, farm labor camps, construction sites) and bar ("B") girls who entertain customers in cocktail lounges and make themselves available for sexual activities for a price.

Popular, political, and scientific opinions on prostitution have changed, no doubt largely because prostitution has changed. Around the turn of the century it probably was true that a large number of prostitutes had been forced into this occupation by unscrupulous men. Indeed, it was that pattern that led to the enactment of the "White Slave Traffic Act" (called the Mann Act, after the senator who proposed the bill), prohibiting the interstate transportation of females for purposes of prostitution. There is some evidence that today the need for money and a dearth of legitimate opportunities to obtain it prompts many young women and men to become prostitutes. The sex researcher Paul Gebhard found in 1969 that only 4 percent of prostitutes were forced into prostitution. More recently Jennifer James found that the majority entered "the life" because of its financial rewards.[75]

Whatever view we take of adult prostitutes as victims of a supposedly victimless criminal activity, one subgroup clearly is a victimized class: children, female and male, who are enticed and sometimes forced into prostitution, especially in large cities. Some are runaways, picked up by procurers at bus depots; some are simply "street children"; and others have been abused and molested by the adults in their lives.[76]

Pornography

Physical sexual contact is a basic component of both sodomy and prostitution. Pornography requires no contact at all. It is a crime that simply portrays sexually explicit material. Statutes in all states make it a criminal offense to produce, offer for sale, sell, distribute, or exhibit pornographic (sometimes called obscene, lewd, or lascivious) material. Federal law prohibits the transportation of such material in interstate commerce and outlaws the use of the mails, the telephone, radio, and television for the dissemination of pornographic material.[77]

The term "pornographic" is derived from the Greek *pornographos* (writing of harlots, or descriptions of the acts of harlots). The term "obscene" comes from the Latin *ob* (against, before) plus *caenum* (filth), or possibly from *obscena* (offstage). In Roman theatrical performances, disgusting and offensive parts of plays took place offstage, out of sight but not out of hearing of the audience.[78] Courts and legislators have used the two terms interchangeably, but nearly all statutes and decisions deal with pornography (with the implication of sexual arousal) rather than with obscenity (with its implication of filth).[79] Scholars generally agree that the statutes in existence appear to be addressed primarily to pornographic materials.[80]

What, then, is the contemporary meaning of **pornography**? The Model Penal Code (1962) says that a publication is pornographic (obscene or indecent) "if, considered as a whole, its predominant appeal is to prurient interests," and if, "in addition, it goes substantially beyond customary limits in describing or representing such matters" (sec. 251.4). This definition, which is full of ambiguities and problems, was to play a major role in several Supreme Court decisions.

Two presidential commissions were no more

successful in defining the term. The Commission on Obscenity and Pornography (1970) avoided defining the term and used instead the term "explicit sexual material."[81] The Attorney General's Commission on Pornography (1986) gave no definition.[82] The definition created by a British parliamentary committee in 1979 seems to describe pornography best:

> A *pornographic* representation combines two features: it has a certain function or intention, to arouse its audience sexually, and also a certain content, explicit representation of sexual materials (organs, postures, activity, etc.).[83]

This definition indicates nothing about any danger inherent in pornography. Indeed, pornography may well be called for when a psychiatrist treats a patient for impotence. Consequently, the law will step in only when pornography is exhibited or distributed in a manner calculated to produce harm. Historically, that harm has been seen as a negative effect on public morals, especially those of children. Indeed, that was the stance taken by many national and local societies devoted to the preservation of public morality in the nineteenth century. More recently the emphasis has shifted to the question of whether the availability and use of pornography produce actual, especially violent, victimization of women, children, or, for that matter, men.

The National Commission on Obscenity and Pornography in 1970 and the Attorney General's Commission on Pornography in 1986 reviewed the evidence of an association between pornography on the one hand and violence and crime on the other. The National Commission provided funding for more than eighty studies to examine public attitudes toward pornography, experiences with pornography, the association between the availability of pornography and crime rates, the experience of sex offenders with pornography, and the relation between pornography and behavior. The commission concluded that

> empirical research designed to clarify the question has found no evidence to date that exposure to explicit sexual materials plays a significant role in the causations of delinquent or criminal behavior among youth or adults. The Commission cannot conclude that exposure to erotic materials is a factor in the causation of sex crimes or sex delinquency.[84]

Between 1970 (when the National Commission reported its findings) and 1986 (when the Attorney General's Commission issued its report) hundreds of studies have been conducted on this question. For example:

• Researchers reported in 1977 that when male students were exposed to erotic stimuli, those stimuli neither inhibited nor had any effect on levels of aggression. When the same research team worked with female students, they found that mild erotic stimuli inhibited aggression and that stronger erotic stimuli increased it.[85]
• Researchers who exposed students to sexually explicit films during six consecutive weekly sessions in 1984 concluded that exposure to increasingly explicit erotic stimuli led to a decrease in both arousal responses and aggressive behavior. In short, these subjects became habituated to the pornography.[86]

After analyzing such studies, the Attorney General's Commission concluded that nonviolent and nondegrading pornography is not significantly associated with crime and aggression. It did conclude, however, that exposure to pornographic materials

> (1) leads to a greater acceptance of rape myths and violence against women; (2) results in pronounced effects when the victim is shown enjoying the use of force or violence; (3) is arousing for rapists and for some males in the general population; and (4) has resulted in sexual aggression against women in the laboratory.[87]

To feminists, these conclusions supported the call for greater restrictions on the manufacture and dissemination of pornographic material. The historian Joan Hoff has coined the term "pornerotic," meaning "any representation of persons that sexually objectifies them and is accompanied by actual or implied violence in ways designed to encourage readers or viewers that such sexual subordination of women (or children or men) is acceptable behavior or an innocuous form of sex education."[88] Hoff's definition also suggests that pornography, obscenity, and erotica may do far more than offend sensitivities. Such material may victimize not only the people who are depicted but all women (or men or children, if they are the people shown). Pornographers have been accused of promoting the exploitation, objectification, and degradation of women. Many people who call for the abolition of violent pornography argue that it also promotes violence toward women. Future legislation may need to focus on violent and violence-producing pornography, not on pornography in general.

Ultimately, defining pornographic acts subject to legal prohibition is a task for the U.S. Supreme Court. The First Amendment to the Constitution guarantees freedom of the press. In a series of decisions culminating in *Miller* v. *California*, however, the Supreme Court articulated the view that obscenity, really meaning pornography, is outside the protection of the Constitution. Following the lead of the Model Penal Code and reinterpreting its own earlier decisions, the Court announced the following standard for judging a representation as obscene or pornographic:

• The average person, applying contemporary community standards, would find that the work, taken as a whole, appeals to prurient interests.
• The work depicts or describes, in a patently offensive way, sexual conduct specifically defined by the applicable state law.
• The work, taken as a whole, lacks serious literary, artistic, political, or scientific value.[89]

While this proposed standard has the merit of being flexible enough to expand or contract its coverage as standards change over time and from place to place, its terms are so vague that they give little guidance to local law enforcement officers or to federal and state courts. In 1987 the Supreme Court addressed this problem and modified the *Miller* decision. In *Pope* v. *Illinois* the court ruled that the third aspect of

Miller (that the work has "no value") may be judged by an objective test rather than by local community standards. Justice Byron White wrote for the majority:

> The proper inquiry is not whether an ordinary person of any given community will find serious literary, artistic, political, or scientific value in the allegedly obscene material, but whether a reasonable person would find such value in the material, taken as a whole.[90]

Whether this test will make juries' tasks easier when they must decide whether a film or magazine is pornographic or obscene is still not clear.

When we examine sexual morality offenses, we note an enormous gap between the goals of law and actual behavior. As long ago as the late 1940s and early 1950s the pioneering Kinsey reports brought us evidence about this gap. According to these studies, of the total white male population in the United States,

• 69 percent had had some experience with prostitutes.
• Between 23 and 37 percent had had extramarital intercourse.
• 37 percent had had at least one homosexual experience.[91]

Among women:

• 26 percent could be expected to have extramarital intercourse by age 40.
• 19 percent had had some physical contact with other females which was deliberately and consciously, at least on the part of one of the partners, intended to be sexual.[92]

Morton Hunt noted that the frequency with which Americans were breaking legally imposed moral standards had increased significantly by the 1970s, yet far fewer American men were buying sex from prostitutes than had done so in the 1940s.[93] This finding raised the question whether the sexual revolution of the 1960s and 1970s made access to sexual partners more freely available.

AT ISSUE

The Congressional Dial-a-Porn Debate

On July 31, 1985, the Subcommittee on Criminal Law of the Committee on the Judiciary of the United States Senate held a hearing on a bill proposed by Senator Jesse Helms of North Carolina (to amend the Communications Act of 1934, Title 47, U.S. Code, Section 223), which proposed to make it a penal offense, subject to a maximum fine of $50,000 and/or six months' imprisonment, to communicate by telephone any "obscene, lewd, lascivious, filthy, or indecent message." The bill sought to curb the dial-a-porn industry. In introducing the bill Senator Helms stated, "...The people who oppose pornography—and this includes the overwhelming majority of Americans in my judgment—have no economic interest at stake. They are simply concerned about humane values and what used to be called common decency."

Following are excerpts from the testimony before the subcommittee:

Mr. Harold COLE [a constituent]. Thank you, Senator Denton and Congressman Bliley, for inviting us here today. I have consented to come as a concerned parent, also, of a 12-year-old son who was involved in a dial-a-porn incident.

I first became aware of the situation when reviewing the telephone bill from C&P Telephone Co. in January 1984. The bill reflected numerous calls to New York City, ranging from 50 to 75 cents each.

After questioning several of the family members, including several of the older children and my wife, about the calls to New York, I finally got down to 12-year-old Andy and he said that he had been calling New York to get information on what concerts would appear on HBO.

I took the answer and, later, after thinking about, I recall reading the paper about the work that Congressman Bliley was doing on the situation of dial-a-porn. I took it upon myself to call one of the numbers on the phone bill and, sure enough, as I anticipated, it was the dial-a-porn number.

I then confronted Andy with the situation and he told me what it was and was obviously very upset. He was reluctant to tell me where he had received the number. He finally said he had received it from John Hunt, and Lee Hunt who is testifying today is a close friend of the family.

I called Lee and discussed it with him and suggested that he check his phone bill. Shortly thereafter he called me back and he was amazed that there were between 50 and 60 phone calls to New York on his phone bill.

Since then, the boys have reimbursed the families for the phone calls. We have had long discussions about it and both boys are aware that Lee and I are both here today and what we are doing here today, sanctioning us being here.

REVIEW

Intoxicating substances have been used for religious, medicinal, and recreational purposes throughout history. The lifestyles of the people who use them are as varied as the drugs they favor.

Governments have repeatedly tried to prevent the abuse of these substances. The drug problem is massive, and it grows more serious every year. Heroin and cocaine in particular are associated with many crimes. A vast international criminal empire has been organized to promote the production and distribution of

To the best of my knowledge and to the best of Lee's knowledge, we have not experienced any further phone calls since that time. After that time, I had talked with other parents and I was appalled to learn from a younger brother who has a 9-year-old daughter who was 9 years old at the time—that she had gotten the number from children at school and had actually called and heard the same things that our boys had heard.

Senator DENTON. You mentioned in your written statement that the 9-year-old daughter may have been involved in making numerous calls to New York.

Mr. COLE. There were numerous calls on my brother's phone bill, also.

STATEMENT OF BARRY W. LYNN, LEGISLATIVE COUNSEL, AMERICAN CIVIL LIBERTIES UNION

Mr. LYNN. Thank you very much. With all due respect, Mr. Chairman, of your own sponsorship of this bill, frankly, efforts to regulate cable television's content or the content of telephone communication are, in our judgment, two more very significant steps in a disturbing rebirth of censorship in the United States.

* * *

I do think that ultimately the answer as far as the values that you are talking about is for people like yourself, for broadcasters like Pat Robertson, the Christian Broadcasting Network, and other people who believe in them and who have the facilities to promote these values to get out there and criticize the images in pornography.

They are exercising the best of first amendment values when they do that, and that forms a competition, a competing idea, which, if we believe in the first amendment, may well drive out "wrong" ideas.

You know, I do not just look at this thing theoretically, Senator. I have two kids, a dog and station wagon. I am a very straight-laced person in many, many ways. But to suggest that the remedy is to abridge any of the free expression guarantees of the Constitution is to set forth on a very dangerous path.

The proposed bill did not pass. What could criminologists have added to the hearings? There was scant scientific evidence before the subcommittee with little apparent effect. The debate centered on the First Amendment's guarantee of free speech. Five years later the dial-a-porn industry has grown into a multimillion-dollar business. Every telephone in America can receive "pornographic" messages for a fee.

Source: Cable-Porn and Dial-a-Porn Control Act. Hearing before the Subcommittee on Criminal Law of the Committee on the Judiciary. United States Senate, Ninety-Ninth Congress, First Session, July 31, 1985. Serial No. J.–99–46. (Washington, D.C.: U.S. Government Printing Office, 1986), pp. 3, 95, 96, 97.

drugs. Efforts of law enforcement and health agencies to control the drug problem take the forms of international cooperation in stemming drug trafficking, treatment of addicts, education of the public, and arrest and incarceration of offenders. Some observers, comparing the drug problem with the wide evasion of the prohibition amendment and the consequent rise in crime, believe that drugs should be legalized.

Legalization of alcoholic beverages, however, has not solved all problems related to alcohol. The abuse of alcohol has been reliably linked to violence, and the incidence of drunk driving has increased so alarmingly that citizen groups have formed to combat the problem.

The legal regulation of sexual conduct has undergone striking changes in recent decades. Many sexual "offenses" once categorized as capital crimes no longer bother our society. In this sphere, research has done much to influence public opinion and consequently legisla-

tion. Pornography, however, remains a hotly debated issue.

KEY TERMS

money laundering
pimp
pornography

prostitution
sodomy
statutory rape

NOTES

1. United States v. Montoya de Hernandez, 473 U.S. 531 (1985).

2. Richard P. Retting, Manuel J. Torres, and Gerald R. Garrett, *Manny: A Criminal-Addict's Story* (Boston: Houghton Mifflin, 1977).

3. "The Drug Gangs," *Newsweek*, March 28, 1988, p. 20.

4. Mark D. Merlin, *On the Trail of the Ancient Opium Poppy* (Rutherford, N.J.: Fairleigh Dickinson University Press, 1984).

5. Howard Abadinsky, *Drug Abuse: An Introduction* (Chicago: Nelson Hall, 1989), pp. 30–31, 54.

6. Michael D. Lyman, *Narcotics and Crime Control* (Springfield, Ill.: Charles C Thomas, 1987), p. 8.

7. W. Z. Guggenheim, "Heroin: History and Pharmacology," *International Journal of the Addictions* 2 (1967): 328.

8. Abadinsky, *Drug Abuse*, p. 52.

9. Ibid., p. 56.

10. Lyman, *Narcotics and Crime Control*, p. 10.

11. Public Law 100-690, of November 18, 1988; 102 Stat. 4187.

12. Lloyd D. Johnston, Patrick M. O'Malley, and Jerald G. Bachman, *National Trends in Drug Use and Related Factors Among American High School Students and Young Adults, 1975–1986,* for U.S. Department of Health and Human Services, National Institute of Drug Abuse (Washington, D.C.: U.S. Government Printing Office, 1987), pp. 48, 179–181.

13. U.S. Department of Health and Human Services, National Institute on Drug Abuse, *National Household Survey on Drug Abuse: Population Estimates, 1985* (Washington, D.C.: U.S. Government Printing Office, 1987), pp. 10–17, 46–49.

14. Lyman, *Narcotics and Crime Control*, p. 21.

15. National Institute on Drug Abuse, *National Household Survey*, p. 9.

16. Abadinsky, *Drug Abuse*, p. 107; Lyman, *Narcotics and Crime Control*, pp. 33–34.

17. Robert J. Michaels, "The Market for Heroin Before and After Legalization," in *Dealing with Drugs*, ed. Ronald Hamowy, pp. 311–318 (Lexington, Mass.: Lexington Books, 1987).

18. For a summary of psychiatric approaches, see Marie Nyswander, *The Drug Addict as a Patient* (New York: Grune & Stratton, 1956), chap. 4.

19. Richard Cloward and Lloyd Ohlin, *Delinquency and Opportunity* (New York: Free Press, 1960), pp. 178–186; see also Jeffrey A. Fagan, "The Social Organization of Drug Use and Drug Dealing Among Urban Gangs," *Criminology* 27 (1989), pp. 633–669.

20. D. F. Musto, "The History of Legislative Control over Opium, Cocaine, and Their Derivatives," in Hamowy, *Dealing with Drugs.*

21. Marsha Rosenbaum, *Women on Heroin* (New Brunswick, N.J.: Rutgers University Press, 1981), pp. 14–15; Jeannette Covington, "Theoretical Explanations of Race Differences in Heroin Use," in *Advances in Crimi-*

nological Theory, vol. 2, ed. William S. Laufer and Freda Adler (New Brunswick: N.J.: Transaction Books).

22. Freda Adler, Arthur D. Moffett, Frederick B. Glaser, John C. Ball, and Diana Horwitz, *A Systems Approach to Drug Treatment* (Philadelphia: Dorrance, 1974).

23. Erich Goode, *Drugs in American Society* (New York: Basic Books, 1972); also Ned Polsky, *Hustlers, Beats, and Others* (Chicago: Aldine, 1967).

24. Norman E. Zinberg, "The Use and Misuse of Intoxicants: Factors in the Development of Controlled Abuse," in Hamowy, *Dealing with Drugs*, p. 262.

25. Abadinsky, *Drug Abuse*, p. 53.

26. National Institute on Drug Abuse, "Cocaine Use in America," *Prevention Networks*, April 1986, pp. 1–10.

27. Patricia A. Adler, *Wheeling and Dealing: An Ethnography of an Upper-Level Drug Dealing and Smuggling Community* (New York: Columbia University Press, 1985).

28. Abadinsky, *Drug Abuse*, p. 83; see also Jeffrey A. Fagan, "Initiation into Crack and Powdered Cocaine: A Tale of Two Epidemics," *Contemporary Drug Problems* 16 (1989): 579–618; Jeffrey A. Fagan, Joseph G. Weis, and Y. T. Cheng, "Drug Use and Delinquency Among Inner City Youth," *Journal of Drug Issues* 20 (1990): 349–400.

29. *New York Times*, July 13, 1989, pp. A1, B3.

30. James Inciardi, "Heroin Use of Street Crime," *Crime and Delinquency* 25 (1979): 335–346; Bruce D. Johnson, Paul J. Goldstein, Edward Preble, James Schmeidler, Douglas S. Lyston, Barry Spunt, and Thomas Miller, *Taking Care of Business: The Economics of Crime by Heroin Abusers* (Lexington, Mass.: D. C. Heath, 1985); James Inciardi, *The War on Drugs: Heroin, Cocaine, Crime, and Public Policy* (Palo Alto, Calif.: Mayfield, 1986); Eric Wish and Bruce Johnson, "The Impact of Substance Abuse on Criminal Careers," in *Criminal Careers and Career Criminals*, ed. Alfred Blumstein, Jacqueline Cohen, Jeffrey A. Roth, and Christy A. Visher, pp. 52–58 (Washington, D.C.: National Academy Press, 1986).

31. Christopher Innes, *Drug Use and Crime*, for Bureau of Justice Statistics (Washington, D.C.: U.S. Government Printing Office, 1988).

32. Stephanie Greenberg and Freda Adler, "Crime and Addiction: An Empirical Analysis of the Literature, 1920–1973," *Contemporary Drug Problems*, Summer 1974, pp. 221–270.

33. George Speckart and M. Douglas Anglin found that criminal records preceded drug use; see their "Narcotics Use and Crime: An Overview of Recent Research Advances," *Contemporary Drug Problems* 13, no. 4 (Winter 1986): 741–769, and "Narcotics and Crime: A Causal Modeling Approach," *Journal of Quantitative Criminology* 2 (1986): 3–28. See also Cheryl Carpenter, Barry Glassner, Bruce D. Johnson, and Julia Louglin, *Kids, Drugs, and Crime* (Lexington, Mass.: D. C. Heath, 1988).

34. David N. Nurco, Thomas E. Hanlon, Timothy W. Kinlock, and Karen R. Duszynski, "Differential Criminal Patterns of Narcotics Addicts over an Addiction Career," *Criminology* 26 (August 1988): 407–423; M. Douglas Anglin and George Speckart, "Narcotics Use and Crime: A Multisample, Multimethod Analysis," *Criminology* 26 (May 1988): 197–233; M. Douglas Anglin and Yin-ing Hser, "Addicted Women and Crime," *Criminology* 25 (May 1987): 359–397.

35. Paul Goldstein, "Drugs and Violent Crime," in *Pathways to Criminal Violence*, ed. Neil Alan Weiner and Marvin E. Wolfgang, pp. 16–48 (Newbury Park, Calif.: Sage, 1989); *Ebony*, August 1989, p. 99.

36. This section is based on James A. Inciardi, *The War on Drugs* (Palo Alto, Calif.: Mayfield, 1986).

37. Royal Canadian Mounted Police, *National Drug Intelligence Estimate* (Ottawa, 1988), p. 47.

38. Royal Canadian Mounted Police, *The Illicit Drug Situation in the United States and Canada* (Ottawa, 1984–1986), p. 19.

39. United Nations, Commission on Narcotic Drugs, *Comprehensive Review of the Activities of the United Nations Fund for Drug Abuse Control in 1985*, E/CN.7/1986/CRP.4 (Febru-

ary 4, 1986). See also Elaine Sciolino, "U.N. Report Links Drugs, Arms, and Terror," *New York Times,* January 12, 1987.

40. John Warner, "Terrorism and Drug Trafficking: A Lethal Partnership," *Security Management* 28 (June 1984): 44–46.

41. See Mark Moore, *Drug Trafficking* (Washington, D.C.: National Institute of Justice, 1988).

42. Adler et al., *Systems Approach to Drug Treatment.*

43. Abadinsky, *Drug Abuse,* p. 170.

44. Ibid., p. 171.

45. Harold I. Hendler and Richard C. Stephens, "The Addict Odyssey: From Experimentation to Addiction," *International Journal of the Addictions* 12 (1977): 25–42.

46. Troy Duster, *The Legislation of Morality: Law, Drugs, and Moral Judgment* (New York: Free Press, 1970), p. 192.

47. Dan Waldorf, "Natural Recovery from Opiate Addiction," *Journal of Drug Issues* 13 (Spring 1983): 237–280.

48. James B. Bakalar and Lester Grinspoon, *Drug Control in a Free Society* (New York: Cambridge University Press, 1984); Lyman, *Narcotics and Crime Control.*

49. James B. Jacobs, *Drunk Driving: An American Dilemma* (Chicago: University of Chicago Press, 1989), p. xiii.

50. Johnson et al., *National Trends in Drug Use.*

51. James Inciardi, *Reflections on Crime* (New York: Holt, Rinehart & Winston, 1978), pp. 8–10.

52. U.S. Department of Justice, *Report to the Nation on Crime and Justice,* 2d ed. (Washington, D.C.: U.S. Government Printing Office, 1988), p. 50.

53. Marvin E. Wolfgang, *Patterns in Criminal Homicide* (New York: Wiley, 1966).

54. P. Linquist, "Criminal Homicides in Northern Sweden, 1970–81: Alcohol Intoxication, Alcohol Abuse, and Mental Disease," *International Journal of Law and Psychiatry* 8 (1986): 19–37.

55. D. Mayfield, "Alcoholism, Alcohol Intoxification, and Assaultive Behavior," *Diseases of the Nervous System* 37 (1976): 288–291; C. K. Meyer, T. Magendanz, B. C. Kieselhorst, and S. G. Chapman, *A Social-Psychological Analysis of Police Assaults* (Norman: Bureau of Government Research, University of Oklahoma, April 1978).

56. S. D. Johnson, L. Gibson, and R. Linden, "Alcohol and Rape in Winnipeg, 1966–1975," *Journal of Studies on Alcohol* 39 (1987): 1877–1894; Menachem Amir, *Patterns of Forcible Rape* (Chicago: University of Chicago Press, 1971), p. 99.

57. D. H. Coleman and M. A. Straus, "Alcohol Abuse and Family Violence," in *Alcohol, Drug Abuse, and Aggression,* ed E. Gottheil, K. A. Druley, T. E. Skoloda, and H. M. Waxman (Springfield, Ill.: Charles C Thomas, 1983). See also C. J. Hamilton and J. J. Collins, "The Role of Alcohol in Wife-Beating and Child Abuse: A Review of the Literature," in *Drinking and Crime: Perspectives on the Relationship Between Alcohol Consumption and Criminal Behavior* (New York: Guiford, 1981). For discussion of the presence of alcohol in victims of homicide, see R. A. Goodman, J. A. Mercy, R. Loya, M. L. Rosenberg, J. C. Smith, M. H. Allen, L. Vargas, and R. Kotts, "Alcohol Use and Interpersonal Violence—Alcohol Detected in Homicide Victims," *American Journal of Public Health* 76 (1986): 144–149.

58. See James J. Collins, "Alcohol and Interpersonal Violence," in Weiner and Wolfgang, *Pathways to Criminal Violence.* For a comprehensive review of aggression and drug abuse, see Jeffrey A. Fagan, "Intoxication and Aggression," in *Crime and Justice: An Annual Review of Research,* vol. 13, *Drugs and Crime,* ed. James Q. Wilson and Michael Tonry (Chicago: University of Chicago Press, 1990).

59. K. E. Leonard, "Alcohol and Human Physical Aggression," *Aggression* 2 (1983): 77–101.

60. C. M. Steele and L. Southwick, "Alcohol and Social Behavior I: The Psychology of Drunken Excess," *Journal of Personality and Social Psychology* 48 (1985): 18–34.

61. S. Ahlstrom-Laakso, "European Drinking

Habits: A Review of Research and Time Suggestions for Conceptual Integration of Findings," in *Cross-Cultural Approaches to the Study of Alcohol*, ed. M. W. Everett, J. O. Waddell, and D. Heath (The Hague: Mouton, 1976).

62. Lawrence A. Greenfeld, *Drunk Driving*, for Bureau of Justice Statistics (Washington, D.C.: U.S. Government Printing Office, February 1988), p. 1; William K. Stevens, "Deaths from Drunken Driving Increase," *New York Times*, October 29, 1987, p. 12; U.S. Department of Justice, Federal Bureau of Investigation, *Crime in the United States, 1988* (Washington, D.C.: U.S. Government Printing Office, 1989), p. 168.

63. Joseph R. Gusfield, "The Control of Drinking-Driving in the United States: A Period of Transition," in *Social Control of the Drinking Driver*, ed. Michael D. Lawrence, John R. Snortum, and Franklin E. Zimring (Chicago: University of Chicago Press, 1988).

64. Jacobs, *Drunk Driving*, p. xvi.

65. Faye Silas, "Gimme the Keys," *American Bar Association Journal* 71 (1985): 36.

66. *Newsweek*, December 21, 1987.

67. Fred Heinzelmann, *Jailing Drunk Drivers* (Washington, D.C.: National Institute of Justice, 1984); Gerald Wheeler and Rodney Hissong, "Effects of Criminal Sanctions on Drunk Drivers: Beyond Incarceration," *Crime and Delinquency* 34 (1988): 29–42; Richard Speezlman, "Issues in the Rise of Compulsion in California's Drinking Drive Treatment System," in *Punishment and Treatment for Driving Under the Influence of Alcohol and Other Drugs*, ed. M. Valverius, pp. 151–180 (Stockholm: International Committee on Alcohol, Drugs, and Traffic Safety, 1985); Dale E. Bergen and John R. Snortum, "A Structural Model of Drinking and Driving: Alcohol Consumption, Social Norms, and Moral Commitments," *Criminology* 24 (1986): 139–152.

68. *The Effectiveness of the Ignition Interlock Device in Reducing Recidivism Among Driving Under the Influence Cases* (Honolulu: Criminal Justice Commission, 1987).

69. Personal communication, 1951.

70. Alfred C. Kinsey, Wardel B. Pomeroy, and Clyde E. Martin, *Sexual Behavior in the Human Male* (Philadelphia: W. B. Saunders, 1948), p. 613.

71. Bowers v. Hardwick, 478 U.S. 186; *reh'g denied*, 478 U.S. 1039 (1986).

72. Robinson v. California, 370 U.S. 660 (1962).

73. Uniform Crime Reports, 1988.

74. Jeremiah Lowney, Robert W. Winslow, and Virginia Winslow, *Deviant Reality—Alternative World Views*, 2d ed. (Boston: Allyn & Bacon, 1981), p. 156.

75. Paul Gebhard, "Misconceptions About Female Prostitution," *Medical Aspects of Human Sexuality* 3 (1969): 28–30; Jennifer James, "Prostitutes and Prostitution," in *Deviants: Voluntary Action in a Hostile World*, ed. Edward Sagarin and F. Montamino (Glenview, Ill.: Scott, Foresman, 1977), p. 384.

76. Daniel S. Campagna and Donald L. Poffenberger, *The Sexual Trafficking in Children* (Dover, Mass.: Auburn House, 1988); Jeffrey J. Haugard and N. Dickon Reppucci, *The Sexual Abuse of Children* (San Francisco: Jossey-Bass, 1988); Edward Donnerstein, Daniel Linz, and Steven Penrod, *The Question of Pornography* (New York: Free Press, 1987).

77. See Gerhard O. W. Mueller, *Legal Regulation of Sexual Conduct* (New York: Oceana, 1961), Tables 9A and 9B, pp. 139–147. Note, however, that some states have amended their statutes since these data were collected.

78. Donnerstein et al., *Question of Pornography*, p. 147.

79. Joel Feinberg, "Pornography and Criminal Law," in *Pornography and Censorship*, ed. D. Copp and S. Wendell (New York: Prometheus, 1979).

80. See Donnerstein et al., *Question of Pornography*, chap. 7; and Gordon Hawkins and Franklin E. Zimring, *Pornography in a Free Society* (Cambridge: Cambridge University Press, 1988), p. 26.

81. *The Report of the Commission on Obscenity and Pornography* (Washington, D.C.: U.S. Government Printing Office, 1970).

82. U.S. Department of Justice, Attorney Gen-

eral's Commission on Pornography, *Final Report*, vols. 1 and 2 (Washington, D.C.: U.S. Government Printing Office, 1986).

83. Home Office, *Report of the Committee on Obscenity and Film Censorship* (London: Her Majesty's Stationery Office, 1979), p. 103.

84. *Report of the Commission on Obscenity and Pornography.*

85. R. A. Barron and P. A. Bell, "Sexual Arousal and Aggression by Males: Effects of Type of Erotic Stimuli and Prior Provocation," *Journal of Personality and Social Psychology* 35 (1977): 79–87.

86. Dolf Zillman and Jennings Bryant, "Pornography, Sexual Callousness, and the Trivialization of Rape," *Journal of Communication* 32 (1984): 10–21.

87. Donnerstein et al., *Question of Pornography; Final Report of the Attorney General's Commis-*

sion on Pornography (Nashville: Rutledge Hill Press, 1986), esp. pp. 38–47.

88. Joan Hoff, "Why Is There No History of Pornography?" in *For Adult Users Only: The Dilemma of Violent Pornography*, ed. Susan Gubar and Joan Hoff (Bloomington: Indiana University Press, 1989), p. 18.

89. Miller v. California, 413 U.S. 15 (1973).

90. Pope v. Illinois, 107 S.Ct. 1918 (1987).

91. Kinsey et al., *Sexual Behavior in the Human Male.*

92. Alfred C. Kinsey, Wardel B. Pomeroy, Clyde E. Martin, and Paul H. Gebhard, *Sexual Behavior in the Human Female* (Philadelphia: W. B. Saunders, 1953), p. 453.

93. Morton Hunt, *Sexual Behavior in the 1970s* (New York: Dell, 1974).

PART IV

A CRIMINOLOGICAL APPROACH TO THE CRIMINAL JUSTICE SYSTEM

When a crime appears to have been committed and authorities, such as the police or prosecutors, have been notified, a legal apparatus is set in motion. This apparatus, called the criminal justice system, and its processes to deal with offenders have come under close criminological scrutiny. Extensive research is available, which makes it possible to understand the system, its component parts, and its processes. This research provides the basis for efforts to render the system more rational, cost-beneficial, and humane (Chapter 14). The law enforcement component of the criminal justice system is by far the most visible and costly one, because it employs the largest proportion of all personnel working in the entire system. The operations and tactics of the police, the images and perceptions of law enforcement, and its successes and failures are explained in terms of contemporary criminological research (Chapter 15). Similarly, the functions and tasks of the judiciary—the second component of the criminal justice system—are examined in light of extant criminological studies (Chapter 16). Much blame for America's high crime rate is bestowed, justly as well as unjustly, on the third component of the criminal justice system: corrections (Chapter 17). Corrections include institutional corrections (namely, prisons and jails), juvenile institutions, and community-based facilities, as well as noninstitutional correctional responses, such as fines, community service sentences, probation, and parole. Increasingly, mixtures of such correctional devices, some of them rather punitive, are being used. The functioning, success, and failure of all the correctional responses are explained on the basis of research findings.

14

PROCESSES AND DECISIONS

The great novelist Franz Kafka, in one of his most famous works, *The Trial*, portrayed the justice process with a profound understanding of the frustrations and despair experienced by a person caught in its machinery. One cannot know what will be the next step or the one after that. Escape doors seem blocked, a step ahead is prevented by a step that one should not have taken earlier. No one has a map to chart the way. One can only submit without hope to a fate that seems arbitrary.

Are today's criminal defendants in America as bewildered and frustrated as Kafka's defendant three-quarters of a century ago, in his native Czechoslovakia? As we explore the criminal justice system in the United States, Kafka will be much on our minds, because many aspects of the U.S. criminal justice process are bewildering to the uninitiated. However, as criminologists have focused their research attention on criminal justice, the system and the interdependency of its components became better understood. Criminology has revealed that the process has a logical structure, but one that can be tolerant of bias, arbitrariness, mistake, and caprice. Moreover, in many large and congested urban areas this system of criminal justice suffers from delay, overcrowding, indifference, and budget shortfall.

THE STAGES OF THE CRIMINAL JUSTICE PROCESS

Until the 1960s criminal justice procedures from arrest to conviction were generally not seen as comprising an orderly process. The various sectors and procedures of the criminal justice system seemed to exist in isolation. Only in the 1960s was criminal justice seen as a system with a process, similar to a production system in the world of industry. In 1967 the President's Commission on Law Enforcement and Criminal Justice first depicted the criminal justice system as an apparatus by which a product is produced in an orderly process.[1] Some people regard that product as justice, others as the reduction of crime; still others recognize both as the system's products.

WINDOW TO THE WORLD

Our Criminal Justice Heritage

The American criminal justice process is largely what the history of England and the United States has made it. Its basic structure was determined in A.D. 1215, when trial by jury became a right in England as a result of the Magna Charta. By the sixteenth century the criminal justice process there had most of the features we find in it today. Even in early sixteenth-century England, for example, legal authorities carefully examined the facts. The suspect was arrested when the authorities were presented with a good deal of evidence indicating that this person was implicated in the crime (today called probable cause). The defendant was entitled to bail and to a trial by jury. Witnesses played a key role in the process. These features are still found intact in twentieth-century American felony cases. In Table 14.1 we have contrasted a

sample common law (English) proceeding with a comparable case of roughly the same era, processed under the continental European rules of procedure. In Germany, the outcome of a case depended primarily on a confession extracted from the defendant. Judges, not a jury, convicted the defendant when they had no doubt that they had learned the absolute truth. The absolute truth, so it was believed, could be known only through the defendant's confession extracted by torture. Only under torture could a person be trusted to tell the truth. Torture was used well into the nineteenth century to extract confessions.

Today's continental criminal procedure still aims at reaching the ultimate truth, though torture is no longer an official practice. The American system of criminal justice is not interested in establishing the ultimate truth; in fact, it places some restrictions on the truth-finding process, for example, by rules that prevent the proof of some facts and that restrict witnesses to testimony relevant to the charges contained in the indictment. Continental procedure still makes little use of ordinary citizens in the criminal justice process, whereas American law maintains the right to trial by jury, and in felony cases to indictment by a grand jury. It is difficult for an

accused person to escape conviction in a continental trial. It is far easier for a defendant in a common law country, such as the United States, to be acquitted. The premise of the common law has always been: Better that ten guilty defendants be acquitted than that one innocent defendant be convicted. Mr. Comport, who was acquitted in England, may well have been guilty, and Father Johann, who was convicted and burned at the stake, may well have been innocent. This is not to suggest that contemporary continental courts convict the innocent at a higher rate than ours do under common law procedure. Rather, our system may acquit more defendants who may in fact be guilty than does the continental process. Our historical examples simply point to different approaches, different concerns, and different rules. The rules established in the United States include the presumption of innocence, the right not to be arrested except upon establishment of probable cause that one has been involved in crime, the right to bail, the right to be confronted by one's accusers, the right to have fellow citizens determine one's guilt or innocence, protection against cruel and unusual punishments, and other constitutional guarantees.

TABLE 14.1   *ENGLISH AND GERMAN MURDER CASES, FIFTEENTH AND SIXTEENTH CENTURIES*

	ENGLAND (common law)	GERMANY (continental law)
Crime	Murder	Attempted Murder
Place	Crowhurst, in a forest	A count's castle
County	Surrey	Katzenelnbogen
Date of crime	Wednesday, August 28, 1532	Week after New Year's, 1474
Facts	Grame, a collier (charcoal maker), is reported missing in the woods. It is rumored that Grame had bragged about cash in his wallet.	The priest Father Johann serves cloudy sacramental wine to the countess. Concerned, she questions him. He gives an unsatisfactory answer. She drinks it anyway, falls ill next day. The priest flees to Cologne.
Criminal justice system enters: investigation of the crime	Justice of the Peace Sir John Gaynesford takes charge of investigation. Body is found, throat cut. Murder is indicated. Sir John summons witnesses, takes them to scene, questions them. All evidence points to one Benson as perpetrator. Possible motive: robbery.	
Arrest or custody?	Sir John puts Benson into stocks (jail), warns material witness (one Comport) not to leave jurisdiction. Sir John hears further witnesses. Benson and Comport both implicated Sir John takes Benson before Privy Council, Westminster. Benson is held in Tower of London. Further witnesses are examined by Sir John and Privy Council. Comport is sent to Tower for detention.	The fiscal (prosecutor) of the church in Cologne issues a clerical (church) warrant for the arrest of Father Johann on the charge of attempted murder. He is arrested and subjected to torture. He confesses his guilt and implicates others, who, he says, acted from political motives. He repeats his confession after torture, but recants the implication of others.
Trial	Summer assizes. Effort to start a trial. Jury of 14 impaneled. Comport and Benson plead not guilty and are released on bail, briefly. Both defendants then in custody of sheriff, pending trial. King's chief counsel prepares case for trial, one year after crime. By writ of mandamus, case is called for trial at Court of King's Bench. Comport and Benson bailed again. Apparently Comport was acquitted. No report on Benson.	Trial begins six months after crime, before a clerical court composed of major jurists and professors. Father Johann found guilty, defrocked on the spot, denied confession, burned at the stake.

Note: The German crime of attempted murder did not exist in England at the time. Attempts were not punishable as such (W. C. Turner, *Kenny's Outlines of Criminal Law*, 17th ed. [Cambridge: Cambridge University Press, 1958], p. 90). In England the act of serving poisoned wine would have been regarded as an assault. If the act of Father Johann had been regarded as an attempt to kill his sovereign's wife, he would have been charged with the capital offense of treason even in England.

Source: William B. Robinson, "Murder at Crowhurst: A Case Study in Early Tudor Law Enforcement," *Criminal Justice History* 9 (1988): 31–62; Max Peter Maass, *Halsgericht* (Darmstadt: Siegfried Toeche-Mittler, 1968), pp. 78–99; photo p. 27.

FIGURE 14.1   The flow of the process in the criminal justice system

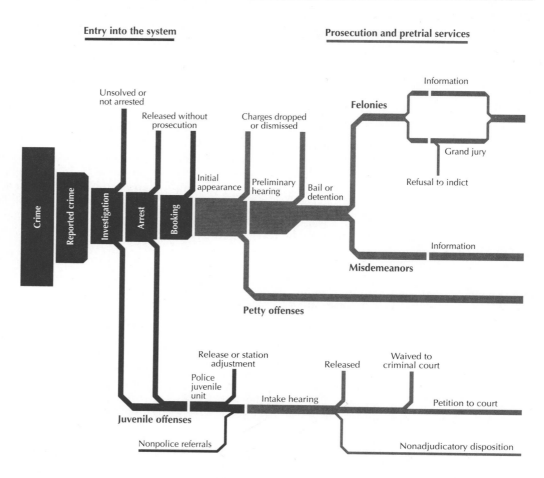

Note: this chart gives a simplified view of caseflow through the criminal justice system. Prodecures vary among jurisdictions. The weights of the lines are not intended to show the actual size of caseloads.

Source: Adapted from the President's Commission on Law Enforcement and Administration of Justice, *The Challenge of Crime in a Free Society*, 1967, pp. 8–9. In U.S. Department of Justice, Bureau of Justice Statistics, *Report to the Nation on Crime and Justice*, 2d ed. (Washington, D.C.: U.S. Government Printing Office, 1988), pp. 56–57.

The President's Commission depicts the criminal justice system as composed of five phases. Every criminal case may potentially flow through all five phases, though most do not, as we shall see.

In the first phase, called "entry into the system," citizens play an important role by bringing criminal events to the attention of the police. The police, by investigating the case and identifying a suspect, play a crucial role. The judiciary participates by issuing search and arrest warrants.

The second phase, prosecution and pretrial services, is dominated by prosecutors, who prepare the charges; grand juries, who indict defendants; and judges, who conduct a series of hearings, including the initial appearance of an arrested person at court and a preliminary hearing.

The third phase, adjudication, begins with

FIGURE 14.1   Continued

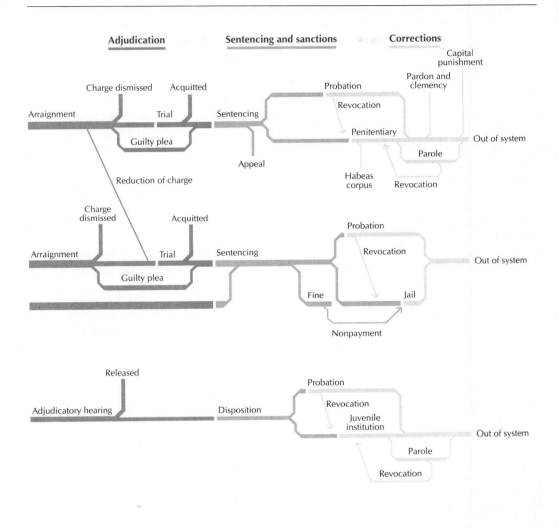

the arraignment, at which the officially accused person pleads to (answers) the indictment or information (formal charges) against him or her, and ends with a judgment of guilty or not guilty. This phase is conducted by a judge, with or without a jury. The prosecutor, representing the state and the people, and the defense lawyer play the most active roles in this phase.

The fourth phase consists of sentencing and sanctions. In most cases, in most states, jurors do not participate in sentencing. The judge alone imposes the sentence, usually after hearing a presentence investigation (PSI) report pre-

pared by a probation officer. Prosecutors, defense lawyers, and defendants have their say, and in some states victims as well.

The fifth and final phase, corrections, is in the hands of the executive branch of government, whose department of corrections executes the sentence imposed by the court. When called upon to do so, however, courts do play a considerable role in probing compliance with law in the correctional phase.

The system flowchart devised by the President's Commission (Figure 14.1) indicates four different paths through the system. The first path is that for major crimes, or felonies; the second is for minor crimes, or misdemeanors. They differ in some respects; misdemeanors normally require no grand jury indictment and no trial by jury, and the sanctions imposed are jail sentences of one year or less or fines rather than imprisonment for more than a year. A third path is for petty offenses, with summary proceedings resulting in minor sanctions, usually fines. The fourth path is that for juveniles. It resembles the paths for adults in many respects, except that the proceedings are less formal and rarely include juries.

As the flowchart indicates, the various paths through the criminal justice system and the juvenile justice system do not end at a single exit; they lead to many exits at various way stations. Thus an offender's path through the system is not inexorable, predestined. The direction an offender's path takes depends on decisions made by people all along the way, including the offender. Michael R. Gottfredson and Don M. Gottfredson point out that decision making throughout the system results in a very large attrition rate. Many more crimes are reported than are adjudicated; many more offenders are arrested than are ultimately sent to prison.[2] In this chapter we shall examine the consequences

of decision making at the various stages of the process.

Entry into the System

Decisions by victims and witnesses   Intake into the criminal justice system begins when a crime becomes known to the police, as Figure 14.1 indicates. As we discussed in Chapter 2, this figure does not correspond with the actual amount of crimes committed. First, many events are reported as crimes which are not crimes—lost wallets are thought to have been stolen, automobiles are reported as stolen when in fact they have been abandoned for purposes of collecting insurance benefits. Such reported events tend to inflate crime statistics. Second, many crimes that are committed are not reported to the police (see Chapter 2). Thus, victims may fail to report a rape for a variety of reasons: 35 percent claim to consider it a "private/personal matter," 18 percent are of the opinion that nothing can be done because they cannot prove they have been victimized, and 16 percent fear reprisals. Decisions to invoke the criminal justice process are related to the seriousness of the crime, a positive attitude toward

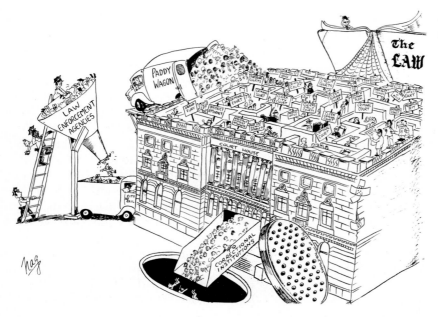

A simplified guide to the Criminal Justice System

the police, the sex of the victim, and other assorted factors.[3]

Decisions by the police   Once information about a possible crime has come to the attention of the police, a decision has to be made whether to investigate the case to determine if a crime has been committed and who committed it. The police cannot possibly investigate every complaint. Under the pressure of heavy caseloads, the police place primary emphasis on the investigation of major crimes. Ordinary petty larcenies are rarely investigated because of the sheer bulk of the cases and the shortage of investigators. Other factors as well are in the minds of police when they decide whether to make an arrest or to seek an arrest warrant. They consider, for example, public ambivalence about the significance of a given statute, the probability that a witness will or will not cooperate with the police, and whether an arrest may be too harsh a response. The police have alternatives to arrest, ranging from outright release to release with a citation to release of a youngster into the custody of parents or guardians.[4]

What are the legal criteria that determine when and whether a suspect can be taken into the criminal justice system? When may the system do something to or about a suspect? There are legal criteria for processing a suspect from one phase to the next in the criminal justice process. The Constitution, as interpreted by the Supreme Court, provides some of these criteria.

The Constitution states that nobody may be "seized" (taken into the criminal justice process) except on a warrant issued on the basis of probable cause of having committed a crime. For almost two centuries the **probable cause** requirement was deemed to establish the point at which potential guilt is clear enough to take a person into custody. Ideally the probable cause determination is made by a judge or magistrate on the basis of the testimony of witnesses (including the police) delivered under oath that a given suspect has committed a given crime. In practice, the probable cause decision more frequently is made by a law enforcement officer at the scene of the crime. Neither magistrates who issue warrants of arrest nor police officers who make an arrest without a warrant are guided by any precise standard of probable cause. The Supreme Court has ruled that the police have probable cause to take a suspect into custody when

> the facts and circumstances within their knowledge and of which they [have] reasonable trustworthy information [are] sufficient to warrant a prudent man in believing that the [suspect] had committed or was committing an offense.[5]

This definition, relying as it does on such vague terms as "reasonable trustworthy information" and "prudent man," lacks precision. Nevertheless, arrests made without probable cause, or not resting on a warrant issued on sworn testimony before a judge and based on a determination of probable cause, are considered to be unreasonable seizures of the person, and so in violation of the Fourth Amendment. Evidence seized in the course of such an illegal arrest can be barred from trial. This is called the **exclusionary rule.** Its intent is to deter the police from engaging in illegal practices and to keep the courts from condoning such conduct. The Supreme Court ruled in 1969, in *Mapp* v. *Ohio*, that all courts in the country must apply the exclusionary rule.[6] This ruling has been hailed by civil libertarians, who view it as a necessary safeguard against police misconduct, and strongly attacked by conservatives, who argue that the rule is an arbitrary measure that "handcuffs" the police. These two positions resemble the fundamental issues that are balanced in a Fourth Amendment analysis, that is, the need for effective law enforcement versus individual rights and liberties. Conservatives call for unhampered law enforcement and liberals ask for the assurance of rights. Research, on the whole, establishes that law enforcement has not been seriously hindered by the exclusionary rule. On the contrary, the result has been improved legal training for law enforcement officers, and consequently, some argue, improved police behavior.[7]

Recent Supreme Court decisions have strengthened police powers—unduly so, some critics say. Faced with mounting public concern over street crime in the 1960s, the Supreme Court was under pressure to legitimize prudent police action for the purpose of preventing a specific crime about to be committed, even when an officer had no probable cause to make an arrest. In 1968 the Supreme Court acknowledged the propriety of police intervention when evidence against a suspect fell short of probable cause. If a police officer has **reasonable suspicion** that a person might be engaged in the commission of a crime, the officer is authorized to stop such a person, to ask questions, and to frisk him or her, so as to make sure that the suspect is not armed and dangerous to the officer.[8]

In some circumstances law enforcement officers can intervene even short of reasonable suspicion. The highest court of New York, the New York Court of Appeals, stated in the case of *People* v. *de Bour* that police officers have the right and duty to approach a person for purposes of making an inquiry on the basis of "articulable facts" that "crime is afoot."[9]

Assume that a police officer or a magistrate has made the decision to arrest a suspect, and a suspect has in fact been arrested. What happens now?

Immediately after the arrest, when the arrestee is in custody, the arresting officer will recite the *Miranda* warning (Figure 14.2). The term derives from one of the Supreme Court's most important rulings, which laid down the standards of procedural fairness mandated by the Fourth, Fifth, and Sixth Amendments to the Constitution.[10] If the warning is not given, the courts may exclude from evidence at trial any statement the arrestee may have made and any evidence that has resulted from it.[11]

Once a suspect has been taken into custody, the processing of the event and of the offender commence, with booking, the taking of fingerprints and mug shots (identifying photographs), the filling out of forms, and waiting in usually sordid holding pens for the next step.

The right to counsel and counsel's decisions
In the case *Gideon* v. *Wainwright* the Supreme Court laid down the rule that every person charged with a crime that may lead to incarceration has the right to an attorney, and that the state must pay for that service if the defendant

---

MIRANDA WARNING

1. You have the right to remain silent.
2. Anything you say can and will be used against you in a court of law.
3. You have the right to talk to a lawyer and have him present with you while you are being questioned.
4. If you cannot afford to hire a lawyer, one will be appointed to represent you before any questioning, if you wish one.
5. You may stop answering questions at any time.
6. Do you understand each of these rights I have explained to you?
7. Having these rights in mind, do you wish to talk to us now?

SUS DERECHOS

1. Usted tiene el derecho de permanecer en silencio y rehusar a contestar preguntas.
2. Cualquier cosa que usted diga puede ser usada en contra de usted en una corte de ley.
3. Usted tiene el derecho de consultar un abogado antes de hablar a la policía, y tener un abogado presente durante alguna pregunta ahora o en el futuro.
4. Si usted no tiene un abogado, usted tiene el derecho de permanecer en silencio hasta que usted tenga la oportunidad de consultar con uno.
5. Si usted no puede pagar un abogado, uno se le proveerá a usted sin ningún costo.

FIGURE 14.2   The *Miranda* warning, in English and in Spanish

cannot afford to do so.[12] This case, involving an indigent Florida defendant, established the universal right to free defense counsel for the poor. It subsequently was reflected in the *Miranda* warning.

The Supreme Court requirement has been implemented nationwide by the provision of

AT ISSUE

Exposé on Police Lockups

In an exposé of New York City's police lockups and courthouse holding pens, William Glaberson, an investigative reporter for the *New York Times*, reported:

> There are no mattresses, no bedding, no clean clothing and no showers. The toilets, where there are toilets at all, are open bowls along the walls and often encrusted and overflowing. Meals usually consist of a single slice of baloney and a single slice of American cheese on white bread.

> Lockups and holding pens were designed half a century or a century ago to hold arrested persons for a few hours. Nowadays the clients of the criminal justice system are confined there for several days before they are taken to court. Rather than the few hundred originally envisaged, thousands are occupying the dingy, dark cells in the basements of police stations and courthouses. Only a third of the people who receive this "pretrial punishment" are ultimately sentenced to prison.

> People who have been through the system say it is not easy to forget. Some were threatened by other prisoners. Others were chained to people who were vomiting and stinking of the streets. With few phone privileges, many felt as if they were lost in a hellish labyrinth far from the lives they had been plucked from.

> The situation is virtually out of control. No one agency is responsible, and no agency's budget provides for the upkeep of these places. Officials alerted to the chaos in the lockups and pens have promised to look into the situation, and a consultant has been engaged to suggest solutions to the problem. Meanwhile hell on earth continues for thousands trapped underneath New York City's police stations and courthouses.

Source: William Glaberson, "Trapped in the Terror of New York's Holding Pens," *New York Times*, March 23, 1990, pp. A1, B4. Copyright © 1990 by The New York Times Company.

assigned counsel, public defenders, contract counsel, or legal aid. As we shall see, however, these defense lawyers, under tremendous caseload pressures, sometimes may be inclined to pressure their clients into unfavorable plea bargains.[13] Thus their decisions, too, have a considerable impact on the flow of the process.

Prosecution and Pretrial Services

During the phase of prosecution and pretrial services, prosecutors and judges make the decisions. Far fewer persons are processed through this phase than are entered into the system. Many arrested persons have been diverted out of the system; others will be diverted at this stage, when charges are dropped or cases dismissed. Charges may be dismissed for many reasons. Perhaps the evidence is not strong enough to support probable cause; perhaps the arrested person is a juvenile who should be dealt with by the juvenile justice system, or a mentally disturbed person who requires hospitalization. Perhaps the judge believes that justice is best served by compassion.

The judicial decision to release   After an arrest, the arrested person must be taken before a magistrate, a local judge, who makes a determination that probable cause exists. As a judge, the magistrate will use a standard of probable cause that is likely to be a bit tougher than the police officer's. The magistrate must also repeat the *Miranda* warning and then decide whether to permit the defendant to be released on bail or on "percentage bail" (the defendant may deposit with the court only a stipulated percentage of the bail set); to "release on recognizance" (ROR, no bail required, on condition that the defendant appear for trial and behave in the meantime); to release the defendant into someone's custody; or to detain the defendant in jail pending further proceedings. In making the decision to release, judges or magistrates are strongly influenced by prosecutors' views as to whether a given defendant is a safe risk for release. In some states, release criteria have been enacted into law (see Chapter 16, Table 16.3). Historically, however, the only criterion for release on bail has been whether the defendant can be relied on to appear for the next court appearance. In practice, judges tend to rely on such factors as the gravity of the charge and the probability that the defendant may commit a crime or harass victims if he or she is released. The District of Columbia and a few other jurisdictions permit preventive detention when there is a high probability that the defendant may commit a crime if he or she is released. Despite the difficulty of predicting anyone's behavior, the Supreme Court has ruled it to be constitutionally proper to deny bail to a person who is considered dangerous.[14]

A large number of studies have been conducted in efforts to assess factors related to release decisions. The seriousness of the charge was found to be the single most important factor in the decision. Both rearrest rates and rates of failure to appear are quite low, especially if trial follows within a short time after pretrial release.[15] This finding might indicate that judges have done well in assessing the risk of releasing defendants. It could also mean that judges might want to liberalize their risk assessments. The issue requires further research.

The preliminary hearing   The next step in the process in many states is the **preliminary hearing,** a preview of the trial in court before a judge, in which the prosecution must produce enough evidence to convince the judge that the case should proceed to trial or to the grand jury. In many jurisdictions the preliminary hearing is officially considered to be another probable cause hearing. But what emerges is more than probable cause. In this proceeding,

conducted with some of the rights afforded at trials, cross-examination of witnesses, and the introduction of evidence under stringent rules, enough evidence must be produced to "bind the defendant over" to the grand jury, to constitute a reasonable inference of guilt or reasonable grounds to believe that the defendant is guilty. In the preliminary hearing, in which the defense presents no evidence, the defendant gains the advantage of finding out how the prosecution's case is being developed. The defense attorney's decision whether to enter a plea or to engage in plea negotiations depends very much on what transpires during the preliminary hearing.

The decision to charge   No matter what the result of the preliminary hearing may be, the decision to charge the defendant with a crime rests predominantly with the prosecutor. Even in states where a grand jury must determine whether a defendant is to be indicted for a felony, it is the prosecutor who decides in the first place whether to place a case before the grand jury. The prosecutor also decides what evidence to present to the grand jury and how to present it.

In a major study based on data from the Prosecutor's Management Information System (PROMIS), researchers found that the prosecutors' reasons not to proceed after an arrest vary by offense. Of all reasons given for not proceeding with robbery cases, 43 percent were "witness problem(s)," 35 percent "insufficiency of evidence," and 22 percent "other." For nonviolent property offenses, the reasons were 25 percent "witness problems," 37 percent "insufficiency of evidence," and 36 percent "other."[16]

As soon as the prosecutor has made a decision to charge the defendant and has informed defense counsel accordingly, the stage is set for plea bargaining. This process is inherent in the Anglo-American system, under which a trial always proceeds in accordance with the prosecution's charge and the defendant's agreement (guilty plea) or disagreement (not-guilty plea) with that charge.

The plea-bargaining process   Every criminal defendant exercises some power over the way the case is to be conducted. A defendant who pleads guilty admits all the facts alleged in the accusation, whether it is an indictment or an information, and all their legal implications: he or she admits to being guilty as charged. No trial has to be conducted. A defendant who pleads not guilty denies all the facts and their legal implications and puts the government—the prosecutor—to great expense to prove guilt in an elaborate criminal trial. The idea arose centuries ago that both sides, prosecution and defense, could benefit if they were to agree on a plea that would save the government the expense of a trial and the defendant the risk of a very severe punishment if he or she were found guilty. By the mid-twentieth century it had become common practice in the United States for prosecutors and defense attorneys to discuss the criminal charges against defendants and to agree on a reduced or modified plea that would spare the state the cost of a trial and guarantee the defendant a sentence more lenient than the original charge warranted. At first such plea negotiations were quite clandestine and officially denied. In fact, when accepting a plea, the judge would always inquire whether the plea was freely made, and the defendant always answered yes, when in fact the plea was the result of a bargain in which the defendant and the prosecutor manipulated each other into a deal. Contemporary legislation, federal and state, fully recognizes the plea-bargaining process, and simply requires guarantees that no one be coerced and that all pleas are voluntarily entered, with full awareness of the consequences.

Nevertheless, the process of plea bargaining invites injustices of many sorts. Defendants who are morally or legally not guilty, for example, may feel inclined to accept a plea bargain in the face of strong evidence. Other defendants may plead guilty to a lesser charge even though the evidence was obtained in violation of constitutional guarantees. In some cases, by "overcharging" (charging murder instead of manslaughter, for example), a prosecutor may in effect coerce a defendant to plead guilty to the lower charge, thus, in effect, forcing him or her to relinquish the right to a jury trial. The practice of plea bargaining is widespread. A Bureau of Justice Statistics report has estimated that in urban areas guilty pleas outnumbered trials by

about 17 to 1, and nearly all of those guilty pleas were negotiated.[17]

Research on why defendants accept plea bargains and on the factors that weigh upon the decisions is inconclusive. Nevertheless, there appears to be agreement that plea bargains

• Are necessary devices to keep the courts from getting hopelessly clogged with criminal cases.
• Are desirable means of compensating for the harshness of the sanctions provided by the penal codes.
• Allow for adjustments of inadequately developed legal rules regarding defenses, such as mistake, insanity, self-defense.
• Reduce the negative effects of "net-widening"—that is, the tendency of our society to include more and more offenders within the sweep of the criminal justice system.
• Allow for consideration of legally irrelevant but factually important factors, ranging from poverty and despair to intense emotional distress.

Abolishing plea bargaining would require broad changes in criminal law and procedure, and thus in the entire criminal justice system. Until such reforms are achieved, if ever, the system will continue to rely on the decisions of prosecutors and defense counsels to agree on a plea.

If the prosecutor and defense counsel have agreed on a plea bargain—for example, by reducing the charge from murder to manslaughter or by reducing the number of charges from four counts of larceny to one—the judge will have to decide whether that bargain is in the interest of justice. Before accepting the defendant's bargained plea, the judge must

• Inform the defendant of the implications of the plea (that the defendant can now be sentenced).
• Ascertain that the facts support the plea.
• Accept the plea.[18]
• Impose sentence.

The second of these requirements is particularly important, as it requires the judge to adjudicate the facts of the case in order to determine whether the plea of guilty is warranted. This determination of fact amounts to a miniature trial.

If no plea bargain is agreed upon, the case will be set for submission to the grand jury whenever a defendant has the right to trial on indictment by a grand jury. Normally this right is restricted to felony cases.

The grand jury's decision to indict   The grand jury is one of the oldest institutions of our criminal justice system. It dates to Magna Charta in A.D. 1215. It has been abolished in England, but in most American states it continues, in serious (felony) cases, to screen the prosecution's evidence in secret hearings and decide whether the defendant should be formally charged with crime.

Federal grand juries are composed of sixteen to twenty-three citizens. An indictment requires the concurrence of at least twelve grand jurors in the federal criminal process.[19] State rules are similar. The indictment must rest on evidence indicating a "prima facie" case against the defendant. A **prima facie case** exists when there seems to be sufficient evidence to convict the defendant. The prima facie case may be defeated by evidence at trial that raises reasonable doubt or constitutes a legal excuse. Since that is a strong evidentiary requirement, most indicted defendants are inclined to make a plea bargain at this point. Indeed, the conviction rate of persons who stand trial is high. Of every sixteen persons indicted, ten plead guilty (usually in a plea bargain), and four go to trial. Three of the four are convicted; only one is acquitted, dismissed by the judge, or dismissed by the prosecutor.[20] If, after the indictment has been presented in open court, the defendant pleads not guilty, the stage is set for trial.

Adjudication Decisions

Defendants may choose to be tried either by a judge (a bench trial) or by a jury (consisting usually of twelve citizens but as few as six in some states for lesser offenses).[21] In a jury trial the judge rules on matters of law, instructs the jurors about relevant legal questions and defini-

tions, and tells them how to apply the law to the facts of the case.

A defendant may prefer either a jury trial or a bench trial for any number of reasons. When a defense is based largely on the application and interpretation of technical legal propositions, a judge is likely to be the preferable choice. If the defense appeals more to sympathy and emotion, a jury is likely to be the better choice. Much research has been done on the functions and functioning of judges and juries, especially since the University of Chicago Jury Project in the 1950s.[22] Much of that research focused on whether juries differ widely in their decisions. Apparently they do not. Most juries come to a unanimous verdict. That was believed to be the general requirement under American law. In a surprise decision in 1972, however, the Supreme Court ruled that a conviction decided upon by fewer than all twelve jurors is constitutionally acceptable.[23]

Sentencing Decisions

If a defendant has not been diverted out of the system, has pleaded not guilty, and has been tried and convicted, the next step in the process is the imposition of a sentence. In some states, with respect to some crimes, the statute leaves the sentencing judge no choice: a fixed sentence is imposed by law. But in most states judges still have some choice. The judge must decide whether to place the defendant on probation, and if so, on what type of probation; whether to impose a sentence of incarceration, for what length of time; whether to impose a minimum or maximum term (or both), or to leave the sentence open-ended (indeterminate) within statutory limits; whether to impose a fine and how much; whether to order compensation for the victims; whether to impose court costs, and so on. Don Gottfredson and Bridget Stecher conducted research on what factors judges take into consideration when they select an "appropriate" sentence. In studying 17 judges who sentenced 982 adult offenders, they found that the main objective in 36 percent of the cases was rehabilitation, followed by 34 percent "other purposes including general deterrence,"

17 percent retribution, 9 percent special deterrence, and 4 percent incapacitation.[24]

In making sentencing decisions, judges are supposed to consider factors pertaining to the offenders' personal characteristics, their past and possibly their potential future, their problems, and their needs. What do judges actually consider when they decide on sentences? The National Academy of Sciences, having reviewed most of the research on sentencing, has found that

> offense seriousness and offender's prior record emerge consistently as the key determinants of sentences. The more serious the offense and the worse the offender's prior record, the more severe the sentence. The strength of this conclusion persists despite the potentially severe problems of pervasive biases arising from the difficulty of measuring—or even precisely defining—either of these complex variables. This finding is supported by a wide variety of studies using data of varying quality in different jurisdictions and with a diversity of measures of offense seriousness and prior record.[25]

In order to avoid bias that results in dissimilar sentences for more or less similar offenders, several researchers have developed the idea of sentencing guidelines. These guidelines assign specific values to the important sentencing criteria—principally the seriousness of the offenses, and possibly prior record and other factors (Chapter 16). Such guidelines are meant to guide judges' selection of the length and type of punishment.

Corrections Decisions

Correctional decisions in the community Probation departments are a part of the court system. They perform investigative and correctional functions under the courts' supervision. A probation officer's presentence report on every convicted offender is designed to help the court find the most appropriate sentence. After evaluating the probation officer's presentence investigation report, the judge may decide to place the convict on probation, usually with specified conditions—that the convict not commit another offense, not leave the county without permission, make payments to the victim,

attend meetings of Alcoholics Anonymous, or whatever. More recently states have experimented with a variety of alternatives to the two traditional choices, incarceration and routine probation. Among them are placement in restitution programs, intensive supervision programs (ISP), shock incarceration, regimented discipline programs (RDP, also called boot camp), and several others. Much research has been done on the success or failure of traditional probation among various types of offenders. The newer programs have not been in existence long enough to permit reliable evaluation. Initial research (discussed in Chapter 17) indicates that some types may be cost-beneficial and somewhat successful in lowering recidivism rates.[26]

Correctional decisions in institutions The correctional sector of the criminal justice system is composed of institutions of varying degrees of security, with varying forms of programs, and of quasi-institutional as well as community-based programs. Within the limitations of law, the correctional staff decides where to place sentenced convicts in view of security requirements, the availability of treatment and rehabilitation programs, and organizational needs. All inmates must be classified in accordance with the placements that are available.[27] Such decisions are not easy. Above all, it is difficult to predict the types of security precautions that an inmate will require. Nor is it possible to predict the success of education, vocational training, or any other treatment program with any accuracy. It is perhaps easier to decide where to place inmates among the institutional jobs that keep the institution running. Inmates do clerical and classification work, provide legal aid, perform maintenance work; they work in the library, the infirmary, the laundry, the kitchen. But even these decisions require consideration of other factors, especially safety concerns. All of these decisions have to be reviewed on the basis of the experience gathered, and new decisions have to be made from time to time.

Release and parole decisions To the extent that the system permits any leeway, the most important decision is whether to release a convict from the institution. There are two types of release from the correctional system. In the first, correctional administrators have little choice. At the expiration of their sentences, inmates must be released. The expiration point depends to some degree on the decisions of correctional administrators, who in the course of disciplinary proceedings must decide whether an inmate must lose "good time" benefits because of violations of the institution's rules. An inmate who violates the rules loses the benefit of the early release that comes with good behavior. Today release decisions are further complicated by policy decisions made at higher governmental levels or by judges, who frequently order prisoners released to make space for new ones, in order to relieve prison overcrowding.

The second way an inmate may be released is through parole. In its original and ideal form, parole was a benefit bestowed on a prisoner for good behavior in prison and a promise of good conduct after discharge. Success on parole was to be achieved with the aid of a parole officer. As parole officers' caseloads increased, however, that ideal faded, until today parole is simply an early release from prison based on the decision of a parole board. Parole boards have little information to rely on in making their decisions. Conduct in the institution, however, has been demonstrated to relate to behavior outside it.[28] Some progress has been made in the development of devices to predict success on parole, called base expectancy scales.[29] Nevertheless, these decisions remain difficult. Statistics show that arrest rates of released inmates are very high, as are rates of reconviction and reincarceration (Chapter 17).[30] Variations in these rates depend on the number of previous incarcerations, the types of crimes committed, ethnic background, education, the length of the prison term served, the time elapsed since release, and other factors. Some states have abolished parole, and others are using it with steadily declining frequency. (Several special forms of parole, such as intensive supervision parole with and without electronic monitoring, are discussed in Chapter 17.)

Diversion Out of the Criminal Justice System

Throughout the flow of the criminal justice process, the number of persons within the system steadily decreases. This phenomenon is called the attrition rate, or the mortality rate. The President's Commission on Law Enforcement and the Administration of Justice depicted the criminal justice system as a funnel. In the mid-1960s 727,000 defendants entered the wide opening at the top of the funnel—roughly one for every four of the 2.78 million Index crimes reported. Slightly more than one in five of the arrestees were convicted.[31] Two decades later, by the mid-1980s, the 1965 numbers had quadrupled or quintupled; yet, the proportion has essentially remained the same (Figure 14.3).

As we have seen, there are two reasons for the enormous amount of diversion from the system at various stages. First, decisionmakers may, for a variety of reasons, deem a case inappropriate for further processing within the normal flow of the criminal justice system. If they

FIGURE 14.3 Funneling effect from reported crimes through prison sentence

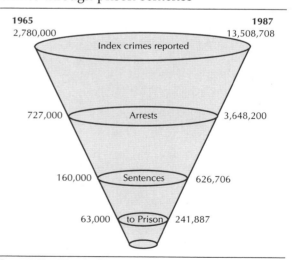

1965		1987
2,780,000	Index crimes reported	13,508,708
727,000	Arrests	3,648,200
160,000	Sentences	626,706
63,000	to Prison	241,887

Source: President's Commission on Law Enforcement and Administration of Justice, *Task Force Report on Science and Technology* (Washington, D.C.: U.S. Government Printing Office, 1967), p. 61; and compiled from the *Sourcebook of Criminal Justice Statistics*, 1988, U.S. Department of Justice (Washington, D.C.: U.S. Government Printing Office, 1989).

did not do so, the system would become clogged and the flow would halt. Moreover, the exercise of discretion in this way keeps our already punitive system from being overly punitive. Thus compassion is added to the mix. Second, in many situations decisionmakers have no choice but to dismiss a case. At each stage of the process the authorities must meet a legal standard of proof. When that standard is not met, the case leaves the criminal justice process. These standards become progressively tighter as the flow proceeds through the various stages of the process (Figure 14.4).

A very broad standard of proof—reasonable suspicion—permits a large intake into the criminal justice system. A very tight standard of proof, guilt beyond a reasonable doubt, permits persons ultimately to be convicted and retained in the system. Various intermediate standards determine whether a defendant should be processed to the next stage.

JUVENILE JUSTICE

The juvenile justice system of today is very large, as it must cope with a very sizable num-

TABLE 14.2   INDEX CRIMES CLEARED BY ARREST OF JUVENILES, 1988 (PERCENT)

INDEX CRIMES	PERCENT OF TOTAL ARRESTS
Murder, nonnegligent manslaughter	6.5%
Forcible rape	9.3
Robbery	10.4
Aggravated assault	8.5
Burglary	18.4
Larceny-theft	21.6
Motor vehicle theft	21.3
Arson	39.5
All violent crime	8.9
All property crime	20.9
All Index crimes	18.1

Source: U.S. Department of Justice, Bureau of Justice Statistics, *Crime in the United States, 1988* (Washington, D.C.: U.S. Government Printing Office, 1989), p. 165.

ber of juvenile offenders.[32] Table 14.2 indicates the proportion of arrests for Index crimes represented by juveniles in 1988. Among the eight UCR Index crimes, the percentage ranges from

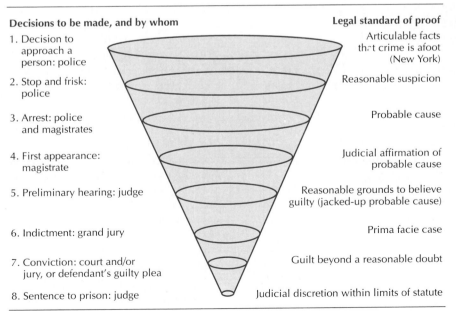

Decisions to be made, and by whom

1. Decision to approach a person: police
2. Stop and frisk: police
3. Arrest: police and magistrates
4. First appearance: magistrate
5. Preliminary hearing: judge
6. Indictment: grand jury
7. Conviction: court and/or jury, or defendant's guilty plea
8. Sentence to prison: judge

Legal standard of proof

Articulable facts that crime is afoot (New York)

Reasonable suspicion

Probable cause

Judicial affirmation of probable cause

Reasonable grounds to believe guilty (jacked-up probable cause)

Prima facie case

Guilt beyond a reasonable doubt

Judicial discretion within limits of statute

FIGURE 14.4
Funneling effect of the standard of proof

a low of 6.5 percent for murder and nonnegligent manslaughter to a high of nearly 40 percent for arson. The juveniles under 18 arrested for all Index crimes represented 18.1 percent of all persons arrested for such crimes. If we take the traditional age of majority, 21 years, as our standard, it turns out that one-third of all crimes of violence are committed by juveniles.[33]

The Development of the Juvenile Justice System

The roots of our system of juvenile justice are two thousand years old. They can be traced to classical Roman law. There are two roots, one clearly punitive, the other supportive and caring. The punitive root brought us the imposition of adult criminal liability on children. In the Middle Ages, under the law of the church, the Roman law classification of children with respect to their criminal liability took definite shape and was taken over by the common law.

This classification system (shown in Table 14.3) subjected children to the rigors of adult criminal liability, proceedings, and punishments. It still affects our thinking. Its impact can be seen in the laws of many states. Theoretically, a 10-year-old can be tried today as an adult in Vermont, a 12-year-old in Montana, and a 13-year-old in Georgia, Illinois, and Missouri. There is indeed a general tendency across the country to reduce the age of criminal liability.

The second root, likewise originating in Roman law, is that of concern for troubled children. We find its traces in the concepts used today in juvenile court proceedings. It was very much present in the concept of **parens patriae,** or "parent of the country," which to the Romans meant that the emperor, and in medieval times the king or queen, could exercise *patria potestas,* or "parental power," *in loco parentis,* "in the place of a parent" deemed incapable or unworthy, over children in trouble or in danger of becoming wayward. The position of the monarch was eventually transferred to the people of the state, as represented by the juvenile court judge, exercising the ancient *patria potestas.* These doctrines guided American practice for dealing with troubled children since 1838, with the case *Ex parte Crouse.* On the petition of her mother, a young girl, Mary Ann Crouse, had been committed by the court to the Philadelphia House of Refuge as wayward and incorrigible. When Mary Ann's father, who was estranged from his wife, learned what had happened, he sought a writ of habeas corpus to secure the release of his daughter, who, so he alleged, had been imprisoned without a jury trial. The Pennsylvania Supreme Court rejected this argument, reasoning that under the *parens patriae* doctrine the state has every right to protect children from improper upbringing.[34]

Houses of refuge were based on an earlier English model, designed to care for the impoverished, "dangerous" street people of the time. In fact, these houses were little more than prisons to which one could be sent without trial. The houses of refuge proved a dismal failure. They neither educated nor reformed anybody.

TABLE 14.3   AGE CATEGORIES FOR CRIMINAL LIABILITY UNDER COMMON LAW

AGE	CATEGORY	LIABILITY AND BURDEN OF PROOF
0–7	*Infantia* (infancy)	None
7–10½	*Infantia proxima* (close to infancy)	Presumed incapable of committing crime but proof of malice makes up for the lack of age
10½–14	*Pubertate proxima* (close to puberty)	Presumed capable of committing crime, but defendant may prove incapacity
14+	Adulthood	Full criminal liability

Children whose parents had failed them were subjected to harsh discipline.

Massachusetts tried a new approach in 1854, with the creation of the Massachusetts Industrial School for Girls. In a cottage-style setting, surrogate families were created, with the goal of reforming girls who were considered wayward and delinquent, terms then virtually synonymous. Other states followed Massachusetts' lead. The problem with this approach was the lack of a judicial determination that a given child had indeed violated the law and therefore was in need of some remedial placement.

The all-important change occurred in Chicago, where Timothy D. Hurley, a judge and former probation officer, and Julia Lathrop, of the Illinois Board of Charities, advocated abandonment of the system that placed child offenders and wayward children in adult jails and prisons and removed children who had been arbitrarily declared wayward from the custody of their parents and placed them in prison-like institutions. Hurley and Lathrop lobbied for the creation of a juvenile court, and with the help of the Catholic Visitation and Aid Society and the Chicago Bar Association, they succeeded. The Illinois legislature created the nation's first juvenile court, in Chicago, in 1899.

The concepts that guided the operation of this and subsequent similar courts were straightforward:

• All dependent, neglected, and delinquent children under 16 years of age could be brought under the jurisdiction of the juvenile court.
• Delinquency included any act that, if committed by an adult, would be a crime.
• The juvenile court did not find youngsters guilty of anything, but simply determined their status as dependent, neglected (in a very broad, sweeping sense), or delinquent.
• The juvenile court judge acted as a surrogate parent, conducting informal proceedings (in contrast to the formal adversarial proceedings in criminal court).
• Exercising much discretion, the juvenile court judge gave first consideration to the best interest of the child.
• Dispositions by the court were not punish-

ments; they might include only friendly probation, in the child's own home, or placement in a suitable foster home or training in an industrial school.

There were two problems with this approach. First, the definition of behavior that brought a child under the jurisdiction of the juvenile court was still extremely broad. "Dependency" and "neglect" are vague terms. Nor are these conditions the youngster's fault; they are the parents' fault. Moreover, the concept of delinquency embraced not only acts that would be crimes if an adult committed them but also behavior that would not be considered deviant in adults, such as truancy or running away from home. When dependency and neglect were included in the definition of delinquency, neglect itself became a status offense. A neglected child was by definition delinquent.

Second, while the motivations for the informality of the proceedings in the juvenile justice system were most praiseworthy, they led to intolerable abuses. Not all children's rights were violated in all cases, but abuses occurred in virtually every case. Most juvenile court judges did not view their practices as abuses, but sincerely regarded the informality of their proceedings as in the best interest of the child.[35]

This system held sway until 1967, when the Supreme Court at last ruled that children, too, have rights that are protected by the Constitution. In the case *In re Gault* the court ruled that virtually all of the guarantees of the Fourth, Fifth, and Sixth Amendments, made applicable to the states under the due process clause of the Fourteenth Amendment, must be extended to juveniles. These guarantees include the right to be informed of the charges brought against one, freedom from unreasonable seizure (arrest), the right to an attorney, and the right to be confronted by and to examine witnesses. Later the Court ruled that proof of juvenile delinquency, like that of a crime charged to an adult, must be established beyond a reasonable doubt. Only the right to a jury trial need not be accorded to juveniles, perhaps so as to preserve some of the informality of the juvenile court.[36] These decisions severely curtailed a juvenile court judge's exercise of *patria potestas*. They subjugated

CRIMINOLOGICAL FOCUS

In re Gault: *The Demise of* Parens Patriae

On June 8, 1964, in Gila County, Arizona, Mrs. Cook complained to Deputy Sheriff Flagg about obscene phone calls she had received, which she attributed to a neighborhood kid, Gerald Francis Gault, aged 15. The deputy sheriff knew Gerry Gault; he was on probation, having been found in the company of another youngster who had lifted a wallet from a woman's handbag.

Deputy Sheriff Flagg promptly went to Gerry's home, arrested him, and placed him in the juvenile detention facility. When Gerry's mother returned home that night and found Gerry gone, she sent her elder son out to find him. He learned from acquaintances that Gerry was in detention. Gerry's mother promptly went to the detention center. She did not get to see Gerry. The deputy told her of Gerry's arrest and informed her that there would be a hearing in juvenile court at 3:00 P.M. next day. On that day the deputy filed an application with the court noting that Gerry, as a minor, is "in need of the protection of the honorable court, as he is delinquent." The application contained no reference to Mrs. Cook's complaint. The hearing took place

before Judge McGhee of juvenile court. Present were Deputy Sheriff Flagg in his capacity as a probation officer, Gerry, and, by chance, his mother and elder brother. Mrs. Cook was absent.

In a formless proceeding Gerry denied ever having made an obscene phone call. The judge returned Gerry to the detention facility. A second hearing was held one week later. Gerry's mother was informed about this hearing by means of a hand-scribbled note that Deputy Sheriff Flagg left at her door. The second hearing was as formless as the first one. There was no complaining witness, and Judge McGhee ruled that none was necessary. The court declared that Gerry's obscene phone call was proved, and that if the act were committed by an adult, it was a misdemeanor subject to a fine of from $5 to $50 and a jail term of up to two months. Juveniles, he declared, could not be punished. Judge McGhee then found Gerry to be a habitual juvenile offender, because three years earlier Gerry had been accused of the theft of a baseball glove (though he had not been charged with an offense), and declared that Gerry had lied when

he denied the accusation. Judge McGhee found Gerry to be a juvenile delinquent, not to be punished, but to be sent to a juvenile correctional facility for six years—until he reached the age of 21.

After Gerry's parents finally engaged an attorney, the case gained widespread publicity. Everything seemed to have gone wrong in the case. Yet all the appeals courts upheld Judge McGhee's disposition. With the help of civil libertarians and members of some of the most prestigious law faculties, the case reached the United States Supreme Court, three years after Gerry had been incarcerated. The Supreme Court's opinion was written by one of the most compassionate men ever to sit on that bench, Justice Abe Fortas. The case was *In re Gault*, and it made history. Children, Fortas wrote, have fully as much right as adults to the protection of the Constitution. Never again would a child be sentenced to six years of incarceration for an act that was never proved, and that if proved against an adult would have warranted a jail term of two months.

Source: *In re Gault*, 387 U.S. 1 (1967).

parens patriae to the rule of law, to constitutional due process.

Juvenile court judges viewed the Supreme Court's decisions with mixed emotions. Some thought the juvenile court movement had come to an end. But as time passed, it became evi-

dent that juvenile courts can function well in administering juvenile justice even while abiding by the due process guarantees of the Constitution. There is some evidence, however, that many children and parents do not claim the procedural rights to which they are constitutionally entitled, frequently out of ignorance. [37]

The transformation of juvenile justice proceedings into a junior model of adult criminal justice seemed to entail a peculiar consequence. If juveniles are to have the rights of adults charged with crime, should they not also have the responsibilities? In 1977 an influential joint committee of the Institute of Judicial Administration at New York University and the American Bar Association formulated a set of standards for juvenile justice. They proposed that juvenile dispositions should be based on the seriousness of the offense committed, and not merely on the court's view of the juvenile's needs. [38] With these standards the punitive movement of the mid-1970s had reached juvenile justice as well. New York passed legislation permitting the incarceration of juveniles over the age of 13 for certain serious felonies, and other states followed suit. Thus, in most states, the juvenile justice system is indeed a junior criminal justice system. Only the offenders are junior, however; the rest of the players are not.

Most states specify an age (16, 17, 18, 21) below which an offender can be brought before a juvenile court. But most states have a provision that permits a juvenile court judge to waive the jurisdiction of the juvenile court and transmit the case to the criminal court. Table 14.4 indicates the youngest age at which a juvenile may be transferred to criminal court. Since the Supreme Court decision in *Breed* v. *Jones* (1975), such a waiver hearing has been a constitutional right. [39] In most states less than 5 percent of juvenile cases are in fact waived to criminal court.

The Juvenile Justice Process

Let us now return to the flowchart of the President's Commission (Figure 14.1). Having entered the juvenile justice system, the juvenile will now be processed according to its procedures.

Entry into the system   It has been said that "citizens...largely determine delinquency

TABLE 14.4   YOUNGEST AGE AT WHICH A JUVENILE MAY BE TRANSFERRED TO CRIMINAL COURT BY JUDICIAL WAIVER IN ALL STATES, THE DISTRICT OF COLUMBIA, AND OTHER FEDERAL DISTRICTS

AGE (years)	STATES
No specific age	Alaska, Arizona, Arkansas, Delaware, Florida, Indiana, Kentucky, Maine, Maryland, New Hampshire, New Jersey, Oklahoma, South Dakota, West Virginia, Wyoming, federal districts
10	Vermont
12	Montana
13	Georgia, Illinois, Mississippi
14	Alabama, Colorado, Connecticut, Idaho, Iowa, Massachusetts, Minnesota, Missouri, North Carolina, North Dakota, Pennsylvania, South Carolina, Tennessee, Utah
15	District of Columbia, Louisiana, Michigan, Nebraska, New Mexico, Ohio, Oregon, Texas, Virginia
16	California, Hawaii, Kansas, Nevada, New York, Rhode Island, Washington, Wisconsin

Note: Many judicial waiver statutes also specify offenses that are waivable. For example, New York has a designated felony rule that permits transfers under 16 years of age for certain violent crimes. This table lists the states by the youngest age for which judicial waiver may be sought without regard to offense.

Source: Adapted from Linda A. Szymanski, *Waiver/transfer/certification of juveniles to criminal court: Age restrictions, Crime restrictions* (Washington, D.C.: National Center for Juvenile Justice, February 1987).

rates," because it is the citizens' tolerance level and perceptions that determine their decision to call the police.[40] Perceptions and tolerance levels vary from area to area and neighborhood to neighborhood, but on the whole, they are more benign in the case of juvenile misconduct than they are in the case of adult misconduct. We noted earlier that the crimes actually committed far outnumber those reported to the police. It appears that as far as crimes committed by juveniles are concerned, the disparity is even greater because of the reluctance of other juveniles, and of adults who remember their own juvenile escapades, to bring juvenile misconduct to the attention of the authorities.

Invoking the juvenile justice process Once juvenile misconduct has been brought to the attention of the authorities, usually the police, the next crucial step is a decision to investigate, to arrest, and to process. There is no uniform standard as to whether the taking of a juvenile into custody is in fact an arrest. In some states it is; in others it is not; in some states the issue is not clear; but in all states the taking of a juvenile into custody requires compliance with the constitutional mandates of *In re Gault*, including the probable cause requirement and the administration of the *Miranda* warning. Generally the police have broad power when a juvenile is taken into custody for reasons other than criminal conduct, such as being in danger, in trouble, or in violation of a juvenile court's order. But police officers are both reluctant and ill prepared to make such decisions.[41]

After an arrest or detention, usually by a patrol officer, the juvenile is ordinarily handed over to a juvenile officer, a member of a specially trained police juvenile unit. Such units exercise far broader discretion than their colleagues who process adult criminal cases. They may decide to release a juvenile into the custody of parents, or otherwise involve parents, who may be called to the stationhouse to discuss the matter.

Once a juvenile has been taken into custody, the police juvenile unit must also decide, guided by law, whether to process the youngster as an adult offender and take him or her

before a magistrate for a first appearance; to choose the juvenile path and take the suspect before a juvenile court judge; or to deal with the case in a less formal manner. Over the years dispositions of juveniles have tended to become increasingly formal. In 1972, half of all juvenile cases were referred to juvenile court. By 1987, two-thirds of all cases reached the juvenile court. In 1972, 45 percent of all cases were handled informally within the department and the suspect was released; by 1987 only 30.3 percent were handled informally (Table 14.5). Referral to a criminal court increased from 1.3 percent in 1972 to 5.2 percent in 1987. This is clear evidence of a trend in the direction of greater punitiveness toward juvenile offenders.

If the case is not informally disposed of by the police or the juvenile probation department, it moves before a juvenile court judge for an intake hearing. In large metropolitan areas the juvenile court judge usually is a specialist in juvenile matters. Perhaps he or she was a juvenile probation officer who went on to obtain a law degree. In the more rural parts of the country the criminal court judge doubles as juvenile court judge.

The juvenile court then decides, on the basis of the report of the intake department (juvenile court officers and probation intake officers), whether sufficient grounds exist for filing a petition requesting an adjudicatory hearing (juvenile court trial); whether the case should be waived to criminal court; whether the juvenile should be transferred to a social agency; or whether the case should be dismissed. Juvenile court judges have broad discretion in making these decisions.

Adjudication If the juvenile court has retained jurisdiction over the alleged delinquent, the case moves into the adjudicatory hearing, which is the equivalent to a trial in criminal court. Under the terms of *In re Gault* the juvenile is entitled to nearly all the procedural guarantees that protect adults charged with crime, as we noted earlier.

In this adjudicatory hearing, the juvenile court judge must decide whether the facts warrant a decision in accordance with the petition.

TABLE 14.5 PERCENT DISTRIBUTION OF JUVENILES TAKEN INTO CUSTODY BY METHOD OF DISPOSITION, UNITED STATES, 1972–87

	REFERRED TO JUVENILE COURT JURISDICTION	HANDLED WITHIN DEPARTMENT AND RELEASED	REFERRED TO CRIMINAL OR ADULT COURT	REFERRED TO OTHER POLICE AGENCY	REFERRED TO WELFARE AGENCY
1972	50.8%	45.0%	1.3%	1.6%	1.3%
1973	49.5	45.2	1.5	2.3	1.4
1974	47.0	44.4	3.7	2.4	2.5
1975	52.7	41.6	2.3	1.9	1.4
1976	53.4	39.0	4.4	1.7	1.6
1977	53.2	38.1	3.9	1.8	3.0
1978	55.9	36.6	3.8	1.8	1.9
1979	57.3	34.6	4.8	1.7	1.6
1980	58.1	33.8	4.8	1.7	1.6
1981	58.0	33.8	5.1	1.6	1.5
1982	58.9	32.5	5.4	1.5	1.6
1983	57.5	32.8	4.8	1.7	3.1
1984	60.0	31.5	5.2	1.3	2.0
1985	61.8	30.7	4.4	1.2	1.9
1986	61.7	29.9	5.5	1.1	1.8
1987	62.0	30.3	5.2	1.0	1.4

Source: U.S. Department of Justice, Office of Justice Programs, Bureau of Justice Statistics, Sourcebook of Criminal Justice Statistics, 1988 (Washington, D.C.: U.S. Government Printing Office, 1989), p. 517.

If the petition alleges that the juvenile has committed an act, which if committed by an adult would be a crime, or that the juvenile is a juvenile-status offender by being a truant, a runaway, or ungovernable (or some other such term), and if the facts support the petition, the court will adjudicate the juvenile to be a delinquent. In order not to stigmatize juveniles with the label "delinquent," some states have created such categories as **"persons in need of supervision"** (**PINS**) or "dependent and neglected children." Juveniles so charged will be adjudicated as such, if the facts warrant it. The judge will then proceed to the second part of the adjudication process, which corresponds to sentencing in criminal court.

The dispositional hearing In finding an appropriate disposition, the court is guided by any relevant information, especially that provided by the juvenile probation officer. The juvenile court judge must reconcile the child's interest with society's interest in protection from dangerous and disruptive children; guide delinquent children into a socially acceptable path; set an example for other children on the path of delinquency; make children responsible for their harmful actions; and set an example of love, care, and forgiveness for children who have transgressed the law.[42] In choosing a disposition, juvenile court judges have broader discretion than criminal court judges. The judge may choose probation, with numerous conditions; commitment to a juvenile correctional facility; restitution; or fines. Placement in a foster home or in a special program may also be decreed.

Juvenile corrections The juvenile court may reject all the alternatives and decide that the only option is to place the juvenile in an institution. There has been considerable debate over whether placement in an institution is ever an appropriate response to juvenile wrongdoing.

Alden Miller, as head of the Massachusetts juvenile correction system, tried to prove the point by closing down all of the Massachusetts juvenile detention facilities.[43] The experiment did not last. Policy makers determined that some juvenile offenders must be segregated for the protection of the community. Although researchers continue to demonstrate that the jailing of juvenile offenders has no appreciable effect on the juvenile crime rate,[44] all states maintain facilities for their confinement and hoped-for rehabilitation. Most inmates of juvenile facilities (74 percent) have committed crimes. Only 12 percent are adjudicated juvenile status offenders. A surprising 14 percent are juveniles classed as nonoffenders, including dependent, neglected, and abused children. Even more surprising, in a single year (1985) 3 percent of America's entire juvenile population were in custody. And the total number of residents in juvenile facilities keeps growing by 6 to 9 percent annually.[45]

A federal government survey revealed that in 1985

49,610 juveniles were committed to state-operated long-term facilities

44,570 juveniles were committed to other long-term facilities

433,579 juveniles were committed to short-term facilities

527,759 for a total of over half a million commitments.

The number of residents on an average day, however, amounts to only about 55,000, of which about half are long-term residents.[46]

Fifty percent of all admissions to juvenile facilities come from only five states, which have 5 percent of the entire juvenile population of theUnited States: California, Ohio, Texas, Washington, and Florida.[47] How can some states manage the juvenile justice problem with few institutionalizations, while others require so many?

The juvenile facilities encompass a wide spectrum: detention centers, training schools, reception or diagnostic centers, shelters, ranches, forestry camps or farms, halfway houses, and group homes. Most of the 3,036 facilities in the nation are privately operated. Yet the majority of juvenile offenders are being held in public facilities, which are far more security-minded than the private facilities.[48] Conditions in juvenile facilities range from serene, campuslike complexes with understanding counselors to deplorable, sordid, prisonlike facilities. Criminologists have argued that incarceration of juveniles will do more harm than good unless the conditions of detention are radically reformed and the population is kept at a minimum through reduced admissions. This is one of the tasks of the science of criminology.

Arguments about the future of juveniles placed in detention facilities have reached an impasse in the courts. In the case of *Schall* v. *Martin* it was argued before the Supreme Court that a New York law permitting the incarceration of juveniles predicted to constitute a danger was unconstitutional, because social science cannot make such predictions. In addressing the question, the Supreme Court made short

One of over half-a-million commitments to juvenile correctional institutions annually.

shrift of social science and affirmed its belief "that there is nothing inherently unattainable about a prediction of future conduct."[49] To many researchers it is still apparent that juvenile correctional treatment is largely unsuccessful.[50] There is general agreement that our juvenile justice system is far from perfect. The real problem, however, inheres not necessarily in the juvenile justice system but in social and economic conditions that produce delinquency in the first place. Reforms, therefore, must aim primarily at the root causes of delinquency.

Having traveled along the path of the juvenile justice process, we have yet one more path to pursue, that of the victims in the criminal justice process.

VICTIMS AND CRIMINAL JUSTICE

Victims of crime play a crucial role in invoking the criminal and juvenile justice processes. An old proverb states: Where there is no complainant, there is no judge. Victims play an equally significant role at the later stages of the process, as witnesses. Without their testimony convictions usually cannot be obtained. Until recently, however, the victims seemed to have been overlooked by the criminal justice system.

The History of the Role of Victims of Crime

The plight of the crime victim was recognized by the earliest legal systems. The Code of Hammurabi in the eighteenth century B.C. provided that the victims of highway robbers had to be compensated for their losses out of the governor's treasury.[51] Until the Middle Ages many acts that are crimes today were considered to be torts—that is, civil wrongs—which entitled the victim to compensation from the wrongdoer. Later on, however, powerful monarchs claimed compensation for themselves for the harm done to the real victim. Fines to the government replaced compensation to actual victims, who were forced to seek compensation in civil court proceedings. Thus started the long

decline of the role of the crime victim in the criminal justice process.

Not until after World War II did concern for the victim become revitalized. In *The Criminal and His Victim,* Hans von Hentig (himself a victim of Nazi persecution) forced us to think of the crucial role of the victim in the criminal justice process.[52] Benjamin Mendelson in 1947 coined the term **victimology,** the scientific study of the victim.[53] The Hungarian-American scholar Stephen Schafer (a victim of Nazi and Stalinist oppression) contributed significantly to victimology in his books *Restitution to Victims of Crime* and *The Victim and His Criminal.*[54] The momentum for focusing on the victim's role in criminal justice processing had been generated.[55] Legislatures responded by enacting victim-compensation legislation. By 1987 forty-four states had such programs (Table 14.6).

A further issue is how to integrate victims into the criminal justice process. Criminologists who specialize in the role and plight of the victim—victimologists—have come to the conclusion that victims have been badly treated in the criminal justice process.[56] The study of victimology now focuses on five goals:

- To understand the extent and nature of crime as victims perceive them.
- To assess the relative risk of victimization.
- To appreciate the nature and extent of losses, injuries, and damages experienced by victims of crime.
- To study the relation between victim and offender.
- To investigate the social reaction of the family, community, and society toward the victim of crime.

Victims' Rights

A strong movement for victims' rights began in the late 1960s and early 1970s with the creation of the first domestic violence and rape crisis centers by feminist activists. These initial efforts were followed by the establishment of victim-witness units in the District of Columbia courts,

TABLE 14.6   FORTY-TWO STATES, THE DISTRICT OF COLUMBIA, AND THE VIRGIN ISLANDS HAVE COMPENSATION PROGRAMS TO HELP VICTIMS OF VIOLENT CRIME

STATE	VICTIM COMPENSATION BOARD LOCATION[a]	FINANCIAL AWARD	TO QUALIFY, VICTIM MUST:		
			SHOW FINANCIAL NEED	REPORT TO POLICE WITHIN:	FILE CLAIM WITHIN:
Alabama	Alabama Crime Victim Compensation Commission	$0–10,000	No	3 days	12 mos.
Alaska	Department of Public Safety	$0–40,000	Yes	5	24
Arizona	Arizona Criminal Justice Commission	**	Yes	3	**
California	State Board of Control	$100–46,000	Yes	*	12
Colorado	Judicial district boards	$25–10,000	No	3	6
Connecticut	Criminal Injuries Compensation Board	$100–10,000	No	5	24
Delaware	Violent Crimes Board	$25–20,000	No	*	12
D.C.	Office of Crime Victim Compensation	$100–25,000	Yes	7	6
Florida	Department of Labor and Employment Security, Workmen's Compensation Division	$0–10,000	Yes	3	12
Hawaii	Department of Corrections	$0–10,000	No	*	18
Idaho	Industrial Commission	$0–25,000	No	3	12
Illinois	Court of Claims	$0–25,000	No	3	12
Indiana	Industrial Board	$100–10,000	No	2	24
Iowa	Department of Public Safety	$0–20,000	No	1	6
Kansas	Executive Department	$100–10,000	Yes	3	12
Kentucky	Victim Compensation Board	$0–25,000	Yes	2	12
Louisiana	Commission on Law Enforcement	$100–10,000	No	3	12
Maryland	Criminal Injuries Compensation Board	$0–45,000	Yes	2	6
Massachusetts	District Court system	$0–25,000	No	2	12
Michigan	Department of Management and Budget	$200–15,000	Yes	2	12
Minnesota	Crime Victims Reparation Board	$100–50,000	No	5	12
Missouri	Division of Workmen's Compensation	$200–10,000	No	2	12
Montana	Crime Control Division	$0–25,000	No	3	12
Nebraska	Commission on Law Enforcement and Criminal Justice	$0–10,000	Yes	3	24
Nevada	Board of Examiners and Department of Administration	$0–15,000	Yes	5	12
New Jersey	Executive Branch	$0–25,000	No	90	24
New Mexico	Executive Branch	$0–12,500	No	30	12
New York	Executive Department	$0–30,000†	Yes	7	12

TABLE 14.6   (Continued)

STATE	VICTIM COMPENSATION BOARD LOCATION[a]	FINANCIAL AWARD	TO QUALIFY, VICTIM MUST:		
			SHOW FINANCIAL NEED	REPORT TO POLICE WITHIN:	FILE CLAIM WITHIN:
North Carolina[b]	Department of Crime Control and Public Safety	$100–20,000		3 days	24 months
North Dakota	Workmen's Compensation Bureau	$0–25,000	No	3	12
Ohio	Court of Claims Commissioners	$0–25,000	No	3	12
Oklahoma	Crime Victims Board	$0–10,000	No	3	12
Oregon	Department of Justice/ Workmen's Compensation Board	$250–23,000	No	3	6
Pennsylvania	Crime Victims Board	$0–35,000	No	3	12
Rhode Island	Superior Court system	$0–25,000	No	10	24
South Carolina	Crime Victims Advisory Board	$100–3,000	No	2	6
Tennessee	Court of Claims Commission	$0–5,000	No	2	12
Texas	Industrial Accident Board	$0–25,000	No	3	6
Utah	Department of Administrative Services	$0–25,000	**	7	12
Virgin Islands	Department of Social Welfare	Up to $25,000	No	1	24
Virginia	Industrial Commission	$0–15,000	No	5	24
Washington	Department of Labor and Industries	$0–15,000†	No	3	12
West Virginia	Court of Claims Commissioner	$0–35,000	No	3	24
Wisconsin	Department of Justice	$0–40,000	No	5	12

[a]If location of the board is not indicated in the State statute, the board itself is noted.
[b]North Carolina's program is administratively established but not funded.
*Must report but no time limit specified.
**No reference in statute.
†Plus unlimited medical expenses.

Source: U.S. Department of Justice, Bureau of Justice Statistics, *Report to the Nation on Crime and Justice,* 2d ed. (Washington, D.C.: U.S. Government Printing Office, March 1988), p. 37.

which ensured respectful treatment for victims and witnesses involved in the criminal justice system. The purpose of such units was (*a*) to assist victims who report crimes; (*b*) to respond at the scene of a crime in order to provide crisis counseling; (*c*) to provide twenty-four-hour telephone hotline service to victims and witnesses; (*d*) to make emergency monetary aid available to victims; (*e*) to provide victims with referral services to appropriate agencies; (*f*) to help victims obtain the return of property; and (*g*) to assist victims and witnesses throughout their court appearances. Similar programs have been established throughout the country to make it easier for crime victims to participate in the criminal justice process, to secure their participation, and ultimately to provide satisfaction for them.

The Victim's Role in the Criminal Justice Process

Entry into the system   One of the most important achievements of victimologists was the development of victimization surveys (Chapter 2), which enabled us to estimate more accurately the extent of crime. The analysis of survey data focused attention on the impact of crime on the victim and demonstrated the importance of the victim's perception of any criminal event and willingness to report it to the authorities. The victim virtually determines the course of the criminal justice process by his or her willingness to report a victimization and to testify before the authorities, especially at trial.[57] Without a victim's complaint, the process normally cannot start.

Prosecution and pretrial services   The victim must appear at a police precinct once or twice. The police may have to interview the victim at home. The victim is likely to have to appear several times at the district attorney's office to answer the same questions. Accommodations for victims are not comfortable. Interview offices are typically dingy and crowded. Confrontations with the accused, however brief, are disquieting. Actual or anticipated harassment by the perpetrator of the crime may instill fear in the victim. Many victims get frustrated and stop showing up for scheduled hearings; many do not appear at the trial.

Adjudication   In most criminal proceedings, a plea negotiation takes the place of a criminal trial. In the past, victims played no role in the plea-bargaining process. More recently the American Bar Association has directed prosecuting attorneys to "make every effort to remain advised of the attitudes and sentiments of victims" before reaching a plea agreement.[58] Several researchers have studied the mode of participation by victims in the plea-bargaining process. One study found that only one-third of victims chose to participate, and their participation was minor.[59] Another researcher, by contrast, found victims to be very active in the plea-bargaining process, as demonstrated by the fact that 46 percent of the victims asked for the maximum punishment.[60]

If a case goes to trial, the victim is likely to be called as a witness. Though the defendant, handcuffed and in a holding pen, may be less comfortable and more anxious than the victim-witness, the anxiety of the victim and the lack of comfort in a courthouse corridor are painful experiences as well. During the trial the victim is subject to cross-examination by defense counsel, whose principal purpose it is to impugn the credibility of the witness.

The victim's rights movement has spurred the development of legislation and services that are responsive to the plight of victims called to testify in court. Several states have increased witness fees from the previous low of $5 a dayto as much as $30 a day. Some states have created procedures to notify victims of court proceedings and guarantee them the right to speedy disposition of their cases. Nine states and the federal government have enacted comprehensive bills of rights for victims. Thirty-nine states and Congress have enacted laws or provided guidelines requiring that victims and witnesses be informed of the scheduling and cancellation of criminal proceedings. Thirty-three states and the federal government permit victims to participate in criminal proceedings by oral or written testimony.[61] These developments have vastly improved the role of the victim in the adjudication process.

Sentencing   In the common law tradition the victim has no input in the imposition of a sentence. In thirty states, however, victims now have the right to state their views at sentencing hearings.[62] Yet on average only 10 percent of victims make use of this right. More important, at this stage it is possible to unite the punishment of the offender with the satisfaction of the victim. Ideally, a sentence can be fashioned to satisfy both the victim's sense of outrage and his or her need to be compensated for the monetary loss caused by the crime.[63] In several states, for example, a defendant may be sen tenced to a community restitution facility instead of a prison. At a sentencing hearing it can be made clear to a victim who demands a stiff prison sentence for the defendant that such a sentence will not result in compensation for any loss the victim has sustained. A sentence to a community restitution facility, however, guarantees that the offender will make installment payments to the victim for the harm inflicted. Victims are likely to agree to this seemingly less punitive but more rewarding sentence.

A promising new strategy for involving victims in the sentencing process is the opportunity of reconciling victim and offender in some cases, with or without compensation for the victim.[64] But the emotional problems involved require further study before such programs can be put into practice on a large scale.

Corrections and release   The correctional system implements any victim-compensation sentence that is imposed. If the sentence makes no provision for compensation, the victim at least

has one more opportunity to affect an important decision in several states: the parole hearing.[65] Parole boards tend to give great weight to a victim's opposition to a prisoner's release on parole.

Victims could be given a far greater opportunity to pursue their legitimate interests, especially to obtain compensation for the harm they have suffered. The continental criminal justice process has always offered the victim an opportunity to "join" the prosecution. The objective is to have the judge award compensation to the victim in conjunction with the sentence imposed on the offender. American law has not yet adopted this practice.

Nevertheless, great improvements have been made in our system to accommodate victims of crime. Victimology's drive for the recognition of the role of the victim in the criminal justice process has had powerful effects. Undoubtedly it will create even further changes in our criminal justice system as criminology continues to widen its focus to include the victim as well as the offender.

REVIEW

The criminal justice system, like any other production system, has components that are related and interdependent. This system has its own processes, which begin with the perception that a crime has been committed. After the crime has been reported, the authorities follow procedures developed for the arrest of suspects and for the presentation of the case to the courts. When the facts warrant a grand jury indictment or a prosecutor's information, the case moves to trial. Yet at this stage a plea agreement may be reached under which the defendant avoids trial and receives a reduced sentence in return for a plea of guilty to a lesser charge or to fewer charges. The conviction rate of defendants who go to trial is high.

A juvenile's path through the criminal justice system differs from an adult's. Juveniles are now granted the constitutional rights that not long ago were denied them, but they have also

been increasingly subjected to some of the rigors of the adult criminal justice system.

The movement through the criminal justice system is not automatic and inevitable. At each stage of the process it is dependent on decisions made by criminal justice officials and by the defendant. These decisions may lead to the diversion of the defendant out of the system at any stage. The criminal justice path has many side roads. These multiple exits explain the high attrition rate: only a fraction of the offenders who enter the criminal justice system wind up in corrections.

The development of victimology as a subdiscipline of criminology has drawn attention to the role of victims. Legislation in most states has eased victims' participation in the criminal justice process and provided compensation for their losses.

KEY TERMS

exclusionary rule
Miranda warning
parens patriae
person in need of supervision (PINS)
preliminary hearing

prima facie case
probable cause
reasonable suspicion
victimology

NOTES

1. President's Commission on Law Enforcement and the Administration of Justice, *The Challenge of Crime in a Free Society* (Washington, D.C.: U.S. Government Printing Office, 1967).

2. Michael R. Gottfredson and Don M. Gottfredson, *Decision Making in Criminal Justice: Toward the Rational Exercise of Discretion*, 2d ed. (New York: Plenum, 1988).

3. Ibid., chap. 2.

4. Ibid., chap. 3.

5. Beck v. Ohio, 379 U.S. 89 (1964).

6. Mapp v. Ohio, 367 U.S. 643 (1969).

7. Comptroller General of the United States, *Impact of the Exclusionary Rule on Federal Criminal Prosecutions* (Washington, D.C.: U.S. General Accounting Office, April 19, 1979); U.S. National Institute of Justice, *The Effects of the Exclusionary Rule: A Study in California* (Washington, D.C., December 1982); but see Malcolm Richard Wilkey, "The Exclusionary Rule: Costs and Viable Alternatives," *Criminal Justice Ethics* 1(2) (1982): 16–27.

8. Terry v. Ohio, 392 U.S. 1 (1968).

9. People v. de Bour, 40 N.Y. 2d 210 (1976).

10. Miranda v. Arizona, 384 U.S. 436 (1966).

11. But there is an exception to this rule: when public safety is at risk, the warning may be postponed. See New York v. Quarles, 467 U.S. 649 (1984).

12. Gideon v. Wainwright, 372 U.S. 335 (1963), as amplified by, *int. al.*, Argersinger v. Hamlin, 407 U.S. 25 (1972), and Strickland v. Washington, 446 U.S. 668 (1984) (counsel must be competent). See also Anthony Lewis, *Gideon's Trumpet* (New York: Vintage, 1966).

13. Robert Hermann, Eric Single, and John Boston, *Counsel for the Poor* (Lexington, Mass.: Lexington Books, 1977), esp. p. 153.

14. United States v. Salerno, 481 U.S. 739 (1987).

15. Gottfredson and Gottfredson, *Decision Making in Criminal Justice*, chap. 4.

16. Brian E. Forst, J. Lucianovic, and S. Cox, *What Happens After Arrest*, Institute for Law and Social Research Publication no. 4 (Washington, D.C.: U.S. Government Printing Office, 1977), p. 67.

17. "Only 3 of every 100 arrests went to trial in 1986, whereas 52 resulted in a guilty plea": U.S. Department of Justice, Bureau of Justice Statistics, *Annual Report, Fiscal 1988* (Washington, D.C.: U.S. Government Printing Office, 1989), p. 49.

18. Federal Rules of Criminal Procedure, Rule 11.

19. Ibid., Rule 6.

20. Forst et al., *What Happens After Arrest*, p. 17.

21. Held constitutional in Williams v. Florida, 399 U.S. 25 (1972).

22. See Harry Kalven, Jr., and Hans Zeisel, *The American Jury* (Chicago: University of Chicago Press, 1966).

23. Apodica v. Oregon, 406 U.S. 404 (1972). The case involved a homicide lesser than first-degree murder.

24. Don Gottfredson and Bridget Stecher, "Sentencing Policy Models," manuscript, School of Criminal Justice, Rutgers University, 1979.

25. Alfred Blumstein, Jacqueline Cohen, Susan E. Martin, and Michael H. Tonry, eds., *Research on Sentencing: The Search for Reform,*

vol. 1 (Washington, D.C.: National Academy Press, 1983), p. 11.

26. Joan Petersilia, *Expanding Options for Criminal Sentencing* (Santa Monica, Calif.: Rand Corporation, 1987).

27. Hans Toch, *Living in Prison* (New York: Free Press, 1977).

28. Michael R. Gottfredson and K. Adams, "Prison Behavior and Release Performance: Empirical Reality and Public Policy," *Law and Policy Quarterly* 4 (1982): 373–391.

29. Gottfredson and Gottfredson, *Decision Making in Criminal Justice*, chap. 8.

30. Allen J. Beck and Bernard E. Shipley, *Recidivism of Young Parolees: Special Report*, U.S. Department of Justice, Bureau of Justice Statistics (Washington, D.C.: U.S. Government Printing Office, 1987).

31. For a discussion of this study, see Charles Silberman, *Criminal Violence, Criminal Justice* (New York: Random House, 1978), pp. 257–261.

32. Readers interested in the subject may wish to consult William B. Sanders, *Juvenile Delinquency* (New York: Holt, Rinehart & Winston, 1976); G. Larry Mays, *Juvenile Delinquency and Juvenile Justice* (New York: Wiley, 1987); Roy Lotz, Eric D. Poole, and Robert M. Regoli, *Juvenile Delinquency and Juvenile Justice* (New York: Random House, 1985); Larry J. Siegel and Joseph J. Senna, *Juvenile Delinquency: Theory, Practice, and Law* (St. Paul, Minn.: West, 1981); Arnold Binder, Gilbert Geis, and Bruce Dickson, *Juvenile Delinquency: Historical Cultural, Legal Perspectives* (New York: Macmillan, 1988).

33. U.S. Department of Justice, Bureau of Justice Statistics, *Criminal Victimization in the United States, 1987* (Washington, D.C.: U.S. Government Printing Office, June 1989), Table 40, p. 47.

34. Ex parte Crouse, 4 Wharton, Pa., 9 (1838). See Steven L. Schlossman, *Love and the American Delinquent: The Theory and Practice of "Progressive" Juvenile Justice, 1825–1920* (Chicago: University of Chicago Press, 1977).

35. On the problems inherent in the concepts that guide the juvenile justice system, see

Sanford Fox, "Juvenile Justice Reform: An Historical Perspective," *Stanford Law Review* 22 (1970): 1187–1239; Anthony M. Platt, *The Child Savers: The Invention of Delinquency*, 2d ed. (Chicago: University of Chicago Press, 1977).

36. In re Winship, 397 U.S. 358 (1970); McKeiver v. Pennsylvania, 403 U.S. 528 (1971).

37. Norman Lefstein, Vaughan Stapleton, and Lee Teitelbaum, "In Search of Juvenile Justice: *Gault* and Its Implementation," *Law and Society Review* 3 (1969): 491; H. Ted Rubin, "The Juvenile Court's Search for Identity and Responsibility," *Crime and Delinquency* 23 (1977): 1–13.

38. Institute of Judicial Administration–American Bar Association, *Juvenile Justice Standards: A Summary and Analysis*, 2d ed., ed. Barbara Danziger Flicker, (Cambridge, Mass.: Ballinger, 1982), p. 47.

39. Breed v. Jones, 421 U.S. 519 (1975).

40. Richard J. Lundman, Richard E. Sykes, and John P. Clark, "Police Control of Juveniles: A Replication," in *Police Behavior: A Sociological Perspective*, ed. Richard J. Lundman, pp. 130–151 (New York: Oxford University Press, 1980).

41. Samuel M. Davis, *Rights of Juveniles: The Juvenile Justice System* 2d ed. (New York: Clark Boardman, 1980), pp. 3–9.

42. State ex. rel. D.D.H. v. Dostert, 165 W. Va. 448, 269 S.E. 2d 401 (1980). See also Institute of Judicial Administration–American Bar Association, *Juvenile Justice Standards*.

43. See Lloyd E. Ohlin, Robert B. Coates, and Alden D. Miller, "Radical Correctional Reform: A Case Study of the Massachusetts Youth Correctional System," *Harvard Educational Review* 44 (1974): 74–111.

44. Richard Allinson, "There Are No Juveniles in Pennsylvania Jails," *Corrections Magazine* 9(3) (1983): 13–20; Paul W. Keve, *The Consequences of Prohibiting the Jailing of Juveniles* (Richmond: Virginia Commonwealth University, 1984).

45. U.S. Department of Justice, Bureau of Justice Statistics, *Report to the Nation on Crime*

and Justice, 2d ed. (Washington, D.C.: U.S. Government Printing Office, 1988), pp. 95, 103, 105.

46. U.S. Department of Justice, Bureau of Justice Statistics, *Correctional Populations in the United States, 1987* (Washington, D.C.: U.S. Government Printing Office, December 1989), pp. 38, 70.

47. Binder et al., *Juvenile Delinquency*, p. 329.

48. Ibid., p. 110.

49. Schall v. Martin, 467 U.S. 253 (1984).

50. Steven P. Lab and John T. Whitehead, "An Analysis of Juvenile Correctional Treatment," *Crime and Delinquency* 34 (1988): 60–83.

51. See Gerhard O. W. Mueller, "Compensation for Victims of Crime: Thought Before Action," *Minnesota Law Review* 50 (1965): 213–221.

52. Hans von Hentig, *The Criminal and His Victim* (New Haven, Conn.: Yale University Press, 1948).

53. Benjamin Mendelson, "The Origin of the Doctrine of Victimology," *Excerpta Criminologica* 3 (1963): 239–244.

54. Stephen Schafer, *Restitution to Victims of Crime* (London: Stevens & Sons Ltd., 1960), and *Victimology: The Victim and His Criminal* (New York: Random House, 1968). See also Gerhard O. W. Mueller and H. H. A. Cooper, *The Criminal, Society, and the Victim*, for Law Enforcement Assistance Administration (Washington, D.C.: U.S. Government Printing Office, 1973).

55. See Symposium, *Minnesota Law Review* 50 (1965): 211–310. See also symposium, "Compensation for Victims of Criminal Violence," *Journal of Public Law* 8 (1959): 191–253, with contributions by G. Williams, J. L. Montrose, F. E. Inbau, F. W. Miller, H. Weihofen, G. O. W. Mueller, and H. Silving.

56. See Mary S. Knudten and Richard P. Knudten, "What Happens to Crime Victims and Witnesses in the Justice System?" in *Perspectives on Crime Victims*, ed. Burt Galaway and Joe Hudson, pp. 52–72 (St. Louis: C. V. Mosby, 1981). See also Wesley G. Skogan, "Citizens' Reporting of Crime: Some National Panel Data," in ibid., pp. 45–51; Michael J. Hindelang and Michael Gottfredson, "The Victim's Decision Not to Invoke the Criminal Process," in *Criminal Justice and the Victim*, ed. William F. McDonald, pp. 57–58 (Beverly Hills, Calif.: Sage, 1976).

57. American Bar Association, *Pleas of Guilty: Approved Draft* (Washington, D.C., February 1979), Standard 14-3, 1 (d).

58. A. M. Heinz and W. A. Kerstetter, "Victim Participation in Plea Bargaining: A Field Experiment," in *Plea Bargaining*, ed. W. F. McDonald and J. A. Cramer (Lexington, Mass.: D. C. Heath, 1979), pp. 167–177.

59. William F. McDonald, "The Victim's Role in the American Administration of Criminal Justice: Some Developments and Findings," in *The Victim in International Perspective*, ed. Hans Joachim Schneider, pp. 397–407 (New York: Walter de Gruyter, 1982). See also Lis Wieht, "Victim and Sentence: Resetting Justice's Scale," *New York Times*, September 29, 1989, p. B5.

60. Bureau of Justice Statistics, *Report to the Nation*, p. 82.

61. Donald J. Hall, "The Role of the Victim in the Prosecution and Disposition of a Criminal Case," in Galaway and Hudson, *Perspectives on Crime Victims*, pp. 318–342.

62. Ibid.

63. Stephen Schafer, "The Victim and Correctional Theory: Integrating Victim Reparation with Offender Rehabilitation," in McDonald and Cramer, *Plea Bargaining*, pp. 227–236.

64. See Dorothy [Edmonds] McKnight, "The Victim-Offender Reconciliation Project," in Galaway and Hudson, *Perspectives on Crime Victims*, pp. 292–298.

65. Hall, "Role of the Victim."

15

ENFORCING THE LAW: PRACTICE AND RESEARCH

Crime is rampant. There are pickpockets and purse snatchers lurking on every street. To protect their money from muggers, people now carry their wallets on a leather strap around their necks. Just the other day a noted wit said: "Only a fool would go out to dinner without having made his will."[1] The police are sparse in the neighborhoods. The city even installed dummy police officers, at highway intersections and school crossings, to serve as an alert to the presence of law enforcement. Citizens bought locks to protect their homes. You have never seen so many "Beware of Dog" signs! The more affluent hired private security agencies to protect their premises. Public officials don't even ride around in public anymore without security agents in front, in back, and on the sides. Neighborhoods have formed citizens' watch groups. And everybody is upset about the lack of police presence.

What city is being described? Chicago? Washington? New York? Or Denver? Seattle? Dallas? Although it could be any of these or other cities in the United States, this was reported about the Rome of two thousand years ago.

No country or city is capable of ensuring an orderly, secure life for its citizens unless it polices itself. This idea is so ancient that the Greeks used the same term for city and for police: *polis*. Through their presence the police, whether the lictors of ancient Rome or the men and women in blue in modern America, are supposed to maintain peace in the community. But their mere presence cannot prevent crime and disorder unless it is backed up by enforcement power. This power cannot be merely reactive. It has to encompass the right and duty to investigate, to assemble facts, and to prepare these facts for judicial disposition. These duties can be categorized as peacekeeping and crimefighting functions. Yet as we shall see, relatively little of police time is devoted to these duties that to citizens are most closely associated with policing. Far more police time is devoted to social services, such as helping people in distress; answering requests for information; responding to emergencies, disasters, and accidents; and maintaining an orderly traffic flow.

There is general agreement that the police are a multifunction service agency equipped to respond to civic problems and to fight crime.

PRÆTORIAN GUARDS   LICTORS

The Praetorian Guards may be likened to the state police, enforcing the law outside the city proper. The Lictors could be likened to the Federal Protection Agency, which guards public officials and diplomats.

But there is disagreement on the political and social role that police should play in a democratic society. This debate is marked by fear that civil liberties may be lost if the police power to take away personal freedom—by arrest, search, or use of force—is abused. As we shall see, this debate, which almost prevented the English from creating their first police force in 1829, has surfaced intermittently in the United States since the early nineteenth century. It reached particular intensity in the 1960s, when aggressive policing against demonstrators and minorities resulted in claims that some police agencies were biased organizations that infringed on the rights of citizens. We shall pay particular attention to this problem.

Their strategic position at the gateway of the criminal justice process, their numerical strength in comparison with that of all other agents of criminal justice, and their constant contact with the public give the police uppermost significance in the criminal justice process.

THE HISTORY OF POLICING

Policing in England

Eleventh to eighteenth centuries   The earliest records of policing in Anglo-American history can be found in the laws of the Danish king Canute (d. 1035), who governed England in the first quarter of the eleventh century, before the Norman Conquest. In a system called **frank-pledge,** members of a **tithing,** an association of ten families, were bound together by a mutual pledge to keep the peace. Every male over age 12 was part of the system. Over time the frankpledge system was strengthened by the establishment of the king's representative, the *reeve*, in each county or shire. The shire reeve, or sheriff, presided over the shire's court, executed summonses, and enforced the laws. A force of able-bodied citizens, called a *posse comitatus* (Latin for "power of the county"), assisted the sheriff and could be convened at his command. (The use of sheriff's posses persisted well into the twentieth century in the western and southern United States.) The Statute of Winchester in 1285 established the office of **constable** (Latin *comes stabuli,* "officer of the stable"), a royal official charged with suppressing riots and violent crimes in each county. By the thirteenth century a night watch system was developed in larger towns and cities. These **night watchmen** were untrained citizens who patrolled at night, on the lookout for disturbances. In 1326 the first **justices of the peace** were commissioned. They were untrained men, usually of the nobility, who investigated and tried minor cases. Law enforcement by sheriffs, constables, hired assistants, justices of the peace, and night watchmen changed very little in England until the eighteenth century.[2]

Eighteenth and nineteenth centuries   The system that had worked in rural and feudal England proved inadequate in the growing cities. At the beginning of the eighteenth century there was little law and order in London. Henry Fielding (1707–1754), the author of *Tom Jones* and a justice of the peace, led efforts to establish a uniformed, armed standing police force. In response to research conducted by Fielding and reported in his *Enquiry into the Causes of the Late Increase of Robbers* (1751), Parliament granted him funds to recruit England's first professional police force. The experiment failed, and it was not until 1829 that a new system was established. In that year an "Act for

In this painting, one of the world's most famous, Rembrandt portrayed the "Nightwatch," a society of wealthy burghers, who banded together to protect the city at night from burglars and other predators.

Improving the Police in and near the Metropolis" was steered through Parliament by England's home secretary, Sir Robert Peel (1788–1850). This bill established the Metropolitan Constabulary, originally composed of one thousand men. These officers were uniformed but unarmed, well disciplined, and taught to "remember, that there is no qualification more indispensable to a police officer, than a perfect command of temper, never suffering himself to be moved in the slightest degree, by any language or threats that may be used."[3] Sir Robert's officers came to be known as little Roberts, or bobbies. The experiment proved such a success in London that by 1856 all counties and boroughs in England were required to have their own professional police forces.[4]

Notwithstanding the rising crime rates, the urban chaos, and the humanitarian reforms instituted by Peel, some scholars believe that the real reason for the establishment of the English police was not in fact the crime problem. They see it as having been motivated by a desire of the elite to control the poor. Vagrants and idle persons, after arrest and conviction, could be a source of cheap labor for the Industrial Revolution's growing number of factories.[5]

By the mid-nineteenth century policing in England had evolved from an association of families to an organized, uniformed metropolitan police force. The successful English experiment quickly spread to the United States and replaced the earlier English system that had been followed up to that time.

Policing in the United States

Colonial America adopted a system of policing much like that of early England. County **sheriffs** were the principal law enforcement officers. They were supplemented by town marshals, constables, and night watchmen. Sheriffs received no salaries, but were paid standard fees for the various services they performed (collecting taxes, supervising elections, and so forth).[6] Sheriffs were assisted by deputies, and in case of need they could convene posses composed of ordinary citizens to aid in law enforcement tasks requiring strength of numbers. This system lasted until the early nineteenth century, when the rapid growth of cities brought a need for a better and more formal law enforcement system.[7] In a time of migration and immigration, rapid industrialization, social unrest, hostility toward minorities, and mob violence, cities were forced to organize their first uniformed police forces. In 1838 Boston established its first force. New York followed in 1844, Philadelphia ten years later.

The police were expected to keep the peace, to prevent crime, and to soothe social conflict. Their duties extended to such nonenforcement activities as caring for orphans and derelicts, operating soup kitchens, and maintaining sanitary conditions in overcrowded neighborhoods. Appointments to the police were made by political bosses. Police commissioners changed with every election, as did many of the men on the force. Often the officers were, in fact, tools of ward politicians, with little accountability to the public. Throughout the nineteenth century, the conduct of police forces in the United States was an ongoing scandal. As a group, they were corrupt, powerful, often poorly trained, without standards for admission to the force (not even health or age), unsupervised, and frequently abusive.[8] (Brutality appeared to be tolerated by the middle class because it was used in large measure against social outcasts.)

At the turn of the twentieth century policing was influenced significantly by the Progressive reformers and the development by August Vollmer of the concept of police professionalism. Vollmer's model of police organization and activity, based on the crime-fighting role of the police, was not challenged until the 1960s. Let us take a closer look at its development.

The era of reform   The Progressives were by and large educated upper- and middle-class Americans determined to stamp out corruption wherever they found it. Among the many places they found it were the police forces. The Progressives worked to professionalize law enforcement by taking it out of politics and introducing modern technology. Their slogan was

"The police have to get out of politics, and politics has to be out of the police."[9] One of the reformers, Theodore Roosevelt, who accepted the presidency of the New York City Board of Police Commissioners in 1895, immediately implemented a change in police standards by failing over half of the applicants on the physical examination and 30 percent on the mental examination in a ten-month period.[10] Despite their many reforms, some historians of criminology have argued that the Progressives' interest in a more efficient police force was grounded less in a desire to reform than in their fear that newer immigrant groups might be gaining too much power in local government and thus too much control in the cities.

August Vollmer, who developed the professional model of policing in the early twentieth century, was a first-generation American with a limited education, yet he became one of the most prominent figures in the history of American policing. He began his career in 1904 as police marshal in Berkeley, California. Within five years he was made chief of police, a position he held until 1932. To Vollmer, a professional police force had to be nonpolitical, well recruited, well trained, well disciplined, and equipped with modern technology. Its members had to be part of the civil service, selected and advanced by merit. The police officers' major role was to be crime fighting. His book *The Police and Modern Society* (1936) remained a guide for police professionals for decades. The American Society of Criminology gave his name to its most prestigious award for outstanding achievement in law enforcement and criminal justice.

Another pioneer in modern policing, Orlando W. Wilson, a student and protégé of Vollmer, stands out for his contribution to the modern management and administrative techniques used in policing. Wilson, who obtained a degree in criminology from the University of California in 1924, became chief of police in Fullerton, California (1924–1928), and Wichita, Kansas (1928–1939). He served as professor of police administration (1939–1960) and as founding dean of the University of California, Berkeley, School of Criminology (1953). He retired in 1967 as superintendent of the Chicago Police

Department, which he had transformed from one of the least reputable in the country to one of the very best.

During the period when the pioneers in policing were professionalizing the police forces, several crime commissioners at the local, state, and national levels began to investigate the extent of crime and the criminal justice system's response to it. Attorney General George W. Wickersham was appointed to head the United States National Commission on Law Observance and Enforcement from 1929 to 1932.[11] The commission retained practitioners and academicians to observe and analyze the state of law enforcement in the country, particularly in connection with the futile attempts to enforce the prohibition laws. The result of the inquiry was devastating: Many police forces were corrupt, training was superficial, and recruitment was inadequate. Communications, statistics, and information sharing were chaotic. Constitutional guarantees were largely ignored. The report of the Wickersham Commission provided solid evidence that American's early reform efforts had not reached far enough or deep enough.

In summary, during the early part of the nineteenth century, the Progressives fought for reform of policing; various commissions detailed the problems; and police advocates put new ideas into practice. The crime-fighting role of officers became dominant. They were supposed to be tough, well-trained members of a highly militaristic organization.

This crime-fighting model of policing lasted until it was challenged in the 1960s, in the wake of civil unrest. Before we discuss how police departments attempted to foster good community relations in order to improve their image and deal more effectively with the public, let us look at their organizational structure.

THE ORGANIZATION OF THE POLICE

There are more than 20,000 separate law enforcement agencies in the United States. Most of them are at the local level—county, city, town, and village forces. These departments may have only a single officer or as many as 33,000 officers. There are about two hundred agencies at the state level and about fifty at the federal level. More than 600,000 full-time law enforcement personnel, including almost 500,000 sworn officers and over 100,000 civilian employees, serve these agencies.[12] American policing differs from that found in most other countries in its diversity of forces and lack of central coordination and command. The idea that federal and state police functions are separate is basic to our system of federalism. Even within the states there has always existed a concern that any central command not only would violate local autonomy but might tend to put a dangerous concentration of power in the hands of the chief executive. Consequently, most policing takes place at the municipal level, where the control rests, for the most part, with an elected police commissioner and an appointed chief, superintendent, or director, who handles the administrative responsibilities. (Window to the World offers a glimpse of policing at the international level.)

Federal Law Enforcement

The framers of the Constitution did not envisage the need for any federal law enforcement agency. But it soon became clear that the federal government had to police its mandated functions. The first federal police force to be established was the United States Coast Guard, which in 1790 was assigned the task of policing the shoreline to prevent smuggling and ensure the collection of import duties. Other federal police forces were added, particularly after 1870, when the Department of Justice became aware of its law enforcement obligations. The agency with the broadest range of duties is the Federal Bureau of Investigation.

The Federal Bureau of Investigation   In 1908 President Theodore Roosevelt, angered by Congress's failure to adopt legislation to regulate political and business corruption, established the Department of Justice's Bureau of Investigations. Initially the bureau was staffed by thirty-five employees, most of whom had been

WINDOW TO THE WORLD

Interpol

With the expansion of international commerce, railroad and steamship transportation, telephone and telegraph communication, and traffic across national borders, Europe experienced a sharp increase in crime in the early twentieth century. Criminals had become internationally mobile; law enforcement had remained local. Against this background, in 1914 Prince Albert I of Monaco organized the First International Criminal Police Congress, which led to the creation of what is now called the International Criminal Police Organization,

known as Interpol. This organization has a unique feature that sets it apart from other police agencies: it has no police officers. Interpol is a complex telecommunication clearinghouse in which 147 governments participate. It provides information on criminals and handles requests for wanted criminals. In the United States, the U.S. National Central Bureau (USNCB), located in the Department of Justice in Washington, handles all Interpol requests. The bureau may be asked to locate a fugitive, check a license, or supply a criminal

record. Interpol maintains its effectiveness by annual meetings of member governments, by jointly devising crime-prevention strategies, by improving the level of training, by research into crime developments, and by maintaining a sophisticated system of tracing firearms. The exclusion of the Eastern European socialist countries had kept Interpol from being a universal organization. But with the recent application of the Soviet Union and other Eastern European countries for membership, that situation is changing.

---

recruited from the ranks of federal investigators. They were empowered to investigate bankruptcy fraud, antitrust violations, and other violations of federal law.

During the late 1920s—the heyday of Prohibition—citizens became frustrated by the inability of local and state law enforcement agencies to stem the proliferation of underworld gangsters. Moreover, incidents such as the Lindbergh kidnapping (Chapter 10) fueled this frustration. But at that point the bureau had no authority to investigate or apprehend fleeing felons who crossed state lines. In the face of arguments favoring establishment of a national or federal police force, J. Edgar Hoover, whom President Calvin Coolidge had appointed to head the bureau in 1924, argued vehemently that state and local police should retain their own jurisdictions and sovereignty, but that new federal legislation was needed to give the bureau jurisdiction over criminals who operate across state lines. In 1934 Congress passed legislation expanding the bureau's jurisdiction. One year later, in 1935, the bureau adopted a

new name—the Federal Bureau of Investigation (FBI).

Over the years the FBI has played a highly publicized role in the investigation and capture of such infamous criminals as Baby Face Nelson, Doc Barker, John Dillinger, Pretty Boy Floyd, Al Capone, Bonnie Parker, and Clyde Barrow. Under the directorship of Hoover, the FBI acquired a sterling image as the chief investigative branch of the Department of Justice. This image was tarnished in the 1960s when it was revealed that FBI agents had been wiretapping such leaders as Martin Luther King, Jr., opening mail, and discrediting political radicals as "enemies of the government."[13]

Since Hoover's death, much of the FBI's reputation has been restored through enlightened leadership. The orientation of the bureau has changed; now it focuses on white-collar crime, public corruption, organized crime, drug offenses, and terrorism. Headquartered in Washington, D.C., the bureau has approximately 8,000 agents in fifty-nine field offices around the United States. The FBI Laboratory and Forensic Science Research and Training Center have stayed at the forefront of technology and training. In 1982 the laboratory conducted nearly 800,000 scientific investigations. By 1985 that number had almost doubled.[14] The laboratory holds the fingerprints of more than 65 million people. In addition, the bureau maintains one of the main sources of crime statistics, the Uniform Crime Reports (Chapter 2). In 1967 the FBI initiated the National Crime Information Center (NCIC), a computerized data base that retains information on criminals and makes it accessible to law enforcement agencies in all fifty states. More than 1.5 million transactions are processed each week. The NCIC also supplies information on stolen guns, stolen vehicles, and wanted persons. The FBI plays a role in police training as the administrator of the National Police Academy, located at the U.S. Marine Corps base in Quantico, Virginia. The academy trains all agents and is responsible for the professional education of more than 1,000 state and local law enforcement administrators every year.

Other federal law enforcement agencies   The Department of Justice maintains other agencies that also fulfill law enforcement duties:

• The Drug Enforcement Administration (DEA), which is charged with the enforcement of laws controlling the use, sale, and distribution of narcotics and other controlled substances.
• The Immigration and Naturalization Service (INS), which has the dual authority of policing U.S. borders so as to prevent aliens from entering illegally and overseeing the admission, naturalization, exclusion, and deportation of aliens.
• The United States Marshal Service, which provides protection for relocated witnesses and administrative support and security services for federal district courts and the United States courts of appeals.

Most of the other departments of the federal government operate law enforcement agencies as well. The Treasury Department maintains a law enforcement agency within the Internal Revenue Service (IRS). This agency is responsible for enforcing laws relating to taxes and their collection. The Treasury also operates the Secret Service, which protects governmental officials and investigates forgery and counterfeiting, and the Bureau of Alcohol, Tobacco, and Firearms (ATF), which enforces the federal laws regulating the importation, distribution, and use of alcohol, tobacco, and firearms. The Federal Trade Commission (FTC), the Securities and Exchange Commission (SEC), the Department of Labor, and the United States Postal Service all maintain their own law enforcement agencies.

State Police

In 1835 the first state police agency, the Texas Rangers, was established. Its purpose was primarily to control the Mexican border. Thirty years later Massachusetts created a similar force. It was not until the turn of the twentieth century that states across the country followed suit—Connecticut in 1903, Arizona and Pennsylvania in 1905, New Jersey in 1921. Today all states have their own police forces. Their primary function is to control traffic on the highways. They also fill gaps in rural and suburban policing, respond to the statewide mobility of crime (for example, by pursuing offenders crossing jurisdictional boundaries), aid in crowd control, and provide centralized services for local police forces (tracing stolen cars, statewide record keeping, laboratory assistance). The distrust of centralized police power has generally kept state police forces from assuming any duties of local officials.

County Police

The sheriff's office, at the county level, is responsible for countywide policing outside municipalities. In Western movies, the sheriff is portrayed as a tough, fearless, fair, and incorruptible official, clearly distinguishable by his five-pointed star and his agility with pistols. He was indeed a powerful figure on the frontier. During the westward expansion in the nineteenth century, the sheriff was often the only legal authority over vast areas. Today sheriff's departments range from small offices with an appointed sheriff to large departments staffed by trained, professional personnel (as in Los Angeles County, California). Most sheriff's forces perform functions that extend beyond crime prevention and control to such traditional county governmental services as tax assessment and collection, court duty, jail administration, various inspection services, serving court orders, and overseeing public buildings, highways, bridges, and parks. In some places the sheriff may even serve as the coroner.

Municipal Police

A prototype for a well-organized municipal police department, developed by the President's Commission on Law Enforcement and the Administration of Justice, has been adopted, at least in part, by most urban agencies (Figure 15.1). A department has basically two types of functions to perform: line functions (operations bureau) and nonline functions (administration and service bureaus). Line functions include patrol duties, investigation, traffic control, and various specialized services (juvenile, vice, domestic dispute). Most officers are assigned to patrol duties. The nonline functions include the staff duties that one finds in most large organizations, public or private, such as planning, research, administration and training, budgeting, purchasing, public relations, inspections. Nonline functions also increasingly include the complex tasks of supporting line functions with high-tech services in communications, identifi-

FIGURE 15.1   One form of a well-organized municipal police department

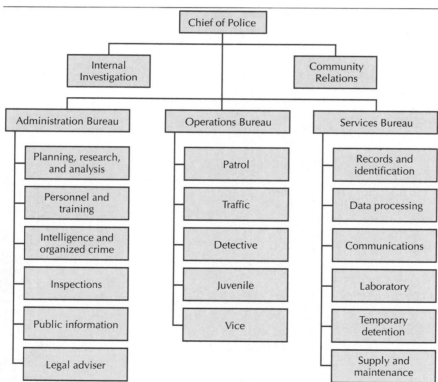

Source: The President's Commission on Law Enforcement and the Administration of Justice, *Task Force Report: The Police* (Washington, D.C.: U.S. Government Printing Office, 1967), p. 47.

cation, laboratory work, and data processing, as well as such routine services as building and grounds maintenance, repair services, supply provisioning, and jail administration.

Police departments are not democratic organizations. They function largely along the lines of a military command structure, with military ranks and insignia. Patrol officers are responsible to their sergeants, sergeants to lieutenants, lieutenants to captains, captains to inspectors, inspectors to their chief or director. The structure of operational units is similar to that of other governmental departments. A bureau is at the highest level (a bureau of police within a department of public safety for instance); divisions (such as a criminal investigation division) are at the next lower level; and sections are at the lowest level (the art theft section, for example). The goal of this type of organization is efficient performance. The day-to-day and night-to-night operations of line officers are carried out in shifts or watches, usually of eight consecutive hours but often lasting longer.

Patrol   Patrol officers on the beat are usually the first law enforcement persons on the scene of a crime. They conduct the initial search, block off the crime scene for later investigation, interview victims and witnesses, and make a report of the facts. Small police agencies may have only patrol officers. In larger agencies, the patrol unit constitutes about two-thirds of the officers. The function of this unit is to deter crime by the presence of officers on the street, to check on suspicious activities, to respond to calls for aid, to enforce laws, and to maintain order. The public is more familiar with patrol officers than with officers of other units because they are the ones who walk or cruise the neighborhoods, constantly coming into contact with the residents. For this reason the patrol officer on the beat is very important to the relations between the police and the community. Since the 1960s the police have been very sensitive to the need to maintain good community relations, for reasons that we shall soon explore.

Investigation   With only a few clues, a magnifying glass, a bumbling friend, and a good bit of intuition, the fictional Sherlock Holmes always solved the crime. Television and motion pictures have carried on this romanticized version of the detective as a tough "loner" stalking suspects until they end up in handcuffs or dead after a hair-raising shoot-out. In reality, however, the role of the detective is quite different. Most detectives are trained in modern techniques of investigation and in the laws of evidence and procedure. They interact with many other individuals or police units, such as the traffic, vice, juvenile, and homicide divisions. And they spend most of their time on rather routine chores involving quite a bit of paperwork and not much excitement. Detectives, however, occupy a more prestigious position in a police department than do patrol officers. They receive better salaries, they have more flexible hours, they do not wear uniforms, and they can act more independently.

After a crime is reported, detectives investigate the facts in order to determine whether a crime has been committed and whether they have enough information to indicate that the case warrants further investigation. This information may come from patrol officers or members of the public. If a full-scale investigation is undertaken, detectives begin the process of reinterviewing witnesses, contacting informants, checking crime files, and so on. Modern detective work sometimes includes **sting operations,** which are undercover operations in which police pretend to involve themselves in illegal acts to trap a suspect. They may pose as fences in order to capture thieves or as wealthy businesspeople offering money to those suspected of taking bribes. Sting operations have been highly criticized by researchers, who find that this particular method of detective work borders on illegal entrapment.[15]

The Rand Corporation has studied how efficient detectives are at clearing cases. Data from 153 large detective bureaus demonstrated that the expertise of detectives was ineffective and too much time was spent on paperwork.[16] Another analysis of 5,336 cases reported to suburban police departments reached a similar conclusion: The solution of most crimes does not require detective work.[17] But a Police Executive Research Forum (PERF) study had contradictory findings: data on 3,360 burglaries and 320 robberies in De Kalb County, Georgia; St. Petersburg, Florida; and Wichita, Kansas, show that both initial investigation by patrol officers and follow-up work by detectives are necessary to find suspects.[18]

Specialized units   Metropolitan police departments have specialized units to deal with specific kinds of problems. The traffic unit, for example, is responsible for investigation of accidents, control of traffic, and enforcement of parking and traffic laws. Since police departments have neither the resources to enforce all traffic laws nor the desire to punish all violators, they have a policy of selective enforcement: They target specific problem intersections or highways with high accident or violation rates for stiffer enforcement. Traffic law enforcement has an important influence on community relations because of the large amount of contact with the public that this task requires. Most large city departments have a vice squad. It enforces laws against such activities as gambling, drug dealing, and prostitution. This type of work requires undercover agents, informants, and training in the legal procedures that govern their duties, including the law on entrapment, which forbids law enforcement officers to induce others to commit crimes.

Every department also needs administrators to recruit officers, to plan, to run the budget, to keep records, and to teach. Training of officers varies from state to state. Before 1969 only ten states required preservice training for their officers.[19]

In summary, there are public law enforcement agencies at many levels, each with its own specialized units and duties. They are, however, often called upon to work together to solve cases. A major narcotics operation, for example, may involve the DEA, the Coast Guard, the FBI, the state police, county sheriffs, and local police authorities. By and large, though, citizens come into contact primarily with local law enforcement officers.

As the most highly visible members of the criminal justice system, local police play a major role in instilling a sense of security among citizens and in maintaining good relations between the police and the community. During the civil unrest of the 1960s, police departments began to look for ways to improve their image in order to establish better public relations. Police administrators realized that officers had to do more than just enforce the law; they needed to concentrate on maintaining order and providing services as well.

THE FUNCTIONS OF THE POLICE

The police have three categories of functions: law enforcement, order maintenance, and community service. The way the police function in communities determines their relationship with their constituents.

The Law Enforcement Function

We have seen why the law enforcement function, which involves intervention in situations in which the law has been broken, became predominant in the early twentieth century under the strong influence of Vollmer, Wilson, and their associates. Crime was to be controlled by concentration on serious offenses, and police performance was assessed by the number of felony arrests. No one felt much concern about the routine, minor violators, such as drunks and groups of noisy teenagers. Crime was to be suppressed in the most efficient way possible, and that way depended on the maximum coverage of an officer's beat. A beat, the argument ran, was covered better in a car than on foot, and one-officer cars were twice as efficient as two-officer cars. So police departments shifted from foot patrol to car patrol and made large investments in communication equipment. As depersonalized as the car-patrolled beats became, they were made even more so by frequent rotation in an effort to minimize the corruption that might tempt officers who got to know their constituents too well. The result of all these changes, suggest James Q. Wilson and George Kelling, was that the personal relationship between the folks in the neighborhood and the cop of former days was lost.[20]

Not all criminologists agree with Wilson and Kelling. Samuel Walker, for example, contends that the "good old days" of policing never ex-

AT ISSUE

Private Policing

Most people do not realize that we depend more on private services for our security than on public police officers. Private policing, or private security, assumed a major role during the westward movement of our nation. Express companies carried valuable cargo under the protection of armed guards. In March 1850 Henry Wells and William G. Fargo founded the American Express Company and two years later they founded Wells Fargo and Company.

One name stands out in the history of private policing in the United States: Allan Pinkerton. In 1849 he became Chicago's first detective. A year later he set himself up as a private detective, and thus started the private detective business in America. During the Civil War he served in the Union army as a major and set up its successful espionage system. After the war Pinkerton's agents became the tools of management in labor disputes. The brutal force used by "the Pinkertons" to break strikes became notorious. By the beginning of World War II, private policing had acquired a very poor image.

That image changed after World War II, however. Industrial plants were involved in the production of nuclear weapons and rocketry; the cold war was in progress; and the need to protect highly dangerous industrial activities against espionage,

sabotage, or accident was keenly felt. The 1950s and 1960s were years of civil unrest, increasing crime rates, and the beginning of terrorism. This was fertile ground for the growth of the private security business. Public law enforcement was not able to keep up with the demand for protection. Voters were unwilling to increase police budgets. Private enterprises, even housing developments, had to provide for their own protection. Today there are nearly twice as many private security personnel as public police officers.

The rapid, uncontrolled growth of the private security industry began to worry the government. Concern was expressed that the security industry served only corporations and the rich. In the 1980s many states and municipalities passed legislation and ordinances to regulate the private security industry, in an effort to ensure the public of reasonably accountable and at least semiprofessional protection.

In the past, few skills were needed to do the work. Different needs prevail today. Sophisticated electronic systems used for plant protection require highly skilled personnel to operate them. The development of security systems and programs requires technical and management skills. Executive protection requires intelligence, agility, training, and often language skills. More and more,

state and municipal agencies require the licensing and bonding of private security personnel. Contract security agencies have vastly upgraded their recruitment and educational standards.

Yet much remains to be done to bring private security under public control and to improve the relationship between private and public security. Of particular concern is the extent to which private security runs its own criminal justice system. For example, will private security always surrender an employee thief or embezzler or a shoplifter, or will the problem somehow be dealt with internally, without reference to public authority? Also worrisome is the increasing exchange of personnel between private security and the police. It has been estimated that 166,000 police officers work in private security in their off-duty hours. Moreover, the wages offered by private security entice many police officers to take the earliest possible retirement in order to enter the private sector. To the extent that the private sector benefits from the expensive training and experience of public police officers, the public sector loses.

Some criminologists are concerned that in the long run the notion that all citizens should be equally protected by the police will suffer. All evidence suggests that private policing will continue to grow, but not without problems.

isted. When communications were primitive, officers could avoid supervision, neglect their responsibilities, and engage in corrupt practices. Walker also points out that at the same time that police were put into patrol cars to depersonalize the system, the widespread use of the telephone resulted in increasing contacts with individuals. When police were on foot patrol, they did indeed have more contact with people, but in public places. They did not often go into private homes, for the good reason that a person in trouble had no way to call for help.[21] Empirical studies have confirmed the importance of the telephone. It is estimated that when citizens ask for police help, close to 90 percent of the requests are made by phone.[22]

The Order Maintenance Function

Besides their law enforcement function, police officers have the responsibility to prevent and control disturbances of the public peace, such as domestic quarrels, aggressive panhandlers soliciting in the streets, noisy drunks, and disorderly demonstrations. In their order maintenance function, police officers usually can exercise discretion in deciding whether a law has been broken. Wilson and Kelling describe this police function in an article titled "Broken Windows: The Police and Neighborhood Safety."[23] Though literally "broken windows" refers to the rundown, burned-out, deteriorated conditions of buildings in many inner-city neighborhoods, the phrase has a more symbolic meaning as well. It refers to the quality of life in a neighborhood and the attitudes of the people who live in it. According to Wilson and Kelling, as policing in America became more professional, increasing emphasis was placed on crime fighting (the law enforcement model) and less on the type of policing that enhances harmonious relationships within the community, reduces fear of crime, and stimulates cooperation between citizens and police (the order maintenance function).[24]

The Service Function

As the government's front-line response to social problems and emergencies, the police are called on to provide community service to those members of the community who by reason of personal, economic, social, or other circumstances are in need of immediate aid.[25] Their duties bring them in contact with knife and gunshot wounds, drug overdoses, alcoholic delirium, and routine medical problems from heart attacks to diabetic comas. They return runaway children to their parents and remove cats from trees. Research done in a city of 400,000 found, in fact, that social service and administrative tasks accounted for 55 percent of officers' time; crime fighting accounted for 17 percent.[26] Another study found that of 18,000 calls to a Kentucky police department over a four-month period, 60 percent were for information, 13 percent concerned traffic, 2.7 percent dealt with violent crime, and 1.8 percent involved property crime.[27]

The successful performance of the law enforcement, order maintenance, and service functions requires that the police have the trust and cooperation of the public. Community relations all but vanished during the era of professionalization. This became apparent during the late 1960s and early 1970s, when citizens, especially in inner-city ghetto areas, revolted against government policy in general and law enforcement in particular. These revolts prompted large-scale reforms in American policing.

THE RULE OF LAW IN LAW ENFORCEMENT

A close examination of the functioning of American policing revealed defects in six distinct areas: constitutional due process, civil rights, use of deadly force, abuse of discretion, corruption, and police–community relations. Restoration and maintenance of the rule of law to which the American system of government is devoted required reforms in all of these areas.

Constitutional Due Process

Largely as a result of the demonstrated systematic lawlessness of some police officers, the United States Supreme Court, under the leadership of Chief Justice Earl Warren, played the leading role in the reform movement. In case after case the Supreme Court reversed convictions that had been obtained in violation of constitutional restraints. The provisions in the Bill of Rights, which had been applied only to federal law enforcement, were extended to cover state actions as well through the Fourteenth Amendment, which guarantees that no one shall be deprived of life, liberty, or property without due process of law (Chapter 14). These rights include protection against unreasonable searches and seizures (Fourth Amendment), protection against self-incrimination (Fifth Amendment), and the right to counsel (Sixth Amendment). Some people hailed these decisions; but others decried them as a means of handcuffing the police in their efforts to enforce the law.

Civil Rights

American policing also suffered from increasing tensions between black citizens who demanded their civil rights and police who tried to maintain the status quo. Police officers gave the appearance of a force removed from the community, encapsulated in their cocoon of elitist professionalism, insensitive to community moods and needs. This was especially the case in the inner city. Tensions mounted. On July 16, 1964, a white New York City officer shot and killed a black teenager. Demonstrators marched to the 28th Precinct headquarters. Two days of rioting followed. The rioting spread to Rochester, Jersey City, and Philadelphia, and in the next year to Los Angeles, Chicago, and San Diego. Then Cleveland, San Francisco, Atlanta, Detroit, and Newark were affected. In the same era, students were demonstrating against the Vietnam War. In all cases, the police were called in to restore order, a process that culminated in many confrontations and some deaths.

During these years of turmoil, in 1966, Lyndon B. Johnson established the President's Commission on Law Enforcement and the Administration of Justice. The commission reported findings of racism, unequal justice, and police brutality. This report led to the enactment of the Omnibus Crime Control and Safe Streets Act of 1968, which created the Law En-

forcement Assistance Administration (LEAA). During its brief existence (1967–1982) the agency spent $7 billion in an effort to upgrade law enforcement and criminal justice in the United States. Though the LEAA has been criticized for its vast expenditures on hardware and on speculative research and development, among other things, it has also been praised for its enormous positive effects on American criminal justice.[28] LEAA funds established advanced training in law enforcement and criminal justice and, directly and indirectly, resulted in the establishment of more than 600 academic programs of criminal justice in the United States.

Use of Deadly Force

In *Tennessee* v. *Garner* the United States Supreme Court was confronted with a tragic situation. A father was suing a Memphis police officer, as well as governmental agencies, for the loss of the life of his 17-year-old son. The son, according to the undisputed facts, had burglarized a home. The police responded instantly to the homeowner's call. An officer spotted the suspect fleeing across the backyard and ordered him to stop. The officer saw that the suspect was unarmed. The youngster made an effort to jump over a high fence. The officer shot and killed him. The common law rule of England and the United States, as well as the law of Tennessee, had always been that the police may use deadly force to stop a fleeing felon whether or not he or she is in possession of a weapon. Consequently, the officer had acted properly when he shot and killed the suspect; and the Supreme Court found that the officer could not be prosecuted or sued for wrongful death.

The Court reached a different conclusion, however, with respect to governmental liability. The Court reasoned that when all felonies in England were capital crimes, perhaps such a rule on the use of deadly force made sense, because an offender found guilty at trial could be sentenced to death. But the taking of the life of a suspect who, if convicted, might receive only a relatively short prison sentence makes no sense and constitutes an unreasonable seizure of the person in violation of the Fourth Amendment. The Police Foundation was allowed to file an *amicus curiae* (friend of the court) brief in which it supported abandonment of the harsh common law rule. The brief demonstrated through research that the shoot-to-kill rule for fleeing felons does not prevent crime or enhance the protection of police officers, and thus is unreasonable as a law enforcement tool. Consequently, the Supreme Court overturned the common law rule as violating the due process clause of the Fourteenth Amendment. Deadly force may not be used unless it is necessary to prevent the escape of a suspect who the officer has probable cause to believe poses a significant threat of death or serious injury to the officer or others.[29]

As we noted, use of deadly force by police officers has been a major issue in police–minority relations. James J. Fyfe writes, "As most police recruits learn in the academy, the cop on the street...carries in his holster more power than has been granted the Chief Justice of the Supreme Court."[30] If this power is used improperly, it can lead to riots, more deaths, litigation against the police, and the downfall of entire city administrations. The issue was confronted by two presidential commissions, the Commission on Civil Disorders (1968) and the President's Commission on Law Enforcement and the Administration of Justice (1967). Both suggested that use of deadly force was the immediate reason for urban riots. Before the work of these commissions, little had been done in the way of empirical research.[31] Since then a number of scientists have studied the issue. John Goldkamp explains that there are two conflicting perspectives. Some people claim that the disproportionately high number of minority persons shot and killed by police can be explained by the irresponsible use of deadly force by some police officers and the differential administration of law enforcement toward minorities. Others claim that the disproportionately high number of minority persons shot and killed by police can be explained by disproportionately high arrest rates among minorities for crimes of violence.[32]

There is evidence to support both claims. Catherine Milton and her associates point out that 70 percent of the people shot by police in the seven cities that they studied were black, although blacks made up about 39 percent of the population.[33] Along the same lines, Betty Jenkins and Adrienne Faison showed that 52 percent of the persons killed by police over a three-year period were black and 21 percent Hispanic.[34] Paul Takagi sums up this side of the controversy: "The news gets around the community when someone is killed by police. It is part of a history—a very long history of extralegal justice that included whippings and lynchings."[35] The other side of the argument—that larger proportions of minorities are shot by police because they live in high-crime areas, are more likely to own guns, and more often commit violent crime—also finds support. James Fyfe's study of New York City shootings, for example, shows that in many incidents in which a shooting took place, police officers themselves were killed or wounded. He also found that minorities were more likely than whites to be involved in incidents in which guns were used.[36]

Official inquiries and empirical studies of police use of deadly force continue. Lawrence Sherman maintains that there have been some positive developments. Data obtained from surveys of killings of civilians by police in fifty-nine cities between 1970 and 1984 show that such killings have decreased by 50 percent.[37]

Abuse of Discretion

Yet another defect in the functioning of American policing has been and still is the potential abuse of discretion in making decisions about whom to arrest. For example, does police discretion work against young, poor, minority males? While discretionary power may indeed be regulated officially, the reality of the patrol situation is such that officers have considerable autonomy. Several studies show that the discretionary nature of police decision making discriminates against blacks.[38] But there is no clear-cut pattern. Some people say the neighborhood is the best predictor of arrest; that is, police make more arrests in low-income areas.[39] Others clarify the importance of neighborhood by adding that in black communities police are more punitive toward whites than blacks. The reverse is also true. In predominantly white neighborhoods, police are more punitive to black offenders.[40] Other determinants of racial disparity in arrests are revealed by an array of studies that have examined such factors as income differences between neighborhood residents and suspects, personal characteristics of the victim, the demeanor (attitude and appearance) of the suspect, real differences in rates of offending, and the choice of the people who make the complaints (blacks more often than whites request that an officer make an arrest).[41] Christy Visher found that police are more likely to arrest a woman whose attitudes and actions differ from the stereotype of a "lady," and that older white women are less likely to be arrested than young black women.[42] Marvin Krohn and his colleagues disagree. In a study conducted between 1948 and 1976 involving 10,723 police contacts, they found a trend toward more equal treatment of girls (compared with boys) for juvenile misdemeanors and of women (compared with men) for both misdemeanors and felonies.[43]

Many efforts have been made to control police abuse of discretion. The courts have placed limits on what police are permitted to do when they investigate and question suspects. Police administrators have tried to establish guidelines for police behavior in the field. But the task is difficult. Police officers perform a wide variety of duties under a wide range of conditions. We have little detailed information on what factors actually influence their decisions.

Corruption

At the turn of the century the Progressives thought that the civil service system would eliminate corruption and incompetence among the police. Yet after a century of reforms, police corruption persists. In the early 1970s a New York City police lieutenant, David Durk, and his partner, Detective Frank Serpico, in the course of their police work discovered massive corruption among fellow officers and superiors. They collected the evidence and reported it to higher authorities within the department. Neither there nor at the highest level of the department was any action taken. Durk and Serpico ultimately reported their findings directly to the

mayor. Still nothing happened. In frustration they released their information to the press. Durk and Serpico were attacked by fellow officers for "dirtying their own nest," "washing dirty laundry in public," "tarnishing their shields," and worse. The result of their revelations was the creation of the Knapp Commission, which unraveled the existing police corruption in New York City and recommended measures to avoid it in the future.[44]

The term "corruption" covers a wide range of conduct patterns. The Knapp Commission itself distinguished—in typical police jargon—between "meat eaters," who solicit bribes or actually cooperate with criminals for personal gain, and "grass eaters," who accept payoffs for rendering police services or for looking the other way when action is called for. Subsequent empirical and analytical studies have provided additional classifications and descriptions of police misconduct, including soliciting and accepting bribes, dereliction of duty, and street crime offenses such as larceny, embezzlement, and coercion.[45]

Despite the efforts of the Knapp Commission in 1972 and the National Advisory Commission on Criminal Justice Standards and Goals in 1973, corruption continues. According to experts, corruption may even be more serious now than it was in the 1970s.[46] In 1988 more than one hundred Miami police officers were implicated in corrupt drug-related activities. A federal grand jury indicted ten of them for their involvement in a $13 million theft of cocaine from a boat anchored in the Miami River. A Philadelphia officer who was heading a corruption investigation was given an eighteen-year prison sentence on evidence that he received $50,000 a month from operators of illegal electronic poker machines.[47]

The ancient Romans had a phrase, *Quis enim custodiet custodes*?—"Who then watches the watchmen?" Modern policing relies on internal and external controls to maintain its professionalism, its integrity. We have discussed some of the external controls. The court system, above all the Supreme Court, plays its role in policing the police by holding law enforcement activities to strict constitutional standards.

Another external control mechanism is the

civilian police review boards that were established to fulfill a review function. From the outset, however, they were opposed both by police unions (such as the Fraternal Order of Police) and by management organizations (such as the International Association of Chiefs of Police). The boards were short-lived in Philadelphia and New York. Voters in other cities defeated proposals to establish such boards; and both the 1967 President's Commission on Law Enforcement and the Administration of Justice and the 1973 National Advisory Commission on Criminal Justice Standards and Goals opposed them as being unworkable and detrimental to morale within departments.

Although civilian police review boards still function in some municipalities, police departments rely primarily on internal controls to police themselves. If internal controls are to be effective, experts argue, law enforcement professionals need to change their thinking about self-policing. In the past, departmental whistle-blowers were regarded with derision, as were David Durk and Frank Serpico. The claim is made that such attitudes need to be replaced by intolerance toward those who abuse the public trust and the power of the shield by engaging in abuses, corruption, and other forms of criminality. Studies indicate, however, that more officers than not are unwilling to report misconduct by fellow officers.[48]

By the mid-1970s, despite the guarantees of due process, the technical advances, the establishment of progressive standards in policing, the effort to eliminate excessive use of force, and attempts to curb discriminatory discretion and corruption among police officers, difficulties still existed. Police departments looked for new ways to deal with their constituencies. Administrators became increasingly aware that police officers were too far removed from the people they served. They began to reach out to the community.

Police–Community Relations

Community policing   Everyone seems to agree that the police should maintain close relations with the community they serve. The idea behind the concept of **community policing** is that public confidence and citizen cooperation will help prevent crime and will make the residents of a neighborhood feel more secure. Many types of programs have been described as community policing, including storefront police stations, home visits by officers, foot patrols, support of athletic leagues, and various strategies that involve citizen self-help groups (see Criminological Focus) and crime-prevention programs, such as Neighborhood Watch groups.[49] In other words, the purpose of community policing is to get neighbors involved in their own security.

The idea of community policing is neither new nor specific to the United States. Several countries around the world, in fact, have much more active programs than we have in this country. In Japan, for example, officers are stationed in a mini-police station (called a *koban*) in each neighborhood. They receive complaints, search for runaways, patrol on bike or foot, and provide security through constant contact. The *koban* has a reception room, a small kitchen, an interview area, and a lost-and-found service; it serves the important function of soliciting recommendations for what the police might do to help the community.[50] Norway and Singapore also have such mini-police stations.[51] The idea behind this approach is that communities have different needs and priorities that the police have to be aware of if efforts to prevent crime are to be effective. New York City, dissatisfied with the traditional, bureaucratic functioning of its law enforcement agencies, established the Community Patrol Officers (CPO) Program in July 1984. Individual officers were taken out of their routine line duties and were appointed CPOs. A CPO was to make his or her own rounds, on foot, and "to function as a planner, problem solver, community organizer, and information link between the community and the police."[52] The CPO evaluation project conducted by the Vera Institute focused on the functioning of CPOs in relation to the command structure of normal policing. It concluded that if the program was to work, changes would need to be made in traditional operational functioning—changes that would take

CRIMINOLOGICAL FOCUS

The Guardian Angels

A well-known citizen self-help group is the Guardian Angels. Founded in 1979 by Curtis Sliwa, this band of young people began "patrolling" subway trains in New York City. They then spread out to other metropolitan areas. Their concept is simple enough: A small platoon of clean-cut youths, distinguishable by their red berets and other insignia, would make their presence felt in various places considered unsafe (such as subway trains) and through their very presence deter crime or aid in preventing crime and apprehending offenders. The citizen response to this added crime-prevention presence was generally favorable. Police management reacted predominantly negatively. It was an interference with

professional crime prevention. Police unions, as well, reacted negatively. The volunteers were taking jobs away from professional police officers. The activities of the Guardian Angels have produced conflict with law enforcement agencies and have resulted in unnecessary deaths.

The lesson is clear that independent crime-fighting groups cannot operate successfully unless they are accepted by the community's law enforcement agencies. They need to coordinate their activities with the public law enforcement agencies. The Guardian Angels have made a strong case for their presence and the need for their services. The National Institute of Justice, after

comprehensive study, concluded that the Guardian Angels are a worthy form of crime prevention, but that they should

- Adhere to national rules and regulations (as to recruitment, screening, uniforms, interactions with police, record keeping, etc.).
- Increase their interaction and coordination with other citizen groups and with the police.
- Raise public awareness regarding the objectives of the group.
- Standardize training.
- Improve recruitment by the national leader's participation in local recruitment drives.
- Meet with community leaders before setting up new patrols to identify the concerns and needs of the citizenry and any similar types of groups already in existence.

into account the aspirations of the residents, the diversity of their problems, and the resources in the neighborhoods patrolled.[53]

Team policing In the early 1970s a strategy called team policing became a popular way to enhance contacts between citizens and police. Team policing was a response to the riots in the inner cities, the perception of the police as an army of occupation, and the limited familiarity on the part of officers with the needs of the neighborhoods they served. It was hoped that if the image of the police were changed from that of enemy to that of friend, law enforcement activities would be a great deal more effective. In **team policing,** a team of officers, rather than individual officers, carries the re-

sponsibilities of policing. The team, a group of officers and a supervisor, is in charge of a specific neighborhood on a twenty-four-hour basis. Team members, within broad guidelines, decide how to divide up the work, what methods to use to cover an area, and how to maximize communication with community members. The communication is accomplished by a variety of measures, including meetings between community leaders and team representatives, storefront mini-police stations that encourage citizens to drop in, programs in which community volunteers work as block watchers to report suspicious situations, and so forth. Team members meet regularly to discuss problems of the neighborhood, to keep each other informed, and to decide on a common policy.

Like most innovations, team policing has its advocates and its critics. Some observers say that it has neither prevented crimes nor increased the number solved.[54] Others question whether it really differs much from routine patrol activities.[55] Nevertheless, other experts argue, team policing has indeed helped to encourage crime control through better police–community relations.[56]

Problem-oriented policing   Another way in which police can enhance community relations is through **problem-oriented policing.** In this approach police work with citizens to identify and respond to community problems. Herman Goldstein warns that police too often focus narrowly on specific incidents. Their object is to get to places fast, to stabilize the situation, and to get back into service quickly. Most administrators want their officers visibly available to respond to emergency calls as rapidly as possible. But, argues Goldstein, police cannot reduce or prevent crime this way. They need to be more problem-oriented and less incident-oriented. They should analyze local social problems, help to design solutions, advocate programs to change the situation, and monitor effects.[57] Goldstein's approach has been tried in many communities. In Madison, Wisconsin, police were called regularly to deal with people behaving strangely at a shopping mall. The press characterized the mall as a haven for vagrants and put their number at one thousand. The public began to stay away. Business suffered. The police looked into the problem over time and discovered that individuals who had been under psychiatric supervision were responsible. They were disruptive when they did not take their medication. The police worked with mental health professionals to set up better supervision. Within a short time the problem was solved, customers returned, and business went back to normal. Similarly, in 1982 the Baltimore County Police Department created three teams of officers to solve recurring problems. The teams, called COPE (Citizen-Oriented Police Enforcement), worked with local patrol officers to pinpoint conditions that appeared to be creating problems. For example, each spring burglaries increased, and one item, baseball gloves, was consistently stolen. When a program was instituted to provide baseball equipment to low-income families, the burglary rate fell significantly.[58]

Foot patrol   Another effort to improve police–community relations involved the reintroduction of pre–World War II "walking the beat." It was felt that patrol cars isolated officers from citizens, and that if police were put back on the streets, people would get to know them and feel a greater sense of security.[59] A number of cities, including Houston, Newark, and Flint, Michigan, carried out experiments to test the effectiveness of foot patrol. They found that crime rates generally did not go down significantly, but citizens' fear of crime did. Moreover, better citizen cooperation resulted in more job satisfaction for officers and fewer calls for assistance.[60]

Preventive patrol   It has long been argued that preventive patrol, which entails an increase in police presence and visibility, deters criminals from carrying out crimes and thereby reduces citizens' fear and fosters good police–community relations. Between October 1, 1972, and September 30, 1973, the Kansas City Police Department conducted the Kansas City Preventive Patrol Experiment. Fifteen police beats covering a population of close to 150,000 inhabitants were divided into three sections. Each section was subjected to a different type of patrol: intensified routine patrol (two to three times more officers on the beat), decrease of officers on a beat (officers came into the area only when they were called for service), and routine patrol (the area maintained its usual number of police). The results were unexpected. Increased patrol levels had no effect on crime rates, citizens' fear of crime, citizens' satisfaction with police, or the amount of time it took to respond to calls.[61]

Lawrence Sherman and David Weisburd decided to replicate the Kansas City Study, but with a different focus. They argued that allocating more police to entire neighborhoods did not have a deterrent effect because not all areas of a neighborhood are at high risk for crime. The police presence, rather than being distributed over the whole neighborhood, should be intensified in hot spots, particular places within neighborhoods that are the source of the most calls to the police. In Minneapolis, for example, 5 percent of the locations were the sources of 64 percent of the calls.[62] Sherman and Weisburd are now testing the effects of an increased police presence in 110 hot spots in this city.[63]

It is evident from the vast number of changes made in policing since the 1960s that the courts are committed to protecting the rights of citizens and that law enforcement agencies realize the necessity of improving their image through improved police–community relations. A great deal of money has been spent to gain the cooperation of the public. The campaign involves not only police practices but also the composition of police departments: Efforts are being made to ensure that they reflect the community as a whole.

POLICE OFFICERS AND THEIR LIFESTYLE

To change the composition of police departments, many reforms have been instituted in recent years. Efforts have been made to recruit college graduates, blacks, and women—groups that were seldom represented in the past.

Qualifications

Most departments require that new recruits be in good physical condition, have no criminal record, and have a high school diploma. Other criteria for selection, used to varying degrees by different departments, are a written exam (78 percent), an interview (97 percent), a lie detector test (40 percent), weight and height standards (42 percent), and a background check (99 percent). Some require intelligence and psychological tests also (68 percent).[64] About 10 percent require some college education, and less than 1 percent a college degree.[65] The question whether police officers should have a college degree, although it has been recommended by national commissions since 1931, is still controversial. In a survey of law enforcement agencies conducted by the Police Executive Research Forum and supported by the Ford Foundation, some consistent themes emerged: those in favor of higher education argued that college-educated officers

- Communicate better with the public.
- Show more initiative.
- Write better reports.
- Make better decisions.
- Have greater sensitivity to minorities.
- In general, perform better.[66]

Those who questioned higher education requirements for police officers argued that college-educated officers

- Might leave police work.
- Are more prone to question orders.
- Expect preferential treatment.
- Cause animosity within the ranks.
- Feel dissatisfied with the job.[67]

Minority Groups in Policing

The first minority police officer was hired in Washington D.C., in 1861.[68] By 1940, only 1 percent of all police officers in the United States came from minority groups; in 1950, only 2 percent.[69] Nicholas Alex wrote in *Black in Blue* (1969) that black officers were pressured in two ways: by racism on the part of white colleagues and by the expectation of black citizens that they would get a break from a black officer.[70] Changes began to occur in the 1960s. Civil unrest at the time showed that if our police officers were recruited from only a limited segment of the overall population, there was a risk of alienating those population groups that were not represented in law enforcement.[71] Recruitment drives to hire minorities began in most major metropolitan police departments. The issue was highly controversial during the initial phase, and progress has been slow.[72] In the face of outright discrimination in examination and appointment procedures, court action had to be resorted to in many instances to open the doors to blacks and Hispanics who wanted to join the ranks.

By 1982 the overall percentage of minorities in the police force was 7.6 percent.[73] In Washington, D.C., where 70.3 percent of the population was black, over half of the officers came from the black community. One-third of Detroit's officers were black; two-thirds of the total population was black. Recruitment and retention of Hispanic officers likewise increased slowly. By 1980, Hispanic officers accounted for 7.2 percent of the police department of the City of New York, where the Hispanic population was 19.9 percent of the total. In Los Angeles the percentage was 13.6 percent; the Hispanic population was 27.5 percent.[74]

Although changes have occurred—many police departments are headed by blacks, for example—the ethnic problem has not yet been resolved.[75] Well-founded discrimination suits continue to be brought by minority-group officers. In 1989 Hispanic police officers in New York City complained about discrimination in the promotion of patrol officers to sergeants.[76] The Federal Bureau of Investigation, found by a federal court to have engaged in discriminatory practices, is revamping its practices so as to be in compliance with the Equal Employment Opportunity Act of 1972. This act prohibits discriminatory hiring practices by state and local governments. It also prohibits job discrimination against women.

Women in Policing

The first American woman to serve as a sworn police officer was Lola Baldwin, who joined the Portland, Oregon, police department in 1905. Like the few police matrons of the nineteenth century, she dealt primarily with women and children. In fact, she was originally granted the police power so that she could manage them at the Ohio State Exposition. Five years later, in 1910 in Los Angeles, Alice Stebbin Wells became the first officially classified policewoman, assigned to "supervising and enforcing laws concerning dance halls, skating rinks, and theaters; monitoring billboard displays; locating missing persons; and maintaining a general bureau for women seeking advice on matters within the scope of the police department."[77] In

Policewomen making an arrest during a police task force for crackdown on drug dealing.

LAW ENFORCEMENT ACROSS CULTURES

No country can do without law enforcers. Police duties are similar around the world, in many respects. Police status, behavior, and uniforms, however, vary according to cultural traditions, political situations, and government ideologies. The English provided the world with the first uniformed police. Respect for "bobbies" has remained high, although terrorism and racial unrest are now commonplace in England. French police officers, sometimes known as "flics," are also still called *gendarmes* (armed gentlemen), even though women are joining the force in increasing numbers. In Italy, one of the major police forces is called the *carabinieri*, in which officers wear elegant and highly visible uniforms every day and change to even more resplendent uniforms for gala occasions. The detective units of the carabinieri have earned great respect for their effectiveness in curbing terrorism. Japan has made a determined effort to station officers in small police boxes *(koban)* dotting the cities and the countrysides. This policy allows officers to get to know the people in their neighborhood, thus increasing the popularity of the police and improving their crime-fighting effectiveness.

Western policing styles have been transplanted to many developing countries. Were it not for his different uniform, the Jaipur, India, traffic police officer might well blow his whistle at Piccadilly Circle in London, and the Lima, Peru, policewoman might well be protecting pedestrians at Porta del Sol in Madrid. Social unrest, ethnic strife and other political factors have prompted many developing countries to militarize their police forces, as evidenced by the photographs shown here, which depict Mexican police officers during a riot control procedure, El Salvador police on parade duty, and Pakistani police at muster for duty to end armed civil conflict.

Around the world, police officers are the most visible agents of formal social control. Until very recently the mere presence of the police in Eastern European countries inspired fear in the population. Ever-present, ever-visible, they imposed their governments' will on the populace, through raids and constant controls. However, the police-state nightmare is ending in Hungary, East Germany (the German Democratic Republic), and most countries of the old socialist bloc. The peoples of Eastern European countries are learning to live with less formal social control—an art long ago mastered by tribal societies that still rely largely on informal social control, as shown in the accompanying photograph of council of Tuareg (Sahel region in northwest Africa) elders.

Two "bobbies" standing guard outside 10 Downing Street in London.

Male and female gendarmes directing traffic in Paris.

A policeman inside a koban on the Ginza, in Japan.

Two policemen outside the Colosseum in Rome.

In Jaipur, India, a policeman is directing traffic.

A policewoman in Lima, Peru.

Mexican police engaged in riot control.

In El Salvador, Treasury Police parading on Independence Day.

Police in Karachi, Pakistan.

Police on patrol at night in East Berlin.

In Azaouak (Sahel), a Tuareg chief holds council.

Two guards on duty in Budapest, Hungary.

1915 she founded the International Association of Police Women.

More than sixty police departments had women on their staffs by 1919; 145 had women by 1925. But women's police roles remained restricted. Women did not attain patrol officer status until the 1960s. There were no female sergeants until 1965, after a successful lawsuit against New York City.[78] With the emergence of the drive for the equality of women in the late 1960s and early 1970s and the passage of Title VII of the Civil Rights Act of 1972, prohibiting discrimination by employers, many departments began to recruit women. Others resisted. Serious obstacles and stereotypes had to be overcome: that women were physically weak, irrational, and illogical; that they lacked the toughness needed to deal with work on the streets. Some people argued that the association of female with male officers would cause complications in both job and family life.

By 1980 the number of policewomen was still low—under 4 percent of all officers. By 1988 that proportion had increased to nearly 8 per-cent (Table 15.1). Most recent surveys of personnel practices have found that eligibility criteria and mechanisms used to recruit, screen, and select candidates have changed dramatically, thus enlarging the pool of eligible women. This change appears to be happening worldwide, not just in the United States, according to an international survey sponsored by the United Nations.[79]

Despite the advances that women have made in policing, they are still not fully accepted by their male colleagues or the public. Most of the resistance stems from the belief that the physical strength of women does not allow them to perform well in violent situations.[80] Responding to these concerns, many police departments continue to assign women to clerical duties or to specific types of problems, such as domestic disputes and runaways. Research has demonstrated, however, that these fears are ungrounded. Female officers make almost as many successful arrests as male officers, their overall work performance has been rated extremely satisfactory by superiors, their level of strength

TABLE 15.1   TOTAL NUMBER AND PERCENTAGE OF WOMEN POLICE OFFICERS IN THE UNITED STATES, 1971–1988

YEAR	POLICE OFFICERS	WOMEN POLICE OFFICERS	PERCENT OF POLICE FORCE
1971	225,474	3,156	1.4%
1972	269,420	4,041	1.5
1973	276,808	4,705	1.7
1974	286,973	5,739	2.0
1975	292,346	6,130	2.1
1976	287,448	6,898	2.4
1977	293,017	7,911	2.7
1978	294,579	9,426	3.2
1979	296,332	10,371	3.5
1980	294,181	11,178	3.8
1981	297,324	13,082	4.4
1982	298,334	14,021	4.7
1983	304,012	15,504	5.1
1984	309,960	17,357	5.6
1985	312,713	19,388	6.2
1986	318,484	21,338	6.7
1987	320,959	22,788	7.1
1988	325,095	24,362	7.5

Source: Uniform Crime Reports relevant to each year.

is well within the acceptable range for the profession, and they may be more pleasant and respectful with the public than their male counterparts.[81] As regards the way policewomen perceive themselves, it appears that they enter the force self-confident and a bit idealistic, but gradually become disillusioned by others' beliefs that they are flirtatious and ineffective.[82] In sum, policewomen have indeed made their mark on the police force; but it may be some time before their male colleagues accept them as equal partners.

While there continue to be many differences—in numbers, seniority, and positions, for example—between black, Hispanic, and female police officers on the one hand and white male police officers on the other, one thing that they all have in common is job-related stress. Where their police work is concerned, they rely heavily on each other as partners.

The Police Subculture

Michael K. Brown describes how police officers stick together when they work the streets because of the constant stress and anxiety that goes along with the job. These working conditions, plus the entry requirements, training, citizen expectations, and behavioral norms (they are required to be respectful yet to be in control of a situation, for instance) combine to produce a similarity of values—a **police subculture**.[83] The process of socialization into the culture begins as soon as new recruits enter the academy. They get to know not only the formal rules of policing but also the informal norms that a person has to abide by in order to be accepted into the group. They learn very quickly that loyalty—the obligation to support a fellow officer—is the first priority. Respect for police authority, honor, individualism, and group solidarity also rank high among esteemed values.[84]

One of the primary reasons for the existence of a subculture that is characterized by very strong in-group ties is the nature of police work. Officers often view the external community as hostile and threatening. They are caught in a bind. Their job calls for them to discipline the people they serve, and they are allowed to use force to do it. The police uniform also isolates officers. Easily recognizable, they are constantly approached on the beat by people who know what is going on (bartenders, waitresses) or who want to complain about the poor quality of law enforcement in the neighborhood. When they are off duty, police officers also tend to isolate themselves from the community, spending most of their time with other officers and their families. William Westley says that police officers are isolated from the rest of society behind a "blue curtain."[85]

Police officers are often viewed as suspicious, authoritative, and cynical.[86] Their working environment may be responsible for the development of these traits.[87] Police work is potentially dangerous, so officers need to be constantly aware of what is happening around them. At the academy they are warned about what happens to officers who are too trusting. They learn about the many fellow officers who have died in the line of duty because they did not exercise proper caution. It would be surprising if they did *not* become suspicious. As George Kirkham, police officer and professor, argues, "Chronic suspiciousness is something that a good cop cultivates in the interest of going home to his family each evening."[88] The second trait, authoritativeness, is another response to the police working environment. Uniforms, badges, and guns signify authority. But even more important is the fact that officers need to gain immediate control of potentially dangerous situations in order to do their job. And what about cynicism? In a study of 220 New York City police officers, Arthur Niederhoffer found that 80 percent of the new recruits believed that the department was a smoothly operating, effective organization. Within a couple of months, fewer than one-third still held that belief. Moreover, cynicism increased with length of service and among those of the more highly educated who did not get promoted.[89]

The working environment that we have described quite often leads to stress, which results in emotional and physical problems. A study of 2,300 officers in twenty departments found that 37 percent had serious marital problems, 36 percent suffered physical ailments, 23 percent abused alcohol, 20 percent indicated problems among their children, and 10 percent abused drugs themselves.[90] Since the 1970s there has been increasing concern over these stress-related problems; and many departments, especially the large ones, are trying to provide more medical attention, more psychological counseling, and a greater range of disability and retirement benefits, and to give higher priority to community-oriented policing, which lessens tension between officer and citizenry.[91]

REVIEW

In tenth-century England, policing was done by all males over age 12, who were bound to keep the peace and track down criminals. Through the centuries the system became more formalized, with sheriffs, night watchmen, and justices of the peace. It was not until 1829 that the first real professional police force came into existence. Colonial America adopted a system similar to the one in England. But as cities began to grow, police departments became pawns of political machines, unaccountable to the public, corrupt, and often brutal. At the turn of the twentieth century, policing began to change as a result of the Progressive reform movement, which was intent on professionalizing law enforcement and removing it from politics. The Wickersham Commission of 1931 and a number of dedicated professionals, among them August Vollmer and O. W. Wilson, continued the efforts to build a police force that was nonpolitical, well trained, and equipped with modern technology.

The crime-fighting role of officers was dominant. But this "law and order" approach alienated the police from the people they served. Tensions grew in the 1960s when riots occurred throughout the country. Police departments sought ways to change their image. They needed closer ties to the community. Community policing became popular as a method to get the public involved in its own security. Innovative projects spread throughout the country—team policing, problem-oriented policing, foot patrol, citizen fear reduction, and so forth. And many police departments opened their doors to researchers so that the effects of the various approaches could be tested.

Although most of us equate the police with law enforcement, they have other important functions. By maintaining order they reduce fear of crime and stimulate the public to cooperate with them to improve the quality of life. They also provide services to members of the community who require aid.

Recently police departments have been reviewing their policies, especially in regard to the recruitment of minorities and women, the discretionary nature of police arrests, corrupt practices of officers, and the use of deadly force. What the police service demands was spelled out by Sir Robert Peel back in 1829: "There is no qualification more indispensable to a police officer, than a perfect command of temper, never suffering himself to be moved in the slightest degree, by any language or threats that may be used."[92] That maxim is valid today, except that we refer to the officer as he or she.

KEY TERMS

community policing
constable
frankpledge
justice of the peace
night watchman
police subculture

problem-oriented policing
sheriff
sting operation
team policing
tithing

NOTES

1. Martin A. Kelly, "Citizen Survival in Ancient Rome," *Police Studies* 11 (1988): 195–201, a delightful historical police vignette, which we recommend to all our readers. The quote is from Juvenal (A.D. 40–120).

2. See Daniel Devlin, *Police Procedure, Administration, and Organization* (London: Butterworth, 1966).

3. Metropolitan Police Force, *Instruction Book* (London, 1829).

4. Patrick Pringle, *Hue and Cry: The Story of Henry and John Fielding & Their Bow Street Runners* (New York: Morrow, 1965).

5. Drew Humphries and David F. Greenberg, "The Dialectics of Crime Control," in *Crime and Capitalism: Readings in Marxist Criminology*, ed. David F. Greenberg, pp. 209–254 (Palo Alto, Calif.: Mayfield, 1981).

6. Samuel Walker, *Popular Justice: A History of American Criminal Justice* (New York: Oxford University Press, 1980), p. 18.

7. Roger Lane, *Policing the City: Boston, 1822–1885* (Cambridge: Harvard University Press, 1967), p. 26.

8. Walker, *Popular Justice*, pp. 61–62.

9. George F. Cole, *The American System of Criminal Justice* (Pacific Grove, Calif.: Brooks/Cole, 1989), p. 177.

10. Samuel Walker, *A Critical History of Police Reform* (Lexington, Mass.: Lexington Books, 1977), pp. 45–46; Bruce Smith, *Police Systems in the United States*, rev. ed. (New York: Harper, 1949). For a complete discussion of Theodore Roosevelt as police commissioner, see Jay Stuart Berman, *Police Administration and Progressive Reform: Theodore Roosevelt as Police Commissioner of New York* (New York: Greenwood, 1987).

11. National Commission on Law Observance and Enforcement, *Report on Lawlessness in Law Enforcement*, no. 11 (Washington, D.C.: U.S. Government Printing Office, 1931).

12. Figures are based on the U.S. Department of Justice, Federal Bureau of Investigation, *Uniform Crime Reports, 1988* (Washington, D.C.: U.S. Government Printing Office, 1989).

13. Walker, *Popular Justice*, p. 238.

14. Donald A. Torres, *Handbook of Federal Police and Investigative Agencies* (Westport, Conn.: Greenwood Press, 1985), pp. 135–144.

15. C. Cotter and J. Burrows, *Proper Crime Program, A Special Report: Overview of the STING Program and Project Summaries*, for U.S. Department of Justice (Washington, D.C.: U.S. Government Printing Office, 1981); Gary Marx, "The New Police Undercover Work," *Urban Life* 8 (1980): 399–446; Carl B. Klockars, "Jonathan Wild and the Modern Sting," in *History and Crime: Implications for Criminal Justice Policy*, ed. James C. Inciardi and Charles Faupel, pp. 225–260 (Beverly Hills, Calif.: Sage, 1980); Henry W. Prunckun, "It's Your Money They're After: Sting Operations in Consumer Fraud Investigations," *Police Studies* 11 (1988): 190–194; Clarence Dickson, "Drug Stings in Miami," *F.B.I. Law Enforcement Bulletin*, January 1988, pp. 1–6.

16. Peter Greenwood and Joan Petersilia, *The Criminal Investigation Process*, vol. 1: *Summary and Policy Implications* (Santa Monica, Calif.: Rand Corporation, 1975).

17. Mark T. Willman and John Snortum, "Detective Work: The Criminal Investigation Process in a Medium-Sized Police Department," *Criminal Justice Review* 9 (Spring 1984): 33–39.

18. John E. Eck, *Solving Crimes: The Investigation of Burglary and Robbery* (Washington, D.C.: Police Executive Research Forum, 1983).

19. Samuel Walker, *The Police in America* (New York: McGraw-Hill, 1983), p. 265.

20. James Q. Wilson and George L. Kelling, "Broken Windows: The Police and Neighborhood Safety," *Atlantic Monthly*, March 1982, pp. 29–38; Mark H. Moore and George L. Kelling, "To Serve and Protect: Learning from Police History," *Public Interest* 70 (1983): 49–65.

21. Samuel Walker, "'Broken Windows' and

Fractured History: The Use and Misuse of History in Recent Police Patrol Analysis," *Justice Quarterly* 1 (March 1984): 76–90.

22. Albert Reiss, *The Police and the Public* (New Haven, Conn.: Yale University Press, 1971), p. 11.

23. Wilson and Kelling, "Broken Windows."

24. George L. Kelling, "Order Maintenance, the Quality of Urban Life, and Police: A Line of Argument," in *Police Leadership,* ed. William A. Gelles (Chicago: American Bar Association, 1985), p. 297.

25. Reiss, *Police and the Public*, pp. 70–72.

26. John Webster, "Police Task and Time Study," *Journal of Criminal Law, Criminology, and Police Science* 61 (1970): 94–100.

27. J. Robert Lilly, "What Are the Police Now Doing?" *Journal of Police Science and Administration* 6 (1978): 51–60. See also James Q. Wilson, *Varieties of Police Behavior* (Cambridge: Harvard University Press), chap. 7; Egon Bittner, *The Function of the Police in Modern Society* (Chevy Chase, Md.: National Institute of Mental Health, 1970).

28. See Richard S. Allinson, "LEAA's Impact on Criminal Justice: A Review of the Literature," *Criminal Justice Abstracts* 11 (1979): 608–648.

29. Tennessee v. Garner, 471 U.S. 887 (1985).

30. James J. Fyfe, "Police Use of Deadly Force: Research and Reform," *Justice Quarterly* 5 (June 1988): 165–205.

31. With the exception of, for example, Gerald D. Robin, "Justifiable Homicide by Police Officers," *Journal of Criminal Law, Criminology, and Police Science* 54 (1963): 225–231, and American Civil Liberties Union, "Police Power vs. Citizens' Rights" (New York, 1966).

32. John S. Goldkamp, "Minorities as Victims of Police Shootings: Interpretations of Racial Disproportionality and Police Use of Deadly Force," *Justice System Journal* 2 (1976): 169–183.

33. Catherine Milton, J. W. Halleck, J. Lardner, and G. L. Abrecht, *Police Use of Deadly Force* (Washington, D.C.: Police Foundation, 1977).

34. Betty Jenkins and Adrienne Faison, *An Analysis of 248 Persons Killed by New York City Policemen* (New York: Metropolitan Applied Research Center, 1974).

35. Paul Takagi, "Death by Police Intervention," in *A Community Concern: Police Use of Deadly Force,* ed. R. N. Brenner and M. Kravitz (Washington, D.C.: U.S. Government Printing Office, 1979), p. 34.

36. James J. Fyfe, "Race and Extreme Police-Citizen Violence," in *Race, Crime, and Criminal Justice,* ed. R. L. McNeely and C. E. Pope, pp. 89–108 (Beverly Hills, Calif.: Sage, 1981). See also Arnold Binder and Peter Scharf, "Deadly Force in Law Enforcement," *Crime and Delinquency* 28 (1982): 1–23; Reiss, *Police and the Public.*

37. Lawrence W. Sherman, *Citizens Killed by Big City Police, 1970–1984* (Washington, D.C.: Crime Control Institute, Crime Control Research Corporation, 1986).

38. Cecil L. Willis and Richard H. Wells, "The Police and Child Abuse: An Analysis of Police Decisions to Report Illegal Behavior," *Criminology* 26 (1988): 695–716; John R. Hepburn, "Race and the Decision to Arrest: An Analysis of Warrants Issued," *Journal of Research in Crime and Delinquency* 15 (January 1978): 54; Douglas A. Smith and Christy A. Visher, "Street-Level Justice: Situational Determinants of Police Arrest Decisions," *Social Problems* 29 (1981): 167–177; Dale Dannefer and Russell K. Schutt, "Race and Juvenile Justice Processing in Court and Police Agencies," *American Journal of Sociology* 87 (1982): 1113–1132.

39. Carl Werthman and Irving Piliavin, "Gang Members and the Police," in *The Police: Six Sociological Essays,* ed. David Bordua, pp. 75–83 (New York: Wiley, 1967).

40. Dennis D. Powell, "Race, Rank, and Police Discretion," *Journal of Police Science and Administration* 9 (1981): 383–389.

41. Douglas Smith and Jody Klein, "Police Control of Interpersonal Disputes," *Social Problems* 21 (1984): 468–481; Richard C.

Hollinger, "Race, Occupational Status, and Pro-Active Police Arrest for Drinking and Driving," *Journal of Criminal Justice* 12 (1984): 173–183; Douglas A. Smith, Christy A. Visher, and Laura A. Davidson, "Equity and Discretionary Justice: The Influence of Race on Police Arrest Decisions," *Journal of Criminal Law and Criminology* 75 (1984): 234–249; Donald Black, "The Social Organization of Arrest," *Stanford Law Review* 23 (1971): 1087–1098; Alfred Blumstein, "On the Racial Disproportionality of United States' Prison Populations," *Journal of Criminal Law and Criminology* 73 (1982): 1259–1281; Richard J. Lundman, Richard E. Sykes, and John P. Clark, "Police Control of Juveniles: A Replication," *Journal of Research in Crime and Delinquency* 15 (1978): 74–91.

42. Christy A. Visher, "Gender, Police Arrest Decisions, and Notions of Chivalry," *Criminology* 21 (1983): 5–28.

43. Marvin D. Krohn, James P. Curry, and Shirley Nelson-Kilger, "Is Chivalry Dead?: An Analysis of Changes in Police Dispositions of Males and Females," *Criminology* 21 (1983): 417–437.

44. Commission to Investigate Allegations of Police Corruption and the City's Anticorruption Procedures (New York City; Whitman Knapp, Chairman), *Commission Report* (1972); *Knapp Commission Report on Police Corruption* (New York: George Braziller, 1973).

45. Herman Goldstein, *Police Corruption: A Perspective on its Nature and Control* (Washington, D.C.: Police Foundation, 1975); Lawrence Sherman, *Police Corruption: A Sociological Perspective* (Garden City, N.Y.: Doubleday, 1974); Ellwyn Stoddard, "Blue Coat Crime," in *Thinking About Police: Contemporary Readings*, ed. Carl Klockars, pp. 338–349 (New York: McGraw-Hill, 1983); Michael Johnston, *Political Corruption and Public Policy in America* (Monterey, Calif.: Brooks/Cole, 1982), p. 75.

46. Robert J. McCormack, "Confronting Police Corruption: Organizational Initiatives for Internal Control," in *Managing Police Corruption: International Perspectives*, ed. Richard H. Ward and Robert McCormack, pp. 151–165 (Chicago: Office of International Criminal Justice, University of Illinois at Chicago, 1987).

47. Cole, *American System of Criminal Justice*, p. 277.

48. William Westley, *Violence and the Police* (Cambridge: MIT Press, 1970); Paul Chevigny, *Police Power: Police Abuses in New York City* (New York: Pantheon Books, 1969); Sherman, *Police Corruption: A Sociological Perspective.*

49. Jerome H. Skolnick and David H. Bayley, *Community Policing: Issues and Practices Around the World* (Washington, D.C.: National Institute of Justice, May 1988). See also Jack R. Greene and Stephen D. Mastrofski, eds., *Community Policing: Rhetoric or Reality?* (New York: Praeger, 1988).

50. Freda Adler, *Nations Not Obsessed with Crime* (Littleton, Colo.: Fred B. Rothman, 1983), p. 101.

51. Skolnick and Bayley, *Community Policing*, p. 8.

52. David Weisburd, Jerome McElroy, and Patricia Hardyman, "Challenges to Supervision in Community Policing: Observations on a Pilot Project," *American Journal of Police* 7, no. 2 (1988): 29–50.

53. David Weisburd and Jerome E. McElroy, "Enacting the CPO Role: Findings from the New York City Pilot Program in Community Policing," in Greene and Mastrofski, *Community Policing*, pp. 89–101. For a discussion of communication between police chiefs and their constituents, see William A Geller, ed., *Police Leadership in America: Crisis and Opportunity* (New York: Praeger, 1985). For a discussion of the use of consumer surveys to evaluate the job that police are doing, see Frank F. Furstenberg, Jr., and Charles F. Wellford, "Calling the Police: The Evaluation of Police Service," *Law and Society Review* 7 (1973): 393–406. For the importance of soliciting and evaluating citizen requirements, problems, and expectations of police, see R. M. Patterson, Jr., and Nancy K. Grant, "Community Mapping: Rationale and Considerations for Implementation," *Journal of Police Science and Administration* 16 (1988): 136–143.

54. William J. Bopp, *Police Personnel Administration* (Boston: Holbrook, 1974), pp. 48–51.

55. Lawrence W. Sherman, Catherine H.

Milton, and Thomas V. Kelly, *Team Policing: Seven Case Studies* (Washington, D.C.: Police Foundation, 1973).

56. John P. Kenney, *Police Administration* (Springfield, Ill.: Charles C Thomas, 1972).

57. Herman Goldstein, *Problem-Oriented Policing* (New York: McGraw-Hill, 1990), pp. 14–31.

58. Gard W. Cordner, "The Baltimore County Citizen-Oriented Police Enforcement (COPE) Project: Final Evaluation," paper presented to the American Society of Criminology, San Diego, 1985.

59. Hubert Williams and Antony M. Pate, "Returning to First Principles: Reducing the Fear of Crime in Newark," *Crime and Delinquency* 33 (1987): 53–70.

60. *The Effects of Police Fear Reduction Studies: A Summary of Findings from Houston and Newark* (Washington, D.C.: Police Foundation, 1986); *The Newark Foot Patrol Experiment* (Washington, D.C.: Police Foundation, 1981); Lee P. Brown and Mary Ann Wycoff, "Policing Houston: Reducing Fear and Improving Service," *Crime and Delinquency* 33 (1987): 71–89; Frans Willem Winkel, "The Police and Reducing Fear of Crime: A Comparison of the Crime-Centered and the Quality of Life Approaches," *Police Studies* 11 (1988): 183–189.

61. George L. Kelling, *What Works—Research and the Police*, Crime File Study Guide, for U.S. Department of Justice, National Institute of Justice (Washington, D.C.: U.S. Government Printing Office, 1988); George L. Kelling, Antony Pate, Duane Dieckman, and Charles E. Brown, *The Kansas City Preventive Patrol Experiment: A Summary Report* (Washington, D.C.: Police Foundation, 1974). See also David F. Greenberg, Ronald C. Kessler, and Colin Loftin, "The Effect of Police Employment on Crime," *Criminology* 21 (1983): 375–394; Charles R. Wellford, "Crime and the Police: A Multivariate Analysis," *Criminology* 12 (1974): 195–213; Craig Uchida and Robert Goldberg, *Police Employment and Expenditure Trends*, for U.S. Department of Justice, Bureau of Justice Statistics (Washington, D.C.: U.S. Government Printing Office, 1986); Colin Loftin and David McDowall, "The Police, Crime, and Economic Theory: An Assessment," *American Sociological Review* 47 (1982): 393–401.

62. Lawrence W. Sherman, *Repeat Calls to Police in Minneapolis* (Washington, D.C.: Crime Control Institute, 1987).

63. Personal communication from David Weisburd; see also David Weisburd, Lisa Maher, Lawrence Sherman, Michael Buerger, Ellen Cohn, and Anthony Petrosino, "Contrasting Crime-General and Crime-Specific Theory: The Case of Hot Spots in Crime," paper presented to the American Sociological Association, San Francisco, 1989.

64. Jack Aylward, "Psychological Testing and Police Selection," *Journal of Police Science and Administration* 13 (1985): 201–210.

65. James J. Fyfe, *Police Personnel Practices*, Baseline Data Reports 15, no. 1 (Washington, D.C.: International City Management Assn., 1983).

66. David L. Carter, Allen D. Sapp, and Darrel W. Stephens, *The State of Police Education: Policy Direction for the 21st Century* (Washington, D.C.: Police Executive Research Forum, 1989). See also Lee H. Bowker, "A Theory of Educational Needs of Law Enforcement Officers," *Journal of Contemporary Criminal Justice* 1 (1980): 17–24. For a discussion of the best type of college education for law enforcement officers, see Lawrence W. Sherman and Warren Bennis, "Higher Education for Police Officers: The Central Issues," *Police Chief* 44 (August 1977): 32. See also Lawrence Sherman et al., *The Quality of Police Education* (San Francisco: Jossey-Bass, 1978).

67. Elizabeth Burbeck and Adrian Furnham, "Police Officer Selection: A Critical Review of the Literature," *Journal of Police Science and Administration* 13 (1985): 58–69.

68. Jack L. Kuykendall and David E. Burns, "The Black Police Officer: An Historical Perspective," *Journal of Contemporary Criminal Justice* 1 (1986): 4–12.

69. Fyfe, *Police Personnel Practices*.

70. Nicholas Alex, *Black in Blue: A Study of the Negro Policeman* (New York: Appleton-Century-Crofts, 1969).

71. Bruce L. Berg, Edmond J. True, and Marc

G. Gertz, "Police, Riots, and Alienation," *Journal of Police Science and Administration* 12 (1984): 186–190.

72. See U.S. Commission on Civil Rights, *Who Is Guarding the Guardians?: A Report on Police Practices* (Washington, D.C.: U.S. Government Printing Office, 1981).

73. Fyfe, *Police Personnel Practices.*

74. Data supplied by the Police Foundation.

75. Ellen Hochstedler, "Impediments to Hiring Minorities in Public Police Agencies," *Journal of Police Science and Administration* 12 (1984): 227–240.

76. David E. Pitt, "Racial Tensions in Police Ranks Work Three Ways Now," *New York Times,* February 19, 1989, p. E6.

77. Daniel J. Bell, "Policewomen: Myths and Reality," *Journal of Police Science and Administration* 10 (1982): 112–120.

78. Samuel S. Janus, Cynthia Janus, Leslie K. Lord, and Thomas Power, "Women in Police Work—Annie Oakley or Little Orphan Annie?" *Police Studies* 11 (1988): 124–127; Susan E. Martin, *Women on the Move?: A Report on the Status of Women in Policing* (Washington, D.C.: Police Foundation, 1989).

79. United Nations Report, A/Conf. 121/17, July 1, 1985, with a comprehensive analysis of women in law enforcement by Edith Flynn, who served as U.N. consultant on the topic.

80. Kenneth W. Kerber, Steven M. Andes, and Michele B. Mittler, "Citizen Attitudes Regarding the Competence of Female Police Officers," *Journal of Police Science and Administration* 5 (1977): 337–347.

81. James A. Davis, "Perspectives of Policewomen in Texas and Oklahoma," *Journal of Police Science and Administration* 12 (1984): 395–403; Peter Bloch and Deborah Anderson, *Policewomen on Patrol: Final Report* (Washington, D.C.: Urban Institute, 1974); Michael T. Charles, "Women in Policing: The Physical Aspect," *Journal of Police Science and Administration* 10 (1982): 194–205; Robert J. Homant and Daniel B. Kennedy, "Police Perceptions of Spouse Abuse: A Comparison of Male and Female Officers," *Journal of Criminal Justice* 13 (1985): 29–47.

82. Sally Gross, "Women Becoming Cops: Developmental Issues and Solutions," *Police Chief* 51, no. 1 (1984): 32–35.

83. Michael K. Brown, *Working the Street* (New York: Russell Sage, 1981).

84. William A. Westley, *Violence and the Police: A Sociological Study of Law, Custom, and Morality* (Cambridge: MIT Press, 1970), p. 226.

85. Ibid.

86. Arthur Niederhoffer, *Behind the Shield: The Police in Urban Society* (Garden City, N.Y.: Doubleday, 1967); Richard Lundman, *Police and Policing* (New York: Holt, Rinehart, and Winston, 1980); Jerome H. Skolnick, *Justice Without Trial* (New York: Wiley, 1966); John P. Crank, Robert M. Regoli, Eric D. Poole, and Robert G. Culbertson, "Cynicism Among Police Chiefs," *Justice Quarterly* 3 (1986): 343–352. For different "types" of officers, see William F. Walsh, "Patrol Officer Arrest Rates: A Study of the Social Organization of Police Work," *Justice Quarterly* 3 (1986): 271–290.

87. Some people believe police work attracts individuals with these characteristics. See Milton Rokeach, Martin Miller, and John Snyder, "The Value Gap Between Police and Policed," *Journal of Social Research* 27 (1971): 155–171; James Teevan and Bernard Dolnick, "The Values of the Police: A Reconsideration and Interpretation," *Journal of Police Science and Administration* 1 (1973): 366–369.

88. George Kirkham, "A Professor's Street Lessons," in *Order under Law,* ed. R. Culbertson and M. Tezak (Prospect Heights, Ill.: Waveland, 1981), p. 81.

89. Niederhoffer, *Behind the Shield.* For changes over time attributed to occupational socialization, see Jesse L. Maghan, "The 21st-Century Cop: Police Recruit Perceptions as a Function of Occupational Socialization" (Ph.D. dissertation, City University of New York, 1988).

90. John Blackmore, "Are Police Allowed to Have Problems of Their Own?" *Police Magazine* 1 (1978): 47–55. See also Clement Mihanovich, "The Blue Pressure Cooker," *Police Chief* 47, no. 2 (1980): 20–21; Mary Hageman, "Occupational Stress and Mari-

tal and Family Relationships," *Journal of Police Science and Administration* 6 (1978): 402–416; Francis T. Cullen, Terrence Lemming, Bruce G. Link, and John F. Wozniak, "The Impact of Social Supports on Police Stress," *Criminology* 23 (1985): 503–522; W. Clinton Terry III, "Police Stress: The Empirical Evidence," *Journal of Police Science and Administration* 9 (1981): 61–75; T. E. Malloy and G. L. Mays, "The Police Stress Hypothesis: A Critical Evaluation," *Criminal Justice and Behavior* 11 (1984): 197–226; B. A. Vulcano, G. E. Barnes, and L. J. Breen, "The Prevalence and Predictors of Psychosomatic Symptoms and Conditions Among Police Officers," *Psychosomatic Medicine* 45 (1983): 277–293; R. C. Trojanowicz, *The Environment of the First-Line Police Supervisor* (Englewood Cliffs, N.J.: Prentice-Hall, 1980); W. Clinton Terry III, "Police Stress as a Professional Self-Image," *Journal of Criminal Justice* 13 (1985): 501–512; Katherine W. Ellison and John L. Genz, *Stress and the Police Officer* (Springfield, Ill.: Charles C Thomas, 1983); William H. Kroes, *Society's Victims—The Police*, 2d ed. (Springfield, Ill.: Charles C Thomas, 1985). An entire organization devoted to the study of police stress (the International Law Enforcement Stress Association) has been founded; it publishes its own journal, *Police Stress.*

91. Jack R. Greene, "Police Officer Job Satisfaction and Community Perceptions: Implications for Community-Oriented Policing," *Journal of Research in Crime and Delinquency* 26 (1989): 168–183.

92. As quoted in William H. Hewitt, Robert S. Getz, and Oscar H. Ibele, *British Police Administration* (Springfield, Ill.: Charles C Thomas, 1965), p. 32.

16

THE NATURE AND FUNCTIONING OF COURTS

I got arraigned before the judge and got ten thousand dollars bail, and then I stayed in jail ever since then.

Now, did you intend to plead not guilty to this charge?

Yes, I was gonna plead not guilty.

So you were arraigned: they gave you a bond you can't make; so you're back in jail.

Right.

What happens then?

I just stayed there and kept going back and forth to court.

What did you go to court for?

For the same charge.

What was happening?

The lawyer didn't seem to be doing nothin. Every time I'd go there he would—he wouldn't, he wasn't sayin nothin.

He was a public defender?

Yes.

Did you appear in circuit court? Did you have the probable cause hearing?

Naw, he said it's better not to have it.

So you were bound over?

Yes. To high court.

So you had a different public defender in superior court?

Yes, I had a different one there.

Now, when was the first time you met him?

It was about three months.

You were taken over to superior court, and you met the public defender?

Yes. See, I had started off with Moore; then they switched me to some other guy. And none was takin interest in—

Did any of them come visit you in jail?

Naw.

The only time you saw them was in the bullpen or around court?

Yes.

Did you eventually plead guilty?

Yes, he told me, "With your record and stuff, you'd better plead guilty."

Who told you that?

The lawyer.[1]

Courts of law are entrusted with the awesome responsibility of resolving controversies arising under civil law and determining the guilt or innocence of a party charged with the violation of a criminal law. To an ordinary citizen charged with a crime, the experience of going to court can be confusing, frightening, and frustrating. Courts follow legal rules and procedures that only lawyers fully understand. The court system is intricate and often complex. Defendants are frightened because they experience a loss of control over their own destiny. The experience is frustrating because the court system does not always function as effectively as it should. In many jurisdictions delay is inevitable. Bargains and deals made by the prosecutor and defense counsel are commonplace. Bias, discrimination, and arbitrariness are now considered part of the system.

In this chapter we will closely examine the structure, function, rules, and procedures of courts. Specifically, we will review their origins, the various types of court systems, the trial court process, and issues relating to the sentencing of offenders.

THE ORIGINS OF COURTS

The word "court" is derived from the Latin of classical Rome. It is a combination of the prefix *co-* ("together") and *hortus* ("garden"). This simply means that all the flowers in the garden are a *co-hortus*, or cohort. Later the term was further contracted to "court," designating the garden or yard, usually surrounded by buildings, where all the cohorts got together. Throughout history, emperors, kings, dukes, and other nobles had estates or castles that were referred to as "courts"—the court of the king of England, the court of the queen of Spain, and so on. Important business was conducted at the court, including the business of

resolving disputes and adjudging the guilt or innocence of persons accused of crime.

The earliest trial methods seem very strange to us today. In trial by combat, for example, the accuser and the accused, or their hired professional fighters, fought on foot or on horseback and in armor until God picked the winner. Trial was a game at court, very much like games played on basketball courts and tennis courts. What all these court games have in common is the fact that they are played in established public places, in accordance with established rules, and are judged by umpires or judges in the presence of the public. A nineteenth-century English cartoonist captured the spirit of an Anglo-American trial court proceeding when he depicted it as if it were a game of tennis. Opposing counsel bounce their arguments back and forth in front of the judge, who makes sure that the game is being played according to the rules. When the game is over, he pronounces the winner.

An American jurist and philosopher, Jerome Frank, questioned the American "game" or "fight" approach to the resolution of disputes in court.[2] Such an approach encourages advocates for the people or state (prosecutors) and the defendant (defense counsel) to adopt and argue extreme positions. A judge is thus re-

A cartoonist's depiction of a trial as a tennis match.

quired to mediate between two inconsistent and often incompatible interpretations of fact and law. Is the truth really discovered when opposing counsel for the prosecution and defense argue it out, sometimes even overstepping the bounds of propriety? Defenders of Anglo-American trial theory hold that a contest between combatants in open court will indeed resolve the issues fairly.

Some changes have been made in criminal procedure over the centuries, but the basic idea still holds: Anglo-American criminal trials are a game played by competitors; the players are combatants defending opposing positions, they are adversaries, and it is at court that the contest is fought out.

As we explained in Chapter 14, the basic premises of the Anglo-American criminal process, having been generated in the thirteenth century, were well established in the fifteenth and sixteenth centuries, and were ready to be imported into the North American colonies in the seventeenth century. At first with reluctance, then with exuberance, the American colonies embraced the common law and its processes. The courts of the colonies were common law courts, applying the common law of England with certain limitations that contributed to the drive for independence. When independence was declared, the courts, which until then had been English common law courts, subject to English sovereignty, now were common law courts of the several states, subject only to the laws of the state legislatures. They still are. We do have fifty state court systems in the United States. The courts of these fifty jurisdictions are common law courts, the heirs of the common law of England as of 1776, applying the law in the common law fashion, as modified and amplified by state legislatures. There is, however, one big difference. In forming the United States, the original colonies granted to the federal government the right to make and enforce, through federal courts, those laws that Congress was empowered to make. Consequently, we find in our society two legal systems, one that is implemented by the state courts and another that is implemented by the federal courts.

THE COURT SYSTEM

State Courts

Most states have three distinct levels of courts of law: courts of limited or special jurisdiction, courts of general jurisdiction, and appellate courts (see Figure 16.1).

Courts of limited or special jurisdiction Courts of limited jurisdiction are limited by law as to the kinds of cases they can hear. Every town or city is likely to have a court with a justice of the peace, magistrate, or judge, not nec-

FIGURE 16.1 State court systems

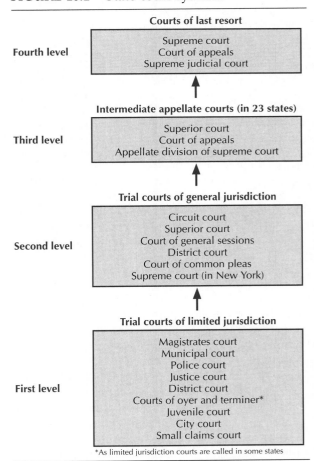

Source: Adapted from Abraham S. Blumberg, *Criminal Justice: Issues and Ironies* (New York: New Viewpoints, 1979), p. 150.

AT ISSUE

Judges as Students

How does one become a brew master? One must graduate from one of the brewing academies in the world, located in Germany, Scotland, and the United States. How does one become a sea captain or ship's officer? One has to graduate from one of six or seven state or federal merchant marine academies and spend plenty of time at sea between semesters. And how does one become a judge? Most judges have graduated from law school and are elected or appointed to the bench. Let us think: Law school prepares one to be a lawyer, not a judge. Then it is solely an election or an appointment that qualifies one for the special profession of the judiciary. Until the 1960s, such was indeed the English and American belief. A mystical transformation from lawyer to judge occurs at the moment the elected or appointed judge takes the oath of office,

dons the judicial robe, rides in an elevator "for judges only," sits on a bench, and is addressed as "your honor."

To a few highly respected judges, that was not enough. Chief Justice Arthur T. Vanderbilt of the New Jersey Supreme Court was instrumental in establishing a school for courts of appeals judges at New York University. And Mr. Justice Robert H. Jackson of the Supreme Court of the United States founded the National Judicial College, which is now located on the campus of the University of Nevada, at Reno. With the help of professors of various disciplines, experienced judges teach other judges all of the subjects that judges must know, from court administration to psychology, opinion casting, developments in the law, innovations in scientific evidence, press relations, and a great deal about crime and

justice in light of new theoretical and practical developments. Unorthodox methods are used in the college's curriculum. In courses on sentencing and correction, convicts from the nearby Nevada penitentiary are working as "cons" (short for consultants or convicts, whichever you choose) so that judges may learn what criminal justice looks like from the receiving end. What is the impact of a sentence on the convict? The cons know. Judges have also volunteered to spend twenty-four-hour periods in prison with the cons, as their cellmates, to learn what a single day, a single night in prison, wearing prison garb, may be like.

Since the founding of the National Judicial College in 1963, 25,707 certificates of course completion have been granted to trial judges from the fifty states, as well as to 211 judges from 114 foreign countries.

essarily trained in law, who handles minor criminal cases (misdemeanors or violations), less serious civil suits (involving small sums of money), traffic and parking violations, and health law violations. These courts are variously called municipal courts, justice of the peace courts, and magistrate's courts. Courts of special jurisdiction include family courts, juvenile courts, and *probate courts* (which deal with estate matters).

Courts of general jurisdiction   At the next level of state courts are the courts of general ju-

risdiction. These courts are a state's major trial courts. They have regular jurisdiction over all cases and controversies involving civil law and criminal law. Courts of general jurisdiction are county courts or, in less populous states, courts of a region that includes several counties. These are called superior courts or district courts. The judges of such courts are law school graduates, often with extensive experience at the bar. They are elected or appointed. In criminal cases, the law grants a defendant the right to a jury trial. When a defendant chooses a jury trial, this court is composed of a judge, to deal with mat ters of law, and a jury, to deal with the facts of the case and to apply to them the law as laid down by the judge.

Appellate courts   All states have developed elaborate procedures of appeal for parties who are unsuccessful at trial. In some states the only appellate court is the state's supreme court, while others provide an intermediate court of appeals. A person convicted of a crime has the right to appeal to an appellate court and ultimately to the court of last resort, the state supreme court, whenever the trial court is alleged to have erred on a point of law.

Federal Courts

The laws   The primary function of the federal courts is to apply and enforce all federal laws created by Congress. These statutes include a large body of federal criminal laws, which range from violations of the Migratory Bird Act to treason and piracy. Most of the federal criminal laws can be found in Title 18 of the U.S. Code. The federal courts have a second and perhaps even more important function: they are continually called upon to test the constitutionality of federal and state legislation and of court decisions.[3] For example, can a state pass and enforce a statute making it a criminal offense for black and white citizens to intermarry? In *Loving* v. *Virginia* (1967) the Supreme Court of the United States resoundingly said no.[4] The states cannot create such a crime because it violates the equal protection clause of the Fourteenth Amendment to the United States Constitution. In other words, the Supreme Court (a federal court) has the power to hold as a matter of law that a state cannot enact a statute that violates the United States Constitution. Consider another example, this time from the realm of criminal procedure: Can a state court receive in evidence at trial an object seized by state or local law enforcement officers in violation of the Fourth Amendment to the United States Constitution, which protects citizens against unreasonable searches and seizures? No, said the Supreme Court, that would be a violation of the due process guarantee of the Fourteenth

Amendment, which protects all people in the United States.[5] Thus federal courts often scrutinize the legal rights of citizens, ensuring that they are afforded the rights that the United States Constitution guarantees them.

Federal magistrates   At the lowest level of jurisdiction are the federal magistrates, called United States commissioners. The commissioners not only have trial jurisdiction over minor federal offenses but they also have the important right to issue warrants, such as arrest warrants.

United States district courts   The trial courts in the federal system, called United States district courts, have both civil and criminal jurisdiction. There are ninety-four federal district courts, including those in Guam, the Virgin Islands, the northern Marianas, and Puerto Rico. Every state has at least one such court, and the populous states have more than one. A total of 576 presidentially appointed judges sit in these courts.

United States circuit courts of appeal   An appeal of a conviction in a federal district court is heard by a United States circuit court of appeals. There are thirteen appeals courts in the country: one in each of eleven areas (circuits) of the country plus one in the District of Columbia and another, also in Washington, D.C., called the Federal Circuit, which handles appeals that originate anywhere in the country when they pertain to such matters as patents and copyrights, some tax disputes, and suits against the federal government. There are 156 federal appeals court judges.

The original designation of states included within the federal circuits was made when most of the business of the federal courts was in the populous East and in the Midwest (Figure 16.2). Because the West Coast has since become very populous, the Ninth Circuit, which covers a vast area, has more business than any of the other courts.

The Supreme Court of the United States   The Supreme Court of the United States occupies a unique position in our system of government. It represents the highest echelon of the third

FIGURE 16.2   United States Circuit Courts of Appeal

branch of government, the judiciary. Our Supreme Court occupies a place of honor in our system of government which is not equaled in any other country. Its chief justice is not just the chief justice of the Supreme Court but the chief justice of the United States. The chief justice and the eight associate justices are appointed by the president of the United States, with the advice and consent of the Senate.

The United States Supreme Court is the ultimate authority in interpreting the Constitution as it applies to both federal and state law; and it also is the final authority in interpreting federal law. Thus, both federal and state cases may reach the Supreme Court.

Interaction between State Courts and Federal Courts

It is important not to view state and federal court systems as wholly independent or mutu-

ally exclusive. A legal controversy that arises in a state court may raise federal constitutional questions. In such a case, a federal court may be asked to resolve the federal question.

Suppose that on the tip of an anonymous informer, with no other corroborating evidence, a local magistrate issues a search warrant authorizing the search of a college dormitory room for marijuana. Let us further suppose that several joints are found in the drawer of a desk that is used by two students. Both are arrested, tried in a local court, and convicted of the crime of possession of a controlled substance. Defense counsel claims that the search warrant was illegally issued, because it was not based on the legally required evidence showing probable cause that a crime was committed. Therefore, the evidence, the joints, should never have been admitted in court. Let us suppose that the state trial judge does not agree with this defense.

WINDOW TO THE WORLD

The International Criminal Court

At one time decisions were made and the law was enforced in very small groupings, namely families. In earliest Roman law the *pater familias,* or father of the family, had power over life and death with respect to every family member. Thus, the family was the jurisdictional unit in criminal law. Later on it became the clan that exercised this jurisdiction. When some wrongs affected people in several clans it became necessary to give criminal jurisdiction to yet higher authority, at the level of tribes, cities, kingdoms, and empires. In America the thirteen newly formed states yielded some of their criminal law jurisdiction to the federal government for crimes affecting the whole country or people in more than one state.

We live in an age when some wrongs are so massive or pervasive that they can affect all people on earth. Warmongers can create world conflict and commit genocide. Criminal negligence in building a nuclear reactor can cause a meltdown with atomic fallout that might kill people all over the world. Narcotic drug producers and traders can cause addiction and crime problems all over the globe. Terrorist organizations can disrupt the peace and tranquility

in many nations. Many government leaders and legal scholars believe the time has come to establish a criminal jurisdiction, resting in an international criminal court, to deal with offenses of an international or transnational nature. There is precedent for an international criminal court. The Congress of Vienna, 1814–1815, declared Napoleon Bonaparte to be an enemy of all mankind and confirmed his banishment to the remote island of St. Helena in the South Atlantic. Following World War II the allied powers established an international war crimes tribunal, at Nuremberg, Germany, which tried and convicted the principal German leaders responsible for World War II on charges of war crimes. After World War II the United Nations tried unsuccessfully to create an international criminal court. Now that the cold war is over, there is a considerable prospect for the establishment of such a court to deal with any or all "international" crimes that affect people as a whole. At the 1989 General Assembly of the United Nations the Prime Minister of Trinidad and Tobago urged the speedy constitution of such a court to deal with international narcotics traffickers. The General Assembly

has now before it the agenda item "International Criminal Responsibility of Individuals and Entities Engaged in the Illegal Trafficking in Drugs across National Frontiers: Establishment of an International Criminal Court with Jurisdiction over Such Offences." It is envisaged that such a court would be composed of distinguished criminal law specialists from all regions of the world. Its effectiveness would depend on the willingness of governments to apprehend drug traffickers and surrender them to the International Criminal Court. Many governments would prefer this option over trying the traffickers in their national courts, or surrendering them to other countries.

Once such an International Criminal Court proves effective in dealing with international drug criminality, its jurisdiction could be widened to include terrorism and other international crimes. As crime becomes globalized, the criminal justice response must become globalized. An International Criminal Court could become the centerpiece of a worldwide criminal justice system, and it likely will be in the not-too-distant future.

Appeal and the writ of certiorari   The students decide to appeal their conviction, claiming that the trial judge committed a legal error by not excluding the evidence. Let us suppose that the state court of appeals (if there is one) rules against the students. They next appeal to

the state supreme court. If the state supreme court rejects the argument as well, the next option is to appeal to the Supreme Court of the United States. The basis of this appeal is that the federal constitutional right to be free from search and seizure except on a warrant issued on the basis of probable cause (Fourth Amendment) was violated. This option is exercised by an application for a **writ of certiorari,** a document issued by a higher court (in this case the U.S. Supreme Court) directing a lower court (the state supreme court) to send to it the records of a case.

The Supreme Court may accept this case because it has established the rule that a search warrant issued on the basis of an unreliable informant's tip does not meet the reasonableness and probable cause requirements of the Fourth Amendment.[6] But the U.S. Supreme Court gets thousands of appeals and applications for writs of certiorari every year; it can consider only a very few. Normally the Supreme Court chooses to review a case only if it involves a substantial unresolved constitutional question, particularly one on which the findings of the various federal courts of appeals have diverged.

Habeas corpus   Having been denied a writ of certiorari by the United States Supreme Court, the students may then apply for a writ of **habeas corpus** at the federal district court. Historically, under the common law of England, a prisoner's detention could be tested by a judicial writ (command) to a jailer for an inquiry.

Written in Latin, the writ contained the crucial words "habeas corpus," which means "you have the body [person] of..." The text of the writ concluded with a request to produce the prisoner before the reviewing judge, and to explain by what lawful authority the prisoner is being detained.[7] Used throughout the history of Anglo-American law, such inquiries still determine whether the Constitution was violated during the trial that resulted in the conviction that led to the imprisonment.

In our hypothetical case, until 1976, the students could indeed have applied to the federal district court for a writ of habeas corpus. But in that year the Supreme Court held that the writ was no longer available in Fourth Amendment search-and-seizure cases because the federal courts were so flooded with applications for the writ that they could not manage the caseload.[8] Whenever the alleged constitutional violation pertains to issues other than search and seizure, the writ is still available. If the district court denies the writ of habeas corpus, the prisoner can appeal that decision to a U.S. circuit court of appeals. If that court does not overrule the district court, the prisoner can appeal again to the U.S. Supreme Court. Figure 16.3 depicts the entire process.

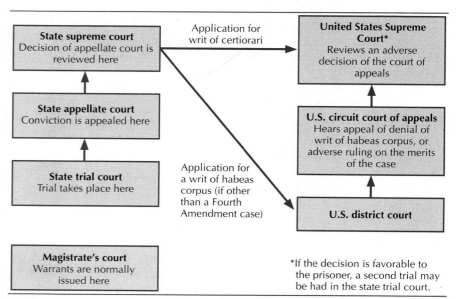

FIGURE 16.3   Path of a state criminal case through state and federal courts

Lawyers in the Court System

In every criminal case an attorney represents the government, whether county, city, or state. That attorney is called a **prosecutor.** On the other side of the case is the lawyer who has been retained by the person charged with an offense or assigned by the court if the defendant is indigent. That attorney is called the **defense counsel.**

Prosecutors and their duties   Prosecutors are government officials who represent the people of a particular jurisdiction. They may be appointed or elected. Prosecutors are responsible for some of the most important initial responses to crime. They screen suspects arrested by the police, decide whether or not to press charges, argue the case on behalf of the government, and often make recommendations regarding sentencing. More than 8,000 state and local agencies are involved in prosecution. They include the offices of district attorney, city corporation counsel, and state attorney general. Federal crimes are prosecuted by United States attorneys, who are appointed by the president.

Prosecutorial discretion   Prosecutors can exercise a variety of options that have far-reaching effects on an individual's freedom, life, property, reputation, and well-being. This power is unmatched by that of any other official in the American criminal justice system. Prosecutors are relatively free to choose their causes, cases, and targets for prosecution.[9] They have complete discretion in three areas of pretrial decision making: (1) whether or not to file a criminal charge; (2) how to set the level of seriousness of the offense to be charged; and (3) when to cease prosecution.[10] In most jurisdictions, prosecutors are empowered by statute to "prosecute for all offenses." As the legal scholar Abraham S. Goldstein has noted, however, this exclusive authority to prosecute does not confer an obligation to do so in every case.[11] Prosecutors have discretion in the way they handle cases, as Figure 16.4 indicates.

Prosecutorial roles   Prosecutors play a variety of functional and occupational roles, which are not necessarily identified by law. Abraham Blumberg has identified several such roles:

- *Collection agent.* In smaller communities, prosecutors collect and dispense money to cover debts, such as family support payments, proceeds from bad checks, and debt arising from fraud.
- *Dispenser of justice/power broker–fixer.* Prosecutors weigh the available penalties associated with certain charges and, in using their discretion, dispense justice. In political situations, they mediate between disputants by the use and threat of sanctions.
- *Political enforcer.* A prosecutor may prosecute a case for reasons and purposes other than a desire to achieve a just conviction—perhaps to get vengeance or notoriety, to deter certain conduct, or to damage a reputation.
- *Overseer of police.* The prosecutor is also known to act as a magistrate, continually reviewing the work of the police.[12]

Defense counsel   All persons accused of a crime for which jail or prison is the possible penalty have a right to counsel under the Sixth Amendment to the United States Constitution.[13] A defense attorney ensures that the legal rights of an accused person are fully protected at every stage in the criminal justice process. Defendants who can afford counsel retain an attorney of their choice, or, very rarely, choose to represent themselves. An accused person who is unable to afford an attorney may be represented free of charge by counsel coming from any of three sources, depending on the jurisdiction (see Figure 16.5):

- *A public defender program.* Statewide and local public defenders belong to public or private nonprofit organizations that provide free legal counsel.
- *An assigned counsel system.* Judges appoint attorneys who are in private practice as they are needed.
- *A contract system.* Contracts are awarded to bar associations, private law firms, or individual attorneys who agree to provide legal counsel on a regular basis.

FIGURE 16.4 Differences in the way prosecutors handle felony cases in four jurisdictions

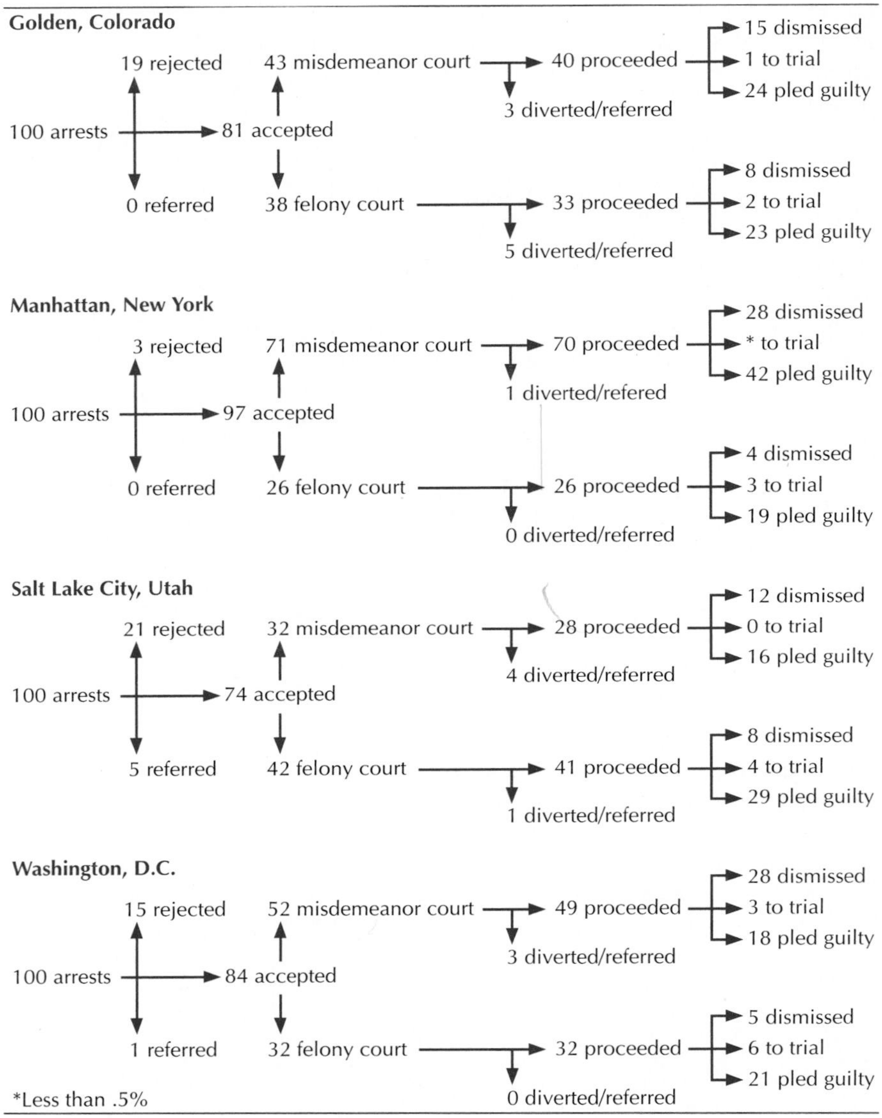

Golden, Colorado

```
                                          ┌──► 15 dismissed
                   19 rejected  43 misdemeanor court ──► 40 proceeded ──┤──► 1 to trial
                        ▲            ▲                       │          └──► 24 pled guilty
                        │            │               3 diverted/referred
100 arrests ──► 81 accepted
                        │            │                                  ┌──► 8 dismissed
                   0 referred   38 felony court ──────────► 33 proceeded ──┤──► 2 to trial
                                                             │          └──► 23 pled guilty
                                                    5 diverted/referred
```

Manhattan, New York

```
                                          ┌──► 28 dismissed
                    3 rejected  71 misdemeanor court ──► 70 proceeded ──┤──► * to trial
                        ▲            ▲                       │          └──► 42 pled guilty
                        │            │               1 diverted/refered
100 arrests ──► 97 accepted
                        │            │                                  ┌──► 4 dismissed
                   0 referred   26 felony court ──────────► 26 proceeded ──┤──► 3 to trial
                                                             │          └──► 19 pled guilty
                                                    0 diverted/referred
```

Salt Lake City, Utah

```
                                          ┌──► 12 dismissed
                   21 rejected  32 misdemeanor court ──► 28 proceeded ──┤──► 0 to trial
                        ▲            ▲                       │          └──► 16 pled guilty
                        │            │               4 diverted/referred
100 arrests ──► 74 accepted
                        │            │                                  ┌──► 8 dismissed
                   5 referred   42 felony court ──────────► 41 proceeded ──┤──► 4 to trial
                                                             │          └──► 29 pled guilty
                                                    1 diverted/referred
```

Washington, D.C.

```
                                          ┌──► 28 dismissed
                   15 rejected  52 misdemeanor court ──► 49 proceeded ──┤──► 3 to trial
                        ▲            ▲                       │          └──► 18 pled guilty
                        │            │               3 diverted/referred
100 arrests ──► 84 accepted
                        │            │                                  ┌──► 5 dismissed
                   1 referred   32 felony court ──────────► 32 proceeded ──┤──► 6 to trial
                                                             │          └──► 21 pled guilty
                                                    0 diverted/referred
```

*Less than .5%

Source: Barbara Boland with Ronald Sones, INSLAW, Inc., *The Prosecution of Felony Arrests, 1981,* Bureau of Justice Statistics, 1986.

THE ROLE OF THE TRIAL JUDGE AT ARRAIGNMENT

In discussing the criminal justice process (Chapter 14) we noted the important role that judges play during proceedings before trial. They grant release at various stages, preside over first appearances of arrested persons in court and over preliminary hearings, issue orders and rule on motions, accept plea bargains, impanel grand juries, and instruct juries in their tasks. The role traditionally associated with a judge is that of a person who presides over trials. A trial begins with the **arraignment**, a formal proceeding in open court at which the grand jury hands down its indictment. Not all

FIGURE 16.5 Predominant system for defense of the indigent in each of the fifty states

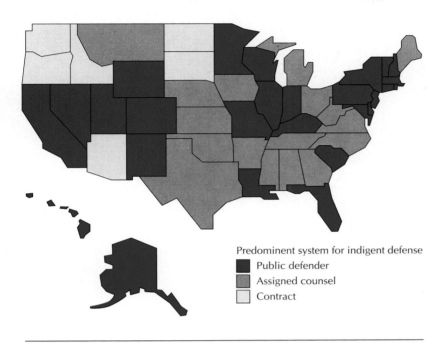

Predominent system for indigent defense
- ◼ Public defender
- ◼ Assigned counsel
- ◻ Contract

Source: Robert L. Spangenberg et al. of Abt Associates, Inc., Bureau of Justice Statistics *National Criminal Defense Systems Study*. October 1986, updated by the Spangenberg Group, March 1987.

states require a grand jury indictment to initiate prosecutions, however, as Table 16.1 indicates.

Arraignment

At the arraignment in open court in the presence of the defendant and the defense counsel, the person named in the **indictment** (accusation by the grand jury) or **information** (accusation by the prosecutor) is asked to plead to the charge. The defendant has two or sometimes three options:

• The defendant may **plead** guilty to the charges contained in the various counts of the indictment, thereby admitting all the facts alleged to have occurred, as well as their legal implications. Under those circumstances no trial need take place. The trial judge need only make certain that the pleas have been advisedly taken and that the facts indeed support the guilt of the defendant. The judge may then accept the plea of guilty and sentence the offender.

• The defendant may plead not guilty, thereby denying everything and putting on the prosecution the burden of proving beyond a reasonable doubt all the facts alleged in the indictment.

• In most jurisdictions, the defendant may also plead no contest, or nolo contendere, with the approval of the prosecution and the court. By this plea the defendant admits criminal liability for the purposes of this proceeding only. That procedure has the practical advantage of avoiding the implications of guilt in other proceedings (a civil suit for damages, for example).

Pretrial Motions

Counsel for either side, defense or prosecution, may make a multitude of **motions,** or official requests to the judge, at any appropriate moment

TABLE 16.1   STATES THAT DO AND DO NOT REQUIRE A GRAND JURY INDICTMENT TO INITIATE PROSECUTIONS

GRAND JURY INDICTMENT REQUIRED	GRAND JURY INDICTMENT OPTIONAL
ALL CRIMES	Arizona
New Jersey	Arkansas
South Carolina	California
Tennessee	Colorado
Virginia	Idaho
	Illinois
ALL FELONIES	Indiana
Alabama	Iowa
Alaska	Kansas
Delaware	Maryland
District of Columbia	Michigan
Georgia	Missouri
Hawaii	Montana
Kentucky	Nebraska
Maine	Nevada
Mississippi	New Mexico
New Hampshire	North Dakota
New York	Oklahoma
North Carolina	Oregon
Ohio	South Dakota
Texas	Utah
West Virginia	Vermont
	Washington
CAPITAL CRIMES ONLY	Wisconsin
Connecticut	Wyoming
Florida	
Louisiana	**GRAND JURY LACKS AUTHORITY TO INDICT**
Massachusetts	Pennsylvania
Minnesota	
Rhode Island	

Note: With the exception of capital cases, a defendant can always waive the right to an indictment. Thus the requirement for an indictment to initiate prosecution exists only in the absence of a waiver.

Source: Deborah Day Emerson, *Grand Jury Reform: A Review of Key Issues,* for National Institute of Justice, U.S. Department of Justice (Washington, D.C.: U.S. Government Printing Office, January 1983).

from arrest until after the trial is over. The bulk of such motions are made before trial; each requires a hearing and sometimes a separate minitrial. Among the many types of motions are the following:

• A *motion for a severance,* by which a defendant claims that it would be prejudicial to his or her case to be tried together with other defendants charged in the indictment.

• A *motion for a change of venue,* when pretrial publicity makes it impossible to get a fair trial in the county where the crime was committed.

• A *motion to quash the indictment* on the grounds that the evidence presented is insufficient to establish probable cause.

• A *motion for a sanity hearing,* when the defendant claims that mental illness deprives him or her of legal responsibility.

• A *motion to suppress illegally obtained evidence.*

- A *motion for discovery of evidence* in the hands of the prosecution.
- A *motion to dismiss the case* for want of adequate evidence or some other cause.

Release Decisions

Once again the trial judge must decide whether to release the defendant, this time for the period between the arraignment and the commencement of the main phase of the trial—a period that may last several weeks. The decision has far-reaching consequences, summarized by the President's Commission on Law Enforcement and the Administration of Justice:

> The importance of this decision to any defendant is obvious. A released defendant is one who can live with and support his family, maintain his ties to his community, and busy himself with his own defense by searching for witnesses and evidence and by keeping close touch with his lawyer. An imprisoned defen-

dant is subjected to the squalor, idleness, and possible criminalizing effect of jail. He may be confined for something he did not do; some jailed defendants are ultimately acquitted. He may be confined while presumed innocent only to be freed when found guilty; many jailed defendants, after they have been convicted, are placed on probation rather than imprisoned. The community also relies on the magistrate for protection when he makes his decision about releasing a defendant. If a released defendant fails to appear for trial, the law is flouted. If a released defendant commits crimes, the community is endangered.[14]

The various types of pretrial release are summarized in Table 16.2.

In view of the large number of indigent defendants today, is it reasonable to base release decisions on defendants' financial means? A movement to ensure fairness in bail decisions began in the early 1960s in response to the perception of discrimination against defendants

TABLE 16.2   TYPES OF PRETRIAL RELEASE

FINANCIAL BOND	ALTERNATIVE RELEASE OPTIONS
Fully secured bail—The defendant posts the full amount of bail with the court.	*Release on recognizance* (ROR)—The court releases the defendant on his promise that he will appear in court as required.
Privately secured bail—A bondsman signs a promissory note to the court for the bail amount and charges the defendant a fee for the service (usually 10% of the bail amount). If the defendant fails to appear, the bondsman must pay the court the full amount. Frequently the bondsman requires the defendant to post collateral in addition to the fee.	*Conditional release*—The court releases the defendant subject to his following of specific conditions set by the court, such as attendance at drug treatment therapy or staying away from the complaining witness.
Percentage bail—The courts allow the defendant to deposit a percentage (usually 10%) of the full bail with the court. The full amount of the bail is required if the defendant fails to appear. The percentage bail is returned after disposition of the case although the court often retains 1% for administrative costs.	*Third-party custody*—The defendant is released into the custody of an individual or agency that promises to assure his appearance in court. No monetary transactions are involved in this type of release.
Unsecured bail—The defendant pays no money to the court but is liable for the full amount of bail should he fail to appear.	

Source: U.S. Department of Justice, Bureau of Justice Statistics, *Report to the Nation on Crime and Justice: The Data* (Washington, D.C.: U.S. Government Printing Office, 1983), p. 58.

who could not afford bail. The Manhattan Bail Project, sponsored by the Vera Institute of Justice, found that it was possible to minimize no-shows and to predict with reasonable accuracy whether an accused would return to court on the basis of the person's offense history, family ties, and employment record. The project's early findings revealed a low default rate. Through the 1960s and early 1970s, similar programs flourished throughout the country. Perhaps the most promising reform attempt may be credited to the criminologist John Goldkamp, who, with the assistance of Michael Gottfredson, designed uniform guidelines for bail decision makers (see Figure 16.6).[15] By creating a two-dimensional grid on which they could plot the severity of the offense against a series of variables, such as type of crime, number of arrests, age, and community ties, these criminologists enabled judges to reduce significantly the disparities in decisions regarding bail.

Despite efforts to make the bail system equitable, the tide has shifted toward placing restraints on pretrial release and instituting provisions for pretrial detention. As Table 16.3 suggests, many states now place significant restrictions on pretrial release decisions. Some jurisdictions, such as Washington, D.C., have instituted preventive detention statutes that authorize judges to deny bail to apparently dangerous offenders and keep them in custody. In fact, the Bail Reform Act of 1984 permits preventive detention where "no condition or combination of conditions will reasonably assure the appearance of the person as required and the safety of any other person, and the community."[16]

Plea Bargaining

The arraignment affords the prosecutor and defense counsel the last significant opportunity to offer the court a negotiated plea. As we noted in Chapter 14, the majority of defendants prefer to plead guilty to a lesser charge, at any step of the process before trial. The inclination to make such a bargain is particularly great at arraignment, when the defendant may perceive a high

probability of conviction. Though an acquittal cannot be ruled out, the assurance of a significant period of incarceration if the defendant is convicted is an incentive to bargain or negotiate with the prosecution. Statistics support such considerations. While the conviction rate in felony cases that go to trial varies from jurisdiction to jurisdiction, it is generally high. Prosecutors are concerned about the expense of a trial, a shortage of staff, and perhaps a long wait for available courtroom space and a trial judge. A study of twenty-six jurisdictions found a median conviction rate of 73 percent.[17]

The National Advisory Commission on Criminal Justice Standards and Goals recommended in 1971 that the practice of plea bargaining be abolished. "As soon as possible, but in no event later than 1978, negotiations between prosecutors and defendants—either personally or through their attorneys—concerning concessions to be made in return for guilty pleas should be prohibited."[18] According to the commission, abolishing plea bargaining would remove the incentive for prosecutors to charge an offender with a crime more serious than they expect to be able to prove; it would increase the number of trials only insignificantly; and, most important, it would increase the rationality and fairness of the criminal trial process.[19] Abolition of plea bargaining would also restore the constitutional right to a trial by jury, which defendants are now manipulated to give up, and it would prevent the prosecution from achieving victory on the basis of insufficient or even illegally obtained evidence, which it can currently hide in a plea bargain.

But would the elimination of plea bargaining really have only an insignificant effect on the caseloads of judges, juries, prosecutors, and defense counsel? Only a 10 percent increase in trials, some experts claim, might cause the court apparatus to stop functioning.[20] But it also has been argued, on the basis of the experience of the few jurisdictions that have abolished plea bargaining—Alaska, New Orleans, El Paso, Blackhawk County in Iowa, Maricopa County in Arizona, Oakland County in Michigan, and Multnomah County in Oregon—that

FIGURE 16.6 Bail guidelines (revised)

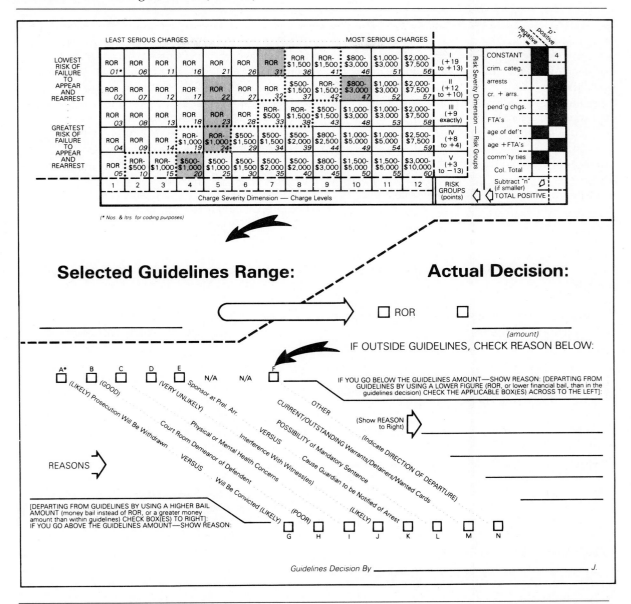

Source: John Goldkamp and Michael Gottfredson, *Judicial Decision Guidelines for Bail: The Philadelphia Experiment* (Washington, D.C.: National Institute of Justice, 1983).

most defendants who consider themselves to be guilty will plead guilty anyway in the hope that they may then receive a lighter sentence (Table 16.4). This hypothesis, however, is largely untested. Rather than abolish plea bar-

gaining, most jurisdictions have made it more open, more regulated, and fairer. The U.S. Supreme Court has insisted that the voluntariness of the plea and an understanding of its implications must be demonstrated in open court and

TABLE 16.3   STATES THAT HAVE ONE OR MORE PROVISIONS TO ENSURE COMMUNITY SAFETY IN PRETRIAL RELEASE

TYPE OF PROVISION	STATES THAT HAVE ENACTED THE PROVISION
Exclusion of certain crimes from automatic bail eligibility	Colorado, District of Columbia, Florida, Georgia, Michigan, Nebraska, Wisconsin
Definition of the purpose of bail to ensure appearance and safety	Alaska, Arizona, California, Delaware, District of Columbia, Florida, Hawaii, Minnesota, South Carolina, South Dakota, Vermont, Virginia, Wisconsin
Inclusion of crime control factors in the release decision	Alabama, California, Florida, Georgia, Minnesota, South Dakota, Wisconsin
Inclusion of release conditions related to crime control	Alaska, Arkansas, Colorado, Delaware, District of Columbia, Florida, Hawaii, Illinois, Iowa, Minnesota, New Mexico, North Carolina, South Carolina, South Dakota, Vermont, Virginia, Washington, Wisconsin
Limitations on the right to bail for those previously convicted	Colorado, District of Columbia, Florida, Georgia, Hawaii, Indiana, Michigan, New Mexico, Texas, Utah, Wisconsin
Revocation of pretrial release when there is evidence that the accused committed a new crime	Arizona, Arkansas, Colorado, District of Columbia, Georgia, Hawaii, Illinois, Indiana, Maryland, Massachusetts, Michigan, Nevada, New Mexico, New York, Rhode Island, Texas, Utah, Vermont, Wisconsin
Limitations on the right to bail for crimes alleged to have been committed while on release	Arizona, Arkansas, Colorado, District of Columbia, Florida, Georgia, Illinois, Indiana, Maryland, Massachusetts, Michigan, Minnesota, Nevada, New Mexico, New York, Rhode Island, Tennessee, Texas, Utah, Vermont, Wisconsin
Provisions for pretrial detention to ensure safety	Arizona, Arkansas, California, Colorado, District of Columbia, Florida, Georgia, Hawaii, Illinois, Indiana, Maryland, Massachusetts, Michigan, Nebraska, Nevada, New Mexico, New York, Rhode Island, South Dakota, Texas, Utah, Vermont, Virginia, Washington, Wisconsin

Source: Elizabeth Gaynes, *Typology of State Laws Which Permit Consideration of Danger in the Pretrial Release Decision* (Washington, D.C.: Pretrial Services Resource Center, 1982), and updated from Barbara Gottlieb, *Public Danger as a Factor in Pretrial Release: A Comparative Analysis of State Laws,* for National Institute of Justice (Washington, D.C.: U.S. Government Printing Office, July 1985).

that the prosecution must stick to its part of the bargain.[21] In federal courts the plea-bargaining process has actually been turned into a mini-trial, consisting of such an "inquiry as shall satisfy [the court] that there is a factual basis for the plea."[22]

THE TRIAL

Setting of the Trial

The trial court is established to find and express the communal judgment under law, as to the

TABLE 16.4   PERCENTAGE OF CASES FILED RESULTING IN GUILTY PLEAS AND IN TRIALS IN SIX MUNICIPAL JURISDICTIONS, 1981

JURISDICTION	GUILTY PLEA	TRIAL
New Orleans	73%	16%
Lansing	68	9
Denver	68	6
Dallas	72	8
San Diego	73	4
Miami	70	3

Source: Barbara Boland with Ronald Sones, INSLAW, Inc., *Prosecution of Felony Arrests, 1981* (Washington, D.C.: Bureau of Justice Statistics, 1986).

guilt or innocence of an accused person. The public, in whose name the judgment is rendered, is supposed to participate actively in the process. Indictments read "The People of the State of...versus John Doe [or Jane Roe]." What specifically is meant by "the people"? One answer is that the judge, who is elected by the people or appointed by somebody who was elected by the people, represents a consensus of the people. Furthermore, when an indictment is handed down and a jury trial held, the people are directly represented by a cross section of the community participating in the grand jury that indicts the defendant and the trial jury that tries the defendant. Any citizen is allowed into the courtroom to witness the proceedings, and seats for spectators are provided (see Figure 16.7). Indeed, in pioneer days, trial day at the county seat was major entertainment. Everybody would be there to see justice being administered. In some states, television coverage of court proceedings has taken the place of direct and total community participation. The experience with televised trials has been positive, on the whole.

Selecting the Jury

After a plea of not guilty, the first step is the impaneling of the jury, which is called the petit or petty jury, in contrast to the grand jury. Twelve is the traditional number of trial jurors. The number 12 has long had a mystical significance in Western civilization—the twelve apostles, the twelve tribes of Israel, the twelve days of Christmas. Some states use fewer than twelve jurors for trials involving crimes of lesser seriousness. Ordinarily several alternate jurors are selected to take the place of any juror who might become disabled during the trial.

Voir dire   Jury selection is usually guided by three objectives. Attorneys have to

"*...and I ask, gentlemen, if this is the face of a villain, a cheat and a parasite?*"

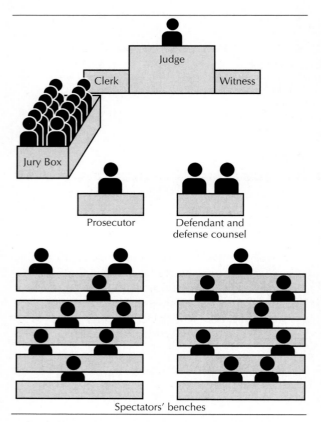

FIGURE 16.7   Contemporary criminal trial setting

unsympathetic by means of **peremptory challenges,** or objections to potential jurors for which no explanation is required. Each side has a certain number of such challenges; usually the defense has more than the prosecution. Either side may use an unlimited number of **challenges for cause,** which are intended to keep persons with a conflict of interest off the jury. A person related by birth or by marriage to any of the parties connected with the case, for example, would almost certainly be challenged for cause.

The jury selection process has yet another aspect. Skilled attorneys believe they can subliminally inject certain biases into potential jurors to ensure that evidence introduced at trial will be understood their particular way. In a sense, they attempt to create sympathetic understanding for the position of the prosecution or the defense, as the case may be. The psychologists David Suggs and Bruce Sales, however, have noted that

> suggestions from the legal literature [on ways to ensure sympathetic jurors] for the most part are based on hypotheses and folklore. Very little, if any, empirical work has been performed to substantiate the reliability and validity of the [jury selection] techniques proposed by legal writers.[23]

- Determine whether prospective jurors meet the minimum qualifications to sit as jurors (e.g., age and residency requirements).
- Determine the impartiality of prospective jurors.
- Obtain sufficient information on prospective jurors to enable them to exclude "for cause" any who may be prejudiced for or against the defendant.

The process by which lawyers and the judge examine a prospective juror to determine his or her acceptability, known as **voir dire,** extends further. Counsel for both the defense and the prosecution have certain strategic considerations. Attorneys for each side attempt to pick jurors who might be just a little more understanding or sympathetic to their argument. They can exclude people they think will be

The proceedings   Once a jury has been chosen or the defendant has waived a jury trial and consented to a trial by the judge alone, the trial proceedings begin. The prosecution makes an opening statement, outlining the case and previewing what it proposes to prove and how. The defense may then make or postpone its opening statement. It is the prosecution's burden to introduce the evidence against the defendant. All evidence necessary to prove the case must be introduced in court directly and in compliance with the rules of evidence.

Evidence   The rules of evidence have evolved over centuries. One prominent rule says that hearsay cannot be used. This rule is based on the fact that when information is repeated, it tends to become distorted. Thus it is unsafe to trust any statement other than the original. The exclusionary rule, as we saw in Chapter 14, prohibits the introduction of any evidence that does not meet the strict standards of the law of evidence.[24] If a suspect is not given the *Miranda* warning, for example, any evidence obtained through police-initiated questioning after arrest may be excluded from trial. The exclusionary rule has become a standard of constitutional law that binds not only the federal courts but all state courts as well.[25] Evidence found as a result of illegally received information cannot be introduced as evidence at trial either. It is regarded to be "the fruit of the poisonous tree," and as Justice Felix Frankfurter stated, "the criminal is to go free because the constable had blundered."[26]

The Supreme Court has been willing to make exceptions to the rigid constitutional exclusionary rule by creating the "inevitable discovery" rule. Under this rule, evidence that was obtained in violation of a constitutional prohibition is admissible if it would inevitably have been discovered anyway.[27]

During the entire evidentiary stage of the trial, the defense watches the prosecution carefully, objecting immediately when it appears that one of the rules of evidence may have been violated to the detriment of the defendant. If the breach of the rule is so grave that the defendant's chance of a fair trial has been prejudiced, the defense may even move for a mistrial. If that motion is granted, the prosecution will have to start over again before a new jury. The judge rules on all motions and objections. If the judge rules against the defendant, defense counsel will have the ruling placed on record as a potential cause to appeal a verdict and judgment of guilty. Every witness called by either party is subject to cross-examination by the other party.

When the prosecution has completed its case, the defense has several options. If the evidence against the defendant is poor, the defense may move for a directed verdict of acquittal or a motion to dismiss. A directed verdict is a verdict that is pronounced by the judge. A motion to dismiss is a request that the proceedings be terminated. The defense can also address the jury in a postponed opening statement to influence an acquittal. The defense is more likely to present its own evidence—alibi witnesses, expert witnesses, character witnesses, even the defendant. The defendant is under no obligation to testify in his or her own behalf. Any defendant who does testify is subject to cross-examination by the prosecution.

The task of the jury   In the normal course of a trial, after both sides have presented their evidence, closing arguments are presented by the defense and the prosecution. The jurors then must apply the law to the facts that they have heard and must determine the guilt or innocence of the defendant. So that they may do so responsibly, the judge gives them instructions—directions concerning the way they should go about deciding the case. Often both the prosecution and the defense will offer instructions to the judge on the law that they propose should be given to the jury. Typically the defense and the prosecution differ on how the jury should be instructed, especially on how the instructions should be phrased. Once again the judge is the arbiter. The judge takes the ultimate responsibility for instructing the jury and may even prefer his or her own version of the instructions to those offered by defense and prosecution. If the defense counsel objects to the proposed instructions on grounds of law, the objections are noted for a potential appeal.

After receiving their instructions, the jurors retire to the jury room for their deliberations, which are guided by a foreman—one of their number whom they select to preside over their deliberations. The majority of juries have little difficulty in arriving at a verdict of guilty, not guilty, guilty of the crime charged in a lesser degree, or guilty of some but not all of the crimes charged. Some juries, however, do have difficulty reaching a verdict. In the celebrated "preppy murder case" (*People* v. *Chambers*), the jury wavered for nine days between overwhelming majorities for and against the defendant, until defense and prosecution both realized the dilemma and agreed on a plea bargain, thus taking the jury out of the picture.[28]

Jury decision making   For several decades psychologists have studied juror decision making, courtroom testimony, and the eyewitness identification and testimony.[29] In examining the power of eyewitness testimony, Elizabeth Loftus conducted a mock-trial experiment in which subjects played the roles of jurors, listened to testimony, and were asked to reach a verdict. The mock jurors received a detailed description of a grocery store robbery in which the store's owner and granddaughter were killed. Loftus presented three versions of the evidence. One group of subjects was informed that there was no eyewitness, only circumstantial evidence. The second group was told a store clerk testified that the defendant shot the two victims. The third group was told of the store clerk's identification, but that on cross-examination his testimony was discredited because he had not been wearing his glasses and his eyesight was poor. Eighteen percent of the first group found the defendant guilty, 72 percent of the second group, and 68 percent of the third group. The results of this research suggest that eyewitness testimony, even if contradicted or impeached, can be very persuasive to jurors.

Psychologists also have studied the influence of personal prejudice and expectations on the validity of eyewitness accounts. To address this question Albert H. Hastorf and Hadley Cantrill showed a film of a football game between Dartmouth and Princeton to students at each school and asked them to note the number of infractions. Princeton students reported twice as many infractions by Dartmouth as their own team had made, and twice the number that Dartmouth students noted about their own team.[30] This study and the hundreds that followed it demonstrate the frailty of eyewitness accounts. Consider the findings of just a few of these other studies:

• The accuracy of older eyewitnesses is reduced in certain situations.[31]
• Both whites and blacks do better at identifying suspects of their own race.[32]
• Experience in recalling details of events witnessed (as a police officer might have, for example) does not necessarily improve recall.[33]
• The credibility of a witness is increased significantly by a display of confidence.[34]

A large body of research has evaluated the process of juror decision making and whether or not extralegal issues influence jurors when they grapple with the facts of a case. Studies have demonstrated that jurors are sometimes influenced by their own personal characteristics (age, race, gender, occupation) and by the characteristics of the defendant and victim, such as the defendant's social attractiveness. In fact, mock jurors who evaluated the culpability of attractive versus unattractive defendants charged with identical crimes ascribed greater guilt to the unattractive ones.[35] Other studies that considered the character of the victim found that such variables as marital status, unorthodox lifestyle, and past sexual experience can play a role in jurors' decision making.

SENTENCING: TODAY AND TOMORROW

Sentencing has been characterized as the most controversial of all the stages in the criminal justice process.[36] This is not surprising. At earlier stages of the administration of justice the defendant benefits from the presumption of innocence, and certain safeguards are built into the adversarial system: notions of due process, fundamental fairness, and impartiality. Once the defendant is convicted, however, the focus shifts away from these concerns to the imposition of a sentence.

Judges can choose from a variety of sentencing options, ranging from the death penalty to the imposition of a fine:

• *Death penalty.* In 37 jurisdictions, judges may impose a sentence of death for any offense designated a capital crime, most commonly murder.
• *Incarceration.* A defendant may be sentenced to serve a term in a state or federal prison or in a local jail.
• *Probation.* A defendant also may be sentenced to a period of community supervision with special limitations. Violation of these conditions may result in incarceration.
• *Split sentence.* A judge may split the sentence between a period of incarceration and a period of probation.

• *Restitution.* An offender may be required to provide financial reimbursement to cover the cost of a victim's losses.
• *Community service.* A judge may require an offender to spend a period of time performing public service work.
• *Fine.* The offender may be required to pay a certain sum of money as a penalty and/or as an alternative to or in conjunction with incarceration.

What determines which sentencing option will be chosen? More often than not, judges are given discretion and thus are guided by a preference for one or more than one sentencing philosophy. Their discretion may be limited by a statute that prescribes a prison term of a specified length or a range of prison terms. Let us review the most prominent philosophies of punishment.

Incapacitation

"Lock 'em up and throw away the key" expresses the frustration people feel about the crime problem. It reflects a belief that, given the frequency with which offenders commit crime, society is best off when criminals are incarcerated for long periods of time. Yet long sentences imposed for the purpose of incapacitation may be unjust, unnecessary, counterproductive, and inappropriate:

• They are unjust if other offenders who have committed the same crime receive shorter sentences.
• They are unnecessary if the offender is not likely to offend again.
• They are counterproductive whenever prison increases the risk of habitual criminal behavior.
• They are inappropriate if the offender has committed an offense entailing insignificant harm to the community.

Research evidence on incapacitation is equivocal. Joan Petersilia and Peter Greenwood, for example, suggest that the crime rate could be reduced by as much as 15 percent if every convicted felon were imprisoned for one year.[37] Earlier investigations provided widely different estimates. Revel Shinnar and his colleagues projected that an 80 percent reduction in violent crime rates was possible if everyone convicted of a violent crime served five years in prison. Another study, however, concluded that only a 4 percent reduction would result from that policy.[38] Most of the empirical research in the area of incapacitation relates to criminality that persists over many years. Such research examines how criminal careers begin, how they progress, and why they terminate. As we saw in Chapter 2, Marvin Wolfgang and his associates determined that two-thirds of all violent crimes and more than one-half of all crimes were committed by 6 percent of the birth cohort they investigated. This evidence, in conjunction with Peter Greenwood's findings that recidivists often manage to stay out of prison by plea bargaining, suggests that if prosecutors could identify recidivists and prosecute them vigorously, and if judges imposed long prison sentences on them, serious crime might be reduced significantly. Some believe that a policy of **selective incapacitation**—that is, the targeting of high-risk, recidivistic offenders for rigorous prosecution and incarceration—may be worth pursuing.[39] Implementation of such a policy, however, is limited by the state of criminological research. In Joan Petersilia's words:

> For an incapacitative crime control strategy to be effective, we need to know, first, whether there is a group of offenders who commit large numbers of offenses over a substantial period, and second, whether we can identify them. The first condition can be met. There is a small group of persistent offenders....The second condition—ability to predict—cannot now be met.[40]

There are other problems as well, such as the false identification of high-risk offenders (false positive) and the release of defenders mistakenly labeled as low-risk (false negative).

Deterrence

According to Philip Cook, if we disbanded all law enforcement agencies and removed all sanctions from the penal laws, the result would be "a crime wave of unprecedented proportions."[41] The very existence of the criminal justice system, he argues, has a strong general deterrent effect, civilizing many people who otherwise would not be civil.

Researchers have investigated instances in which policing was terminated, and others in which policing was significantly strengthened. A classic example of the former situation occurred in Denmark in 1944, when the German occupation forces arrested the entire Danish police force. An examination of insurance claims showed that fraud crimes and embezzlement did not increase, but that larcenies and burglaries increased tenfold.[42] During a strike by the Montreal police force in 1969, crimes of revenge and vandalism increased significantly.[43] Yet research on the effect of police strikes in the 1970s on the crime rates of eleven American cities provided very little support for the hypothesis that removal of the police presence increases crime rates.[44] The evidence on the effects of intensified policing is no clearer. In 1982, New York City's Transit Police force was strengthened to combat subway crime. Additional officers were posted in subway stations on virtually all trains between 8 P.M. and 4 A.M. The results were inconclusive.[45]

Researchers have studied the effects of increasing the threatened punishments for some crimes. Massachusetts mandated a minimum prison term of one year for carrying a firearm without a permit. This law had a measurable deterrent effect.[46] But the deterrent effect of criminal sanctions is limited. In a study of deterrence by the Criminal Law Education and Research Center at New York University, three types of warning stickers were attached to parking meters in three comparable areas. One sticker threatened a $50 fine for the use of slugs in parking meters. The second threatened a $250 fine and three months' imprisonment. The third threatened one year in prison and a $1,000 fine. Slug use decreased substantially where the threatened sanction was lowest and thus realistic. The highest sanction appeared so unrealistic that slug use actually increased, although only slightly. In another area, where new parking meters had been installed which were equipped with coin-view windows that revealed what had been inserted into the meter, slug use decreased substantially.[47]

Overall, research on **deterrence** is still inconclusive, largely because the opportunities for making controlled studies are extremely limited, but also because some crimes and some criminals are more easily deterrable than others. It is important to note that deterrence presupposes rational choice. Supporters of deterrence-based strategies argue that criminals weigh the relative benefits and risks of engaging in crime and choose not to do so because they are deterred by an increased possibility of apprehension.

Retribution

In preliterate societies victims retaliated fiercely against anybody or anything that had caused them harm—another person, an animal, a tree. In early literate societies such uncontrolled revenge gave way to a measured response to wrongdoing. In the Mosaic laws we find a limitation on revenge: the punishment should be comparable to the harm inflicted ("an eye for an eye"). This *lex talionis* ("retaliation law") marks the onset of the concept of **retribution**.[48]

Under the retributive system of the nineteenth and early twentieth centuries, all punishments were determined by legislative act, so that the judge had little choice in sentencing. Every type of crime commanded a fixed punishment in accordance with the legislative mandate. In fixing punishments, legislatures took into account the perceived gravity of each type of crime. Thus murder commanded a more severe punishment than robbery, and robbery a more severe punishment than larceny.

In the early part of this century attitudes began to change. This was a period of great expectations, of learning, of advances in medicine and in psychology. Especially in the United States, anything seemed possible, even changing criminals into law-abiding citizens. In this climate the classical retributive idea of punishment seemed to be inherently flawed. The idea of punishment as retribution was based on the assumption that all offenders who had violated the same provision of the penal law were alike and thus deserved the same punishment. But behavioral scientists point out that no two offenders who have committed the same crime are completely alike in capacity, depravity, intelligence, and potential for rehabilitation.

Rehabilitation

Dissatisfaction with the retributive approach to punishment led to a new emphasis on the rehabilitative ideal. As a sentencing strategy or option, **rehabilitation** is based on the premise that through correctional intervention (educational and vocational training and psychotherapeutic programs), an offender may be changed. This change should result in an ability to return to society in some productive, meaningful capacity. Consequently, punishment became individualized. The court could select a sentence ranging from a minimum to a maximum length of incarceration or could impose an indeterminate sentence. The parole board was established to decide when the convict should be released and under what conditions.

Although correctional systems did experiment with rehabilitation, more often than not the efforts were perfunctory. Yet judges believed in the promise of rehabilitation and sentenced offenders accordingly. In the 1970s, researchers increasingly attacked the rehabilitative ideal as a failure. In 1974 Robert Martinson wrote that "with few and isolated exceptions, the rehabilitative efforts that have been reported so far have had no appreciable effect on recidivism."[49] After Martinson's devastating analysis of rehabilitation, a number of criminologists and research organizations responded with comparable findings and conclusions.[50] The result was a temporary vacuum in sentencing theory. In practice, however, most states had adopted the sentencing policies of the Model Penal Code and tried to abide by them.

Model Penal Code Sentencing Purposes

The Model Penal Code describes the general purposes of the provisions governing the sentencing of offenders as follows:

1. To prevent and condemn the commission of offenses.

2. To promote the correction and rehabilitation of offenders.

3. To ensure the public safety by preventing the commission of the offenses through the deterrent influence of sentences imposed and the confinement of offenders when required in the interest of public protection.

4. To safeguard offenders against excessive, disproportionate, or arbitrary punishment.

5. To give fair warning of the nature of the sentences that may be imposed on conviction of an offense.

6. To differentiate among offenders with a view to a just individualization in their treatment.

7. To advance the use of generally accepted scientific methods and knowledge in sentencing offenders.[51]

Thus the Model Penal Code set as goals the prevention of crime through *deterrence* and *incapacitation*; *condemnation* of the commission of offenses, which may be referred to as *vindication* of the law; *correction* and *rehabilitation* of the offender; and also *retribution* if sentences are justly individualized.

These various sentencing objectives have been with us for a long time. Each objective has been given more or less emphasis at various times. As we have noted, some objectives have been supported or even partially validated by research. The difficulty comes in trying to combine objectives. Legislatures, in providing appropriate punishments for the various offenses in the code, are supposed to consider the interplay of these multiple goals. Judges, acting within the legislative framework, likewise are supposed to consider all the goals when they mete out individual sentences. However, the goals are not necessarily compatible; indeed, they may be contradictory. For example, a long prison term may be necessary to remove an offender from society (incapacitation). But a long prison sentence can be incompatible with the goal of rehabilitation.

Just Deserts

In the wake of the perceived failure of the rehabilitative ideal, the wide-ranging differences in

CRIMINOLOGICAL FOCUS

Andrew von Hirsch on Just Deserts

A desert rationale's central principle is that of *commensurate deserts*: the severity of punishments should be proportionate to the seriousness of the offender's criminal conduct.

The commensurate-deserts principle rests on the condemnatory implications of punishment. Punishment is a *censuring* institution. It treats the act as reprehensible and the actor as someone to be blamed for the act. The more severe the penalty, the greater the resulting reproof. That is why the severity of punishments should fairly reflect the degree of blame worthiness of the offender's criminal behavior.

A desert rationale makes the penalty depend chiefly on the seriousness of the crime of conviction, with only a modest adjustment for the previous criminal record. The seriousness of crime, in turn, depends on two factors: the *harmfulness* of the conduct (i.e., how injurious the conduct typically is), and the *culpability* of

the actor (e.g., the actor's degree of purpose and knowledge).

Does a desert rationale exclude crime control in sentencing? Not necessarily. A desert-based scheme of graded penalties will have significant deterrent and incapacitative effects—and it is not realistically likely that those effects can much be increased by departing from desert requirements. Rehabilitation may be sought while the offender undergoes his penalty—so long as it is not used to decide the penalty's severity. Excluded are only such strategies as selective incapacitation, which would decide sanctions' severity on the basis of factors alien to crime-seriousness, such as social history, frequency of arrests, and early offending.

A desert rationale can be implemented in a variety of ways. The least promising way is through legislatively mandated penalties—as politics, rather than proportionality concerns, tend to dominate such legislative decisions. A pre

ferable way is through sentencing guidelines: A rulemaking agency, such as a sentencing commission, establishes a table of normally prescribed sentences based mainly on the seriousness of crimes. Judges ordinarily are expected to follow these presumptions, but can deviate in aggravating or mitigating circumstances. (Minnesota and Washington State have been experimenting with this approach, with some success.) Still another way, now tried in Sweden, is to have the sentencing law set forth general desert principles, which judges apply in their sentencing decisions.

For a general introduction to desert theory, see Andrew von Hirsch, *Doing Justice*, reprint ed. (Boston: Northeastern University Press, 1986). For more detailed discussion, see Andrew von Hirsch, *Past or Future Crimes* (New Brunswick, N.J.: Rutgers University Press, 1985).

---

sentences for like crimes under indeterminate sentencing laws became apparent. In light of such inconsistencies, Andrew von Hirsch, Richard Singer, and other scholars began to promote a return to retribution.[52] Their model is called **just deserts.** Underlying the concept of just deserts is the proposition that the punishment must be based on the gravity of the offense and the culpability of the perpetrator. The introduction of utilitarian aims, such as general or individual deterrence, incapacitation, and rehabilitation, can only result in variations among the sentences imposed on offenders who have

deserved identical punishments and therefore is unjust. Moreover, it can indeed be established that such extralegal factors as the characteristics of judges, race, socioeconomic status, sex, age, geographical area of the trial, and type of defense counsel cause wide divergences in sentences imposed.[53] The just-deserts advocates further hold that courts simply do not have the capacity to discriminate between those who can be deterred, reformed, or incapacitated and those who cannot. Parole boards likewise have been found to be ill prepared to make sound decisions as to which offenders are good risks for release and which are not. The system of rehabilitation was premised on the capacity of prisons—"correctional" institutions—to correct or rehabilitate; demonstrably, they did not do so in most cases. There is therefore no choice but to return to a system of retribution, which at least guarantees just or like sentences for like crimes. Any rehabilitative efforts in prisons should be made only within the terms of the fixed sentence, and with the consent of the convict.[54]

The just-deserts approach has been successful in minimizing disparity in sentences and in curbing judicial arbitrariness. But it has its problems as well. It has been blamed for prison overcrowding. It has been attacked for its insensitivity to the social problems that lead a large proportion of offenders to crime. It has been criticized for its refusal to acknowledge the fact that education, in the broadest sense, can affect values, attitudes, and behavior. It also has been called unscientific because of its rejection of scientific efforts to identify types of offenders whose leanings toward crime are said to be demonstrable. Critics have complained that the just-deserts concept is superficial in its rejection of the rehabilitative ideal, that it ignores the fact that rehabilitation has been condemned on the basis of flawed evaluations. Recently, legislatures and courts have demonstrated a willingness to search for new sentencing orientations that take into account the scholarly disputes over the rehabilitative ideal, the incapacitative approach, and just deserts, and yet also satisfy popular demands.

Presumptive and Mandatory Sentencing

In at least twelve states judges are virtually deprived of the power to determine the lengths of sentences. The law determines what the punishment ought to be, often by a "presumptive" (presumed to be most appropriate) sentence. Such a sentence has its length constrained by a statute—a definite sentence for each class of crimes, which cannot ordinarily be adjusted to account for mitigating or aggravating circumstances. In some limited cases, however, the judge may modify the sentence slightly on the basis of such circumstances, provided the reasons for deviating from the presumptive sentence are detailed in a written explanation. When sentences are mandatory, judges have no discretion to alter them. Thus presumptive and mandatory sentencing leaves judges with little power to respond to the needs of the individual offender. More recently this situation has been eased somewhat by the institution of sentencing guidelines.

Sentencing Guidelines

In 1972 Federal District Judge Marvin E. Frankel made a plea for an independent sentencing commission to study sentences and assist in the formulation and enactment of detailed guidelines for use by judges in sentencing.[55] Since then, thirteen states have adopted sentencing guidelines and three states (Minnesota, Washington, and Pennsylvania) have created sentencing commissions. In 1984 the United States Sentencing Commission was established by Congress, and in 1987 it delivered its guidelines.[56]

At the heart of all guidelines is a sentencing matrix in which a defendant's criminal history or other characteristic is plotted against a ranking of the severity of the offense (Figure 16.8). A judge simply calculates a defendant's history and the severity of the offense and, with the exactness of a computer, has a sentence to impose.

Sentencing guidelines can trace their ancestry to, among others, the *lex talionis* of Exodus 21 (the Mosaic law); the tariffs found in the laws of the ancient Germanic tribes, including the Saxons; the 1926 Social Defense (penal) Code of Cuba; and the current Spanish Penal Code.[57] Each of these systems uses a fixed punishment, which corresponds with prevailing notions of harm and allows for upward or downward adjustment of the sentence on the basis of certain specific aggravating or mitigating circumstances.

CAPITAL PUNISHMENT

Capital punishment is a controversial issue, and one that poses particular challenges to the judiciary. After all, it is the only sentence that is

FIGURE 16.8   The dispositional line on Minnesota's sentencing grid

Seriousness of Conviction Offense	Criminal History Score						
	0	1	2	3	4	5	6 or more
10 (e.g., 2d-degree murder)							
9 (e.g., felony-murder)							
8 (e.g., rape)			IN				
7 (e.g., armed robbery)							
6 (e.g., burglary of occupied dwelling)							
5 (e.g., burglary of unoccupied dwelling)							
4 (e.g., nonresidential burglary)							
3 (e.g., theft of $250 to $2,500)		OUT					
2 (e.g., lesser forgeries)							
1 (e.g., marijuana possession)							

Source: Andrew von Hirsch, Kay A. Knapp, and Michael Tonry, *The Sentencing Commission and Its Guidelines* (Boston: Northeastern University Press, 1987), p. 91.

irreversible and final: it deprives the convict of an ultimate appeal.

Daniel Frank's execution in 1622 was the first to be recorded on American soil. He was executed in the colony of Virginia for the crime of theft.[58] Criminologists have estimated that since that year, between 18,000 and 20,000 people have suffered state-sanctioned execution for crimes including train wrecking, aggravated murder, and rape.[59] Countless others have died at the hands of lynch mobs.[60] During the last century, Western countries have employed six methods of execution: firing squad, lethal gas, hanging, decapitation by ax or guillotine, electrocution, and lethal injection. Decapitation is the only one of these methods that has never been used in the United States (see Table 16.5).

Since 1976, when the death penalty was reinstated after a short moratorium, 110 convicted criminals have been executed. Thirty-seven states now have death penalty laws in effect (see Figure 16.9). The United States is the only Western democratic country that retains the death penalty. All other Western European countries have abolished it. Public opinion polls in the United States over the last several decades have indicated clearly that citizens support the death penalty overwhelmingly, and this support has been increasing.

The arguments surrounding capital punishment are deceptively simple. What makes them deceptive is that abolitionist or retentionist views toward the death penalty often influence assessments of the penalty's utility and effec-

Convicts on death row facing the electric chair.

TABLE 16.5   METHODS OF EXECUTION USED BY THE VARIOUS STATES, 1985

LETHAL INJECTION	ELECTROCUTION	LETHAL GAS	HANGING	FIRING SQUAD
Arkansas[a]	Alabama	Arizona	Delaware	Idaho[a]
Idaho[a]	Arkansas[a]	California	Montana[a]	Utah[a]
Illinois	Connecticut	Colorado	New Hampshire	
Mississippi[a,b]	Florida	Maryland	Washington[a]	
Montana[a]	Georgia	Mississippi[a,b]		
Nevada	Indiana	Missouri		
New Jersey	Kentucky	North Carolina[a]		
New Mexico	Louisiana	Wyoming[a]		
North Carolina[a]	Nebraska			
Oklahoma[c]	Ohio			
Oregon	Pennsylvania			
South Dakota	South Carolina			
Texas	Tennessee			
Utah[a]	Vermont			
Washington[a]	Virginia			
Wyoming[a]				

[a]Authorizes two methods of execution.
[b]Mississippi authorizes lethal injection for persons convicted after 7/1/84; executions of persons convicted before that date are to be carried out with lethal gas.
[c]Should lethal injection be found to be unconstitutional, Oklahoma authorizes use of electrocution or firing squad.

Source: *Capital Punishment, 1985*, BJS Bulletin, November 1986, p. 98.

FIGURE 16.9   The death penalty in the fifty states, 1985.

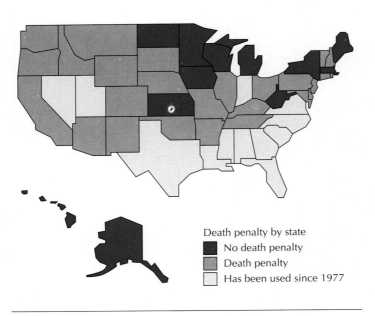

Death penalty by state
- ■ No death penalty
- ▨ Death penalty
- ☐ Has been used since 1977

Source: *Capital Punishment, 1985.* BJS Bulletin, November 1986.

tiveness. Abolitionists find little empirical evidence of a deterrent effect, and retentionists claim that sophisticated studies can be conducted only after executions have been resumed at a steady pace. They argue, in other words, that it is impossible to tell whether deterrence is fact or fiction until we execute, as a matter of course, all inmates sentenced to death.

The Deterrence Argument

Criminologists have long debated whether and to what extent executions deter murder. The debate focuses on two questions. Do would-be murderers decide not to kill out of fear of being put to death? If the threat of execution is in fact a deterrent, would the threat of life imprisonment be just as effective? The results of studies designed to answer these questions are inconclusive. Thorsten Sellin, Hans Zeisel, and William C. Bailey, for example, have found little evidence that homicide rates are affected by executions.[61] On the other hand, Isaac Ehrlich, an economist, has found what does appear to be a deterrent effect; specifically, that each exe-

cution prevents between eight and twenty murders.[62] His work, however, is controversial. The legal scholar Charles L. Black has noted that it is difficult, if not impossible, to design methodologically sound deterrence studies. For instance, how can one estimate the number of people who did not commit murder in a given jurisdiction with a death penalty or in one without a death penalty? How can we know that a would-be killer decided against the act of murder? According to Black,

> After all possible inquiry, we do not know, and for systematic and easily visible reasons cannot know, what the truth about this "deterrent" effect may be.... A "scientific"—that is to say, a soundly based—conclusion is simply impossible, and no methodological path out of this tangle suggests itself.[63]

The Discrimination Argument

In the early 1970s Marvin Wolfgang and Mark Riedel identified an anomaly in the use of the death penalty. Since the 1950s it had become clear that death sentences in some southern states fell disproportionately on blacks who had been convicted of the rape of white women. Wolfgang and Riedel noted, "Of the 3,859 persons executed for all crimes since 1930, 54.6 percent have been black or members of other racial minority groups. Of the 455 executed for rape alone, 89.5 percent have been non-white."[64]

Though the discrimination question has been at the core of legal challenges to the constitutionality of many death sentences, it remained in the background until the legal scholar David Baldus and his colleagues conducted a comprehensive and methodologically sound analysis of discrimination in capital sentencing in Fulton County, Georgia.[65] This study, which clearly and unequivocally demonstrated that a black defendant is eleven times more likely to be sentenced to death for killing a white person than a white for killing a black, was presented to the United States Supreme Court in *McKlesky* v. *Kemp*.[66] Warren McKlesky asked the Supreme Court to invalidate the Georgia capital punishment statute because of this proven discrimination. The Court refused to do so because defense attorneys had not shown that McKlesky himself had been discriminated against. Further, the Court opined that if there is such racial bias, it is at a tolerable level. But a level that is tolerable is difficult to specify. For over fifty years research on sentencing disparity has found racial discrimination in both capital and noncapital cases. This is not to suggest that all judges discriminate. Rather, as it has been said, some judges discriminate and some do not.[67]

Other arguments for and against the death penalty have been advanced. They are based on everything from religious concerns to hardheaded calculation of the cost of imprisonment.

Against the Death Penalty

The arbitrary use argument   With over 2,200 inmates on death row, the process by which an inmate is selected to die is entirely arbitrary; it is not determined by the seriousness of the crime committed or on any other objective measure.

The mistakes argument   Studies have documented cases in which individuals were wrongly convicted and thus executed in error. Since it is impossible to be entirely certain that a person is truly guilty, are we willing to permit such mistakes? Islamic law allows the execution only of persons proved to be guilty beyond *any* doubt, not just beyond a reasonable doubt (though for some acts we do not consider crimes).

The religious argument   Religious organizations representing most of the major religions have called for an end to the death penalty. Interreligious task forces have voiced concern over issues of ethics and guilt in the putting to death of fellow human beings.

The morality argument   Examinations of the relation between moral development and attitudes toward capital punishment show that the more developed one's sense of morality is, the less likely one is to favor the death penalty.

For the Death Penalty

The economic argument   The cost of maintaining an inmate in prison for life places an unfair burden on taxpayers and the state.[68]

The retribution argument   Any individual who kills another human being deserves the condemnation of society, and must pay for the crime committed.

The community protection argument   It is always possible that a person on death row may escape and kill again, or may kill another inmate or correctional officer. Thus the community cannot be fully protected unless the person is executed.[69]

The public opinion argument   Standards of decency, the criteria by which courts judge the humaneness of a punishment, are continually evolving. Two decades ago public opinion was not in favor of the death penalty. Over the last decade, the number of Americans favoring capital punishment has increased from 65 percent to 75 percent. (Much of the rest of the world has shown the opposite trend. Democratic countries have abolished the death penalty. The trend in the socialist countries is toward abolition.)[70]

REVIEW

Since earliest times society has used courts to resolve disputes arising under its rules, or laws. With the emergence of government under strong rulers, or kings, the establishment of courts became a sovereign prerogative. In the common law family of legal systems, to which the United States belongs, the adversary system prevails. In criminal cases the prosecution, as one of the adversaries, presents evidence against the defendant in an effort to establish guilt beyond a reasonable doubt. The defendant, as the other adversary, has the right to contest the prosecution's evidence. The judge ensures the fairness of the proceedings.

In the United States criminal cases are tried in state courts when the crime charged is one violative of state law, and in federal courts when a violation of federal law is charged. Both state and federal convictions may be appealed within each system, with federal review of state cases when certain federal constitutional issues are raised.

The roles and decision-making processes of all participants in the criminal process—defendants and defense counsel, prosecutors, judges and jurors—have been subjected to increasing criminological scrutiny. Such research reveals that the system does not measure up to expectations. Plea bargaining, in particular, undermines confidence in the court process, yet it may well be the only way to deal with vastly increased caseloads that make it impossible to grant a jury trial in most cases.

Legislative and judicial policies in sentencing convicted offenders are in a state of turmoil. Evidence of grossly disproportionate punishments meted out for comparable offenders has led to a large scale abandonment of the rehabilitative goal in sentencing, and to a return of retributive (just-deserts) and incapacitative approaches. But sentencing continues to be in a state of flux, with some signs of a rebirth of the rehabilitative goal. At the moment, many states operate with sentencing guidelines which seek to curb abuses of judicial discretion, incorporate just-deserts ideas, and allow some degree of flexibility for considering aggravating and mitigating circumstances.

Capital punishment as a sentencing option preoccupies the thinking of policy makers and the general public. The United States is the last remaining major democratic country to have returned to capital punishment, without any clear evidence that it promotes public safety.

The judiciary will continue to play the key role in the administration of criminal justice, within policy limits set by legislatures, and subject to continuing scrutiny by criminological research.

KEY TERMS

arraignment
certiorari, writ of
challenges for cause
defense counsel
deterrence
habeas corpus
indictment
information
just deserts

motions
peremptory challenges
plead
prosecutor
rehabilitation
retribution
selective incapacitation
voir dire

NOTES

1. Jonathan D. Casper, *American Criminal Justice: The Defendant's Perspective* (Englewood Cliffs, N.J.: Prentice-Hall, 1972).

2. See, for example, Jerome Frank, *Courts on Trial: Myth and Reality in American Justice* (Princeton, N.J.: Princeton University Press, 1949).

3. In the epochal case Marbury v. Madison, 1 Cr. 137 (1803), the Supreme Court, in an opinion by Chief Justice John Marshall, established the power of judicial review over all legislation, and thus the primacy of the judiciary in our system of government.

4. Loving v. Virginia, 388 U.S. 1 (1967).

5. Mapp v. Ohio, 367 U.S. 643 (1961).

6. Draper v. United States, 358 U.S. 307 (1961). The Draper rule was modified in Illinois v. Gates, 462 U.S. 213 (1983), upholding the issuance of a search warrant even on the basis of an anonymous informant's tip, as long as, under all the circumstances, the magistrate had a "substantial basis for concluding...that probable cause existed."

7. "Praecipibus tibi quod *corpus* A.B. in custodia vestra detentum, ut dicitur, una cum causa captionis et detentionis suae, quocumque nomine idem A.B. censeatur in eadem *habeas* coram nobis apud Westm..." (emphasis supplied).

8. In Stone v. Powell, 428 U.S. 465 (1976), the court ruled that in Fourth Amendment cases (search and seizure), federal habeas corpus is not available to a state prisoner when the alleged due process violation has been fully and fairly litigated in the state court system.

9. See, for example, Elizabeth Anne Stanko, "The Impact of Victim Assessment on Prosecutor's Screening Decisions: The Case of the New York County District Attorney's Office," *Law and Society Review* 16 (1982): 225–239; James Eisenstein and Herbert Jacob, *Felony Justice: An Organizational Analysis of Criminal Courts* (Boston: Little, Brown, 1977); W. Boyd Littrell, *Bureaucratic Justice: Police, Prosecutors, and Plea Bargaining* (Beverly Hills, Calif.: Sage, 1979); Victoria Swigert and Ronald A. Farrell, *Murder, Inequality, and the Law* (Lexington, Mass.: D. C.

Heath, 1976); Frank Miller, *Prosecution: The Decision to Charge a Suspect with a Crime* (Boston: Little, Brown, 1969); Martha Myers and John Hagan, "Private and Public Trouble: Prosecutors and the Allocation of Court Resources," *Social Problems* 26 (1979): 439–451; David Neubauer, "After the Arrest: The Charging Decision in Prairie City," *Law and Society Review* 8 (1974): 495–517.

10. Celesta A. Albonetti, "Prosecutorial Discretion: The Effects of Uncertainty," *Law and Society Review* 21 (1987): 291–313.

11. Abraham S. Goldstein, *The Passive Judiciary: Prosecutorial Discretion and the Guilty Plea* (Baton Rouge: Louisiana State University Press, 1981).

12. Abraham S. Blumberg, *Criminal Justice: Issues and Ironies* (New York: New Viewpoints, 1979), p. 123.

13. Gideon v. Wainright, 375 U.S. 335 (1963); Argersinger v. Hamlin, 407 U.S. 25 (1972).

14. President's Commission on Law Enforcement and Administration of Justice, *Task Force Report: Courts* (Washington, D.C.: U.S. Government Printing Office, 1967), p. 131.

15. John S. Goldkamp, *Two Classes of Accused: A Study of Bail and Detention in American Justice* (Cambridge, Mass.: Ballinger, 1979).

16. Bail Reform Act of 1984, 18 U.S.C. §§ 3141–3150 (1984).

17. U.S. Department of Justice, Bureau of Justice Statistics, *Report to the Nation on Crime and Justice* (Washington, D.C.: U.S. Government Printing Office, 1988), p. 24.

18. National Advisory Commission on Criminal Justice Standards and Goals, *A National Strategy to Reduce Crime* (Washington, D.C.: U.S. Government Printing Office, 1971), p. 43.

19. See Douglas Smith, "The Plea Bargaining Controversy," *Journal of Criminal Law and Criminology* 77 (1986): 949–967.

20. Barbara Boland, *Prosecution of Felony Arrests*, for Bureau of Justice Statistics (Washington, D.C.: U.S. Government Printing Office, 1986).

21. Boykin v. Alabama, 395 U.S. 238 (1964); Santobello v. New York, 404 U.S. 257 (1971).

22. Rule 11 (f), Federal Rules of Criminal Procedure.

23. David Suggs and Bruce Sales, "The Art and Science of Conducting the Voir Dire," *Professional Psychology* 9 (1978): 362–388.

24. Mapp v. Ohio, 410 U.S. 19 (1973).

25. The Mapp decision made the Fourth Amendment's exclusionary rule applicable to the states through the Fourteenth Amendment's due process clause.

26. See, for example, Wong Sun v. United States, 371 U.S. 471 (1923); People v. Defore, 242 N.Y. 13 (1926), at 21.

27. Nix v. Williams, 467 U.S. 431 (1984).

28. Linda Wolfe, *Wasted: The Preppie Murder* (New York: Simon & Schuster, 1989).

29. See Reid Hastie, *Inside the Jury* (Cambridge, Mass.: Harvard University Press, 1983); Elizabeth F. Loftus, "Reconstructing Memory: The Incredible Eyewitness," *Psychology Today*, August 1974, pp. 116–119; Elizabeth F. Loftus, "Leading Questions and the Eyewitness Report," *Cognitive Psychology* 7 (1975): 560–572; Elizabeth F. Loftus, *Eyewitness Testimony* (Cambridge, Mass.: Harvard University Press, 1979); Elizabeth F. Loftus, "Eyewitness Testimony: Psychological Research and Legal Thought," in *Crime and Justice: An Annual Review of Research*, ed. Michael Tonry and Norval Morris, 3:105–151 (Chicago: University of Chicago Press, 1981); Elizabeth F. Loftus and James M. Doyle, *Eyewitness Testimony: Civil and Criminal* (New York: Kluwer, 1987); Elizabeth F. Loftus and G. Zanni, "Eyewitness Testimony: The Influence of the Wording of a Question," *Bulletin of the Psychonomic Society* 5 (1975): 86–88.

30. Albert H. Hastorf and Hadley Cantrill, "They Saw the Game: A Case Study," *Journal of Abnormal and Social Psychology* 49 (1954): 129–134.

31. J. C. Bartlett and J. E. Leslie, "Aging and Memory for Faces Versus Single Views of Faces," *Memory and Cognition* 14 (1986): 371–381.

32. Kenneth A. Deffenbacher and Elizabeth F. Loftus, "Do Jurors Share a Common Understanding Concerning Eyewitness Behavior?" *Law and Human Behavior* 6 (1982): 15–30.

33. J. C. Yuille, "Research and Teaching with Police: A Canadian Example," *International Review of Applied Psychology* 33 (1984): 5–23.

34. R. K. Bothwell, J. Brigham, and M. A. Piggott, "An Exploratory Study of Personality Differences in Eyewitness Memory," *Journal of Social Behavior and Personality* 2 (1987): 335–343.

35. C. A. Visher, "Juror Decision-Making: The Importance of Evidence," *Law and Human Behavior* 11 (1987): 1–17.

36. See Gerhard O. W. Mueller, *Sentencing: Process and Purpose* (Springfield, Ill.: Charles C Thomas, 1977).

37. See, for example, Joan Petersilia, Peter Greenwood, and Marvin Lavin, *Criminal Careers of Habitual Felons*, for LEAA (Washington, D.C.: U.S. Government Printing Office, 1978).

38. Revel Shinnar and S. Shinnar, "The Effects of the Criminal Justice System on the Control of Crime: A Quantitative Approach," *Law and Society Review* 9 (1975): 581–611.

39. See, for example, Peter Greenwood, *Selective Incapacitation* (Santa Monica, Calif.: Rand Corporation, 1982).

40. Petersilia et al., *Criminal Careers of Habitual Felons*, p. 5.

41. Philip Cook, "The Demand and Supply of Criminal Opportunities," in Tonry and Morris, *Crime and Justice*, vol. 7.

42. Johannes Andenaes, *Punishment and Deterrence* (Ann Arbor: University of Michigan Press, 1974), p. 51.

43. William G. Bailey, ed., *The Encyclopedia of Police Science* (New York: Garland, 1989), p. 600.

44. Edwin H. Pfuhl, Jr., "Police Strikes and Conventional Crime," *Criminology* 21 (1983): 489–503.

45. Ari L. Goldman, "In Spite of Dip, Subway Crime Nears a Record," *New York Times*, November 20, 1982, pp. 1, 26.

46. James A. Beha II, "And Nobody Can Get You Out: The Impact of a Mandatory Prison Sentence for the Illegal Carrying of a Firearm and on the Administration of Criminal Justice in Boston," *Boston University Law Review* 57 (March 1977): 96–146.

47. Robert P. Barry, "To Slug a Meter: A Study of Coin Fraud," *Criminology* 4, no. 4 (1969): 40–47; John F. Decker, "Curbside Deterrence," *Criminology* 10 (1972): 127–142.

48. Immanuel Kant, *Critique of Pure Reason* (1781).

49. Robert Martinson, "What Works? Questions and Answers About Prison Reform," *Public Interest* 35 (Spring 1974): 25; see also, James Q. Wilson, "'What Works?' Revisited: New Findings on Criminal Rehabilitation," *Public Interest* 61 (Fall 1980): 1.

50. National Research Council.

51. Model Penal Code, Section 1.02b.

52. Andrew von Hirsch, *Doing Justice: The Choice of Punishments* (New York: Hill & Wang, 1976). And see Andrew von Hirsch, *Past or Future Crimes: Deservedness and Dangerousness in the Sentencing of Criminals* (New Brunswick, N.J.: Rutgers University Press, 1985).

53. Willard Gaylin, *Partial Justice* (New York: Knopf, 1974).

54. Norval Morris, *The Future of Imprisonment* (Chicago: University of Chicago Press, 1974).

55. Marvin E. Frankel, *Criminal Sentences: Law Without Order* (New York: Hill & Wang, 1972).

56. See Andrew von Hirsch, Kay A. Knapp, and Michael Tonry, *The Sentencing Commission and Its Guidelines* (Boston: Northeastern University Press, 1987).

57. (Spanish) Código Penal of 23 Dec. 1944, art. 9 (mitigating circumstances), 10 (aggravating circumstances), 11 (circumstances that can be either mitigating or aggravating), 58–67 (on the application of mitigating and aggravating circumstances). Authors' translation.

58. Sara T. Dike, "Capital Punishment in the United States, Part I: Observations on the Use and Interpretation of the Law," *Criminal Justice Abstracts* 13 (1981): 283–311; Hugo A. Bedau, *The Death Penalty in America* (New York: Oxford University Press, 1984).

59. William Bowers, *Executions in America* (Lexington, Mass.: Lexington Books, 1974).

60. S. Nicolai et al., *The Question of Capital Punishment* (Lincoln, Nebr.: Contact, 1980).

61. Thorsten Sellin, *The Death Penalty* (Philadelphia: American Law Institute, 1959); Thorsten Sellin, *Capital Punishment* (New York: Harper & Row, 1967); Thorsten Sellin, *The Penalty of Death* (Beverly Hills, Calif.: Sage, 1980); Hans Zeisel, "The Deterrent Effect of the Death Penalty: Facts v. Faith," in *The Supreme Court Review,* ed. P. E. Kurland, pp. 317–343 (Chicago: University of Chicago Press, 1976); William C. Bailey, "A Multivariate Cross-sectional Analysis of the Deterrent Effect of the Death Penalty," *Sociology and Social Research* 64 (1980): 183–207.

62. Isaac Ehrlich, "The Deterrent Effect of Capital Punishment: A Question of Life and Death," *American Economic Review* 65 (1975): 397–417.

63. Charles L. Black, *Capital Punishment: The Inevitability of Caprice and Mistake* (New Haven, Conn.: Yale University Press, 1984).

64. Marvin Wolfgang and Mark Riedel, "Race, Judicial Discretion, and the Death Penalty," *Annals of the American Academy of Political and Social Sciences* (1973): 119–133. See also Joseph E. Jacoby and Raymond Paternoster, "Sentencing Disparity and Jury Packing: Further Challenges to the Death Penalty," *Journal of Criminal Law and Criminology* 73 (1982): 379–387; Joseph E. Jacoby, "The Deterrence and Brutalizing Effects of the Death Penalty," in *The Death Penalty in South Carolina,* ed. Bruce L. Pearson (Columbia, S.C.: Acluse Press, 1981).

65. David Baldus, Charles Pulaski, and George Woodworth, "Comparative Review of Death Sentences: An Empirical Study of the Georgia Experience," *Journal of Criminal Law and Criminology* 74 (1983): 661–678.

66. McKlesky v. Kemp, 478 U.S. 1019 (1985).

67. Blumberg, *Criminal Justice.*

68. Actually, the cost of appeals and maintenance of a person on death row is far higher than the cost of maintaining a prisoner sentenced to life imprisonment—approximately $3 million. See Andrew H. Malcolm, "Capital Punishment Is Popular, but So Are Its Alternatives," *New York Times*, September 10, 1989, p. E4.

69. Thorsten Sellin demonstrated by research that this argument is specious. Convicted murderers behave exceedingly well in prison, and if released have very good parole records. Repeat homicides are statistically rare. See Sellin, *Death Penalty*, pp. 69–79. Conceivably, with greater militancy among prisoners, the situation has changed during the last thirty years.

70. Antoinette D. Viccica, "Political Recourse to Capital Punishment" (Ph.D. dissertation, Rutgers University, 1982).

17

A RESEARCH FOCUS ON CORRECTIONS

To the uninitiated observer, the sentencing of the convicted person is the end of the judiciary's role in the process of reacting to crime and the beginning of the role of the executive branch of government—the execution of the court-imposed sentence. Such a view was official doctrine as late as 1958, when Justice Felix Frankfurter, in *Gore* v. *United States,* pronounced that "in effect, we are asked to enter the domain of penology....This Court has no such power."[1] Much has changed since then. Prisoners have acquired the right to appeal judgment and sentence and the conditions of their confinement. In many states, courts have intervened by ordering changes in the way sentences are being executed. In some jurisdictions the courts have actually assumed control and management of prison systems, through court-appointed masters. The tasks of the courts never end. From the moment a sentence has been imposed until the last minutes of the execution of a sentence, the courts have the power and duty to intervene in the correctional system. Courts and corrections may be separate organizational entities and represent different branches of government, yet they are quite interdependent, in that corrections executes and implements the orders of courts—the sentences. Corrections must do so in compliance with standards of law, as monitored by the courts.

There was yet another anachronism in Frankfurter's pronouncement. He referred to *penology* as the domain of those who deal with offenders after sentence has been imposed. "Penology" was a term used in the nineteenth century and the first half of the twentieth to designate the science of applying punishment for social or utilitarian purposes. The term has become virtually obsolete. Today criminologists speak of **corrections** when they refer to the implementation and execution of sentences imposed by courts, and to the system that administers those sentences. The switch from "penology" to "corrections" was more than a change of name. It was a change of outlook and approach, from a punitive to a rehabilitative philosophy.

The meaning of "corrections" varies with the context. Professors make corrections on term papers. Eyeglasses or contact lenses make corrections in vision. Ignorance may be corrected by education. In each of these contexts, "correction" implies some form of improvement. After centuries of exploiting and punishing criminals, the penologists of the nineteenth century concluded that criminals were imperfect and therefore needed correction more than punishment. "Penologists" became "correctional specialists," and the "penal system" became a "correctional system."

PUNISHMENT AND CORRECTIONS THROUGH THE AGES

From Antiquity to the Eighteenth Century: Slavery and Brutality

It is common to equate corrections with a prison system. That equation is not accurate today, nor was it ever accurate in times past. Nomadic people have no prisons, because buildings cannot be carried on the trek. Yet nomadic people do have means of correcting or punishing offenders. The Roman people, once nomads, did not use prisons for punishment even after they settled and built the city and state of Rome. They believed *carcer enim ad continendos non ad puniendos,* which means that "prison serves to contain people, not to punish them." Roman convicts were punished primarily by being sentenced to hard labor for a specified period of time or for life. The Romans also had capital punishment of various forms for very serious crimes that offended not only the Roman state but also the gods. Roman prisons were simply places of detention for offenders awaiting trial or convicts about to be transported to the place where their sentence was to be carried out.

The limited information we have about Germanic punishment comes from the Roman historian Tacitus, who reported in the first century A.D. that the ancient Germans hanged traitors and deserters. Cowards were drowned in swamps. The Goths, a nomadic Germanic people, declared a convicted offender to be a wolf and sent him to the wilderness to live if he could (Chapter 1). Under Germanic law, however, most wrongs were compensated by *bot,* a money or property compensation, to which, in serious cases, a *wite*—that is, a fine—could be added.

From the fifth to the eleventh centuries, homicides, under Germanic law, were dealt with by blood feuds, revenge killings by the victimized family against the offender's family. These feuds were not viewed as private revenge. In fact, the law demanded and sanctioned the feud as punishment. But the feud was lawful only if it was completed in a timely manner and if it did not exceed in measure the harm done. Any revenge committed thereafter or any that exceeded the limit was considered to be unlawful and would lead to legal proceedings.[2] Some unlawful killings could also be compensated by payment of *wergeld,* money to compensate for the loss of a warrior.[3]

The late Middle Ages were marked by the emergence of strong rulers who gained increasing control over the punishment of wrongdoers. Punishment, except that inflicted within the family, became a function of the state. By converting compensation money into fines and by claiming the estates of persons sentenced to death, the rulers enriched themselves. Consequently, the number of capital offenses and of executions increased sharply. During the reign of Henry VIII in England (1509–1547), the number of executions rose rapidly, though apparently not to the 72,000 that some writers have claimed.[4] The forms of punishment became ever more cruel. Persons sentenced to death were hanged, burned at the stake, drawn and quartered, disemboweled, boiled, broken on the wheel, stoned to death, impaled, drowned, pressed to death in a spiked container, and torn by red-hot tongs. Noncapital punishments also rose to a level of unprecedented cruelty; prisoners were branded, dismembered, flogged, and tortured by devilishly designed instruments, even for offenses that today are considered trivial. This state-sanctioned brutality apparently did not reduce the crime rate, but it did condition the population to accept cruelty as part of daily life.

During the reign of Queen Elizabeth I (1558–1603) the English began to experiment with additional forms of punishment. In 1598 galley was introduced in England.[5] Queen ... characterized it as a "more merciful" ... unishment.[6] Many city-states on the ... also used this form of punishment, ... ir convicts as galley slaves to the ... alian city-states.[7] Slave galleys were ... tained by France, Spain, Denmark, ... er European countries well into the ... ith century. The conditions on the gal- ... re anything but merciful. Chained to ... ed rowing benches, exposed to all kinds ... ather conditions, whipped by brutal over- ... s, and fed on hard rations, the galley slaves ... en welcomed death.

During that period imprisonment was not yet a principal means of punishment in England or on the Continent. The penal code of the Holy Roman Emperor Charles V (1532) mentions punitive incarceration only once. Gradually, however, punitive incarceration evolved from the practice of forced labor, a popular punishment because it supplied rulers with cheap workers. It was necessary to confine forced laborers at night in dungeons, fortresses, and other secure places. Ultimately, imprisonment came to be the primary punishment and forced labor the secondary punishment. By the mid-sixteenth century, the old English castle of Bridewell had been converted into a "house of occupations, or rather a house of correction— for repression of the idle and sturdy vagabond

and common strumpet."[8] "Bridewells" were later established in all counties of England.

Reformers in other countries created similar institutions. The Dutch, for example, established a *tuchthuis,* a house of discipline, in 1589. Germany, Denmark, and Sweden soon followed. The concept was generally accepted. The purpose of imprisonment was to make offenders useful members of the community through hard labor and religious worship. But soon after prisons were established, they became overcrowded. The English addressed the problem by establishing the prison hulk. Decommissioned and deteriorated warships were converted into prisons, most of which were docked in the river Thames. In the 1840s the British government had about twelve hulks that housed up to 4,000 inmates.[9] These hulks made no contribution to the correction of offenders. They offered no opportunity for work or exercise. They were overcrowded, unsanitary places of confinement, with high death rates due to communicable diseases. Today the world community is in agreement that no prisoners of war should be confined on prison ships,[10] yet New York City has commissioned a fleet of prison barges for ordinary convicts.

The Bridewells and the houses of correction never measured up to the ideals of the reformers. In fact, they became slave-labor camps in which cheap convict labor contributed to the

Left: One of the dreaded prison hulks, a decommissioned battleship of the Royal Navy, 1826. Right: The Bibby Resolution, *which served the Royal Navy as a barracks ship in the Falkland Islands War between the United Kingdom and Argentina, now in use as a prison barge of the New York City Department of Corrections.*

CRIMINOLOGICAL FOCUS

The Punishment Response: Public Ridicule

Benjamin Keach, a young Baptist minister in Winslow, England, wrote a book in 1664 titled *The Child's Instructor; or, A New and Easy Primmer*. He was charged with and convicted of writing and publishing a seditious book (one opposed to lawful authority). In passing sentence on the Reverend Mr. Keach, the judge remarked:

Benjamin Keach, you are here convicted of writing and publishing a seditious and scandalous Book, for which the Court's judgement is this, and the Court doth award, That you shall [next Saturday] stand upon the pillory at Ailsbury for the space of two hours, from eleven o'clock to one, with a Paper on your head with this inscription, *For writing, printing and publishing a schismatical book, entitled, The Child's Instructor, or a New and Easy Primmer*. And the next Thursday to stand in the same manner, and for the same time in the market of Winslow; and there your book shall be openly burnt before your face by the common hangman, [and you] shall remain in gaol [jail], until you find sureties for your good behavior and doctrine, and make such public submission as shall be enjoined to you.

How can we interpret the punishment imposed on Benjamin Keach? What was its purpose? The pillory imposed little physical suffering, yet it did subject the convict to public exposure and ridicule. The punishments of that time distributed the convict's burden between public exposure and physical suffering. The ducking stool, for example, exposed convicts to the fear of drowning, but also exposed them to public ridicule and condemnation. Benjamin Keach was to be shamed before his neighbors.

Source: W. Andrews, *Old Time Punishments* (London: Tabard, 1891), pp. 96–98.

---

wealth of the rulers or of the counties. In 1832 prison inmates still worked on treadmills, holding on to a wooden bar above their heads and treading steadily as the steps went round to produce power to move millstones.[11]

In the eighteenth century England invented yet another way to deal with convicts: it sentenced them to be "transported" to the colonies. Virginia and the other southern colonies received many convicts who labored for the development of the towns and plantations. After the American colonies won their independence, England could no longer ship convicts to North America, so it transported them to Australia, which is proud to acknowledge its debt to convict labor.[12]

Throughout that period, English justice used punishments of ridicule and fright for minor offenders. The pillory and ducking stool were used in England as well as on the Continent, and these instruments of punishment made their way to the New World.

Punishment in the New World

The first settlers of New England were Puritans, opposed to the primacy of the Church of England. Rejecting English law, they nevertheless imported the English means of punishment, including the stocks and the pillory. Their religious beliefs were similar to those of the Calvinists of the Netherlands, the country in which the *Mayflower* group prepared for the crossing to America. The *tuchthuis*, which they saw in the Netherlands, must have stuck in their minds as a means of correcting wrongdoers.

It was not in New England, however, but in Pennsylvania that the American correctional movement began. It started there with William Penn's "Great Law" of December 4, 1682, which provided for the establishment of houses of correction. Penn's law restricted corporal and capital punishment greatly, though it retained whipping for the more severe offenses.[13] After the colonies declared their independence, Pennsylvania continued the liberal spirit of William Penn. In Philadelphia the physician William Rush (1745–1813) took up the cause of penal reform. He worked to abolish capital punishment and introduce penitentiaries. In 1787 Rush published *An Enquiry into the Effects of Public Punishment upon Criminals*. He helped organize the Pennsylvania Society for the Abolition of Slavery, and became instrumental in the creation of the Philadelphia Society for Alleviating the Miseries of Public Prisons (1787). As a result of Dr. Rush's inquiry, a small **penitentiary** wing was added to the Walnut Street Jail in 1790. Extended solitary confinement in a cell, it was thought, would bring the offender to penitence. Even at work prisoners were not allowed to communicate with one another. The Quaker idea of penitence and labor in lieu of capital punishment seemed persuasive. For a few years after the creation of the Walnut Street penitentiary wing, the crime rate appeared to drop. New York (1791), Virginia (1800), Kentucky (1800), New Jersey (1798), and other states later on adopted the penitentiary concept and reduced the use of capital punishment. These reforms reflected the Quaker philosophy of redemption through penitence. They must also be viewed as an extension of the Enlightenment reforms advocated by Cesare Beccaria in Italy and by John Howard, Jeremy Bentham, and Elizabeth Fry in England (Chapter 3).

Although the experiment at first seemed to be successful, barely a decade after the penitentiary wing was constructed at the Walnut Street Jail, the visiting committee of the Philadelphia Society for Alleviating the Miseries of Public Prisons reported "Idleness, Dirt, and Wretchedness" in the facility.[14] These conditions were the result of overcrowding and management's failure to cope with it. Prisoners were not at all penitent, useful labor could not be provided, and the authorities were unable to maintain the institution in a condition conducive to the improvement of prisoners. New solutions were sought—better prisons, with better conditions and better management. Dr. Rush was in the forefront of the search. After his death in 1813 and after much lobbying by the Philadelphia Society, the Pennsylvania legislature approved the construction of two new penitentiaries, the Western in Pittsburgh and the Eastern in Philadelphia. They received their first inmates in 1826 and 1829, respectively.

The Pennsylvania system: separate confinement   The Western Penitentiary was a round building, permitting control of all cells from a central point. It was constructed more sturdily than any fortress then in existence. The prisoners were housed in small, tomblike cells that were furnished with Bibles. They had to work in their cells and were permitted only one hour of exercise daily. Even then they were not allowed to communicate with one another. This system of separate confinement proved disastrous. Anxiety increased. Psychoses were rampant. The prison soon had to be rebuilt at great cost to allow some daylight to flow into the cells.

The Eastern Penitentiary functioned in accordance with similar principles. Solitary confinement, work in cells, religious instruction, and penitence were the principal features. Yet harsh discipline was not tolerated.

The Auburn system: congregate labor   An alternative approach to imprisonment was developed in New York at the Auburn Penitentiary. Silence and labor, key features of the Pennsylvania system, were adopted. But one innovation was added—congregate labor. Younger offenders were permitted to work and eat in groups. But they were not allowed to talk to or even to glance at one another. Since the Pennsylvania system, which permitted inmates to work only in their cells, also proved extremely expensive, most states adopted the Auburn system. Congregate labor was cost-beneficial. Many penitentiaries even made a profit. European countries, which studied both American models, opted mostly for Pennsylvania's system, which was endorsed by the World's First International Prison Congress, held at Frankfurt, Germany, in 1846.

The Reformatory Movement

After the Civil War, Americans became disenchanted with both types of penitentiaries. Penitence rarely resulted from incarceration. Brutality and corruption were common. Operating costs rose. In 1870 a group of prison administrators met in Cincinnati to discuss their problems. Two English penal reformers, Captain Alexander Maconochie and Sir Walter Crafton, traveled across the Atlantic to address the gathering. Their ideas were received with enthusiasm by corrections leaders, who included Gaylord Hubbell, warden of Sing Sing Prison in New York; Enoch C. Wines, secretary of the New York Prison Association; Franklin Sanborn, Massachusetts correctional administrator; and Zebulon Brockway, of the Michigan House of Corrections, Detroit. Maconochie and Crafton called for an end to the vindictive imposition of suffering and embraced the ideas of treatment, moral regeneration, and reformation. The approach had to be scientific, starting with classification of inmates. Sentences had to be indeterminate, and release was to be the reward for having reformed in the "reformatory." The new reform spirit was to be kept alive by the National Prison Association, founded at that conference. Within a few years, nearly all states had constructed reformatories, primarily for younger prisoners. The Elmira Penitentiary in New York (1876) was used as a model. Optimism disappeared, however, as it became apparent that reformatories did not reform.

The Medical Treatment Model and Community Involvement

After World War I a new philosophy entered corrections. During the war draftees had been subjected to psychological testing. A psychological approach to dealing with convicts seemed to be indicated. Psychiatry was widely accepted as a means of dealing with individual and social problems. Psychiatrists (especially psychoanalysts) and psychologists became involved in the treatment of criminals and the reform of the penal system. Individual and group therapy were practiced in American prisons. This medical model flourished until World War II.

Despite the good intentions to treat convicts as if they were medical patients, the conditions of their imprisonment changed very little. They were permitted to leave their cells only for exercise, congregate work, chapel, therapy, and meals. Silence was enforced. Movements from cell to yard, to mess hall, to chapel took place in controlled groups that marched in lockstep. A particularly harsh form of military discipline had taken over. Indeed, many members of the prison staff were recruited from the military. The slightest infraction of the rules was severely punished, often by flogging.

After World War II the medical model lingered on under such rubrics as the therapeutic approach and the rehabilitative model. California was the leader in this movement, but nearly all states instituted group and individual therapy programs, counseling services, and behavior modification programs of various sorts, including shock therapy and revulsion therapy. Many of these programs raised serious civil liberties issues. Most were underfunded and inadequately staffed. They reached only a small number of inmates. The results of most programs were disappointing.

At the same time American corrections experienced yet another change. With the realization that prisons seemingly did not rehabilitate offenders and at best rendered them fit to survive in a prison environment, efforts were made to integrate the offender into the community. Representatives of the community came into prisons, and convicts were diverted out of prisons. Increasing use was made of probation, parole, and halfway houses. Later on work-release and community projects became popular. Yet in all these approaches prisoners were simply the objects of the system and had to take what came to them. That situation was bound to lead to confrontation.

The Prisoners' Rights Movement

The mid- and late 1960s witnessed rapid social change all over the world. In the United States minority groups demanded equality, women wanted equal treatment in public and private life, students rebelled against complacent educational systems, and the young rebelled against their elders. Prisoners, too, demanded their rights. But the correctional system was not prepared to respond. A riot broke out on September 9, 1971, at New York's Attica State Prison, an institution holding 2,200 inmates. Prisoners took over most of the facility. They held correctional officers as hostages. Governor Nelson Rockefeller ordered an attack by the state police. Helicopters dropped bombs and gas canisters. After four days and forty-three lives lost, "peace" was restored.[15]

Why had the prisoners revolted? As a list of their demands revealed, they had been denied many of the fundamental rights guaranteed them under the Constitution. Douglas J. Besharov and G. O. W. Mueller compared the list of demands by the inmates with the United Nations Standard Minimum Rules for the Treatment of Prisoners, to which all countries, including the United States, had agreed. These standards pertain to diet, the handling of complaints, hygiene, religious freedom, contact with the outside world, treatment, education, legal assistance, recreation, medical treatment, minority-group personnel, inmate funds, resentencing and parole, and discipline. Most of the prisoners' demands were justified by the minimum standards guaranteed to them.[16]

The experience of Attica was a shock for correctional administrators. Prisoners' rights litigation had been initiated in the early 1960s, but the Attica rebellion opened the floodgates to lawsuits by prisoners, testing not only the right of access to the courts but the particular conditions of their confinement.[17]

Until the middle of the twentieth century, the penal codes of many states provided that felony imprisonment amounted to civil death: The felon lost virtually all civil rights, including the right to vote; the spouse of the prisoner was even entitled to have the marriage annulled. The courts refrained from interfering with the management of prisons. In 1951 a federal circuit court ruled in the case of the "Birdman of Alcatraz," a prisoner who had become a highly respected ornithologist in prison, that "it is not the function of the courts to superintend the treatment and discipline of persons in penitentiaries."[18] This was called the "hands-off" doctrine.

In the 1960s the National Prison Project of the American Civil Liberties Union, the NAACP Legal Defense and Educational Fund, and the Legal Services of the federal government's Office of Economic Opportunity, as well as countless volunteers from the legal profession and hundreds of self-trained jailhouse lawyers, succeeded in overturning the hands-off doctrine. Since then, hundreds of decisions establishing various rights of prisoners have been handed down. Prisoners now have the right to humane living conditions, legal assistance and law libraries, and freedom of religious practice. The rights guaranteed by the Constitution were finally granted to prisoners. Prisoners' rights litigation had a profound impact on the American correctional system. Some correctional administrators welcomed these decisions. Under court order, or the threat of court order, they could finally make improvements they had long considered necessary. Others regarded court-ordered changes in prison management as undue interference with their authority (see Table 17.1).

During the 1980s the number of prisoners' rights suits reaching the Supreme Court declined, for five reasons. First, the Supreme Court has taken a more restrictive view of prisoners' rights litigation. Second, prison administrators, whether directly affected by lawsuits or not, have made an effort to comply with mandated standards. Third, many prison systems have instituted alternative means to improve conditions, such as grievance procedures, mediation, and review boards. Fourth, while trial courts are as busily ruling for prisoners' rights as ever, most administrators prefer to comply rather than to take the costly route of appeal. Fifth, most state correctional systems are under court order to improve conditions of confinement. In many (but not all) cases court-appointed special masters with expertise in corrections are monitoring compliance with court orders.

TABLE 17.1   BENCHMARKS IN RIGHTS FOR PRISONERS

YEAR	CASE	RULING
1958	*Gore* v. *United States*, 357 U.S. 386, 393	The "hands-off" doctrine. The court has no right to enter the domain of penology.
1964	*Cooper* v. *Pate*, 378 U.S. 546	End of the "hands-off" doctrine. Prisoners may bring civil action for violation of their civil rights under the Civil Rights Act of 1871.
1964	*Rouse* v. *Cameron*, 373 F.2d 452 (D.C. Cir.)	Right to treatment. A person imprisoned for "treatment" has a right to such treatment; otherwise he or she must be discharged.
1968	*Lee* v. *Washington*, 390 U.S. 333	Equal protection (Fourteenth Amendment). Racial discrimination in prison is unconstitutional.
1969	*Johnson* v. *Avery*, 393 U.S. 499	Right to legal defense. Prisoners have a right to assistance from jailhouse lawyers.
1970 1974	*Palmigiano* v. *Trevisano*, 317 F.Supp. 776 (D.R.I.); *Procunier* v. *Martinez*, 416 U.S. 396	Freedom of speech (First Amendment). Prisoners' mail may be opened only by "legitimate," "least restrictive" means. Relative freedom from censorship.
1970	*Goldberg* v. *Kelly*, 397 U.S. 254	Due process rights (Fourteenth Amendment). Prisoners have a right to due process when threatened with a loss resulting from arbitrary or erroneous official decisions.
1972	*Cruz* v. *Beto*, 415 U.S. 319	Freedom of religion (First Amendment) must be granted equally to inmates of all faiths.
1973	*Hutto* v. *Finney*, 437 U.S. 678	Prohibition of cruel and unusual punishment (Eighth Amendment). Confinement in a segregation cell for 30 days is cruel and unusual punishment. (Totality of circumstances test.)
1974	*Wolf* v. *McDonnell*, 418 U.S. 539	Due process in disciplinary proceedings. When faced with serious disciplinary action, prisoners are entitled to procedural due process.
1976	*Estelle* v. *Gamble*, 429 U.S. 97	Medical treatment. Deliberate indifference to prisoners' serious medical needs is cruel and unusual punishment.
1977	*Bounds* v. *Smith*, 430 U.S. 817	Legal assistance. Prison law libraries must be adequately staffed to provide legal assistance to inmates in need.

Source: Based on Geoffrey P. Albert, ed., *Legal Rights of Prisoners* (Beverly Hills, Calif.: Sage, 1980).

The Rebirth of the Retributive Philosophy and the Selective Incapacitation Response

The prisoners' rights movement was one of two factors that changed the nature of American corrections. The other factor was the rebirth in the mid-1970s of the retributive philosophy (discussed in the sentencing section of Chapter 16) in the form of the just-deserts model. This rebirth had an immediate effect on corrections. As sentencing became oriented toward punitive and proportionate prison sentences, corrections became punitive and custodial. Most rehabilitation programs in prisons, already discredited, were abandoned. Prisoners were doing time proportionate to the gravity of their crime. They were not engaged in efforts to rehabilitate themselves or to be reformed. This more punitive attitude toward offenders had an unfortunate consequence: legislators passed more punitive sentencing laws, and parole boards either became more reluctant to grant parole or were abolished altogether. The result was a steep increase in prison populations.

This situation posed a challenge to the just-deserts model. Some scholars argued that the focus should be shifted from distributing just deserts to all prisoners to identifying those few who contribute the most to the crime rate. These individuals should be identified and selectively incapacitated by incarceration, but not the others.[19] The increasing incarceration rates and the accompanying costs to the taxpayer also forced policy makers to search for other options, as we shall see.

Table 17.2 identifies the significant stages in the evolution of corrections and their relation to important criminological phenomenon.

CORRECTIONS TODAY

The Size and Cost of the Correctional Enterprise

The correctional enterprise encompasses a very large number of people and requires a huge budget. In 1988 there were 627,402 prisoners in about 640 state and federal prisons; this is the highest number in our history. There were also 343,569 persons in locally administered jails.[20] If we add the number of children in custody, which stood at 83,402,[21] over one million persons were incarcerated in the United States, or about 1 in every 250 residents. That figure does not include the 37,842 persons arrested daily for Index crimes or the many more arrested for misdemeanors and disorderly charges, most of whom were being detained on any given day (usually for several days) in the country's 13,500 police lockups, holding pens, and other local facilities operated by police and sheriffs' departments.[22] Thus well over a million people may be incarcerated at any given moment. Most of the prisoners are male. State and federal correctional facilities held only 32,691 female prisoners in 1988, as compared with 594,711 male prisoners. Female imprisonment, however, increased at a faster rate (12.5 percent) than male imprisonment (7.1 percent) from 1987 to 1988. Since 1981 the number of women incarcerated has risen from 4.2 percent to 5.2 percent of the total prison population.

In addition to the offenders in correctional institutions, there are those who are sentenced to noninstitutional or community corrections. Principally, this means persons on probation, which provides for the sentence to be served in the community in lieu of imprisonment, and on parole, which permits a convict to serve the tail end of a prison sentence in the community. At the end of 1987, 2,242,053 adults were on probation and 362,192 on parole. Consequently, an estimated 3.6 million adult men and women, or an estimated 1 in 52 United States residents aged 18 or older, were being serviced by the correctional system.[23]

Our rate of incarceration is higher than that of comparable countries. In the United States 25.8 people per 100,000 of the population are incarcerated for robbery; Canada incarcerates 15.5 people, England only 4.3, and the Federal Republic of Germany 3. For burglary and theft the disparities are similar. If the incarceration rate is based not on the population as a whole but on the number of persons arrested, it turns out that we do not incarcerate substantially more robbers or thieves than do the Canadians

TABLE 17.2   SIGNIFICANT STAGES IN THE EVOLUTION OF CORRECTIONS

DATE	STAGE OF CORREC-TIONAL DEVELOP-MENT	SIGNIFICANT INFLUENCE OR EVENT	THEORY OF CRIME CAUSATION	INTERVENTION USED	PURPOSE OF INTERVENTION	SCHOOL OF CRIMI-NOLOGY	LEADERSHIP ROLE
5000 B.C.	Private vengeance	Beginning of government and rise of the tribe	Criminality unanalyzed, but treated as if caused by immediate personal motivation	Direct, unprescribed individual response	Personal vengeance and atonement to propitiate gods or God	None	Tribal leaders
2200 B.C.	Group retaliation	Code of Hammurabi Justice controlled by church leaders, lawgivers		Compensation of person and property "Eye for eye," etc.			Church leaders, divine rulers, and their advisers and agents
400 B.C.	Individual determinism	Sophocles, Plato, and Aristotle	Unstated, but apparently "free will" Pleasure-pain	Sentences of: torture branding maiming banishment public shaming fines death	Reformation by expiation	Preclassical	
30 A.D.	Personal expiation	Death of Christ and spread of Christianity	Possession or manip-ulation of man by the Devil against sins vs. God and Man				
1215	Inquisition and intimidation (Dawn of the change)	Magna Charta forbids arbitrary imprisonment Spanish Inquisition reaches despotic heights	Personal responsibility for actions, coupled with influence of the inequali-ties of the feudal system		Repression and intimidation		Feudal lords and church or political leaders
1550	Incarceration for punish-ment	King of England designates Bridewell as "Hospital of the City"		Galley labor Workhouse imprisonment			

TABLE 17.2   (Continued)

DATE	STAGE OF CORREC- TIONAL DEVELOP- MENT	SIGNIFICANT INFLUENCE OR EVENT	THEORY OF CRIME CAUSATION	INTERVENTION USED	PURPOSE OF INTERVENTION	SCHOOL OF CRIMI- NOLOGY	LEADERSHIP ROLE
1700	Incarceration for social protection and discipline	Pope Clement XI opens a house for profligate youth in Rome Houses of correction on Continent	Vicious association, bad habits, laziness	Penal colonies Imprisonment	Protection		
1770	Segregated incarceration and isolation	Howard's survey of English jails French humanitarian movement Quaker influence in England	Bentham's free will theory enunciated Pleasure vs. pain	Penal colonies Solitary confinement for personal reformation		Classical	
1800	Varied punishments for varied responsibility	French Revolution and the rise of the middle class Quaker influence in America	Free choice of evil Children, insane, lunatics exempt from responsibility		Rehabilitation with penitence	Neoclassical*	
1876	Incarceration for refor- mation	Lombroso's studies of criminal types Development of refor- matory and grading of prisoners	Return to idea of sin and willful corruption	Confinement with Bible Hard labor under strict discipline		Positive or Italian	The "people" and the politicians
1913	Clinical criminology [individual treatment]	Goring disproves Lombroso's theory American Association of Clinical Criminology formed	Focus on unitary causes: physical disabilities, mental defects, psychopathic states, character anomalies	Individual diagnosis with clinically prescribed and extramural treatment Probation system in America	Reformation	[Positive] Analytical or individualistic	

TABLE 17.2 SIGNIFICANT STAGES IN THE EVOLUTION OF CORRECTIONS (Continued)

DATE	STAGE OF CORRECTIONAL DEVELOPMENT	SIGNIFICANT INFLUENCE OR EVENT	THEORY OF CRIME CAUSATION	INTERVENTION USED	PURPOSE OF INTERVENTION	SCHOOL OF CRIMINOLOGY	LEADERSHIP ROLE
1929	Confusion and revolt	American prison riots, 1929–1932 Politicians and civil servants struggle for penal positions					Professionally trained clinicians
1936	Cultural therapy [subsequently called the Rehabilitative Model]	Professional social case work and correctional approach Collegiate research in crime, especially ecologic	Multiple factors	Correctional and social education in institutions Community prisons "Classification"	Education, adjustment, and prevention	[Positive] Multiple factors	
1945	Humane approach to sanctions	Brutalities of Hitler era, World War II U.N. standard minimum rules, 1957	Strain, cultural deviance, subcultural	Indeterminate sentence, parole, probation Vocational, educational, or psychological treatment	Rehabilitation	Positive (Sociological factors)	Parole boards, psychiatrists, social workers
1960s	Concern for prisoners' rights; beginning of diversion	Civil rights movement, prison riots	Strain, cultural deviance, subcultural, social control, labeling				
1975 — 1990	Incarceration for retribution Diversion continued	Disenchantment with rehabilitative model and inequality of sentences; prison overcrowding	Strain, cultural deviance, subcultural, social control, labeling, conflict, radical	Fixed sentences, community-based corrections, short-term shock programs, electronic surveillance, restitution	Retribution, Incapacitation; diversion for overcrowding	Return to classical	Lawyers, politicians, legislatures, econometricians, sociologists

*Barnes' and Teeters' classification, "Neoclassical" refers to the revival of the classical thinking of Beccaria and his contemporaries.

Source: (5000 B.C.–1936): Harry Elmer Barnes and Negley K. Teeters, *New Horizons in Criminology*, rev. ed. (New York: Prentice-Hall, 1945), pp. 640–643, as supplemented by authors.

TABLE 17.3   RATES OF IMPRISONMENT FOR PROPERTY OFFENSES, UNITED STATES, CANADA, ENGLAND, AND WEST GERMANY, 1985

OFFENSE	UNITED STATES		CANADA	
	PRISONERS PER 100,000 POPULATION	PERCENT OF ARRESTEES INCARCERATED	PRISONERS PER 100,000 POPULATION	PERCENT OF ARRESTEES INCARCERATED
Robbery	25.8	49%	15.5	52%
Burglary	53.7	35	43.2	23
Theft	117.0	18	81.5	14

OFFENSE	ENGLAND		WEST GERMANY	
	PRISONERS PER 100,000 POPULATION	PERCENT OF ARRESTEES INCARCERATED	PRISONERS PER 100,000 POPULATION	PERCENT OF ARRESTEES INCARCERATED
Robbery	4.3	48%	3.0	23–58%
Burglary	36.9	30	—	
Theft	70.6	14	21.0	4–9

Source: U.S. Department of Justice, Bureau of Justice Statistics, *Imprisonment in Four Countries* (Washington, D.C.: U.S. Government Printing Office, 1987), Tables 3 and 1.

or English, but we probably incarcerate more thieves than the Germans do (see Table 17.3).

In 1988 the cost of running the overall federal and state correctional enterprise was over $19 billion. This may sound like a lot of money, but it is actually only 1.0 percent of all government spending. Over 480,000 persons were employed in the corrections systems in 1988, at a total payroll cost of more than $1 billion. The annual cost of incarcerating an offender varies from state to state. It is $10,873 in Nevada and $24,700 in New Mexico (1985). The cost of constructing a new cell ranged from $29,599 for minimum security state prisons to $70,768 for maximum security state prisons.[24] Some jail cells cost as much as $100,000 to construct; this figure doubles when financing is taken into consideration.[25]

Types of Incarceration

There are two categories of prison facilities: detention facilities and correctional facilities. Detention facilities normally do not house con-victs; they are not, technically, correctional facilities. They only house persons arrested and undergoing processing, awaiting trial, or awaiting transfer to a correctional facility after conviction. Correctional facilities include county jails and state and federal prisons. In county jails, persons convicted of misdemeanors normally serve sentences of not more than one year. State and federal prisons house convicts sentenced for felonies to terms of longer than one year. But there are many exceptions to the rules. Many jails operated by counties and cities serve two purposes. They house persons awaiting trial or transfer, and they also hold convicts serving misdemeanor sentences. Moreover, since so many state prisons are overcrowded, many states have found it necessary to house convicts sentenced to state prison for felonies in county jails. Local variations cloud the distinctions even further. Riker's Island in New York City serves not only as the jail for all of the boroughs of the city but also as a prison for the serving of longer state sentences. Finally, a few states call some of their prisons "houses of detention," but the basic differences remain. County jails are intended for the temporary detention of prisoners and for persons serving sentences for misdemeanors; federal and state prisons are intended for felons, whose sentences are for longer than one year.

Jails   Criminologists generally consider the conditions in jails to be inferior to those in prisons. Most jails are unsanitary, have few services or programs for inmates, and do not separate dangerous from nondangerous prisoners.[26] They are often overcrowded and underfunded.

There are 3,338 jails in the United States. A jail in one state may be as large as the entire prison system of another state. The men's central jail of Los Angeles has a rated capacity of 5,136 inmates; it usually holds more. Cook County Jail in Chicago, with a rated capacity of 4,600, holds many more than that. It is under court order to reduce its inmate population to 4,600. Many jails in rural counties, by contrast, are small and operate under a **fee system,** by which the county government pays a modest amount of money for each prisoner per day. That amount usually constitutes the entire operating budget of the jail. As a result, there are movements to create central jails for contiguous counties, which share the cost of operation.

The movement to deinstitutionalize mental patients, begun in the 1960s, added an additional burden to the criminal justice system, especially to jails. It was demonstrated in a study of county jails in New Jersey that 10.9 percent of inmates had a history of mental hospitalization. That figure did not include those inmates who were confined on special tiers reserved for inmates exhibiting grossly bizarre, irrational, or violent behavior patterns that the jail staff considered a threat to researchers.[27] The inmates on the segregated tiers were even more likely to have some history of mental institutionalization. Jail staff, whether law enforcement or corrections employees, cannot be expected to have the expertise required to deal with such a massive mental health problem.[28] Experts argue that if public policy dictates that jails deal with emotionally disturbed and mentally ill offend-

ers, a far better program of identification, diagnosis, crisis intervention, and case management at release is called for.[29] In sum, the major problems with jails are overcrowding, lack of proper classification systems, and underfunding.

Prisons   Whatever they are called, whether state or federal prisons, penitentiaries, or correctional institutions, prisons have for the most part been blessed with better management than jails and with better education, recreation, and employment programs.[30] A prison normally has three distinct custody levels for inmates, based on an assessment of their perceived dangerousness: maximum danger, medium danger, and minimum danger.

Maximum security prisons are designed to hold the most dangerous and aggressive inmates. Their structure is often imposing. They have high concrete walls or double-perimeter fences, gun towers with armed guards, and strategically placed electronic monitors.

Medium security prisons house inmates who are considered less dangerous or escape-prone than those in maximum security facilities. These less imposing structures typically have no outside wall, only a series of fences. Many medium security inmates are housed in dormitories rather than cells.

Minimum security prisons hold inmates who are considered the lowest security risks. Very often these institutions operate without armed guards and without perimeter walls or fences. The typical inmate in such an institution has proved to be trustworthy in the correctional setting, is nonviolent, and/or is serving a short prison term.

The Problem of Prison Overcrowding

At a recent international conference of criminal justice specialists, a Japanese correctional administrator asked, "With half of our prison cells being empty and our prisoner population declining, do I have a future in my chosen profession, corrections?" American corrections specialists do not have that worry. The U.S. prison population increased sharply in 1971 and again in 1979–80 (Figures 17.1 and 17.2), precisely at times when the crime rate was fairly stable or even declining. For example, the number of Index offenses committed had been 199.4 million in 1968 and 208.2 million in 1972. This increase was not extraordinary. Between 1979 and the early 1980s, the crime rate even declined. Thus, it cannot have been an increase in the crime rate that prompted the sharp rise in the prison population. Some experts argue that punitiveness had increased, perhaps fueled by increasing

fear of drug criminality and crime in general, supported by increasing media attention to crime. Once this fear was generated, it had a snowball effect. Scholars began to argue in favor of punitiveness, against the rehabilitative idea, and in support of just deserts. These arguments prompted legislative programs that severely curtailed judicial discretion in sentencing by mandating specific sentences for specific crimes.

An alternative hypothesis seeks to explain

FIGURE 17.1 Number of state and federal prisoners, 1925–1987: (*a*) total; (*b*) per 100,000 population

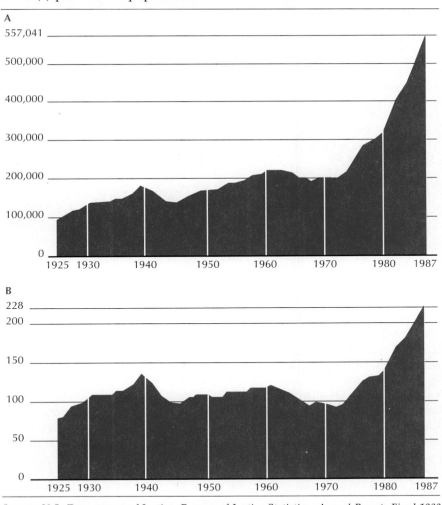

Source: U.S. Department of Justice, Bureau of Justice Statistics, *Annual Report, Fiscal 1988* (Washington, D.C.: U.S. Government Printing Office, 1989), p. 60.
2nd color

FIGURE 17.2   U.S. prison incarceration rates, 1930–1985

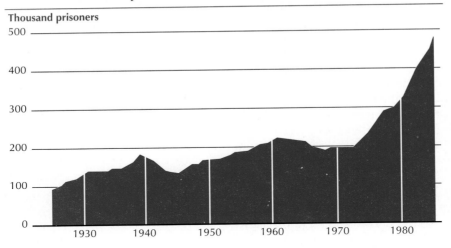

Thousand prisoners

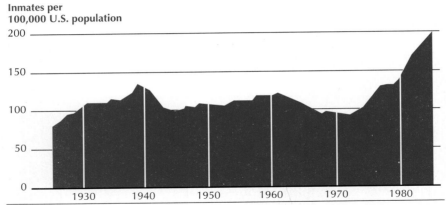

**Inmates per
100,000 U.S. population**

Source: U.S. Department of Justice, Bureau of Justice Statistics, *Report to the Nation on Crime and Justice*, 2d ed. (Washington, D.C.: U.S. Government Printing Office, March 1988), p. 104.

the escalating prison population in demographic terms. The most crime-prone population group is made up of 18-to-25-year-old males, a group whose population has grown rapidly since 1960. But the effects of that group on the prison population were delayed by the fact that offenders generally are not imprisoned until after several years of noninstitutional dispositions. Arrest rates peak around age 18; imprisonment rates peak around age 25. But this explanation is not entirely satisfactory, since the increase in the prison population was greater than the increase in the prison-prone population group.[31]

Several researchers have studied this question. Charles F. Wellford and Laure Weber Brooks investigated possible explanations for the rise in the prison population between 1970 and 1979. They found that from 54 to 76 percent of the rise could be explained by changes in demographic, structural, and legal (tougher sentencing laws) characteristics, strongly associated with regional location in the South, the percentage of the population aged 18 to 29, unemployment rates, and changes in prison capacity and use of parole.[32]

The enormous prison overcrowding over the last two decades contributed significantly to the increase in prisoners' rights litigation. The populations of institutions in twenty-nine state and local jurisdictions currently exceed the institutions' capacity. All jurisdictions are nearing their breaking points. The National Prison Project of the American Civil Liberties Union has reported that forty-four states, the District of Columbia, Puerto Rico, and the Virgin Islands are under some form of court order to reduce prison populations. On federal litigation arising out of this "crisis in corrections," Stephen D. Gottfredson and Sean McConville noted:

> The issue of crowding and other atrocious conditions is central to the overwhelming majority of these suits, and under present interpretation, the U.S. Constitution forbids the kind of treatment prison inmates in almost all states presently receive. Most of these states have been unable to meet the terms of the court orders, and despite action (such as refusals to accept new prison admissions or wholesale release of inmates), the situation in most jurisdictions is daily getting worse. As a result, we are facing a far-reaching constitutional crisis.[33]

Prison Culture and Society

For over half a century social scientists have studied the prison as a social entity that has its own traditions, norms, language, and roles. Donald Clemmer, who has described the prison subculture and how inmates adapt to it, uses the term **prisonization** to describe the complex process by which new prisoners learn the ways of the prison society and what is expected of them. Inmates are first reduced in status from civilians to anonymous figures, numbers in a common uniform, subject to institutional rules and the prison's rigid hierarchy. After a while they begin to accept the inferior role; to take on new habits of eating, sleeping, and working; and to learn that they do not owe anything to anybody for their subsistence.[34]

Building on Clemmer's work, Gresham M. Sykes has described the "pains of imprisonment" that new inmates suffer.[35] First, inmates are deprived of liberty and are cut off from their friends and family. The results are lost emotional relationships, boredom, and loneliness. Second, inmates are deprived of goods and services. While it is true that an inmate will get "three squares and clean sheets," the standard of living inside a prison is very low. Prisoners have no chance to retain or to obtain material possessions. Third, inmates are deprived of heterosexual relations. Criminologists have identified a number of psychological problems that result from this deprivation. The worst of these problems expresses itself in the homosexual enslavement of younger prisoners by older, aggressive inmates. For heterosexual inmates the deprivation of a partner of the opposite sex is one of the worst forms of punishment. Precisely for that reason, many correctional systems have instituted programs of **conjugal visits,** allowing inmates to have contact with their loved ones and family. At the Eastern Correctional Facility in Napanoch, New York, inmates are given the opportunity to stay with their spouse for forty-four hours every three or four months.[36] Fourth, convicts are deprived of their personal autonomy. Their lives are regulated and controlled twenty-four hours a day. But the control by corrections staff is selective. Staff are likely to look the other way when prisoners enforce, often brutally, their own code of conduct among themselves. The fifth pain of imprisonment is the deprivation of security. When a prisoner shares a small space with other inmates, some of whom are likely to be violent, aggression, violence, and sexual exploitation are inevitable.

To cope with these pains of imprisonment, an inmate needs to live by the **inmate code,** a set of rules that reflects the values of the prison society ("Don't interfere with inmate interests," "Don't trust the guards," "Don't weaken," etc.).[37] The prison culture is a distinct culture that develops because of the nature of confinement.

Clarence Schrag has offered an opposing explanation of prison cultures. In his view, the values that one finds within the prison are precisely those values found on the streets from which the offenders come.[38] This model, called the *importation model*, suggests, then, that the inmate subculture is not formed within the prison but is brought in from the outside.

Many researchers have tested the ideas of Clemmer, Sykes, and Schrag. Charles W. Thomas, for example, found support for the importation model.[39] Stanton Wheeler tested Clemmer's prisonization concept empirically and found that prisonization follows a U-shaped pattern during a period of incarceration: it is mild at the beginning, increases in intensity, and then decreases as release becomes imminent.[40] More recent research on Swedish prisoners by Ulla V. Bondeson comes to the opposite conclusion: Prisonization, with all its detrimental aspects, increases with the length of the term. She concludes that prisons are schools of crime.[41] Race and economic marginality, as a study by Kevin N. Wright found, are not related to prison adjustment.[42] The psychologist Hans Toch and his colleagues determined that most inmates serve trouble-free terms and that prison misbehavior is characteristic of youthful convicts sentenced to long terms. Their misbehavior dissipates as they age. To Toch, the goal of any prison system is to reduce violence through the creation of a climate that defuses it and to deal with residual violence through a person-centered approach.[43] The anthropologist Mark S. Fleisher's research on life in the Lompoc Federal Penitentiary in California supports Toch's postulate. An institutional culture that fosters and rewards peace and quiet can maintain a peaceful prison life, even for violent offenders.[44]

Reformers traditionally have been concerned with the physical environment in which prisoners serve their sentences. They have expressed the belief that prisoners cannot be reformed unless they are provided with more decent, more humane, and more refined settings. The findings of a study by James F. Houston, Don C. Gibbons, and Joseph F. Jones contradicted this premise. The physically more attractive settings and facilities of a new jail made prisoners feel no better about their surroundings and made the correctional staff feel only slightly better.[45]

Prison life is governed by the relationships among inmates, and between inmates and the rest of the world, mostly as represented by the correctional officers or guards. Race plays the dominant role in inmate relationships.[46] In many state prison systems competition among black, Hispanic, Native American, and white power blocs often leads to alliances that resemble international treaties among nations. Robert G. Leger concludes:

> Whites, who represent the dominant race outside prison, find themselves [to be] a distinct minority group on the inside. Whites' apparent realization of their minority position seems to affect their perception of their living space, levels of aggression, and attitudes towards the dominant racial group—blacks.[47]

The popular perception is that the correctional staff must control prisoners by brute force. Yet guards rarely carry weapons inside the prison because inmates might take the weapons away from them if they did. They survive by earning respect and resorting, whenever necessary, to unarmed coercion.

James W. Marquart designed an innovative study to address this issue. In order to understand inmate coercion by guards, Marquart became a correctional officer for nineteen months in a prison housing nearly 3,000 inmates. He worked throughout the institution, collecting data on social control and order. He was able to observe how the guards meted out official and unofficial punishments, coopted inmate elites to act as convict guards, cultivated snitches, and engaged in other activities.

Marquart observed the routines of prison life carefully. He developed relations with more than twenty key informants, who helped him interpret events. He found that

> guard violence was not idiosyncratic nor a form of self-defense and was relatively unprovoked. Instead, force was used against inmates as a means of physical punishment by a small but significant percentage of the guards. These officers were primarily hall officers and sergeants with relatively low-ranking positions in the guard hierarchy. It also demonstrated that force served not only as a control mechanism, but also induced group cohesion, maintained status and deference, and facilitated promotions.[48]

The life of a corrections officer is not easy. In some communities, such as Moundsville, West Virginia, and Elmira, New York, it is a tradition for sons, and now daughters as well, to follow in a father's footsteps and seek employment with the state correctional authority. In many towns the prison is the principal employer. Most guards, however, take the job for lack of better opportunities.

The stressful quality of the job determines the types of personalities that serve in correctional institutions. Kelsey Kaufman describes five personality types, based on their attitudes toward inmates and fellow officers:

- Pollyannas (optimists): positive to both groups.
- Burnouts: negative to both groups.
- Functionaries: ambivalent toward both groups.
- Hard asses: negative toward inmates, positive toward fellow officers.
- White hats: positive to inmates, negative toward fellow officers.[49]

Similarly, Barbara A. Owen found that at San Quentin, in California, correctional officers are molded by the interactions between themselves and prisoners and among themselves. She ranks the personality types on a continuum:

- John Waynes (disciplinarians)
- Wishy-washy
- Lazy/laid back
- All right
- Dirty officers.[50]

Programs in Penal Institutions

Labor   With this understanding of prison life and institutional culture, it is possible to assess contemporary programs in American corrections. The overpowering demand to save taxpayers' money has led to massive programs to employ prisoners for profit. We have seen that in antiquity prisoners were exploited as cheap labor on ships. In the nineteenth century, American convicts were farmed out to private entrepreneurs. The products of the prisoners' labors were sold at a profit, which was shared by the entrepreneur and the state. In Alabama until 1862, Burrows, Holt & Co. used prison labor for the manufacture "of sack, blinds, doors, russet, brogans, cabinet furniture, wagons,

wheat fans, well buckets, five and ten gallon kegs."[51] Alabama was still leasing inmates to private mining companies as recently as 1928.

When the lease system was abolished in the 1920s, the legislatures of southern states enacted statutes permitting the state highway authorities to use prison labor in chain gangs on the roads. Several southern states established plantation prisons, where, to save money, armed convict trusties replaced guards. Conditions were brutal. Flogging was a common response to infractions of the rules.

The exploitation of prison labor came to a gradual halt in the early 1930s when federal legislation prohibited the interstate sale of prison-made goods.[52] Some prison administrators disregarded federal restraints on inmate labor and defiantly maintained their own prison industries. In other states, however, prison labor was restricted to government services, such as the manufacture of license plates and the repair of state vehicles. But there was not enough of this kind of work to keep all inmates busy, and many prisoners spent their days in idleness.

In the 1970s prison administrators once again realized the potential profitability of prison industries. The U.S. Department of Justice now certifies state prison systems that have met certain standards and are authorized to ship prison-made goods in interstate commerce. At present the resistance to inmate labor has lessened. In fact, more than thirty private-sector industry projects are in operation. Companies such as Best Western International (hotels), Wahlers Company (office furniture), and Utah Printing and Graphics have set up shops in prisons around the country. Prisoners manufacture such products as disk drives, airplane parts, light metal products, and condensing units. Many prisoners also operate computer terminals. In several other states, private, nonprofit corporations operate all or parts of prison industries. The wages paid to most prisoners, however, are less than those paid to free workers.[53]

Among the states that have successfully experimented with productive prison labor are New York and Florida. New York State created Corcraft, a corporation empowered to run its prison industries. It has proved economically

WINDOW TO THE WORLD

Prisons Abroad

On the outskirts of the world's largest metropolitan area, Mexico City (population over 20 million), lies the little town of Toluca. It is the site of the prison for the Federal District of Mexico. People who visit this prison with preconceived notions about corrections south of the border are in for a surprise. The complex is pleasantly landscaped. There are rows of cottage-style dormitories. Loudspeakers softly play classical music outside the buildings. Prisoners are usefully employed at tasks that may equip them for employment on the outside. A resident judge disposes of needed court orders, release decisions, and prisoners' complaints. Six months before discharge, prisoners move into cottages outside the walls, from which they commute to town for work.

At one time the director had distributed a copy of the United Nations Standard Minimum Rules for the Treatment of Prisoners to each new arrival. When he discovered that most prisoners were illiterate, a talented prisoner was commissioned to prepare the Standard Minimum Rules in comic-book form. Now every prisoner can understand his rights.

When a group of prisoners was asked how they liked it there, one responded, "Señor, this could be paradise except for that"—and he pointed to the loudspeaker, which was playing Prokofiev's *Peter and the Wolf.*

What does the Toluca story tell us? Perhaps that correctional administrators do not always know what inmates perceive as punishment and what is an effort at cultural uplifting. But above all, it tells us that even in a poor country an imaginative and dedicated administrator can create a correctional environment that is humane and minimizes the burdens that come with confinement. Unhappily, in the world of confinement the Tolucas are the exception. In some countries, during certain periods, brutal treatment of prisoners—or of some categories of prisoners—has been the official policy. In many more countries, incompetence and neglect on the part of government have created inhumane conditions.

Several international organizations have been monitoring prison conditions worldwide. The reports from Amnesty International, the organization which was awarded the Nobel Peace Prize, have been particularly candid and objective. One of its recent reports documented that in Sierra Leone (West Africa) prisoners are dying not because of a calculated plan but rather because of governmental neglect. The torture and disappearance of prisoners were documented for Ecuador and many other Latin American countries. In Somalia (East Africa) prisoners of conscience have been detained without trial for eleven years or longer. In Pakistan prisoners have been kept in bar fetters and shackles. In Spain Basques charged with terrorist crimes have been tortured in detention facilities. In the United Kingdom (Northern Ireland) Amnesty International continued to receive reports about ill treatment of suspects incarcerated under the antiterrorist legislation.

We have mentioned the names of but a few countries from Amnesty's report. In fact, prison conditions in these countries may well be better than those in many other countries. The fact is that there is no country in which prison conditions are ideal and free from abuses.

Source: Based on Amnesty International Report 1987 (London: Amnesty International Publications, 1987).

beneficial for the state, and jobs displaced in the private sector were more than offset by new civilian employment opportunities created by Corcraft.[54] Similarly, Florida created PRIDE (Prison Rehabilitative and Diversified Enterprises), a nonprofit corporation that since 1982 has operated all prison industries at double the income that was made before it took over ($4 million in 1987). It has increased prisoner employment rates by 70 percent and seemingly has lowered the recommitment rate for prisoners who participate in the program.[55] However, when Kathleen E. Maguire, Timothy J. Flanagan, and Terence P. Thornberry compared the recidivism rate of former prisoners who had participated in prison industry programs and that of nonparticipants, they found that when differences among the two groups in regard to other characteristics associated with imprisonment were taken into account, the rates were virtually identical.[56] The question of convict labor is intricate and bothersome, and correctional policy makers must be alert to its pitfalls.[57]

The return to prison industry seemed to offer a means to deal with the budget crisis in which American corrections found itself. As yet there is no indication that the correctional system can be made to pay for itself by prison industry. It is doubtful as well that useful work in a commercial industry can prepare prisoners for gainful employment in free society. Moreover, troublesome questions persist about such issues as the adequacy of compensation for prison labor, industrial safety, unionization, and the absence of benefits.

Treatment and rehabilitation Few criminologists disagree about the need for prisons. But they also generally agree that the number of people imprisoned is far greater than necessary. They disagree about the criteria for determining which inmates should be incarcerated and which should not. Some criminologists suggest the need for educational, psychological, and vocational programs for prisoners. Progressive criminologists regard the principal objective of the correctional system to be reformation, the voluntary, self-initiated transformation of an individual, lacking in social or vocational skills, into a productive, normally functioning citizen. Offenders are, according to this view, in need of rehabilitation. They may be psychologically disturbed, addicted to alcohol or drugs, or simply lacking in the basic skills necessary to survive in a complex society.

Other criminologists either have little faith in the efficacy of rehabilitation programs or are philosophically opposed to placing the primary emphasis on treating and correcting behavior. With the recent emphasis on the retributive and just-deserts philosophies, some criminologists have promoted the incarceration of offenders in humane conditions with few (if any) efforts to change them, either through work or through involvement in therapeutic programs. But even those opposed to compulsory rehabilitation programs would not deny prisoners the right to participate in voluntary programs.

Rehabilitation has been broadly defined as the result of any social or psychological intervention intended to reduce an offender's further criminal activity.[58] By this standard, the true test of rehabilitative success is noninvolvement in crime following an offender's participation in an intervention program. For this reason, criminologists traditionally have examined recidivism rates of offenders who have and have not been exposed to rehabilitative intervention. Supporters of rehabilitation hope to see decreased recidivism rates, while those who seek nonreformative warehousing of inmates anticipate no such change. Three types of programs are typically in use in prisons in the United States: psychological (e.g., psychotherapy and behavior therapy), educational (e.g., general equivalency diploma), and vocational (e.g., food preparation) programs.

Evaluation of Rehabilitation Efforts

Innovative rehabilitation programs are generally instituted with great enthusiasm, but disillusionment sets in when they are subjected to critical examination. Most programs promise more than they can deliver, as new techniques of evaluation have demonstrated. In 1964 Daniel Glaser established that vocational rehabilitation programs have virtually no effect on postrelease behavior.[59] In 1966, after evaluating one hundred correctional treatment programs, Walter C. Bailey concluded that "evidence supporting the efficacy of correctional treatment is slight, inconsistent and of questionable reliability."[60] Roger Hood came to similarly disappointing conclusions in England.[61] James Robison and Gerald Smith evaluated California correctional and treatment programs and found evidence of success inconclusive.[62] Freda Adler and her colleagues, after evaluating all Pennsylvania drug-treatment programs, including all prison-based programs, concluded that virtually none could claim any significant successes and that the system as a whole was in a chaotic condition.[63] The most devastating evaluation was that by Douglas Lipton, Robert Martinson, and Judith Wilks, published in 1975, with a preview article proclaiming that nothing works.[64] As a result, the treatment philosophy was discredited, programs were dismantled, and the vacuum in corrections was filled by the just-deserts approach.

Subsequently, some criminologists scrutinized Martinson's evaluations and found them methodologically flawed.[65] Martinson himself recanted to some extent and later confirmed that some programs have some success in curbing recidivism.[66] Paul Gendreau and Robert R. Ross presented impressive evidence of successful treatment programs.[67] After a thorough review of treatment programs initiated between 1981 and 1987, they concluded that

> it is downright ridiculous to say "nothing works." This review attests that much is going on to indicate that offender rehabilitation has been, can be, and will be achieved.[68]

Their analysis of biomedical, diversion, family intervention, education, get-tough, and work programs gives reasons for hope. The expectation that appropriate rehabilitation efforts may yield some success in curbing recidivism rates has thus been rekindled.[69]

Presently criminologists are ambivalent about the future of the rehabilitative approach. They agree only that therapy can never again be forced. The types and forms of future correc-

tional treatment are not yet clear. Integration of the treatment approach with the widely accepted just-deserts model seems hard to achieve. Matching offenders with available treatment programs has been difficult in the past and will continue to be a problem. Above all, criminologists must be wary of viewing treatment of offenders as the solution to the crime problem. The rehabilitative approach nevertheless is gaining support because, as Francis T. Cullen and Karen E. Gilbert aptly remark, it is "the only justification of criminal sanctioning that obligates the state to care for an offender's needs or welfare."[70] It is a humanitarian approach.

Treatment and Medical Needs in the AIDS Crisis

When the rehabilitative model was created, and even as late as 1982, when Cullen and Gilbert spoke of the state's obligation to care for an offender's need and welfare, nobody could anticipate the enormous financial burden that the crisis of AIDS (acquired immune deficiency syndrome) would impose on correctional budgets. As of March 1988, 525 prisoners in New York State alone had died of AIDS, which is transmitted through blood and semen. Drug addicts who share hypodermic needles and homosexuals are particularly at risk, as are the female partners and children of addicts and bisexual men. Contaminated blood transfusions account for additional cases. The New York Department of Correctional Services estimated in 1988 that from 60 to 70 percent of all prisoners (some 24,000 to 28,000) have histories of drug use and are therefore at risk for AIDS.[71] The cost of caring for a terminal AIDS patient has been estimated to be $500,000. There are large management problems as well. AIDS patients are shunned by other prisoners and by officers. How can the system control prisoners dying of AIDS, who have nothing to lose? Prison hospitals are not equipped to provide adequate care for terminal AIDS patients. Their placement in community hospitals poses grave risks. Successful treatment has not yet been achieved. The system is still searching for solutions.

Women in Prison

Most prisons are male institutions in which male offenders are guarded and receive services by a male staff, although women have begun to enter the staff of the male prison world, first as clerical and professional personnel and more recently as correctional officers. Until the latter part of the nineteenth century there were no separate prisons for women in the United States. The small number of women prisoners were housed in male institutions, though usually in segregated sections. The first prison for women was opened in 1873 in Indiana. During the next century, women convicts were exclusively imprisoned in women's prisons. These institutions have tended to be smaller, and less threatening in appearance and operation than male prisons (e.g., absence of high walls and guard towers, and less regimentation). Yet, being smaller, they also lack many of the facilities of male institutions.

Currently, the population in women's prisons resembles that in men's prisons. The prisoners come predominantly from the uneducated, urban, poor sections of the population. Women in prison often adapt to prison life by creating surrogate families amongst themselves and assume the roles of father, mother, brother, or sister. And programs available in women's prisons tend to emphasize society's traditional stereotype of "women's work": cooking, sewing, cosmetology, and office work, to which more recently computer programming has been added.

A century after the first U.S. prison for women was opened, an effort to use facilities in a cost-effective manner led to the establishment of the first co-correctional institutions in which men and women, segregated at night, participate in joint daytime programs of work, recreation, and meals. Physical contact is limited to handholding. Infraction of the rules leads to transfer of the offenders to separate institutions. The federal system has played a leading role in operating co-correctional prisons. Nearly two-thirds of federal women convicts serve their sentences in such facilities. For the country as a whole, however, the majority of the women prisoners are serving their time in institutions for women.

There is an additional burden on women in institutions. Over two-thirds of women prisoners are mothers, with an average of two children. Many give birth in prison. The mother-child relationship poses problems to mothers that the correctional system has not resolved. Programs for facilitating mother-child contacts are woefully inadequate. Mothers may keep their newborns only for a few weeks. And children's visits to prisons are typically limited because of the distance of prisons from the children's homes and the restrictions placed on visiting hours.

Privatization of Corrections

So far we have viewed punishment as the sole prerogative of the state, and the correctional system as a governmental institution for dealing with convicted offenders. This state monopoly of the penal system has existed since the Middle Ages. In the current era of free enterprise, state monopolies in many areas of governmental functioning are gradually giving way to private enterprise. The delivery of letters is no longer exclusively in the hands of a government agency, the U.S. Postal Service; much of it has been taken over by private courier companies. In Chapter 15 we noted that much of government's police function has been taken over by private security firms. A similar movement is discernible in corrections.[72]

Frustration over the low success rates of prisons, usually measured by recidivism rates, coupled with an incredibly high expense to the taxpayers, has prompted policy makers to search for alternatives to government-operated prisons. One alternative is to turn over the administration of prisons to private entrepreneurs, who expect to run prisons at a profit rather than at the expense of the taxpayer.[73] The first private-enterprise prison was established in 1975, when RCA, under contract with the Commonwealth of Pennsylvania, opened a training school for delinquents in Weaversville. When James O. Finckenauer evaluated this facility, he found it "better staffed, organized, and equipped than any other program of its size" that he knew.[74] By 1987, approximately 3,000 adults were incarcerated in privately run prisons, and private juvenile facilities were in operation in twelve states.[75] Although it still has not been conclusively shown that private facilities are indeed more cost-beneficial than public ones, the privatization of corrections is continuing. This movement raises some troubling questions, which have been summarized by Ira P. Robbins:

• What standards will govern the operation of the institution?
• Who will monitor the implementation of the standards?
• Will the public still have access to the facility?
• What recourse will members of the public have if they do not approve of how the institution is operated?
• Who will be responsible for maintaining security if the private personnel go on strike?
• Where will the responsibility for prison disciplinary procedures lie?
• Will the company be able to refuse to accept certain inmates, such as those who have contracted AIDS?
• What options will be available to the government if the corporation substantially raises its fees?
• What will happen if the company declares bankruptcy or simply goes out of business because there is not enough profit?[76]

These questions underline the massive legal problems inherent in the privatization of corrections. Robbins has suggested appropriate remedies and procedures.[77] The most disturbing and basic question that must be addressed is whether the sovereign right of the people, as represented by their government, to punish those found guilty of violating the people's code should ever be transferred to private hands.

A report prepared for the National Institute of Justice, based on a survey of private-sector corrections in all states, is fairly optimistic about the future of private prisons. Idleness is reduced at low cost, prisons have access to private-sector economic expertise, the prison environment is improved, prisoners may earn real wages and obtain vocational training useful after their release, taxpayers benefit because the wages of prisoners help offset the cost of incarceration, and victims have a better chance of obtaining compensation out of prisoners' earnings.[78] As for the inmates themselves, by and large they do not care who runs the prison.[79]

The general reluctance to accept the concept of private correctional institutions may perhaps be offset by a reminder that noninstitutional corrections owes its origin largely to private entrepreneurship, private concern for convicts, and community action in caring for convicted offenders in the community itself.

COMMUNITY ALTERNATIVES TO PRISONS

The public equates punishment and corrections with prisons and jails. Incarceration is, in fact, the most painful contemporary punishment. In terms of the number of sentenced offenders, however, incarceration is far less significant than noninstitutional control of offenders through probation, parole, and other alternatives to confinement in an institution.

Probation

John Augustus was a humble man. Born in Woburn, Massachusetts, in 1784, he moved to Lexington at the age of 21, learned the shoemaking trade, and by 1827 had become a successful craftsman in Boston. He often visited the courts, and he was appalled by what he saw. Judges filled the jails with petty criminals simply because the miscreants could not pay the small fines imposed. So Augustus stepped forward to pay the fines himself. Sheldon Glueck, nearly a century later, described how John Augustus worked:

> His method was to bail the offender after conviction, to utilize this favor as an entering wedge to the convict's confidence and friendship, and through such evidence of friendliness as helping the offender to obtain a job and aiding his family in various ways, to drive the

wedge home. When the defendant was later brought into court for sentence, Augustus would report on his progress toward reformation, and the judge would usually fine the convict one cent and costs, instead of committing him to an institution.[80]

John Augustus promoted his new approach through his Washington Total Abstinence Society, and the Boston courts endorsed the idea. Thus was born the idea of **probation,** the release of a prison-bound convict into the community under the supervision of a trustworthy person and bound by certain conditions, such as not to violate the law, not to leave the jurisdiction, and to maintain employment. Probation was greeted as a welcome alternative to prisons in the mid-nineteenth century, when demand for prison space was greater than the supply, the first disenchantment about the capacity of penitentiaries to reform their inmates had set in, and the exorbitant cost of imprisonment was first perceived.

The purpose of probation has always been to integrate offenders, under supervision, into law-abiding society. By 1956 all states had established a probation system. Most systems operate throughout a county, but some are statewide.[81] Probation is now one of the most widely used correctional dispositions. In fact, approximately four times as many offenders are placed on probation as are sent to prison. Probation serves the dual purpose of protecting the community through continued court supervision and rehabilitating the offender. Only minor restrictions are imposed on the probationer's life. The benefits of probation are large: (1) not all types of offenses are serious enough to require costly incarceration; (2) probationers can obtain or maintain employment and pay taxes; and (3) offenders can care for their families and comply with their other financial responsibilities without becoming burdens on the state.

As we noted in Chapter 16, the trial judge, in order to determine a convicted defendant's eligibility for probation, requests a presentence investigation (PSI) report. This report is prepared by a probation officer, who focuses on such factors as the nature of the offense (violent or non-violent), the defendant's version of the offense,

prior criminal record, employment history, family background, financial situation, health, religious involvement, length of current residence, and community ties.[82] On the basis of such factors, the judge then decides whether to impose a prison sentence or probation.

The probation concept as it works in practice has two major flaws. (1) Judges generally do not have the time, the information, or the predictive capacity to determine whether a given convict is a good prospect for probation. They frequently view probation simply as a means to control the prison population by keeping less serious offenders out of prison or jail. (2) The probationer (the person put on probation) does not have the assistance and guidance that John Augustus considered essential for the success of probation. There are 20,236 probation officers in the United States, each with an average caseload of 111 probationers at any given moment. Some officers supervise as many as 250 probationers.[83] The cases are constantly changing. Under such circumstances, the officer has no chance to provide meaningful guidance and assistance. Consequently, one would expect probation failure rates to be very high. But such is not the case. In 1987, 77 percent of probationers completed their terms successfully.[84] In 1984 the success rate had been as high as 80.9 percent.[85] The unmet challenge is to exclude from routine probation those 20 to 23 percent of offenders who constitute a danger. Better presentence screening may provide an answer, since probationers (except property offenders) for whom the PSI recommends probation are less likely to offend than those placed on probation against the investigator's recommendation.

Some scholars have suggested that probation would work best if the convict had "a taste of prison," so that he or she would be motivated to behave well during the probation period. This approach, which some legislatures have enacted into law, has two versions. **Shock probation** is probation granted after a short period of incarceration; **split sentence** is a sentence partly to prison or jail and partly to probation. Edward J. Latessa and Gennaro F. Vito have conducted a series of important studies on the comparative value of shock probation and regular probation. In 1981 they reported on the reincarceration rates of 585 shock and 938 regular probationers. Regular probationers had an 11 percent rate of reincarceration versus 17 percent for shock probationers. This study was replicated successfully in 1985.[86] Apparently knowing the brutal realities of prison life does not make a difference to probationers—or, for that matter, to delinquents. James O. Finckenauer, in evaluating a New Jersey program intended to make juvenile delinquents "scared straight" by subjecting them to the harsh realities of prison life for a day, found that over time the program did not succeed in curbing delinquency rates.[87] Thus the shock approach is not supported by research.

Treatment programs in general and probation programs in particular depend greatly on the personality of the person providing the service. The relative success of probation programs may be attributable to the people who have joined the probation service. An evaluation of the Massachusetts probation system found the quality of probation staff to be outstanding, with a strong and common desire to ensure public safety while providing rehabilitative support for offenders.[88] Probation officers have relatively low levels of job stress. They like what they are doing, except for the endless preoccupation with administrative procedures.[89]

Parole

The concept of **parole** was first introduced about the same time as that of probation. Captain Alexander Maconochie administered an English penal colony in the 1840s on Norfolk Island, a speck of land in the Pacific Ocean, 900 miles east of Australia. He observed that

> a man under a time sentence thinks only how he is to cheat that time and while it away; he evades labor, because he has no interest in it whatsoever, and he has no desire to please the officers under whom he is placed, because they cannot serve him essentially; they cannot in any way promote his liberation.

Maconochie conceived a solution. He created a "scheme of marks awarded for industry, labor, and good conduct, [which] gave prisoners an opportunity to earn their way out of confinement."[90] Under Maconochie's scheme, release from confinement proceeded through several stages of ever greater freedom from control.

On the surface parole may appear to be similar to probation. Both programs provide periods in which an offender lives in the community instead of serving time in a prison. Both programs require that the convict be under supervision to ensure his or her good conduct. When the condition is violated, confinement results. But here the similarity ends (see Table 17.4).

The idea of parole was introduced in the United States at the first National Prison Association Congress in Cincinnati in 1870. Warden Zebulon Brockway of the Elmira Reformatory began using parole in 1876. Promising convicts were released into the care of private reform groups before their terms had expired. Later on, corrections officers were assigned to supervise the parolees. By 1900 twenty states and the federal government had parole systems in place. Ultimately all jurisdictions instituted parole.

Parole success rates have never been great. Perhaps parole has usually been granted too late. Don M. Gottfredson and his colleagues of the National Council on Crime and Delinquency found that success on parole diminishes as the length of time served in prison increases.[91] In 1987 only 59 percent of parolees had completed their terms successfully.[92] The high failure rate is not the only reason that parole has come under attack in recent years. First, parole is supposed to be a reward for rehabilitation in prison, yet prisons do not rehabilitate inmates. Thus prisoners are denied rewards because of the prison's failure. Second, the parole system has long been plagued by a lack of valid criteria that parole boards can use when they decide whether to release a prisoner, and their hearings have long been known for their arbitrariness. Though nineteen jurisdictions have had guidelines for parole decisions since federal guidelines were instituted in 1973, parole decision making nevertheless remains a mysterious process that increases the anxiety of inmates. Moreover, the system is subject to political manipulation and lobbying.

TABLE 17.4   PROBATION VS. PAROLE

PROBATION	PAROLE
A convict is sentenced to a period of probation *in lieu of prison*.	A prisoner is *released from prison* and placed on parole.
Probation is a front-end measure.	Parole is a tail-end measure.
The court imposes the sentence of probation.	A parole board grants release on parole.
The court retains jurisdiction.	A parole board retains jurisdiction.
A probation officer is an officer of the court and is employed by a county or district.	A parole officer is a state officer employed by the state government.
Probation is an alternative sentence for less serious cases.	Originally serious offenders earned parole through good conduct in prison.
Eligibility depends on a favorable PSI report.	Eligibility depends on successful service of a specific part of the prison sentence.

For example, the governor may pressure the parole board to grant more parole releases when prisons are overcrowded. Lobbyists may exert pressure against a parole decision when a notorious convict comes up for parole. Third, parole, like probation, depends for its success on assistance and supervision. Yet caseloads are so great that such assistance is not available in the ordinary case.[93]

In a broad attack on the parole system, Andrew von Hirsch and Kathleen J. Hanrahan argued for its abolition. The decision to release an offender, they argue, should not be based on questions of treatment or likelihood of offending again; rather, prison time should be correlated with the offender's blameworthiness for the current offense. Parole supervision and the potential for revocation of parole disturb von Hirsch and Hanrahan particularly on grounds of fairness and appropriateness. They propose instead a fixed release date, rather than one that can change after a large portion of the sentence has been served.[94]

Such criticisms have led some jurisdictions to terminate discretionary parole releases by parole boards. They have substituted mandatory release, either through determinate sentencing (Alaska, Arizona, Colorado, Indiana, Maine, Missouri, New Jersey, New Mexico, North Carolina, Tennessee) or through parole guidelines (Florida, Georgia, Hawaii, Louisiana, Maryland, Michigan, New York, Ohio, Oregon, Rhode Island, South Carolina, Virginia, Washington, West Virginia, Wisconsin, and the federal system). Some jurisdictions use both methods (California, Minnesota, Pennsylvania), and some have returned to the "good time" system.[95] The **good time system** entails a procedure by which the length of the sentence is shortened by specific periods if the prisoner performs in accordance with the expectations of the prison authorities. Many risks, especially to public safety, may inhere in the good time system, and much has yet to be learned about it before it can be considered a viable means of dealing with prison overcrowding.[96] An opinion survey has found strong public approval for the use of good time and community-based corrections; construction of more prisons received only moderate support; and shortening sentences and increasing parole boards' authority were disapproved.[97]

The Search for Cost-Beneficial Alternatives

Probation and parole have always been regarded as cost-beneficial alternatives to imprisonment.[98] As we noted, however, their success rates are mixed. In an era when drug-related and other crimes of violence are increasing, policy makers and the public view routine probation and parole as unsuitable solutions to the problem of prison overcrowding. Conservative legislators have generally been willing to fund the construction of new prisons, but construction costs and the frequency with which new facilities have to be built have put such a strain on state budgets that many conservatives have joined their liberal colleagues in opposing the expansion of the prison system. Thus has begun the search for cost-beneficial alternatives consistent with the public's demand for security and the punitive philosophy that marks the current era.[99] The search has focused on penal or correctional measures that

- Are less costly than confinement in a prison or jail.
- Are not perceived by the population as a copout, a lessening of the message conveyed by a jail or prison term.
- Do not pose a threat to the community.
- Do not have the negative effect on convicts that prison terms normally entail, but may actually benefit the convicts, their families, and their communities.

Experimentation has shown some promising possibilities, among them intensive supervision programs, home jail programs, shock programs, restitution programs, and fines.

Intensive supervision programs As originally conceived, probation programs were aimed at prison-bound convicts for whom it was thought that safety considerations did not require confinement and for whom association with other prisoners in confinement would do more harm than good. As we have seen, traditional probation required intensive supervision. But such supervision has become impossible because the number of probationers is so enormous. Some states continue to use token or routine probation for low-risk cases, but many have also introduced **intensive supervision probation (ISP)** for convicts who do not qualify for routine probation. The experience of the New Jersey ISP program has been particularly encouraging. The New Jersey ISP program, directed by the

Administrative Office of the Courts since 1983, is designed to handle 500 convicts, the equivalent of the population of one prison. Only nonviolent offenders are eligible for the program, so it excludes robbers, murderers, and all sex offenders. Convicts who want to be considered for the program must apply after thirty days and before sixty days from the day of imprisonment. This period is considered to be a desirable shock incarceration period.

Each applicant must develop a personal plan, describing his or her own problems, plans, community resources, and contacts. A community sponsor must be identified with whom the offender will live during the early months after release and who will help the offender to fulfill the program's objectives. Applicants for the program must also identify several other people in the community who can be relied on for help. These people are called the network team.

The offender's ISP plan and the persons identified in it are closely checked. All information is placed before the ISP screening board, which includes the ISP director, correctional staff, and community representatives. If the screening board's decision is positive, the application goes to a three-judge resentencing panel. A positive decision by this panel results in a ninety-day placement in the ISP program; the placement is renewable after ninety days. Each ISP participant must serve a minimum of one year, including time on parole after release, in the program, during which period he or she is on a bench warrant status and thus subject to immediate arrest should a violation occur.

The program conditions are punitive and onerous, centering on employment and hard work. They include the following:

- At least sixteen hours of community service per week.
- Multiple weekly contacts with the ISP officer and the community sponsor.
- Maintenance of a daily diary detailing accomplishments.
- Immediate notification of the ISP officer of any police contact or arrest.
- Participation in weekly counseling activities, if ordered.

• Maintenance of employment or participation in a vocational training program.
• Participation in any treatment program (e.g., drug, alcohol) designated by the ISP officer.
• Adherence to curfew requirements (normally 10:00 P.M. to 6:00 A.M.).
• Subjection to electronic monitoring, if ordered.
• Payment of all obligations, such as the cost of electronic monitoring ($5 to $18 daily), court costs, fines, victim compensation payments, and child support, to the extent ordered by the court.

The failure rate in the New Jersey ISP program has been far lower than anybody expected. As of 1987, of the 600 participants accepted into the program, 27 percent had been expelled, most of them for technical violations, for use of drugs or alcohol, or for disorderly conduct. Only 5 percent of ISP participants committed a felony during the average one and one-half years of the program's duration. This failure rate is considered a success rate, as it tends to prove that intensive supervision is capable of detecting those who have abused the privilege of participating in the ISP program.

Among the program's greatest benefits are these:

• Rather than costing the state $17,000 per year, ISP costs $7,000, thus saving the state $10,000 yearly per convict.
• The offender earns a living, pays taxes, pays the cost of electronic monitoring, fines, fees, and other obligations.
• Though it is too soon to make definite pronouncements, there is an indication that ISP program participants can do better after discharge than comparable prison inmates, thus saving the community some of the costs of crime.[100]

The criminologist Frank Pearson recently evaluated the New Jersey ISP program. Using data collected on ISP participants from 1983 to 1987, he found that the ISP program resulted in only a slight improvement in recidivism rates over ordinary imprisonment and parole. The program did save on prison space, however, and was more cost-effective than other correctional interventions.[101]

New Jersey's program is particularly punitive and demanding, and thus more costly than any other state's ISP program. The Illinois program, for instance, aims at offenders who constitute a lesser risk and costs only $2,500 per convict. ISP programs in some other jurisdictions have proved to be similarly cost-beneficial

TABLE 17.5   *ANNUAL COST PER PRISONER OF SENTENCING OPTIONS, EXCLUSIVE OF CONSTRUCTION COSTS*

OPTION	ANNUAL COST
Routine probation	$ 300–2,000
Intensive probation	1,500–7,000
House arrest	
without electronics	1,350–7,000
with telephone callback system	2,500–5,000
with passive electronic monitoring	2,500–6,500
with active electronic monitoring	4,500–8,500
Local jail	8,000–12,000
Local detention center	5,000–15,000
State prison	9,000–20,000

Source: Joan Petersilia, *Expanding Options for Criminal Sentencing* (Santa Monica, Calif.: Rand Corporation, 1987), p. 32.

(see Table 17.5). The ISP program in Montgomery County (Dayton), Ohio, was found to be operating at an acceptable level for a program of its kind.[102] But the evaluation of a similar Ohio county program indicated that it did not lower recidivism rates.[103] The effectiveness of ISP programs in other jurisdictions is inconclusive.[104]

Intensive supervision has also proved to be effective and cost-beneficial as a tail-end measure when convicts eligible for parole might pose undue risks and are therefore denied release on routine parole. In such cases, release into an ISP parole program, structured along the same lines as front-end programs, releases prison bed space and provides the same financial rewards to the community as front-end programs. New Jersey's Intensive Supervision and Surveillance Program (ISSP), operated by the Bureau of Parole, assigns high-risk offenders to ISSP for ninety days. Following a case evaluation, the parolee may then be assigned to standard parole.

Home confinement programs   In view of the high cost of incarcerating a convict in a public prison, many states have considered whether it might not be cheaper to "imprison" a person at a place where the "rent" is cheaper. The convict's home, or an alternative such as a group home or shelter, has been viewed as a viable option. Thus was introduced the concept of house arrest, to which some 50,000 American convicts have already been sentenced.

> House arrest is a sentence imposed by the court whereby offenders are legally ordered to remain confined in their own residences for the duration of their sentence. House arrestees may be allowed to leave their homes for medical reasons, employment, and approved religious services. They may also be required to perform community service and to pay victim restitution and probation supervising fees. In selected instances, electronic monitoring equipment may be used to monitor an offender's presence in a residence where he or she is required to remain.[105]

Technical problems in the original electronic monitoring systems had caused some initial dif-

ficulties. These have now been largely resolved. As to psychological difficulties, it appears that fellow householders can accept their family member's house arrest, but many people have a civil libertarian aversion to electronic monitoring of human beings.[106]

Michigan, Nevada, and Oklahoma have experimented with residential confinement programs whose participants are drawn from the prison population. Most states with such programs use them for front-end diversion from prison. In the Maryland program, which has operated successfully for several years, the sentencing judge, together with the Department of Corrections, makes the decision to use the defendant's home rather than a prison cell as the place of confinement. This twofold approval requirement is designed to ensure that dangerous or high-risk offenders are not placed in the program. The total cost of the Prince Georges County, Maryland, Home Detention Program, including staff, transportation, and equipment, is $7 per day per prisoner, contrasted with the $45 it costs to maintain a prisoner in the County Detention Center for a day. In the first two years of this program, 188 convicts successfully completed their period of confinement on home detention, at a savings to the county of well over $1 million.

The advantages of home confinement programs are that they are seen as sufficiently punitive, that the retribution and deterrence goals of punishment are satisfied, and that the offender is still allowed to maintain employment as well as close family ties, which can be particularly important when the family includes young children who need the offender at home. But it is too early to claim that home confinement programs are a total success.[107]

Shock programs and other options   Both under the retribution theory of the past and under the current just-deserts theory, punishment is measured by the length of time to be spent in confinement, a period that is determined by the gravity of the offense and the guilt or culpability of the perpetrator. Some corrections specialists believe that punishment should be measured not by time alone but also by the punitiveness and severity of incarceration.

AT ISSUE

Boot Camp: A Military Option for Corrections

Germany was thoroughly militarized in the days of the Kaiser (until 1918). This militarization included the prison system. Prisoners wore military-style uniforms, marched in lock-step from place to place, had orders barked at them by drill sergeants, and their education was confined to military manuals. The story goes—and it was retold in several books and movies—that one prisoner, upon discharge, bought himself an infantry captain's worn uniform in a second-hand clothing store, donned the uniform at the toilet of the railroad station, and emerged as a man of authority. He promptly assumed command of a passing platoon of soldiers, marched them to city hall, arrested the mayor, and retrieved his confiscated passport, just to get out of the country. This is the story of the captain of Koepenik,

and it may have some implications for Americans' latest fascination for a correctional approach called RID (Regimented, or Regimental, Inmate Discipline), popularly known as boot camp. Young prison-bound convicts—most of them undisciplined high school dropouts with histories of alcohol and drug abuse—are selected for these programs and subjected to Marine Corps-style drill, hard work, absence of spare time, and character-building exercises. The Oklahoma RID program, its participants carefully selected, has a failure rate of only 15 percent and a success rate (crimefree twelve months after discharge) of 85 percent. Georgia's program has a success rate of 90 percent. The cost of such programs, at $26.43 per day in Georgia, is lower than the cost of secure incarceration.

These programs have been used only for young male offenders, but there are a lot of offenders in this category. Boot camp programs have been attacked as creators of Rambos and praised as character builders. It may be too early to assess the value of boot camps to the correctional system, but the legislatures of several states, including Mississippi, Louisiana, Michigan, Florida, Colorado, and Nevada, have been willing to experiment with this alternative form of confinement. The faith of legislatures in these programs, demonstrated by their willingness to fund them, in view of scant evaluation research, is surprising. It remains to be seen whether American boot camps will produce disciplined and productive members of the community, Rambos, mercenaries, or captains of Koepenik.

Thus the intensity of a short, sharp shock incarceration may be as severe as a longer, "easy-time" confinement in a prison. Moreover, the shorter incarceration may avoid the detrimental prisonization effects that a longer prison sentence entails. As we have noted, some ISP programs include shock incarceration. Other types of programs are based entirely on the shock model. Much experimentation has been done throughout the country.

Restitution programs In theory, victims of crime always have some recourse against their victimizers, traditionally in the form of a civil suit. Most offenders, however, are too poor to

pay damages. Their incarceration aggravates the situation by depriving them of the employment that could provide the money for restitution. Policy makers have begun to recognize this anomaly. Restitution programs have become increasingly popular since 1973, when a team of American corrections specialists visited Radbruch Haus in Frankfurt, West Germany, a former prison that had been converted into an employment-detention facility. Half of the district's prison inmates had been selected at random to reside in this no-security facility. They were obligated to go to work every day. Their wages were carefully budgeted by correctional staff (guards retrained as accountants) to pay for court costs, confinement costs, victim restitution, support of their families, transportation to work, and so forth. The walk-away rate was low. Inmates who did walk off were placed in a secure prison.[108] Among the American visitors was Kenneth C. Schoen, who, as head of the Minnesota correctional system, pioneered the first American restitution program at the Minnesota Restitution Center. Offenders lived at a community correctional center after making a contractual agreement with the victim, which itemized the amount, schedule, and form of restitution.

By now several jurisdictions have experimented successfully with **employment prisons,** or minimum security restitution centers. Low-risk offenders bound for prison may be placed in such facilities, which are usually located in or near the cities where they live and work. At night, the prisoners must remain in the facility. During working hours they have to pursue their employment. The wages are administered by the correctional staff and applied to the cost of incarceration and to all other financial obligations, including compensation to the victim when it has been ordered.

Research has confirmed the feasibility and success of restitution programs. Burt Galaway reviewed the development of restitution programs and research on them from the 1970s through 1988. He concluded:

• Restitution programs are feasible in both juvenile and adult correctional systems.
• Victims and the public at large strongly support restitution programs.
• Restitution may achieve the utilitarian goal of punishment as well as the goal of ensuring just deserts.[109]

Research conducted in Canada by Joe Hudson and Burt Galaway, however, established that restitution programs there have a much higher rate of failure. Yet even there, only one-quarter of the offenders fail to live up to their restitution orders.[110]

Straight fines, day fines, and community service   Forced labor to pay the treasury and fines to reimburse the government for its troubles in dealing with or punishing an offender have been part of the system since the Middle Ages. Most offenders today are too poor to pay fines. Even a dollar is a lot for a person who has no income. A straight fine can be a burden to a factory worker but no burden to a manager. A fixed sum of money means different things to persons in different income brackets. To compensate for income differentials among offenders, the Scandinavian countries (Sweden, Denmark, Norway, Finland, and Iceland) have long used the "day fine" system, according to which the amount of the fine is measured in days of earnings. For a drunk-driving offense, the fine may be ten days' earnings. For the corporate executive, the fine may amount to ten times $500, or $5,000. For a factory worker it may amount to ten times $50, or $500. This scheme, which approximates that of the graduated income tax, helps the public treasury. The offender is in the community and is able to meet other obligations, such as supporting his or her children and making the car payments. And the offender is not subjected to prisonization. Fines are predicted to play a far greater role in American corrections than they have done in the past. In view of the large number of unemployed and unemployable minor offenders, however, fines have their limitations. Whether vocational training can bring these people into the group of finable offenders is yet to be seen.

When the payment of money is inappropriate, perhaps for reasons of indigency, an order of community service may be a viable alternative. One of the first jurisdictions in the United States to use community service orders was Alameda County, California. In October 1966 the Alameda County court agreed to permit misdemeanants to serve their sentences as volunteers for community organizations. Since the initiation of that program, thousands of minor offenders have served their time by performing many hours of service for health and welfare organizations. The benefits of such programs are clear:

• Offenders have opportunities to engage in constructive activities.
• Offenders may undergo a change of attitude through the experience of volunteer work.

- Community service is a sentence uniquely appropriate to indigent offenders.
- It can also be an appropriate sentence for persons in higher income brackets whose offenses merit a public humbling.

Evaluation of Community Alternatives to Prison

Prison overcrowding in America has become such a problem both socially and financially that the established correctional system can no longer cope with it. Many legislatures tolerated prison construction and extension of the capacity of existing penal institutions for a while. Then a countertrend set in. As both liberal and conservative legislators became reluctant to commit ever-increasing portions of state budgets to prison expansion, criminologists were challenged to devise cost-beneficial alternatives to incarceration and the standard forms of probation and parole which met the contemporary demand for punitiveness and public security. In an amazingly short time, several such alternatives were developed and instituted across the country. Heralded as cost-beneficial, punitive, and secure, these programs were accepted at face value and replicated in other states on very little evidence of their success in achieving the stated goals. We have pointed to some of the early evaluations, fully aware that they do not provide an accurate measure of the success of these programs.

James M. Byrne has assessed the entire body of evaluation research on these new programs. He concludes that traditional probation remains cost-beneficial and that the other intermediate sanctions currently involve only about 5 percent of the correctional population, although they constitute a "growth area." He finds that intensive supervision programs do not significantly reduce the risk of recidivism, that house arrest programs cannot yet be evaluated successfully, that boot camp programs do not yet offer evidence of success, and that new approaches to the fine system cannot yet be evaluated. Byrne's research has led him to several challenging conclusions about the future of American corrections:

- It makes good sense to do something about the problem of prison overcrowding.
- Innovative programs must be evaluated before they are replicated elsewhere.
- "The available evidence points toward a renewed awareness of the importance of treatment and the futility of simply increasing the level of offender surveillance and/or control."[111]

REVIEW

Throughout history systems of punishment have often served the economic purposes of the state, first as a source of slave labor, later as a source of fines. Many of the well-meaning efforts of reformers to rehabilitate offenders during the last two centuries turned out to be fruitless, but they shaped the correctional system into the form it has today, a mix of punishment and reform efforts.

Prison overcrowding is a particularly American phenomenon, resulting from punitiveness fueled by the drug problem and resulting violence. The traditional forms of alternative corrections, probation and parole, are still viable, but recognition of their limitations has led to the development of innovative forms of intermediate corrections, such as intensive supervision programs, home confinement programs, shock programs, restitution programs, fine systems, and community service programs.

In the midst of the prison overcrowding crisis, legislators have rushed to adopt alternative programs that have not yet been thoroughly evaluated. Curiously, this phenomenon has marked the history of corrections. Programs have often been adopted without proof of their effectiveness. Criminologists have a great role to play in shaping humane and cost-beneficial reactions to crime which do not extend the net of control to ever-growing numbers of citizens.[112]

There is no end to experimentation in the search for alternatives to prison. So far we have been accustomed to measuring punishment in terms of time—time forfeited for the criminal harm inflicted. It has not always been that way. In Biblical times the measure was an eye for an eye. At other times it was recompense for the criminally inflicted harm: I lost one man, you give me one of yours; you injured my kinsman, nurse him back to health. Later the measure of response to crime was service: work as a galley slave or in the salt mines or on a public construction project. In the Middle Ages physical suffering was the measure of punishment: torture and death. Only since the time of Beccaria (Chapter 3) has straight time been the measure of punishment. Having recently gone through an era in which the need for rehabilitation nearly determined the measure of punishment, and after a brief return to straight time (the just-deserts movement), we seem to be headed for a new era in which the measure of punishment is likely to be a composite of the following:

• The need to protect society (by, among other things, reintegrating the offender into society).
• The need to compensate society for its loss through crime.
• The need to compensate the victims of crime for their losses.

Whatever the developments, it will remain the task of criminologists to monitor and evaluate those developments.

KEY TERMS

conjugal visits
corrections
employment prisons
fee system
good time system
inmate code
intensive supervision probation (ISP)

parole
penitentiary
prisonization
probation
rehabilitation
shock probation
split sentence

NOTES

1. Gore v. United States, 357 U.S. 386 (1958), at 393.

2. Rudolf His, *Deutsches Strafrecht bis zur Karolina* (Munich and Berlin: R. Oldenbourg, 1928), pp. 58–60.

3. Georg Rusche and Otto Kirchheimer, *Punishment and Social Structure* (New York: Columbia University Press, 1939), p. 9. The book has a foreword by Thorsten Sellin.

4. Thorsten Sellin, "Two Myths in the History of Capital Punishment," *Journal of Criminal Law and Criminology* 50 (1959): 114–117.

5. Thorsten Sellin, *Slavery and the Penal System* (New York: Elsevier, 1976), p. 54.

6. George Ives, *A History of Penal Methods* (1914; Montclair, N.J.: Patterson Smith, 1970), p. 104.

7. Sellin, *Slavery and the Penal System*, pp. 54–55.

8. Ibid., p. 71.

9. Ibid., pp. 77, 101.

10. Geneva Convention Relative to the Treatment of Prisoners of War, of August 12, 1949, art. 22.

11. Sellin, *Slavery and the Penal System*, p. 101.

12. It is estimated that 100,000 convicts were transported from England to the American colonies and Australia over a period of nearly two hundred years: J. J. Tobias, *Nineteenth-Century Crime: Prevention and Punishment* (Newton, Mass.: David & Charles, 1972); C. R. Henderson, *Penal and Reformatory Institutions* (New York: Charities, 1910).

13. Graeme R. Newman, *The Punishment Re-*

sponse (Philadelphia: Lippincott, 1978), p. 121.

14. Harry Elmer Barnes and Negley K. Teeters, *New Horizons in Criminology*, rev. ed. (New York: Prentice-Hall, 1945), p. 505.

15. *Attica: The Official Report of the New York Special Commission on Attica* (McKay Commission report) (New York: Bantam, 1972); Herman Badillo and Milton Haynes, *A Bill of No Rights: Attica and the American Prison System* (New York: Outerbridge & Lazard, 1972). For an astute analysis of conditions leading to prison riots and management proposals for the future, see Edith E. Flynn, "From Conflict Theory to Conflict Resolution: Controlling Collective Violence in Prisons," *American Behavioral Scientist* 23 (1980): 745–776. For an overall account of prison riots, see Bert Useem and Peter Kimball, *States of Siege: U.S. Prison Riots, 1971–1986* (New York: Oxford University Press, 1989).

16. "Standard Minimum Rules for the Treatment of Prisoners," in Center for Human Rights, *Human Rights: A Compilation of International Instruments* (New York: United Nations, 1988), pp. 190–209; Douglas J. Besharov and Gerhard O. W. Mueller, "The Demands of the Inmates of Attica State Prison and the United Nations Standard Minimum Rules for the Treatment of Prisoners: A Comparison," *Buffalo Law Review* 21 (1972): 839–854.

17. In Cooper v. Pate, 378 U.S. 546 (1964), the Supreme Court declared that prisoners may sue "the system" for infringement of their civil rights under the Civil Rights Act of 1871. For an account of the prisoners' rights movement, see James B. Jacobs, *New Perspectives on Prisons and Imprisonment* (Ithaca, N.Y.: Cornell University Press, 1983); Geoffrey P. Repert, ed. *Legal Rights of Prisoners* (Beverly Hills, Calif.: Sage, 1980); Penelope D. Clute, *The Legal Aspects of Prisons and Jails* (Springfield, Ill.: Charles C Thomas, 1980); Leonard Orland, *Prisons: Houses of Darkness* (New York: Free Press, 1975).

18. Stroud v. Swope, 187 F.2d 850 (9th Cir. 1951).

19. Peter W. Greenwood, "Controlling the Crime Rate Through Imprisonment," in *Crime and Public Policy*, ed. James Q. Wilson (San Francisco: Institute for Contemporary Studies, 1983), pp. 251–269; Peter W. Greenwood and Allan Abrahams, *Selective Incapacitation* (Santa Monica, Calif.: Rand Corporation, 1982).

20. U.S. Department of Justice, Bureau of Justice Statistics, *Annual Report, Fiscal 1988* (Washington, D.C.: U.S. Government Printing Office, 1989).

21. Up 12 percent since 1975. See U.S. Department of Justice, Bureau of Justice Statistics, *Children in Custody, 1975–85* (Washington, D.C.: U.S. Government Printing Office, 1989). There were 1.2 million admissions in 1984. But see Allen J. Beck, Susan A. Kline, and Lawrence A. Greenfield, *Survey of Youth in Custody, 1987* (Washington, D.C.: U.S. Government Printing Office, 1988), p. 2, which gives a 1985 census of 51,402 residents in juvenile facilities.

22. Todd R. Clear and George F. Cole, *American Corrections* (Monterey, Calif.: Brooks/Cole, 1986), p. 198.

23. U.S. Department of Justice, Bureau of Justice Statistics, *Prisoners in 1988* (Washington, D.C.: U.S. Government Printing Office, 1989).

24. U.S. Department of Justice, Bureau of Justice Statistics, *Report to the Nation on Crime and Justice*, 2d ed. (Washington, D.C.: U.S. Government Printing Office, 1988), p. 124.

25. Clear and Cole, *American Corrections*, p. 226.

26. Hans Mattick, "The Contemporary Jail in the United States," in *Handbook of Criminology*, ed. Daniel Glaser (Chicago: Rand McNally, 1974).

27. Freda Adler, "Jails as a Repository for Former Mental Patients," *International Journal of Offender Therapy and Comparative Criminology* 30 (1986): 225–236.

28. See John J. Gibbs, "Symptoms of Psychopathology among Jail Prisoners: The Effects of Exposure to the Jail Environment," *Criminal Justice and Behavior* 14 (1987): 288–310. John R. Belcher, "Are Jails Replacing the Mental Health System for the Homeless Mentally Ill?" *Community Mental*

Health Journal 24 (1988): 185–195, recommending changes in the mental health system so as to prevent the criminalization of the homeless mentally ill. See also State of Illinois, *Mentally Retarded and Mentally Ill Offender Task Force Report* (Springfield, 1988).

29. Henry J. Steadman, Dennis W. McCarty, and Joseph P. Morrissey, *The Mentally Ill in Jail: Planning for Essential Services* (New York: Guilford, 1989); see also Peter Finn, "Coordinating Services for the Mentally Ill Misdemeanor Offender," *Social Service Review* 63 (1989): 127–141.

30. The literature on imprisonment is vast. For some of the most challenging assessments (besides those mentioned elsewhere in this section), see Benedict S. Alper, *Prisons Inside Out* (Cambridge, Mass.: Ballinger, 1974); Richard Hawkins and Geoffrey P. Alpert, *American Prison Systems: Punishment and Justice* (Englewood Cliffs, N.J.: Prentice-Hall, 1989).

31. See Clear and Cole, *American Corrections*, p. 279.

32. Charles F. Wellford and Laure Weber Brooks, *Correlates of Incarceration Rates: Explaining the Pattern of Incarceration Between 1970 and 1979* (College Park: Institute of Criminal Justice and Criminology, University of Maryland, 1984).

33. Stephen D. Gottfredson and Sean McConville, eds., *America's Correctional Crisis: Prison Populations and Public Policy* (New York: Greenwood, 1987), p. 3, with contributions by Barton L. Ingraham and Charles F. Wellford, Todd R. Clear and Patricia Harris, Ralph B. Taylor, Joan Mullen, Eryl Hall Williams, Don Gottfredson, Alfred Blumstein, Alan T. Harland, and Philip W. Harris and M. Kay Harris. For overcrowding problems of jails see John M. Klofus, "The Jail and the Community," *Justice Quarterly* 7 (1990): 69–102.

34. Donald Clemmer, *The Prison Community* (New York: Holt, Rinehart & Winston, 1965).

35. Gresham M. Sykes, *The Society of Captives: A Study of a Maximum Security Prison* (Princeton, N.J.: Princeton University Press, 1974).

36. J. Q. Burstein, *Conjugal Visits in Prison: Psychological and Social Consequences* (Lexington, Mass.: Lexington Books, 1977); Ann Goetting, "Conjugal Association in Prison: Issues and Perspectives," *Crime and Delinquency* 28 (1982): 52–71; Randolph Davis, "Education and the Impact of the Family Reunion Program in a Maximum Security Prison," *Journal of Offender Counseling, Services, and Rehabilitation* 12, no. 2 (1988): 153–159.

37. Gresham M. Sykes and Sheldon L. Messinger, "The Inmate Social System," in Richard A. Cloward et al., *Theoretical Studies in Social Organization of the Prison* (New York: Social Science Council, 1960).

38. Clarence Schrag, "Some Foundations for a Theory of Corrections," in *The Prison: Studies in Institutional Organization and Change,* ed. Donald R. Cressey (New York: Holt, Rinehart & Winston, 1961). For a comparative analysis see William G. Archambeault and Charles Fenwick, "A Comparative Analysis of Culture, Safety, and Organizational Management Factors in Japan and U.S. Prisons," *Prison Journal* 68 (1988): 3–23.

39. Charles W. Thomas, "Prisonization or Resocialization: A Study of External Factors Associated with the Impact of Imprisonment," *Journal of Research in Crime and Delinquency* 10 (1973): 13–21.

40. Stanton L. Wheeler, "Socialization in Correctional Institutions," in *Handbook of Socialization Theory and Research,* ed. D. A. Goslin (Chicago: Rand McNally, 1969).

41. Ulla V. Bondeson, *Prisoners in Prison Societies* (New Brunswick, N.J.: Transaction, 1989). For a discussion of the failure of prisons, see Gerhard O. W. Mueller, "Economic Failures in the Iron Womb: The Birth of Rational Alternatives to Imprisonment," in *Sentencing: Process and Purpose* (Springfield, Ill.: Charles C Thomas, 1977), pp. 110–143.

42. Kevin N. Wright, "Race and Economic Marginality in Explaining Prison Adjustment," *Journal of Research in Crime and Delinquency* 26 (1989): 67–89.

43. Hans Toch, Kenneth Adams, and Douglas J. Grant, *Coping: Maladaptation in Prisons*

(New Brunswick, N.J.: Transaction, 1989). See Ester Heffernan, *Making It in Prison: The Square, the Cool, and the Life* (New York: Wiley-Interscience, 1972), for an analysis of adaptation processes in women's prisons.

44. Mark S. Fleisher, *Warehousing Violence* (Newbury Park, Calif.: Sage, 1989). See also Albert K. Cohen, George F. Coke, and Robert G. Bailey, eds., *Prison Violence* (Lexington, Mass.: Lexington Books, 1976).

45. James F. Houston, Don C. Gibbons, and Joseph F. Jones, "Physical Environment and Jail Social Climate," *Crime and Delinquency* 34 (1988): 449–466.

46. Frank S. Pearson, "Evaluation of New Jersey's Intensive Supervision Program," *Crime and Delinquency* 34 (1988): 437–448.

47. R. G. Leger, "Perception of Crowding, Racial Antagonism, and Aggression in a Custodial Prison," *Journal of Criminal Justice* 16 (1988): 167–181, at p. 178.

48. James W. Marquart, *Cooptation of the Kept: Maintaining Control in a Southern Penitentiary* (Ann Arbor, MI: University Microfilms, 1983).

49. Kelsey Kaufman, *Prison Officers and Their World* (Cambridge, Mass.: Harvard University Press, 1988).

50. Barbara A. Owen, *The Reproduction of Social Control: A Study of Prison Workers at San Quentin* (New York: Praeger, 1988).

51. Sellin, *Slavery and the Penal System*, p. 143.

52. Barnes and Teeters, *New Horizons in Criminology*, p. 702.

53. Clear and Cole, *American Corrections*, pp. 333–338.

54. Institute for Economic and Policy Studies, *The Economic Impact of Corcraft Correctional Industries in New York State* (Alexandria, Va., 1988).

55. Florida, House of Representatives, Committee on Corrections, Probation & Parole, *Oversight Report on PRIDE* (Tallahassee, 1988).

56. Kathleen E. Maguire, Timothy J. Flanagan, and Terence P. Thornberry, "Prison Labor and Recidivism," *Journal of Quantitative Criminology* 4 (1988): 3–18.

57. See Rusche and Kirchheimer, *Punishment and Social Structure*; Torsten Eriksson, *The Reformers: An Historical Survey of Pioneer Experiments in the Treatment of Criminals* (New York: Elsevier, 1976); and Sellin, *Slavery and the Penal System*.

58. L. Sechrest, S. O. White, and E. D. Brown, eds., *The Rehabilitation of Criminal Offenders: Problems and Prospects* (Washington, D.C.: National Academy of Sciences, 1979).

59. Daniel Glaser, *The Effectiveness of a Prison and Parole System* (Indianapolis: Bobbs-Merrill, 1964).

60. Walter C. Bailey, "Correctional Outcome: An Evaluation of 100 Reports," *Journal of Criminal Law, Criminology, and Police Science* 57 (1966): 153–160, at p. 157.

61. Roger Hood, "Research on the Effectiveness of Punishments and Treatments," in Council of Europe, European Committee on Crime Problems, *Collected Studies in Criminological Research* (Strasbourg, 1967).

62. James Robison and Gerald Smith, "The Effectiveness of Correctional Programs," *Crime and Delinquency* 17 (1971): 67–80.

63. Freda Adler, Arthur D. Moffett, Frederick B. Glaser, John C. Ball, and Diane Horwitz, *A Systems Approach to Drug Treatment* (Philadelphia: Dorrance, 1974).

64. Douglas Lipton, Robert Martinson, and Judith Wilks, *The Effectiveness of Correctional Treatment: A Survey of Treatment Evaluation Studies* (New York: Praeger, 1975); Robert Martinson, "What Works?: Questions and Answers About Prison Reform," *Public Policy* 35 (1974): 22–54.

65. Carl B. Klockars, "The True Limits of the Effectiveness of Correctional Treatment," *Prison Journal* 55, no. 1 (1975): 53–64; Ted Palmer, "Martinson Revisited," *Journal of Research in Crime and Delinquency* 12 (1975): 133–152.

66. Robert Martinson, "New Findings, New Views: A Note of Caution Regarding Sentencing Reform," *Hofstra Law Review* 7 (1979): 254–258.

67. Paul Gendreau and Bob Ross, "Effective Correctional Treatment: Bibliotherapy for Cynics," *Crime and Delinquency* 25 (1979): 463–489. See also Michael R. Gottfredson, "Treatment Destruction Techniques," *Journal of Research in Crime and Delinquency* 16 (1979): 39–54.

68. Paul Gendreau and Robert R. Ross, "Revivification of Rehabilitation: Evidence from the 1980s," *Justice Quarterly* 4 (1987): 395; Francis T. Cullen and Paul Gendreau, "The Effectiveness of Correctional Rehabilitation: Reconsidering the 'Nothing Works' Debate," in *The American Prison: Issues in Research and Policy,* ed. Lynne Goodstein and Doris Layton Mackenzie, pp. 23–44 (New York: Plenum, 1989).

69. Carol J. Garrett, "Effects of Residential Treatment on Adjudicated Delinquents: A Meta-analysis," *Journal of Research in Crime and Delinquency* 22 (1985): 287–308; Alexander B. Smith and Louis Berlin, *Treating the Criminal Offender,* 3d ed. (New York: Plenum, 1988); Cullen and Gendreau, "Effectiveness of Correctional Rehabilitation."

70. Francis T. Cullen and Karen E. Gilbert, *Reaffirming Rehabilitation* (Cincinnati: Anderson, 1982), p. 247.

71. Cathy Potler, *AIDS in Prison: A Crisis in New York State Corrections* (New York: Correctional Association of New York, 1988).

72. For a general overview, see "Privatization of Corrections," special issue of *Corrections Today* 50 (1988), with articles by Samuel F. Saxton, Bob Turner, T. Don Hulto and James D. Henderson, Edward J. Loughran, Merle E. Springer, and Michael J. Mahoney.

73. For the lesson to be learned from our experience with private prisons in the nineteenth and early twentieth centuries (namely, caution), see Alexis M. Durham III, "Origins of Interest in the Privatization of Punishment: The Nineteenth and Twentieth Century American Experience," *Criminology* 27 (1989): 107–139.

74. Quoted in Kevin Krajick, "Punishment for Profit," *Across the Road* 21 (1984): 25.

75. J. C. Hackett, H. P. Hatry, R. B. Levinson, J. Allen, K. Chi, and E. D. Feigenbaum, *Issues in Contracting for the Operation of Prisons and Jails,* for National Institute of Justice (Washington, D.C.: U.S. Government Printing Office, 1986).

76. Ira P. Robbins, "Privatization of Corrections: Defining the Issues," *Federal Probation* 50, no. 3 (1986): 24–30.

77. Ira P. Robbins, *The Legal Dimensions of Private Incarceration* (Washington, D.C.: American Bar Association, 1988), including a model contract form and a model statute.

78. Barbara J. Auerbach et al., *Work in American Prisons: The Private Sector Gets Involved,* for National Institute of Justice (Washington, D.C.: U.S. Government Printing Office, 1988).

79. Samuel Jan Broker, "Prison Management, Private Enterprise Style: The Inmates' Evaluation," *New England Journal on Criminal and Civil Confinement* 14 (1988): 175–244.

80. Sheldon Glueck, Introduction to *John Augustus, First Probation Officer* (N.p.: National Probation Association, 1939), p. xvi.

81. R. M. Carter and L. T. Wilkins, *Probation and Parole: Selected Readings* (New York: Wiley, 1970).

82. Gennaro F. Vito, "Developments in Shock Probation: A Review of Research Findings and Policy Implications," *Federal Probation* 48 (1984): 22–27.

83. Calculated from Contact Center, Inc., *Corrections Compendium* (Lincoln, Nebr., 1987), pp. 9–13.

84. U.S. Department of Justice, Bureau of Justice Statistics, *Correctional Population in the United States, 1987* (Washington, D.C.: U.S. Government Printing Office, 1989), p. 22.

85. Lawrence Greenfield, *Probation and Parole, 1984* (Washington, D.C.: U.S. Government Printing Office, 1986).

86. Edward J. Latessa and Gennaro F. Vito, "The Effects of Intensive Supervision on Shock Probationers," *Journal of Criminal Justice* 16 (1988): 319–330. See also Doris Layton Mackenzie and James W. Shaw,

"Inmate Adjustment and Change During Shock Incarceration: The Impact of Correctional Boot Camp Programs," *Justice Quarterly* 7 (1990): 125–150.

87. J. O. Finckenauer, *Scared Straight and the Panacea Phenomenon* (Englewood Cliffs, N.J.: Prentice-Hall, 1982).

88. Robert L. Spangenberg et al., *Assessment of the Massachusetts Probation System* (Newton, Mass.: Spangenberg Group, 1987).

89. Robert L. Thomas, "Stress Perception Among Select Federal Probation and Pretrial Services Officers and Their Supervisors," *Federal Probation* 52, no. 3 (1988): 48–58.

90. Alexander Maconochie as quoted in Barnes and Teeters, *New Horizons in Criminology,* p. 548.

91. Don M. Gottfredson, M. G. Neithercutt, Joan Nuffield, and Vincent O'Leary, *Four Thousand Lifetimes: A Study of Time Served and Parole Outcomes* (Davis, Calif.: National Council on Crime and Delinquency, Research Center, 1973).

92. U.S. Department of Justice, Bureau of Justice Statistics, *Correctional Populations in the United States* (Washington, D.C.: U.S. Government Printing Office, 1989), p. 124.

93. M. K. Harris, "Disquisition on the Need for a New Model for Criminal Sanctioning Systems," *West Virginia Law Review* 77 (1975): 263–301.

94. Andrew von Hirsch and Kathleen J. Hanrahan, *The Question of Parole: Retention, Reform, or Abolition?* (Cambridge, Mass.: Ballinger, 1979).

95. U.S. Department of Justice, Bureau of Justice Statistics, *Parole Today* (Washington, D.C.: U.S. Government Printing Office, 1980), p. 11. It is noteworthy, however, that though parole releases declined from 72 percent to 43 percent of prison discharges between 1977 and 1985, they rose again by 47 percent from August 1983 through 1987: Bureau of Justice Statistics, *Annual Report, Fiscal 1988,* p. 59.

96. Norval Morris and Michael H. Tonry, *Between Prison and Probation* (New York: Oxford University Press, 1990); David Weisburd and Ellen F. Chayet, "Good Time: An Agenda for Research," *Criminal Justice and Behavior* 16 (1989): 183–195.

97. Sandra Evans Skovron, Joseph E. Scott, and Francis T. Cullen, "Prison Crowding: Public Attitudes Toward Strategies of Population Control," *Journal of Research in Crime and Delinquency* 25 (1988): 150–169.

98. This section is based on Edna McConnel Clark Foundation, *Overcrowded Time: Why Prisons Are So Crowded and What Can Be Done* (New York, 1982).

99. See William B. Lawless and Gerhard O. W. Mueller, *Report of the Commission to Advise the Nevada Legislature on the Question of Prison Overcrowding* (Reno, Nev.: National Judicial College, 1989).

100. New Jersey Criminal Disposition Commission, "Report to the Governor and Legislature, 1987," on file at NCCD Library, Rutgers University.

101. Frank S. Pearson, *Research on New Jersey's Intensive Supervision Program: Final Report* (New Brunswick, N.J.: Institute for Criminological Research, Rutgers, The State University of New Jersey, 1987).

102. Susan B. Noonan and Edward J. Latessa, "Intensive Probation: An Examination of Recidivism and Social Adjustment for an Intensive Supervision Program," *American Journal of Criminal Justice* 12 (1987): 45–61.

103. Latessa and Vito, "Effects of Intensive Supervision."

104. Virginia, Department of Corrections, Research and Evaluation Unit, *Intensive Supervision Program: Final Evaluation Report Client Characteristics and Supervision Outcomes: A Caseload Comparison* (Richmond, 1988).

105. Joan Petersilia, *Expanding Options for Criminal Sentencing* (Santa Monica, Calif.: Rand Corporation, 1987), p. 32; and see Joan Petersilia, *Exploring the Option of House Arrest* (Santa Monica, Calif.: Rand Corporation, 1986).

106. See Barton L. Ingraham and Gerald W.

Smith, "The Use of Electronics in the Observation and Control of Human Behavior and Its Possible Use in Rehabilitation and Parole," *Issues in Criminology* 7, no. 2 (1972): 35–53; George E. Rush, "Electronic Surveillance: An Alternative to Incarceration," *American Journal of Criminal Justice* 12 (1989): 219–242. For a detailed discussion of psycholegal effects of home confinement, see Dorothy K. Kagehiro and Ralph Taylor, "A Social Psychological Analysis of Home Electronic Confinement," in *Handbook of Psychology and Law*, ed. D. K. Kagehiro and W. S. Laufer (New York: Springer-Verlag, in press).

107. For a pilot study on a limited number of home confinement offenders, see Paulette Hatchett, *The Home Confinement Program: An Appraisal of the Electronic Monitoring of Offenders in Washtenaw County, Michigan* (Lansing: Community Programs Evaluation Unit, Michigan Department of Corrections, 1987).

108. Criminal Law Education and Research Center, *International Conference of Correctional Policy Makers* (New York: New York University School of Law, 1973).

109. Burt Galaway, "Restitution as Innovation or Unfulfilled Promise?" *Federal Probation* 52, no. 3 (1988): 3–14.

110. Joe Hudson and Burt Galaway, "Financial Restitution: Toward an Evaluable Program Model," *Canadian Journal of Criminology* 31 (1989): 1–18.

111. James M. Byrne, "Assessing What Works in the Adult Community Corrections Systems," p. 10 (paper presented at the 1990 Annual Meeting of the Academy of Criminal Justice Sciences, Denver, March 16, 1990). We thank Mr. Byrne for permission to cite his work here.

112. James Austin and Barry Krisberg, "The Unmet Promise of Alternatives to Incarceration," *Crime and Delinquency* 28 (1982): 374–409.

EPILOGUE

Few criminologists have attempted to predict the development and future of criminology. Those who have done so have often failed. Forecasts made in the 1970s about the situation in the early 1990s have proved largely incorrect. A single scientific breakthrough, such as the discovery of nuclear energy, or the emergence of a single individual, such as a Napoleon or a Gorbachev, can drastically and suddenly alter the course of history. For example, the socioeconomic and political changes that began in Eastern Europe in 1989 could not have been predicted. Yet these developments have had a profound impact in many areas, including criminology, because of the changes they have brought about in employment patterns, worldwide communication and transportation, international cooperation, and increased international economic interdependency. Let us nevertheless consider what the near future may hold in relation to the topics covered in the four parts of *Criminology*.

PART I: UNDERSTANDING CRIMINOLOGY

Criminology will continue to study the making of laws, the breaking of laws, and reactions to the breaking of laws. However, in view of an increasing understanding of the interdependency of crime with social, economic, political, biological, psychological, and environmental factors, it is inescapable that the relationship between criminologists and their colleagues in other disciplines will become more integrated. The conditions that seemed to add up to a sociological monopoly in criminology are not likely to persist.

Moreover, criminology will become far more international than it has been in the past. The growing openness in east-west relations bodes well for joint and cooperative criminological research. However, the developing countries are not likely to benefit from this cooperative spirit for some time, because the developed western countries have not yet made any major investment in crime prevention and criminal justice efforts in these third-world countries. Unassisted, these countries may not have the capacity to cope effectively with their crime problems. Research

4 international

has demonstrated that the crime problems of developed and developing countries are interdependent. This situation poses a major challenge to criminology.

Over the last few decades criminologists have made great progress in measuring the characteristics of crime, criminals, and victims. Among the most promising advances in the measurement of crime is the National Incident Based Reporting System (NIBRS). New methods of gathering data, such as the NIBRS, will enhance our ability to test criminological theories more precisely. Such methods will also enhance our understanding of the situational characteristics of crimes, with a view toward development of more effective prevention strategies, and will help us to make more efficient use of the criminal justice system.

There is, however, another side to the increasing sophistication of criminological research methods: the danger that practitioners in the field (legislators, police officials, judges, and correctional administrators) may not fully appreciate the implications of the findings. A major challenge for the field of criminology is to bridge the gap between theory and practice.

PART II: EXPLANATIONS OF CRIMINAL BEHAVIOR

The midtwentieth century has been an era of theory construction in criminology. Some criminologists deem it unlikely that there will be additional theoretical breakthroughs in explaining criminal behavior. They are searching for further advances in criminological theory through refinement of existing theories with improved state-of-the-art statistical techniques.

What is more likely is that there will be significant advances in biological theory, especially genetics. The implications of the findings in biological research for understanding criminality are considerable. Just as the discovery of social causes of crime (e.g., poverty, inequality, and racial discrimination) has led to social efforts to prevent crime, the discovery of biological causes of crime may lead to biogenetic approaches to crime prevention. This possibility and its ethical implications are awesome.

PART III: TYPES OF CRIME

The focus is likely to continue shifting from the characteristics of criminals to the characteristics of crimes. We can expect that research on intrafamily crime, political offenses (especially assassinations), and terrorist events will receive high priority, because these crimes have not yet received the same degree of attention as traditional crimes of violence. Rapid developments in the mode of conducting commercial transactions are likely to afford new opportunities for criminals to commit property crimes, as well as posing new challenges to criminologists. Credit card fraud and computer crime are examples.

In organizational crime two developments are expected. Criminologists will likely, first, pay increasing attention to the measurement and nature of this type of crime and, second, play an increasing role in fashioning responses to it. Criminologists have long explained that organizations function through the decisions of individuals. In recent years prosecutors have singled out for prosecution those persons most responsible for organizational crimes. The apparent success of these prosecutions may well lead to further research on the criminal behavior of individuals within organizations. Yet whether this research will lead to a consensus on how organizational crime can best be controlled—by prosecuting individuals or by prosecuting corporations—remains to be resolved. Corporate criminal liability may remain the preferred approach for some forms of organizational crime (e.g., violation of environmental protection statutes), and individual criminal liability may prove to be the most effective prevention strategy for other types of organizational crime (e.g., RICO violations, bribery, political corruption).

Despite all the attention given to the drug problem in the United States and throughout the world, there is as yet no agreement on a realistic policy for preventing drug-related crime. Until significant criminological research can demonstrate the potential success of any given strategy, drug-related crime is likely to remain a major problem in all parts of the world.

PART IV: A CRIMINOLOGICAL APPROACH TO THE CRIMINAL JUSTICE SYSTEM

Less than a generation ago, criminologists discovered that criminal justice is in fact a system. The functioning of this system has come under strong criminological scrutiny. Many criminologists have focused their attention on how it deals with conventional criminality, predominantly "street crime." It seemed as if criminal justice were concerned solely with conventional criminality. Yet, as we have demonstrated throughout this book, there are also many forms of nonconventional crimes, such as securities violations, tax offenses, and environmental crimes, which are not of the street-crime variety and which, for the most part, have not been dealt with by the criminal justice system.

There is, in fact, a parallel justice system—much less visible, far less understood, and rarely studied—that deals with these types of offenses. In this system, the process is not invoked by officers at police precincts but rather by officials in federal, state, and local administrative agencies. This system consists of hearing panels, commissions, and administrative tribunals, with or without intervention of criminal courts. The sanctions of this parallel system also tend to vary, ranging from forfeitures, damages, and fines to occasional confinement in a minimum-security correctional facility. The enormous outreach of this parallel system is gradually becoming apparent. During the next decade and beyond, criminologists are likely to focus their research on it in order to make it as visible and manageable as the principal criminal justice system. There is a great potential for innovative research in this area.

The next decade is likely also to witness the emergence of a third criminal justice system: international criminal justice. As already indicated, the globalization of crime makes such a system necessary. Nations acting separately cannot possibly cope with the various forms of transnational and international crime. Emergence of an international criminal justice system is unavoidable, and criminologists will play a major role in constructing this system and in evaluating its functioning.

In all probability the police will receive far greater criminological attention in the future than it has in the past. In particular, with the emergence of private policing, criminologists are likely to study the distribution of public and private policing responsibilities and the consequences of that distribution. Moreover, with the rapid advance of technology in crime detection and prevention, policing and research on policing will come under additional scrutiny because of the danger to civil liberties posed by electronic policing. This issue is closely tied to effective functioning of the police within the community, another subject likely to receive continuing interest from researchers.

Both the courts and the correctional system will continue to search for cost-beneficial and humane methods for dealing with offenders. A large part of criminological research will be focused on this problem. For example, while states have adopted a variety of sentencing methods, including fixed sentences, indeterminate sentences, and guideline sentences, relatively little research has been conducted on the impact of the divergent approaches. Legislatures in the future are likely to insist on evaluative research in this area. Likewise, because of increasing use of alternatives to imprisonment, legislators are becoming insistent about the necessity of obtaining evaluations of the various choices.

We began *Criminology* by looking at the enormous reach of criminological curiosity. We suggested that very little happens anywhere in the world that does not have criminological implications. We have probed these implications throughout and have pointed to the future with its continuing challenge to explain the making of laws, the breaking of laws, and society's reaction to the breaking of laws.

GLOSSARY

Accomplice
A person who helps another to commit a crime.

Aggravated assault
An attack on another person in which the perpetrator inflicts serious harm on the victim or uses a deadly weapon.

Aging-out phenomenon
A concept which holds that offenders commit less crime as they get older because they have less strength, initiative, stamina, and mobility.

Anomic suicide
A suicide that occurs in a time of economic change when the individual experiences a dramatic change in lifestyle and is thrown into an unfamiliar and personally unsatisfying way of life.

Anomie
A societal state marked by "normlessness," in which disintegration and chaos have replaced social cohesion.

Arraignment
First stage of the trial process, at which the indictment or information is read in open court and the defendant is requested to respond thereto.

Arson
At common law, the malicious burning of the dwelling house of another. This definition has been broadened by state statutes and criminal codes to cover the burning of other structures or even personal property.

Assassination
The murder of a head of state or government, or other highly important public figure.

Assault
At common law, an unlawful offer or attempt with force or violence to do a corporal hurt to another.

Atavistic stigmata
Physical features of a human being at an earlier stage of development, which—according to Cesare Lombroso—distinguish a born criminal from the general population.

Attachment
A variable used by Travis Hirschi to describe the bond between individuals and their family, friends, and school.

Bankruptcy fraud
A scam in which an individual falsely attempts to claim bankruptcy (and thereby erase financial debts) by taking advantage of loopholes in the laws.

Bank Secrecy Act
Federal Statute protecting the confidentiality of banking transactions, but which makes certain information available to the government in connection with criminal proceedings.

Battery
Common law crime consisting of the intentional touching or inflicting of hurt on another.

Behavioral modeling
Learning how to behave by fashioning one's behavior after that of others.

Belief
A variable used by Travis Hirschi to describe the extent to which an individual subscribes to society's values.

Biocriminology
The subdiscipline of criminology that investigates biological and genetic factors and their relation to criminal behavior.

Birth cohort
A group consisting of all individuals born in the same year.

Boiler room
An operation run by one or more stock manipulators who, through deception and misleading sales techniques, seduce the unsuspecting and uninformed public into buying stocks in obscure and often poorly financed corporations.

Burglary
At common law, the nighttime breaking and entering of the dwelling house of another, with the intention to commit a crime or larceny therein. A felony.

Career criminal
An individual who repeatedly engages in criminal activity and whose life revolves around crime.

Case study
An analysis of all pertinent aspects of one unit of study.

Certiorari, writ of
A writ issued by a higher court directing a lower court to prepare the record of a case and send it to the higher court for review.

Challenge for cause
A challenge to remove a potential juror because of his or her inability to render a fair and impartial decision in a case. *See also* Peremptory challenges; Voir dire.

Check forging
The criminal offense of making or altering a check with intent to defraud.

Chromosomes
Basic cellular structures containing genes, i.e., biological material that creates individuality.

Churning
Frequent trading, by a broker, of a client's shares of stock, for the sole purpose of generating large commissions.

Classical school of criminology
A criminological perspective suggesting that: (1) people have free will to choose criminal or conventional behavior; (2) people choose to commit crime for rea-

sons of greed or personal need; and (3) crime can be controlled by criminal sanctions, which should be proportionate to the guilt of the perpetrator.

Commitment
A variable used by Travis Hirschi to describe an individual's support of and participation in a program, cause, or social activity, which ties the individual to the moral or ethical codes of society.

Community policing
A strategy that relies on public confidence and citizen cooperation to help prevent crime and make the residents of a community feel more secure.

Computer espionage
Activities by which unauthorized computer access yields information from data bases belonging to government or private parties, for purposes of exploitation.

Computer fraud
Falsification of stored data or deception in legitimate transactions by manipulation of data or programming, including the unlawful acquisition of data or programs for purposes of financial gain.

Computer hacking
In criminology, activities that include the gaining of unauthorized access to data banks for malicious though not necessarily destructive purposes, and for neither financial gain nor purposes of espionage.

Computer sabotage
The tampering with, or destruction or scrambling of, data or software through unlawful access to data banks.

Conditioning
The process of developing a behavior pattern through a series of repeated experiences.

Conduct norms
Norms that regulate the daily lives of people and that reflect the attitudes of the groups to which they belong.

Confidence game
A deceptive means of obtaining money or property from a victim who is led to trust the perpetrator.

Conflict theory
A model of crime in which the criminal justice system is seen as being used by the ruling class to control the lower class. Criminological investigation of the conflicts of society is emphasized.

Conformity
Correspondence of an individual's behavior to society's patterns, norms, or standards.

Conjugal visits
A program that permits prisoners to have contact with their spouses or significant others in order to maintain their relationships.

Consensus model
A model of criminal lawmaking that assumes that members of society agree on what is right and wrong, and that law is the codification of agreed-upon social values.

Constable
An officer, established by the Statute of Winchester in 1285, who was responsible for suppressing riots and violent crimes in each county. Later, a local law enforcement officer.

Consumer fraud
Causing a consumer to surrender money through deceit or a misrepresentation of a material fact.

Containment theory
A theory that posits that every person possesses a containing external structure and a protective internal structure, both of which provide defense, protection, or insulation against delinquency.

Corrections
Implementation and execution of sentences imposed by the courts; the system that administers those sentences.

Cortical arousal

Activation of the cerebral cortex, a structure of the brain which is responsible for higher intellectual functioning, information processing, and decision making.

Criminal attempt

An act or omission constituting a substantial step in a course of conduct planned to culminate in the commission of a crime.

Cross-sectional study

An analysis that focuses on a particular group conducted at a single point in time.

Cultural deviance theories

Theories that posit that crime results from cultural values that permit, or even demand, behavior in violation of the law.

Cultural transmission

A theory that views delinquency as a socially learned behavior transmitted from one generation to the next in disorganized urban areas.

Culture conflict theory

A theory that posits that two groups may clash when their conduct norms differ.

Culture of poverty

A culture characterized by helplessness, cynicism, and mistrust of authority as represented by schools and police.

Data

Collected facts, observations, and other pertinent information from which conclusions can be drawn.

Defense counsel

A lawyer retained by an individual accused of committing a crime, or assigned by the court if the individual is unable to pay.

Deterrence

The theory of punishment that envisages that potential offenders will refrain from committing crimes for fear of punishment (sometimes called general prevention).

Deviance

A broad concept encompassing both illegal behavior and behavior that departs from the social norm.

Differential association–reinforcement

A theory of criminality based on an incorporation of psychological learning theory and differential association with social learning theory; criminal behavior, the theory claims, is learned through associations and is contained or discontinued as a result of positive or negative reinforcements.

Differential association theory

A theory of criminality based on the principle that an individual becomes delinquent because of an excess of definitions learned that are favorable to violation of law over definitions learned that are unfavorable to violation of law.

Differential opportunity theory

A theory that attempts to join the concept of anomie and differential association by analyzing both legitimate and illegitimate opportunity structures available to individuals. It posits that illegitimate opportunities, like legitimate opportunities, are unequally distributed.

Direct control

An external control which depends on rules, restrictions, and punishments.

Drift

According to David Matza, a state of limbo in which youths move in and out of delinquency and in which their lifestyles can embrace both conventional and deviant values.

Due process

According to the Fourteenth Amendment of the U.S. Constitution, a fundamental mandate that a person should not be deprived of life, liberty, or property without reasonable and lawful procedures.

Dizygotic (DZ) twins

Fraternal twins, who develop from two separate eggs fertilized at the same time. *See also* Monozygotic twins.

Ego

The part of the psyche which, according to psychoanalytic theory, governs rational behavior. The moderator between the superego and the id.

Embezzlement

The crime of withholding or withdrawing, without consent, funds entrusted to an agent, e.g., a bank teller as officer.

Employment prison

A prison for low-risk offenders. Prisoners work at jobs outside the prison during the day but return to prison after work.

Equal protection

A clause of the Fourteenth Amendment to the U.S. Constitution that guarantees equal protection of the law to everyone, without regard to race, economic class, gender, religion, etc.

Eugenics

A science, based on the principle of heredity, that has for its purpose the improvement of the race.

Exclusionary rule

A rule prohibiting use of illegally obtained evidence in a court of law.

Experiment

A research technique in which an investigator introduces a change into a process in order to make measurements or observations that evaluate the effects of the change.

Extraversion

According to Hans Eysenck, a dimension of the human personality. Describes individuals who are sensation-seeking, dominant, and assertive.

False pretense, obtaining property by

Leading a victim to part with property on a voluntary basis through trickery, deceit, or misrepresentation.

Federal Corrupt Practices Act

A federal statute that restricts lobbying, especially by prohibiting the making of gifts and contributions in expectation of political support for commercial and/or similar activities.

Federal Election Campaign Act

A federal statute regulating campaign contributions and making it criminal to make contributions in violation of the act.

Federal Witness Protection Program

A program, established under the Organized Crime Control Act of 1970, designed to protect witnesses who testify in court by relocating them and assigning to them new identities.

Fee system

A system used in some rural areas in which the county government pays a modest amount of money for each prisoner per day as operating budget.

Felony

A severe crime, subject to punishment of one year or more in prison, or to capital punishment.

Felony murder

The imposition of criminal liability for murder upon one who participates in commission of a felony that is dangerous to life and that causes the death of another.

Fence

A receiver of stolen property who resells the goods for profit.

Field experiment

An experiment conducted in a real-world setting as opposed to one conducted in a laboratory.

Frankpledge

An ancient system whereby members of a tithing, an association of ten families, were bound together by a mutual pledge to keep the peace. Every male over age twelve was part of the system. *See also* Tithing.

Fraud

An act of trickery or deceit, especially involving misrepresentation.

Good time system

A system under which time is deducted from a prison sentence for good behavior within the institution.

Habeas corpus

A writ requesting that a person or institution that is detaining a named prisoner bring him or her before a judicial officer and give reasons for the prisoner's capture and detention, so that the lawfulness of the imprisonment may be determined.

Homicide

The killing of one person by another.

Hypoglycemia

A condition that may occur in susceptible individuals when the level of blood sugar falls below an acceptable range, causing anxiety, headaches, confusion, fatigue, and aggressive behavior.

Hypothesis

A proposition set forth as an explanation for some specified phenomenon.

Id

The part of the personality that, according to psychoanalytic theory, contains powerful urges and drives for gratification and satisfaction.

Index crimes

The eight major crimes included in Part One of the Uniform Crime Reports: criminal homicide, forcible rape, robbery, aggravated assault, burglary, larceny-theft, auto theft, and arson.

Indictment

Accusation against a criminal defendant rendered by a grand jury on the basis of evidence constituting a prima facie case.

Indirect control

Behavioral influences that arise from an individual's identification with noncriminals and desire to conform to societal norms.

Information

Accusation against a defendant prepared by a prosecuting attorney.

Inmate code

An informal set of rules that reflects the values of the prison society.

Insider trading

Use of material nonpublic financial information to obtain an unfair advantage in trading securities.

Intensive supervision probation (ISP)

An alternative to prison for convicted nonviolent offenders who do not qualify for routine probation.

Internalized control

Self-regulation of behavior and conformity to societal norms as a result of guilt feelings arising in the conscience.

Involuntary manslaughter

Unintentionally but recklessly causing the death of another person by consciously taking a grave risk that endangers the person's life.

Involvement

A variable used by Travis Hirschi to describe an individual's participation in conventional activities.

Just deserts

Philosophy of justice which asserts that the punishment should fit the crime and the culpability of the offender. *See also* Retribution.

Justice of the peace

Originally (established in 1326), an untrained man, usually of the lower nobility, who was assigned to investigate and try minor cases. Presently, a judge of a lower local or municipal court with limited jurisdiction.

Justifiable homicide

A homicide, permitted by law, in defense of a legal right or mandate.

Kidnapping

A felony consisting of the seizure and abduction of a person by force or threat of force and against the victim's will; under federal law, the victim of a kidnapping is one who has been taken across state lines and held for ransom.

Labeling theory

Explanation of deviance in terms of the process by which a person acquires a negative identity, such as "addict" or "ex-con," and is forced to suffer the consequences of outcast status.

Larceny

A trespassory taking and carrying away of personal property belonging to another with the intent to deprive the owner of the property permanently.

Laws of imitation

An explanation of crime as learned behavior; individuals are thought to emulate behavior patterns of others with whom they have contact.

Longitudinal study

An analysis that focuses on studies of a particular group conducted repeatedly over a period of time.

Macrosociological study

The study of overall social arrangements, their structures, and their long-term effects.

Mafia

Sicilian families which, in both the United States and Sicily, are loosely associated with one another in op-erating criminal activities. Synonymous with "organized crime."

Malice aforethought

The mens rea requirement for murder, consisting of the intention to kill with the awareness that there is no right to kill. *See also* mens rea.

Manslaughter

Criminal homicide without malice, committed intentionally (voluntary manslaughter) or recklessly (involuntary manslaughter).

Mass murder

The murder of several persons, in one act or transaction, by one perpetrator or a group of perpetrators.

Mens rea

(Latin) Guilty mind; awareness of wrongdoing. Intention to commit a criminal act, or recklessness.

Microsociological study

The study of everyday patterns of behavior and personal interactions.

Minimal brain dysfunction

An attention-deficit disorder that may produce such asocial behavior as impulsivity, hyperactivity, and aggressiveness.

Miranda warning

A warning that explains the rights of an arrestee, and that an arresting officer is required by law to recite at the time of the arrest.

Misdemeanor

A crime less serious than a felony and subject to a maximum sentence of one year in jail or a fine.

Money laundering

The process by which money derived from illegal activities (especially drug sales) is unlawfully taken out of the United States, placed in a numbered account overseas, and then transferred as funds no longer traceable to crime.

Monozygotic (MZ) twins
Identical twins, who develop from a single fertilized egg that divides into two embryos. *See also* Dizygotic twins.

Motion
An oral or written request to a judge, asking the court to make a specified ruling, finding, decision, or order; may be presented at any appropriate moment from arrest until the end of the trial.

Murder
An unlawful (usually intentional) killing of a human being with malice aforethought.

Murder in the first degree
A killing done with premeditation and deliberation or, by statute, in the presence of other aggravating circumstances.

Murder in the second degree
A killing done with intent to cause death but without premeditation and deliberation.

Night watchman
Originally, a thirteenth-century untrained citizen who patrolled at night on the lookout for disturbances.

Nonparticipant observation
A study whereby investigators observe behavior closely but do not become participants.

Occupational crime
A crime committed by an individual for his or her own benefit, in the course of rendering a service.

Parens patriae
(Latin, "father of the fatherland") Assumption by the state of the role of guardian over children whose parents are deemed incapable or unworthy.

Parole
Supervised conditional release of a convicted prisoner before expiration of the sentence of imprisonment.

Participant observation
Collection of information through involvement in the social life of the group a researcher is studying.

Penitentiary
A prison or place of confinement and correction for persons convicted of committing criminal acts; originally a place where convicts did penance.

Penologist
A social scientist who studies and applies the theory and methods of punishment for crime.

Peremptory challenges
Challenges (limited in number) by which a potential juror may be dismissed by either the prosecution or the defense without assignment of reason. *See also* Challenge for cause; Voir dire.

Person in need of supervision (PINS)
A juvenile (or adult) requiring supervision but usually not incarceration.

Phrenology
A nineteenth-century theory based on the hypothesis that human behavior is localized in certain specific brain and skull areas. According to this theory, criminal behavior can be determined by the "bumps" on the head.

Physiognomy
The study of facial features and their relation to human behavior.

Pimp
A procurer or manager of prostitutes who provides access to prostitutes and protects and exploits them, living off their proceeds.

Plead

To respond to a criminal charge. Forms of pleas are guilty, not guilty, and nolo contendere.

Police subculture

The result of socialization and bonding among police officers due to the stress and anxiety produced on the job.

Population

A large group of persons in a study.

Pornography

The portrayal, by whatever means, of lewd or obscene material prohibited by law.

Positivist school of criminology

A criminological perspective that uses the scientific methods of the natural sciences and suggests that human behavior is a product of social, biological, psychological, or economic forces.

Preliminary hearing

A preview of a trial held in court before a judge, in which the prosecution must produce sufficient evidence for the case to proceed to trial.

Prima facie case

A case in which there is as much evidence as would warrant the conviction of the defendant unless otherwise contradicted; a case that meets evidentiary requirements for grand jury indictment.

Primary data

Facts and observations that researchers gather by conducting their own measurements for a study.

Principals

Joint perpetrators of a criminal act.

Prisonization

A socialization process in which new prisoners learn the ways of prison society, including rules, hierarchy, customs, and culture.

Probable cause

A set of facts that would induce a reasonable person to believe that an accused person committed the offense in question; the minimum evidence requirement for an arrest, according to the Fourth Amendment to the U.S. Constitution.

Probation

An alternative to imprisonment, allowing a person found guilty of an offense to stay in the community, under conditions and with supervision.

Problem-oriented policing

A strategy to enhance community relations whereby police work with citizens to identify and respond to community problems.

Prosecutor

An attorney and government official who represents the people against persons accused of committing criminal acts.

Prostitution

Engaging in sexual activities for hire.

Psychoanalytic theory

In criminology, a theory of criminality that attributes delinquent and criminal behavior to a conscience that is either so overbearing that it arouses excessive feelings of guilt or so weak that it cannot control the individual's impulses.

Psychopathy

A condition in which a person appears to have mental health but in reality has no sense of responsibility; shows disregard for truth; is insincere; and feels no sense of shame, guilt, or humiliation.

Psychosis

A mental illness characterized by a loss of contact with reality.

Psychoticism

According to Hans Eysenck, a dimension of the human personality describing individuals who are aggressive, egocentric, and impulsive.

Racketeer Influenced and Corrupt Organizations (RICO) Act

A federal statute which provides for forfeiture of assets derived from a criminal enterprise.

Radical criminology

A criminological perspective that studies the relationship between economic disparity and crime, avers that crime is the result of a struggle between owners of capital and workers for the distribution of power and resources, and posits that only when capitalism is abolished will crime disappear.

Random sample

A sample chosen in such a way as to assure that each person in the population to be studied has an equal chance of being selected. *See also* Sample.

Rape

At common law, a felony consisting of the carnal knowledge (intercourse), by force and violence, by a man of a woman (not his wife). The stipulation that the woman not be the man's wife is omitted in modern statutes.

Rational choice

A perspective which states that crime is the result of a decision-making process in which the offender weighs the potential penalties and rewards of committing a crime.

Reaction formation

An individual response to anxiety in which the person reacts to a stimulus with abnormal intensity or inappropriate conduct.

Reasonable suspicion

Warranted suspicion (short of probable cause) that a person may be engaged in the commission of a crime.

Rehabilitation

A punishment philosophy which asserts that through proper correctional intervention, a criminal can be reformed into a law-abiding citizen.

Retribution

An "eye for an eye" philosophy of justice. *See also* Just deserts.

Robber barons

Originally, European barons who, unemployed after the Crusades, waylaid merchant convoys. Later, used to describe nineteenth-century entrepreneurs who amassed great fortunes in the United States through cunning and sharp dealing.

Robbery

The taking of the property of another, or out of his or her presence, by means of force and violence or the threat thereof.

Routine activities

A term used in explaining an increase or decrease in crime rates by changes in the daily habits of potential victims; based on the expectation that crimes will occur where there is a suitable target unprotected by guardians.

Sample

A selected subset of a population to be studied. *See also* Random sample.

Secondary data

Facts and observations that were previously collected for a different study.

Selective incapacitation

The targeting of high-risk and recidivistic offenders for rigorous prosecution and incarceration.

Self-report survey

A survey in which respondents answer in a confidential interview or, most often, by completing an anonymous questionnaire.

Serial murders

Killing of several victims over a period of time.

Sheriff
The principal law enforcement officer of a county.

Sherman Antitrust Act
An act (1890) of Congress prohibiting any contract, conspiracy, or combination of business interests in restraint of foreign or interstate trade.

Shock probation
A sentence that allows for brief incarceration followed by probation, in an effort to induce law abidance by shocking the offender.

Shoplifting
Stealing goods from stores or markets.

Simple assault
An attack that inflicts little or no physical harm on the victim.

Social control theory
An explanation of criminal behavior that focuses on control mechanisms, techniques, and strategies for regulating human behavior, leading to conformity or obedience to society's rules, and that posits that deviance results when social controls are weakened or break down, so that individuals are not motivated to conform to them.

Social disorganization theory
A theory of criminality in which the breakdown of effective social bonds, primary group associations, and social controls in neighborhoods and communities is held to result in development of high-crime areas.

Social interactionists
Scholars who view the human self as formed through a process of social interaction.

Social learning theory
A theory of criminality which maintains that delinquent behavior is learned through the same psychological processes as nondelinquent behavior, e.g., through reinforcement.

Sociopathy
See Psychopathy.

Sodomy
Sexual intercourse by mouth or anus; a felony at common law.

Somatotype school of criminology
A criminological perspective which relates body build to behavioral tendencies, temperament, susceptibility to disease, and life expectancy.

Split sentence
A sentence that requires the convicted criminal to serve time in jail followed by probation.

Statutory rape
Sexual intercourse with a person incapable of giving legally relevant consent, because of immaturity (below age), mental condition, or, occasionally, physical condition.

Sting operation
An undercover operation in which police officers trap suspects by posing as criminals.

Stock manipulation
An illegal practice of brokers, in which they lead their clients to believe the price of a particular stock will rise, thus creating an artificial demand for it.

Strain theory
A criminological theory positing that a gap between culturally approved goals and legitimate means of achieving them causes frustration which leads to criminal behavior.

Stranger homicide
Murder and nonnegligent manslaughter committed by a person unknown and unrelated to the victim.

Strict liability
Liability for a crime or violation imposed without regard for the actor's guilt; criminal liability without mens rea. *See also* Mens rea.

Subculture

A subdivision within the dominant culture that has its own norms, beliefs, and values.

Subculture of violence

A subculture with values that demand the overt use of violence in certain social situations.

Superego

In psychoanalytic theory, the conscience, or those aspects of the personality that threaten the person or impose a sense of guilt or psychic suffering and thus restrain the id.

Survey

The systematic collection of information by asking questions in questionnaires or interviews.

Synnomie

A societal state, opposite of anomie; marked by social cohesion achieved through the sharing of values.

Target hardening

A crime-prevention technique that seeks to make it more difficult to commit a given offense, by better protecting the threatened object or person.

Team policing

A strategy for improving contacts between citizens and police, whereby a team of officers is responsible for a specific neighborhood on a twenty-four-hour basis.

Techniques of neutralization

A rationalization of defense mechanism used by a youthful offender which releases the youth from the constraints of the moral order. Methods include denial of responsibility, denial of injury, denial of victim, condemnation of the condemner, and appeal to higher loyalties.

Terrorism

Use of violence against a target, to create fear, alarm, dread, or coercion for the purpose of obtaining concessions or rewards or commanding public attention for a political cause.

Theft of computer time, software, and hardware

Unauthorized use of computer time and software services; also, unauthorized copying of software programs.

Theory

A coherent group of propositions used as principles in explaining or accounting for known facts or phenomena.

Tithing

In Anglo-Saxon law, an association of ten families bound together by a frankpledge. *See also* Frankpledge.

Tort

An injury or wrong committed against a person or a person's property, subject to compensation; an infringement of the rights of an individual not founded on either contract or criminal law prohibition.

Utilitarianism

A criminological perspective positing that crime prevention and criminal justice must serve the end of providing the most good for the greatest number; based on the rationality of lawgivers, law enforcers, and the public at large.

Variables

Changeable factors.

Victim precipitation

Opening oneself up, by either direct or subliminal means, to a criminal response.

Victimization survey

A survey that measures the extent of crime by interviewing individuals about their experiences as vic

Victimology

A criminological subdiscipline that examines the role played by the victim in a criminal incident and in the criminal process.

Violations

Minor criminal offenses, usually under city ordinances, commonly subject only to fines.

Voir dire

A process in which lawyers and a judge question potential jurors in order to select those who are acceptable, that is, those who are unbiased and objective in relation to the particular trial. *See also* Challenge for cause; Peremptory challenges.

Voluntary manslaughter

Intentionally but without malice causing the death of another person, as in the heat of passion, in response to strong provocation, or possibly under severe intoxication.

White-collar crime

A sociological concept, encompassing any corporate or individual criminal activity marked by fraud and deception.

PHOTO CREDITS

Photo Essays

Insert I:
"The Universe of the Criminologist's Interest"

2 top left: Kevin Vandivier/TexaStock. **2 top right:** J. L. Barkan/Picture Cube. **2 center:** Richard Hutchings/ Photo Researchers. **2 bottom:** Omar Bradley/Picture Group. **3 top left:** Peter Morgan/Picture Group. **3 top right:** Chuck Nacke/Picture Group. **3 center:** UPI/ Bettmann Newsphotos. **3 bottom:** Reuters/Bettmann Newsphotos. **4 top left:** AP/Wide World. **4 top right:** J. L. Atlan/Sygma. **4 bottom left:** Peter Turnley/Black Star. **4 bottom right:** R. Bossu/Sygma.

Insert II:
"Mass-Media Stereotyping of Crime and Criminals"

2 top: Photofest. **4 top right:** John Seakwood/ Sygma. **4 bottom:** Henry Gris/FPG International.

Insert III:
"The International Drug Cycle"

2 top left: Les Stone/Sygma. **2 top right:** S. Rickey Rogers/Black Star. **2 bottom:** Susan Meiselas/ Magnum. **3 top:** Boroff/TexaStock. **3 bottom left:** Miami Herald. **3 bottom right:** Ruiz/Picture Group. **4 top left:** John Coletti/Picture Cube. **4 top right:** Tony O'Brien/Picture Group. **4 bottom:** Randy Taylor/ Sygma.

Insert IV:
"Law Enforcement Across Cultures"

2 top left: Ed Pieratt/Comstock. **2 top right:** Ellis Herwig/Picture Cube. **2 bottom left:** Adam Tanner/ Comstock. **2 bottom right:** John Spragens, Jr./Photo Researchers. **3 top left:** Paolo Koch/Photo Researchers. **3 top right:** E. Williamson/Picture Cube. **3 bottom left:** Donna Binder/Impact Visuals. **3 bottom right:** Donna De Cesare/Impact Visuals. **4 top left:** Francis J. Dean/The Image Works. **4 top right:** Bastienne Schmidt/Impact Visuals. **4 bottom left:** Victor Englebert/Photo Researchers. **4 bottom right:** Adam Tanner/Comstock.

Text Photos

Chapter 1

2: Stephen L. Feldman/Photo Researchers. **7:** Bill Leiddner/TexaStock. **9:** From *Cinderella and Other*

Tales from Perrault. Illustrated by Michael Hague. Henry Holt & Co., New York, 1989. **10:** Giraudon/Art Resource. **18:** Courtesy of the authors.

Chapter 2

22: AP/Wide World. **36:** AP/Wide World. **42:** Culver Pictures. **46:** UPI/Bettmann Newsphotos.

Chapter 3

56: Maass, Max Peter. Halsgericht, *Kriminalitat und Strafjustiz in alter Zeit.* Darmstadt: S. Toeche-Mittler Verlag, 1968. **60:** The Bettmann Archive.

Chapter 4

80: Judith D. Sodwick/The Picture Cube. **84:** Olive R. Pierce/Stock, Boston. **86:** Michael Weisbrot/Stock, Boston. **90 left:** AP/Wide World. **90 right:** AP/Wide World.

Chapter 5

108: Harvey Stein. **112:** Paolo da Silva/Sygma. **114:** Joel Gordon.

Chapter 6

134: Mary Ellen Mark/Library. **137:** Bruce Davidson/Magnum. **144:** Thelma Shumsky/The Image Works.

Chapter 7

156: Les Stone/Impact Visuals. **158:** Culver Pictures. **160:** Temple University Libraries Photojournalism Collection.

Chapter 8

176: Jon Kral/Miami Herald. **186:** Mark Antman/The Image Works. **188 top:** Steve Kagan/Photo Researchers. **188 center:** AP/Wide World Photos. **188 bottom:** UPI/Bettmann Newsphotos. **194:** Eugene Richards/Magnum.

Chapter 9

202: Courtesy of Joaquin Arriaga. **208:** AP/Wide World. **211:** Sygma. **216:** Culver Pictures.

Chapter 10

224: Maass, Max Peter. Halsgericht, *Kriminalitat und Strafjustiz in alter Zeit.* Darmstadt: S. Toeche-Mittler Verlag, 1968. **230:** UPI/Bettmann. **237:** UPI/Bettmann Newsphotos. **248:** AP/Wide World.

Chapter 11

260: Barbara Alper/Stock, Boston. **264:** Frank Siteman/Jeroboam. **265:** International Foundation for Art Research. **276:** UPI/Bettmann Newsphotos.

Chapter 12

282: Barbara Alper/Stock, Boston. **293:** UPI/Bettmann Newsphotos. **298:** Bob Clay/Jeroboam.

Chapter 13

310: Jim Anderson/Black Star. **315:** AP/Wide World Photos. **324:** Allan Tannenbaum/Sygma.

Chapter 14

342: The Bettmann Archive. **344:** Culver Pictures. **364:** Charles Harbutt/Actuality.

Chapter 15

374: Rick Mansfield/The Image Works. **376:** Morey, William C. Outlines of Roman History, 1901. (American Book Company), p. 51. **377:** Bildarchiv Foto Marburg/Art Resource. **394:** AP/Wide World.

Chapter 16

404: Spencer Grant/The Picture Cube. **406:** Illustrated by George Cruikshank. "The Comic Blackstone" by Gilbert Abbott Beckett. Chicago: Callaghan & Cockroft, 1869, pp. 112–113. **431:** George Mars Cassidy/The Picture Cube.

Chapter 17

440: Alan Pogue/TexaStock. **443 left:** Culver Pictures. **443 right:** F. M. Kearney/Impact Visuals. **444:** "Old Time Punishments" by William Andrews, F.R.H.S. London: The Talard Press Limited.

ILLUSTRATION AND TEXT CREDITS

Chapter 1

12: "Soccer Hooliganism Still Plagues Europe." Reprinted with permission from *CJ International*, Vol. 4, No. 6, 1988, 1333 S. Wabash Ave., Box 55, Chicago, IL 60605. **14:** Drawing by W. B. Park; © 1988 The New Yorker Magazine, Inc. **15 Figure 1.1:** From *The Sociology of Deviance* by Jack D. Douglas and Frances C. Waksler, Little, Brown and Company, 1982. Reprinted by permission of the authors.

Chapter 2

27: From *The Professional Thief* by Edwin H. Sutherland. Copyright 1937. Reprinted by permission of The University of Chicago Press. **32 Cartoon:** From *Investigating Deviance* by Stephen Moore, reproduced by kind permission of Unwin Hyman Ltd. © Stephen Moore, 1988. **33 Figure 2.1:** From *Surveying Victims: A Study of the Measurement of Criminal Victimization, Perceptions of Crime, and Attitudes to Criminal Justice* by R. F. Sparks, H. G. Genn, and D. J. Dodd. Copyright © 1977. Reprinted by permission of John Wiley & Sons, Ltd. **45:** Drawing by Alain; © 1933, 1961 The New Yorker Magazine, Inc.

Chapter 3

59: From Timothy Stroup, "Crime and Punishment in German History." Reprinted with permission from *CJ International*, Vol. 4, No. 6, 1988, 1333 S. Wabash Ave., Box 55, Chicago, IL 60605. **66:** From J. Miller, "The Mismeasure of Man," from *Newsweek*, November 9, 1981, © 1981, Newsweek, Inc. All rights reserved. Reprinted by permission.

Chapter 4

88: Cartoon © 1990 by Sidney Harris. **90–91:** From *The Trial of John W. Hinckley, Jr.: A Case Study in the Insanity Defense* by P. W. Low, J. C. Jeffries, and R. J. Bonnie. Copyright © 1986. Reprinted by permission of The Foundation Press. **94:** Drawing by Chas. Addams; © 1981 The New Yorker Magazine, Inc.

Chapter 5

112: "Aid for an Ancient Tribe" from *Newsweek*, April 9, 1990, © 1990 Newsweek, Inc. All rights reserved. Reprinted by permission. **113 Table 5.1:** Reprinted with permission of The Free Press, a Division of Macmillan, Inc. from *Social Theory and Social Structure*, Revised and Enlarged Edition by Robert K. Merton. Copyright © 1967, 1968 by Robert K. Merton. **118:** From Lee A. Daniels, "Youths Leave Foster Care for Campus," *The New York Times*, April 6, 1988. Copyright © 1988 by The New York Times Company. Reprinted by permission. **120 Figure 5.2:** From *Theories of Delinquency: An Examination of Expla-*

Chapter 11

267: From Michael DeCourcy Hinds, "Follow This Car! I'm Being Stolen!" *The New York Times*, September 2, 1989. Copyright © 1989 by The New York Times Company. Reprinted by permission. **268 Figure 11.4:** From *Outlaws of the Ocean—The Complete Book of Contemporary Crime on the High Seas* by G. O. W. Mueller and Freda Adler. Copyright © 1985 by G. O. W. Mueller and Freda Adler. By permission of Hearst Marine Books, a division of William Morrow & Co. **270:** From *Outlaws of the Ocean—The Complete Book of Contemporary Crime on the High Seas* by G. O. W. Mueller and Freda Adler. Copyright © 1985 by G. O. W. Mueller and Freda Adler. By permission of Hearst Marine Books, a division of William Morrow & Co. **272:** Drawing by Dana Fradon; © 1971 The New Yorker Magazine, Inc. **273 Figure 11.6:** From G. Rengert and J. Wasilchick, *Suburban Burglary: A Time and a Place for Everything*, 1985. Courtesy of Charles C Thomas, Publisher, Springfield, Illinois. **274:** From G. Rengert and J. Wasilchick, *Suburban Burglary: A Time and a Place for Everything*, 1985. Courtesy of Charles C Thomas, Publisher, Springfield, Illinois.

Chapter 12

283–284: Excerpt (1) from *New Developments and Perspectives on Corporate Crime Law Enforcement in America* edited by Leonard Orland and Harold R. Tyler, Practicing Law Institute, 1987. (2) Reprinted with permission of The Free Press, a division of Macmillan, Inc. from *Corporate Crime* by Marshall B. Clinard and Peter C. Yeager. Copyright © 1980 by The Free Press. (3) From Gordon Hawkins, "God and the Mafia," *Public Interest* 14, 1969, Institute of Criminology, Sydney University Law School, Sydney, Australia. **286–287:** "A Penny Scam That Adds Up to Millions." Reprinted from January 23, 1989 issue of *Business Week* by special permission, copyright © 1989 by McGraw-Hill, Inc. **290–291:** From Joseph R. Biden, "Foreword," *American Criminal Law Review* 23, 1986, Georgetown University Law Center. **297:** Drawing by Stevenson; © 1970 The New Yorker Magazine, Inc. **304:** "Chinese Triads Develop International Ties." Reprinted with permission from *CJ International*, Vol. 5, No. 4, 1989, 1333 S. Wabash Ave., Box 55, Chicago, IL 60605.

Chapter 13

322–323 Figures 13.1, 13.2, 13.3, and 13.4: From *The Illicit Drug Situation in the United States and Canada, 1984–1986*. Reprinted by permission of the Royal Canadian Mounted Police, Drug Enforcement Director-ate Strategic Intelligence Branch, Ottawa, Ontario, Canada; and the Drug Enforcement Administration, Washington, D.C.

Chapter 14

348: Cartoon from A Commission Report. *State–Local Relations in the Criminal Justice System.* Advisory Commission on Intergovernmental Relations (Washington, D.C., 1971). **351:** From William Glaberson, "Trapped in the Terror of New York's Holding Pens," *The New York Times*, March 23, 1990. Copyright © 1990 by The New York Times Company. Reprinted by permission. **361 Table 14.4:** From Linda A. Szymanski, "Waiver/Transfer/Certification of Juveniles to Criminal Court: Age Restrictions, Crime Restrictions, Washington, D.C.: National Center for Juvenile Justice, February 1987.

Chapter 16

405–406: Excerpt from *American Criminal Justice: The Defendant's Perspective* by Jonathan Casper. © 1972. Used by permission of Prentice-Hall, Inc. **407 Figure 16.1:** From *Criminal Justice: Issues and Ironies* by Abraham S. Blumberg. Copyright © 1979 by Abraham S. Blumberg. Reprinted with permission of the publisher, Franklin Watts, Inc. **414 Figure 16.4:** From Barbara Boland with Ronald Sones, INSLAW, Inc., *The Prosecution of Felony Arrests, 1981*, Bureau of Justice Statistics, 1986. Reprinted by permission of the authors. **421 Table 16.4:** From Barbara Boland with Ronald Somes, INSLAW, Inc., *The Prosecution of Felony Arrests, 1981*, Bureau of Justice Statistics, 1986. Reprinted by permission of the authors. **421:** Cartoon by Starke, from *The Best Cartoons from Punch*, Simon & Schuster, Inc., 1952. Copyright © 1952, by Bradbury, Agnew & Company, Ltd. Reproduced by permission of *Punch*. **430 Figure 16.8:** From *The Sentencing Commission and Its Guidelines* by Andrew von Hirsch, Kay A. Knapp, and Michael Tonry. Copyright © 1987 by Andrew von Hirsch, Kay A. Knapp, and Michael Tonry. Reprinted with the permission of the Northeastern University Press.

Chapter 17

450–452 Table 17.2: From *New Horizons in Criminology*, Revised Edition, by Harry Elmer Barnes and Negley K. Tetters. Copyright © 1945. Reprinted by permission of Prentice-Hall, Inc., 1945. **469 Table 17.5:** From Joan Petersilia, *Expanding Options for Criminal Sentencing*, The Rand Corporation, 1987.

NAME INDEX

SUBJECT INDEX